Advances of AI in Neuroimaging

Advances of AI in Neuroimaging

Guest Editors

Iman Beheshti
Daichi Sone
Carson K. Leung

MDPI

Basel • Beijing • Wuhan • Barcelona • Belgrade • Novi Sad • Cluj • Manchester

Guest Editors
Iman Beheshti
Department of Human
Anatomy and Cell Science
University of Manitoba
Winnipeg
Canada

Daichi Sone
Department of Psychiatry
Jikei University School
of Medicine
Tokyo
Japan

Carson K. Leung
Department of
Computer Science
University of Manitoba
Winnipeg
Canada

Editorial Office
MDPI AG
Grosspeteranlage 5
4052 Basel, Switzerland

This is a reprint of the Special Issue, published open access by the journal *Brain Sciences* (ISSN 2076-3425), freely accessible at: https://www.mdpi.com/journal/brainsci/special_issues/AI_Neuroimaging.

For citation purposes, cite each article independently as indicated on the article page online and as indicated below:

Lastname, A.A.; Lastname, B.B. Article Title. *Journal Name* **Year**, *Volume Number*, Page Range.

ISBN 978-3-7258-4054-0 (Hbk)
ISBN 978-3-7258-4053-3 (PDF)
https://doi.org/10.3390/books978-3-7258-4053-3

© 2025 by the authors. Articles in this book are Open Access and distributed under the Creative Commons Attribution (CC BY) license. The book as a whole is distributed by MDPI under the terms and conditions of the Creative Commons Attribution-NonCommercial-NoDerivs (CC BY-NC-ND) license (https://creativecommons.org/licenses/by-nc-nd/4.0/).

Contents

About the Editors

Iman Beheshti

Dr. Iman Beheshti, Ph.D., is a Senior Research Scientist and a Guest Lecturer in the Department of Human Anatomy and Cell Science at the University of Manitoba, Winnipeg, Canada. He earned his Ph.D. in Electrical and Electronic Engineering from Eastern Mediterranean University in 2016 on a full-ride scholarship in Turkey, specializing in biomedical engineering with AI applications. Since then, he has made significant contributions to the field as a postdoctoral researcher at prestigious institutions, including the National Center of Neurology and Psychiatry (Japan), Laval University (Canada), and the University of Manitoba (Canada). He has coordinated four national research projects across Japan and Canada. His research focuses on developing innovative AI models specifically designed for real-world clinical settings.

Daichi Sone

Dr. Daichi Sone, M.D., Ph.D., has been a Senior Lecturer of Psychiatry at Jikei University School of Medicine, Tokyo, Japan, since 2021. After graduating with an M.D. from the Faculty of Medicine at the University of Tokyo in 2008, he began his clinical career as a neuropsychiatrist through basic and specialized training. From 2012, he started working at the National Center of Neurology and Psychiatry, Tokyo, Japan, specializing in neuropsychiatry, epileptology, and neuroimaging. Most of his research topics focus on epilepsy imaging, although his interests are also involved in other neuropsychiatric disorders including dementia. He obtained his Ph.D. from the Graduate School of Medicine at the University of Tokyo in 2017. In 2018, to develop expertise in neuroimaging for epilepsy, he moved to London and launched his next career in the Department of Clinical and Experimental Epilepsy, UCL Queen Square Institute of Neurology, under the supervision of Prof. Matthias J. Koepp. His research projects have provided novel findings for seizure focus detection and new potential imaging biomarkers, using structural diffusion and perfusion MRI and PET with advanced methods, such as network analysis and machine learning.

Carson K. Leung

Prof. Dr. Carson K. Leung, Ph.D., is currently a Professor in the Department of Computer Science at the University of Manitoba, Winnipeg, Canada. He received his B.Sc.(Hons.), M.Sc., and Ph.D. degrees, all in computer science, from the University of British Columbia, Vancouver, Canada. He has contributed more than 400 refereed publications on the topics of analytics, artificial intelligence (AI), big data, bioinformatics, brain sciences, data analytics, data mining, data science, health informatics, knowledge discovery, machine learning, social network analysis, and visual analytics. These include publications in refereed international journals and conferences such as *ACM Transactions on Database Systems* (*TODS*), *ACM Transactions on Knowledge Discovery from Data* (*TKDD*), IEEE ICDE, IEEE ICDM, and PAKDD. Moreover, he has served as the Editor-in-Chief for *Advances in Data Science and Adaptive Analysis* (*ADSAA*) and for MDPI's *Analytics*, as well as an Associate Editor for international journals like Springer's *Social Network Analysis and Mining* (*SNAM*). He has served on the Organizing Committees of the ACM CIKM, ACM KDD, ACM SIGMOD, DaWaK, IEEE DSAA, IEEE ICDM, and other conferences; he has also served as a PC member of numerous conferences including ACM KDD, ECML/PKDD and PAKDD. He is a Senior Member of both the ACM and the IEEE; he is also an IEEE Computer Society Distinguished Contributor.

brain sciences

Editorial

Advances of Artificial Intelligence in Neuroimaging

Iman Beheshti [1,*], Daichi Sone [2] and Carson K. Leung [3]

1 Department of Human Anatomy and Cell Science, University of Manitoba, Winnipeg, MB R3E 0J9, Canada
2 Department of Psychiatry, Jikei University School of Medicine, Tokyo 105-8461, Japan; daichisone@gmail.com
3 Department of Computer Science, University of Manitoba, Winnipeg, MB R3T 2N2, Canada; carson.leung@umanitoba.ca
* Correspondence: iman.beheshti@umanitoba.ca

1. Introduction

Neuroimaging [1–3] is a rapidly evolving field that involves the use of non-invasive imaging techniques to visualize and study the structure and function of the human brain. This field has experienced transformative progress—as well as significant breakthroughs in terms of the accuracy, speed, and efficiency of identifying various brain disorders—over the past decade, largely driven by technological advancements and computational innovations. Among these, artificial intelligence (AI) has emerged as a pivotal tool, offering researchers and clinicians novel approaches to explore the brain's structure and function [4–10]. AI models have been widely applied in the analysis and interpretation of neuroimaging data, aiding researchers and clinicians in diagnosing, treating, and monitoring patients with neurological and psychiatric disorders. This Special Issue, titled "Advances of AI in Neuroimaging", was conceived to provide a platform for cutting-edge research at the intersection of AI and neuroimaging, aiming to revolutionize neuroscience and healthcare.

The primary motivation behind this Special Issue was the increasing demand for innovative solutions to address the complexity of neuroimaging data, especially in the context of neurological and psychiatric disorders. AI techniques, such as machine learning (ML) [11,12] and deep learning (DL) [13], offer unparalleled potential for biomarker discovery, disease prediction, and personalized treatment strategies. With the prevalence of brain disorders increasing, the need for accurate and efficient diagnostic tools is more pressing than ever.

This Special Issue sought to highlight both technical advancements and their practical implications for patient care and healthcare systems. The contributions span a range of neuroimaging modalities, including magnetic resonance imaging (MRI), positron emission tomography (PET), computed tomography (CT), and electroencephalography (EEG). By addressing challenges such as data complexity, model interpretability, and cost-efficiency, the featured research underscores the indispensable role of AI in advancing neuroimaging and its applications.

2. Summary of Accepted Papers

This Special Issue attracted widespread attention, receiving over 30 submissions from researchers from around the world. Each submission underwent rigorous quality control by the editorial team and the journal, ensuring adherence to the highest academic standards. The final selection of 17 accepted papers—consisting of 14 research articles, 1 review, 1 perspective, and 1 systematic review—represents cutting-edge research that successfully passed evaluations by expert peer reviewers in the field. Below is a synthesized overview of the published works.

Several studies (Contributions 1–3) focused on the application of ML and DL in medical imaging and surgical outcomes. For example, Ghanem et al. (Contribution 1) produced a *systematic review* examining the use of ML and DL models in predicting outcomes such as length of stay, readmissions, and mortality in spine surgery, revealing data imbalances and variations in evaluation metrics. Similarly, Rasheed et al. (Contribution 2) introduced a novel image enhancement methodology to improve the classification of brain tumors, achieving superior results compared with pre-trained models such as VGG16 and ResNet50, which are convolutional neural networks (CNNs) made up of 16 and 50 layers, respectively. The *review* by Shah and Heiss (Contribution 3) provided an in-depth look at AI's applications in neurology, emphasizing its potential to predict neurological impairments, intracranial hemorrhage expansion, and outcomes for comatose patients, showcasing its diagnostic utility across diverse data sources.

Neuroimaging played a pivotal role in several contributions (Contributions 4–8). For instance, Rudroff (Contribution 4) provided his *perspective* on AI's potential to analyze neuroimaging data, such as PET scans, to optimize treatment protocols and contribute to Long Coronavirus Disease (long COVID) research. Xiong et al. (Contribution 5) utilized support vector machines (SVMs) to classify Parkinson's disease subtypes using arterial spin labeling MRI, while Wang et al. (Contribution 6) proposed a diagnostic model integrating multiple imaging modalities—namely, diffusion tensor imaging (DTI), structural MRI (sMRI), and functional MRI (fMRI)—to enhance the diagnosis of major depressive disorder (MDD). Similarly, Liu et al. (Contribution 7) introduced a low-rank tensor fusion algorithm to improve brain age estimation by integrating multimodal neuroimaging data, demonstrating enhanced accuracy. Yamao et al. (Contribution 8) proposed a deep learning method for directly predicting the centiloid scale based on amyloid PET images.

Several papers addressed neurodegenerative diseases and cognitive impairment (Contributions 9–12). For example, Saha et al. (Contribution 9) investigated baseline MRI data to predict the response of Alzheimer's disease patients to repetitive transcranial magnetic stimulation (rTMS) treatment, while Grigas et al. (Contribution 10) demonstrated how super-resolved MRI images and optimized DL models improved mild cognitive impairment detection. Cerna et al. (Contribution 11) explored the neural mechanisms underlying Tai Chi's benefits for cognitive and physical function, highlighting its potential to mitigate age-related declines in functional connectivity. Sone et al. (Contribution 12) examined disease progression patterns in temporal lobe epilepsy by using diffusion tensor imaging, revealing associations between white matter damage and clinical metrics.

Advancements in virtual reality (VR) and collaborative technologies also featured prominently. For instance, Tadayyoni et al. (Contribution 13) examined EEG data to classify user immersion in VR training environments, achieving high accuracy rates in distinguishing cognitive states and offering insights into real-time user engagement. Similarly, Shih et al. (Contribution 14) assessed inter-brain synchrony patterns in collaborative design tasks, comparing co-located and distributed settings to better understand team performance dynamics. This Special Issue also delves into cutting-edge methodologies, such as generative adversarial networks (GANs) (Contribution 15) and novel brain activity mapping (Contribution 16). Huynh et al. (Contribution 15) applied GANs to diagnose neurological conditions using functional connectivity data, while Huang (Contribution 16) introduced a method for analyzing task-evoked whole-brain activity, providing a unique lens to study individual brain variability during tasks. Lastly, Manabe et al. (Contribution 17) focused on skill assessment in laparoscopic surgery by comparing EEG-based models, revealing that a three-dimensional CNN approach significantly outperformed traditional methods in classifying expertise levels. This curated collection of papers underscores the transformative potential of AI-driven research in neuroimaging and its ability to address clinical and scientific challenges.

3. Statistics on the Special Issue

The accepted papers were authored by 67 researchers from 14 countries, emphasizing the global collaboration underlying these advancements (Figure 1). Submissions were led by contributors from the USA (43 authors), China (22 authors), and Canada (16 authors), among others. The selected studies reflect diverse areas of expertise and applications, unified by their focus on leveraging AI to advance neuroimaging. The research featured in this Special Issue reflects prominent themes through its keywords: ML (17 keywords), neuroimaging techniques (8 keywords), brain functions and disorders (9 keywords), advanced methodologies (10 keywords), and practical applications (12 keywords) (Figure 2). Together, these works illustrate the breadth and depth of interdisciplinary innovation showcased in this Special Issue.

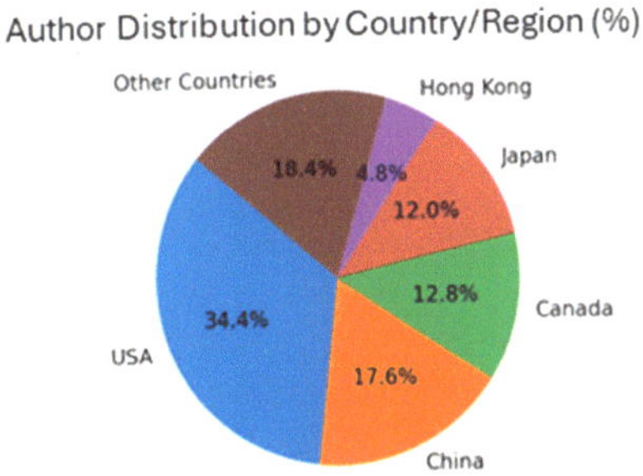

Figure 1. Geographic distribution of authors contributing to this Special Issue.

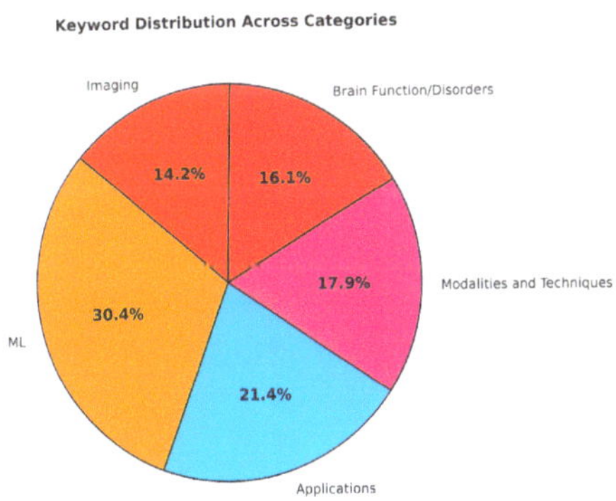

Figure 2. Distribution of keywords across research categories in this Special Issue.

4. Conclusions

This Special Issue received significant attention, with the volume of submissions and the quality of accepted papers far exceeding our initial expectations. The rigorous selection process and peer review ensured that only the most impactful and innovative contributions were published. By highlighting the convergence of AI and neuroimaging, this issue lays the groundwork for future breakthroughs, fostering collaboration and advancing research at the intersection of neuroscience and technology.

Author Contributions: I.B., D.S. and C.K.L. have all significantly contributed to the development of this Special Issue, providing meaningful, direct, and intellectual input equally. All authors have read and agreed to the published version of the manuscript.

Funding: This research was partially supported by the Natural Sciences and Engineering Research Council of Canada (NSERC) (C.K.L.) and the University of Manitoba (C.K.L.).

Acknowledgments: As Guest Editors of this Special Issue, we had the privilege of evaluating an array of compelling articles. We extend our heartfelt gratitude to the authors for their valuable submissions and to the reviewers for their thorough and constructive evaluations of the manuscripts. We also thank editors and staff at MDPI for their assistance in processing this Special Issue.

Conflicts of Interest: The authors confirm that this research was carried out without any commercial or financial interests.

Abbreviations

The following abbreviations are used in this manuscript:

AI	Artificial intelligence
CNN	Convolutional neural network
COVID	Coronavirus disease
CT	Computed tomography
DL	Deep learning
DTI	Diffusion tensor imaging
EEG	Electroencephalography
fMRI	Functional magnetic resonance imaging
GAN	Generative adversarial network
MDD	Major depressive disorder
ML	Machine learning
MRI	Magnetic resonance imaging
PET	Positron emission tomography
rTMS	Repetitive transcranial magnetic stimulation
sMRI	Structural magnetic resonance imaging
SVMs	Support vector machines
VR	Virtual reality

List of Contributions:

1. Ghanem, M.; Ghaith, A.K.; El-Hajj, V.G.; Bhandarkar, A.; de Giorgio, A.; Elmi-Terander, A.; Bydon, M. Limitations in evaluating machine learning models for imbalanced binary outcome classification in spine surgery: A systematic review. *Brain Sci.* **2023**, *13*, 1723. https://doi.org/10.3390/brainsci13121723.
2. Rasheed, Z.; Ma, Y.-K.; Ullah, I.; Ghadi, Y.Y.; Khan, M.Z.; Khan, M.A.; Abdusalomov, A.; Alqahtani, F.; Shehata, A.M. Brain tumor classification from MRI using image enhancement and convolutional neural network techniques. *Brain Sci.* **2023**, *13*, 1320. https://doi.org/10.3390/brainsci13091320.
3. Shah, S.P.; Heiss, J.D. Artificial intelligence as a complementary tool for clincal [clinical] decision-making in stroke and epilepsy. *Brain Sci.* **2024**, *14*, 228. https://doi.org/10.3390/brainsci14030228.
4. Rudroff, T. Artificial intelligence's transformative role in illuminating brain function in long COVID patients using PET/FDG. *Brain Sci.* **2024**, *14*, 73. https://doi.org/10.3390/brainsci14010073.
5. Xiong, J.; Zhu, H.; Li, X.; Hao, S.; Zhang, Y.; Wang, Z.; Xi, Q. Auto-classification of Parkinson's disease with different motor subtypes using arterial spin labelling MRI based on machine learning. *Brain Sci.* **2023**, *13*, 1524. https://doi.org/10.3390/brainsci13111524.
6. Wang, J.; Li, T.; Sun, Q.; Guo, Y.; Yu, J.; Yao, Z.; Hou, N.; Hu, B. Automatic diagnosis of major depressive disorder using a high- and low-frequency feature fusion framework. *Brain Sci.* **2023**, *13*, 1590. https://doi.org/10.3390/brainsci13111590.

7. Liu, X.; Zheng, G.; Beheshti, I.; Ji, S.; Gou, Z.; Cui, W. Low-rank tensor fusion for enhanced deep learning-based multimodal brain age estimation. *Brain Sci.* **2024**, *14*, 1252. https://doi.org/10.3390/brainsci14121252.
8. Yamao, T.; Miwa, K.; Kaneko, Y.; Takahashi, N.; Miyaji, N.; Hasegawa, K.; Wagatsuma, K.; Kamitaka, Y.; Ito, H.; Matsuda, H. Deep learning-driven estimation of centiloid scales from amyloid pet images with ^{11}C-PiB and ^{18}F-labeled tracers in Alzheimer's disease. *Brain Sci.* **2024**, *14*, 406. https://doi.org/10.3390/brainsci14040406.
9. Saha, C.; Figley, C.R.; Lithgow, B.; Fitzgerald, P.B.; Koski, L.; Mansouri, B.; Anssari, N.; Wang, X.; Moussavi, Z. Can brain volume-driven characteristic features predict the response of Alzheimer's patients to repetitive transcranial magnetic stimulation? a pilot study. *Brain Sci.* **2024**, *14*, 226. https://doi.org/10.3390/brainsci14030226.
10. Grigas, O.; Damaševičius, R.; Maskeliūnas, R. Positive effect of super-resolved structural magnetic resonance imaging for mild cognitive impairment detection. *Brain Sci.* **2024**, *14*, 381. https://doi.org/10.3390/brainsci14040381.
11. Cerna, J.; Gupta, P.; He, M.; Ziegelman, L.; Hu, Y.; Hernandez, M.E. Tai chi practice buffers aging effects in functional brain connectivity. *Brain Sci.* **2024**, *14*, 901. https://doi.org/10.3390/brainsci14090901.
12. Sone, D.; Sato, N.; Shigemoto, Y.; Beheshti, I.; Kimura, Y.; Matsuda, H. Estimated disease progression trajectory of white matter disruption in unilateral temporal lobe epilepsy: A data-driven machine learning approach. *Brain Sci.* **2024**, *14*, 992. https://doi.org/10.3390/brainsci14100992.
13. Tadayyoni, H.; Campos, M.S.R.; Quevedo, A.J.U.; Murphy, B.A. Biomarkers of immersion in virtual reality based on features extracted from the EEG signals: A machine learning approach. *Brain Sci.* **2024**, *14*, 470. https://doi.org/10.3390/brainsci14050470.
14. Shih, Y.-T.; Wang, L.; Wong, C.H.Y.; Sin, E.L.L.; Rauterberg, M.; Yuan, Z.; Chang, L. The effects of distancing design collaboration necessitated by COVID-19 on brain synchrony in teams compared to co-located design collaboration: A preliminary study. *Brain Sci.* **2024**, *14*, 60. https://doi.org/10.3390/brainsci14010060.
15. Huynh, N.; Yan, D.; Ma, Y.; Wu, S.; Long, C.; Sami, M.T.; Almudaifer, A.; Jiang, Z.; Chen, H.; Dretsch, M.N.; et al. The use of generative adversarial network and graph convolution network for neuroimaging-based diagnostic classification. *Brain Sci.* **2024**, *14*, 456. https://doi.org/10.3390/brainsci14050456.
16. Huang, J. The commonality and individuality of human brains when performing tasks. *Brain Sci.* **2024**, *14*, 125. https://doi.org/10.3390/brainsci14020125.
17. Manabe, T.; Rahul, F.N.U.; Fu, Y.; Intes, X.; Schwaitzberg, S.D.; De, S.; Cavuoto, L.; Dutta, A. Distinguishing laparoscopic surgery experts from novices using EEG topographic features. *Brain Sci.* **2023**, *13*, 1706. https://doi.org/10.3390/brainsci13121706.

References

1. Ombao, H.; Lindquist, M.; Thompson, W.; Aston, J. (Eds.) *Handbook of Neuroimaging Data Analysis*; Chapman and Hall/CRC: New York, NY, USA, 2016.
2. Scott, M. (Ed.) *Encyclopedia of Neuroimaging: Volume VI (Advances and New Frontiers)*; Hayle Medical: New York, NY, USA, 2015.
3. Yen, C.; Lin, C.-L.; Chiang, M.-C. Exploring the frontiers of neuroimaging: A review of recent advances in understanding brain functioning and disorders. *Life* **2023**, *13*, 1472. [CrossRef] [PubMed]
4. Berson, E.R.; Aboian, M.S.; Malhotra, A.; Payabvash, S. Artificial intelligence for neuroimaging and musculoskeletal radiology: Overview of current commercial algorithms. *Semin. Roentgenol.* **2023**, *58*, 178–183. [CrossRef] [PubMed]
5. Borchert, R.J.; Azevedo, T.; Badhwar, A.; Bernal, J.; Betts, M.; Bruffaerts, R.; Burkhart, M.C.; Dewachter, I.; Gellersen, H.M.; Low, A.; et al. Artificial intelligence for diagnostic and prognostic neuroimaging in dementia: A systematic review. *Alzheimer's Dement.* **2023**, *19*, 5885–5904. [CrossRef] [PubMed]
6. Brahma, N.; Vimal, S. Artificial intelligence in neuroimaging: Opportunities and ethical challenges. *Brain Spine* **2024**, *4*, 102919. [CrossRef] [PubMed]
7. Choi, K.S.; Sunwoo, L. Artificial intelligence in neuroimaging: Clinical applications. *Investig. Magn. Reson. Imaging (iMRI)* **2022**, *26*, 1–9. [CrossRef]

8. Dalboni da Rocha, J.L.; Lai, J.; Pandey, P.; Myat, P.S.M.; Loschinskey, Z.; Bag, A.K.; Sitaram, R. Artificial intelligence for neuroimaging in pediatric cancer. *Cancers* **2025**, *17*, 622. [CrossRef] [PubMed]
9. Hao, B.; Leung, C.K.; Camorlinga, S.; Reed, M.H.; Bunge, M.K.; Wrogemann, J.; Higgins, R.J. A computer-aided change detection system for paediatric acute intracranial haemorrhage. In Proceedings of the C3S2E 2008, Montreal, QC, Canada, 12–13 May 2008; pp. 109–111. [CrossRef]
10. Monsour, R.; Dutta, M.; Mohamed, A.-Z.; Borkowski, A.; Viswanadhan, N.A. Neuroimaging in the era of artificial intelligence: Current applications. *Fed. Pract.* **2022**, *39* (Suppl. S1), S14–S20. [CrossRef] [PubMed]
11. Damer, A.; Chaudry, E.; Eftekhari, D.; Benseler, S.M.; Safi, F.; Aviv, R.I.; Tyrrell, P.N. Neuroimaging scoring tools to differentiate inflammatory central nervous system small-vessel vasculitis: A need for artificial intelligence/machine learning?—A scoping review. *Tomography* **2023**, *9*, 1811–1828. [CrossRef] [PubMed]
12. Pierre, K.; Turetsky, J.; Raviprasad, A.; Razavi, S.M.S.; Mathelier, M.; Patel, A.; Lucke-Wold, B. Machine learning in neuroimaging of traumatic brain injury: Current landscape, research gaps, and future directions. *Trauma Care* **2024**, *4*, 31–43. [CrossRef]
13. Xu, M.; Ouyang, Y.; Yuan, Z. Deep learning aided neuroimaging and brain regulation. *Sensors* **2023**, *23*, 4993. [CrossRef] [PubMed]

Disclaimer/Publisher's Note: The statements, opinions and data contained in all publications are solely those of the individual author(s) and contributor(s) and not of MDPI and/or the editor(s). MDPI and/or the editor(s) disclaim responsibility for any injury to people or property resulting from any ideas, methods, instructions or products referred to in the content.

brain sciences

MDPI

Article

Brain Tumor Classification from MRI Using Image Enhancement and Convolutional Neural Network Techniques

Zahid Rasheed [1], Yong-Kui Ma [1], Inam Ullah [2,*], Yazeed Yasin Ghadi [3], Muhammad Zubair Khan [4], Muhammad Abbas Khan [5], Akmalbek Abdusalomov [6], Fayez Alqahtani [7] and Ahmed M. Shehata [8]

1 School of Electronics and Information Engineering, Harbin Institute of Technology, Harbin 150001, China
2 Department of Computer Engineering, Gachon University, Sujeong-gu, Seongnam-si 13120, Republic of Korea
3 Department of Computer Science, Al Ain University, Abu Dhabi P.O. Box 112612, United Arab Emirates
4 Faculty of Basic Sciences, Balochistan University of Information Technology Engineering and Management Sciences, Quetta 87300, Pakistan
5 Department of Electrical Engineering, Balochistan University of Information Technology, Engineering and Management Sciences, Quetta 87300, Pakistan
6 Department of Artificial Intelligence, Tashkent State University of Economics, Tashkent 100066, Uzbekistan; bobomirzaevich@gmail.com
7 Software Engineering Department, College of Computer and Information Sciences, King Saud University, Riyadh 12372, Saudi Arabia
8 Computer Science and Engineering Department, Faculty of Electronic Engineering, Menoufia University, Menofia 32511, Egypt
* Correspondence: inam@gachon.ac.kr

Abstract: The independent detection and classification of brain malignancies using magnetic resonance imaging (MRI) can present challenges and the potential for error due to the intricate nature and time-consuming process involved. The complexity of the brain tumor identification process primarily stems from the need for a comprehensive evaluation spanning multiple modules. The advancement of deep learning (DL) has facilitated the emergence of automated medical image processing and diagnostics solutions, thereby offering a potential resolution to this issue. Convolutional neural networks (CNNs) represent a prominent methodology in visual learning and image categorization. The present study introduces a novel methodology integrating image enhancement techniques, specifically, Gaussian-blur-based sharpening and Adaptive Histogram Equalization using CLAHE, with the proposed model. This approach aims to effectively classify different categories of brain tumors, including glioma, meningioma, and pituitary tumor, as well as cases without tumors. The algorithm underwent comprehensive testing using benchmarked data from the published literature, and the results were compared with pre-trained models, including VGG16, ResNet50, VGG19, InceptionV3, and MobileNetV2. The experimental findings of the proposed method demonstrated a noteworthy classification accuracy of 97.84%, a precision success rate of 97.85%, a recall rate of 97.85%, and an F1-score of 97.90%. The results presented in this study showcase the exceptional accuracy of the proposed methodology in accurately classifying the most commonly occurring brain tumor types. The technique exhibited commendable generalization properties, rendering it a valuable asset in medicine for aiding physicians in making precise and proficient brain diagnoses.

Keywords: deep learning; brain tumor; magnetic resonance imaging; classification; neural network; pre-trained models; healthcare

1. Introduction

The development of a brain tumor can occur when there is an abnormal proliferation of cells within the brain tissues. Tumors have been identified by the World Health Organization (WHO) as the second most significant contributor to global mortality [1,2]. Brain tumors can be categorized into two main types: benign and malignant. In most instances, benign tumors are not considered a substantial risk to an individual's health. It is primarily due to their comparatively slower growth rate than malignant tumors, lack of ability to infiltrate adjacent tissues or cells, and inability to metastasize. Their recurrence is generally uncommon after the surgical removal of benign tumors.

Compared to benign tumors, malignant tumors can infiltrate adjacent tissues and organs, and if not promptly and effectively managed, they can result in significant physiological dysfunction. Detecting brain tumors in their earliest stages is crucial for optimizing the survival rate of patients. Gliomas, meningioma, and pituitary tumors are the three most frequently diagnosed types of brain tumors. Glioma is a neoplasm originating from the glial cells that encompass and provide support to neurons. The cellular composition of these structures includes astrocytes, oligodendrocytes, and ependymal cells. A pituitary tumor is formed within the pituitary gland. A meningioma is a tumor originating within the meninges, the three layers of tissue between the skull and the brain. According to the cited source, it has been established that meningiomas are classified as benign tumors, while gliomas are categorized as malignant tumors. Additionally, pituitary tumors have been identified as benign. The dissimilarity above represents the most notable differentiation among these three cancer variants [3–5].

Various symptoms can be produced by benign and malignant brain tumors, depending on factors such as their size, location, and growth rate. The symptoms of primary brain tumors may exhibit variability among individual patients. Glioma has the potential to induce various symptoms, including aphasia, visual impairments or loss, cognitive impairments, difficulties with walking or balance, and other associated manifestations. A meningioma is often associated with mild symptoms, including visual disturbances and morning migraines. Pituitary tumors can exert pressure on the optic nerve, leading to symptoms such as migraines, vision disorders, and diplopia [6,7].

Hence, it is imperative to distinguish among these diverse tumor classifications to precisely diagnose a patient and determine the optimal course of treatment. The expertise of radiologists significantly influences the speed at which they can detect brain malignancies. Although magnetic resonance imaging (MRI) presents challenges due to its dependence on human interpretation and the complexity of processing large volumes of data, it is commonly employed to categorize different forms of cancer. Biopsies are commonly employed in identifying and managing brain lesions, although their utilization before definitive brain surgery is infrequent. Developing a comprehensive diagnostic instrument for detecting and classifying tumors based on MR images is imperative [8]. The implementation of this approach will effectively mitigate the occurrence of excessive operations and uphold the impartiality of the diagnostic procedure. The healthcare industry has been significantly influenced by recent technological advancements, particularly in the fields of artificial intelligence (AI) and machine learning (ML) [9–12]. Solutions to various healthcare challenges, such as imaging, have been successfully identified [13–18]. Various machine-learning techniques have been developed to provide radiologists with unusual insights into the recognition and classification of MR images. Medical imaging techniques are widely recognized as highly effective and widely utilized modalities for cancer detection. These methodologies facilitate the identification and detection of malignant neoplasms. The methodology holds significance due to its non-invasive nature, as it does not require invasive procedures [19,20].

MRI and other imaging modalities are commonly employed in medical interventions because they produce distinct visual representations of brain tissue, facilitating the identification and categorization of diverse brain malignancies. Brain tumors exhibit various sizes, dimensions, and densities [21]. Moreover, it is worth noting that tumors can exhibit similar appearances, even when they possess distinct pathogenic characteristics. A substantial quantity of images within the database posed a significant challenge in classifying MR images utilizing specialized neural networks. Due to the ability to generate MR images in multiple planes, there is a potential for increased database sizes. In order to obtain the desired classification outcome, it is necessary to preprocess MR images before integrating them into different networks. The Convolutional Neural Network (CNN) is employed to solve this problem, benefiting from several advantages, such as reduced preprocessing and feature engineering requirements. A network with lower complexity necessitates a reduced allocation of resources for implementation and training compared to one with higher complexity. Resource limitations hinder the utilization of the system for medical diagnostics or on mobile platforms. The method must be relevant to brain disorders for daily regular clinical diagnosis.

The main contributions to this investigation are delineated as follows:

- This study presents a novel methodology integrating Gaussian-blur-based sharpening and Contrast-Limited Adaptive Histogram Equalization (CLAHE) with the proposed model to facilitate more precise diagnostic procedures for identifying glioma, meningioma, pituitary tumors, and cases without malignancies.
- This investigation aims to demonstrate the superiority of the proposed methodology above existing methodologies while highlighting its ability to achieve comparable results with fewer resources. Additionally, an assessment is conducted on the network's potential for integration into clinical research endeavors.
- The results obtained from this analysis demonstrate that the novel strategy surpasses previous methodologies, as indicated by its ability to attain the highest levels of accuracy on benchmark datasets. Further, we evaluate the prediction capabilities of this strategy by comparing it to pre-trained models and other established strategies.

The subsequent sections of this work delineate the literature review in Section 2. Section 3 explores the dataset, methodology, optimization techniques, and pre-trained models. Section 4 presents the findings obtained from the conducted experiments. Section 5 involves a discussion. Lastly, Section 6 provides a conclusive summary.

2. Literature Review

It is challenging to distinguish between various varieties of brain tumors. The authors [22] examined the clinical applications of DL in radiography and outlined the processes necessary for a DL project in this discipline. They also discussed the potential clinical applications of DL in various medical disciplines. In a few radiology applications, DL has demonstrated promising results, but the technology is not yet developed enough to replace the diagnostic occupation of a radiologist [23]. There is a possibility that DL algorithms and radiologists will collaborate to enhance diagnostic effectiveness and efficiency. Numerous studies have investigated the capability of MRI to identify and classify brain tumors utilizing a variety of research methodologies. Afshar et al. developed a modified version of the CapsNet architecture for categorizing the primary brain tumor consisting of 3064 images using tumor boundaries as supplementary inputs to increase effort, surpass previous techniques, and achieve a classification rate of 90.89% [24]. Gumaei et al. proposed a brain tumor classification method using hybrid feature extraction techniques and RELM. The authors preprocessed brain images using min–max normalization, extracted features using the hybrid method, classified them using RELM, and achieved a maximum accuracy of 94.23% [25].

Kaplan et al. proposed brain tumor classification models using nLBP and αLBP feature extraction methods. These models accurately classified the most common brain tumor types, including glioma, meningioma, and pituitary tumors, and achieved a high accuracy of 95.56% using the nLBPD = 1 feature extraction method and KNN model [19]. Rezaei et al. developed an integrated approach for segmenting and classifying brain tumors in MRI images. The methods included noise removal, SVM-based segmentation, feature extraction, and selection using DE. Tumor slices were classified using KNN, WSVM, and HIK-SVM classifiers. Combined with MODE-based ensemble techniques, these classifiers achieved a 92.46% accuracy rate [26]. Fouad et al. developed a brain tumor classification method using HDWT-HOG feature descriptors and the WOA for feature reduction. The approach utilized the Bagging ensemble techniques and achieved an average accuracy of 96.4% with Bagging, and, when used, Boosting attained 95.8% [27].

Ayadi et al. presented brain tumor classification techniques using normalization, dense speeded-up robust features, and the histogram of gradient approaches to enhance the image quality and generate a discriminative feature. In addition, they used SVM for classification and achieved a 90.27% accuracy on the benchmarked dataset [28]. Srujan et al. built a DL system with sixteen layers of CNN to classify the tumor types by leveraging activation functions like ReLU and Adam optimizer, and the system achieved a 95.36% accuracy [29]. Tejaswini et al. proposed a CNN model to detect meningioma, glioma, and pituitary brain tumors with an average training accuracy of 92.79% and validation accuracy of 87.16%; in addition, the tumor region segmentation was performed using Otsu thresholding, Fuzzy c-means, and watershed techniques [30]. Huang et al. developed a CNNBCN to classify brain tumors. The network structure was generated using a random graph algorithm, achieving an accuracy of 95.49% [31].

Ghassemi et al. suggested a DL framework for brain tumor classification. The authors used pre-trained networks as GAN discriminators to extract robust features and learn MR image structures. By replacing the fully connected layers and incorporating techniques like data augmentation and dropout, the method achieved a 95.6% accuracy using fivefold cross-validation [32]. Deepak et al. combined the CNN feature with SVM for the medical image classification of brain tumors. The automated system achieved an accuracy of 95.82% evaluated on the fivefold cross-validation procedure, outperforming the state-of-the-art method [33]. Noreen et al. adapted fine-tuned pre-trained networks, such as InceptionV3 and Xception, for identifying brain tumors. The models were integrated with various ML methods, namely Softmax, SVM, Random Forest, and KNN, and achieved a 94.34% accuracy with the InceptionV3 ensemble [34]. Shaik et al. addressed the challenging task of brain tumor classification in medical image analysis. The authors introduced a multi-level attention mechanism, MANet, which combined spatial and cross-channel attention to prioritize tumors and maintain cross-channel temporal dependencies. The method achieved a 96.51% accuracy for primary brain tumor classification [35].

Ahmad et al. proposed a deep generative neural network for brain tumor classification. The method combined variational auto encoders and generative adversarial networks to generate realistic brain tumor MRI images and achieved an accuracy of 96.25% [36]. Alanazi et al. proposed a deep transfer learning model for the early diagnosis of brain tumor subtypes. The method involved constructing isolated CNN models and adjusting the weights of a 22-layer CNN model using transfer learning. The developed model obtained 95.75- and 96.89-percent accuracies on MRI images [37]. Almalki et al. used an ML approach with MRI to promptly diagnose brain tumor severity (glioma, meningioma, pituitary, and no tumor). They extracted Gaussian and nonlinear scale features, capturing small details by breaking MRIs into 8×8-pixel images. The strongest features were selected and segmented into 400 Gaussian and 400 nonlinear scale features, and they were hybridized with each MRI. They obtained a 95.33% accuracy using the SVM classifier [38]. Kumar et al. compared three CNN models (AlexNet, ResNet50, and InceptionV3) to classify the primary tumor types and employed data augmentation techniques. The results showed that AlexNet achieved an accuracy of 96.2%, surpassing the other models [39].

Swati et al. employed a pre-trained deep CNN model and proposed a block-wise fine-tuning technique using transfer learning. This approach was evaluated using a standardized dataset consisting of T1-weighted images. Using minimal preprocessing techniques and excluding handcrafted features, the strategy demonstrated an accuracy of 94.82% with VGG19, VGG16 achieved 94.65%, and AlexNet achieved 89.95% when evaluated using a fivefold cross-validation methodology [40]. Ekong et al. integrated depth-wise separable convolutions with Bayesian techniques to precisely classify and predict brain cancers. The recommended technique demonstrated superior performance compared to existing methods in terms of an accuracy of 94.32% [41].

Asiri et al. enhanced computer-aided systems and facilitated physician learning using artificially generated medical imaging data. A deep learning technique, a Generative Adversarial Network (GAN), was employed, wherein a generator and a discriminator engage in a competitive process to generate precise MRI data. The proposed methodology demonstrated a notable level of precision, with an accuracy rate of 96%. The evaluation of this approach was conducted using a dataset comprising MRI scans collected from various Chinese hospitals throughout the period spanning from 2005 to 2020 [42]. Shilaskar et al. proposed a system comprising three main components: preprocessing, HOG for feature extraction, and classification. The results indicated varying levels of accuracy when employing multiple machine learning classifiers, including SVM, Gradient Boosting, KNN, XG Boost, and Logistic Regression, with the XG Boost classifier attaining the highest accuracy rate of 92.02% [43].

3. Materials and Methods

This section presents the proposed method, which consists of two primary components: image preprocessing and model training. The flowchart illustrating the suggested system is presented in Figure 1. To enhance the quality of the image, the preprocessing stage incorporated Gaussian-blur-based sharpening and Adaptive Histogram Equalization techniques using CLAHE. Subsequently, labeled images were resized while maintaining the aspect ratio, normalized, and divided into three sets, as shown in Figure 2. Furthermore, the model underwent training using 5-fold cross-validation [44] using the Adam optimizer and incorporated the ReduceLROnPlateau callbacks to dynamically regulate the learning rate throughout the training process. The effectiveness of the proposed model was evaluated using metrics such as accuracy, precision, recall, and F1-score.

This study employed a publicly accessible MRI dataset Msoud [45], obtained from the Kaggle repository. This dataset combines three publicly accessible datasets, including Figshare [46], SARTAJ [47], and BR35H [48]. It consists of 7023 MRIs of the human brain provided in grayscale and jpg format. The dataset includes primary types of brain tumors, namely glioma, meningioma, pituitary tumors, and images without tumors.

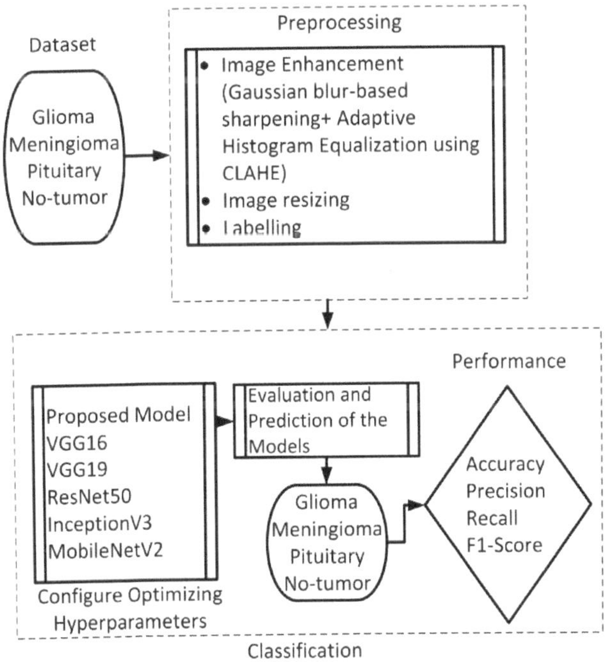

Figure 1. Flow chart of the suggested scheme.

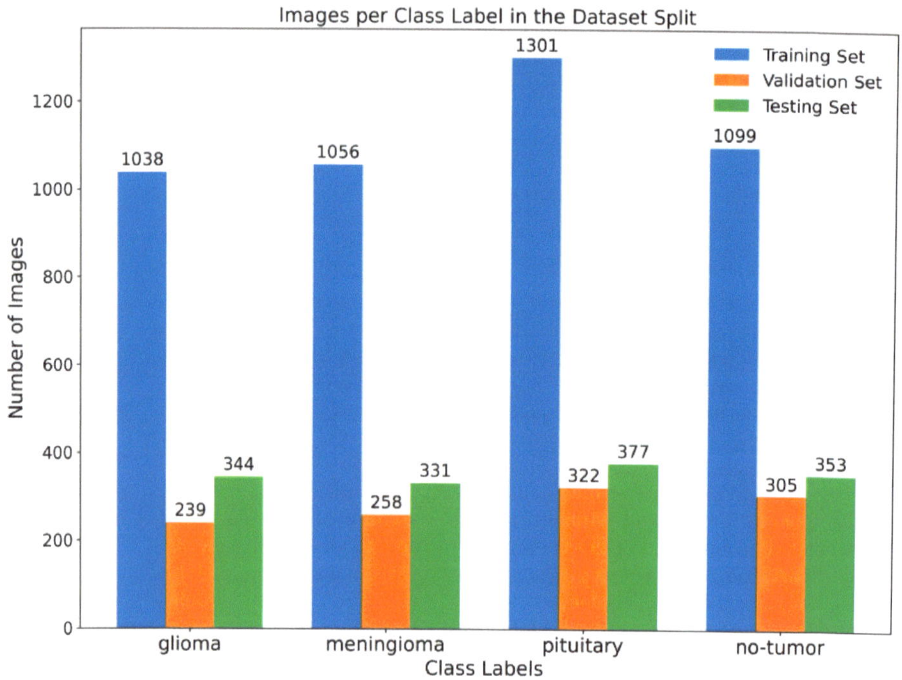

Figure 2. Illustration of the distribution of images among various class labels throughout the training, validation, and testing dataset splits. The bar graph displays the distribution of images across different classes, with the training set at 64%, the validation set at 16%, and the testing set at 20%.

3.1. Preprocessing

We implemented a preprocessing framework to improve image quality by integrating sharpening and Contrast-Limited Adaptive Histogram Equalization (CLAHE) approaches. The process of sharpening commenced by implementing a Gaussian blur through the utilization of a specific technique. The utilization of a 5×5 kernel was suitable in the process of attenuating high-frequency noise. The resultant enhanced image was determined using the formula:

$$Sharpened\ Image = 1.5 \times Original\ Image - 0.5 \times Blurred\ Image \tag{1}$$

Subsequently, the image underwent a conversion process to grayscale, facilitating a precise enhancement of contrast. To achieve this, CLAHE was utilized, characterized by an 8×8-tile grid and a clip limit of 2.0. Distinct from global histogram equalization, CLAHE adopts a localized strategy by partitioning the image into discrete tiles and performing individual equalizations, encapsulated by

$$H_{local}(i) = CLAHE(H_{tile}(i)) \tag{2}$$

In order to ensure accordance with the specifications of the subsequent deep learning framework, the enhanced grayscale image was transformed into the RGB color space [49,50]. Figure 3 illustrates the several stages of enhancing picture quality, from the initial image to the CLAHE-enhanced image. This depiction showcases the effectiveness of our preprocessing method and its notable impact on improving the overall quality of the image.

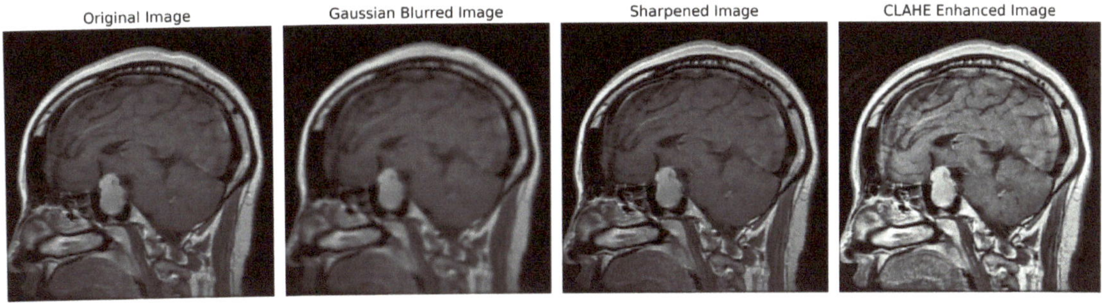

Figure 3. Sequential image improvement as part of the preprocessing framework. The stages progress from the unaltered original image through Gaussian blurring for noise suppression, sharpening the emphasized edge definition to the final enhancement using CLAHE.

3.2. Proposed Architecture

Figure 4 depicts the proposed model, which acquires MRI data with input dimensions of 224 × 224 and reveals its operational characteristics. The model consists of multiple server blocks. A convolutional layer [51] was employed in the initial stage, consisting of 16 filters. Each filter was employed with a kernel size of 3 × 3 and a stride size of 1 × 1. A normalizing layer [52] and a 2D (two-dimensional) max pooling layer with a size of 2 × 2 were employed to maximize the information among the intermediate layer's output. Similarly, we integrated additional convolutional layers into the model, utilizing 32, 64, 128, and 256 filter sizes. Each filter utilized in this study had a kernel size of 3 × 3 and a stride size of 1 × 1, and the same and valid padding was suitable for the experiment. As illustrated in Figure 4, skip connections were employed within each block to facilitate the information flow by concatenating the outputs of specific convolutional layers. Subsequently, a dense layer of 512 neurons was employed, accompanied by global average pooling and activation through the rectified linear unit (ReLU) function.

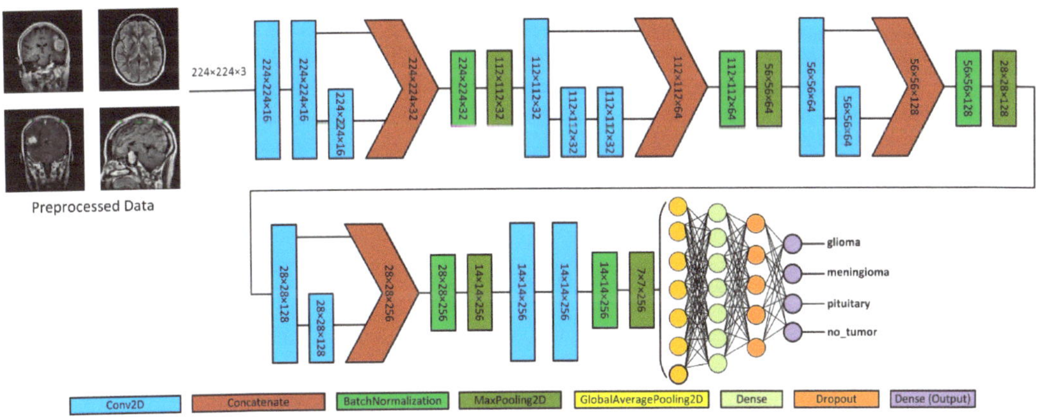

Figure 4. Illustration of the proposed architecture and various forms of brain tumors.

To mitigate the issue of overfitting, the dense layer was subjected to regulation using L1 (10^{-5}) and L2 (10^{-4}) regularization techniques [53]. During the training process, the neurons within a dropout layer [54] were randomly deactivated at a rate of 0.5% to enhance regularization implementation further. Finally, the output layer employed the softmax algorithm [51] to compute the probability score for each class and classify whether the input image exhibited a glioma, meningioma, pituitary, or no tumor. In addition, the model employed the Adam optimizer [55,56], categorical cross-entropy for loss functions, and the ReduceLROnPlateau callback to optimize the learning rate [57]. The model was trained with a batch size of 8 for 30 epochs.

Convolutional neural networks are widely used for image classification tasks. In the proposed model, 2D convolution involved applying a kernel to the input data to extract features. The convolution operation captures spatial dependencies and hierarchies within the data. The convolution operation in a 2D CNN can be mathematically defined as follows:

$$Y_{ij} = \sum_m \sum_n X_{(i+m)(j+n)} \cdot K_{mn} \tag{3}$$

where Y_{ij} represents the output element at the position i, j; $X_{(i+m)(j+n)}$ denotes the input elements at the position $(i + m, j + n)$; and $K_{(mn)}$ signifies the kernel element at the position (m, n). The equation involves summing the element-wise multiplication of the input element and corresponding kernel element across the indices m and n. This operation is applied across the entire input to compute the element of the output feature map. The convolution operation efficiently captures local patterns and interactions between neighboring elements, enabling the network to learn the hierarchical representation and extract meaningful features from the input data. Furthermore, the convolutional operation involved applying the kernel to input using a sliding window. The kernel size determines the local region considered, and the stride size controls the movement of the kernel. Padding preserves spatial dimensions. The output size can be calculated using the following equation.

$$O = \left\lfloor \frac{I - K + 2P}{S} \right\rfloor + 1 \tag{4}$$

where O represents the output size, I denotes the input size, K represents the kernel size, S denotes the stride size, and P represents the padding size [51].

3.2.1. Batch Normalization

Batch normalization (BN) is used in deep neural networks to normalize the intermediate layers' outputs. It suits internal covariate shifts, improving training, stability, and performance. In our proposed model, we incorporated the BN layer, following the skip connections and preceding the Max Pooling layer. The rationale behind this design was attributed to the function of skip connections, which involves the concatenation of feature maps originating from distinct layers. Including the BN layer immediately after ensures that the aggregated feature maps undergo normalization, preserving a uniform scale and distribution before pooling. In addition to normalization, the positioning of BN also provides regularization, hence mitigating the potential issue of overfitting and ensuring that the pooling layer functions on standardized activations. The equation can represent the normalization process.

$$y = \frac{x - \mu}{\sigma} . \gamma + \beta \tag{5}$$

where x is the input; μ and σ; are the mean and standard deviation computed over a mini-batch size, respectively; and γ and β are learnable scaling and shifting parameters, respectively.

3.2.2. Pooling Layers

The pooling operation is used in a CNN for downsampling, and the input feature map is divided into non-overlapping regions or pooling windows. The purpose is to calculate the maximum value of each window, resulting in a downscaled output feature map. The following equation represents the max pooling operation at the position (i, j) in the output feature map.

$$Maxpooling(x)(i, j) = (\forall m, n) \max(x)(i + m, j + n) \tag{6}$$

Max pooling $(x)(i, j)$ denotes the value at the position (i, j) in the output feature map after max pooling. The term $\forall m, n$ represents the double summation over the indices m and n and covers all possible values within the pooling windows. $\max(x)(i + m, j + n)$ represents the maximum value among the neighboring elements in the input feature map, specifically at positions $(i + m, j + n)$. The global average pooling (GAP) operation reduces the spatial dimension of a feature map while capturing the average representation of the entire feature map. The GAP can be formulated as follows:

$$GobalAvgPooling(x) = \frac{1}{k \times 1} \sum_{i=1}^{k} \sum_{j=1}^{l} x_{i,j} \tag{7}$$

The equation illustrates the operational mechanism of GAP applied to a feature map (x). The feature map is characterized by l dimensions for height, width, and channels (k). The symbol $\sum$ denotes the mathematical operation of summation and the variables i and j are employed to iterate through the spatial dimensions of the feature map. The k values in the resulting vector correspond to the mean activation of the relevant channel across all spatial positions in the feature map [53].

3.2.3. Activation and Loss Functions

ReLU is an activation function that introduces nonlinearity into a neural network [58]. It takes an input value and returns the maximum value and 0. Mathematically the ReLU function can be defined as

$$ReLU(x) = max(0, x) \tag{8}$$

where x is the input value; if the input value is positive, *ReLU* outputs the same value. If the input value is negative, *ReLU* outputs 0.

The utilization of the softmax function occurs in the output layer of the proposed model planned for multi-classification tasks. The process converts a vector of real input values into a probability distribution across different classes. The mathematical expression for the softmax role is as follows:

$$Softmax(x_i) = \frac{exp(x_i)}{\sum_{j=1}^{4} exp(x_j)}, for\ i = 1, 2, 3, 4 \tag{9}$$

The equation x_i represents the i-th element of the input vector, and the softmax function normalizes each probability by dividing it by the sum of the exponential value of all probabilities in the vector. Furthermore, the loss function was utilized to measure the discrepancy between the algorithm's predictions and actual values. Various optimization techniques can be applied to minimize this error. In addition, categorical cross-entropy was chosen as the loss function. Categorical cross-entropy can be calculated as the error rate using the equation.

$$Categorical\ Cross\ Entropy = -\sum_{i}^{N} y_{true}[i].log(y_{pred}[i]) \tag{10}$$

where N is the number of classes, $y_{true}[i]$ represents the true class probabilities, and $y_{pred}[i]$ denotes the predicted probabilities of each class.

3.2.4. Optimization Techniques

Several regularization strategies were used in the proposed model, including dropout, L1, L2, and ReduceLROnPlateau callbacks to reduce the overfitting in neural networks. Dropout arbitrarily changes a small portion of the input units (neurons) to zero during the training phase [59]. By preventing the network from being overly dependent on particular units and encouraging generalization, this dropout process aids in the network learning redundant representations. The model becomes more resilient and enhances its capacity to perform effectively on unknown data by injecting this unpredictability through the 50%

dropout rate, thereby improving its overall performance. The 50% dropout example is shown in Figure 5.

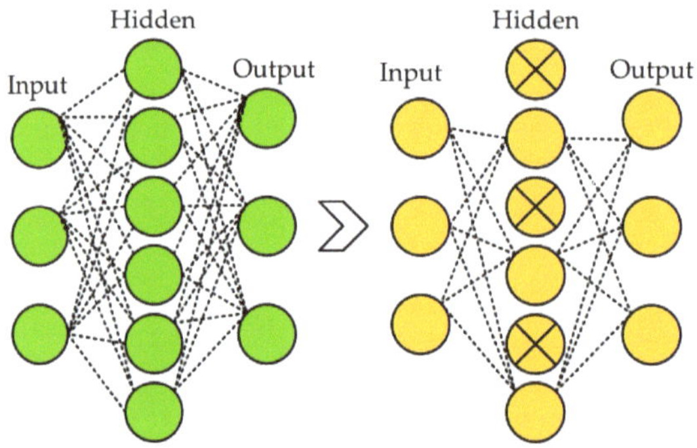

Figure 5. The right side of the diagram visually depicts a dropout layer characterized by a dropout rate of 50%.

L1 and L2 strategies are employed in the neural network to mitigate the issue of overfitting and enhance the accuracy when activated with novel data from the problem domain [60]. These techniques were employed in the proposed model due to their effectiveness among the standard regularization methods. L1 regularization is also known as Lasso regression, and L2 regularization is known as weight decay or ridge regression. The cost drives for L1 and L2 can be defined as follows:

$$\begin{array}{c} L1Regularization(LassoRegression): \\ Cost\ Function = Loss\ Funtion + \lambda\sum_{i=1}^{N}|w_i| \\ L2Regularization(Weight\ Decay\ or\ RidgeRegression): \\ Cost\ Function = Loss\ Funtion + \lambda\sum_{i=1}^{N}|w_i^2| \end{array} \tag{11}$$

where λ is the hyperparameter that regulates the strength of regularization, N is denoted as the model factors, w_i embodies i-th parameters, and $\sum$ denotes the sum of all parameters. The cost function combines the loss, representing the error between predicted and target values, with a regularization term to form the overall objective function.

In the proposed model, we utilized the ReduceLROnPlateau from Keras [61]. This callback is crucial in reducing the learning rate (LR) during the model training phase, specifically when validation losses showed no further improvement. Incorporating this callback enabled the optimization process to take smaller steps toward minimizing the loss function, resulting in a more efficient model. During the training phase, the ReduceLROnPlateau callback monitored the chosen metric, such as validation loss. The system recorded the optimal observed value for this metric and assessed whether the current value demonstrated improvement over a predetermined number of epochs. If the monitored metric did not exhibit improvement, the callback triggered a reduction in the learning rate. We employed a factor that was set while configuring the ReduceLROnPlateau callbacks to achieve the learning rate reduction. In the proposed model, we initially set the learning rate to 0.001 and utilized a reduction factor (F) of 0.4; the new learning rate (New LR) can be calculated by applying the given equation.

$$New\ LR = LR \times F \tag{12}$$

3.3. Pre-Trained Model

Pre-trained neural networks are ML models that have undergone training on extensive datasets like ImageNet, consisting of various images belonging to various classes. Pre-trained models have proven highly advantageous in various tasks, including image classification and object detection. Pre-trained models are employed because of their ability to graph data patterns, allowing them to be used as a starting point for new tasks without having to start the training process from scratch. This investigation included five pre-trained models, namely VGG16, ResNet50, MobileNetV2, InceptionV3, and VGG19.

3.3.1. VGG16

The VGG16 model was initially presented in 2014 by Simonyan and Zisserman [62], scholars affiliated with the Visual Geometry Group at the University of Oxford. The architectural design incorporates filters of dimensions 3 × 3, a stride of 1, and 16 layers, consisting of three fully connected layers and thirteen convolutional layers. The maximum pooling layers employ pooling windows with dimensions of 2 by 2 and a stride of 2. VGG16, a widely recognized choice for efficient feature extraction in transfer learning, boasts a substantial parameter count of 138 million.

3.3.2. ResNet50

Deep neural networks demonstrate improved performance as their depth increases, as evidenced in the literature [63]. The challenges related to this improvement arise from vanishing or exploding gradients, manifesting as the neural network expands. To overcome this impediment, the authors of [64] have proposed ResNet50, an innovative approach that utilizes residual modules to facilitate the learning of residual mapping instead of conventional input–output mapping. This innovative approach involves incorporating the input into the output of the modules through shortcut connections that circumvent certain levels. Consequently, including residual blocks effectively mitigates the problem of vanishing gradients, thereby preventing a decline in performance as the network depth increases. The ResNet50 architecture incorporates convolutional layers of varying filter sizes (1 × 1, 3 × 3, 1 × 1) within bottleneck blocks interspersed with max pooling and average pooling layers to facilitate extracting features from the input.

3.3.3. MobileNetV2

The architectural design aims to provide mobile and embedded applications, achieving a remarkable balance between high accuracy, lightweight computation, and optimal memory usage. The employed model utilized three primary strategies: the inverted residual, the linear bottleneck, and the width multiplier parameters. Using convolutional layers in the inverted residual technique increases network capacity while concurrently reducing the computational requirements and memory usage. The input is improved by increasing the number of channels and applying convolution using a small kernel size to achieve this objective. Subsequently, the resulting output is projected onto a reduced number of channels. In contrast, linear bottlenecks employ a linear activation function instead of a non-linear one, aiming to minimize the number of parameters needed. Furthermore, utilizing width multiplier parameters can adjust the number of channels within a network, thereby introducing enhanced adaptability [65].

3.3.4. InceptionV3

The InceptionV3 architecture is a CNN that belongs to the inception series. It is recognized for its significant advancements compared to previous iterations. The proposed approach employs an advanced design strategy wherein the network's capacity is expanded by incorporating multiple kernel sizes at a given level instead of increasing depth through stacked layers. The proposed methodology employs inception modules, which integrate a max pooling layer with varying kernel sizes of 1 × 1, 3 × 3, and 5 × 5 to effectively capture a wide range of features at different scales. The resulting output is obtained by concatenating the outputs of these layers, which is achieved by including a 1 × 1 convolution layer before the 3 × 3 and 5 × 5 convolutional layers. This additional layer decreases the number of input channels and optimizes the utilization of computational resources [66].

3.3.5. VGG19

The VGG19 architecture modified the VGG16 architecture, encompassing nineteen layers. This included sixteen convolutional layers, three fully connected layers, a compact filter with dimensions of 3 × 3, and a stride size 1. Additionally, the model incorporated max pooling layers that employ a pooling of size 2 × 2 and a stride size of 2. With a parameter count of 144 million, this model surpasses VGG16 in terms of power, although at the cost of increased computational requirements [62].

4. Experimental Results

This study employed the proposed model to categorize a substantial MRI dataset comprising 7023 images. The dataset encompassed glioma, meningioma, pituitary cases, and cases with no tumor. Initially, a preprocessing stage was incorporated to enhance the feature extraction. In this stage, image enhancement techniques with Gaussian blur and CLAHE were applied to improve the quality of the images. The dataset was divided into subsets, namely training, validation, and testing. The dataset was trained using the Adam optimizer and subsequently assessed through a fivefold cross-validation method. Algorithm 1 presents the procedure for the training and evaluation process.

Algorithm 1: Training and Evaluation Process with 5-fold Cross-Validation

1. Initialize Metrics List
. final_test_metrics = []
2. Combine Training and Validation sets
. S = N train + N val where S represents the dataset
3. 5-Fold Cross - Validation
. For i in {1, 2, 3, 4, 5}:
3.1. Data Splitting
. $Train_i = S - S_i$
. $Val_i = S_i$
3.2. Train Model
.Train the model on $Train_i$ *and validate on* Val_i
.Setup Callbacks and Optimizer
3.3. Evaluate on Test set (T) where T represents the testing data
.temp_metrics = Model. Evaluate (T)
.Append temp_metrics to final_test_metrics
4. Calculate Average Test Metrics
.Metrics final = $\frac{1}{5}\sum_{i=1}^{5} final\_test\_metrics[i]$
5. Output
. Metrics final contains the average values on the set T

The learning rates were optimized using the ReduceLROnPlateau callbacks, and a batch size of 8 was utilized. Figure 6 presents the average accuracy and losses of the model proposed in this study. During the initial stage of training, the graphs display fluctuations, which can be attributed to the utilization of the ReduceLROnPlateau callback. The primary objective of this callback is to dynamically modify the learning rate of the optimizer during the training process, specifically when the loss function reaches a plateau. After completing 12 epochs, the optimizer demonstrates a gradual convergence toward an optimal configuration of weights, resulting in diminished fluctuations observed in the accuracy and loss curves.

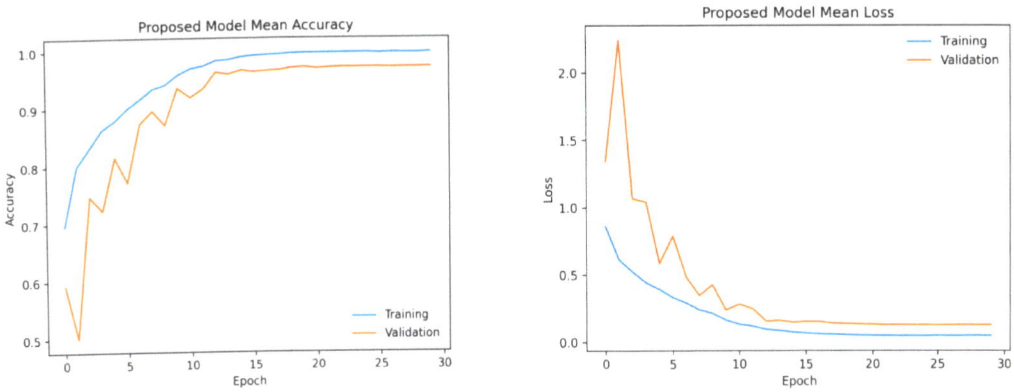

Figure 6. Mean accuracy and losses of the proposed model during 5-fold cross-validation. (**Left**): mean accuracy progression across training folds. (**Right**): corresponding mean loss trend. This demonstrates consistent accuracy improvement and decreasing loss, highlighting effective model training.

Furthermore, the platform utilized several libraries, such as Numpy, Pandas, Matplotlib, Sklearn, Keras, and TensorFlow, to enhance the efficiency of data processing and model development. The computation was performed on an Intel Core i7-7800 CPU operating at a clock speed of 3.5 GHz. The model training and tuning were managed using an NVIDIA GeForce GTX 1080 Ti GPU. The selection of Python 3.7 as the primary programming language for this study was based on its comprehensive set of tools for data manipulation, analysis, and visualization. The platform successfully preserved the data employed in this study due to its substantial RAM capacity of 32 GB.

Model Evaluation Matrices

The suggested framework was subjected to a thorough evaluation, which involved an analysis of its precision, recall, F1-score, and accuracy. Precision evaluates the model's ability to minimize the misclassification of negative examples as positive, and the term "is derived from" refers to the calculation of a specific metric, which is obtained by dividing the number of true positives by the sum of true positives and false positives. However, it is important to note that recall is a metric that measures the model's capacity to classify the appropriate tumor type accurately. This is calculated by dividing the number of true positives by the sum of true positives and false negatives. The F1-score is a metric used in evaluation that quantifies the balance between precision and recall. It is calculated as the harmonic mean of precision and recall, obtained by multiplying precision and recall and dividing the result by their sum, multiplied by two. In the context of classification models, accuracy measures the model's overall performance by quantifying the proportion of correct classifications. It is calculated by dividing the number of accurate predictions by the total number of predictions made. Equations (13)–(16) indicate the mathematical representations of precision, recall, F1-score, and accuracy [67].

$$Precision = \frac{TP}{TP + FP} \tag{13}$$

$$Recall = \frac{TP}{TP + FN} \tag{14}$$

$$F1 - Score = 2 \times \frac{Recall \times Precision}{Recall + Precision} \tag{15}$$

$$Accuracy = \frac{TP + TN}{TP + TN + FP + FN} \tag{16}$$

The evaluation results, including the average precision, recall, F1-score, and accuracy for both the proposed and pre-trained models, are presented in Table 1. The suggested framework demonstrated a notable accuracy rate of 97.84%. Moreover, it achieved precision and recall values of 97.85% and an F1-score of 97.90%. On the contrary, the InceptionV3 model exhibited the lowest performance, achieving an accuracy of 88.15%, a precision rate of 87.70%, a recall rate of 87.89%, and an F1-score rate of 87.60%. The observed variation in the performance of InceptionV3 can be ascribed to its utilization of multiple and parallel modules, which may not be well suited for the specific characteristics of this dataset, as supported by our research findings. The pre-trained models VGG16, ResNet50, and VGG19 exhibited superior performance compared to MobileNetV2. Furthermore, the pre-trained models employed the standard input dimensions, including VGG16, VGG19, ResNet50, and MobileNetV2 with dimensions of 224 × 224 and InceptionV3 with dimensions of 299 × 229. In order to preserve the pre-existing weights, the layers of the base model were designated as non-trainable.

Table 1. Evaluation results of proposed and pre-trained models.

Models Name	Total Params:	Precision Average (%)	Recall Average (%)	F1-Score Average (%)	Accuracy Average (%)	Testing Time Average (s)
VGG16	14,979,396	95.00	94.85	94.90	95.00	2.29
ResNet50	24,638,852	94.59	94.64	94.55	94.75	1.91
InceptionV3	55,362,340	87.70	87.89	87.60	88.15	2.61
MobileNetV2	2,915,908	91.65	91.40	91.60	91.73	0.99
VGG19	20,289,092	94.80	94.65	94.70	94.83	2.64
Proposed Model	1,708,356	97.85	97.85	97.90	97.84	0.83

The utilization of the confusion matrix is a fundamental assessment instrument for classification models [68]. The proposed network demonstrated robust capabilities in accurately classifying various types of brain tumors, effectively identifying each type during the examination. Figure 7 presents a visual representation of the results obtained from the testing data, enabling a comparison between the proposed and pre-trained models. The comparison reveals that the proposed model outperformed the pre-trained models in performance. The proposed model demonstrated high accuracy in predicting glioma, achieving 97%, and meningioma, achieving a 96% accuracy rate. Additionally, it achieved a 99% accuracy rate in predicting pituitary and no-tumor cases. These results surpass the performance of pre-trained models. However, it is crucial to emphasize that the efficacy of treatment for glioma and meningioma in this study did not achieve comparable levels of success. This finding underscores the necessity for additional research and investigation in subsequent studies.

Furthermore, the Receiver Operating Characteristics (ROC) curve is a visual representation of the performance of a classification model across different classification thresholds [69]. The True Positive Rate (TPR) and False Positive Rate (FPR) are graphically represented. The ROC curve illustrates the balance between correctly identifying positive and incorrectly classifying negative instances as positive at all classification thresholds on the testing set. The ROC curve provides insights into the model's ability to differentiate between different thresholds effectively.

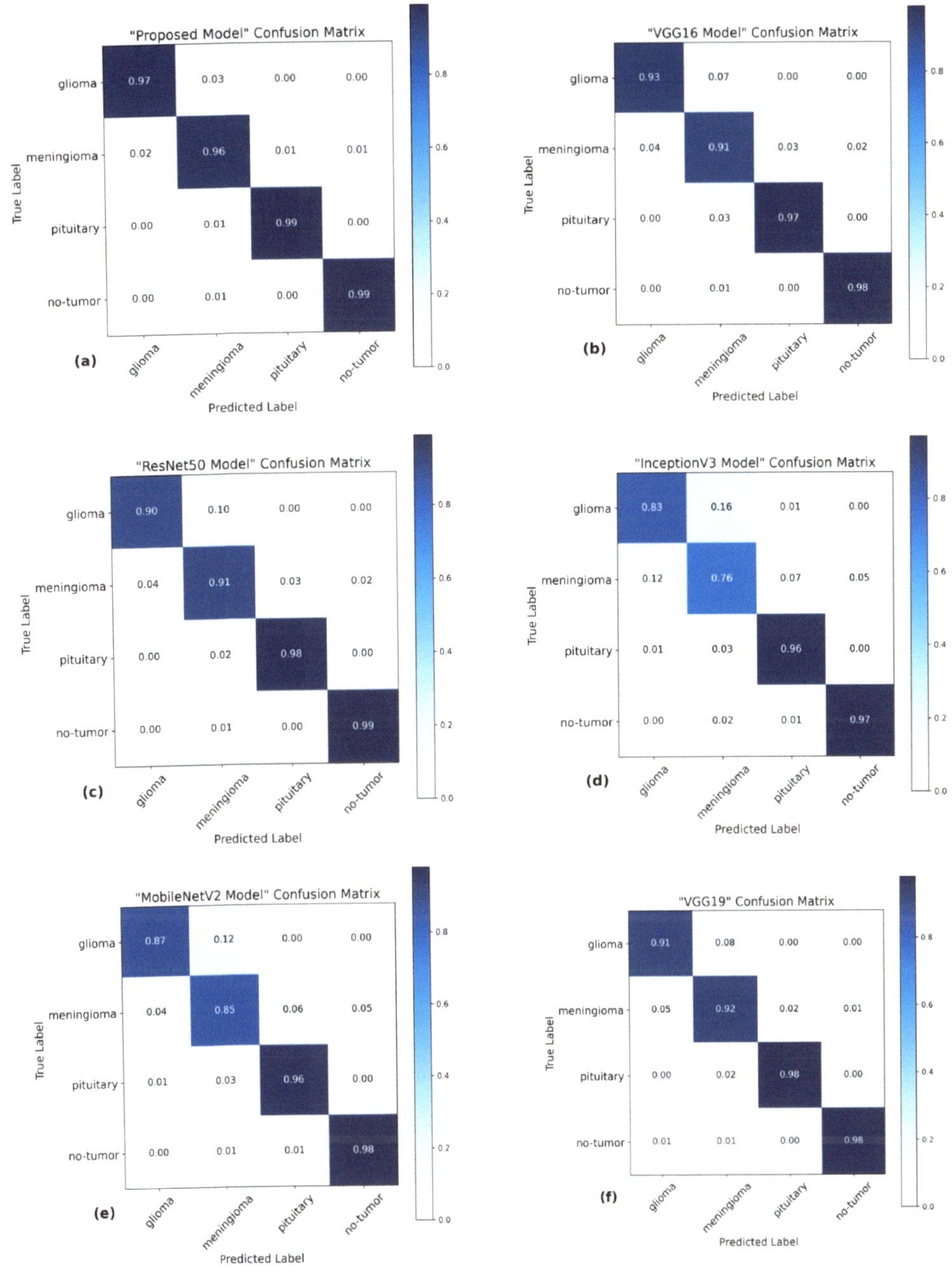

Figure 7. Confusion matrices of several models using the testing data. (**a**) The proposed model has a high level of accuracy, achieving a score of 97.84%. (**b**) VGG16 model achieved a classification accuracy of 95.00%. (**c**) ResNet50 model achieved an accuracy of 94.75%. (**d**) The accuracy of InceptionV3 is 88.15%. (**e**) MobileNetV2 model achieved a classification accuracy of 91.73%. (**f**) VGG19 model achieved a classification accuracy of 94.83%.

The present investigation demonstrates the proposed framework's superior diagnostic efficacy compared to pre-trained designs. The findings of this study provide evidence supporting the suggested model's higher diagnostic accuracy compared to state-of-the-art methodologies. When comparing the performance of the VGG16 architecture, it was observed that it achieved scores of 0.95 for glioma, 0.93 for meningioma, 0.97 for pituitary, and 0.98 for the no-tumor category. The ResNet50 architecture achieved classification scores of 0.92, 0.93, 0.97, and 0.98 for the glioma, meningioma, pituitary, and no-tumor classes, respectively. The InceptionV3 model yielded predictive scores of 0.84 for glioma, 0.81 for meningioma, 0.96 for pituitary, and 0.97 for the no-tumor category. The MobileNetV2 design achieved scores of 0.90, 0.86, 0.97, and 0.98 for the glioma, meningioma, pituitary, and no-tumor categories, respectively. Additionally, the VGG19 architecture demonstrated classification scores of 0.92 for glioma, 0.93 for meningioma, 0.98 for the pituitary, and 0.98 for the no-tumor category.

The model under consideration demonstrates notable performance regarding ROC scores. The achieved classification accuracies are as follows: 0.98 for glioma, 0.97 for meningioma, 0.99 for pituitary, and a flawless accuracy of 1.00 for the no-tumor category. The robust performance of the model is supported by a collective ROC score of 98.50%, as depicted in Figure 8, compared to pre-trained models.

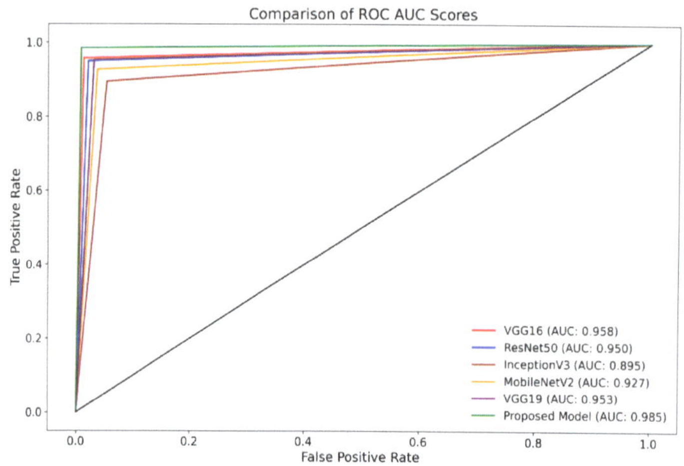

Figure 8. Illustration of a comprehensive visual representation that compares the proposed model's overall ROC score with other pre-trained models.

5. Discussion

This investigation introduces a novel methodology for categorizing the Msoud dataset, which consists of a varied assortment of 7023 brain images. The efficacy of the proposed system is demonstrated by its capacity to attain highly precise prediction outcomes, surpassing prior research endeavors with comparable aims. Moreover, this study proposes a method that does not rely on segmenting brain tumor images for classification purposes. The primary advantage of our approach resides in its capacity to substantially diminish the requirement for manual procedures, such as feature extraction and tumor localization. These processes are not only time-intensive but also susceptible to inaccuracies. By employing various enhancement techniques, including sharpening with Gaussian blur and Contrast-Limited Adaptive Histogram Equalization (CLAHE), notable enhancements are achieved in the quality of the brain images. The enhancement process plays a crucial role in the refinement of edges and improving the overall image clarity, reducing the manual effort needed for feature extraction.

Furthermore, our proposed model incorporates distinctive concatenation concepts within the convolutional layers, demonstrating superior performance compared to alternative methods, as shown in Table 2. By incorporating these enhancement techniques, the proposed model has demonstrated exceptional performance, surpassing the existing state-of-the-art model in classifying brain tumors. The successful accomplishment is evidence of the proposed model's resilience and capacity to apply to a wide range of brain image classification tasks, highlighting its potential for achieving precise and dependable results. Integrating decreased manual intervention, enhanced image quality, and the suggested model architecture renders our approach highly promising for practical implementations in classifying brain tumors.

Table 2. Comprehensive comparison of the obtained and previous studies' results.

Authors	Year	Methods	Dataset	Classes	Precision	Recall	F1-Score	Accuracy
Gumaei et al. [25]	2019	Hybrid PCA-NGIST-RELM	Figshare 3064 Images	3	X	X	X	94.23
Swati et al. [40]	2019	VGG16 Fine tune	Figshare 3064 Images	3	89.17	X	91.50	94.65
Swati et al. [40]	2019	VGG19 Fine Tune	Figshare 3064 Images	3	89.52	X	91.73	94.82
Ghassemi et al. [32]	2019	CNN-based GAN	Figshare 3064 Images	3	95.29	X	95.10	95.60
Huang et al. [31]	2020	CNNBCN	Figshare 3064 Images	3	X	X	X	95.49
Fouad et al. [27]	2020	HDWT-HOG-Bagging	Figshare 3064 Images	3	X	X	X	96.40
Kaplan et al. [19]	2020	NLBP-αLBP-KNN	Figshare 3064 Images	3	X	X	X	95.56
Ayadi et al. [28]	2020	DSURF-HOG -SVM	Figshare 3064 Images	3	X	88.84	89.37	90.27
Noreen et al. [34]	2021	InceptionV3 Ensemble	Figshare 3064 Images	3	93.00	92.00	92.00	94.34
Almalki et al. [38]	2022	SURF-KAZE-SVM	Kaggle 2870 Images	4	X	X	X	95.33
Ekong et al. [41]	2022	Bayesian-CNN	Benchmark BRATS 2015 4000 Images	4	94	95	94	94.32
Asiri et al. [42]	2023	GAN-Softmax	Kaggle 2870 Images	4	92	93	93	96.00
Shilaskar et al. [43]	2023	HOG-XG Boost	Figshare, SARTAJ and Br35H 7023 images	4	92.07	91.82	91.85	92.02
Our work	-	Image Enhancement + Proposed Model	Figshare, SARTAJ and Br35H 7023 images	4	97.85	97.85	97.90	97.84

The methodology of Gumaei et al. [25] introduced a combination of PCA, NGIST, and RELM. While this hybrid approach attempted to capture a comprehensive feature set, PCA might not always capture non-linear patterns inherent in brain images, potentially missing crucial tumor-specific details and resulting in less accuracy. The methodologies of Swati et al. [40] and Noreen et al. [34] relied on refining generic architectures, specifically state-of-the-art models. Such fine-tuning of deep architectures can be resource-intensive. The intricate process necessitates substantial computational resources and proves time-consuming, given the need to adjust many parameters in these extensive networks. Contrarily, our model is purposefully designed for brain tumor classification. It captures tumor-specific attributes efficiently without the excessive computational demands typically associated with deep architectures. As corroborated by Table 1, our method requires fewer parameters than the state of the art and delivers faster testing times.

Ghassemi et al. [32] ventured into the territory of Generative Adversarial Networks, leveraging CNN-based GANs. While GANs are adept at generating synthetic images, their direct application to classification might introduce synthetic nuances that deviate from real-world MRI variations, potentially affecting classification accuracy. Huang et al. [31] introduced the CNNBCN, a model rooted in randomly generated graph algorithms, achieving an accuracy of 95.49% and demonstrating advancements in neural network design. In contrast, our methodology performs superior classification on extensive tumor and no-tumor images.

Techniques like HDWT-HOG-Bagging and NLBP-αLBP-KNN, as presented by Fouad et al. [27] and Kaplan et al. [19], rely heavily on traditional feature extraction. While computationally intensive, such methods might still miss subtle details and patterns in the MRI scans, resulting in less accuracy. Ayadi et al. [28] employed DSURF-HOG combined with SVM for classification, a method that might overlook hierarchical and spatial patterns in MRI images, which deep learning models can capture more effectively.

Ekong et al. [41] introduced a Bayesian-CNN approach, and while Bayesian methods offer probabilistic insights, they might not always capture the intricate features of brain tumors. While the GAN-Softmax approach by Asiri et al.'s [42] model offers certain advancements, it is computationally more demanding. Moreover, the efficacy of methodologies such as HOG-XG Boost by Shilaskar et al. [43] and the SURF-KAZE technique by Almalki et al. [38] might be constrained, particularly in their ability to capture spatial and hierarchical MRI patterns—areas where contemporary deep learning models exhibit proficiency as proved in this study.

Limitations

The usefulness of the proposed methodology for extracting features has been proven by using a specific dataset obtained from MRI scans. In order to enhance the clarity of the images, various techniques for image enhancement were employed. Although these strategies can enhance visibility, it is crucial to acknowledge that, in specific circumstances, it may impact classification accuracy. Therefore, comprehensive evaluations are necessary to test the method's suitability for different imaging modalities and clinical scenarios and its flexibility for image enhancements.

6. Conclusions

The present study introduced a novel approach to classify various categories of brain tumors, such as primary, meningioma, pituitary, and instances with no tumor. This is achieved by combining image enhancement techniques, namely, Gaussian-blur-based sharpening and Contrast-Limited Adaptive Histogram Equalization (CLAHE), with a proposed convolutional neural network. The findings of our study demonstrate a remarkable level of accuracy, specifically 97.84%, which was achieved through a diligent evaluation of the effectiveness of the suggested framework. The outcome of this study showcases the model's robust capacity for generalization, rendering it a valuable and dependable tool within the medical field. The capacity of this method to facilitate expeditious and accurate decision making by medical professionals in the realm of brain tumor diagnosis is evident. To enhance patient care in the future, we intend to revolutionize medical imaging methods. This will be accomplished by creating real-time brain tumor detection systems and establishing three-dimensional networks to analyze other medical images.

Author Contributions: Conceptualization, Z.R.; data curation, M.Z.K.; formal analysis, Y.-K.M.; funding acquisition, I.U., F.A. and A.M.S.; investigation, Y.Y.G.; methodology, Z.R.; project administration, I.U., F.A. and A.M.S.; resources, Y.Y.G., M.Z.K., A.A. and A.M.S.; software, Z.R.; supervision, Y.-K.M.; validation, Z.R., I.U., M.A.K. and A.A.; visualization, M.A.K. and F.A.; writing—original draft, Z.R.; writing—review and editing, Y.-K.M. and I.U. All authors have read and agreed to the published version of the manuscript.

Funding: This work was funded by the Researchers Supporting Project Number (RSP2023R509), King Saud University, Riyadh, Saudi Arabia.

Institutional Review Board Statement: Not applicable.

Informed Consent Statement: Not applicable.

Data Availability Statement: The data will be available on reasonable request from the corresponding author.

Acknowledgments: This work was funded by the Researchers Supporting Project Number (RSP2023R509), King Saud University, Riyadh, Saudi Arabia.

Conflicts of Interest: The authors declare no conflict of interest.

Abbreviations

DE	Differential Evolution	AI	Artificial Intelligence
SVM	Support Vector Machine	KNN	K-Nearest Neighbors
WSVM	Weight Kernel Width SVM	DL	Deep learning
HIK-SVM	Histogram Intersection Kernel SVM	ML	Machine learning
HDWT	Haar Discrete Wavelet Transforms	MRI	Magnetic Resonance Imaging
HOG	Histogram of Oriented Gradients	LPB	Local Binary Pattern
MODE	Multi-Objective Differential Evolution	SURF	Speeded Up Robust Feature
GAN	Generative Adversarial Network	WOA	Whale Optimization Algorithm
CNNBCN	Convolutional Neural Network based on Complex Network	PCA	Principal Component Analysis
RELM	Regularized Extreme Learning Machine	CNN	Convolutional Neural Network
CLAHE	Contrast-Limited Adaptive Histogram Equalization	CPU	Central Processing Unit

References

1. Khazaei, Z.; Goodarzi, E.; Borhaninejad, V.; Iranmanesh, F.; Mirshekarpour, H.; Mirzaei, B.; Naemi, H.; Bechashk, S.M.; Darvishi, I.; Ershad Sarabi, R.; et al. The association between incidence and mortality of brain cancer and human development index (HDI): An ecological study. *BMC Public Health* **2020**, *20*, 1696. [CrossRef]
2. GLOBOCAN. The Global Cancer Observatory—All Cancers. *Int. Agency Res. Cancer—WHO* **2020**, *419*, 199–200. Available online: https://gco.iarc.fr/today/home (accessed on 12 February 2023).
3. Johns Hopkins Medicine. Gliomas. Available online: https://www.hopkinsmedicine.org/health/conditions-and-diseases/gliomas (accessed on 12 February 2023).
4. Mayo Clinic. Pituitary Tumors—Symptoms and Causes. Available online: https://www.mayoclinic.org/diseases-conditions/pituitary-tumors/symptoms-causes/syc-20350548 (accessed on 12 February 2023).
5. Johns Hopkins Medicine. Meningioma. Available online: https://www.hopkinsmedicine.org/health/conditions-and-diseases/meningioma (accessed on 12 February 2023).
6. Merck Manuals Consumer Version. Overview of Brain Tumors—Brain, Spinal Cord, and Nerve Disorders. Available online: https://www.merckmanuals.com/home/brain,-spinal-cord,-and-nerve-disorders/tumors-of-the-nervous-system/overview-of-brain-tumors (accessed on 17 May 2022).
7. American Brain Tumor Association. American Brain Tumor Association Mood Swings and Cognitive Changes. 2014. Available online: https://web.archive.org/web/20160802203516/http://www.abta.org/brain-tumor-information/symptoms/mood-swings.html (accessed on 11 December 2022).
8. Tiwari, A.; Srivastava, S.; Pant, M. Brain tumor segmentation and classification from magnetic resonance images: Review of selected methods from 2014 to 2019. *Pattern Recognit. Lett.* **2020**, *131*, 244–260. [CrossRef]
9. Iwendi, C.; Khan, S.; Anajemba, J.H.; Mittal, M.; Alenezi, M.; Alazab, M. The use of ensemble models for multiple class and binary class classification for improving intrusion detection systems. *Sensors* **2020**, *20*, 2559. [CrossRef] [PubMed]
10. Ahmad, S.; Ullah, T.; Ahmad, I.; Al-Sharabi, A.; Ullah, K.; Khan, R.A.; Rasheed, S.; Ullah, I.; Uddin, M.N.; Ali, M.S. A Novel Hybrid Deep Learning Model for Metastatic Cancer Detection. *Comput. Intell. Neurosci.* **2022**, *2022*, 8141530. [CrossRef] [PubMed]
11. Zhuang, Y.; Chen, S.; Jiang, N.; Hu, H. An Effective WSSENet-Based Similarity Retrieval Method of Large Lung CT Image Databases. *KSII Trans. Internet Inf. Syst.* **2022**, *16*, 2359–2376. [CrossRef]
12. Li, C.; Lin, L.; Zhang, L.; Xu, R.; Chen, X.; Ji, J.; Li, Y. Long noncoding RNA p21 enhances autophagy to alleviate endothelial progenitor cells damage and promote endothelial repair in hypertension through SESN2/AMPK/TSC2 pathway. *Pharmacol. Res.* **2021**, *173*, 105920. [CrossRef]
13. Deng, X.; Liu, E.; Li, S.; Duan, Y.; Xu, M. Interpretable Multi-Modal Image Registration Network Based on Disentangled Convolutional Sparse Coding. *IEEE Trans. Image Process.* **2023**, *32*, 1078–1091. [CrossRef]

14. Zhang, K.; Yang, Y.; Ge, H.; Wang, J.; Lei, X.; Chen, X.; Wan, F.; Feng, H.; Tan, L. Neurogenesis and Proliferation of Neural Stem/Progenitor Cells Conferred by Artesunate via FOXO3a/p27Kip1 Axis in Mouse Stroke Model. *Mol. Neurobiol.* **2022**, *59*, 4718–4729. [CrossRef]
15. Wang, F.; Wang, H.; Zhou, X.; Fu, R. A Driving Fatigue Feature Detection Method Based on Multifractal Theory. *IEEE Sens. J.* **2022**, *22*, 19046–19059. [CrossRef]
16. Gao, Z.; Pan, X.; Shao, J.; Jiang, X.; Su, Z.; Jin, K.; Ye, J. Automatic interpretation and clinical evaluation for fundus fluorescein angiography images of diabetic retinopathy patients by deep learning. *Br. J. Ophthalmol.* **2022**, 1–7. [CrossRef] [PubMed]
17. Xu, H.; Van Der Jeught, K.; Zhou, Z.; Zhang, L.; Yu, T.; Sun, Y.; Li, Y.; Wan, C.; So, K.M.; Liu, D.; et al. Atractylenolide I enhances responsiveness to immune checkpoint blockade therapy by activating tumor antigen presentation. *J. Clin. Investig.* **2021**, *131*, e146832. [CrossRef] [PubMed]
18. Ao, J.; Shao, X.; Liu, Z.; Liu, Q.; Xia, J.; Shi, Y.; Qi, L.; Pan, J.; Ji, M. Stimulated Raman Scattering Microscopy Enables Gleason Scoring of Prostate Core Needle Biopsy by a Convolutional Neural Network. *Cancer Res.* **2023**, *83*, 641–651. [CrossRef] [PubMed]
19. Kaplan, K.; Kaya, Y.; Kuncan, M.; Ertunç, H.M. Brain tumor classification using modified local binary patterns (LBP) feature extraction methods. *Med. Hypotheses* **2020**, *139*, 109696. [CrossRef]
20. Rathi, V.G.P.; Palani, S. Brain Tumor Detection and Classification Using Deep Learning Classifier on MRI Images. *Res. J. Appl. Sci. Eng. Technol.* **2015**, *10*, 177–187. [CrossRef]
21. Cheng, J.; Huang, W.; Cao, S.; Yang, R.; Yang, W.; Yun, Z.; Wang, Z.; Feng, Q. Enhanced Performance of Brain Tumor Classification via Tumor Region Augmentation and Partition. *PLoS ONE* **2015**, *10*, e0140381. [CrossRef]
22. McBee, M.P.; Awan, O.A.; Colucci, A.T.; Ghobadi, C.W.; Kadom, N.; Kansagra, A.P.; Tridandapani, S.; Auffermann, W.F. Deep Learning in Radiology. *Acad. Radiol.* **2018**, *25*, 1472–1480. [CrossRef]
23. Lu, S.; Yang, J.; Yang, B.; Yin, Z.; Liu, M.; Yin, L.; Zheng, W. Analysis and Design of Surgical Instrument Localization Algorithm. *Comput. Model. Eng. Sci.* **2022**, *137*, 669–685. [CrossRef]
24. Afshar, P.; Plataniotis, K.N.; Mohammadi, A. Capsule Networks for Brain Tumor Classification Based on MRI Images and Coarse Tumor Boundaries. In Proceedings of the ICASSP 2019—2019 IEEE International Conference on Acoustics, Speech and Signal Processing (ICASSP), Brighton, UK, 12–17 May 2019; pp. 1368–1372. [CrossRef]
25. Gumaei, A.; Hassan, M.M.; Hassan, M.R.; Alelaiwi, A.; Fortino, G. A Hybrid Feature Extraction Method with Regularized Extreme Learning Machine for Brain Tumor Classification. *IEEE Access* **2019**, *7*, 36266–36273. [CrossRef]
26. Rezaei, K.; Agahi, H.; Mahmoodzadeh, A. A Weighted Voting Classifiers Ensemble for the Brain Tumors Classification in MR Images. *IETE J. Res.* **2020**, *68*, 3829–3842. [CrossRef]
27. Fouad, A.; Moftah, H.M.; Hefny, H.A. Brain diagnoses detection using whale optimization algorithm based on ensemble learning classifier. *Int. J. Intell. Eng. Syst.* **2020**, *13*, 40–51. [CrossRef]
28. Ayadi, W.; Charfi, I.; Elhamzi, W.; Atri, M. Brain tumor classification based on hybrid approach. *Vis. Comput.* **2020**, *38*, 107–117. [CrossRef]
29. Srujan, K.S.; Shivakumar, S.; Sitnur, K.; Garde, O.; Pk, P. Brain Tumor Segmentation and Classification using CNN model. *Int. Res. J. Eng. Technol.* **2020**, *7*, 4077–4080.
30. Tejaswini, G.P.; Sreelakshmi, K. Brain Tumour Detection using Deep Neural Network. *Wutan Huatan Jisuan Jishu* **2020**, *XVI*, 27–40.
31. Huang, Z.; Du, X.; Chen, L.; Li, Y.; Liu, M.; Chou, Y.; Jin, L. Convolutional Neural Network Based on Complex Networks for Brain Tumor Image Classification with a Modified Activation Function. *IEEE Access* **2020**, *8*, 89281–89290. [CrossRef]
32. Ghassemi, N.; Shoeibi, A.; Rouhani, M. Deep neural network with generative adversarial networks pre-training for brain tumor classification based on MR images. *Biomed. Signal Process. Control* **2020**, *57*, 101678. [CrossRef]
33. Deepak, S.; Ameer, P.M. Automated Categorization of Brain Tumor from MRI Using CNN features and SVM. *J. Ambient Intell. Humaniz. Comput.* **2020**, *12*, 8357–8369. [CrossRef]
34. Noreen, N.; Palaniappan, S.; Qayyum, A.; Ahmad, I.; Alassafi, M.O. Brain Tumor Classification Based on Fine-Tuned Models and the Ensemble Method. *Comput. Mater. Contin.* **2021**, *67*, 3967–3982. [CrossRef]
35. Shaik, N.S.; Cherukuri, T.K. Multi-level attention network: Application to brain tumor classification. *Signal Image Video Process.* **2022**, *16*, 817–824. [CrossRef]
36. Ahmad, B.; Sun, J.; You, Q.; Palade, V.; Mao, Z. Brain Tumor Classification Using a Combination of Variational Autoencoders and Generative Adversarial Networks. *Biomedicines* **2022**, *10*, 223. [CrossRef]
37. Alanazi, M.F.; Ali, M.U.; Hussain, S.J.; Zafar, A.; Mohatram, M.; Irfan, M.; Alruwaili, R.; Alruwaili, M.; Ali, N.H.; Albarrak, A.M. Brain Tumor/Mass Classification Framework Using Magnetic-Resonance-Imaging-Based Isolated and Developed Transfer Deep-Learning Model. *Sensors* **2022**, *22*, 372. [CrossRef] [PubMed]
38. Almalki, Y.E.; Ali, M.U.; Ahmed, W.; Kallu, K.D.; Zafar, A.; Alduraibi, S.K.; Irfan, M.; Basha, M.A.A.; Alshamrani, H.A.; Alduraibi, A.K. Robust Gaussian and Nonlinear Hybrid Invariant Clustered Features Aided Approach for Speeded Brain Tumor Diagnosis. *Life* **2022**, *12*, 1084. [CrossRef] [PubMed]
39. Kavin Kumar, K.; Dinesh, P.M.; Rayavel, P.; Vijayaraja, L.; Dhanasekar, R.; Kesavan, R.; Raju, K.; Khan, A.A.; Wechtaisong, C.; Haq, M.A.; et al. Brain Tumor Identification Using Data Augmentation and Transfer Learning Approach. *Comput. Syst. Sci. Eng.* **2023**, *46*, 1845–1861. [CrossRef]
40. Swati, Z.N.K.; Zhao, Q.; Kabir, M.; Ali, F.; Ali, Z.; Ahmed, S.; Lu, J. Brain tumor classification for MR images using transfer learning and fine-tuning. *Comput. Med. Imaging Graph.* **2019**, *75*, 34–46. [CrossRef] [PubMed]

41. Ekong, F.; Yu, Y.; Patamia, R.A.; Feng, X.; Tang, Q.; Mazumder, P.; Cai, J. Bayesian Depth-Wise Convolutional Neural Network Design for Brain Tumor MRI Classification. *Diagnostics* **2022**, *12*, 1657. [CrossRef]
42. Asiri, A.A.; Shaf, A.; Ali, T.; Aamir, M.; Usman, A.; Irfan, M.; Alshamrani, H.A.; Mehdar, K.M.; Alshehri, O.M.; Alqhtani, S.M. Multi-Level Deep Generative Adversarial Networks for Brain Tumor Classification on Magnetic Resonance Images. *Intell. Autom. Soft Comput.* **2023**, *36*, 127–143. [CrossRef]
43. Shilaskar, S.; Mahajan, T.; Bhatlawande, S.; Chaudhari, S.; Mahajan, R.; Junnare, K. Machine Learning Based Brain Tumor Detection and Classification using HOG Feature Descriptor. In Proceedings of the International Conference on Sustainable Computing and Smart Systems, ICSCSS, Coimbatore, India, 14–16 June 2023; pp. 67–75.
44. Yadav, S. Analysis of k-fold cross-validation over hold-out validation on colossal datasets for quality classification. In Proceedings of the 2016 IEEE 6th International Conference on Advanced Computing (IACC), Bhimavaram, India, 27–28 February 2016. [CrossRef]
45. Nickparvar, M.; Brain_Tumor_MRI Dataset. Kaggle. *Dataset*. 2021. Available online: https://www.kaggle.com/datasets/masoudnickparvar/brain-tumor-mri-dataset (accessed on 10 May 2023).
46. Cheng, J.; Brain Tumor Dataset. Figshare. 2017. Available online: https://figshare.com/articles/dataset/brain_tumor_dataset/1512427 (accessed on 10 May 2023).
47. Kaggle. Brain Tumor Classification (MRI). Available online: https://www.kaggle.com/datasets/sartajbhuvaji/brain-tumor-classification-mri (accessed on 10 July 2023).
48. Hamada, A. Br35H: Brain Tumor Detection. 2020. Available online: https://www.kaggle.com/datasets/ahmedhamada0/brain-tumor-detection (accessed on 10 May 2023).
49. Wang, W.; Chen, Z.; Yuan, X. Simple low-light image enhancement based on Weber–Fechner law in logarithmic space. *Signal Process. Image Commun.* **2022**, *106*, 116742. [CrossRef]
50. Wang, Y.; Su, Y.; Li, W.; Xiao, J.; Li, X.; Liu, A.A. Dual-path Rare Content Enhancement Network for Image and Text Matching. *IEEE Trans. Circuits Syst. Video Technol.* 2023; *Early Access*. [CrossRef]
51. Goodfellow, I.; Bengio, Y.; Courville, A. *Deep Learning*; MIT Press: Cambridge, MA, USA, 2016; pp. 1–10. Available online: https://www.deeplearningbook.org (accessed on 10 May 2023).
52. Ioffe, S.; Szegedy, C. Batch normalization: Accelerating deep network training by reducing internal covariate shift. In Proceedings of the 32nd International Conference on Machine Learning, Lille, France, 6–11 July 2015; Volume 1, pp. 448–456.
53. Alzubaidi, L.; Zhang, J.; Humaidi, A.J.; Al-Dujaili, A.; Duan, Y.; Al-Shamma, O.; Santamaría, J.; Fadhel, M.A.; Al-Amidie, M.; Farhan, L. *Review of Deep Learning: Concepts, CNN Architectures, Challenges, Applications, Future Directions*; Springer International Publishing: Cham, Switzerland, 2021; Volume 8, ISBN 4053702100444.
54. Bin Tufail, A.; Ullah, I.; Rehman, A.U.; Khan, R.A.; Khan, M.A.; Ma, Y.K.; Hussain Khokhar, N.; Sadiq, M.T.; Khan, R.; Shafiq, M.; et al. On Disharmony in Batch Normalization and Dropout Methods for Early Categorization of Alzheimer's Disease. *Sustainability* **2022**, *14*, 14695. [CrossRef]
55. Kingma, D.P.; Ba, J. Adam: A Method for Stochastic Optimization. In Proceedings of the 3rd International Conference on Learning Representations, San Diego, CA, USA, 7–9 May 2015; Conference Track Proceedings. 2014; pp. 1–15.
56. Robbins, H.; Monro, S. A Stochastic Approximation Method. *Ann. Math. Stat.* **1951**, *22*, 400–407. [CrossRef]
57. Rasheed, Z.; Ma, Y.-K.; Ullah, I.; Al Shloul, T.; Bin Tufail, A.; Ghadi, Y.Y.; Khan, M.Z.; Mohamed, H.G. Automated Classification of Brain Tumors from Magnetic Resonance Imaging Using Deep Learning. *Brain Sci.* **2023**, *13*, 602. [CrossRef]
58. Nair, V.; Hinton, G.E. Rectified linear units improve Restricted Boltzmann machines. In Proceedings of the 27th International Conference on Machine Learning, Haifa, Israel, 21–24 June 2010; Association for Computing Machinery: New York, NY, USA, 2010.
59. Srivastava, N.; Hinton, G.; Krizhevsky, A.; Sutskever, I.; Salakhutdinov, R. Dropout: A Simple Way to Prevent Neural Networks from Overfitting. *J. Mach. Learn. Res.* **2014**, *15*, 1929–1958.
60. Moradi, R.; Berangi, R.; Minaei, B. A Survey of Regularization Strategies for Deep Models. *Artif. Intell. Rev.* **2020**, *53*, 3947–3986. [CrossRef]
61. ReduceLROnPlateau. Available online: https://keras.io/api/callbacks/reduce_lr_on_plateau/ (accessed on 24 May 2023).
62. Simonyan, K.; Zisserman, A. Very deep convolutional networks for large-scale image recognition. In Proceedings of the 3rd International Conference on Learning Representations, San Diego, CA, USA, 7–9 May 2015. Conference Track Proceedings.
63. Glorot, X.; Bengio, Y. Understanding the difficulty of training deep feedforward neural networks. *J. Mach. Learn. Res.* **2010**, *9*, 249–256.
64. He, K.; Zhang, X.; Ren, S.; Sun, J. Deep residual learning for image recognition. In Proceedings of the IEEE Conference on Computer Vision and Pattern Recognition (CVPR), Las Vegas, NV, USA, 27–30 June 2016; Volume 2016, pp. 770–778. [CrossRef]
65. Sandler, M.; Howard, A.; Zhu, M.; Zhmoginov, A.; Chen, L.C. MobileNetV2: Inverted Residuals and Linear Bottlenecks. In Proceedings of the 2018 IEEE Conference on Computer Vision and Pattern Recognition (CVPR), Salt Lake City, UT, USA, 18–23 June 2018; pp. 4510–4520. [CrossRef]
66. Szegedy, C.; Vanhoucke, V.; Ioffe, S.; Shlens, J.; Wojna, Z. Rethinking the Inception Architecture for Computer Vision. In Proceedings of the 2016 IEEE Computer Society Conference on Computer Vision and Pattern Recognition, Las Vegas, NV, USA, 27–30 June 2016; IEEE Computer Society. pp. 2818–2826.

67. Kuraparthi, S.; Reddy, M.K.; Sujatha, C.N.; Valiveti, H.; Duggineni, C.; Kollati, M.; Kora, P.; Sravan, V. Brain tumor classification of MRI images using deep convolutional neural network. *Trait. Signal* **2021**, *38*, 1171–1179. [CrossRef]
68. Ting, K.M. Confusion Matrix. In *Encyclopedia of Machine Learning and Data Mining*; Springer: Boston, MA, USA, 2017; p. 260. [CrossRef]
69. Hajian-Tilaki, K. Receiver operating characteristic (ROC) curve analysis for medical diagnostic test evaluation. *Casp. J. Intern. Med.* **2013**, *4*, 627–635.

Disclaimer/Publisher's Note: The statements, opinions and data contained in all publications are solely those of the individual author(s) and contributor(s) and not of MDPI and/or the editor(s). MDPI and/or the editor(s) disclaim responsibility for any injury to people or property resulting from any ideas, methods, instructions or products referred to in the content.

brain sciences

MDPI

Article

Auto-Classification of Parkinson's Disease with Different Motor Subtypes Using Arterial Spin Labelling MRI Based on Machine Learning

Jinhua Xiong [1], Haiyan Zhu [2], Xuhang Li [3], Shangci Hao [1], Yueyi Zhang [1], Zijian Wang [3,*] and Qian Xi [1,*]

1 Department of Radiology, Shanghai East Hospital, Tongji University School of Medicine, No. 150 Jimo Road, Pudong New Area, Shanghai 200120, China; xjh941116@sina.com (J.X.)

2 Department of Radiology, Shanghai Tongji Hospital, Tongji University School of Medicine, No. 389 Xincun Road, Putuo District, Shanghai 200065, China

3 School of Computer Science and Technology, Donghua University, No. 2999 North Renmin Road, Songjiang Area, Shanghai 200000, China

* Correspondence: wang.zijian@dhu.edu.cn (Z.W.); 96125007@sina.com (Q.X.); Tel.: +139-1822-2536 (Q.X.); Fax: +021-3880-4518 (Q.X.)

Abstract: The purpose of this study was to automatically classify different motor subtypes of Parkinson's disease (PD) on arterial spin labelling magnetic resonance imaging (ASL-MRI) data using support vector machine (SVM). This study included 38 subjects: 21 PD patients and 17 normal controls (NCs). Based on the Unified Parkinson's Disease Rating Scale (UPDRS) subscores, patients were divided into the tremor-dominant (TD) subtype and the postural instability gait difficulty (PIGD) subtype. The subjects were in a resting state during the acquisition of ASL-MRI data. The automated anatomical atlas 3 (AAL3) template was registered to obtain an ASL image of the same size and shape. We obtained the voxel values of 170 brain regions by considering the location coordinates of these regions and then normalized the data. The length of the feature vector depended on the number of voxel values in each brain region. Three binary classification models were utilized for classifying subjects' data, and we applied SVM to classify voxels in the brain regions. The left subgenual anterior cingulate cortex (ACC_sub_L) was clearly distinguished in both NCs and PD patients using SVM, and we obtained satisfactory diagnostic rates (accuracy = 92.31%, specificity = 96.97%, sensitivity = 84.21%, and AUCmax = 0.9585). For the right supramarginal gyrus (SupraMarginal_R), SVM distinguished the TD group from the other groups with satisfactory diagnostic rates (accuracy = 84.21%, sensitivity = 63.64%, specificity = 92.59%, and AUCmax = 0.9192). For the right intralaminar of thalamus (Thal_IL_R), SVM distinguished the PIGD group from the other groups with satisfactory diagnostic rates (accuracy = 89.47%, sensitivity = 70.00%, specificity = 6.43%, and AUCmax = 0.9464). These results are consistent with the changes in blood perfusion related to PD subtypes. In addition, the sensitive brain regions of the TD group and PIGD group involve the brain regions where the cerebellothalamocortical (CTC) and the striatal thalamocortical (STC) loops are located. Therefore, it is suggested that the blood perfusion patterns of the two loops may be different. These characteristic brain regions could become potential imaging markers of cerebral blood flow to distinguish TD from PIGD. Meanwhile, our findings provide an imaging basis for personalised treatment, thereby optimising clinical diagnostic and treatment approaches.

Keywords: Parkinson's disease; motor subtypes; arterial spin labelling; machine learning; support vector machine

1. Introduction

Parkinson's disease (PD) is a common neurodegenerative disorder that becomes increasingly prevalent with age [1]. The typical symptoms of PD are rigidity, bradykinesia, tremor, and postural instability [2], which are caused by a profound loss of dopaminergic neurons from the basal ganglia [3]. Additionally, many environmental and genetic factors exert an influence on the risk of PD, with different factors predominating in different patients. These factors converge on specific pathways, including mitochondrial dysfunction, oxidative stress, protein aggregation, impaired autophagy, and neuroinflammation [4]. Several pathophysiological concepts, pathways, and mechanisms, including the presumed roles of α-synuclein misfolding and aggregation, Lewy bodies, oxidative stress, iron and melanin, deficient autophagy processes, insulin and incretin signalling, T-cell autoimmunity, the gut–brain axis, and the evidence that microbial (viral) agents, may induce molecular hallmarks of neurodegeneration [5]. The Unified Parkinson's Disease Rating Scale (UPDRS) is the most commonly used scale to assess the motor symptoms of PD patients [6]. Based on the UPDRS score, Jankovic was the first person who proposed classifying idiopathic PD into tremor-dominant (TD) and postural instability and gait difficulty (PIGD) subtypes [7]. PD patients with different motor subtypes have different disease progression and prognoses. The PIGD subtype has more severe motor and cognitive impairment and worse response to drug treatment than the TD subtype [7,8]. Therefore, it is of great significance to improve the clinical classification of PD for individualised treatment. Meanwhile, there is an increasing interest in the analysis of variability in clinical presentation, which reflects the existence of multiple subtypes of, and heterogeneous progression in, PD. The identification of patient subgroups within PD has significant implications for generating hypotheses on defining the heterogeneity of PD, understanding etiopathogenic mechanisms, and developing treatments [9].

At present, the classification of PD subtypes is mainly based on the UPDRS. The brain imaging neural markers of PD are far from reaching a consensus. Excavating the neural mechanism under the imaging is conducive to promoting the differential diagnosis of PD subtypes so as to optimise the clinical diagnosis and treatment. In recent years, neuroimaging studies have shown that cerebrovascular lesions are common in PD patients. Therefore, PD is considered a disease related to abnormal cerebrovascular function [10]. This issue was also described in the context of atypical parkinsonisms, such as corticobasal syndrome (CBS), characterised by both motor and higher cortical dysfunctions. Furthermore, ischemia is the primary risk factor for vascular CBS. Cerebral hypoperfusion can play a significant role in neuropathological changes in neurodegenerative diseases, CBS included [11]. Previous studies have confirmed that dopaminergic neurons are attached to brain microvessels and cerebral blood flow (CBF) changes due to metabolic reduction caused by neuronal degeneration and death [12]. However, this basic pathological change reflected in cerebral blood perfusion in patients with different motor subtypes of PD has not been confirmed by definite studies.

Arterial spin labelling (ASL) is a magnetic resonance imaging (MRI) perfusion technique that enables the quantification of CBF without the use of intravenous gadolinium contrast [13]. Regional CBF measured by ASL is relatively stable and is considered to reflect the functional activity of the brain directly [14]. Studies have shown that ASL technology can detect signs of neurodegeneration at an earlier stage and can be used to monitor changes in CBF during the progression of the disease [15]. There was no difference in whole-brain CBF in TD patients compared to PIGD patients. The prolonged arterial arrival time appeared more diffuse in the TD group than in the PIGD group. The PIGD group had a more predominantly posterior pattern of hypoperfusion and, indeed, basal ganglia hyperperfusion than the more temporo-parieto-frontal hypoperfusion of the TD group (which did not show areas of hyperperfusion) [16]. To our knowledge, the PD subtypes differences revealed in specific brain regions of CBF have not been previously investigated. Currently, resting-state functional MRI is widely utilised in the study of PD motor subtypes [17–20], while there are few studies on ASL-MRI. It is necessary to consider an imaging marker of CBF to distinguish TD from PIGD.

With the development of machine learning technology, support vector machine (SVM) has been widely used in the early diagnosis and classification of PD due to its excellent performance [21–24]. SVM aims to find the maximum interval between classes, which is known as the optimal decision boundary. This helps enhance the generalisation performance of classification, which is particularly important for medical data classification, where accuracy is paramount. SVM has shown excellent performance for the classification of PD motor subtypes using neuroimaging data or 3D kinematic data [25,26]. The aim of this study was to use SVM to perform automatic classification on ASL-MRI data and explore the neuroimaging markers of PD subtypes in cerebral blood perfusion.

2. Materials and Methods

2.1. Subjects

We enrolled 38 subjects in this study, including 17 normal controls (NCs). Based on the Unified Parkinson's Disease Rating Scale (UPDRS) subscores, there were 11 TD and 10 PIGD patients among the 21 PD patients. This study was reviewed and approved by the Ethics Review Committee of Shanghai East Hospital. Written informed consent was obtained from all subjects. All subjects underwent by the following tests: (1) Mini-Mental State Examination (MMSE); (2) Modified Hoehn and Yahr clinical grading scale; (3) Movement Disorder Society-Sponsored Revision UPDRS.

The inclusion criteria of PD patients were as follows: (1) age 50–75 years old, tremor was the main symptom, Hoehn and Yahr stages II–IV; (2) clear and effective treatment with dopaminergic drugs; (3) no other systemic malignant tumours. The inclusion criteria for the NCs were as follows: (1) sex and age matching those of participants in the PD group (there was no statistically significant difference ($p > 0.05$)); (2) the patients were healthy without nervous system diseases. The exclusion criteria were as follows: (1) history of recurrent stroke, transient ischemic attack, brain injury, and encephalitis; (2) symptoms during the use of antipsychotic drugs; (3) serious heart, liver, and kidney diseases and mental disorders; (4) severe autonomic nervous dysfunction occurring in the early stage of the disease; (5) inability to cooperate with the examination due to various reasons (such as illiteracy, advanced age, hearing impairment, claustrophobia, etc.).

2.2. Magnetic Resonance Imaging

All subjects were scanned with a M750w 3.0T GE Signa MRI system (GE Healthcare, Chicago, IL, USA) equipped with a 32-channel phased-array head coil. The subjects were in a resting state during the acquisition of ASL-MRI data. During the scanning, the subjects were in the supine position with their head fixed using a fixed band, and earplugs were placed in both ears to reduce scanner noise. All subjects were asked to limit their head movements as much as possible. The three groups of subjects were scanned with the same sequence under the same parameters. The sequences included conventional MRI sequences (T1WI and T2WI), DWI, and ASL sequences. Other nervous system lesions, such as multiple cerebral infarctions, hydrocephalus, and intracranial tumours, can be excluded by conventional MRI scans in selected subjects.

Conventional MRI scans were performed, including cross-sectional T1WI (repetition time (TR) = 2000 ms, echo time (TE) = 20 ms, field of view (FOV) = 250 × 221 mm, matrix = 400 × 250, and slice thickness/slice distance = 7 mm/0.6 mm); T2WI (TR = 3000 ms, TE = 80 ms, FOV = 250 × 221 mm, matrix = 436 × 295, and slice thickness/slice distance = 7 mm/0.6 mm); FLAIR (TR = 11,000 ms, TE = 120 ms, FOV = 250 × 221 mm, matrix =240 × 160, and slice thickness/pitch = 7 mm/0.6 mm); and DWI (TR = 2634 ms, TE = 58 ms, FOV = 230 × 230 mm, matrix = 140 × 136, and slice thickness/slice distance = 6 mm/0.6 mm). The ASL scanning parameters were as follows: TR = 4854 ms; TE = 10.7 ms; post-labelling delay time = 2025 ms; spiral arm = 8; sampling point = 512; flip angle (FA) = 111°; FOV = 240 mm × 240 mm; reconstruction matrix = 128 × 128; slice thickness = 4 mm, no septum; slice number = 36, axial position; number of excitations (NEX) = 3. The intraslice resolution was 1.9 mm × 1.9 mm, and the scan time was 282 s.

2.3. Statistical Analysis

We analysed the general information and clinical scale data of the subjects using the Statistical Package for the Social Sciences version 26.0 (IBM Corp., Armonk, NY, USA) and compared the gender distribution of the groups by performing a chi-square test. For quantitative data, we first performed a normality test (Shapiro–Wilk test) and homogeneity of variance test. We expressed normally distributed data as the means ± standard deviations. We compared the three groups using one-way analysis of variance and compared pairs of groups using a two-sample *t*-test. We expressed non-normally distributed data as M (P25, P75). The Kruskal–Wallis test was used for comparisons among the three groups, and a two-sample nonparametric *t*-test was used for comparisons between the two groups. $p < 0.05$ was considered statistically significant.

2.4. Data Preprocessing

2.4.1. Feature Extraction

Due to the long time required for MR image acquisition, it is difficult for PD patients with a tremor to avoid head movement, which can affect the subsequent data analysis. Therefore, the brain images in the first 10 time points of each subject were discarded to ensure the stability of the data signals. The brain images in the remaining time series were corrected by interlayer time correction, strict head movement correction, brain normalization, and image smoothing using the SPM spatial template to minimise the possible influence of head movement.

After correction, the automated anatomical atlas 3 (AAL3) brain region template (including 170 brain regions) was selected. We used SPM to register the AAL3_1 mm template with the ASL image to obtain images with the same size and shape. According to the brain regions defined by AAL3, we obtained the location coordinates contained by each brain region in the AAL3 image and then obtained the voxel values of the corresponding brain region location of the subject. A csv file was generated for each brain region containing the voxel values of that region for all subjects, so we obtained the voxel values for 170 brain regions. Due to the different size of each brain region, the number of corresponding voxel values also varied. Before the data were entered into the SVM classifier, we only normalised the voxel data of the current brain region without changing the data size. Consequently, the length of the feature vector depended on the number of voxel values in each brain region. The length of these feature vectors varied from brain region to brain region. However, the length of the feature vectors was consistent for each brain region. For example, in Acc_pre_L, the number of voxels for per patient was 626, while, in Angular_R, the number of voxels was 1751.

2.4.2. Model Classification and Validation

Patients were classified according to the obtained voxel values in each brain region. The data of NC, PIGD patients, and TD patients were referred to the classification methods of previous similar studies [27], and three binary classification models were proposed: "NC vs. others", "PIGD vs. others", and "TD vs. others".

The data were normalised and used to construct SVM classifiers based on the Sklearn library. We adopted the leave-one-out cross-validation (LOOCV) method to estimate the performance of the classifiers. Given a set of data samples, the classifier removed one data sample in each trial, and the classifier was trained on the remaining data samples. The removed samples were used for model testing [28]. Since the feature vector size of each brain region is different, we trained the model for the same brain region of all subjects in each experiment to test the diagnostic effect under the current brain region. According to the classification standard of the AAL3 brain region template, a total of 170 brain regions were shown. Therefore, experiments were conducted for all 170 brain regions. In the experiment, each subject's current brain region would be used as the test set in turns due to adopting the LOOCV. For example, when we targeted the Thal_VA_L in the AAL3 template for the experiment, the voxel value of Thal_VA_L for each subject was taken as a sample. When we performed experiments on other brain regions, since the number of voxel values in each brain region was different, the length of the feature vector in each experiment depended on the number of voxel values in each brain region. The model performance indicators of accuracy, sensitivity, specificity, and maximum area under the curve (AUCmax) in the receiver operating characteristic (ROC) analysis were used to evaluate the classification performance of the SVM model. The overall procedure of data preprocessing, feature extraction, model classification, and validation is displayed in Figure 1.

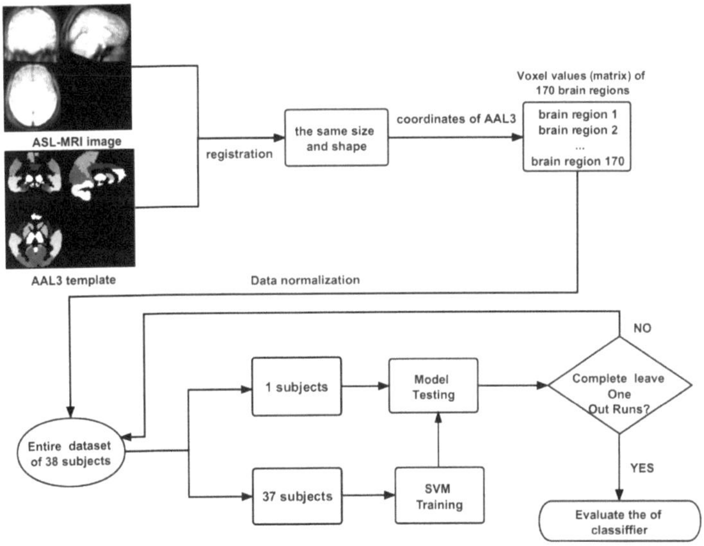

Figure 1. The flowchart of data preprocessing, feature extraction, model classification, and validation.

3. Results

3.1. Demographic and Clinical Study

There was no significant difference in age, sex, or disease duration among the three groups ($p > 0.05$, Table 1). There was no significant difference in UPDRS score or H&Y grade between the TD group and PIGD group ($p > 0.05$, Table 1). There was no significant difference in MMSE scores between the TD group and the PIGD group ($p > 0.05$, Table 1).

Table 1. Comparison of general clinical data among the three groups.

Groups	NC	TD	PIGD	*p*-Value
Number of subjects	17	11	10	-
Age (year)	64 (52~68)	68 (55~70)	69.500 (67.25~68.75)	0.052
Sex (M/F)	5/12	5/6	4/6	0.671
Disease duration (year)	-	6 (4~6)	4/6	0.152
H&Y	-	1.500 (1~2)	1.500 (1.375~2)	0.809
UPDRS	-	36.730 ± 15.021	39.700 ± 11.870	0.623
MMSE	-	27.820 ± 3.682	26.000 ± 3.582	0.260

H&Y: Hoehn and Yahr stage; UPDRS: Unified Parkinson's Disease Rating Scale; MMSE: Mini-Mental State Examination; NC: normal control; TD: tremor-dominant; PIGD: postural instability and gait difficulty.

3.2. Classifier Performance Assessment

After SVM screening, a total of 4 brain regions with high accuracy were selected from 170 brain regions in the AAL3 template. According to the performance analysis of three binary classification models, we found that the left subgenual anterior cingulate cortex (ACC_sub_L) of the NCs was more sensitive to classification than that of the PD patients. The proposed classifier differentiated PD patients and NCs with diagnostic accuracy, sensitivity, and specificity of 81.58%, 76.47%, and 85.71%, respectively. At the same time, the ROC analysis showed that the AUCmax reached 0.8992.

For the right supramarginal gyrus (SupraMarginal_R), SVM distinguished the TD group from the other groups with diagnostic accuracy, sensitivity, and specificity of 84.21%, 63.64%, and 92.59%, respectively, and the AUC value was 0.9192. For the right intralaminar of the thalamus (Thal_IL_R), SVM could distinguish the PIGD group from the other groups with a diagnostic accuracy, sensitivity, and specificity of 89.47%, 70.00%, and 96.43%, respectively, and the AUC value was 0.9464. For the left lateral geniculate of the thalamus (Thal_LGN_L), the accuracy of the TD and PIGD classification was above 75%, but the AUC value was relatively low (Table 2 and Figure 2).

Table 2. The diagnostic performance of sensitive brain regions for the three binary classifications.

Brain Regions	Groups	Accuracy	Sensitivity	Specificity	AUC
ACC_sub_L	NC vs. others	81.58%	76.47%	85.71%	89.92%
	PIGD vs. others	65.79%	40.00%	75.00%	63.57%
	TD vs. others	68.42%	54.55%	74.07%	64.98%
SupraMarginal_R	NC vs. others	76.32%	76.47%	76.19%	80.67%
	PIGD vs. others	73.68%	50.00%	82.14%	70.00%
	TD vs. others	84.21%	63.64%	92.59%	91.92%
Thal_IL_R	NC vs. others	73.68%	70.59%	76.19%	81.79%
	PIGD vs. others	89.47%	70.00%	96.43%	94.64%
	TD vs. others	81.58%	63.64%	88.89%	75.42%
Thal_LGN_L	NC vs. others	57.89%	64.71%	52.38%	60.50%
	PIGD vs. others	76.32%	30.00%	92.86%	52.14%
	TD vs. others	78.95%	45.45%	92.59%	67.34%

ACC_sub_L: the left subgenual of anterior cingulate cortex; SupraMarginal_R: the right supramarginal gyrus; Thal_IL_R: the right intralaminar of the thalamus; Thal_LGN_L: the left lateral geniculate of the thalamus; NC: normal control; TD: tremor-dominant; PIGD: postural instability and gait difficulty.

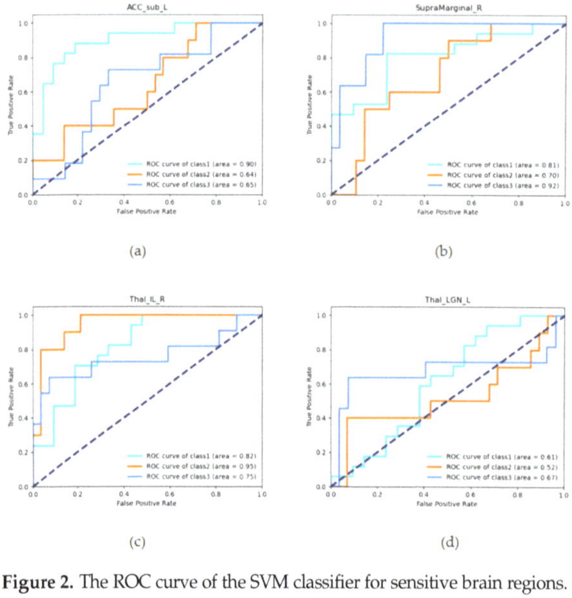

Figure 2. The ROC curve of the SVM classifier for sensitive brain regions. (**a**) ROC of ACC_sub_L in three binary classification models; (**b**) ROC of SupraMarginal_R in three binary classification models; (**c**) ROC of Thal_IL_R in three binary classification models; (**d**) ROC of Thal_LGN_L in three binary classification models; Class 1 = "NC vs. others", Class 2 = "PIGD vs. others", and Class 3 = "TD vs. others".

3.3. Visualisation of the Most Sensitive Features

According to the sensitive brain regions screened by SVM, we input four related sensitive brain regions into BrainNetViewer for visualisation [29] and displayed the related brain regions intuitively (Figure 3).

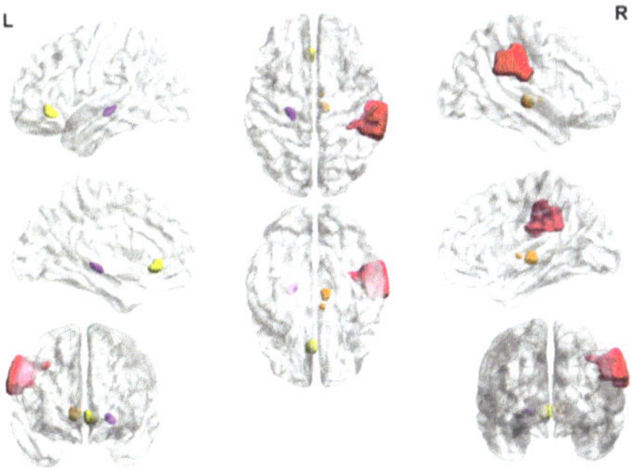

Figure 3. Visualisation of the relevant brain regions. Red region = SupraMarginal_R; orange region = Thal_IL_R, yellow region = ACC_sub_L, and purple region = Thal_LGN_L.

4. Discussion

This study introduces a SVM-based classifier for the differential diagnosis of PD patients with different motor subtypes using ASL-MRI data for the first time. In general, the proposed classifier has high classification performance in the four brain regions, showing a satisfactory classification ability. The diagnostic accuracy, sensitivity, specificity, and AUCmax value are high, which are almost consistent with the evaluation of the clinical scales. This indicates the feasibility of using ASL-MRI data for the automatic classification of PD subtypes. We also find that the voxel values of the four related brain regions are the most sensitive classification features, which can be used as potential neuroimaging markers for PD subtypes in cerebral blood perfusion.

The AAL3 brain template used in this study helped to further divide the brain regions into detailed subregions [30]. These regions are of interest in many neuroimaging studies and studies of psychiatric and neurological disorders [31–34]. Compared to radiomics features extracted from ROIs (left and right caudate and putamen) in MRI images and DAT SPECT images [35], we paid more attention to the extraction and selection of the features of the whole brain. Numerous new data-driven methods, such as biclustering or triclustering, seem to have been proposed for subtyping from neuroimaging data [36]. Unlike data-driven methods applied to schizophrenia research [37,38], SVM has gained significant popularity for the early diagnosis and classification of PD. The SVM algorithm in machine learning was used for the classification model. We utilised a linear kernel SVM, which is also a linear classifier. This classifier has demonstrated exceptional classification performance and interpretability, rendering it extensively utilised in various research endeavours. In our data sample, the number of subjects in the control group was large, while the number of subjects in the other categories was relatively small, and the categories were unbalanced. SVM can handle unbalanced data by adjusting the regularisation parameter C to ensure that the model is not biased toward the dominant category. In the conducted experiment, a range of regularisation parameter C values from 1 to 1000 were explored. Based on the obtained experimental results, it was determined that the current value of C exhibited optimal efficacy. Compared to deep learning and random forest, SVM is more suitable for the research of small samples. Due to the existence of a "black box", deep learning is not as interpretable as SVM. LOOCV was used as the validation method instead of k-fold cross-validation, because it is suitable for small sample studies. Future research could explore the application of unsupervised machine learning for the data-driven identification of motor subtypes in PD. Previous studies have employed clustering methods such as unsupervised hierarchical clustering, KMeans, and random forest clustering to identify subtypes of PD [35,39,40].

Voxel-based morphometry (VBM) is a neuroimaging technique that investigates focal differences in brain anatomy [41]. Furthermore, VBM is widely used for neurodegenerative and psychiatric diseases [41–45]. In previous studies using VBM to distinguish idiopathic PD patients from normal subjects, the analysis was based on multiple machine learning classifiers. The results indicated that the logistic method and support vector machine showed the best performance [46]. However, a possible problem with these approaches is that the evaluated regions are not the most relevant to the pathogenesis of PD. We found that SVM could distinguish the NC group from the PD group in ACC_sub_L, which was consistent with a previous study on the cingulate cortex in PD. Evidence has been provided for a new conceptualisation of the connectivity and functions of the cingulate cortex in emotion, action, and memory [47]. In addition, VBM has been used in many studies of mild cognitive impairment in PD to show reduced thickness in the anterior cingulate cortex and posterior cingulate cortex. Regional CBF is altered in association with the verbal intelligence quotient in the posterior cingulate cortex and anterior midcingulate cortex and in association with executive impairments in the anterior cingulate cortex [48].

In particular, a structural MRI study showed decreased cerebellar grey matter and increased Sulc (a measure of sulcal depth) in the right supramarginal gyrus in the TD subtype [49,50]. SupraMarginal_R has been shown to play an important role in various cognitive functions [51]. The intralaminar nuclei, through extensive projections to the striatum and cortex, participates in a range of behaviours, including sensorimotor coordination, pain modulation, arousal, and cognition [52]. In general, PIGD subtypes mainly involve changes in the basal ganglia output-related circuitry (striatal thalamocortical loop, STC loop), while TD subtypes involve an additional downstream compensation mechanism consisting of the cerebellothalamocortical (CTC) loop [53]. Based on the more than 30 quantitative PD studies performed to date, it seems safe to conclude that the resting state in PD patients is characterised by various degrees of hypoperfusion and hypometabolism in cerebral cortical structures (mostly frontoparietal) and possibly also in certain subcortical structures [54]. A recent study using ASL revealed that TD exhibited more hypoperfusion in the temporo–parieto–frontal network, while PIGD showed hypoperfusion in a predominantly posterior pattern, as well as hyperperfusion in the basal ganglia [55]. The TD group showed a higher classification performance in SupraMarginal_R, while the PIGD group showed the highest classification performance in Thal_IL_R. This is consistent with the changes in blood perfusion related to the PD subtype. The sensitive brain regions of the TD group and PIGD group were in the brain regions involved in the CTC and STC loops, so it is suggested that the blood perfusion patterns of the two pathways may be different.

This study still had several limitations. First, the sample size included in this study was small. Additionally, the relatively wide age range of participants may have had an impact on the results due to the small sample. Therefore, the conclusions of this study need to be further verified by large-sample and multicentre data. Second, the detection results of cerebral blood flow perfusion by ASL are easily affected by the post-labelling delay (PLD) time, slice thickness, matrix, and other parameters; thus, people of different ages need different PLD times. The 2025 ms PLD time interval selected in this study conforms to the requirements of the 2014 expert consensus for a single PLD time of pseudo-continuous arterial spin labelling to minimise its influence in most adults [56]. Third, the reliability of the classification model would be further improved if a multimodal comparative study were to be carried out by combining biological markers; other modalities such as MRI, PET, or SPECT; and other imaging methods. In the future, on the basis of expanding the sample size and integrating other modality images, we further will optimise the algorithm for quantitative research to enhance the accuracy of the sensitive features and provide multidimensional neuroimaging markers for clinical diagnosis and treatment.

5. Conclusions

In conclusion, we introduced a classification method based on machine learning to classify ASL-MRI images of PD patients with different motor subtypes and found that the classification efficiency was high in four brain regions. In addition, ACC_sub_L can be used as a neuroimaging marker for the classification of PD and NCs. SupraMarginal_R and Thal_IL_R are within the range of the CTC and STC loops, which is helpful for investigating the cerebral blood perfusion patterns of the two loops. These characteristic brain regions could become potential imaging markers of CBF to distinguish TD from PIGD. It can help to explain the differences in the anatomical and clinical symptoms of different PD motor subtypes and provide an imaging basis for research on the neuropathological mechanism and personalised treatment, thereby optimising clinical diagnostic and treatment approaches.

Author Contributions: Conceptualisation, Q.X.; Data curation, Z.W., X.L. and S.H.; Formal analysis, J.X. and Z.W.; Funding acquisition, Q.X.; Investigation, Y.Z.; Methodology, J.X. and X.L.; Project administration, Q.X.; Resources, Q.X., S.H. and Y.Z.; Software, Z.W. and X.L.; Supervision, Q.X. and H.Z.; Validation, X.L.; Visualisation, Z.W. and X.L.; and Writing—original draft, J.X. All authors have read and agreed to the published version of the manuscript.

Funding: This work was supported by the Science and Technology Commission of Shanghai Municipality (Grant No. 20Y11911700) and the Outstanding Leaders Training Program of Pudong Health Bureau of Shanghai (Grant No. PWRl2022-05).

Institutional Review Board Statement: The study was approved by the Ethics Review Committee of Shanghai East Hospital (No. 2022-206).

Informed Consent Statement: Informed consent was obtained from all subjects involved in the study. Written informed consent was obtained from the participants to publish this paper.

Data Availability Statement: All data reported in this manuscript will be made available from the corresponding author upon reasonable request.

Conflicts of Interest: The authors declare no conflict of interest.

References

1. Hirsch, L.; Jette, N.; Frolkis, A.; Steeves, T.; Pringsheim, T. The Incidence of Parkinson's Disease: A Systematic Review and Meta-Analysis. *Neuroepidemiology* **2016**, *46*, 292–300. [CrossRef] [PubMed]
2. Chiu, W.T.; Chan, L.; Wu, D.; Ko, T.H.; Chen, D.Y.-T.; Hong, C.-T. Cerebral Microbleeds are Associated with Postural Instability and Gait Disturbance Subtype in People with Parkinson's Disease. *Eur. Neurol.* **2018**, *80*, 335–340. [CrossRef]
3. Peters, O.M.; Weiss, A.; Metterville, J.; Song, L.; Logan, R.; Smith, G.A.; Schwarzschild, M.A.; Mueller, C.; Brown, R.H.; Freeman, M. Genetic diversity of axon degenerative mechanisms in models of Parkinson's disease. *Neurobiol. Dis.* **2021**, *155*, 105368. [CrossRef] [PubMed]
4. Simon, D.K.; Tanner, C.M.; Brundin, P. Parkinson Disease Epidemiology, Pathology, Genetics, and Pathophysiology. *Clin. Geriatr. Med.* **2020**, *36*, 1–12. [CrossRef]
5. Wüllner, U.; Borghammer, P.; Choe, C.-U.; Csoti, I.; Falkenburger, B.; Gasser, T.; Lingor, P.; Riederer, P. The heterogeneity of Parkinson's disease. *J. Neural Transm.* **2023**, *130*, 827–838. [CrossRef] [PubMed]
6. Ramaker, C.; Marinus, J.; Stiggelbout, A.M.; van Hilten, B.J. Systematic evaluation of rating scales for impairment and disability in Parkinson's disease. *Mov. Disord.* **2002**, *17*, 867–876. [CrossRef] [PubMed]
7. Jankovic, J.; McDermott, M.; Carter, J.; Gauthier, S.; Goetz, C.; Golbe, L.; Huber, S.; Koller, W.; Olanow, C.; Shoulson, I.; et al. Variable expression of Parkinson's disease: A base-line analysis of the DAT ATOP cohort. The Parkinson Study Group. *Neurology* **1990**, *40*, 1529–1534. [CrossRef]
8. Postuma, R.B.; Berg, D.; Stern, M.; Poewe, W.; Olanow, C.W.; Oertel, W.; Obeso, J.; Marek, K.; Litvan, I.; Lang, A.E.; et al. MDS clinical diagnostic criteria for Parkinson's disease. *Mov. Disord.* **2015**, *30*, 1591–1601. [CrossRef] [PubMed]
9. Cubo, E.; Martínez-Martín, P.; González-Bernal, J.; Casas, E.; Arnaiz, S.; Miranda, J.; Gámez, P.; Santos-García, D.; Coppadis Study Group. Effects of Motor Symptom Laterality on Clinical Manifestations and Quality of Life in Parkinson's Disease. *J. Park. Dis.* **2020**, *10*, 1611–1620. [CrossRef]
10. Nanhoe-Mahabier, W.; de Laat, K.F.; Visser, J.E.; Zijlmans, J.; de Leeuw, F.-E.; Bloem, B.R. Parkinson disease and comorbid cerebrovascular disease. *Nat. Rev. Neurol.* **2009**, *5*, 533–541. [CrossRef]
11. Dunalska, A.; Pikul, J.; Schok, K.; Wiejak, K.A.; Alster, P. The Significance of Vascular Pathogenesis in the Examination of Corticobasal Syndrome. *Front. Aging Neurosci.* **2021**, *13*, 668614. [CrossRef]

12. Rane, S.; Koh, N.; Oakley, J.; Caso, C.; Zabetian, C.P.; Cholerton, B.; Montine, T.J.; Grabowski, T. Arterial spin labeling detects perfusion patterns related to motor symptoms in Parkinson's disease. *Park. Relat. Disord.* **2020**, *76*, 21–28. [CrossRef] [PubMed]
13. Ho, M.-L. Arterial spin labeling: Clinical applications. *J. Neuroradiol.* **2018**, *45*, 276–289. [CrossRef] [PubMed]
14. Grade, M.; Tamames, J.A.H.; Pizzini, F.B.; Achten, E.; Golay, X.; Smits, M. A neuroradiologist's guide to arterial spin labeling MRI in clinical practice. *Neuroradiology* **2015**, *57*, 1181–1202. [CrossRef]
15. Takahashi, H.; Ishii, K.; Hosokawa, C.; Hyodo, T.; Kashiwagi, N.; Matsuki, M.; Ashikaga, R.; Murakami, T. Clinical Application of 3D Arterial Spin-Labeled Brain Perfusion Imaging for Alzheimer Disease: Comparison with Brain Perfusion SPECT. *Am. J. Neuroradiol.* **2014**, *35*, 906–911. [CrossRef]
16. Al-Bachari, S.; Vidyasagar, R.; Emsley, H.C.; Parkes, L.M. Structural and physiological neurovascular changes in idiopathic Parkinson's disease and its clinical phenotypes. *J. Cereb. Blood Flow Metab.* **2017**, *37*, 3409–3421. [CrossRef]
17. Wang, Q.; Yu, M.; Yan, L.; Xu, J.; Wang, Y.; Zhou, G.; Liu, W. Altered functional connectivity of the primary motor cortex in tremor dominant and postural instability gait difficulty subtypes of early drug-naive Parkinson's disease patients. *Front. Neurol.* **2023**, *14*, 1151775. [CrossRef]
18. Chen, Z.; He, C.; Zhang, P.; Cai, X.; Huang, W.; Chen, X.; Xu, M.; Wang, L.; Zhang, Y. Abnormal cerebellum connectivity patterns related to motor subtypes of Parkinson's disease. *J. Neural Transm.* **2023**, *130*, 549–560. [CrossRef]
19. Wang, Q.; Yu, M.; Yan, L.; Xu, J.; Wang, Y.; Zhou, G.; Liu, W. Aberrant inter-network functional connectivity in drug-naive Parkinson's disease patients with tremor dominant and postural instability and gait difficulty. *Front. Hum. Neurosci.* **2023**, *17*, 1100431. [CrossRef] [PubMed]
20. Lan, Y.; Liu, X.; Yin, C.; Lyu, J.; Xiaoxaio, M.; Cui, Z.; Li, X.; Lou, X. Resting-state functional magnetic resonance imaging study comparing tremor-dominant and postural instability/gait difficulty subtypes of Parkinson's disease. *Radiol. Medica* **2023**, *128*, 1138–1147. [CrossRef] [PubMed]
21. Amoroso, N.; La Rocca, M.; Monaco, A.; Bellotti, R.; Tangaro, S. Complex networks reveal early MRI markers of Parkinson's disease. *Med. Image Anal.* **2018**, *48*, 12–24. [CrossRef]
22. Tang, Y.; Meng, L.; Wan, C.-M.; Liu, Z.-H.; Liao, W.-H.; Yan, X.-X.; Wang, X.-Y.; Tang, B.-S.; Guo, J.-F. Identifying the presence of Parkinson's disease using low-frequency fluctuations in BOLD signals. *Neurosci. Lett.* **2017**, *645*, 1–6. [CrossRef] [PubMed]
23. Gu, Q.; Zhang, H.; Xuan, M.; Luo, W.; Huang, P.; Xia, S.; Zhang, M. Automatic Classification on Multi-Modal MRI Data for Diagnosis of the Postural Instability and Gait Difficulty Subtype of Parkinson's Disease. *J. Park. Dis.* **2016**, *6*, 545–556. [CrossRef] [PubMed]
24. Abós, A.; Baggio, H.C.; Segura, B.; García-Díaz, A.I.; Compta, Y.; Martí, M.J.; Valldeoriola, F.; Junqué, C. Discriminating cognitive status in Parkinson's disease through functional connectomics and machine learning. *Sci. Rep.* **2017**, *7*, 45347. [CrossRef] [PubMed]
25. Jin, C.; Qi, S.; Yang, L.; Teng, Y.; Li, C.; Yao, Y.; Ruan, X.; Wei, X. Abnormal functional connectivity density involvement in freezing of gait and its application for subtyping Parkinson's disease. *Brain Imaging Behav.* **2023**, *17*, 1–11. [CrossRef]
26. Gong, N.J.; Clifford, G.D.; Esper, C.D.; Factor, S.A.; McKay, J.L.; Kwon, H. Classifying Tremor Dominant and Postural Instability and Gait Difficulty Subtypes of Parkinson's Disease from Full-Body Kinematics. *Sensors* **2023**, *23*, 8330. [CrossRef] [PubMed]
27. Xu, J.; Xu, Q.; Liu, S.; Li, L.; Li, L.; Yen, T.-C.; Wu, J.; Wang, J.; Zuo, C.; Wu, P.; et al. Computer-Aided Classification Framework of Parkinsonian Disorders Using 11C-CFT PET Imaging. *Front. Aging Neurosci.* **2022**, *13*, 792951. [CrossRef]
28. Larrañaga, P.; Calvo, B.; Santana, R.; Bielza, C.; Galdiano, J.; Inza, I.; Lozano, J.A.; Armañanzas, R.; Santafé, G.; Pérez, A.; et al. Machine learning in bioinformatics. *Briefings Bioinform.* **2006**, *7*, 86–112. [CrossRef]
29. Xia, M.; Wang, J.; He, Y. BrainNet Viewer: A Network Visualization Tool for Human Brain Connectomics. *PLoS ONE* **2013**, *8*, e68910. [CrossRef] [PubMed]
30. Rolls, E.T.; Huang, C.-C.; Lin, C.-P.; Feng, J.; Joliot, M. Automated anatomical labelling atlas 3. *NeuroImage* **2020**, *206*, 116189. [CrossRef]
31. Long, Z.; Li, J.; Liao, H.; Deng, L.; Du, Y.; Fan, J.; Li, X.; Miao, J.; Qiu, S.; Long, C.; et al. A Multi-Modal and Multi-Atlas Integrated Framework for Identification of Mild Cognitive Impairment. *Brain Sci.* **2022**, *12*, 751. [CrossRef]
32. Bai, X.; Wang, W.; Zhang, X.; Hu, Z.; Zhang, Y.; Li, Z.; Zhang, X.; Yuan, Z.; Tang, H.; Zhang, Y.; et al. Cerebral perfusion variance in new daily persistent headache and chronic migraine: An arterial spin-labeled MR imaging study. *J. Headache Pain* **2022**, *23*, 156. [CrossRef] [PubMed]
33. Cheng, W.; Rolls, E.T.; Qiu, J.; Xie, X.; Wei, D.; Huang, C.-C.; Yang, A.C.; Tsai, S.-J.; Li, Q.; Meng, J.; et al. Increased functional connectivity of the posterior cingulate cortex with the lateral orbitofrontal cortex in depression. *Transl. Psychiatry* **2018**, *8*, 90. [CrossRef] [PubMed]
34. Trutti, A.C.; Mulder, M.J.; Hommel, B.; Forstmann, B.U. Functional neuroanatomical review of the ventral tegmental area. *NeuroImage* **2019**, *191*, 258–268. [CrossRef] [PubMed]
35. Salmanpour, M.R.; Shamsaei, M.; Rahmim, A. Feature selection and machine learning methods for optimal identification and prediction of subtypes in Parkinson's disease. *Comput. Methods Programs Biomed.* **2021**, *206*, 106131. [CrossRef] [PubMed]
36. Castanho, E.N.; Aidos, H.; Madeira, S.C. Biclustering fMRI time series: A comparative study. *BMC Bioinform.* **2022**, *23*, 192. [CrossRef]

37. Rahaman, A.; Damaraju, E.; Turner, J.A.; van Erp, T.G.; Mathalon, D.H.; Vaidya, J.; Muller, B.; Pearlson, G.; Calhoun, V.D. Tri-Clustering Dynamic Functional Network Connectivity Identifies Significant Schizophrenia Effects Across Multiple States in Distinct Subgroups of Individuals. *Brain Connect.* **2022**, *12*, 61–73. [CrossRef]
38. Rahaman, A.; Mathalon, D.; Lee, H.J.; Jiang, W.; Mueller, B.A.; Andreassen, O.; Agartz, I.; Sponheim, S.R.; Mayer, A.R.; Stephen, J.; et al. N-BiC: A Method for Multi-Component and Symptom Biclustering of Structural MRI Data: Application to Schizophrenia. *IEEE Trans. Biomed. Eng.* **2020**, *67*, 110–121. [CrossRef]
39. Yang, H.-J.; Kim, Y.E.; Yun, J.Y.; Kim, H.-J.; Jeon, B.S. Identifying the Clusters within Nonmotor Manifestations in Early Parkinson's Disease by Using Unsupervised Cluster Analysis. *PLoS ONE* **2014**, *9*, e91906. [CrossRef] [PubMed]
40. Albrecht, F.; Poulakis, K.; Freidle, M.; Johansson, H.; Ekman, U.; Volpe, G.; Westman, E.; Pereira, J.B.; Franzén, E. Unraveling Parkinson's disease heterogeneity using subtypes based on multimodal data. *Park. Relat. Disord.* **2022**, *102*, 19–29. [CrossRef] [PubMed]
41. Nemoto, K. Understanding Voxel-Based Morphometry. *Brain Nerves* **2017**, *69*, 505–511. [CrossRef]
42. Pezzoli, S.; Sánchez-Valle, R.; Solanes, A.; Kempton, M.J.; Bandmann, O.; Shin, J.I.; Cagnin, A.; Goldman, J.G.; Merkitch, D.; Firbank, M.J.; et al. Neuroanatomical and cognitive correlates of visual hallucinations in Parkinson's disease and dementia with Lewy bodies: Voxel-based morphometry and neuropsychological meta-analysis. *Neurosci. Biobehav. Rev.* **2021**, *128*, 367–382. [CrossRef]
43. Matsuda, H. MRI morphometry in Alzheimer's disease. *Ageing Res. Rev.* **2016**, *30*, 17–24. [CrossRef]
44. Nemoto, K. Voxel-Based Morphometry for Schizophrenia: A Review. *Brain Nerves* **2017**, *69*, 513–518.
45. Keramatian, K.; Chakrabarty, T.; Saraf, G.; Pinto, J.V.; Yatham, L.N. Grey matter abnormalities in first—Episode mania: A systematic review and meta—analysis of voxe—based morphometry studies. *Bipolar Disord.* **2021**, *23*, 228–240. [CrossRef] [PubMed]
46. Solana-Lavalle, G.; Rosas-Romero, R. Classification of PPMI MRI scans with voxel-based morphometry and machine learning to assist in the diagnosis of Parkinson's disease. *Comput. Methods Programs Biomed.* **2021**, *198*, 105793. [CrossRef]
47. Rolls, E.T. The cingulate cortex and limbic systems for emotion, action, and memory. *Brain Struct. Funct.* **2019**, *224*, 3001–3018. [CrossRef]
48. Vogt, B.A. Cingulate cortex in Parkinson's disease. *Handb. Clin. Neurol.* **2019**, *166*, 253–266. [CrossRef]
49. Piccinin, C.C.; Campos, L.S.; Guimarães, R.P.; Piovesana, L.G.; dos Santos, M.C.A.; Azevedo, P.C.; Campos, B.M.; de Rezende, T.J.R.; Amato-Filho, A.; Cendes, F.; et al. Differential Pattern of Cerebellar Atrophy in Tremor-Predominant and Akinetic/Rigidity-Predominant Parkinson's Disease. *Cerebellum* **2017**, *16*, 623–628. [CrossRef]
50. Li, J.; Zhang, Y.; Huang, Z.; Jiang, Y.; Ren, Z.; Liu, D.; Zhang, J.; La Piana, R.; Chen, Y. Cortical and subcortical morphological alterations in motor subtypes of Parkinson's disease. *NPJ Park. Dis.* **2022**, *8*, 167. [CrossRef]
51. Guidali, G.; Pisoni, A.; Bolognini, N.; Papagno, C. Keeping order in the brain: The supramarginal gyrus and serial order in short-term memory. *Cortex* **2019**, *119*, 89–99. [CrossRef] [PubMed]
52. Vertes, R.P.; Linley, S.B.; Rojas, A.K.P. Structural and functional organization of the midline and intralaminar nuclei of the thalamus. *Front. Behav. Neurosci.* **2022**, *16*, 964644. [CrossRef]
53. Lopez, A.M.; Trujillo, P.; Hernandez, A.B.; Lin, Y.; Kang, H.; Landman, B.A.; Englot, D.J.; Dawant, B.M.; Konrad, P.E.; Claassen, D.O. Structural Correlates of the Sensorimotor Cerebellum in Parkinson's Disease and Essential Tremor. *Mov. Disord.* **2020**, *35*, 1181–1188. [CrossRef] [PubMed]
54. Borghammer, P. Perfusion and metabolism imaging studies in Parkinson's disease. *Dan. Med. J.* **2012**, *59*, B4466. [PubMed]
55. Boonstra, J.T.; Michielse, S.; Temel, Y.; Hoogland, G.; Jahanshahi, A. Neuroimaging Detectable Differences between Parkinson's Disease Motor Subtypes: A Systematic Review. *Mov. Disord. Clin. Pract.* **2020**, *8*, 175–192. [CrossRef] [PubMed]
56. Siger, M.; Schuff, N.; Zhu, X.; Miller, B.L.; Weiner, M.W. Regional Myo-inositol Concentration in Mild Cognitive Impairment Using 1H Magnetic Resonance Spectroscopic Imaging. *Alzheimer Dis. Assoc. Disord.* **2009**, *23*, 57–62. [CrossRef]

Disclaimer/Publisher's Note: The statements, opinions and data contained in all publications are solely those of the individual author(s) and contributor(s) and not of MDPI and/or the editor(s). MDPI and/or the editor(s) disclaim responsibility for any injury to people or property resulting from any ideas, methods, instructions or products referred to in the content.

brain sciences

MDPI

Article

Automatic Diagnosis of Major Depressive Disorder Using a High- and Low-Frequency Feature Fusion Framework

Junyu Wang [1,2], Tongtong Li [1,2], Qi Sun [1,2], Yuhui Guo [2,3], Jiandong Yu [1,2], Zhijun Yao [1,2,*], Ning Hou [4,*] and Bin Hu [1,2,5,6,*]

1 School of Information Science and Engineering, Lanzhou University, Lanzhou 730000, China; wangjy22@lzu.edu.cn (J.W.); ttli2022@lzu.edu.cn (T.L.); sunq2023@lzu.edu.cn (Q.S.); 220220942541@lzu.edu.cn (J.Y.)
2 Gansu Provincial Key Laboratory of Wearable Computing, Lanzhou University, Lanzhou 730000, China; guoyh2022@lzu.edu.cn
3 School of Mathematics and Statistics, Lanzhou University, Lanzhou 730000, China
4 Medical Department, The Third People's Hospital of Tianshui, Tianshui 741000, China
5 School of Medical Technology, Beijing Institute of Technology, Beijing 100081, China
6 CAS Center for Excellence in Brain Science and Intelligence Technology, Shanghai Institutes for Biological Sciences, Chinese Academy of Sciences, Shanghai 200031, China
* Correspondence: yaozj@lzu.edu.cn (Z.Y.); 15337010167@163.com (N.H.); bh@lzu.edu.cn (B.H.)

Abstract: Major Depressive Disorder (MDD) is a common mental illness resulting in immune disorders and even thoughts of suicidal behavior. Neuroimaging techniques serve as a quantitative tool for the assessment of MDD diagnosis. In the domain of computer-aided magnetic resonance imaging diagnosis, current research predominantly focuses on isolated local or global information, often neglecting the synergistic integration of multiple data sources, thus potentially overlooking valuable details. To address this issue, we proposed a diagnostic model for MDD that integrates high-frequency and low-frequency information using data from diffusion tensor imaging (DTI), structural magnetic resonance imaging (sMRI), and functional magnetic resonance imaging (fMRI). First, we designed a meta-low-frequency encoder (MLFE) and a meta-high-frequency encoder (MHFE) to extract the low-frequency and high-frequency feature information from DTI and sMRI, respectively. Then, we utilized a multilayer perceptron (MLP) to extract features from fMRI data. Following the feature cross-fusion, we designed the ensemble learning threshold voting method to determine the ultimate diagnosis for MDD. The model achieved accuracy, precision, specificity, F1-score, MCC, and AUC values of 0.724, 0.750, 0.882, 0.600, 0.421, and 0.667, respectively. This approach provides new research ideas for the diagnosis of MDD.

Keywords: major depressive disorder; magnetic resonance imaging; multi-modal; deep learning; high and low frequencies; feature fusion

1. Introduction

Major depressive disorder (MDD) is a prevalent mental health disorder that has a significant impact on both the individual and society [1]. It often presents as a severe and enduring depression that is accompanied by a variety of physical and mental symptoms. The utilization of clinical data and advanced imaging techniques in the investigation of depression [2,3] can aid healthcare professionals in achieving a precise diagnosis. Presently, imaging technology continues to advance at a rapid rate. Due to their non-invasive ability to provide a more comprehensive insight into the mechanistic abnormalities associated with disease pathology, both diffusion tensor imaging (DTI) and functional magnetic resonance imaging (fMRI) have become prominent tools in the field of MDD research and diagnosis. Specifically, DTI can illuminate the structural and anisotropic attributes of the brain's white matter fibers by tracking the diffusion patterns of water molecules, which provides a more profound understanding of the brain's communication system. Additionally, using BOLD signals for studying changes in brain function is one of the fundamental methods of fMRI.

Traditional machine learning techniques are capable of extracting information from pre-processed data sources, including gray matter (GM) [4] and functional connectivity (FC) matrices, among others, for disease diagnosis. Meanwhile, deep learning is particularly adept at the automated extraction of higher-level features and has demonstrated excellent performance across a range of computer vision tasks [5]. Deep learning has been extensively employed in various data feature extraction applications, including encompassing computed tomography (CT) [6], positron emission tomography (PET) [7], and magnetic resonance imaging (MRI). Moreover, deep learning models for multimodal data exhibit superior capabilities in capturing qualitative data features compared to unimodal approaches, and they offer robust model interpretability. For instance, Song et al. [8] designed multicenter and multichannel pooling GCN to diagnose Alzheimer's disease using fMRI and DTI modalities, with an average classification accuracy of 93.05% in their binary classification tasks. Wang et al. [9] proposed an adaptive multimodal neuroimage integration (AMNI) framework for automatic MDD detection using both functional and structural MRI modalities, which demonstrated the effectiveness of the proposed method. While researchers make use of various modal features for disease diagnosis, there is often a missed opportunity to leverage cross-fusion between different scale features from different modalities, resulting in the potential oversight of valuable information.

Wang et al. [10] used the depth model 3D-Densenet for MDD diagnosis with only unimodal information from MRI. Gao et al. [11] proposed an attention-guided, unified deep learning framework using only local structural characteristics for classification. Marwa et al. [12] utilized shallow deep learning architecture to extract only local feature information from brain MRI for identifying a multi-class Alzheimer's disease. However, they only considered local or global information. Jang et al. [13] proposed a spach transformer to accomplish image denoising for PET modalities using local and global information, but few modalities were involved.

It is observed that convolutional neural networks (CNN) [14] predominantly emphasize local receptive fields during convolution, which vary in texture, shape, and size across various features. CNN leverages its robust capability in extracting effective local information to further harness more intricate, high-frequency local details. Nevertheless, fully concentrating on the entire dataset can be challenging, potentially resulting in the loss of information pertaining to long-range dependencies. Transformers [15] with self-attention mechanisms can minimize this shortcoming to capture global low-frequency information about data. In medical imaging, high-frequency components often convey specific details and edge information, including features like the border of brain sulci and gyri, the subtle texture of the cerebral cortex, and more, while low-frequency components typically reflect information at a larger scale, including things like tissue distribution and brain morphology. Qiu et al. [16] fused long-range dependencies and global context information to alleviate the problem of over-smoothing and over-fitting. Qin et al. [17] found that long-range transformers have a great advantage in content selection. From a particular perspective, the transformer's capability to extract information over extensive distances is showcased.

Recently, Su et al. [18] proposed a convolutional model of 3DMKDR of electroencephalogram (EEG) signals for depression disorder recognition. Teng et al. [19] proposed a transformer-based modeling approach for depression prediction. Nonetheless, their emphasis was confined to either low-frequency or high-frequency information, potentially neglecting the comprehensive explorations of data.

To address the issue of information loss attributed to the absence of either high-frequency or low-frequency data, we have introduced a cross-fusion, which harnesses multiple modalities to encode low- and high-frequency feature representations for MDD diagnosis. This approach strengthens the adversarial robustness of the extracted feature model. The model consists of three core components: the meta-high-frequency encoder, the meta-low-frequency encoder, and integrated learning. Specifically, the meta-high-frequency encoder, which consists of a simple fully convolutional network (SFCN) [20], is better able to extract the modality's high-frequency information with fewer parameters. The meta-low-frequency encoder, comprising the 4-head attention and cls_token with positional encoding added (positional encoding has the ability to learn to differentiate between positions and cls_token serves as a learnable embedding vector, which is pre-encoded to end up with a feature vector that can be used for classification), proves more efficient and expeditious in extraction of the modality's low-frequency information. Consequently, it endeavors to steer our model towards a more comprehensive exploration of both localized specific features and global structural characteristics. Additionally, we designed MLP for feature extraction of the FC matrix and designed the cross-fusion of all the extracted different features of different modalities to obtain a deeper feature representation. To delve deeper into understanding the information loss attributed to the constraints of high-frequency and high-frequency fusion, as well as low-frequency and low-frequency fusion, we tried to explore this phenomenon in greater detail. Finally, the ensemble learning voting idea was used for classification. Compared with individual modules, ensemble learning provided greater improvements in classification performance. We summarize our contributions as follows:

- We proposed a novel multi-modality deep learning framework for automatic diagnosis of MDD;
- We developed a feature extractor to mine global dependencies and local responses using transformer and CNN architectures, respectively;
- We designed an ensemble learning voting mechanism to obtain predictions.

The rest of this paper is organized as follows: Section 2 describes the source of the subjects' data and preprocessing. Section 3 exhibits the proposed model and experimental details. Section 4 shows the ablation experiment and comparison with other deep learning models. Section 5 provides the results of this study, limitations, and future improvements. Section 6 presents a summary.

2. Material

2.1. Subjects

We collected information on three modalities—DTI, fMRI, and sMRI—from 128 participants, and all patients with MDD in this study received a clinical diagnosis based on the structured clinical interview for diagnostic and statistical manual of mental disorders, fourth edition (DSM-IV) axis i disease (SCID). HCs (healthy controls) were recruited using the non-patient edition of the structured clinical interview for DSM-IV.

All participants were within the age range of from 18 to 65 and did not manifest any other mental illnesses. Furthermore, we obtained approval from the Ethics Committee of Gansu Provincial Hospital, China (Approval No. 2017-071, 6 July 2017). Prior to participation, individuals provided informed consent after attaining a comprehensive understanding of the study's objectives, potential risks, and benefits.

2.2. Data Processing

The rs-fMRI images underwent preprocessing, utilizing the unified data processing assistant for the resting-state fMRI (DPARSF) pipeline within the DPARSF V6.2_220915 toolbox [21]. These preprocessing steps primarily encompassed head motion correction, slice timing correction, spatial normalization, and spatial smoothing. We proceeded to extract the time series data from 116 brain regions using the automated anatomical labeling (AAL) templates. Subsequently, by calculating the Pearson correlation coefficients between pairs of these brain regions, we derived the final FC matrix.

We applied the PANDA 1.3.1 software (http://www.nitrc.org/projects/panda) to preprocess the raw DTI data. Ultimately, the fractional anisotropy mapping (FAM) was generated by mapping from the MNI space to the AAL template.

For sMRI, we used the CAT12 toolbox (http://dbm.neuro.uni-jena.de/vbm/) implemented in the SPM12 software (http://www.fil.ion.ucl.ac.uk/spm/) to extract normalized gray matter volumes.

Following data preprocessing, the data size of the FAM was 91 × 109 × 91, while the size of the sMRI gray matter image was 113 × 137 × 113. To match the model inputs, we used simpleITK (simpleITK is an open source tool library for medical image processing) in the sitkNearestNeighbor to modify the size of the input data.

The clinical diagnostic characteristics of the participants are shown in Table 1. Excessive head movement (rotation degree > 2°, translation distances > 2 mm, or mean FD (Jenkinson) > 0.2) and missing modalities were excluded from the analysis. Patients clinically diagnosed with MDD and possessing HAMD scores > 7 were included. A total of 116 subjects were eventually further analyzed, including 54 MDDs and 62 HCs.

Table 1. The clinical diagnosis characteristics of the participants.

	MDD	HCs
Number of participants	54	62
HAMA	17.19 ± 7.58	-
HAMD (17-item)	17.62 ± 5.95	-

Abbreviations: MDD = Major Depressive Disorder, HCs = healthy controls, HAMA = Hamilton anxiety scale, HAMD = Hamilton depression rating scale.

Following the processing, we obtained a 3D medical image size of 112 × 112 × 112 for both FAM and sMRI, while the FC matrix size from fMRI remained unchanged at 116 × 116. As a final step, we introduced a minute value of 1×10^{-9} to normalize all the data, thereby preventing division by zero.

3. Methods

This paper introduces an approach that integrates both CNN and transformer architectures to extract features encompassing global low-frequency information and local high-frequency information and then fuses these features.

3.1. Overview

The proposed model primarily consisted of encoders for extracting high- and low-frequency features. These encoders encompassed the meta-low-frequency encoder (MLFE) and the meta-high-frequency encoder (MHFE). The MLFE was designed as an encoder for extracting low-frequency information, adapted to capture features in medical images that encapsulate global information. This proficiency was valuable for comprehending the overarching characteristics of the data. Conversely, MHFE was designed as an encoder to extract high-frequency depth features from the image. These features represented the local key attributes of the image, enabling the removal of redundant information and the representation of a unique and stable data structure to a significant extent. Additionally, the model incorporated a MLP for the extraction of functional features from the FC matrix, as illustrated in Figure 1.

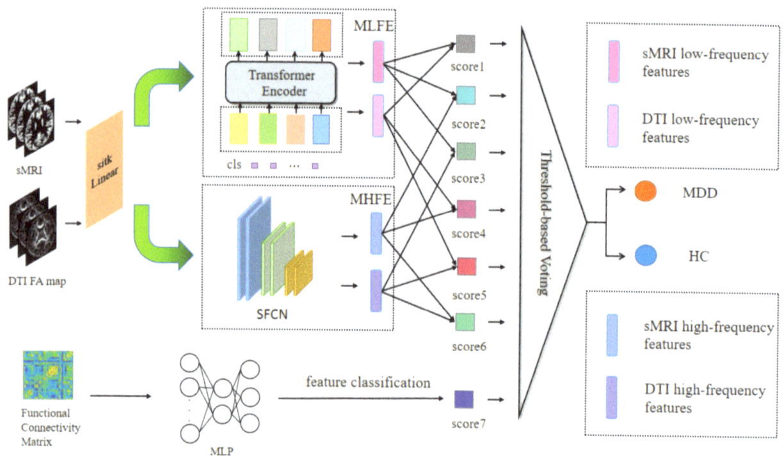

Figure 1. Overall structure of the proposed model. Abbreviations: MLFE = meta-low-frequency encoder, MHFE = meta-high-frequency encoder, MDD = major depressive disorder, HC = healthy control.

3.2. Meta-Low-Frequency Encoder

Low-frequency information typically signifies slowly evolving structural characteristics and global patterns, corresponding to alterations occurring over longer spatial or temporal scales. This enables the capture of macroscopic brain structural features. In this module, we devised the meta-component for low-frequency feature extraction responsible for acquiring low-frequency feature information from FAM and sMRI, as depicted in Figure 2. The transformer encoder [22] element served as the foundation for our design in this module.

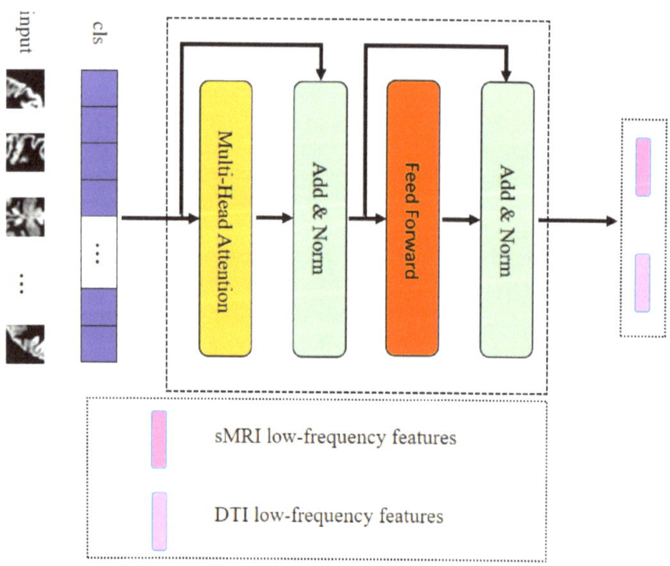

Figure 2. Meta-low-frequency encoder.

To enhance computational efficiency, we selected 4 heads of attention in the transformer encoder, set the individual word vector to 512, and set num_layers to 6. This method was utilized to develop lightweight models, which were useful for implementing models in resource-constrained situations and could improve model utility. Initially, we generated a positional encoding vector for the cls_token in a random manner. Prior to this, we selected a convolutional layer rather than a linear layer to boost the module's performance, and finally, positional encoding was added to the input data.

Through the implementation of MLFE, we could subsequently acquire information pertaining to the low-frequency features within the corresponding modalities.

3.3. Meta-High-Frequency Encoder

High-frequency information typically conveys localized details with rapidly changing characteristics, corresponding to changes on shorter spatial or temporal scales. This makes local subtleties and minute changes in the brain's architecture easier to capture. In this module, we designed the meta-module, which was made up of SFCN to extract sMRI and FAM high-frequency features.

This module comprised a convolutional layer in combination with an average pooling layer. The channel sizes of the convolutional layers were configured as [32, 64, 128, 64, 32]. Notably, the last layer did not contain a max-pooling operation and used a $1 \times 1 \times 1$ convolutional kernel, whereas all the previous layers contained a max-pooling layer and a $3 \times 3 \times 3$ convolution with a padding value of 1. Then, it went through the sequence of convolutional, BatchNorm, and ReLU layers, ending with the average pooling layer, shown in Figure 3.

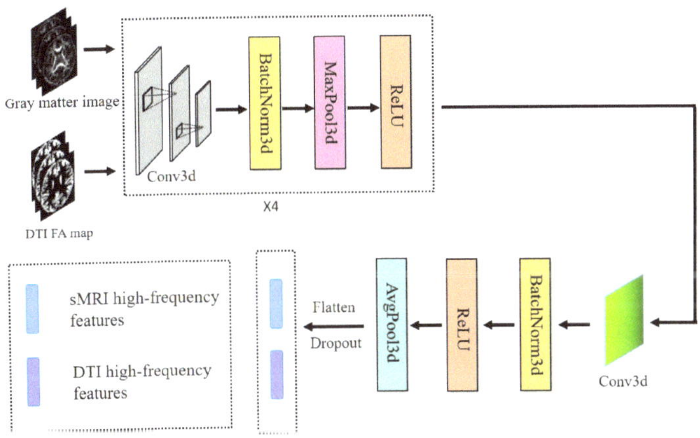

Figure 3. Meta-high-frequency encoder.

We then could acquire high-frequency data describing the modalities' microscopic characteristics using MHFE.

3.4. Multilayer Perceptron

To obtain the FC matrix information, we first calculated the integrating time series extracted from the fMRI, which could reveal the internal functional characteristics of the brain, and help to better obtain useful information and explore the difference between disease and normal state. Finally, we let the FC matrix go through MLP for further analysis.

This module extracted the high-level abstract FC matrix features from fMRI. The MLP included an input layer, a hidden layer, and an output layer. Each layer was accompanied by a ReLU activation layer and a dropout layer with a rate of 20%. The final output consisted of a single logit value obtained from the MLP.

3.5. Feature Fusion

We fused the extracted sMRI and FAM, corresponding to the low-frequency features and high-frequency features, respectively, according to the high-high-frequency fusion, low-low-frequency fusion, and high-low-frequency fusion. The micro- and macro-features of each modality could be extracted via high-high-frequency fusion and low-low-frequency fusion. High-low-frequency fusion serves as compensation for the potential loss of features in each modality encountered in the initial two approaches. We amalgamated the six features using three feature fusion methods, which proved more effective in capturing the potential interactions between multimodal sources and within each modality. As a result, we obtained six logit values corresponding to the fusion process.

The six logit values, along with the single logit value extracted from the fMRI data features, were each subjected to a sigmoid activation layer to yield the seven values essential for the final voting process.

3.6. Ensemble Learning Voting

Ensemble learning seeks to enhance a model's performance and stability by combining predictions from multiple weak learners. This approach mitigates the risk of overfitting, boosts the model's generalization capabilities, enhances its robustness, and ultimately leads to more precise prediction or classification outcomes. Furthermore, ensemble learning helps diminish misclassification attributed to data noise or uncertainty.

Each model in this approach predicted the sample and then this was compared to the threshold we set. The final prediction was determined through the use of the majority vote principle.

3.7. Experiment Detail

The experiments were compiled with pytorch-1.8.2 and run on GPUs of NVIDIA Tesla V100 based on Ubuntu 18.04. The model was trained for a number of 200 epochs, utilizing a binary cross-entropy (BCE) loss function with a small batch size of 4. We used the Adam optimizer [23] with a learning rate of 9×10^{-4} and a weight decay of 1×10^{-8}. To evaluate the model's performance, we implemented a 4-fold cross-validation on the dataset, partitioning the data into four subsets. In each fold, one subset served as the testing set, while the other three subsets were utilized for model training. Ultimately, the mean $\pm$ SD was used as the result.

3.8. Evaluation Metrics

The accuracy (ACC) (Equation (1)), precision (PREC) (Equation (2)), recall (REC) (Equation (3)), specificity (SPE) (Equation (4)), F1-score (F-1), Matthew's correlation coefficient (MCC), and area under the receiver operating characteristic (ROC) curve (AUC) were used to evaluate classification performance,

$$\mathrm{ACC} = \frac{\mathrm{TP}+\mathrm{TN}}{\mathrm{TP}+\mathrm{TN}+\mathrm{FP}+\mathrm{FN}} \tag{1}$$

$$\mathrm{PREC} = \frac{\mathrm{TP}}{\mathrm{TP}+\mathrm{FP}} \tag{2}$$

$$\mathrm{REC} = \frac{\mathrm{TP}}{\mathrm{TP}+\mathrm{FN}} \tag{3}$$

$$\mathrm{SPE} = \frac{\mathrm{TN}}{\mathrm{TN}+\mathrm{FP}} \tag{4}$$

$$\mathrm{F}-1 = 2 \times \frac{\mathrm{PREC} \times \mathrm{REC}}{\mathrm{PREC}+\mathrm{REC}} \tag{5}$$

$$\mathrm{MCC} = \frac{\mathrm{TN} \times \mathrm{TP} - \mathrm{FN} \times \mathrm{FP}}{\sqrt{(\mathrm{TN}+\mathrm{FP})(\mathrm{FN}+\mathrm{TP})(\mathrm{TN}+\mathrm{FN})(\mathrm{TP}+\mathrm{FP})}} \tag{6}$$

where TP, FN, FP, and TN represent True Positive, False Negative, False Positive, and True Negative, respectively.

4. Results

In this section, we set up ablation experiments as well as comparisons with others with the aim of verifying the validity of our proposed models. These comparison experiments included experiments with individual modal combination situations as inputs, experiments with high- and low-frequency sub-modules, and experiments comparing classical CNN as well as transformer models. To ensure the reliability of our results, we used the same standard for dividing the datasets in all experiments. We non-overlappingly divided the datasets into the training set (87) and the test set (29) in a ratio of 3:1, where the training set was used to train the weights of the models and the test set was used to test the models.

4.1. Ablation Experiments

To validate the robustness of the model, we systematically deconstructed it and analyzed its components individually. First, we assessed the cross-fusion of various modalities by validating the performance of each modality in isolation and in various paired combinations. The data size division used in this experiment remained the same as above. All assessment indicators were consistent, and the assessed results are presented in Table 2.

Table 2. Comparisons of different multi-modal inputs in the proposed model.

Modalities	ACC	PREC	REC	SPE	F-1	AUC	MCC
sMRI	0.620 ± 0.088	0.550 ± 0.043	0.500 ± 0.121	0.710 ± 0.082	0.520 ± 0.101	0.667 ± 0.023	0.209 ± 0.021
fMRI	0.517 ± 0.061	0.444 ± 0.068	0.667 ± 0.042	0.412 ± 0.116	0.533 ± 0.038	0.593 ± 0.042	0.080 ± 0.042
DTI	0.517 ± 0.052	0.400 ± 0.031	0.333 ± 0.153	0.647 ± 0.095	0.364 ± 0.069	0.618 ± 0.061	−0.020 ± 0.066
sMRI + fMRI	0.690 ± 0.079	0.667 ± 0.074	0.500 ± 0.086	0.824 ± 0.112	0.571 ± 0.076	0.711 ± 0.077	0.344 ± 0.115
sMRI + DTI	0.655 ± 0.044	0.583 ± 0.069	0.583 ± 0.098	0.706 ± 0.137	0.583 ± 0.124	0.642 ± 0.054	0.289 ± 0.023
fMRI + DTI	0.586 ± 0.056	0.500 ± 0.049	0.500 ± 0.078	0.647 ± 0.063	0.500 ± 0.073	0.652 ± 0.035	0.147 ± 0.121
sMRI + fMRI + DTI	0.724 ± 0.021	0.750 ± 0.028	0.500 ± 0.054	0.882 ± 0.044	0.600 ± 0.034	0.667 ± 0.029	0.421 ± 0.033

Next, we validated the fusion effect of different low- and high-frequencies. The division of the data for this experiment remained as previously described. Then, we validated the three modules of low- and high-frequency and fMRI blocks, respectively, so as to verify the advantages of the proposed fusion method, and the evaluation metrics are shown in Table 3.

Table 3. Comparison of different branches of the proposed model using sMRI, fMRI, and DTI as inputs.

Models	ACC	PREC	REC	SPE	F-1	AUC	MCC
MHFE	0.690 ± 0.053	0.670 ± 0.048	0.500 ± 0.031	0.820 ± 0.065	0.570 ± 0.074	0.650 ± 0.024	0.344 ± 0.011
MLFE	0.517 ± 0.023	0.438 ± 0.034	0.583 ± 0.029	0.471 ± 0.053	0.500 ± 0.062	0.542 ± 0.051	0.053 ± 0.213
Only fMRI block	0.517 ± 0.061	0.444 ± 0.068	0.667 ± 0.042	0.412 ± 0.116	0.533 ± 0.038	0.593 ± 0.042	0.080 ± 0.042
Proposed model	0.724 ± 0.021	0.750 ± 0.028	0.500 ± 0.054	0.882 ± 0.044	0.600 ± 0.034	0.667 ± 0.029	0.421 ± 0.033

4.2. Comparison with Other Models

In this section, a comprehensive comparison was made between the proposed model and four currently popular deep learning models (LeNet, ResNet, DenseNet, and Vision Transformer). In this experiment, we used the same data size division as before. Using the same model settings, the purpose of this comparison was to evaluate the validity of the proposed model. Table 4 shows further details. The proposed model extracted data features more comprehensively and performed feature fusion differently from other models for the extracted features, which was advantageous to the final classification diagnosis.

Table 4. Comparison of different encoders between the proposed model and classical CNN models using sMRI, fMRI, and DTI as inputs.

Models	ACC	PREC	REC	SPE	F-1	AUC	MCC
LeNet *	0.620 ± 0.028	0.533 ± 0.022	0.667 ± 0.041	0.588 ± 0.048	0.593 ± 0.067	0.662 ± 0.049	0.251 ± 0.022
ResNet *	0.621 ± 0.042	0.545 ± 0.039	0.500 ± 0.047	0.706 ± 0.053	0.522 ± 0.035	0.613 ± 0.052	0.209 ± 0.041
DenseNet *	0.655 ± 0.012	0.583 ± 0.055	0.583 ± 0.102	0.706 ± 0.076	0.583 ± 0.042	0.637 ± 0.023	0.289 ± 0.053
Vision Transformer [24] *	0.552 ± 0.089	0.467 ± 0.042	0.583 ± 0.057	0.529 ± 0.039	0.519 ± 0.085	0.500 ± 0.097	0.111 ± 0.037
Proposed model	0.724 ± 0.021	0.750 ± 0.028	0.500 ± 0.054	0.882 ± 0.044	0.600 ± 0.034	0.667 ± 0.029	0.421 ± 0.033

Notes: * denotes classical deep learning model.

5. Discussion

MDD is a complex and common disorder with an uncertain cause. Deep learning models for the diagnosis of MDD have been widely proposed with the advancement of medical imaging technology and algorithms. However, previous studies have mostly concentrated on single-scale modal feature data used as disease diagnostic criteria and have overlooked the possible influence of cross-fusion between various modalities. Simultaneously, during the modal feature extraction process, a singular focus on either local high-frequency or global low-frequency information is prevalent. Traditional fusion techniques employed in these situations may inadvertently mask potential interactions between high- and low-frequency information. As a result, this may further reduce the available data features and ultimately diminish the effectiveness of the model in disease diagnosis. Thus, our completed experiments substantiated significantly improved results when employing multimodal input for extracting high- and low-frequency features, as opposed to using fewer modalities for this purpose. These results could be attributed to the broader representational capacity of multimodal data and the enhanced utilization of valuable information. Furthermore, the results derived from the exclusive use of high- or low-frequency fusion techniques exhibited substantial differences when compared to the results obtained through the three fusion methods for high- and low-frequency. This discrepancy underscored the idea that the effective integration of high- and low-frequency features yields more favorable diagnostic results.

We compared current approaches for diagnosing MDD based on deep learning models. Zhu et al. [25] proposed the only deep graph convolutional neural network (DGCNN) method for brain network classification between 830 MDD patients and 771 normal controls (NC), with a final accuracy of 72.1%. Venkatapathy et al. [26] proposed an ensemble model for the classification between 821 patients with MDD and 765 HCs, and the final model achieved 71.18% accuracy in upsampling and 70.24% accuracy in downsampling. Hu et al. [27] proposed a transformer-based BrainNPT model for brain network classification on a large dataset of REST-meta-MDD, and the accuracy of the model after pre-training reached 70.25%. The reason that these models are less accurate than ours is likely due to the focus on more particular details or the reality that the long- and short-distance information are not sufficiently mined for fusion, even though the amount of this data is much larger than ours.

The integration of high- and low-frequency information represents a crucial approach in clinical diagnosis, encompassing image features across various scales and providing a robust foundation for disease diagnosis and analysis. Specifically, the extraction of the high-frequency component in images is concentrated on the intricate details within the image. These details are essential for identifying diseases because they assist in recognizing subtle changes in pathology. Conversely, the extraction of low-frequency components in images characterizes the macroscopic structures and features that exist within the image. This global perspective complements the local details, providing a vital component of information that proves critical in the final evaluation of the disease. High-frequency and low-frequency information can have distinct features in a variety of medical problems. This integrated method enables healthcare practitioners to selectively emphasize important components, allowing them to conduct a full assessment that easily moves from micro to macro and vice versa. This comprehensive evaluation improves their ability to determine the patients' health status, evaluate therapy outcomes, and develop a more personalized treatment strategy.

We proposed a model for cross-fusion of multimodal features based on high and low frequency, aiming at a better and more thorough utilization of high and low frequency information and an effective resolution of the prior issue. In the case of high- and low-frequency features, the fusion of high-frequency and low-frequency data presented a distinct perspective compared to other feature information. This approach aims to comprehensively bridge the gaps between the overlooked features, gain a deeper understanding of feature interactions, and enhance the diagnosis of MDD. The addition of our cross-fusion method to a previous fusion scheme fully explored this further and made up for the missing information between the neglected features and achieved a more comprehensive feature interaction.

We believe that the proposed model is of great generalization and migration ability. Although our study focuses on specific disease detection, the essential principles and approaches of the model are applicable to other medical image-based disease diagnoses. We believe that if the structural properties of the data are similar, the model can produce similar results in related domains. However, every domain faces its own set of challenges that need adaptation and validation for better use in other fields. Future study might investigate the model's potential for use and evaluation in other fields.

Although our model achieved satisfactory results, there are still some shortcomings. On the one hand, the dataset we used was relatively small, and the size of the dataset affects the effect of the deep learning model to a certain extent. On the other hand, we only used the more common modal features as inputs to the model, and whether there are other features that can further improve the classification ability of our model needs to be further verified.

In future research, we aim to enhance the diagnostic efficacy of the model through the pursuit of two key avenues. (1) Enriching modal data information: our goal is to add the number of modalities of the data to improve the diversity and quality of the data. The work being performed will allow for a deeper and more comprehensive understanding of the features of the illness. (2) Enhancing encoder design: our goal is to design a more efficient encoder that can quickly, accurately, and deeply extract underlying data features. This enhancement will elevate the quality of features deployable in disease diagnosis.

6. Conclusions

In this paper, we proposed a multimodal cross-fusion MDD diagnostic model based on high- and low-frequency information. We designed MHFE and MLFE to capture more profound local high-frequency and global low-frequency information from multimodal magnetic resonance imaging data. By cross-fusing these extracted features, we aimed to address the issue of potential feature loss. Upon extracting the profound functional features from the FC matrix through the MLP, we uniformly classified them utilizing the ensemble learning voting strategy. This approach has the potential to enhance classification performance beyond that of a single module. The model achieved a 72.4% accuracy rate, which highlighted the necessity to study the interactions between multimodal high and low frequencies information.

Author Contributions: Conceptualization, J.W. and T.L.; Methodology, J.W.; Writing—original draft, J.W.; Formal analysis, T.L.; Investigation, T.L.; Project administration, Q.S.; Resources, Y.G.; Software, J.Y.; Supervision, Z.Y. and N.H.; Funding acquisition, B.H. All authors have read and agreed to the published version of the manuscript.

Funding: This work was supported in part by the National Key Research and Development Program of China (Grant No. 2019YFA0706200), in part by the National Natural Science Foundation of China (Grant No. U21A20520, and No.62227807), and in part by the Science and Technology Program of Gansu Province (Grant No. 23YFGA0004).

Institutional Review Board Statement: The study was conducted in accordance with the Declaration of Helsinki, and approved by the Ethics Committee of Gansu Provincial Hospital, China (Approval No. 2017-071, 6 July 2017).

Informed Consent Statement: Informed consent was obtained from all subjects involved in the study.

Data Availability Statement: The data presented in this study are available on request from the corresponding author.

Acknowledgments: The authors thank all participants for their assistance with this research.

Conflicts of Interest: The authors declare no conflict of interest.

References

1. Vos, T.; Lim, S.S.; Abbafati, C.; Abbas, K.M.; Abbasi, M.; Abbasifard, M.; Abbasi-Kangevari, M.; Abbastabar, H.; Abd-Allah, F.; Abdelalim, A. Global burden of 369 diseases and injuries in 204 countries and territories, 1990–2019: A systematic analysis for the Global Burden of Disease Study 2019. *Lancet* **2020**, *396*, 1204–1222. [CrossRef] [PubMed]
2. Chen, Q.; Bi, Y.; Zhao, X.; Lai, Y.; Yan, W.; Xie, L.; Gao, T.; Xie, S.; Zeng, T.; Li, J. Regional amplitude abnormities in the major depressive disorder: A resting-state fMRI study and support vector machine analysis. *J. Affect. Disord.* **2022**, *308*, 1–9. [CrossRef] [PubMed]
3. Van Velzen, L.S.; Kelly, S.; Isaev, D.; Aleman, A.; Aftanas, L.I.; Bauer, J.; Baune, B.T.; Brak, I.V.; Carballedo, A.; Connolly, C.G. White matter disturbances in major depressive disorder: A coordinated analysis across 20 international cohorts in the ENIGMA MDD working group. *Mol. Psychiatry* **2020**, *25*, 1511–1525. [CrossRef]
4. Sacchet, M.D.; Livermore, E.E.; Iglesias, J.E.; Glover, G.H.; Gotlib, I.H. Subcortical volumes differentiate major depressive disorder, bipolar disorder, and remitted major depressive disorder. *J. Psychiatr. Res.* **2015**, *68*, 91–98. [CrossRef] [PubMed]
5. Wang, Y.; Han, Y.; Wang, C.; Song, S.; Tian, Q.; Huang, G. Computation-efficient Deep Learning for Computer Vision: A Survey. *arXiv* **2023**, arXiv:2308.13998.
6. Lell, M.M.; Kachelrieß, M. Recent and upcoming technological developments in computed tomography: High speed, low dose, deep learning, multienergy. *Investig. Radiol.* **2020**, *55*, 8–19. [CrossRef]
7. Reader, A.J.; Corda, G.; Mehranian, A.; da Costa-Luis, C.; Ellis, S.; Schnabel, J.A. Deep learning for PET image reconstruction. *IEEE Trans. Radiat. Plasma Med. Sci.* **2020**, *5*, 1–25. [CrossRef]
8. Song, X.; Zhou, F.; Frangi, A.F.; Cao, J.; Xiao, X.; Lei, Y.; Wang, T.; Lei, B. Multicenter and Multichannel Pooling GCN for Early AD Diagnosis Based on Dual-Modality Fused Brain Network. *IEEE Trans. Med. Imaging* **2022**, *42*, 354–367. [CrossRef]
9. Wang, Q.; Li, L.; Qiao, L.; Liu, M. Adaptive Multimodal Neuroimage Integration for Major Depression Disorder Detection. *Front. Neuroinform.* **2022**, *16*, 856175. [CrossRef]
10. Wang, Y.; Gong, N.; Fu, C. Major depression disorder diagnosis and analysis based on structural magnetic resonance imaging and deep learning. *J. Integr. Neurosci.* **2021**, *20*, 977–984. [CrossRef]
11. Gao, J.; Chen, M.; Xiao, D.; Li, Y.; Zhu, S.; Li, Y.; Dai, X.; Lu, F.; Wang, Z.; Cai, S. Classification of major depressive disorder using an attention-guided unified deep convolutional neural network and individual structural covariance network. *Cereb. Cortex* **2023**, *33*, 2415–2425. [CrossRef]
12. Marwa, E.-G.; Moustafa, H.E.-D.; Khalifa, F.; Khater, H.; AbdElhalim, E. An MRI-based deep learning approach for accurate detection of Alzheimer's disease. *Alex. Eng. J.* **2023**, *63*, 211–221.
13. Jang, S.-I.; Pan, T.; Li, Y.; Heidari, P.; Chen, J.; Li, Q.; Gong, K. Spach Transformer: Spatial and channel-wise transformer based on local and global self-attentions for PET image denoising. *arXiv* **2022**, arXiv:2209.03300.
14. Liu, Z.; Mao, H.; Wu, C.-Y.; Feichtenhofer, C.; Darrell, T.; Xie, S. A convnet for the 2020s. In Proceedings of the IEEE/CVF Conference on Computer Vision and Pattern Recognition, New Orleans, LA, USA, 18–24 June 2022; pp. 11976–11986.
15. Shamshad, F.; Khan, S.; Zamir, S.W.; Khan, M.H.; Hayat, M.; Khan, F.S.; Fu, H. Transformers in medical imaging: A survey. *Med. Image Anal.* **2023**, *88*, 102802. [CrossRef]
16. Qiu, N.; Gao, B.; Tu, H.; Huang, F.; Guan, Q.; Luo, W. LDGC-SR: Integrating long-range dependencies and global context information for session-based recommendation. *Knowl.-Based Syst.* **2022**, *248*, 108894. [CrossRef]
17. Qin, G.; Feng, Y.; Van Durme, B. The nlp task effectiveness of long-range transformers. *arXiv* **2022**, arXiv:2202.07856.
18. Su, Y.; Zhang, Z.; Cai, Q.; Zhang, B.; Li, X. 3DMKDR: 3D Multiscale Kernels CNN Model for Depression Recognition Based on EEG. *J. Beijing Inst. Technol.* **2023**, *32*, 230–241.
19. Teng, S.; Chai, S.; Liu, J.; Tomoko, T.; Huang, X.; Chen, Y.-W. A Transformer-based Multimodal Network for Audiovisual Depression Prediction. In Proceedings of the 2022 IEEE 11th Global Conference on Consumer Electronics (GCCE), Osaka, Japan, 18–21 October 2022; pp. 761–764.
20. Peng, H.; Gong, W.; Beckmann, C.F.; Vedaldi, A.; Smith, S.M. Accurate brain age prediction with lightweight deep neural networks. *Med. Image Anal.* **2021**, *68*, 101871. [CrossRef]
21. Yan, C.; Zang, Y. DPARSF: A MATLAB toolbox for "pipeline" data analysis of resting-state fMRI. *Front. Syst. Neurosci.* **2010**, *4*, 1377. [CrossRef]

22. Vaswani, A.; Shazeer, N.; Parmar, N.; Uszkoreit, J.; Jones, L.; Gomez, A.N.; Kaiser, Ł.; Polosukhin, I. Attention is all you need. *Adv. Neural Inf. Process. Syst.* **2017**, *30*, 1–11.
23. Kingma, D.P.; Ba, J. Adam: A method for stochastic optimization. *arXiv* **2014**, arXiv:1412.6980.
24. Dosovitskiy, A.; Beyer, L.; Kolesnikov, A.; Weissenborn, D.; Zhai, X.; Unterthiner, T.; Dehghani, M.; Minderer, M.; Heigold, G.; Gelly, S. An image is worth 16x16 words: Transformers for image recognition at scale. *arXiv* **2020**, arXiv:2010.11929.
25. Zhu, M.; Quan, Y.; He, X. The classification of brain network for major depressive disorder patients based on deep graph convolutional neural network. *Front. Hum. Neurosci.* **2023**, *17*, 1094592. [CrossRef] [PubMed]
26. Venkatapathy, S.; Votinov, M.; Wagels, L.; Kim, S.; Lee, M.; Habel, U.; Ra, I.-H.; Jo, H.-G. Ensemble graph neural network model for classification of major depressive disorder using whole-brain functional connectivity. *Front. Psychiatry* **2023**, *14*, 1125339. [CrossRef]
27. Hu, J.; Huang, Y.; Wang, N.; Dong, S. BrainNPT: Pre-training of Transformer networks for brain network classification. *arXiv* **2023**, arXiv:2305.01666.

Disclaimer/Publisher's Note: The statements, opinions and data contained in all publications are solely those of the individual author(s) and contributor(s) and not of MDPI and/or the editor(s). MDPI and/or the editor(s) disclaim responsibility for any injury to people or property resulting from any ideas, methods, instructions or products referred to in the content.

brain sciences

MDPI

Article

Low-Rank Tensor Fusion for Enhanced Deep Learning-Based Multimodal Brain Age Estimation

Xia Liu [1], Guowei Zheng [2], Iman Beheshti [3,*], Shanling Ji [4], Zhinan Gou [1] and Wenkuo Cui [1]

1 School of Management Science and Information Engineering, Hebei University of Economics and Businesses, Shijiazhuang 050061, China; liux@hueb.edu.cn (X.L.); zhinan.gou@hotmail.com (Z.G.); wenkuo@tongji.edu.cn (W.C.)
2 School of Computer Science and Technology, Harbin Institute of Technology, Weihai 264209, China; zhenggw@stu.hit.edu.cn
3 Department of Human Anatomy and Cell Science, University of Manitoba, Winnipeg, MB R3T 2N2, Canada
4 Institute of Mental Health, Jining Medical University, Jining 272111, China; jishanling@mail.jnmc.edu.cn
* Correspondence: iman.beheshti@umanitoba.ca

Abstract: Background/Objectives: A multimodal brain age estimation model could provide enhanced insights into brain aging. However, effectively integrating multimodal neuroimaging data to enhance the accuracy of brain age estimation remains a challenging task. **Methods:** In this study, we developed an innovative data fusion technique employing a low-rank tensor fusion algorithm, tailored specifically for deep learning-based frameworks aimed at brain age estimation. Specifically, we utilized structural magnetic resonance imaging (sMRI), diffusion tensor imaging (DTI), and magnetoencephalography (MEG) to extract spatial–temporal brain features with different properties. These features were fused using the low-rank tensor algorithm and employed as predictors for estimating brain age. **Results:** Our prediction model achieved a desirable prediction accuracy on the independent test samples, demonstrating its robust performance. **Conclusions:** The results of our study suggest that the low-rank tensor fusion algorithm has the potential to effectively integrate multimodal data into deep learning frameworks for estimating brain age.

Keywords: brain age; spatial–temporal; multimodal; low-rank tensor fusion; machine learning; deep learning

1. Introduction

Brain aging is the gradual decline of mental function. The "brain age" biomarker measures the aging status of the brain [1]. Advanced machine and deep learning techniques, combined with brain imaging scans, are used to derive brain age [2–7]. Studying brain aging can help identify markers that indicate its progression.

Functional magnetic resonance imaging (fMRI), structural magnetic resonance imaging (sMRI), diffusion tensor imaging (DTI), and magnetoencephalography (MEG) have been instrumental in detecting age-related changes in the brain [8–10]. Among these modalities, sMRI is commonly used to estimate brain age due to its high-resolution images that enable tracking of structural brain changes [10–12]. Moreover, sMRI data are more widely available than other modalities, enhancing the reproducibility of brain age research [13]. For instance, Cao et al. applied the least absolute shrinkage and selection operator (LASSO) algorithm to longitudinal sMRI data from 303 healthy controls (HCs) for predicting individual brain maturity [14]. Beheshti et al. introduced a unique 3D patch-based grading procedure for estimating cortical aging using sMRI data [15,16]. Franke et al. presented a framework for efficiently estimating the brain age of 650 HCs from their sMRI scans using a kernel method for regression [17]. Valizadeh et al. employed sMRI data from 3144 HCs to extract various anatomical features and using them to predict age through different statistical techniques [18]. Cole et al. used convolutional neural networks to estimate brain age using raw sMRI data from 2001 HCs [19]. Lancaster et al. trained a Bayesian optimization framework with data from 2003 HCs to predict age [20]. Liu et al. constructed a multi-feature-based network (MFN) to estimate the brain age of 2501 HCs by describing structural similarities between traditional cortical morphological features [21]. Liem et al. assessed functional connectomes and mean time series from both cortical and subcortical regions, using support vector regression and regression based on random forest methodology to predict brain age [22]. Martina J. Lund employed resting-state fMRI data from 1126 HCs to estimate functional connectivity between brain networks, using these as features to predict brain age [23].

In addition to the aforementioned techniques, DTI enables the identification of diffusion and topological patterns across diverse brain regions, thereby aiding in the prediction of aging [24]. Benson Mwangi et al. applied a multivariate technique, relevance vector regression, to predict age using features extracted from diffusion tensor imaging [25].

Previous studies have primarily estimated brain age using single-modal neuroimaging data. Research has demonstrated that data fusion among data from various imaging methods could provide a more robust machine learning model and also provide a more comprehensive understanding of brain function, structure, and connectivity [26,27]. In the area of brain age estimation, recent research studies have also focused on integrating features from multiple modalities, demonstrating improved accuracy in brain age prediction [28–31]. For instance, D.A. Engemann et al. combined MRI, fMRI, and MEG features to estimate brain age [32].

It is well known that the T1 signal intensity of brain structures varies with age due to changes in brain tissue composition [33,34]. DTI helps to detect changes in diffusion and topological patterns in the brain associated with aging [24]. Thus, studies using unimodal features often fail to simultaneously account for age-related functional and structural changes in spatial and temporal domains, which could potentially improve prediction performance. Therefore, the combination of sMRI and diffusion images with functional metrics (such as EEG/MEG or fMRI) holds promise for enhancing brain age prediction. However, a key challenge in developing multimodal brain age estimation frameworks is the effective integration of data from diverse sources. This integration is crucial for improving prediction performance and providing a comprehensive view of structural and functional brain features throughout the brain aging process.

Recently, fusion techniques for brain age estimation have integrated information from neuroimaging modalities. Traditional methods like concatenation and early fusion may overlook modality specifics, leading to overfitting [35]. Middle fusion, like canonical correlation analysis (CCA), seeks common representations but may miss critical information [36]. Late fusion reduces overfitting but may limit performance by ignoring modality interactions [37]. Advanced deep learning, like autoencoders and variational autoencoders (VAEs), models complex interactions but faces generalizability challenges [38]. Tensor-based fusion captures higher-order relationships but is computationally demanding [39].

To overcome these challenges, our study introduces a low-rank tensor fusion approach. This approach employed low-rank tensors for multimodal fusion, enhancing the accuracy of brain age predictions by integrating structural and functional features. Specifically, we assessed the low-rank tensor fusion technique on both structural and functional brain features, comparing the effects of fused versus non-fused features within our brain age prediction model. Our findings demonstrated that our model performs comparably to state-of-the-art models across three multimodal tasks evaluated on public datasets.

2. Materials and Methods

2.1. Dataset and Data Availability

We used data from the Cambridge Center for Aging Neuroscience (Cam-CAN) [40,41]. Further details are available at https://camcan-archive.mrc-cbu.cam.ac.uk//dataaccess/; accessed on 15 February 2024. Table 1 summarizes the imaging parameters.

Table 1. The imaging parameters of different neuroimaging data used for brain age modeling.

Scans Type	Sequence	TR (ms)	TE (ms)	Flip Angle (°)	FOV (mm)	Voxel Size (mm)
sMRI	MPRAGE	2250	2.99	9	256 × 240 × 192	1 × 1 × 1
Diffusion-weighted		9100	104		192 × 192	2 × 2 × 2
	Sampling rate (HZ)		Duration (min:s)		Task	
Resting-state MEG	1000		08:40		Rest with eyes closed	

Abbreviations: sMRI, structural magnetic resonance imaging. TR, the Alzheimer's Disease Neuroimaging Initiative. TE, Echo Time. MPRAGE, Magnetization Prepared-Rapid Gradient Echo imaging.

In this study, we utilized neuroimaging data from three modalities: sMRI, MEG, and DTI. A total of 521 HCs (270 males, 251 females, aged 18–88, mean age: 52.3 ± 17.7) underwent MR imaging using a 3T scanner. Figure 1 illustrates the age distribution of the participants included in the study. Resting-state MEG data were acquired using a 306-channel system (102 magnetometers, 204 planar gradiometers) with a sampling rate of 1 kHz for 8 min and 40 s with eyes closed. The acquisition parameters were as follows: Flip angle = 9°, field of view = 256 × 240 × 192 mm^3, voxel size = 1 mm.

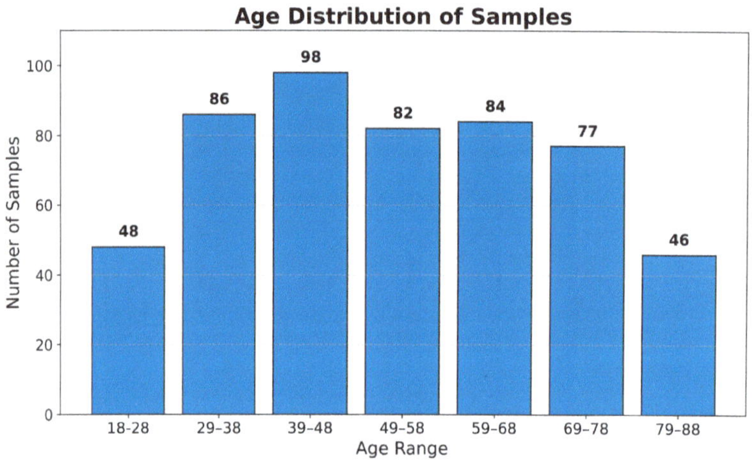

Figure 1. The age distribution of the participants.

2.2. Neuroimaging Data Processing

2.2.1. sMRI Data Preprocessing

sMRI images were preprocessed using SPM12 for affine registration, realignment, bias correction, and white matter (WM)/gray matter (GM)/cerebrospinal fluid (CSF) segmentation. CAT12 toolbox (Version 12.9; https://neuro-jena.github.io/cat/index.html accessed on 9 December 2024) was used for estimating WM and GM probability maps with default settings [42]. Skull stripping and registration to standard space were performed using the Montreal Neurological Institute (MNI) 152 template. Following tissue segmentation and bias correction, probability maps of WM, GM, and CSF [43] were generated.

2.2.2. MEG Data Preprocessing

The MEG data were preprocessed using temporal extension (tSSS) in Elekta Neuromag MaxFilter v2.2 for independent head motion correction and noise reduction, with a correlation limit of 0.98 and a 10-s correlation window [44]. Subsequently, Brainstorm [45] was utilized for further MEG data processing, following the procedure described in Niso et al. [46]. High-pass and notch filters were applied at 0.3 Hz and 60 Hz and harmonics, respectively. Cortical surface reconstruction from sMRI was performed using the recon-all algorithm in FreeSurfer (Version 6; https://surfer.nmr.mgh.harvard.edu/ accessed on 9 December 2024) [47–49]. After the completion of source reconstruction, the computation of the power spectral density (PSD) was performed encompassing the entire duration of the resting-state scan.

2.2.3. Diffusion MRI Data Preprocessing

The diffusion MRI (dMRI) analyses were conducted using SPM12 with the aa 4.2 pipelines [50] and modules [51]. In the DTI stream, the data underwent skull-stripping using the Brain Extraction Tool (BET) utility in FMRIB's Software Library (FSL; https://fsl.fmrib.ox.ac.uk/fsl/docs/#/ accessed on 9 December 2024). Later, a parallel branch was employed to nonlinearly estimate the second-order diffusion tensor and its metrics (i.e., fractional anisotropy (FA), mean diffusion (MD), axial diffusion (AD), etc.).

2.3. *Multimodal Fusion Model*

2.3.1. Problem Modeling

As shown in Figure 2, we first extracted high-level abstract features for multiple modalities. For the extraction of DTI and sMRI features, in order to save computational resources and adapt to neuroimaging datasets with less data, we utilized two identical simple fully convolutional networks (SFCNs) [52] to obtain DTI and sMRI features. Each SFCN comprised six parts. The first five parts contained a 3D convolutional layer with $3 \times 3 \times 3$ convolutional kernels (with channel numbers 32, 64, 128, 256, 256), followed by a batch normalization layer, a $2 \times 2 \times 2$ maximum pooling layer, and was activated using the Rectified Linear Unit (ReLU) function. The sixth part consisted of a 3D convolutional layer with a $1 \times 1 \times 1$ convolutional kernel size and 64 channels, a batch normalization layer, activated using the ReLU function, and finally, a $3 \times 4 \times 3$ average pooling layer. To extract MEG features, we incorporated different attention values for each brain region using the Transformer Encoder [53]. Next, we employed two 1-dimensional convolutional layers with a convolutional kernel size of 1 and channel numbers of 128 and 32, respectively, as well as an average pooling layer to capture the local information from neighboring time points and summarize them [54,55]. Then, a fully connected layer with 64 neurons was used for dimensionality reduction to obtain the extracted MEG features. Finally, a layer with low-rank tensor fusion was added before the fully connected layer. Brain age was estimated from brain images of subjects by feature extraction, low-rank tensor fusion of multimodal features, and mapping with chronological age as label.

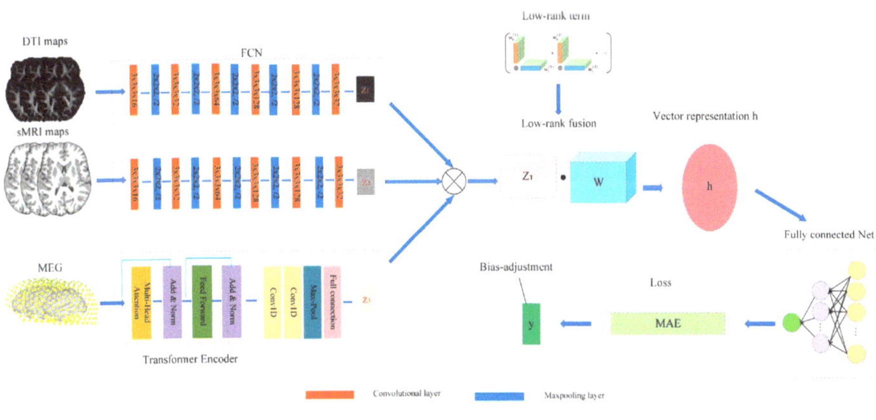

Figure 2. The overview of our proposed approach to fusing multimodal features to predict brain age.

2.3.2. Tensor Fusion and Representation

Tensor representation is a successful approach for multimodal fusion. Prior research has indicated that this method outperforms basic concatenation or pooling strategies in capturing multimodal interactions [56,57]. The tensor Z is computed by the following:

$$Z = \bigotimes_{m=1}^{M} z_m,\ z_m \in R^{d_m} \tag{1}$$

M represents the total number of input modalities and z_i (i = 1, 2, 3, ..., M) represents the features extracted from the multimodal data. The tensor outer product is denoted by $\bigotimes_{m=1}^{M}$. The resulting feature after fusion is denoted by Z_T. The tensor Z is then fed into a linear layer g (·), which produces a vector representation as follows:

$$h = g\,(\mathcal{Z};\, \mathcal{W},\, b) = \mathcal{W}\cdot\mathcal{Z} + b \tag{2}$$

where $\mathcal{W}$ is the weight of this layer and b is the bias. With $\mathcal{Z}$ being an order-M tensor. In the tensor dot product $\mathcal{W}\cdot\mathcal{Z}$, the weight $\mathcal{W}$ can be partitioned into $\widetilde{\mathcal{W}}_k$, k = 1, ..., d_m. Each $\widetilde{\mathcal{W}}_k$ contributes to one dimension in the output vector h, i.e., $h_k = \widetilde{\mathcal{W}}_k\cdot\mathcal{Z}$.

The specific process is as Algorithm 1:

Algorithm 1. Multimodal low-rank tensor fusion algorithm.

Input: sMRI maps; DTI maps; MEG; label: chronologic age y
Output: brain age $\hat{y}$
Parameters: rank, drop rate η

1: sMRI maps and DTI maps were processed using FCN to extract the spatial structure features z_1 and z_2
2: The PSD extracted using MEG are passed through the Encoder of Transformer to extract brain temporal features z_3
3: Low-rank fusion Z_T
4: The fusion feature vector expressed as $h = g\,(\mathcal{Z};\, \mathcal{W},\, b) = \mathcal{W}\cdot\mathcal{Z} + b$
5: Access a fully connected network
6: Minimize the loss function MAE
7: Output bias corrected values for brain age

2.4. Model Implementation and Validation

To reduce the reliance on the disparity in brain age (brain age gap = predict brain age − chronological age) on age, a bias correction was applied [58]. To evaluate the model, we used R^2, root mean square error ($RMSE$), and MAE as metrics.

$$MAE = \frac{1}{n}\Big(\sum_{i=1}^{n} |y_i - Y_i|\Big) \tag{3}$$

$$RMSE = \sqrt{\frac{1}{n}\sum_{i=1}^{n}(y_i - Y_i)^2} \tag{4}$$

$$R^2 = 1 - \frac{\sum_{i=1}^{n}(y_i - Y_i)^2}{\sum_{i=1}^{n}(y_i - \overline{y})^2} \tag{5}$$

The model is implemented in Python 3.7 and Pytorch1.11.0 library and was executed on the Ubuntu 18.04 operating system. Throughout the training period, we utilized MAE as the loss function with the Adam optimizer [59] using a learning rate of 1×10^{-4} and weight decay of 1×10^{-8}. Additionally, we employed a mini-batch size of 12 and trained for a total of 300 epochs. When the model performs best on the validation set, we save it as the final model and use it for testing.

To evaluate the model, 521 subjects were randomly divided into training (416), validation (52), and testing (53) groups.

3. Results

3.1. Estimation Based on Different Features and Fusion Methods

The results of different features and fusion methods on the dataset are presented in Table 2. In summary, our multimodal low-rank fusion method generally outperforms the unimodality. Specifically, we designed the low-rank fusion module to combine multimodal features, resulting in a lower *MAE* and higher R^2, while the competing unimodal-based methods achieved an optimal *MAE* of 4.54 and R^2 = 0.92, respectively. Our multimodal low-rank fusion model achieves smaller age errors compared to other non-fusion models.

Table 2. Performance metrics for various features and fusion methods.

	Strategies	Feature	*MAE* (y)	*RMSE* (y)	R^2	*p*
Training set	Unimodal	DTI	11.67	12.13	0.74	<0.001
		MEG	-	-	-	-
		sMRI	3.83	4.72	0.94	<0.001
	Traditional fusion	Add	2.89	4.30	0.96	<0.001
		Concat	3.11	4.43	0.96	<0.001
	Low-rank tensor fusion	sMRI + AD + PSD	2.30	2.94	0.96	<0.001
		sMRI + MD + PSD	3.04	3.82	0.95	<0.001
		sMRI + FA + PSD	**2.25**	**2.85**	**0.98**	<0.001
Validation set	Unimodal	DTI	12.69	14.56	0.71	<0.001
		MEG	-	-	-	-
		sMRI	4.91	5.61	0.91	<0.001
	Traditional fusion	Add	7.91	9.29	0.89	<0.001
		Concat	10.65	12.17	0.79	<0.001
	Low-rank tensor fusion	sMRI + AD + PSD	5.32	6.67	0.90	<0.001
		sMRI + MD + PSD	4.80	6.18	0.90	<0.001
		sMRI + FA + PSD	**4.49**	**5.72**	**0.92**	<0.001
Testing set	Unimodal	DTI	13.52	15.68	0.57	<0.001
		MEG	-	-	-	-
		sMRI	4.54	5.52	0.92	<0.001
	Traditional fusion	Add	8.56	10.13	0.90	<0.001
		Concat	11.36	13.46	0.72	<0.001
	Low-rank tensor fusion	sMRI + AD + PSD	4.59	5.90	0.91	<0.001
		sMRI + MD + PSD	4.47	5.45	0.92	<0.001
		sMRI + FA + PSD	**4.20**	**5.43**	**0.93**	<0.001

Abbreviations: *MAE*, mean absolute error. *RMSE*, root mean square error. R^2, the coefficient of determination. DTI, diffusion tensor imaging. MEG, magnetoencephalography. sMRI, structural magnetic resonance imaging. AD, axial diffusivity. MD, mean diffusivity. FA, fractional anisotropy. PSD, power spectral density. The symbol "-" indicates that this result is not reported. Add: a parallel strategy to combine the two feature vectors into a compound vector. Concat: a series of feature fusion methods, directly linking the features. The prediction results using MEG data are not reported because the depth prediction model did not converge.

We employ various combinations of multimodal features to predict brain age. As depicted in Table 2, the prediction model achieves optimal performance when fusing sMRI, FA, and PSD. The subsequent analyses are based on the prediction results from the fusion model that utilized the optimal feature combination. Moreover, we compared traditional feature fusion methods, such as addition or concatenation of these features, and found that our low-rank tensor fusion outperformed these traditional methods in predicting brain age.

3.2. Estimation Based on Low-Rank Tensor Fusion Method

In Table 2, the results demonstrate the effectiveness of our low-rank tensor fusion approach for age prediction. In the training set, we achieved an R^2 value of 0.98, with a *MAE* of 2.25 years and *RMSE* of 2.85 years (refer to Figure 3A). This indicates the successful fusion of features in improving age prediction accuracy. Furthermore, on the validation set, our method yielded an *MAE* of 4.49 years, R^2 of 0.92, and *RMSE* of 5.72 years (refer to Figure 3B). On the test set, we obtained an *MAE* of 4.20 years, R^2 of 0.93, and *RMSE* of 5.43 years (refer to Figure 3C).

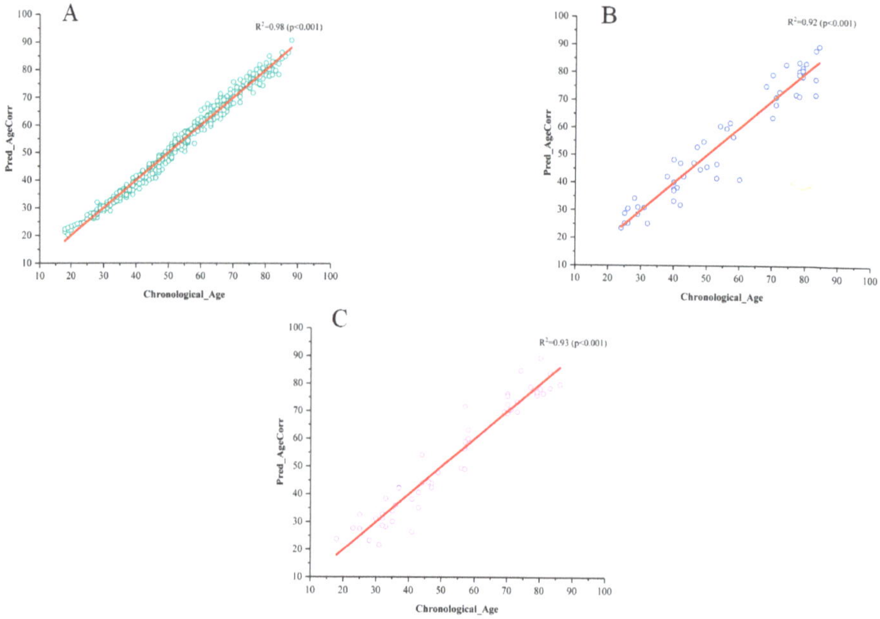

Figure 3. Model performance on each dataset. (**A**) Is the model performance on the training set. (**B**) Is the model performance on the validation set. (**C**) Is the model performance on the test set.

4. Discussion

Multimodal brain imaging data are extensively utilized for estimating brain age across various contexts. Niu et al. explored different analysis strategies for brain age prediction using large datasets encompassing sMRI, DTI, and fMRI data [60]. Similarly, De Lange et al. utilized machine learning and multimodal imaging data to predict brain age, encompassing gray matter, white matter, and resting-state functional connectivity [61]. Their findings highlighted improved prediction accuracy with the inclusion of multimodal features in the model. Rokicki et al. utilized T1 and T2 structural imaging data, along with cerebral blood flow data from arterial spin labeling, to develop a multimodal model for estimating brain age [62]. Their study demonstrated that integrating multiple types of data can enhance the accuracy of brain age prediction.

We aimed to test whether the use of multimodal neuroimaging data can improve the accuracy of predicting brain age and how to fuse features more effectively. As shown in Table 2, when single-mode features were used to predict brain age, sMRI performed better than either DTI or MEG data (*MAE* = 4.54 years, *RMSE* = 5.52 years, R^2 = 0.92 based on structural data vs. *MAE* = 13.52 years, *RMSE* = 15.68 years, R^2 = 0.57 based on DTI data). When predicting brain age based on MEG data, the depth prediction model did not converge, so the prediction results were not reported. As a result, multimodal data improved prediction performance, as we hypothesized. Specifically, when unimodal data were used to predict brain age, sMRI performed best. This may be because sMRI can more easily capture brain anatomical changes and structural variations in the brain [11], which may better reflect aging [63–66]. Therefore, the majority of studies used sMRI data to estimate brain age [30,67].

Despite the macroscopic nature of morphological features derived from sMRI data, their sensitivity to neurodevelopmental microstructural changes is limited [68,69]. To enhance model predictive performance, integration of additional modalities is crucial. For example, diffusion MRI techniques, which are adept at capturing tissue microstructure by tracking water molecule diffusion and probing cellular-level environments, offer promising insights [70]. While numerous studies have effectively utilized DTI data to predict brain age, dMRI faces technical challenges and exhibits higher variability compared to conventional modalities like T1- and T2-weighted imaging [71,72]. These intricacies can introduce nonlinear distortions in the original images, affecting diffusion metrics like MD and FA [72], which can reduce the performance of the prediction model. This may also be one of the reasons why the *MAE* is larger when using DTI prediction alone. In the application of functional data, improvements in the prediction of brain age using fMRI are limited by the hysteresis of the hemodynamic response function [73]. However, the MEG with high spatial and temporal resolution can provide complementary features related to normal aging. In exploring MEG data for brain age estimation, we found that the prediction model failed to converge stably, highlighting common challenges in deep learning with complex feature sets, especially during extraction and training. In a previous study, PSD features combined with a machine learning regression model were used to predict brain age, and the *MAE* value was obtained [30]. This is something we need to consider improving in the future.

In this study, we use resting-state MEG (magnetoencephalography), which is preferred over task-based MEG for studying age-related brain changes because it captures the brain's spontaneous neural activity without the influence of external tasks [74]. This provides a clearer picture of the brain's intrinsic functional organization and baseline neural efficiency. Unlike task-based paradigms, which can introduce variability due to individual differences in task performance and cognitive strategies, resting-state MEG offers a more stable and reliable measure of brain connectivity, especially in key frequency bands like alpha and beta, which are sensitive to aging.

Compared to fMRI, resting-state MEG has several advantages. First, MEG offers high temporal resolution, capturing brain activity on the millisecond scale, while fMRI operates on a much slower, second-level timescale, potentially missing important rapid oscillatory patterns [75]. MEG also directly measures neuronal activity through magnetic fields, while fMRI relies on the slower BOLD signal, which is influenced by hemodynamic processes rather than direct neural firing [76]. Furthermore, MEG is less sensitive to motion artifacts, providing clearer data, especially for older adults who may have difficulty remaining still. These advantages make MEG particularly well-suited for detecting age-related functional changes in the brain [74].

During the feature extraction phase, we opted for the SFCNs technique to extract features from sMRI and DTI data due to its exceptional ability to capture both local and hierarchical spatial patterns necessary for analyzing brain structure. SFCNs can identify detailed patterns in both gray and white matter across different brain regions, which is crucial for detecting age-related changes. Unlike traditional CNNs, SFCNs preserve spatial resolution throughout the network, meaning they can extract fine-grained features without losing information during down sampling. This ability makes SFCNs particularly well-suited for working with sMRI and DTI data, where maintaining spatial accuracy is important. Research has shown that SFCNs outperform other methods, like traditional CNNs, in extracting structural features from brain imaging data [77].

When FCN and Transformer Encoder were used to process the data and then used to predict brain age after low-rank tensor fusion, the prediction performance of the model was significantly improved. Notably, the fusion of sMRI, FA, and PSD features achieved the highest prediction ability. This is inseparable from the advantages of FCN. Moreover, the Transformer method was introduced by [53], which is mainly based on self-attention and has been applied to many tasks, such as natural language processing, classification tasks [78,79], and brain age prediction [80–83]. This is because the feature extraction capability of the Transformer method is superior to that of the Recurrent Neural Network, and the source and target sequences can be "self-associated" with each other. In this way, the information contained in the representation of the source and target sequences is richer, and subsequent layers of feed-forward networks improve the representation of the model. These advantages have enhanced the performance of our models.

Our fusion mechanism, which employs low-rank tensor fusion, allows us to utilize tensor rank minimization to learn tensors that more precisely capture the true correlations and underlying structures within multimodal data, effectively reducing input errors [84,85]. Studies have shown that FA is the most age-sensitive of the conventional DTI metrics [86]. This may be one of the reasons why our prediction model with FA performs better in feature fusion. In contrast to the conventional approach of fusing multiple modes of features, the *MAE* value is reduced, and the prediction result is more desirable. Table 3 summarizes the current studies using Cam-CAN data to predict brain age as well as our proposed method. Specifically, Xifra-Porxas, Alba, et al. [30] used dimensionality reduction techniques and Gaussian process regression (GPR) to predict brain age. Using MEG features (*MAE* = 9.60 years) produced worse performance than using MRI features (MA =5.33 years), but a stacked model combining the two features improved age prediction performance (*MAE* = 4.88 years). Popescu, Sebastian G et al. [87] have trained a U-Net model that utilizes deep learning techniques to generate individualized 3D brain maps at a local level for age prediction, which could provide spatial information about anatomical patterns of brain aging. The Cam-CAN data were then tested on the model and the *MAE* was 9.5 years. Han, Juhyuk et al. [88] trained and compared the predictive performance of 27 machine learning models for brain age prediction and applied the trained models to the Cam-CAN dataset. The *MAE* and R^2 were 7.08–10.50 years and 0.64–0.85, respectively. A brain age prediction model was constructed by using the transfer learning method and a large dMRI dataset as the source domain. Then, the trained model was used to test Cam-CAN data, and the *MAE* was 4.68–5.71 years [89]. From Table 3, we can see that our proposed method has achieved a better performance than that of other previous studies.

Table 3. Comparative results of brain age estimation on Cam-CAN data.

Studies	Modal	*MAE* (y)	R^2
[30]	sMRI, MEG	4.88–9.6	-
[87]	sMRI	9	-
[88]	sMRI	7.08–10.50	0.64–0.85
[89]	dMRI	4.68–5.71	-
Our method	sMRI, MEG, DTI	**4.20**	**0.93**

Abbreviations: *MAE*, mean absolute error. R^2, the coefficient of determination. DTI, diffusion tensor imaging. MEG, magnetoencephalography. sMRI, structural magnetic resonance imaging. dMRI, diffusion magnetic resonance imaging.

Recently, with the broad application of multimodal data in brain age prediction, numerous advanced multimodal fusion methods have been proposed and have achieved promising results. For instance, Clements RG et al. leveraged a multimodal 3D convolutional neural network and magnetic resonance elastography (MRE) technology to predict brain age. The advantages of their method lie in the innovative combination of these two technologies, achieving high-precision brain age prediction, and further enhancing prediction accuracy through multimodal fusion, offering possibilities for the early diagnosis of neurodegenerative diseases. However, this method also has some drawbacks, including high model complexity, substantial computational resource requirements, strong data dependency, and limitations such as no performance improvement when incorporating damping ratio into the model [90]. The multimodal Transformer-based architecture proposed by Wang J and his team demonstrates notable advantages in biological age prediction, including improved prediction accuracy through the fusion of facial, tongue, and retinal images, as well as its potential application in risk stratification and progression prediction of chronic diseases. However, this method also faces some challenges, such as the heterogeneity of the aging process limiting prediction accuracy, deployment difficulties due to technical complexity, and considerations regarding personal privacy and ethical issues [91].

Compared with these methods, our proposed low-rank tensor fusion approach demonstrates notable advantages in multimodal brain age prediction tasks. First, our method leverages low-rank tensor decomposition to effectively reduce redundant information within multimodal data, thus enhancing computational efficiency. Second, due to the automatic selection of salient features between modalities afforded by low-rank tensor decomposition, our method exhibits greater robustness under data imbalances [92]. Additionally, in terms of cross-dataset generalization, the low-rank tensor fusion method adapts better to feature differences across datasets, demonstrating high adaptability [93]. Additionally, by utilizing the low-rank tensor fusion technique, the likelihood of overfitting is minimized, while interpretability is enhanced through the extraction of crucial shared features instead of learning noise specific to each modality. This method has proven to be successful in various multimodal learning tasks, including the classification of neurodegenerative diseases [39], underscoring its resilience and efficacy.

In terms of potential clinical applications, our multimodal neuroimaging approach for brain age prediction holds promise in identifying individuals at risk of neurodegenerative diseases or monitoring disease progression. For instance, deviations between predicted and chronological brain age, known as brain age gaps, have been shown to serve as biomarkers for various neurological conditions, including dementia and other conditions [4,63]. By leveraging the improved prediction accuracy achieved through multimodal data integration, our model could potentially offer earlier and more accurate insights into brain health, facilitating timely interventions and personalized treatment strategies. We plan to explore these clinical implications in future studies.

Our study has several limitations. First, the sample size and the lack of an independent dataset for assessing the generalizability of our model are notable constraints. Our primary aim was to test the low-rank tensor fusion algorithm tailored for deep learning-based frameworks in brain age estimation. We used the Cambridge Center for Aging Neuroscience (Cam-CAN) dataset, which includes sMRI, DTI, and resting-state MEG data. While validating our results on an independent dataset could strengthen the findings, it is challenging to find a dataset that includes all three modalities, especially resting-state MEG data. Therefore, future studies should validate the proposed algorithm on larger, independent datasets. Another limitation involves the failure of our deep learning model to converge during training when using MEG data. This may have been due to issues such as improper weight initialization, inappropriate learning rates, insufficient data, overfitting, or a non-convex loss function. Despite adjusting factors like learning rate and weight initialization, the model did not converge using MEG data alone. However, the model did show convergence when combining MEG features with DTI and sMRI data. Future research with larger sample sizes is needed to investigate these convergence issues and propose solutions for deep learning models applied to brain imaging data. Additionally, in this study, we compared our low-rank tensor fusion algorithm with single-input data and traditional feature fusion methods, such as addition or concatenation. Our results demonstrated that the low-rank tensor fusion method provided better prediction accuracy than traditional feature fusion methods. Future studies could focus on developing more accurate deep learning-based data fusion methods and comparing them to existing techniques. It is important to note that the choice of data fusion method in deep learning models depends on factors such as data characteristics (e.g., structured, unstructured, multimodal), model complexity, and computational resources [94,95]. Finally, we intended to assess our low-rank fusion method using combinations of all feature maps but were limited by computational resources. Future studies may be able to explore this approach further.

5. Conclusions

In this study, we presented a novel low-rank tensor fusion algorithm developed to integrate multimodal brain imaging data for the purpose of brain age estimation. Our strategy involves integrating three different imaging techniques—sMRI, DTI, and resting-state MEG—in order to offer a more thorough understanding of brain aging. We evaluated the method using the Cambridge Centre for Aging Neuroscience (Cam-CAN) dataset. The results indicated that incorporating both structural and functional brain features enables our model to offer a deeper understanding of the brain's aging process. Our data fusion method exhibited performance that rivals state-of-the-art techniques in different multimodal tasks, as tested on datasets that are publicly accessible.

Author Contributions: Conceptualization, X.L., I.B., W.C. and G.Z.; methodology, G.Z. and S.J.; software, X.L., G.Z., S.J., Z.G. and W.C.; validation, S.J. and W.C.; formal analysis, X.L.; data curation, X.L., G.Z., S.J. and Z.G.; writing—review and editing, I.B.; supervision, I.B.; funding acquisition, Z.G. and W.C. All authors have read and agreed to the published version of the manuscript.

Funding: This research was partially funded by the Science Research Project of the Hebei Education Department (Grant No. BJK2024092), the Hebei Natural Science Foundation (Grant No. F2023207003), and the Scientific Research and Development Program of Hebei University of Economics and Business (2024YB23).

Institutional Review Board Statement: This study utilized a publicly available dataset, which does not require IRB approval.

Informed Consent Statement: Written informed consent was obtained from all participants who attended The Cambridge Centre for Ageing and Neuroscience (Cam-CAN) study.

Data Availability Statement: We used data from the Cambridge Center for Aging Neuroscience (Cam-CAN): https://camcan-archive.mrc-cbu.cam.ac.uk//dataaccess/ (15 February 2024).

Acknowledgments: This work was supported in part by the Science Research Project of Hebei Education Department (Grant No. BJK2024092), in part by Hebei Natural Science Foundation (Grant No. F2023207003), in part by Hebei University of Economics and Business Scientific Research and Development Program (2024YB23).

Conflicts of Interest: We declare that there are no conflicts of interest regarding the publication of this paper, and the manuscript is approved by all authors for publication.

References

1. Cullen, N.C.; Mälarstig, A.; Stomrud, E.; Hansson, O.; Mattsson-Carlgren, N. Accelerated inflammatory aging in Alzheimer's disease and its relation to amyloid, tau, and cognition. *Sci. Rep.* **2021**, *11*, 1965. [CrossRef]
2. Cole, J.H.; Franke, K. Predicting age using neuroimaging: Innovative brain ageing biomarkers. *Trends Neurosci.* **2017**, *40*, 681–690. [CrossRef] [PubMed]
3. Ballester, P.L.; da Silva, L.T.; Marcon, M.; Esper, N.B.; Frey, B.N.; Buchweitz, A.; Meneguzzi, F. Predicting Brain Age at Slice Level: Convolutional Neural Networks and Consequences for Interpretability. *Front. Psychiatry* **2021**, *12*. [CrossRef] [PubMed]
4. Franke, K.; Luders, E.; May, A.; Wilke, M.; Gaser, C. Brain maturation: Predicting individual BrainAGE in children and adolescents using structural MRI. *Neuroimage* **2012**, *63*, 1305–1312. [CrossRef] [PubMed]
5. Su, L.; Wang, L.; Shen, H.; Hu, D. Age-related classification and prediction based on MRI: A sparse representation method. *Procedia Environ. Sci.* **2011**, *8*, 645–652. [CrossRef]
6. Baecker, L.; Dafflon, J.; Da Costa, P.F.; Garcia-Dias, R.; Vieira, S.; Scarpazza, C.; Calhoun, V.D.; Sato, J.R.; Mechelli, A.; Pinaya, W.H. Brain age prediction: A comparison between machine learning models using region-and voxel-based morphometric data. *Hum. Brain Mapp.* **2021**, *42*, 2332–2346. [CrossRef]
7. Mishra, S.; Beheshti, I.; Khanna, P. A Review of Neuroimaging-driven Brain Age Estimation for identification of Brain Disorders and Health Conditions. *IEEE Rev. Biomed. Eng.* **2021**, *16*, 371–385. [CrossRef] [PubMed]
8. Matsuda, H.; Mizumura, S.; Nemoto, K.; Yamashita, F.; Imabayashi, E.; Sato, N.; Asada, T. Automatic voxel-based morphometry of structural MRI by SPM8 plus diffeomorphic anatomic registration through exponentiated lie algebra improves the diagnosis of probable Alzheimer Disease. *Am. J. Neuroradiol.* **2012**, *33*, 1109–1114. [CrossRef] [PubMed]

9. Franke, K.; Clarke, G.D.; Dahnke, R.; Gaser, C.; Kuo, A.H.; Li, C.; Schwab, M.; Nathanielsz, P.W. Premature brain aging in baboons resulting from moderate fetal undernutrition. *Front. Aging Neurosci.* **2017**, *9*, 92. [CrossRef] [PubMed]
10. Farokhian, F.; Yang, C.; Beheshti, I.; Matsuda, H.; Wu, S. Age-Related Gray and White Matter Changes in Normal Adult Brains. *Aging Dis* **2017**, *8*, 899–909. [CrossRef] [PubMed]
11. Matsuda, H. Voxel-based morphometry of brain MRI in normal aging and Alzheimer's disease. *Aging Dis.* **2013**, *4*, 29. [PubMed]
12. Madan, C.R.; Kensinger, E.A. Cortical complexity as a measure of age-related brain atrophy. *NeuroImage* **2016**, *134*, 617–629. [CrossRef] [PubMed]
13. Sone, D.; Beheshti, I. Neuroimaging-based brain age estimation: A promising personalized biomarker in neuropsychiatry. *J. Pers. Med.* **2022**, *12*, 1850. [CrossRef]
14. Cao, B.; Mwangi, B.; Hasan, K.M.; Selvaraj, S.; Zeni, C.P.; Zunta-Soares, G.B.; Soares, J.C. Development and validation of a brain maturation index using longitudinal neuroanatomical scans. *Neuroimage* **2015**, *117*, 311–318. [CrossRef]
15. Beheshti, I.; Gravel, P.; Potvin, O.; Dieumegarde, L.; Duchesne, S. A novel patch-based procedure for estimating brain age across adulthood. *Neuroimage* **2019**, *197*, 618–624. [CrossRef] [PubMed]
16. Beheshti, I.; Potvin, O.; Duchesne, S. Patch-wise brain age longitudinal reliability. *Hum. Brain Mapp.* **2021**, *42*, 690–698. [CrossRef]
17. Franke, K.; Ziegler, G.; Klöppel, S.; Gaser, C.; Alzheimer's Disease Neuroimaging Initiative. Estimating the age of healthy subjects from T1-weighted MRI scans using kernel methods: Exploring the influence of various parameters. *Neuroimage* **2010**, *50*, 883–892. [CrossRef] [PubMed]
18. Valizadeh, S.; Hänggi, J.; Mérillat, S.; Jäncke, L. Age prediction on the basis of brain anatomical measures. *Hum. Brain Mapp.* **2017**, *38*, 997–1008. [CrossRef] [PubMed]
19. Cole, J.H.; Poudel, R.P.; Tsagkrasoulis, D.; Caan, M.W.; Steves, C.; Spector, T.D.; Montana, G. Predicting brain age with deep learning from raw imaging data results in a reliable and heritable biomarker. *NeuroImage* **2017**, *163*, 115–124. [CrossRef] [PubMed]
20. Lancaster, J.; Lorenz, R.; Leech, R.; Cole, J.H. Bayesian optimization for neuroimaging pre-processing in brain age classification and prediction. *Front. Aging Neurosci.* **2018**, *10*, 28. [CrossRef]
21. Liu, X.; Beheshti, I.; Zheng, W.; Li, Y.; Li, S.; Zhao, Z.; Yao, Z.; Hu, B. Brain age estimation using multi-feature-based networks. *Comput. Biol. Med.* **2022**, *143*, 105285. [CrossRef] [PubMed]
22. Liem, F.; Varoquaux, G.; Kynast, J.; Beyer, F.; Masouleh, S.K.; Huntenburg, J.M.; Lampe, L.; Rahim, M.; Abraham, A.; Craddock, R.C. Predicting brain-age from multimodal imaging data captures cognitive impairment. *Neuroimage* **2017**, *148*, 179–188. [CrossRef] [PubMed]
23. Lund, M.J.; Alnæs, D.; de Lange, A.-M.G.; Andreassen, O.A.; Westlye, L.T.; Kaufmann, T. Brain age prediction using fMRI network coupling in youths and associations with psychiatric symptoms. *NeuroImage Clin.* **2022**, *33*, 102921. [CrossRef] [PubMed]
24. Le Bihan, D.; Mangin, J.F.; Poupon, C.; Clark, C.A.; Pappata, S.; Molko, N.; Chabriat, H. Diffusion tensor imaging: Concepts and applications. *J. Magn. Reson. Imaging Off. J. Int. Soc. Magn. Reson. Med.* **2001**, *13*, 534–546. [CrossRef]
25. Mwangi, B.; Hasan, K.M.; Soares, J.C. Prediction of individual subject's age across the human lifespan using diffusion tensor imaging: A machine learning approach. *Neuroimage* **2013**, *75*, 58–67. [CrossRef]
26. Cole, J.H. Multimodality neuroimaging brain-age in UK biobank: Relationship to biomedical, lifestyle, and cognitive factors. *Neurobiol. Aging* **2020**, *92*, 34–42. [CrossRef]
27. Li, L.; Wang, Y.; Zeng, Y.; Hou, S.; Huang, G.; Zhang, L.; Yan, N.; Ren, L.; Zhang, Z. Multimodal Neuroimaging Predictors of Learning Performance of Sensorimotor Rhythm Up-Regulation Neurofeedback. *Front. Neurosci* **2021**, *15*, 699999. [CrossRef]
28. Irimia, A.; Torgerson, C.M.; Goh, S.-Y.M.; Van Horn, J.D. Statistical estimation of physiological brain age as a descriptor of senescence rate during adulthood. *Brain Imaging Behav.* **2015**, *9*, 678–689. [CrossRef] [PubMed]
29. Lin, L.; Jin, C.; Fu, Z.; Zhang, B.; Bin, G.; Wu, S. Predicting healthy older adult's brain age based on structural connectivity networks using artificial neural networks. *Comput. Methods Programs Biomed.* **2016**, *125*, 8–17. [CrossRef] [PubMed]
30. Xifra-Porxas, A.; Ghosh, A.; Mitsis, G.D.; Boudrias, M.-H. Estimating brain age from structural MRI and MEG data: Insights from dimensionality reduction techniques. *NeuroImage* **2021**, *231*, 117822. [CrossRef]
31. Beheshti, I.; Maikusa, N.; Matsuda, H. The accuracy of T1-weighted voxel-wise and region-wise metrics for brain age estimation. *Comput. Methods Programs Biomed* **2022**, *214*, 106585. [CrossRef] [PubMed]
32. Engemann, D.A.; Kozynets, O.; Sabbagh, D.; Lemaître, G.; Varoquaux, G.; Liem, F.; Gramfort, A. Combining magnetoencephalography with magnetic resonance imaging enhances learning of surrogate-biomarkers. *Elife* **2020**, *9*, e54055. [CrossRef]
33. Cho, S.; Jones, D.; Reddick, W.E.; Ogg, R.J.; Steen, R.G. Establishing norms for age-related changes in proton T1 of human brain tissue in vivo. *Magn. Reson. Imaging* **1997**, *15*, 1133–1143. [CrossRef] [PubMed]
34. Salat, D.H.; Lee, S.Y.; Van der Kouwe, A.; Greve, D.N.; Fischl, B.; Rosas, H.D. Age-associated alterations in cortical gray and white matter signal intensity and gray to white matter contrast. *Neuroimage* **2009**, *48*, 21–28. [CrossRef]
35. Liu, M.; Cheng, D.; Wang, K.; Wang, Y. Multi-Modality Cascaded Convolutional Neural Networks for Alzheimer's Disease Diagnosis. *Neuroinformatics* **2018**, *16*, 295–308. [CrossRef]
36. Hardoon, D.R.; Szedmak, S.; Shawe-Taylor, J. Canonical correlation analysis: An overview with application to learning methods. *Neural. Comput.* **2004**, *16*, 2639–2664. [CrossRef]
37. Sui, J.; Adali, T.; Yu, Q.; Chen, J.; Calhoun, V.D. A review of multivariate methods for multimodal fusion of brain imaging data. *J. Neurosci. Methods* **2012**, *204*, 68–81. [CrossRef] [PubMed]

38. Martinez-Murcia, F.J.; Arco, J.E.; Jimenez-Mesa, C.; Segovia, F.; Illan, I.A.; Ramirez, J.; Gorriz, J.M. Bridging Imaging and Clinical Scores in Parkinson's Progression via Multimodal Self-Supervised Deep Learning. *Int. J. Neural. Syst.* **2024**, *34*, 2450043. [CrossRef] [PubMed]
39. Miao, X.; Zhang, X.; Zhang, H. Low-rank tensor fusion and self-supervised multi-task multimodal sentiment analysis. *Multimed Tools Appl.* **2024**, *83*, 63291–63308. [CrossRef]
40. Shafto, M.A.; Tyler, L.K.; Dixon, M.; Taylor, J.R.; Rowe, J.B.; Cusack, R.; Calder, A.J.; Marslen-Wilson, W.D.; Duncan, J.; Dalgleish, T. The Cambridge Centre for Ageing and Neuroscience (Cam-CAN) study protocol: A cross-sectional, lifespan, multidisciplinary examination of healthy cognitive ageing. *BMC Neurol.* **2014**, *14*, 1–25. [CrossRef]
41. Taylor, J.R.; Williams, N.; Cusack, R.; Auer, T.; Shafto, M.A.; Dixon, M.; Tyler, L.K.; Henson, R.N. The Cambridge Centre for Ageing and Neuroscience (Cam-CAN) data repository: Structural and functional MRI, MEG, and cognitive data from a cross-sectional adult lifespan sample. *Neuroimage* **2017**, *144*, 262–269. [CrossRef] [PubMed]
42. Farokhian, F.; Beheshti, I.; Sone, D.; Matsuda, H. Comparing CAT12 and VBM8 for Detecting Brain Morphological Abnormalities in Temporal Lobe Epilepsy. *Front. Neurol.* **2017**, *8*, 428. [CrossRef]
43. Ashburner, J.; Friston, K.J.J.N. Unified segmentation. *Neuroimage* **2005**, *26*, 839–851. [CrossRef]
44. Taulu, S.; Simola, J. Spatiotemporal signal space separation method for rejecting nearby interference in MEG measurements. *Phys. Med. Biol.* **2006**, *51*, 1759. [CrossRef]
45. Tadel, F.; Bock, E.; Niso, G.; Mosher, J.C.; Cousineau, M.; Pantazis, D.; Leahy, R.M.; Baillet, S. MEG/EEG group analysis with brainstorm. *Front. Neurosci.* **2019**, *13*, 76. [CrossRef]
46. Niso, G.; Tadel, F.; Bock, E.; Cousineau, M.; Santos, A.; Baillet, S. Brainstorm pipeline analysis of resting-state data from the open MEG archive. *Front. Neurosci.* **2019**, *13*, 284. [CrossRef]
47. Dale, A.M.; Fischl, B.; Sereno, M.I. Cortical surface-based analysis: I. Segmentation and surface reconstruction. *Neuroimage* **1999**, *9*, 179–194. [CrossRef] [PubMed]
48. Fischl, B.; Van Der Kouwe, A.; Destrieux, C.; Halgren, E.; Ségonne, F.; Salat, D.H.; Busa, E.; Seidman, L.J.; Goldstein, J.; Kennedy, D. Automatically parcellating the human cerebral cortex. *Cereb. Cortex* **2004**, *14*, 11–22. [CrossRef]
49. Fischl, B.; Salat, D.H.; Busa, E.; Albert, M.; Dieterich, M.; Haselgrove, C.; Van Der Kouwe, A.; Killiany, R.; Kennedy, D.; Klaveness, S. Whole brain segmentation: Automated labeling of neuroanatomical structures in the human brain. *Neuron* **2002**, *33*, 341–355. [CrossRef] [PubMed]
50. Cusack, R.; Vicente-Grabovetsky, A.; Mitchell, D.J.; Wild, C.J.; Auer, T.; Linke, A.C.; Peelle, J.E. Automatic analysis (aa): Efficient neuroimaging workflows and parallel processing using Matlab and XML. *Front. Neuroinformatics* **2015**, *8*, 90. [CrossRef] [PubMed]
51. Smith, S.M.; Jenkinson, M.; Woolrich, M.W.; Beckmann, C.F.; Behrens, T.E.; Johansen-Berg, H.; Bannister, P.R.; De Luca, M.; Drobnjak, I.; Flitney, D.E. Advances in functional and structural MR image analysis and implementation as FSL. *Neuroimage* **2004**, *23*, S208–S219. [CrossRef] [PubMed]
52. Peng, H.; Gong, W.; Beckmann, C.F.; Vedaldi, A.; Smith, S.M. Accurate brain age prediction with lightweight deep neural networks. *Med. Image Anal.* **2021**, *68*, 101871. [CrossRef] [PubMed]
53. Vaswani, A.; Shazeer, N.; Parmar, N.; Uszkoreit, J.; Jones, L.; Gomez, A.N.; Kaiser, Ł.; Polosukhin, I. Attention is all you need. *Adv. Neural Inf. Process. Syst.* **2017**, *30*. Available online: https://papers.nips.cc/paper_files/paper/2017/hash/3f5ee243547dee91fbd053c1c4a845aa-Abstract.html (accessed on 9 December 2024).
54. Roy, S.; Kiral-Kornek, I.; Harrer, S. ChronoNet: A deep recurrent neural network for abnormal EEG identification. In Proceedings of the Conference on Artificial Intelligence in Medicine in Europe, Poznan, Poland, 26–29 June 2019; pp. 47–56.
55. Yan, W.; Calhoun, V.; Song, M.; Cui, Y.; Yan, H.; Liu, S.; Fan, L.; Zuo, N.; Yang, Z.; Xu, K. Discriminating schizophrenia using recurrent neural network applied on time courses of multi-site FMRI data. *EBioMedicine* **2019**, *47*, 543–552. [CrossRef] [PubMed]
56. Zadeh, A.; Chen, M.; Poria, S.; Cambria, E.; Morency, L.-P. Tensor fusion network for multimodal sentiment analysis. *arXiv* **2017**, arXiv:1707.07250.
57. Fukui, A.; Park, D.H.; Yang, D.; Rohrbach, A.; Darrell, T.; Rohrbach, M. Multimodal compact bilinear pooling for visual question answering and visual grounding. *arXiv* **2016**, arXiv:1606.01847.
58. Beheshti, I.; Nugent, S.; Potvin, O.; Duchesne, S. Bias-adjustment in neuroimaging-based brain age frameworks: A robust scheme. *NeuroImage* **2019**, *24*, 102063. [CrossRef] [PubMed]
59. Kingma, D.P.; Ba, J. Adam: A method for stochastic optimization. *arXiv* **2014**, arXiv:1412.6980.
60. Niu, X.; Zhang, F.; Kounios, J.; Liang, H. Improved prediction of brain age using multimodal neuroimaging data. *Hum. Brain Mapp.* **2020**, *41*, 1626–1643. [CrossRef]
61. De Lange, A.-M.G.; Anatürk, M.; Suri, S.; Kaufmann, T.; Cole, J.H.; Griffanti, L.; Zsoldos, E.; Jensen, D.E.; Filippini, N.; Singh-Manoux, A. Multimodal brain-age prediction and cardiovascular risk: The Whitehall II MRI sub-study. *NeuroImage* **2020**, *222*, 117292. [CrossRef] [PubMed]
62. Rokicki, J.; Wolfers, T.; Nordhøy, W.; Tesli, N.; Quintana, D.S.; Alnæs, D.; Richard, G.; de Lange, A.M.G.; Lund, M.J.; Norbom, L. Multimodal imaging improves brain age prediction and reveals distinct abnormalities in patients with psychiatric and neurological disorders. *Hum. Brain Mapp.* **2021**, *42*, 1714–1726. [CrossRef]
63. Cole, J.H.; Leech, R.; Sharp, D.J.; Alzheimer's Disease Neuroimaging Initiative. Prediction of brain age suggests accelerated atrophy after traumatic brain injury. *Ann. Neurol.* **2015**, *77*, 571–581. [CrossRef] [PubMed]

64. Cole, J.H.; Annus, T.; Wilson, L.R.; Remtulla, R.; Hong, Y.T.; Fryer, T.D.; Acosta-Cabronero, J.; Cardenas-Blanco, A.; Smith, R.; Menon, D.K. Brain-predicted age in Down syndrome is associated with beta amyloid deposition and cognitive decline. *Neurobiol. Aging* **2017**, *56*, 41–49. [CrossRef] [PubMed]
65. Pardoe, H.R.; Cole, J.H.; Blackmon, K.; Thesen, T.; Kuzniecky, R.; Human Epilepsy Project Investigators. Structural brain changes in medically refractory focal epilepsy resemble premature brain aging. *Epilepsy Res.* **2017**, *133*, 28–32. [CrossRef] [PubMed]
66. Kaufmann, T.; van der Meer, D.; Doan, N.T.; Schwarz, E.; Lund, M.J.; Agartz, I.; Alnæs, D.; Barch, D.M.; Baur-Streubel, R.; Bertolino, A. Common brain disorders are associated with heritable patterns of apparent aging of the brain. *Nat. Neurosci.* **2019**, *22*, 1617–1623. [CrossRef]
67. Beheshti, I. Cocaine destroys gray matter brain cells and accelerates brain aging. *Biology* **2023**, *12*, 752. [CrossRef]
68. Deipolyi, A.R.; Mukherjee, P.; Gill, K.; Henry, R.G.; Partridge, S.C.; Veeraraghavan, S.; Jin, H.; Lu, Y.; Miller, S.P.; Ferriero, D.M. Comparing microstructural and macrostructural development of the cerebral cortex in premature newborns: Diffusion tensor imaging versus cortical gyration. *Neuroimage* **2005**, *27*, 579–586. [CrossRef]
69. Weston, P.S.; Simpson, I.J.; Ryan, N.S.; Ourselin, S.; Fox, N.C. Diffusion imaging changes in grey matter in Alzheimer's disease: A potential marker of early neurodegeneration. *Alzheimer's Res. Ther.* **2015**, *7*, 1–8. [CrossRef] [PubMed]
70. Kincses, Z.T.; Vécsei, L. Is diffusion magnetic resonance imaging the future biomarker to measure therapeutic efficacy in multiple sclerosis? *Eur. J. Neurol.* **2018**, *25*, 707–708. [CrossRef]
71. Malyarenko, D.I.; Newitt, D.; Wilmes, L.J.; Tudorica, A.; Helmer, K.G.; Arlinghaus, L.R.; Jacobs, M.A.; Jajamovich, G.; Taouli, B.; Yankeelov, T.E. Demonstration of nonlinearity bias in the measurement of the apparent diffusion coefficient in multicenter trials. *Magn. Reson. Med.* **2016**, *75*, 1312–1323. [CrossRef] [PubMed]
72. Mirzaalian, H.; Pierrefeu, A.d.; Savadjiev, P.; Pasternak, O.; Bouix, S.; Kubicki, M.; Westin, C.-F.; Shenton, M.E.; Rathi, Y. Harmonizing diffusion MRI data across multiple sites and scanners. In Proceedings of the International Conference on Medical Image Computing and Computer-Assisted Intervention, Munich, Germany, 5–9 October 2015; pp. 12–19.
73. Smith, S.M.; Miller, K.L.; Salimi-Khorshidi, G.; Webster, M.; Beckmann, C.F.; Nichols, T.E.; Ramsey, J.D.; Woolrich, M.W. Network modelling methods for FMRI. *Neuroimage* **2011**, *54*, 875–891. [CrossRef] [PubMed]
74. Schoonhoven, D.N.; Briels, C.T.; Hillebrand, A.; Scheltens, P.; Stam, C.J.; Gouw, A.A. Sensitive and reproducible MEG resting-state metrics of functional connectivity in Alzheimer's disease. *Alzheimers Res. Ther.* **2022**, *14*, 38. [CrossRef]
75. Zhang, X.; Lei, X.; Wu, T.; Jiang, T. A review of EEG and MEG for brainnetome research. *Cogn Neurodyn.* **2014**, *8*, 87–98. [CrossRef]
76. Baillet, S. Magnetoencephalography for brain electrophysiology and imaging. *Nat. Neurosci.* **2017**, *20*, 327–339. [CrossRef]
77. Hosseini-Asl, E.; Gimel'farb, G.; El-Baz, A. Alzheimer's disease diagnostics by a 3D deeply supervised adaptable convolutional network. *Front. Biosci. (Landmark Ed.)* **2018**, *23*, 584–596.
78. Li, C.; Cui, Y.; Luo, N.; Liu, Y.; Bourgeat, P.; Fripp, J.; Jiang, T. Trans-ResNet: Integrating Transformers and CNNs for Alzheimer's disease classification. In Proceedings of the 2022 IEEE 19th International Symposium on Biomedical Imaging (ISBI), Kolkata, India, 28–31 March 2022; pp. 1–5.
79. Zheng, G.; Zhang, Y.; Zhao, Z.; Wang, Y.; Liu, X.; Shang, Y.; Cong, Z.; Dimitriadis, S.I.; Yao, Z.; Hu, B. A transformer-based multi-features fusion model for prediction of conversion in mild cognitive impairment. *Methods* **2022**, *204*, 241–248. [CrossRef]
80. Cai, H.; Gao, Y.; Liu, M. Graph Transformer Geometric Learning of Brain Networks Using Multimodal MR Images for Brain Age Estimation. *IEEE Trans. Med. Imaging* **2022**, *42*, 456–466. [CrossRef] [PubMed]
81. Dahan, S.; Xu, H.; Williams, L.Z.; Fawaz, A.; Yang, C.; Coalson, T.S.; Williams, M.C.; Newby, D.E.; Edwards, A.D.; Glasser, M.F. Surface Vision Transformers: Flexible Attention-Based Modelling of Biomedical Surfaces. *arXiv* **2022**, arXiv:2204.03408.
82. Dahan, S.; Williams, L.Z.; Fawaz, A.; Rueckert, D.; Robinson, E.C. Surface Analysis with Vision Transformers. *arXiv* **2022**. [CrossRef]
83. Yang, Y.; Guo, X.; Chang, Z.; Ye, C.; Xiang, Y.; Lv, H.; Ma, T. Estimating Brain Age with Global and Local Dependencies. In Proceedings of the IEEE International Conference on Image Processing (ICIP), Bordeaux, France, 16–19 October 2022.
84. Liang, P.P.; Liu, Z.; Tsai, Y.-H.H.; Zhao, Q.; Salakhutdinov, R.; Morency, L.-P. Learning representations from imperfect time series data via tensor rank regularization. *arXiv* **2019**, arXiv:1907.01011.
85. Shen, X.; Huang, J.; Sun, Y.; Li, M.; Pan, B.; Ding, W. Parallel Pathway Convolutional Neural Network with Low-rank Fusion for Brain Age Prediction. In Proceedings of the 2021 IEEE 1st International Conference on Digital Twins and Parallel Intelligence (DTPI), Beijing, China, 15 July–15 August 2021; pp. 434–437.
86. Beck, D.; de Lange, A.-M.G.; Maximov, I.I.; Richard, G.; Andreassen, O.A.; Nordvik, J.E.; Westlye, L.T. White matter microstructure across the adult lifespan: A mixed longitudinal and cross-sectional study using advanced diffusion models and brain-age prediction. *NeuroImage* **2021**, *224*, 117441. [CrossRef] [PubMed]
87. Popescu, S.G.; Glocker, B.; Sharp, D.J.; Cole, J.H. Local brain-age: A U-net model. *Front. Aging Neurosci.* **2021**, *13*, 761954. [CrossRef] [PubMed]
88. Han, J.; Kim, S.Y.; Lee, J.; Lee, W.H.J.S. Brain Age Prediction: A Comparison between Machine Learning Models Using Brain Morphometric Data. *Hum. Brain Mapp.* **2022**, *22*, 8077. [CrossRef]
89. Chen, C.-L.; Hsu, Y.-C.; Yang, L.-Y.; Tung, Y.-H.; Luo, W.-B.; Liu, C.-M.; Hwang, T.-J.; Hwu, H.-G.; Tseng, W.-Y.I. Generalization of diffusion magnetic resonance imaging–based brain age prediction model through transfer learning. *NeuroImage* **2020**, *217*, 116831. [CrossRef]

90. Clements, R.G.; Claros-Olivares, C.C.; McIlvain, G.; Brockmeier, A.J.; Johnson, C.L. Mechanical Property Based Brain Age Prediction using Convolutional Neural Networks. *bioRxiv* **2023**, *13*, 2023.2002.2012.528186.
91. Wang, J.; Gao, Y.; Wang, F.; Zeng, S.; Li, J.; Miao, H.; Wang, T.; Zeng, J.; Baptista-Hon, D.; Monteiro, O.; et al. Accurate estimation of biological age and its application in disease prediction using a multimodal image Transformer system. *Proc. Natl. Acad. Sci. USA* **2024**, *121*, e2308812120. [CrossRef] [PubMed]
92. Zhou, P.; Lu, C.; Feng, J.; Lin, Z.; Yan, S. Tensor Low-Rank Representation for Data Recovery and Clustering. *IEEE Trans. Pattern Anal. Mach. Intell.* **2021**, *43*, 1718–1732. [CrossRef]
93. Wan, X.; Wang, Y.; Wang, Z.; Tang, Y.; Liu, B. Joint low-rank tensor fusion and cross-modal attention for multimodal physiological signals based emotion recognition. *Physiol. Meas.* **2024**, *45*, 075003. [CrossRef] [PubMed]
94. Gao, J.; Li, P.; Chen, Z.; Zhang, J. A survey on deep learning for multimodal data fusion. *Neural. Comput.* **2020**, *32*, 829–864. [CrossRef]
95. Li, W.; Peng, Y.; Zhang, M.; Ding, L.; Hu, H.; Shen, L. Deep model fusion: A survey. *arXiv* **2023**, arXiv:2309.15698.

Disclaimer/Publisher's Note: The statements, opinions and data contained in all publications are solely those of the individual author(s) and contributor(s) and not of MDPI and/or the editor(s). MDPI and/or the editor(s) disclaim responsibility for any injury to people or property resulting from any ideas, methods, instructions or products referred to in the content.

brain sciences

MDPI

Article

Deep Learning-Driven Estimation of Centiloid Scales from Amyloid PET Images with ^{11}C-PiB and ^{18}F-Labeled Tracers in Alzheimer's Disease

Tensho Yamao [1], Kenta Miwa [1,*], Yuta Kaneko [2], Noriyuki Takahashi [1], Noriaki Miyaji [1], Koki Hasegawa [1], Kei Wagatsuma [3], Yuto Kamitaka [4], Hiroshi Ito [5] and Hiroshi Matsuda [6]

1 Department of Radiological Sciences, School of Health Science, Fukushima Medical University, Fukushima 960-8516, Japan; t.yamao0522@gmail.com (T.Y.)
2 Department of Radiology, Fukushima Medical University Hospital, Fukushima 960-1295, Japan
3 School of Allied Health Sciences, Kitasato University, Tokyo 252-0373, Japan
4 Research Team for Neuroimaging, Tokyo Metropolitan Institute for Geriatrics and Gerontology, Tokyo 173-0015, Japan
5 Department of Radiology and Nuclear Medicine, Fukushima Medical University, Fukushima 960-1295, Japan
6 Department of Biofunctional Imaging, Fukushima Medical University, Fukushima 960-1295, Japan
* Correspondence: kenta5710@gmail.com

Abstract: Background: Standard methods for deriving Centiloid scales from amyloid PET images are time-consuming and require considerable expert knowledge. We aimed to develop a deep learning method of automating Centiloid scale calculations from amyloid PET images with ^{11}C-Pittsburgh Compound-B (PiB) tracer and assess its applicability to ^{18}F-labeled tracers without retraining. Methods: We trained models on 231 ^{11}C-PiB amyloid PET images using a 50-layer 3D ResNet architecture. The models predicted the Centiloid scale, and accuracy was assessed using mean absolute error (MAE), linear regression analysis, and Bland–Altman plots. Results: The MAEs for Alzheimer's disease (AD) and young controls (YC) were 8.54 and 2.61, respectively, using ^{11}C-PiB, and 8.66 and 3.56, respectively, using ^{18}F-NAV4694. The MAEs for AD and YC were higher with ^{18}F-florbetaben (39.8 and 7.13, respectively) and ^{18}F-florbetapir (40.5 and 12.4, respectively), and the error rate was moderate for ^{18}F-flutemetamol (21.3 and 4.03, respectively). Linear regression yielded a slope of 1.00, intercept of 1.26, and R^2 of 0.956, with a mean bias of −1.31 in the Centiloid scale prediction. Conclusions: We propose a deep learning means of directly predicting the Centiloid scale from amyloid PET images in a native space. Transferring the model trained on ^{11}C-PiB directly to ^{18}F-NAV4694 without retraining was feasible.

Keywords: amyloid PET; deep learning; centiloid scale

1. Introduction

Alzheimer's disease (AD) is a major cause of dementia characterized by amyloid-β plaques, hyperphosphorylated tau protein, and brain atrophy [1,2]. Amyloid-β, a key hallmark of AD, begins to accumulate over two decades before the onset of symptoms. Non-invasive amyloid positron emission tomography (PET) allows the early detection of amyloid-β accumulation, which is critical for a differential diagnosis of AD. Fluorine-18-labeled amyloid tracers, such as ^{18}F-florbetaben, ^{18}F-flutemetamol, and ^{18}F-florbetapir, are currently available for routine clinical amyloid PET imaging. On the other hand, ^{11}C-PiB and ^{18}F-NAV4694 are available for research only. These amyloid PET tracers visualize the distribution of amyloid-β despite different chemical architectures. Confirmation of amyloid pathology by amyloid PET or cerebrospinal fluid (CSF) tests is essential for the timely administration of disease-modifying drugs [3].

While amyloid PET results are often visually assessed as negative or positive in clinical practice, quantitative evaluations are essential for clinical investigations and the development of drugs to treat AD. The standardized uptake value ratio (SUVR) is a common quantitative measure, but it varies depending on the region of interest and the tracer. The Global Alzheimer's Association Interactive Network (GAAIN) introduced the Centiloid scale to address these inconsistencies [4]. The Centiloid scale is defined by linearly scaling the average SUVR value to 0 for subjects with a high certainty of being amyloid-negative and to 100 for typical AD patients. The reproducibility of the Centiloid scale calculation can be verified by quality control using available PET and MRI datasets on the GAAIN website. Although the Centiloid scale is defined based on ^{11}C-PiB data, conversion of the SUVR of ^{18}F-labeled amyloid tracers to the ^{11}C-PiB equivalent of the Centiloid scale allows the direct comparison of quantitative values between different tracers. However, the calculation of the Centiloid scale requires several conditions. First, a three-dimensional T1-weighted image covering the region from the vertex to the whole cerebellum is required from the same subject. Then, manual image analysis is required to calculate the Centiloid scale. It involves co-registration of the PET and MRI images of the same subject, anatomical standardization, VOI analysis using specific VOIs, and the conversion process from SUVR to the Centiloid scale. To overcome this, a simple method of calculating the Centiloid scale using low-dose CT instead of MRI has been reported [5–7]. However, manual image analysis and acquisition of anatomical images are still required, and no studies have been reported that automatically calculate the Centiloid scale using only PET images. Quantitative analysis using only PET images allows the evaluation of subjects without the corresponding MRI data.

Recently, deep learning methods in amyloid PET have shown exceptional performance in areas such as classification [8], visual interpretation support [9], the prediction of cognitive decline [10], and image restoration [11]. In addition, deep learning has been applied to predict quantitative values from amyloid PET images. Deep learning-based anatomical standardization method for ^{18}F-florbetaben or ^{18}F-flutemetamol PET without MRI has been proposed [12]. A deep learning model was developed to quantify SUVR from ^{18}F-florbetapir or ^{18}F-florbetaben PET images in a native space [13]. A deep learning quantification of the SUVR of an ^{18}F-florbetapir PET image using a pretrained 2D CNN has also been reported [14]. The use of generative adversarial network model to generate structural MRI image from ^{18}F-florbetapir PET image has been proposed for the quantification of PET alone [15]. However, most of these techniques still rely on PET and MRI preprocessing. In particular, the Centiloid scale has not been directly predicted using deep learning. Since the Centiloid scale is converted from the SUVR calculated with the specific volume of interest (VOI), a deep learning model for the Centiloid scale appears to be of importance. The advantages of 3D convolutional neural network (CNN), which can account for continuity between slices, are significant for an accurate Centiloid scale prediction. The direct comparison of the different tracers is also an important part of the Centiloid scale. Therefore, it is necessary to evaluate the model using a number of amyloid tracers, not just a single one.

In this study, we aimed to fill this gap by directly predicting the Centiloid scale from amyloid PET images without MRI using a 3D CNN. In addition, we investigated whether a 3D CNN constructed with ^{11}C-PiB could be applied to ^{18}F-NAV4694, ^{18}F-florbetaben, ^{18}F-flutemetamol, and ^{18}F-florbetapir without retraining. These PET tracers have the common feature of binding to amyloid-β deposition, suggesting the potential applicability of the deep learning model to different amyloid tracers. These PET data are available from GAAIN and conversion methods to the ^{11}C-PiB-equivalent Centiloid scale have been reported. The ability to apply various amyloid tracers enhances the utility of the Centiloid scale calculation methods, which is a significant advantage in their adoption for research and clinical use.

2. Materials and Methods

2.1. Dataset

We downloaded 79 amyloid ^{11}C-PiB [4] and 210 amyloid ^{18}F-NAV4694 [16], ^{18}F-Florbetaben [17], ^{18}F-Flutemetamol [18], and ^{18}F-Florbetapir [19] PET images from the GAAIN database (https://www.gaain.org/centiloid-project accessed on 6 October 2022). Table 1 shows details of the amyloid PET dataset. The ground truth of the Centiloid scale value for deep learning prediction is published on the GAAIN website. A Centiloid scale value calibrated to ^{11}C-PiB is provided for ^{18}F-labeled amyloid PET. We employed these PET datasets to construct a predictive model for the Centiloid scale and to evaluate its applicability across multiple tracers. In the dataset of ^{18}F-labeled amyloid PET, ^{11}C-PiB PET imaging was also conducted on same subjects. Therefore, we utilized a total of 289 amyloid ^{11}C PiB images from different repositories. ^{11}C-PiB PET scans were performed on 34 healthy subjects and 45 patients with AD, for a total of 79 participants [4,20–26]. ^{11}C-PiB PET image was acquired 50 to 70 min after injection. The acquisition time for ^{11}C-PiB was consistent across all datasets. The PET scanners used a BioGraph TruePoint TrueV (Siemens Healthineers, Erlangen, Germany), an ECAT Exact HR+ (Siemens), an ECAT Exact HR (Siemens), and an Allegro PET camera (Philips Medical Systems, Eindhoven, The Netherlands). Images were reconstructed using the filtered back projection (FBP), the 3D row-action maximum likelihood algorithm (RAMLA), and the ordered subsets expectation maximization (OSEM). ^{11}C-PiB and ^{18}F-NAV4694 PET scans were performed on 10 young controls, 25 elderly controls, 10 patients with mild cognitive impairment (MCI), 7 patients with mild AD, and 3 patients with frontotemporal dementia (FTD). The ^{18}F-NAV4694 PET image was acquired 50 to 70 min after injection using an Allegro PET camera in the 3D mode. Images were reconstructed using the 3D RAMLA [16]. ^{11}C-PiB and ^{18}F-florbetaben PET images were performed on 10 young controls, 6 elderly controls, 10 patients with MCI, 7 patients with AD, and 3 patients with FTD. ^{18}F-florbetaben PET image was acquired 90 to 110 min after injection using an Allegro PET camera [27]. Images were reconstructed using the 3D RAMLA and the line of response (LOR) RAMLA. ^{11}C-PiB and ^{18}F-flutemetamol PET images were performed on 24 young controls, 10 elderly controls, 20 patients with MCI, and 20 patients with AD. ^{18}F-flutemetamol PET images were acquired 90 to 110 min after injection using a 16-slice Biograph (Siemens), an ECAT EXACT HR+, a GE Advance scanner (GE Healthcare, Milwaukee, WI, USA), a Discovery RX, and a Discovery RXT (GE Healthcare) [18,28,29]. Images were reconstructed by the FBP and the OSEM. ^{18}F-florbetapir PET image was obtained for 13 young controls, 6 elderly controls, 3 at-risk elderly controls, 7 patients with MCI, 3 patients with possible AD, and 14 patients with AD. ^{18}F-florbetapir PET image was acquired 50 to 60 min after injection using an ECAT Exact HR+ in the 2D mode with 2D-OSEM, a Gemini TF 64 (Philips) in the 3D mode with LOR-RAMLA, and a GE Advance scanner in the 2D mode with Fourier rebinning iterative reconstruction algorithm [19].

Table 1. Clinical demographics of GAAIN dataset for amyloid PET. ^{18}F-labeled and ^{11}C-PiB amyloid PET images were acquired in one subject each.

PET Tracer	Total	Controls	Patients
^{11}C-PiB	79	34	45
^{18}F-NAV4694 and ^{11}C-PiB	55	10	45
^{18}F-Florbetaben and ^{11}C-PiB	35	10	25
^{18}F-Flutemetamol and ^{11}C-PiB	74	24	50
^{18}F-Florbetapir and ^{11}C-PiB	46	13	33

2.2. Deep Learning Model Architecture for Predicting Centiloid Scale

The Centiloid scale was predicted from amyloid PET images using the 50-layer three-dimensional (3D) ResNet architecture (https://github.com/xmuyzz/3D-CNN-PyTorch accessed on 6 December 2023). This deep learning model was modified from the standard

3D ResNet to address the specific complexities of processing PET images for AD. ResNet facilitates effective learning in the deepest models through skip connection. In addition, the ability of 3D CNN to process volumetric data makes it particularly useful for PET data analysis in AD, where it can effectively capture the spatial complexity of local amyloid deposition. It features a comprehensive design that includes 3D convolutional layers for spatial data processing, batch normalization to accelerate training and improve model performance, and rectified linear units (ReLUs) for nonlinear transformations. The architecture also includes a max-pooling layer to reduce dimensionality and improve feature extraction, followed by four sequential layer blocks carefully constructed with bottleneck blocks. These blocks are designed to deepen the network without increasing its complexity or computational load through a combination of 3D convolution, batch normalization, ReLUs, and down sampling layers. This allows the model to learn more complex features from the PET images with greater efficiency. Sequential layer blocks consisting of 3, 4, 6, and 3 bottleneck blocks allow the model to adaptively refine its predictions, making it highly effective for medical imaging tasks. An average-pooling layer follows these blocks, leading to a fully connected layer that culminates the network architecture and facilitates the final prediction of the Centiloid scale. Figure 1 shows the structure of our deep learning model. A network model was implemented on the following system environment: Intel(R) Xenon Gold 5222 3.80 GHz; NVIDIA RTX A6000 video card with 24 GB of video memory; CUDA v. 11.6; PyTorch v. 1.12.1; Python v. 3.8.13; and Ubuntu 18.04 LTS.

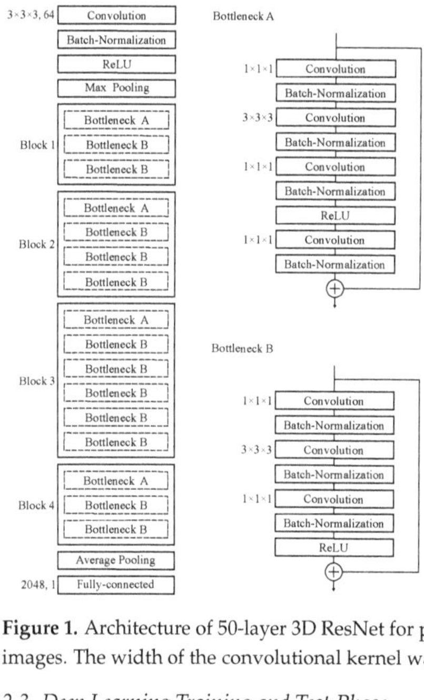

Figure 1. Architecture of 50-layer 3D ResNet for predicting Centiloid scale from native amyloid PET images. The width of the convolutional kernel was set to $1 \times 1 \times 1$ or $3 \times 3 \times 3$.

2.3. Deep Learning Training and Test Phase

Figure 2 shows the comprehensive training and testing processes of our deep learning analysis. The deep learning model was trained on 231 (80%) of the 289 available ^{11}C-PiB amyloid PET images and tested on 58 (20%) of the 289 images, with ^{18}F-amyloid PET images included in the testing phase without further training. It has been demonstrated that deep learning models trained on ^{18}F-florbetapir PET images can be accurately applied to ^{18}F-florbetaben images without the need for retraining [13]. This study extends this approach by applying a model trained on ^{11}C-PiB to four types of ^{18}F-labeled amyloid tracers.

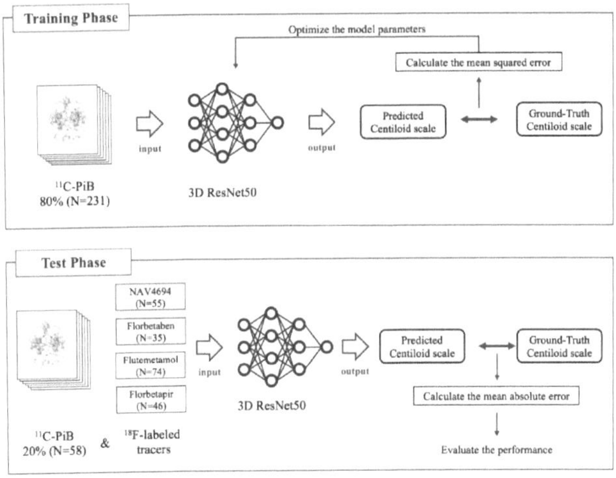

Figure 2. Scheme of deep learning training and testing phases.

All pixel values of less than 0 were adjusted to 0 because PET images reconstructed using the FBP algorithm were included. The training images were randomly rotated (between $-10°$ and $10°$) and scaled to increase the robustness of the model. Since the original matrix size were not uniform, the images were resized to $128 \times 128 \times 128$ voxels. In order to ensure uniformity across the dataset and enhance the model's ability to learn from the PET images effectively, the voxel intensity was normalized using min–max normalization for model input.

The mean square error (MSE) was used for the loss function and adaptive moment (Adam) estimation of the optimization algorithm.

$$MSE = \frac{1}{n}\sum_{i=1}^{n}(y_i - \hat{y}_i)^2$$

where n is the number of PET images, y_i is the ground truth Centiloid scale, and $\hat{y}_i$ is the Centiloid scale computed by our deep learning model. The use of the MSE as the loss function is advantageous because it emphasizes larger errors by squaring the error values, thus causing the model to focus more on reducing these errors during training. The learning rate was 0.0001, and the batch size was 4. To avoid overfitting, the training phase was terminated when performance did not improve over 20 consecutive epochs. Thus, the number of epochs was 73.

The ability to predict the Centiloid scale was evaluated using the mean absolute error (MAE) on the test dataset.

$$MAE = \frac{1}{n}\sum_{i=1}^{n}|y_i - \hat{y}_i|$$

where n is the number of PET images, y_i is the ground truth Centiloid scale, and $\hat{y}_i$ is the Centiloid scale computed by our deep learning model. Using the MAE as a performance metric has the advantage of providing a direct interpretation of the average prediction error in the same units as the predicted value.

2.4. Statistical Analysis

The difference in predictive performance between ADs and YCs was tested using the Mann–Whitney U test with a significance level of 0.05. One-way analysis of variance (ANOVA) was used to evaluate differences in predictive performance between different tracers. In cases where one-way ANOVA indicated significant differences, Bonferroni-corrected post hoc tests were used to identify specific groups. The correlation between the deep learning approach and the ground truth was assessed using Pearson correlation analysis. The slope, intercept, and coefficient of determination were obtained using linear regression analyses of the ground truth and predicted values of the test set. Centiloid scale concordance between deep learning prediction and ground truth was assessed using Bland–Altman plots. All data were statistically analyzed using Python v. 3.8.13, scikit-learn v. 1.1.2, and SciPy v. 1.8.13.

3. Results

The evaluation of the predictive accuracy of deep learning was carefully performed using the designated test set. Figure 3 shows a detailed comparison of the MAE for both ^{11}C-PiB and various ^{18}F-labeled amyloid tracers, delineating the results for young controls (YCs) and AD patients. The MAEs for AD and YC were 8.54 and 2.61, respectively, using ^{11}C-PiB, and 8.66 and 3.56, respectively, using ^{18}F-NAV4694. The MAEs for AD and YC were higher with ^{18}F-florbetaben (39.8 and 7.13, respectively) and ^{18}F-florbetapir (40.5 and 12.4, respectively), and the error rate was moderate for ^{18}F-flutemetamol (21.3 and 4.03, respectively). AD patients had higher MAE values for all tracers compared to YC, indicating a divergence in predictive accuracy between these groups. The MAE was significantly higher for AD than YC for all tracers (^{11}C-PiB, U = 570.0 and $p < 0.001$; ^{18}F-NAV4694, U = 319.0 and $p < 0.05$; ^{18}F-florbetaben, U = 217.0 and $p < 0.001$; ^{18}F-flutemetamol, U = 958.0 and $p < 0.001$; ^{18}F-florbetapir, U = 342.0 and $p < 0.05$;). Significant differences between groups were found for the amyloid PET tracers by one-way ANOVA (F = 17.8 and $p < 0.001$). Significant differences between groups were found for the amyloid PET tracers by one-way ANOVA (F = 17.8 and $p < 0.001$). Post hoc tests confirmed a significant difference in the following six groups: ^{11}C-PiB and ^{18}F-florbetaben ($p < 0.001$), ^{11}C-PiB and ^{18}F-florbetapir ($p <$ 0. 001), ^{18}F-NAV4694 and ^{18}F-florbetaben ($p < 0.001$), ^{18}F-NAV4694 and ^{18}F-florbetapir ($p < 0.001$), ^{18}F-florbetaben and ^{18}F-flutemetamol ($p < 0.001$), and ^{18}F-florbetapir and ^{18}F-flutemetamol ($p < 0.001$).

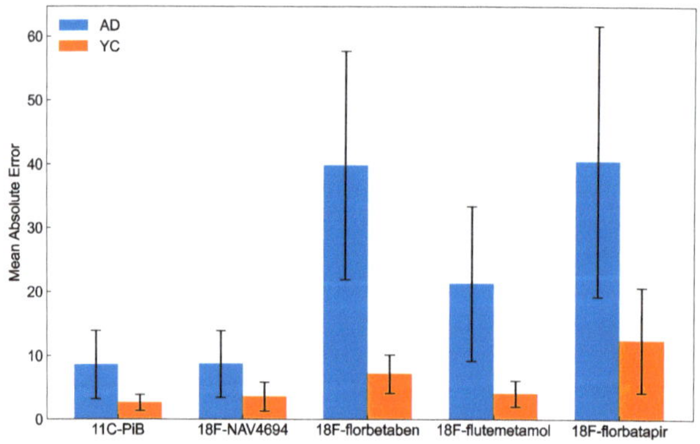

Figure 3. Performance of deep learning ability to predict the Centiloid scale.

Figure 4 shows scatter plots of Pearson correlation analyses. The correlation between deep learning prediction and the ground truth of the Centiloid scale was significant (r = 0.978; $p < 0.001$). Linear regression analysis yielded the following values: slope, 1.00; intercept, 1.26; and coefficient of determination, 0.956. The Centiloid scale calculated by our deep learning model was equivalent to that of the GAAIN Centiloid Project (slope, 0.98–1.02; intercept, −2–2; R^2 correlation coefficient > 0.98). The prediction accuracy of 11C-PiB (r = 0.978), ^{18}F-NAV4694 (r = 0.967), and ^{18}F-flutemetamol (r = 0.957) without retraining was comparable. The correlation between the ground truth and the predicted Centiloid scale was lower for ^{18}F-florbetaben (r = 0.883) and ^{18}F-florbetapir (r = 0.707) than for the other tracers.

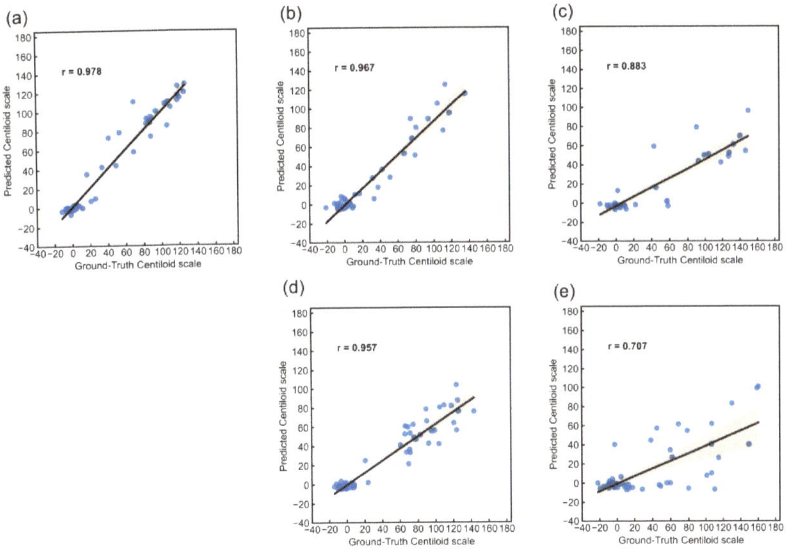

Figure 4. Scatter plot between the ground truth and the predicted Centiloid scale. The results of the linear regression analysis are shown with a black line, and r is the correlation coefficient: (**a**) ^{11}C-PiB, (**b**) ^{18}F-NAV4694, (**c**) ^{18}F-florbetaben, (**d**) ^{18}F-flutemetamol, and (**e**) ^{18}F-florbetapir.

Figure 5 shows Bland–Altman plots in which the mean bias of the Centiloid scale between deep learning prediction and ground truth was −1.31, with 95% acceptable limits of −21.10 and 18.49.

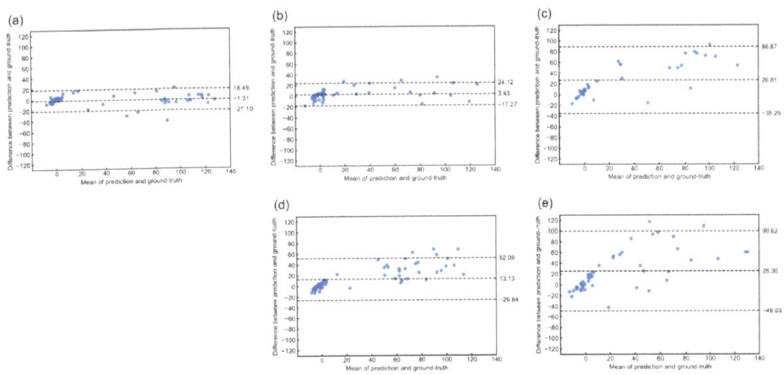

Figure 5. Bland-Altman plot comparing the ground truth and the predicted Centiloid scale. Blue circles represent an individual measurement. The middle-dashed line represents the mean difference, while the upper and lower dashed lines indicate the limits of agreement (mean difference ± 1.96 standard deviations): (**a**) ^{11}C-PiB, (**b**) ^{18}F-NAV4694, (**c**) ^{18}F-florbetaben, (**d**) ^{18}F-flutemetamol, and (**e**) ^{18}F-florbetapir.

4. Discussion

Our team has developed a deep learning system specifically designed to predict the Centiloid scale from amyloid PET images using an advanced 50-layer 3D ResNet architecture. Since the conventional calculation of the Centiloid Scale requires MR images and complex quantitative analysis, our deep learning-based approach offers significant clinical advantages and streamlines the assessment process. To our knowledge, this is the first application of deep learning to derive the Centiloid scale directly from ^{11}C-PiB amyloid PET images in their native space, marking a significant milestone in neuroimaging analysis. In addition, we investigated the feasibility of applying models trained on ^{11}C-PiB data to ^{18}F-labeled amyloid tracers without the need for further training. Our exploration extended to evaluating the model's performance across a spectrum of individuals with normal cognitive function to those diagnosed with Alzheimer's disease, with the goal of demonstrating the versatility and potential of our deep learning system to improve diagnostic processes for neurodegenerative diseases.

The Centiloid scale was directly and accurately computed from ^{11}C-PiB amyloid PET images in a native space using deep learning (Figure 3). The prediction accuracy was significantly higher in the YC than the AD group ($p < 0.05$). The reported cut-off for the Centiloid scale for normal cognition and AD is 10–35 [6,30–33]. The present findings showed that the respective Centiloid ranges for YC and AD were −18.26–28.7 and −22.2–160.7. The AD group included patients with frontotemporal dementia (FTD) and mild cognitive impairment (MCI) who had to recognize various feature patterns from images. Thus, we assumed that such patients would have a higher learning difficulty than cognitively typical people.

The prediction performance of the Centiloid scale using deep learning differed among the amyloid tracers (Figures 4 and 5). This might have been due to the structure or dynamic range of each tracer (Figure 6). The deep learning prediction for ^{18}F-NAV4694 was almost identical to that of ^{11}C-PiB. Time–activity curves and blood clearance of ^{18}F-NAV4694 and ^{11}C-PiB are similar [34] and have the same dynamic range [16,35]. Furthermore, ^{18}F-NAV4694 has higher specific and lower non-specific accumulation than other ^{18}F-labeled amyloid tracers [36–38]. The predictive performance of ^{18}F-flutemetamol was the same as that of PiB for YC, but the error for AD was high. The slightly wider dynamic range of ^{18}F-flutemetamol compared with ^{18}F-florbetaben and ^{18}F-florbetapir [39,40] resulted in better prediction accuracy. High non-specific binding in white matter might affect prediction accuracy. Errors were the highest for ^{18}F-florbetapir and ^{18}F-florbetaben. A quantitative value prediction model trained with ^{18}F-florbetapir can be applied to ^{18}F-florbetaben without retraining [13]. The structures of the thioflavin derivatives ^{11}C-PiB, ^{18F}-NAV4694, and ^{18}F-flutemetamol are similar [41]. On the other hand, ^{18}F-florbetapir and ^{18}F-florbetaben are stilbene derivatives of Congo red [41]. Their distribution in the brain varies due to these structural differences. The model that learned with ^{11}C-PiB had high predictive performance with ^{18}F-NAV4694 and ^{18}F-flutemetamol. In contrast, the model that learned with ^{18}F-florbetapir had high predictive performance with ^{18}F-florbetaben. Therefore, the translucency of the model might differ depending on the chemical structure and the distribution of each drug in the brain even when the amyloid PET tracer is the same. When building deep learning models for multiple tracers, chemical structure and dynamic range have a significant impact on model performance. Therefore, not only the deep learning model but also the knowledge of the tracers become critical in model development and application. When using a model with tracers other than those used in training, it is important to be careful about quantitative accuracy. It has been shown that the higher the structural or imagistic similarity between the tracers, the higher the applicability of the deep learning model. This is not limited to amyloid PET imaging but is also expected to apply to other PET imaging modalities, such as tau PET.

The correlation and linearity between the ground truth Centiloid scale and the deep learning predictions show excellent accuracy (Figure 5). Deep learning methods significantly streamline the calculation of the Centiloid scale by eliminating the need for extensive PET and MRI image analysis and, thus, are not affected by variations in image analysis processes such as co-registration and anatomical standardization. In addition, this deep learning-based Centiloid prediction minimizes quantification variability due to reference region selection and efficiently computes the Centiloid scale from native-space amyloid PET images in just 0.10 s. The absence of preprocessing bias in the Centiloid scale computed by deep learning, due to its reliance on native-space PET images, and the elimination of variation due to slice selection, unlike in 2D models, by using a 3D model, highlight the robustness and precision of this innovative approach. A 3D model has a much larger number of parameters than a 2D model. A 2D ResNet50, with an input size of 224 × 224 × 3 pixels, has approximately 2.56 million parameters, while a 3D ResNet50, with an input size of 224 × 224 × 224 pixels, has approximately 48 million parameters. The number of 3D ResNet50 parameters used in this study is consistent with those of the previous studies [42]. Therefore, we consider the structure of our 3D ResNet to be standard in the field.

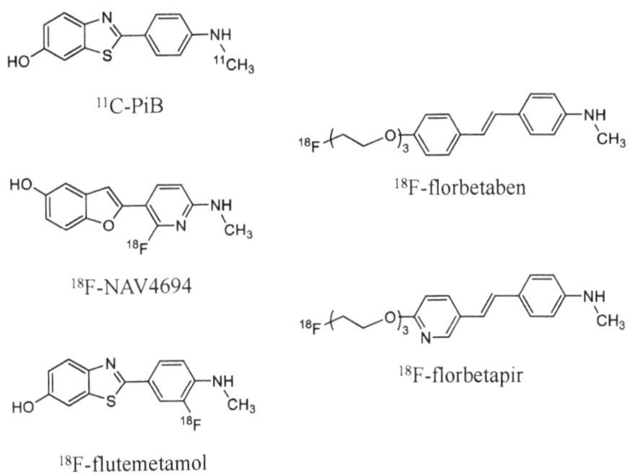

Figure 6. Chemical architecture of amyloid imaging tracers.

This study has several limitations. The dataset was relatively small. More data regarding ^{18}F-labeled amyloid tracers and amyloid PET-positive individuals are needed from larger samples. The predictive performance can potentially be improved, particularly in the 12–30 Centiloid range. A transparent explanation for the decision making process used by deep learning models is essential. The disadvantage of black-box deep learning is that the underlying decision basis must be determined by visualization using means such as heat maps. The model must be specific to each type of amyloid tracer and carefully selected to avoid inaccurate predictions. In this study, there was a duplication of subjects across different amyloid PET tracers. Subjects who underwent PET imaging with ^{18}F-labeled amyloid tracers also underwent imaging with ^{11}C-PiB. The ^{11}C-PiB PET images were used to train the model, while the ^{18}F-labeled images were used to test the model. The possible overestimation of predictive results is due to the duplication of subjects. However, despite the similar distribution patterns of several amyloid tracers, the images are not identical. In fact, differences in predictive performance were observed among the tracers in ^{18}F-labeled amyloid PET, and no overestimation by the model was found. In order to improve predictive performance, ensuring a sufficient amount of data for model training was considered critical. In future research, the use of larger datasets could improve the prediction accuracy of the model. Subjects with different cognitive status and multiple amyloid PET tracers must be included.

5. Conclusions

We developed a deep learning method with 3D CNN to predict the Centiloid scale from amyloid PET images without MRI images. In addition, the applicability of a 3D CNN constructed with ^{11}C-PiB to ^{18}F-NAV4694, ^{18}F-florbetaben, ^{18}F-flutemetamol, and ^{18}F-florbetapyr without retraining was investigated. Our method eliminates manual image analysis and provides consistent, reproducible quantitative results. The advanced redirection of deep learning models for tracers with similar properties was feasible. The current findings may not be limited to amyloid PET but may be applicable to the deep learning approach for any PET imaging.

Author Contributions: Conceptualization, T.Y., K.M., H.I. and H.M.; methodology, T.Y., Y.K. (Yuta Kaneko) and N.T.; image analysis, T.Y.; writing—original draft preparation, T.Y.; writing—review and editing, K.M., N.M., K.H., K.W., Y.K. (Yuto Kamitaka), H.I. and H.M.; supervision, H.I. and H.M. All authors have read and agreed to the published version of the manuscript.

Funding: This work was supported in part by a KAKENHI Grant-in-Aid for Young Scientists (No. 21K18097) from the Ministry of Education, Culture, Sports, Science and Technology (MEXT), the Japanese Government.

Institutional Review Board Statement: Not applicable.

Informed Consent Statement: Not applicable.

Data Availability Statement: The datasets used and/or analyzed during the current study are available from the corresponding author upon reasonable request. The data are not publicly available due to copyright policy of the institutions.

Conflicts of Interest: The authors declare no conflicts of interest.

References

1. Jack, C.R., Jr.; Bennett, D.A.; Blennow, K.; Carrillo, M.C.; Dunn, B.; Haeberlein, S.B.; Holtzman, D.M.; Jagust, W.; Jessen, F.; Karlawish, J.; et al. NIA-AA Research Framework: Toward a biological definition of Alzheimer's disease. *Alzheimer's Dement. J. Alzheimer's Assoc.* **2018**, *14*, 535–562. [CrossRef] [PubMed]
2. Serrano-Pozo, A.; Frosch, M.P.; Masliah, E.; Hyman, B.T. Neuropathological alterations in Alzheimer disease. *Cold Spring Harb. Perspect. Med.* **2011**, *1*, a006189. [CrossRef] [PubMed]
3. Cummings, J.; Apostolova, L.; Rabinovici, G.D.; Atri, A.; Aisen, P.; Greenberg, S.; Hendrix, S.; Selkoe, D.; Weiner, M.; Petersen, R.C.; et al. Lecanemab: Appropriate Use Recommendations. *J. Prev. Alzheimers Dis.* **2023**, *10*, 362–377. [CrossRef] [PubMed]
4. Klunk, W.E.; Koeppe, R.A.; Price, J.C.; Benzinger, T.L.; Devous, M.D., Sr.; Jagust, W.J.; Johnson, K.A.; Mathis, C.A.; Minhas, D.; Pontecorvo, M.J.; et al. The Centiloid Project: Standardizing quantitative amyloid plaque estimation by PET. *Alzheimer's Dement. J. Alzheimer's Assoc.* **2015**, *11*, 1–15.e4. [CrossRef] [PubMed]
5. Matsuda, H.; Yamao, T. Software development for quantitative analysis of brain amyloid PET. *Brain Behav.* **2022**, *12*, e2499. [CrossRef] [PubMed]
6. Matsuda, H.; Yamao, T.; Shakado, M.; Shigemoto, Y.; Okita, K.; Sato, N. Amyloid PET quantification using low-dose CT-guided anatomic standardization. *EJNMMI Res.* **2021**, *11*, 125. [CrossRef]
7. Presotto, L.; Iaccarino, L.; Sala, A.; Vanoli, E.G.; Muscio, C.; Nigri, A.; Bruzzone, M.G.; Tagliavini, F.; Gianolli, L.; Perani, D.; et al. Low-dose CT for the spatial normalization of PET images: A validation procedure for amyloid-PET semi-quantification. *Neuroimage Clin.* **2018**, *20*, 153–160. [CrossRef] [PubMed]
8. Lee, S.Y.; Kang, H.; Jeong, J.H.; Kang, D.Y. Performance evaluation in [18F]Florbetaben brain PET images classification using 3D Convolutional Neural Network. *PLoS ONE* **2021**, *16*, e0258214. [CrossRef] [PubMed]
9. Kim, J.Y.; Oh, D.; Sung, K.; Choi, H.; Paeng, J.C.; Cheon, G.J.; Kang, K.W.; Lee, D.Y.; Lee, D.S. Visual interpretation of [(18)F]Florbetaben PET supported by deep learning-based estimation of amyloid burden. *Eur. J. Nucl. Med. Mol. Imaging* **2021**, *48*, 1116–1123. [CrossRef]
10. Choi, H.; Jin, K.H.; Alzheimer's Disease Neuroimaging Initiative. Predicting cognitive decline with deep learning of brain metabolism and amyloid imaging. *Behav. Brain Res.* **2018**, *344*, 103–109. [CrossRef]
11. Jeong, Y.J.; Park, H.S.; Jeong, J.E.; Yoon, H.J.; Jeon, K.; Cho, K.; Kang, D.Y. Restoration of amyloid PET images obtained with short-time data using a generative adversarial networks framework. *Sci. Rep.* **2021**, *11*, 4825. [CrossRef] [PubMed]
12. Kang, S.K.; Kim, D.; Shin, S.A.; Kim, Y.K.; Choi, H.; Lee, J.S. Fast and Accurate Amyloid Brain PET Quantification Without MRI Using Deep Neural Networks. *J. Nucl. Med. Off. Publ. Soc. Nucl. Med.* **2023**, *64*, 659–666. [CrossRef] [PubMed]
13. Kim, J.Y.; Suh, H.Y.; Ryoo, H.G.; Oh, D.; Choi, H.; Paeng, J.C.; Cheon, G.J.; Kang, K.W.; Lee, D.S.; Alzheimer's Disease Neuroimaging Initiative. Amyloid PET Quantification Via End-to-End Training of a Deep Learning. *Nucl. Med. Mol. Imaging* **2019**, *53*, 340–348. [CrossRef] [PubMed]
14. Reith, F.; Koran, M.E.; Davidzon, G.; Zaharchuk, G.; Alzheimer's Disease Neuroimaging Initiative. Application of Deep Learning to Predict Standardized Uptake Value Ratio and Amyloid Status on (18)F-Florbetapir PET Using ADNI Data. *AJNR Am. J. Neuroradiol.* **2020**, *41*, 980–986. [CrossRef]
15. Choi, H.; Lee, D.S.; Alzheimer's Disease Neuroimaging Initiative. Generation of Structural MR Images from Amyloid PET: Application to MR-Less Quantification. *J. Nucl. Med. Off. Publ. Soc. Nucl. Med.* **2018**, *59*, 1111–1117. [CrossRef]
16. Rowe, C.C.; Jones, G.; Dore, V.; Pejoska, S.; Margison, L.; Mulligan, R.S.; Chan, J.G.; Young, K.; Villemagne, V.L. Standardized Expression of 18F-NAV4694 and 11C-PiB beta-Amyloid PET Results with the Centiloid Scale. *J. Nucl. Med. Off. Publ. Soc. Nucl. Med.* **2016**, *57*, 1233–1237. [CrossRef]

17. Melzer, T.R.; Stark, M.R.; Keenan, R.J.; Myall, D.J.; MacAskill, M.R.; Pitcher, T.L.; Livingston, L.; Grenfell, S.; Horne, K.L.; Young, B.N.; et al. Beta Amyloid Deposition Is Not Associated with Cognitive Impairment in Parkinson's Disease. *Front. Neurol.* **2019**, *10*, 391. [CrossRef]
18. Battle, M.R.; Pillay, L.C.; Lowe, V.J.; Knopman, D.; Kemp, B.; Rowe, C.C.; Dore, V.; Villemagne, V.L.; Buckley, C.J. Centiloid scaling for quantification of brain amyloid with [(18)F]flutemetamol using multiple processing methods. *EJNMMI Res.* **2018**, *8*, 107. [CrossRef]
19. Navitsky, M.; Joshi, A.D.; Kennedy, I.; Klunk, W.E.; Rowe, C.C.; Wong, D.F.; Pontecorvo, M.J.; Mintun, M.A.; Devous, M.D., Sr. Standardization of amyloid quantitation with florbetapir standardized uptake value ratios to the Centiloid scale. *Alzheimer's Dement. J. Alzheimer's Assoc.* **2018**, *14*, 1565–1571. [CrossRef]
20. Aizenstein, H.J.; Nebes, R.D.; Saxton, J.A.; Price, J.C.; Mathis, C.A.; Tsopelas, N.D.; Ziolko, S.K.; James, J.A.; Snitz, B.E.; Houck, P.R.; et al. Frequent amyloid deposition without significant cognitive impairment among the elderly. *Arch. Neurol.* **2008**, *65*, 1509–1517. [CrossRef]
21. Mathis, C.A.; Wang, Y.; Holt, D.P.; Huang, G.F.; Debnath, M.L.; Klunk, W.E. Synthesis and evaluation of 11C-labeled 6-substituted 2-arylbenzothiazoles as amyloid imaging agents. *J. Med. Chem.* **2003**, *46*, 2740–2754. [CrossRef] [PubMed]
22. Mintun, M.A.; Larossa, G.N.; Sheline, Y.I.; Dence, C.S.; Lee, S.Y.; Mach, R.H.; Klunk, W.E.; Mathis, C.A.; DeKosky, S.T.; Morris, J.C. [11C]PIB in a nondemented population: Potential antecedent marker of Alzheimer disease. *Neurology* **2006**, *67*, 446–452. [CrossRef] [PubMed]
23. Oh, H.; Madison, C.; Haight, T.J.; Markley, C.; Jagust, W.J. Effects of age and beta-amyloid on cognitive changes in normal elderly people. *Neurobiol. Aging* **2012**, *33*, 2746–2755. [CrossRef] [PubMed]
24. Oh, H.; Mormino, E.C.; Madison, C.; Hayenga, A.; Smiljic, A.; Jagust, W.J. beta-Amyloid affects frontal and posterior brain networks in normal aging. *Neuroimage* **2011**, *54*, 1887–1895. [CrossRef] [PubMed]
25. Rabinovici, G.D.; Furst, A.J.; O'Neil, J.P.; Racine, C.A.; Mormino, E.C.; Baker, S.L.; Chetty, S.; Patel, P.; Pagliaro, T.A.; Klunk, W.E.; et al. 11C-PIB PET imaging in Alzheimer disease and frontotemporal lobar degeneration. *Neurology* **2007**, *68*, 1205–1212. [CrossRef] [PubMed]
26. Rowe, C.C.; Ng, S.; Ackermann, U.; Gong, S.J.; Pike, K.; Savage, G.; Cowie, T.F.; Dickinson, K.L.; Maruff, P.; Darby, D.; et al. Imaging beta-amyloid burden in aging and dementia. *Neurology* **2007**, *68*, 1718–1725. [CrossRef] [PubMed]
27. Rowe, C.C.; Dore, V.; Jones, G.; Baxendale, D.; Mulligan, R.S.; Bullich, S.; Stephens, A.W.; De Santi, S.; Masters, C.L.; Dinkelborg, L.; et al. 18F-Florbetaben PET beta-amyloid binding expressed in Centiloids. *Eur. J. Nucl. Med. Mol. Imaging* **2017**, *44*, 2053–2059. [CrossRef] [PubMed]
28. Vandenberghe, R.; Van Laere, K.; Ivanoiu, A.; Salmon, E.; Bastin, C.; Triau, E.; Hasselbalch, S.; Law, I.; Andersen, A.; Korner, A.; et al. 18F-flutemetamol amyloid imaging in Alzheimer disease and mild cognitive impairment: A phase 2 trial. *Ann. Neurol.* **2010**, *68*, 319–329. [CrossRef] [PubMed]
29. Lowe, V.J.; Lundt, E.; Knopman, D.; Senjem, M.L.; Gunter, J.L.; Schwarz, C.G.; Kemp, B.J.; Jack, C.R., Jr.; Petersen, R.C. Comparison of [(18)F]Flutemetamol and [(11)C]Pittsburgh Compound-B in cognitively normal young, cognitively normal elderly, and Alzheimer's disease dementia individuals. *Neuroimage Clin.* **2017**, *16*, 295–302. [CrossRef]
30. Amadoru, S.; Dore, V.; McLean, C.A.; Hinton, F.; Shepherd, C.E.; Halliday, G.M.; Leyton, C.E.; Yates, P.A.; Hodges, J.R.; Masters, C.L.; et al. Comparison of amyloid PET measured in Centiloid units with neuropathological findings in Alzheimer's disease. *Alzheimer's Res. Ther.* **2020**, *12*, 22. [CrossRef]
31. Bullich, S.; Roe-Vellve, N.; Marquie, M.; Landau, S.M.; Barthel, H.; Villemagne, V.L.; Sanabria, A.; Tartari, J.P.; Sotolongo-Grau, O.; Dore, V.; et al. Early detection of amyloid load using (18)F-florbetaben PET. *Alzheimer's Res. Ther.* **2021**, *13*, 67. [CrossRef] [PubMed]
32. Jack, C.R., Jr.; Wiste, H.J.; Weigand, S.D.; Therneau, T.M.; Lowe, V.J.; Knopman, D.S.; Gunter, J.L.; Senjem, M.L.; Jones, D.T.; Kantarci, K.; et al. Defining imaging biomarker cut points for brain aging and Alzheimer's disease. *Alzheimer's Dement. J. Alzheimer's Assoc.* **2017**, *13*, 205–216. [CrossRef] [PubMed]
33. La Joie, R.; Ayakta, N.; Seeley, W.W.; Borys, E.; Boxer, A.L.; DeCarli, C.; Dore, V.; Grinberg, L.T.; Huang, E.; Hwang, J.H.; et al. Multisite study of the relationships between antemortem [(11)C]PIB-PET Centiloid values and postmortem measures of Alzheimer's disease neuropathology. *Alzheimer's Dement. J. Alzheimer's Assoc.* **2019**, *15*, 205–216. [CrossRef] [PubMed]
34. Cselenyi, Z.; Jonhagen, M.E.; Forsberg, A.; Halldin, C.; Julin, P.; Schou, M.; Johnstrom, P.; Varnas, K.; Svensson, S.; Farde, L. Clinical validation of 18F-AZD4694, an amyloid-beta-specific PET radioligand. *J. Nucl. Med. Off. Publ. Soc. Nucl. Med.* **2012**, *53*, 415–424. [CrossRef]
35. Rowe, C.C.; Pejoska, S.; Mulligan, R.S.; Jones, G.; Chan, J.G.; Svensson, S.; Cselenyi, Z.; Masters, C.L.; Villemagne, V.L. Head-to-head comparison of 11C-PiB and 18F-AZD4694 (NAV4694) for beta-amyloid imaging in aging and dementia. *J. Nucl. Med. Off. Publ. Soc. Nucl. Med.* **2013**, *54*, 880–886. [CrossRef]
36. Mountz, J.M.; Laymon, C.M.; Cohen, A.D.; Zhang, Z.; Price, J.C.; Boudhar, S.; McDade, E.; Aizenstein, H.J.; Klunk, W.E.; Mathis, C.A. Comparison of qualitative and quantitative imaging characteristics of [11C]PiB and [18F]flutemetamol in normal control and Alzheimer's subjects. *Neuroimage Clin.* **2015**, *9*, 592–598. [CrossRef] [PubMed]
37. Villemagne, V.L.; Mulligan, R.S.; Pejoska, S.; Ong, K.; Jones, G.; O'Keefe, G.; Chan, J.G.; Young, K.; Tochon-Danguy, H.; Masters, C.L.; et al. Comparison of 11C-PiB and 18F-florbetaben for Abeta imaging in ageing and Alzheimer's disease. *Eur. J. Nucl. Med. Mol. Imaging* **2012**, *39*, 983–989. [CrossRef] [PubMed]

38. Wolk, D.A.; Zhang, Z.; Boudhar, S.; Clark, C.M.; Pontecorvo, M.J.; Arnold, S.E. Amyloid imaging in Alzheimer's disease: Comparison of florbetapir and Pittsburgh compound-B positron emission tomography. *J. Neurol. Neurosurg. Psychiatry* **2012**, *83*, 923–926. [CrossRef]
39. Jeong, Y.J.; Yoon, H.J.; Kang, D.Y.; Park, K.W. Quantitative comparative analysis of amyloid PET images using three radiopharmaceuticals. *Ann. Nucl. Med.* **2023**, *37*, 271–279. [CrossRef]
40. Landau, S.M.; Thomas, B.A.; Thurfjell, L.; Schmidt, M.; Margolin, R.; Mintun, M.; Pontecorvo, M.; Baker, S.L.; Jagust, W.J.; Alzheimer's Disease Neuroimaging Initiative. Amyloid PET imaging in Alzheimer's disease: A comparison of three radiotracers. *Eur. J. Nucl. Med. Mol. Imaging* **2014**, *41*, 1398–1407. [CrossRef]
41. Juréus, A.; Swahn, B.M.; Sandell, J.; Jeppsson, F.; Johnson, A.E.; Johnström, P.; Neelissen, J.A.; Sunnemark, D.; Farde, L.; Svensson, S.P. Characterization of AZD4694, a novel fluorinated Abeta plaque neuroimaging PET radioligand. *J. Neurochem.* **2010**, *114*, 784–794. [CrossRef] [PubMed]
42. Ebrahimi, A.; Luo, S.; Alzheimer's Disease Neuroimaging Initiative. Convolutional neural networks for Alzheimer's disease detection on MRI images. *J. Med. Imaging* **2021**, *8*, 024503. [CrossRef] [PubMed]

Disclaimer/Publisher's Note: The statements, opinions and data contained in all publications are solely those of the individual author(s) and contributor(s) and not of MDPI and/or the editor(s). MDPI and/or the editor(s) disclaim responsibility for any injury to people or property resulting from any ideas, methods, instructions or products referred to in the content.

brain sciences

MDPI

Article

Can Brain Volume-Driven Characteristic Features Predict the Response of Alzheimer's Patients to Repetitive Transcranial Magnetic Stimulation? A Pilot Study

Chandan Saha [1,*], Chase R. Figley [2], Brian Lithgow [1,3], Paul B. Fitzgerald [3], Lisa Koski [4], Behzad Mansouri [5], Neda Anssari [5], Xikui Wang [6] and Zahra Moussavi [1]

1 Biomedical Engineering Program, University of Manitoba, Winnipeg, MB R3T 5V6, Canada
2 Department of Radiology, University of Manitoba, Winnipeg, MB R3T 2N2, Canada
3 Department of Psychiatry (MAPRC), Monash University, Melbourne VIC 3004, Australia
4 Department of Psychology, Faculty of Science, McGill University, Montreal, QC H3A 1G1, Canada
5 Brain, Vision and Concussion Clinic-iScope, Winnipeg, MB R2M 2X9, Canada
6 Warren Center for Actuarial Studies and Research, University of Manitoba, Winnipeg, MB R3T 5V4, Canada
* Correspondence: sahac@myumanitoba.ca

Abstract: This study is a post-hoc examination of baseline MRI data from a clinical trial investigating the efficacy of repetitive transcranial magnetic stimulation (rTMS) as a treatment for patients with mild–moderate Alzheimer's disease (AD). Herein, we investigated whether the analysis of baseline MRI data could predict the response of patients to rTMS treatment. Whole-brain T1-weighted MRI scans of 75 participants collected at baseline were analyzed. The analyses were run on the gray matter (GM) and white matter (WM) of the left and right dorsolateral prefrontal cortex (DLPFC), as that was the rTMS application site. The primary outcome measure was the Alzheimer's disease assessment scale—cognitive subscale (ADAS-Cog). The response to treatment was determined based on ADAS-Cog scores and secondary outcome measures. The analysis of covariance showed that responders to active treatment had a significantly lower baseline GM volume in the right DLPFC and a higher GM asymmetry index in the DLPFC region compared to those in non-responders. Logistic regression with a repeated five-fold cross-validated analysis using the MRI-driven features of the initial 75 participants provided a mean accuracy of 0.69 and an area under the receiver operating characteristic curve of 0.74 for separating responders and non-responders. The results suggest that GM volume or asymmetry in the target area of active rTMS treatment (DLPFC region in this study) may be a weak predictor of rTMS treatment efficacy. These results need more data to draw more robust conclusions.

Keywords: Alzheimer's disease (AD); rTMS treatment; DLPFC; MRI analysis; efficacy prediction

1. Introduction

Repetitive transcranial magnetic stimulation (rTMS) has been investigated as a treatment for Alzheimer's disease (AD) in the last decade. Several rTMS studies have reported its effectiveness for AD treatment [1–4]. However, the treatment protocols of rTMS for AD are demanding for the families and patients as they usually involve 2–6 weeks of daily treatment [5,6], and some also continue maintenance treatment for up to 6 months [4,7]. However, not everyone responds positively to rTMS treatment. Furthermore, in our recent large clinical trial [8], we observed that a number of patients declined after rTMS treatment. Therefore, there is uncertainty regarding the efficacy of rTMS. Given that rTMS is an expensive and resource-intensive technology with a demanding treatment protocol for patients, the ability to predict a patient's response before the commencement of rTMS would be very beneficial and could lead to the development of a more individualized therapeutic strategy.

In this study, we analyzed magnetic resonance imaging (MRI) images of participants with AD obtained at baseline in a recent clinical trial [8] to investigate whether brain volume estimates have the potential to predict the patient's response to rTMS treatment. MRI is commonly used to examine gray matter (GM) and white matter (WM) volume anomalies in AD brains [9,10]. In addition, its potential to predict tissue loss in distinct brain regions has been reported in dementia studies [11,12]. Another application of MRI in rTMS clinical trials, including in [13], is for the neuronavigation of the magnetic coil during treatment, in which MRI scans of AD participants are utilized to localize a target area of the brain, in the case of our study, to target stimulation to the dorsolateral prefrontal cortex (DLPFC) bilaterally. The DLPFC is the most common brain region for the treatment of AD using rTMS [14] due to its broad and complex connections with cortical and deeper subcortical brain structures [15] and its executive role in planning and decision -making, most notably in working memory [16,17]. However, to date, no study has investigated the potential of baseline MRI analysis to predict rTMS treatment efficacy in the AD population.

The left and right DLPFC were the target sites of rTMS intervention for AD participants in our clinical trial [8]; thus, in this study, we investigated whether the volume of the DLPFC region estimated from the baseline MRI scans differed between responders and non-responders to rTMS treatment. We investigated this hypothesis in AD participants undergoing rTMS treatment separately by measuring (1) the GM or WM volume of each side of the DLPFC and (2) the magnitude of the asymmetry index of the DLPFC from its GM or WM volume. In addition, we explored baseline structural differences between responders and non-responders in other brain regions using whole-brain analysis. Furthermore, we examined whether the abovementioned DLPFC measures correlated with baseline cognitive scores.

2. Materials and Methods

2.1. Participants

Initially, 128 participants with AD from our rTMS clinical trial [8] who had MRI data at baseline and completed either active (n = 86) or sham (n = 42) rTMS treatment with follow-up post-treatment assessments were included. Subsequently, 18 subjects were excluded owing to inadequate image quality and different MRI scanning parameters; the remaining 110 participants' MRIs (75 in the active group and 35 in the sham group) were included. All participants with AD and their primary caregivers provided written consent prior to enrollment in the study, which was approved by the local ethics committee at each site of the rTMS treatment study (Winnipeg, Montreal, and Melbourne) [17]. The diagnosis of AD was made by a neurologist or neuropsychiatrist based on the participants' clinical history and neuroimaging results from MRI and/or fluorodeoxyglucose positron emission tomography (PET) scans. Using the Super Rapid-2 Magstim system (manufactured by the Magstim Company Limited, Spring Gardens, Whitland, UK), the protocol of rTMS application was to deliver 25 1.5 s trains of pulses at 20 Hz with an intertrain interval of 10 s applied to the DLPFC bilaterally (750 pulses to each side, serially) for either 2 or 4 consecutive weeks (5 days/week) [8]. The pulses were neuronavigated using the MRI scan of each participant and were applied at 100% of the resting motor threshold of each participant. The protocol of sham and active stimulations was exactly the same.

The primary outcome measure of the clinical trial [8] was the Alzheimer's disease assessment scale—cognitive subscale (ADAS-Cog), and the secondary outcome measures were the Neuropsychiatric Inventory–Questionnaire (NPI-Q) and Alzheimer's Disease Cooperative Study—Activities of Daily Living Inventory (ADCS-ADL) to evaluate rTMS treatment efficacy. Each participant's response to rTMS was measured by comparing the baseline ADAS-Cog, NPI-Q, and ADCS-ADL scores with those at either week 5 or post-treatment after week-8 assessments, as detailed in [13]. In brief, a marked response is defined as an ADAS-Cog improvement with a score of 3+. A moderate response is referred to as an improvement (<3 scores) in ADAS-Cog **AND** the same score **OR** improvement in ADCS-ADL **OR** NPI-Q scores. The response is considered small if the **AND** part does not hold in the previous moderate response criterion. A small/stabilized response is also defined as a non-substantial decline in ADAS-Cog (<3 score decline) **AND** an improvement in both ADCS-ADL and NPI-Q scores by 1. If the **AND** part does not meet the previous small/stabilized response criterion, it is considered non-responsive. Notably, in all response criteria mentioned above, the **AND** represents a Boolean logical AND operator (it is only "true" if both statements are true and otherwise "false"), and **OR** is a Boolean logical OR operator (it is "true" if either one of the statements or both statements is true and otherwise "false").

In this study, we focused on predicting the response in the active rTMS group (n = 75), in which 42, 13, 10, and 10 participants had marked, moderate, small, and no responses, respectively. To perform a response group-wise comparison with a sufficiently large sample size, we combined them into binary response groups under active treatment: responders (participants with marked and moderate responses, n = 42 + 13 = 55) and non-responders (participants with small/stabilized and non-responses, n = 10 + 10 = 20).

2.2. MRI Data Acquisition

T1-weighted structural MRI scans were acquired using a 3D magnetization-prepared rapid acquisition gradient-echo (MPRAGE) imaging sequence. Our rTMS efficacy study on AD [17] was run at three different sites: Winnipeg (3T Siemens Verio/Verio Dot MRI system), Montreal (3T Siemens Prisma/Prisma-fit MRI system), and Melbourne (3T Siemens Skyra/Skyra-fit MRI system). The imaging sequence parameters from all sites were as follows: slice thickness = 0.9–1.2 mm, echo time = 2.22–2.98 ms, repetition time = 1800–2300 ms, inversion time = 900/1100 ms, and flip angle = 8–10 degree.

2.3. MRI Data Analysis

Structural MRI data were analyzed by Voxel-Based Morphometry (VBM) using the Computational Anatomy Toolbox (CAT12, v12.7, The Structural Brain Mapping Group, University of Jena, Germany, http://www.neuro.uni-jena.de/cat/, accessed on 3 May 2021) [18] and Statistical Parametric Mapping software (SPM12, v7771,The Wellcome Centre for Human Neuroimaging, University College, London, UK, https://www.fil.ion.ucl.ac.uk/spm/, accessed on 3 May 2021). A standard "unified segmentation" approach of SPM [19] segmented the denoised [20], bias field-corrected, and affine-registered T1-weighted MRI data into tissue maps of GM, WM, and cerebrospinal fluid (CSF). This segmentation was then passed through the refining process to attain the final stage of the adaptive maximum a posteriori segmentation [21]. Subsequently, the T1-weighted image and GM, WM, and CSF masks were non-linearly normalized to the Montreal Neurological Institute (MNI) template using geodesic shooting [22]. Simultaneously, CAT12 performed several automated quality assurance checks and estimated the total intracranial volume (TIV). Finally, the segmented images were modulated to control for the amount of deformation due to differences in brain size [23] and were used in the following region-of-interest (ROI) analysis and whole-brain voxel-wise comparisons.

Since the participants received rTMS treatments targeting both the left and right DLPFC, we created bilateral ROI masks using two 8 mm radius spheres centered at MNI coordinates x = 30, y = 43, and z = 23 (right DLPFC), and x = −30, y = 43, and z = 23 (left DLPFC) in the MarsBar [24] toolbox (v0.45, http://marsbar.sourceforge.net/, accessed on 28 March 2022). These MNI coordinates of the DLPFC, reported in previous studies [25,26], are slightly deeper than the Talairach coordinates (x = ±50, y = 30, and z = 36), in which the coil position and direction are specified using the BrainSight 2 software (Rogue Research, Montreal, QC, Canada) in the clinical trial of rTMS [17]. Instead of using these Talairach coordinates, because of their proximity to the skull, we used the MNI coordinates of the DLPFC [25,26] mentioned above to develop the two ROI masks. These masks were resliced, and the volumes from the modulated and warped GM and WM images were then calculated using the get_totals.m script by G. Ridgeway (http://www0.cs.ucl.ac.uk/staff/g.ridgway/vbm/get_totals.m, accessed on 1 April 2022). The overlays of these masks on a participant's modulated and warped GM and WM images are shown in Figure 1 using the MRIcron [27] software (v1.0.20190902, University of South Carolina, Columbia, SC, USA, https://people.cas.sc.edu/rorden/mricron/, accessed on 15 August 2023).

a. b.

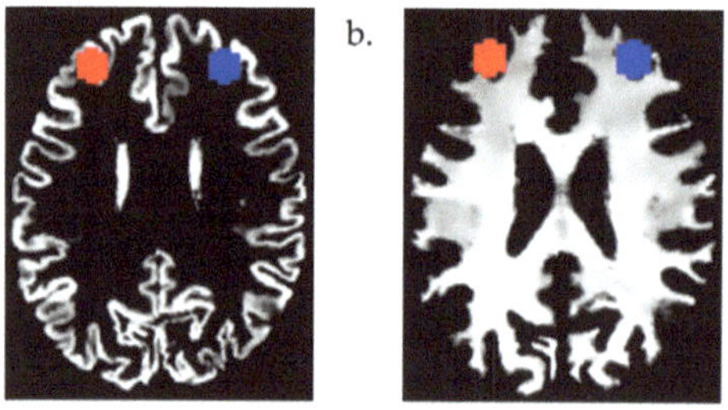

Figure 1. The left (red) and right (blue) dorsolateral prefrontal cortex (DLPFC) masks are shown on the modulated and warped (**a**) gray matter and (**b**) white matter images (axial view) of a participant.

Left and right asymmetries are cardinal features of the brain [28]. In this study, we investigated whether there was a difference in volumetric asymmetry between responder and non-responder groups. GM asymmetry using the VBM technique with T1-weighted MRI data has been widely studied [29]; however, WM asymmetry incorporating this method is less consistent [30]. Nevertheless, prior studies [9,10,31] have performed VBM on T1-weighed MRI data, and Good et al. [32] also used it for WM asymmetry analysis. This study analyzed left GM or WM volumetric asymmetry between bilateral DLPFC regions for each population, where the asymmetry index was calculated separately for GM and WM volumes, using the following formula [33,34]:

$$Asymmetry\ index = \frac{|(left - right)|}{left + right} * 100 \quad (1)$$

Note that the raw volume estimates of the GM or WM were used to calculate the asymmetry index, and lower values indicate more symmetry (i.e., less asymmetry) between the bilateral DLPFC ROIs.

The extracted volumes and asymmetry indices of the responders and non-responders were statistically analyzed (described below). More exploratory post-hoc whole-brain comparisons were then conducted using group-wise (2nd level) statistical analysis in SPM12 to investigate whether any other brain regions (in addition to the bilateral DLPFC) might be useful for rTMS response prediction. To achieve this, the modulated and spatially normalized images (GM and WM) were smoothed using an 8 mm isotropic full width at half-maximum Gaussian kernel to account for potential differences in segmentation and non-linear normalization accuracy between participants. The 2nd level statistical analysis was then set up in SPM12 using a two-sample t-test with two contrasts (responders > non-responders and responders < non-responders) and participants' age, sex, TIV, MRI site, and Cornell Scale for Depression in Dementia (CSDD) scores as covariates. GM and WM analyses were run separately, and family-wise error (FWE) in multiple comparisons was corrected to $p < 0.05$. The extent of the threshold, k > 50 voxels, was set to consider a cluster significant.

2.4. Statistical Analysis

A two-proportion test was used to examine statistical differences in baseline categorical data between the two response groups under active treatment. The independent samples t-test or Wilcoxon rank-sum test was also used depending on whether specific continuous data were normally distributed (checked by the Shapiro–Wilk test).

Analysis of covariance (ANCOVA) was employed to find differences in ROI data between responders and non-responders under active treatment. ANCOVA is a blended version of the analysis of variance and regression [35] that allows for the control of the influences of covariates, including age, sex, TIV, MRI site, and CSDD scores. GM or WM volume in each ROI was used as a dependent variable.

To further investigate the possible lateralization of the DLPFC region in responders and non-responders under active treatment, we performed a paired t-test to compare the normalized (divided by TIV) left and right volumes of GM and WM. Moreover, we used ANCOVA to compare the magnitude of the GM or WM asymmetry index in the DLPFC region between responders and non-responders. The asymmetry index of the GM or WM as a dependent variable and age, sex, TIV, MRI site, and CSDD scores as covariates were used to build the ANCOVA model. Statistical analysis was performed using the R platform after installing the required packages in RStudio (ver. 1.4.1106) [36,37]. To control for multiple comparisons across the two ROIs (left and right DLPFC), we employed Bonferroni correction to control for family-wise error ($p < 0.05/2 = 0.025$, significance threshold).

We employed logistic regression as a predictive classification model and evaluated its performance using a five-fold cross-validation with five repetitions. Additionally, we employed the synthetic minority oversampling technique (SMOTE) [38], as our two response groups' sizes were imbalanced, and the predictive model might be biased toward the over-represented group, that is, responders. In SMOTE, new and non-replicated instances are generated in the minority group, whereas the conventional oversampling scheme has an overfitting issue [39].

Of the 35 participants in the sham group, 12 individuals (responders = 8 and non-responders = 4) received active treatment after the study period (6 months) in an open-label study. Their data were added to the active treatment group, and the analyses were repeated.

3. Results

3.1. Baseline Characteristics of Participants

Table 1 presents the demographic data of the study participants and baseline CSDD, Montreal Cognitive Assessment (MoCA), Clinical Dementia Rating (CDR), and ADAS-Cog scores of the active treatment group. Responders and non-responders did not show significant differences in sex, age, or handedness. These participants had no major depressive disorder, and there was no substantial difference in CSDD scores between the response groups. In cognitive scores, similarity was demonstrated in MoCA and CDR scores between responders and non-responders, while the responders had significantly higher ADAS-Cog scores (implying more cognitive impairment) than the non-responders.

Table 1. Demographic and pretreatment baseline clinical data of responders and non-responders under active treatment.

	Responders	Non-Responders	Two-Tailed p
n	55	20	-
Sex (male, female)	32, 23	12, 8	0.902 †
Age	72.5 ± 7.9	76.2 ± 5.7	0.055 ††
Handedness (left, right) *	2, 52	1, 19	0.680 †
CSDD	4.3 ± 3.7	4.6 ± 2.6	0.362 ‡
MoCA	15.3 ± 5.2	16.2 ± 4.5	0.541 ††
CDR	1.1 ± 0.3	1.2 ± 0.4	0.535 ‡
ADAS-Cog	25.2 ± 9.3	20.8 ± 7.0	0.031 ‡

Vales are reported as mean ± SD. Cornell Scale for Depression in Dementia (CSDD), Montreal Cognitive Assessment (MoCA), Clinical Dementia Rating (CDR), and Alzheimer's disease assessment scale—cognitive subscale (ADAS-Cog). * One responder had unknown handedness. † Two-proportion test. †† Independent samples t-test. ‡ Wilcoxon rank-sum test.

3.2. Region of Interest (ROI) Analyses

3.2.1. GM and WM Volume

After adjusting for covariates, the analysis of covariance showed that the responders in the active treatment group had significantly lower GM volume in the right DLPFC region

($p = 0.004$) than non-responders (Table 2). No significant differences were observed between responders and non-responders in the GM of the left DLPFC or in the WM of either the left or right DLPFC.

Table 2. Gray matter (GM) and white matter (WM) volumes (cm^3) in regions of interest for responders vs. non-responders of the active treatment group.

ROIs	Responders Mean ± SE	Non-Responders Mean ± SE	F * (1, 67)	*p* *
		GM		
Left DLPFC	0.73 ± 0.02	0.72 ± 0.03	0.15	0.698
Right DLPFC	0.64 ± 0.02	0.72 ± 0.02	8.82	**0.004**
		WM		
Left DLPFC	0.51 ± 0.02	0.51 ± 0.03	0.03	0.859
Right DLPFC	0.59 ± 0.02	0.57 ± 0.03	0.14	0.713

* ANCOVA statistics with covariates of age, sex, TIV, MRI site, and CSDD scores. The significance level was $p < 0.05/2 = 0.025$, following the Bonferroni correction for the comparison of two ROIs. DLPFC = dorsolateral prefrontal cortex; SE = standard error. The bold font of *p* values denotes a significant difference between responders and non-responders.

3.2.2. Lateralization and Asymmetry Index

Responders under active treatment had significant leftward lateralization (left > right) in the GM volume and rightward lateralization (left < right) in the WM volume of the DLPFC region, as shown in Figure 2 (paired *t*-test). In contrast, non-responders only had significant rightward lateralization (left < right) in the WM volume of the DLPFC. No significant lateralization was observed in the GM volumes of non-responders in the active treatment group.

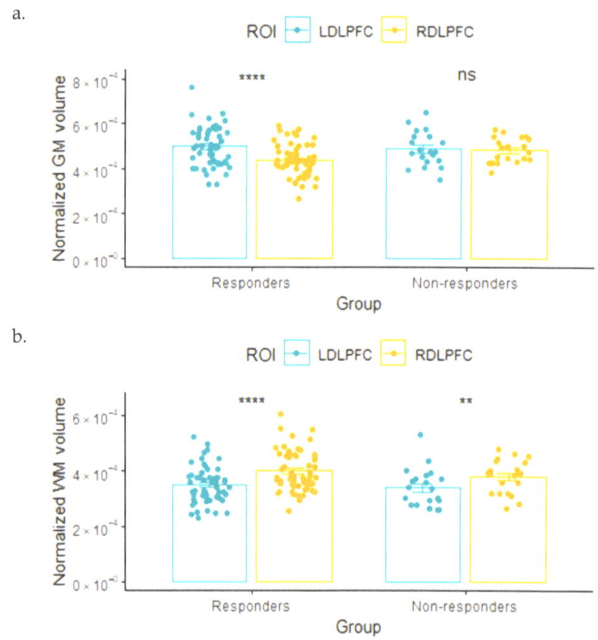

Figure 2. Comparison of normalized (**a**) gray matter (GM) or (**b**) white matter (WM) volumes (mean ± SE) between left DLPFC and right DLPFC for responders and non-responders under active treatment. Normalized volume is calculated by dividing each region's raw volume of GM or WM by the total intracranial volume (TIV). Results of the two-tailed paired *t*-test are shown (**** $p \leq 0.0001$, ** $p \leq 0.01$, and ns: $p > 0.05$).

In the comparative analysis of the volumetric asymmetry index using ANCOVA, the responders showed a significantly higher GM volumetric asymmetry index ($p = 0.009$) in the DLPFC region compared to non-responders (Table 3). However, the asymmetry index in WM was not significantly different between the groups.

Table 3. Asymmetry index of the GM and WM in the DLPFC region for two response groups under active treatment.

Volumes	Responders Mean ± SE	Non-Responders Mean ± SE	F * (1, 67)	*p* *
GM	9.52 ± 0.86	5.06 ± 0.79	7.17	**0.009**
WM	9.24 ± 1.09	7.58 ± 1.39	0.99	0.324

* ANCOVA statistics with covariates of age, sex, TIV, MRI site, and CSDD scores. The bold font of *p* values denotes a significant difference between responders and non-responders.

3.3. Predictive Classification Results

We assessed the performance of logistic regression for classifying responders and non-responders (75 participants) utilizing each significant GM feature of the ROI (GM volume of the right DLPFC and GM asymmetry index of the DLPFC) alone and their combinations (Table 4). As expected, when both GM features of the ROI were used in the logistic regression model, it provided the highest accuracy (0.69), with an area under the curve (AUC) of 0.74 for separating responders and non-responders receiving active treatment.

Table 4. The logistic regression results for classifying responders and non-responders using significant MRI-driven features. Mean values of area under curve (AUC), sensitivity, specificity, and accuracy are presented.

Features	AUC	Sensitivity	Specificity	Accuracy
GM volume	0.71	0.67	0.62	0.65
Asymmetry index	0.70	0.63	0.72	0.66
GM volume and asymmetry index	0.74	0.65	0.77	0.69

3.4. Whole-Brain Analysis Results

The exploratory whole-brain analysis of GM and WM volumes did not reveal any other areas with statistically significant differences between responders and non-responders in the active treatment group after accounting for age, sex, TIV, MRI site, and CSDD as covariates and applying FWE correction for multiple comparisons. Even the right DLPFC region, which demonstrated a significant outcome in the ROI analysis of participants under active treatment, did not survive FWE correction in the whole-brain analysis.

3.5. Correlations between ROI Volumes and Baseline ADAS-Cog Scores

Spearman's correlation analysis for non-normally distributed data was computed between raw data points of GM volume in the ROIs of responders and non-responders and their baseline ADAS-Cog scores. As shown in Figure 3, a significant correlation was observed between baseline ADAS-Cog scores and GM volume in the left DLPFC (rho = −0.26, $p = 0.026$) and right DLPFC (rho = −0.29, $p = 0.013$). After controlling for age, sex, and TIV in the partial correlation analysis, GM volume in the right DLPFC of responders and non-responders showed a significant correlation (rho = −0.23, $p = 0.048$) with baseline ADAS-Cog scores.

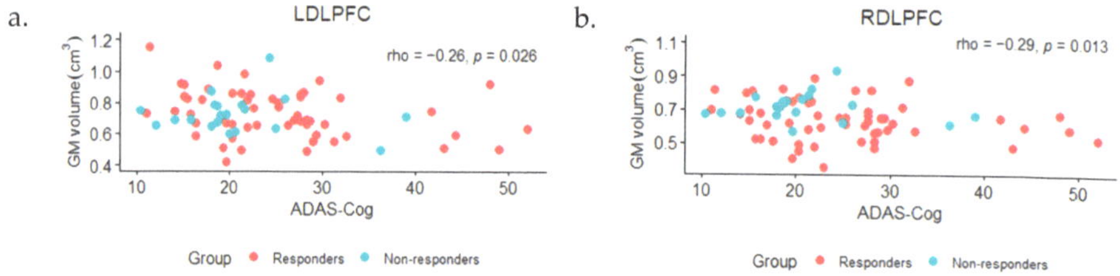

Figure 3. Scatter plots of baseline ADAS-Cog scores of responders and non-responders under active treatment and their raw GM volumes (cm^3) of (**a**) left and (**b**) right dorsolateral prefrontal cortex (DLPFC).

3.6. Results after Adding the 12 Participants Who Received Active Treatment after the Sham 6–7 Months after the Baseline

After adding the baseline data of the 12 participants who received active treatment after sham treatment (~7 months after the baseline) to the initial active treatment group (now, n = 87), the ANCOVA showed significant differences [F (1, 79) = 5.55, p = 0.021] between responders and non-responders in the GM asymmetry index of the DLPFC.

4. Discussion

In this study, we investigated whether baseline structural brain MRI data could predict the efficacy of rTMS treatment for cognitive impairment in patients with mild-to-moderate AD. We herein estimated the GM or WM volumes and asymmetry index in the DLPFC region of the brain and compared those measures between responders and non-responders to rTMS treatment.

The main findings of this study were a significantly lower GM volume in the right DLPFC and higher GM asymmetry of the DLPFC among responders compared to non-responders under active treatment. The responders and non-responders under active treatment did not differ significantly in either CDR or MoCA scores; however, the ADAS-Cog score was significantly higher, representing worse cognitive performance in responders than in non-responders. An important point is that a "ceiling effect" could explain the results of this study. The responders had higher ADAS-Cog scores at baseline and more GM asymmetry in the DLPFC area. Therefore, it was easier to observe a benefit in them after rTMS. It was harder to see a benefit in the non-responders because of the "ceiling effect" (they had baseline ADAS-Cog scores closer to normal).

In general, GM atrophies in the DLPFC areas [40] and GM asymmetry [29] have been reported to be associated with AD. In this study, we focused on the rTMS treatment target area, that is, the DLPFC, and it is possible that in comparison to non-responders, the responders to active treatment at baseline might have been more affected in the pathogenesis of amyloid-beta, tau tangles, and neurodegeneration, particularly in the areas of the DLFPC. We also speculate that the response to treatment is affected by the presence of GM asymmetry in the DLPFC, caused by the neuropathology of AD. Iaccarino et al. [41] reported that amyloid beta accumulates in the association cortex (surrounding sensory and motor regions) in the early stage of dementia, and the distribution of tau tangles may extend up to the lateral occipital and areas of the DLPFC. Amyloid-beta plaques indirectly affect GM volume, while tau tangles are regionally and tightly associated with GM volume reduction, leading to neurodegeneration [41]. GM atrophic patterns in the AD population may alter rTMS response because cortical current density is contingent on the type and extent of atrophy [42]. A correlation was found in a previous study [43] between GM atrophy in subjects with mild cognitive impairment (MCI) or AD and their changes in scores on the word part of the Stroop test after high-frequency (HF) rTMS of the superior temporal gyrus. After applying rTMS (five days/week) for four weeks, a previous study [44] did not find a substantial longitudinal difference in GM across six months between the active and sham intervention groups of patients with MCI.

The difference in WM volume or DLPFC asymmetry was insignificant in responders and non-responders in the active rTMS group at baseline, suggesting that WM volumetric patterns in the DLPFC are not predictors of treatment efficacy. However, both response groups showed rightward lateralization (left < right) in the WM of the DLFPC. Given that greater lateralization is related to declined cognitive abilities [33,45], this extreme lateralization in the WM of the DLPFC was expected at baseline in the two response groups. It is worth mentioning that we investigated these WM volumetric patterns using T1-weighted MRI data; however, T1 signal intensities are not sufficiently associated with WM integrity. Instead, fractional anisotropy with diffusion tensor imaging has been applied in the asymmetric pattern analysis of WM [30,46], and previous studies have also reported the impact of rTMS on alternations in WM fractional anisotropy in individuals with post-stroke aphasia and depression [47,48].

In the classification analysis of responders and non-responders to active treatment, our logistic regression model yielded an accuracy of 0.69 with an AUC of 0.74 using the GM volume in the right DLPFC and the asymmetry index of the DLPFC. These two GM features of the ROI could be used as predictive markers for rTMS efficacy, although the AUC was not in the range from 0.8 to 1, perhaps because of the small sample size.

The analysis within multiple regions throughout the brain did not yield significant differences in GM or WM between the responder and non-responder groups under active treatment. No region, including the DLPFC, reached the threshold for FWE correction ($p < 0.05$, with $k > 50$). A setting cut-off point of $p < 0.05$ for FWE correction seems strict in this study when our two groups of subjects had similar types of AD pathophysiology and might have subtle changes to be detected. Although FWE correction at threshold $p < 0.05$, a reference point, is highly recommended in neuroimaging research [49], several studies have also reported its stringent behavior in subtle lesion detection and instead suggested a liberal uncorrected threshold of p [50,51]. Supplementary Table S1 provides the whole-brain analysis results using an uncorrected p of 0.001.

In the correlation analysis, we noticed a significant negative correlation between the raw GM volumes of the left and right DLPFC and ADAS-Cog scores at the baseline of active treatment. This suggests that in general, the lower GM of the DLPFC increased the disease severity of our participants in the active treatment group. Such a significant correlation also exists in the right DLPFC when controlling for age, sex, and TIV. As noted in previous studies [9,52], a similar relationship between cognitive decline and GM volume also exists in other brain regions in people with AD/MCI.

When the data of the 12 participants in the sham group who received active treatment after the study period (6 months) were analyzed, the responders and non-responders (now 87 subjects) still showed a significant difference in the GM asymmetry index of the DLPFC. However, we ran the logistic regression only on the initial dataset (75 who were in the active rTMS group) for two main reasons: (1) the additional 12 subjects received active treatment in an open-label study, and (2) these 12 participants received active treatment 6–7 months after the baseline MRI.

This study has some limitations that should be considered when interpreting the results. First, the sample size was small, and the response group sizes were imbalanced. Second, this study obtained MRI scans from the participants at three sites scanned on different models of MRI scanners; although from the same manufacturer, a few scanning parameters differed from site to site. Third, the depression level of participants was not measured after treatment, and without having post-treatment measurements, we could not thoroughly investigate the effect of depression on MRI-driven features. Fourth, other factors, such as the distribution of CSF in the brain [53] and the degree and location of microvascular ischemic pathology, may act as confounding variables in treatment responses. Lastly, the lack of amyloid PET or fluid biomarkers to verify the amyloid status of these participants was a limitation of this study; it is also essential for future rTMS studies to include either imaging or fluid AD biomarkers to be sure of the participants' biological diagnosis.

5. Conclusions

To the best of our knowledge, this study is the first to use volumetric measures of MRI data to predict rTMS treatment response for AD at baseline. GM volume in the right DLPFC or the asymmetry index in the GM of the DLPFC have shown potential, albeit weak, as predictive markers of the efficacy of active rTMS treatment. GM volumes in the DLPFC region were significantly associated with baseline ADAS-Cog scores of participants under active treatment.

Supplementary Materials: The following supporting information can be downloaded at https://www.mdpi.com/article/10.3390/brainsci14030226/s1, Table S1: Whole-brain voxel-based morphometry (VBM) results using an uncorrected p of 0.001 to find the differences between responders and non-responders in gray matter (GM) and white matter (WM).

Author Contributions: Conceptualization, C.S., B.L. and Z.M.; methodology, C.S. and C.R.F.; software, C.S. and C.R.F.; formal analysis, C.S.; investigation, C.S.; resources, Z.M., P.B.F. and L.K.; data curation, Z.M., P.B.F. and L.K.; writing—original draft preparation, C.S.; writing—review and editing, C.S., C.R.F., B.L., P.B.F., L.K., B.M., N.A., X.W. and Z.M.; visualization, C.S.; supervision, C.R.F., B.L. and Z.M.; project administration, C.S.; funding acquisition, P.B.F., L.K., B.M., X.W. and Z.M. All authors have read and agreed to the published version of the manuscript.

Funding: This research was funded by the Weston Brain Institute (CT140075). The co-author, P.B.F., was supported by a grant from the National Health and Medical Research Council of Australia (1193596).

Institutional Review Board Statement: This study was conducted in accordance with the Declaration of Helsinki and approved by the Biomedical Research Ethics Boards of the University of Manitoba (reference no: HS19998 (B2016:077); approval date: 5 October 2016), McGill University (reference no: 2017-2749; approval date: 16 December 2016), and Monash University (reference no: 480/16; approval date: 14 June 2017).

Informed Consent Statement: All participants and primary caregivers provided written consent before enrolling in the study. Written informed consent was obtained from all participants to publish this paper.

Data Availability Statement: The data will be available upon a reasonable request from the PI of the study (ZM). Data are not yet available for the public due to ensuring all public data are fully de-identified.

Acknowledgments: The PI (co-author, Z.M.) acknowledges the support of Puchniak's family for their generous donation.

Conflicts of Interest: The co-author, PBF, received research equipment from Nexstim, Neurosoft, and Brainsway Ltd. He has acted as a scientific advisory board member for LivaNova and Magstim and is a founder of Clinics Australia and Resonance Therapeutics. He also received speaker fees from Otsuka, Japan.

References

1. Cotelli, M.; Manenti, R.; Cappa, S.F.; Geroldi, C.; Zanetti, O.; Rossini, P.M.; Miniussi, C. Effect of Transcranial Magnetic Stimulation on Action Naming in Patients with Alzheimer Disease. *Arch. Neurol.* **2006**, *63*, 1602. [CrossRef]
2. Cotelli, M.; Calabria, M.; Manenti, R.; Rosini, S.; Zanetti, O.; Cappa, S.F.; Miniussi, C. Improved Language Performance in Alzheimer Disease Following Brain Stimulation. *J. Neurol. Neurosurg. Psychiatry* **2011**, *82*, 794–797. [CrossRef] [PubMed]
3. Rutherford, G.; Lithgow, B.; Moussavi, Z. Short and Long-Term Effects of RTMS Treatment on Alzheimer's Disease at Different Stages: A Pilot Study. *J. Exp. Neurosci.* **2015**, *9*, JEN.S24004. [CrossRef] [PubMed]
4. Koch, G.; Casula, E.P.; Bonnì, S.; Borghi, I.; Assogna, M.; Minei, M.; Pellicciari, M.C.; Motta, C.; D'Acunto, A.; Porrazzini, F.; et al. Precuneus Magnetic Stimulation for Alzheimer's Disease: A Randomized, Sham-Controlled Trial. *Brain* **2022**, *145*, 3776–3786. [CrossRef]
5. Rutherford, G.; Gole, R.; Moussavi, Z. RTMS as a Treatment of Alzheimer's Disease with and without Comorbidity of Depression: A Review. *Neurosci. J.* **2013**, *2013*, 679389. [CrossRef] [PubMed]
6. Weiler, M.; Stieger, K.C.; Long, J.M.; Rapp, P.R. Transcranial Magnetic Stimulation in Alzheimer's Disease: Are We Ready? *eNeuro* **2020**, *7*, ENEURO.0235-19.2019. [CrossRef]

7. Rabey, J.M.; Dobronevsky, E.; Aichenbaum, S.; Gonen, O.; Marton, R.G.; Khaigrekht, M. Repetitive Transcranial Magnetic Stimulation Combined with Cognitive Training Is a Safe and Effective Modality for the Treatment of Alzheimer's Disease: A Randomized, Double-Blind Study. *J. Neural Transm.* **2013**, *120*, 813–819. [CrossRef]
8. Moussavi, Z.; Uehara, M.; Rutherford, G.; Lithgow, B.; Millikin, C.; Wang, X.; Saha, C.; Mansouri, B.; Omelan, C.; Fellows, L.; et al. Repetitive Transcranial Magnetic Stimulation as a Treatment for Alzheimer's Disease: A Randomized Placebo-Controlled Double-Blind Clinical Trial. *Neurotherapeutics* **2024**, e00331. [CrossRef]
9. Baxter, L.C.; Sparks, D.L.; Johnson, S.C.; Lenoski, B.; Lopez, J.E.; Connor, D.J.; Sabbagh, M.N. Relationship of Cognitive Measures and Gray and White Matter in Alzheimer's Disease. *J. Alzheimers Dis.* **2006**, *9*, 253–260. [CrossRef]
10. Guo, X.; Wang, Z.; Li, K.; Li, Z.; Qi, Z.; Jin, Z.; Yao, L.; Chen, K. Voxel-Based Assessment of Gray and White Matter Volumes in Alzheimer's Disease. *Neurosci. Lett.* **2010**, *468*, 146–150. [CrossRef]
11. Frisoni, G.B.; Bocchetta, M.; Chetelat, G.; Rabinovici, G.D.; de Leon, M.J.; Kaye, J.; Reiman, E.M.; Scheltens, P.; Barkhof, F.; Black, S.E.; et al. Imaging Markers for Alzheimer Disease: Which vs. How. *Neurology* **2013**, *81*, 487–500. [CrossRef] [PubMed]
12. Fleisher, A.S.; Sun, S.; Taylor, C.; Ward, C.P.; Gamst, A.C.; Petersen, R.C.; Jack, C.R.; Aisen, P.S.; Thal, L.J. Volumetric MRI vs Clinical Predictors of Alzheimer Disease in Mild Cognitive Impairment. *Neurology* **2008**, *70*, 191–199. [CrossRef]
13. Moussavi, Z.; Koski, L.; Fitzgerald, P.B.; Millikin, C.; Lithgow, B.; Jafari-Jozani, M.; Wang, X. Repeated Transcranial Magnetic Stimulation for Improving Cognition in Alzheimer Disease: Protocol for an Interim Analysis of a Randomized Controlled Trial. *JMIR Res. Protoc.* **2021**, *10*, e31183. [CrossRef]
14. Guo, Y.; Dang, G.; Hordacre, B.; Su, X.; Yan, N.; Chen, S.; Ren, H.; Shi, X.; Cai, M.; Zhang, S.; et al. Repetitive Transcranial Magnetic Stimulation of the Dorsolateral Prefrontal Cortex Modulates Electroencephalographic Functional Connectivity in Alzheimer's Disease. *Front. Aging Neurosci.* **2021**, *13*, 679585. [CrossRef] [PubMed]
15. Hertrich, I.; Dietrich, S.; Blum, C.; Ackermann, H. The Role of the Dorsolateral Prefrontal Cortex for Speech and Language Processing. *Front. Hum. Neurosci.* **2021**, *15*, 645209. [CrossRef] [PubMed]
16. Chan, R.C.K.; Shum, D.; Toulopoulou, T.; Chen, E.Y.H. Assessment of Executive Functions: Review of Instruments and Identification of Critical Issues. *Arch. Clin. Neuropsychol.* **2008**, *23*, 201–216. [CrossRef]
17. Moussavi, Z.; Rutherford, G.; Lithgow, B.; Millikin, C.; Modirrousta, M.; Mansouri, B.; Wang, X.; Omelan, C.; Fellows, L.; Fitzgerald, P.; et al. Repeated Transcranial Magnetic Stimulation for Improving Cognition in Patients with Alzheimer Disease: Protocol for a Randomized, Double-Blind, Placebo-Controlled Trial. *JMIR Res. Protoc.* **2021**, *10*, e25144. [CrossRef]
18. Gaser, C.; Dahnke, R. CAT—A Computational Anatomy Toolbox for the Analysis of Structural MRI Data. *HBM* **2016**, *2016*, 336–348.
19. Ashburner, J.; Friston, K.J. Unified Segmentation. *Neuroimage* **2005**, *26*, 839–851. [CrossRef]
20. Manjón, J.V.; Coupé, P.; Martí-Bonmatí, L.; Collins, D.L.; Robles, M. Adaptive Non-Local Means Denoising of MR Images with Spatially Varying Noise Levels. *J. Magn. Reson. Imaging* **2010**, *31*, 192–203. [CrossRef]
21. Rajapakse, J.C.; Giedd, J.N.; Rapoport, J.L. Statistical Approach to Segmentation of Single-Channel Cerebral MR Images. *IEEE Trans. Med. Imaging* **1997**, *16*, 176–186. [CrossRef]
22. Ashburner, J.; Friston, K.J. Diffeomorphic Registration Using Geodesic Shooting and Gauss–Newton Optimisation. *Neuroimage* **2011**, *55*, 954–967. [CrossRef]
23. Pletzer, B.; Harris, T.A.; Hidalgo-Lopez, E. Subcortical Structural Changes along the Menstrual Cycle: Beyond the Hippocampus. *Sci. Rep.* **2018**, *8*, 8–13. [CrossRef]
24. Brett, M.; Anton, J.-L.L.; Valabregue, R.; Poline, J.-B. Region of Interest Using an SPM Toolbox [Abstract]. In Proceedings of the 8th International Conferance on Functional of the Human Brain, Sendai, Japan, 2–6 June 2002; Available on CD-ROM in NeuroImage. Volume 16. No. 2.
25. Masina, F.; Vallesi, A.; Di Rosa, E.; Semenzato, L.; Mapelli, D. Possible Role of Dorsolateral Prefrontal Cortex in Error Awareness: Single-Pulse TMS Evidence. *Front. Neurosci.* **2018**, *12*, 179. [CrossRef] [PubMed]
26. Cieslik, E.C.; Zilles, K.; Caspers, S.; Roski, C.; Kellermann, T.S.; Jakobs, O.; Langner, R.; Laird, A.R.; Fox, P.T.; Eickhoff, S.B. Is There One DLPFC in Cognitive Action Control? Evidence for Heterogeneity from Co-Activation-Based Parcellation. *Cereb. Cortex* **2013**, *23*, 2677–2689. [CrossRef] [PubMed]
27. Rorden, C.; Brett, M. Stereotaxic Display of Brain Lesions. *Behav. Neurol.* **2000**, *12*, 191–200. [CrossRef] [PubMed]
28. Kong, X.Z.; Postema, M.C.; Guadalupe, T.; de Kovel, C.; Boedhoe, P.S.W.; Hoogman, M.; Mathias, S.R.; van Rooij, D.; Schijven, D.; Glahn, D.C.; et al. Mapping Brain Asymmetry in Health and Disease through the ENIGMA Consortium. *Hum. Brain Mapp.* **2022**, *43*, 167–181. [CrossRef] [PubMed]
29. Minkova, L.; Habich, A.; Peter, J.; Kaller, C.P.; Eickhoff, S.B.; Klöppel, S. Gray Matter Asymmetries in Aging and Neurodegeneration: A Review and Meta-Analysis. *Hum. Brain Mapp.* **2017**, *38*, 5890–5904. [CrossRef] [PubMed]
30. Büchel, C.; Raedler, T.; Sommer, M.; Sach, M.; Weiller, C.; Koch, M.A. White Matter Asymmetry in the Human Brain: A Diffusion Tensor MRI Study. *Cereb. Cortex* **2004**, *14*, 945–951. [CrossRef] [PubMed]
31. Geng, Z.; Liu, H.; Wang, L.; Zhu, Q.; Song, Z.; Chang, R.; Lv, H. A Voxel-Based Morphometric Study of Age- and Sex-Related Changes in White Matter Volume in the Normal Aging Brain. *Neuropsychiatr. Dis. Treat.* **2016**, *12*, 453–465. [CrossRef]
32. Good, C.D.; Johnsrude, I.; Ashburner, J.; Henson, R.N.A.; Friston, K.J.; Frackowiak, R.S.J. Cerebral Asymmetry and the Effects of Sex and Handedness on Brain Structure: A Voxel-Based Morphometric Analysis of 465 Normal Adult Human Brains. *Neuroimage* **2001**, *14*, 685–700. [CrossRef] [PubMed]

33. Sarica, A.; Vasta, R.; Novellino, F.; Vaccaro, M.G.; Cerasa, A.; Quattrone, A. MRI Asymmetry Index of Hippocampal Subfields Increases through the Continuum from the Mild Cognitive Impairment to the Alzheimer's Disease. *Front. Neurosci.* **2018**, *12*, 576. [CrossRef] [PubMed]
34. Lehtola, S.J.; Tuulari, J.J.; Karlsson, L.; Parkkola, R.; Merisaari, H.; Saunavaara, J.; Lähdesmäki, T.; Scheinin, N.M.; Karlsson, H. Associations of Age and Sex with Brain Volumes and Asymmetry in 2–5-Week-Old Infants. *Brain Struct. Funct.* **2019**, *224*, 501–513. [CrossRef]
35. Kim, H.-Y. Statistical Notes for Clinical Researchers: Analysis of Covariance (ANCOVA). *Restor. Dent. Endod.* **2018**, *43*, e43. [CrossRef]
36. *R Core Team: A Language and Environment for Statistical Computing*; R Foundation for Statistical Computing: Vienna, Austria, 2021.
37. RStudio Team. *RStudio: Integrated Development Environment for R 2021*; RStudio, Inc.: Boston, MA, USA, 2021.
38. Chawla, N.V.; Bowyer, K.W.; Hall, L.O.; Kegelmeyer, W.P. SMOTE: Synthetic Minority over-Sampling Technique. *J. Artif. Intell. Res.* **2002**, *16*, 321–357. [CrossRef]
39. He, H. Imbalanced Learning. In *Self-Adaptive Systems for Machine Intelligence*; John Wiley & Sons, Inc.: Hoboken, NJ, USA, 2011; pp. 44–107.
40. Rabinovici, G.D.; Seeley, W.W.; Kim, E.J.; Gorno-Tempini, M.L.; Rascovsky, K.; Pagliaro, T.A.; Allison, S.C.; Halabi, C.; Kramer, J.H.; Johnson, J.K.; et al. Distinct MRI Atrophy Patterns in Autopsy-Proven Alzheimer's Disease and Frontotemporal Lobar Degeneration. *Am. J. Alzheimer's Dis. Other Dement.* **2008**, *22*, 474–488. [CrossRef] [PubMed]
41. Iaccarino, L.; Tammewar, G.; Ayakta, N.; Baker, S.L.; Bejanin, A.; Boxer, A.L.; Gorno-Tempini, M.L.; Janabi, M.; Kramer, J.H.; Lazaris, A.; et al. Local and Distant Relationships between Amyloid, Tau and Neurodegeneration in Alzheimer's Disease. *Neuroimage Clin.* **2018**, *17*, 452–464. [CrossRef]
42. Wagner, T.; Eden, U.; Fregni, F.; Valero-Cabre, A.; Ramos-Estebanez, C.; Pronio-Stelluto, V.; Grodzinsky, A.; Zahn, M.; Pascual-Leone, A. Transcranial Magnetic Stimulation and Brain Atrophy: A Computer-Based Human Brain Model Study. *Exp. Brain Res.* **2008**, *186*, 539–550. [CrossRef]
43. Anderkova, L.; Eliasova, I.; Marecek, R.; Janousova, E.; Rektorova, I. Grey Matter Atrophy in Mild Alzheimer's Disease Impacts on Cognitive Effects of Noninvasive Brain Stimulation. *Clin. Neurophysiol.* **2016**, *127*, e28. [CrossRef]
44. Esposito, S.; Trojsi, F.; Cirillo, G.; de Stefano, M.; Di Nardo, F.; Siciliano, M.; Caiazzo, G.; Ippolito, D.; Ricciardi, D.; Buonanno, D.; et al. Repetitive Transcranial Magnetic Stimulation (RTMS) of Dorsolateral Prefrontal Cortex May Influence Semantic Fluency and Functional Connectivity in Fronto-Parietal Network in Mild Cognitive Impairment (MCI). *Biomedicines* **2022**, *10*, 994. [CrossRef]
45. Catani, M.; Allin, M.P.G.; Husain, M.; Pugliese, L.; Mesulam, M.M.; Murray, R.M.; Jones, D.K. Symmetries in Human Brain Language Pathways Correlate with Verbal Recall. *Proc. Natl. Acad. Sci. USA* **2007**, *104*, 17163–17168. [CrossRef]
46. Zhou, H.; Tang, Y.; Yuan, Z. White Matter Asymmetries in Patients with Cerebral Small Vessel Disease. *J. Integr. Neurosci.* **2018**, *17*, 159–167. [CrossRef]
47. Allendorfer, J.B.; Storrs, J.M.; Szaflarski, J.P. Changes in White Matter Integrity Follow Excitatory RTMS Treatment of Post-Stroke Aphasia. *Restor. Neurol. Neurosci.* **2012**, *30*, 103–113. [CrossRef]
48. Peng, H.; Zheng, H.; Li, L.; Liu, J.; Zhang, Y.; Shan, B.; Zhang, L.; Yin, Y.; Liu, J.; Li, W.; et al. High-Frequency RTMS Treatment Increases White Matter FA in the Left Middle Frontal Gyrus in Young Patients with Treatment-Resistant Depression. *J. Affect. Disord.* **2012**, *136*, 249–257. [CrossRef] [PubMed]
49. Roiser, J.P.; Linden, D.E.; Gorno-Tempini, M.L.; Moran, R.J.; Dickerson, B.C.; Grafton, S.T. Minimum Statistical Standards for Submissions to Neuroimage: Clinical. *Neuroimage Clin.* **2016**, *12*, 1045–1047. [CrossRef]
50. Wang, W.Y.; Yu, J.T.; Liu, Y.; Yin, R.H.; Wang, H.F.; Wang, J.; Tan, L.; Radua, J.; Tan, L. Voxel-Based Meta-Analysis of Grey Matter Changes in Alzheimer's Disease. *Transl. Neurodegener* **2015**, *4*, 6. [CrossRef] [PubMed]
51. Martin, P.; Winston, G.P.; Bartlett, P.; de Tisi, J.; Duncan, J.S.; Focke, N.K. Voxel-Based Magnetic Resonance Image Postprocessing in Epilepsy. *Epilepsia* **2017**, *58*, 1653–1664. [CrossRef]
52. Wei, C.; Gong, S.; Zou, Q.; Zhang, W.; Kang, X.; Lu, X.; Chen, Y.; Yang, Y.; Wang, W.; Jia, L.; et al. A Comparative Study of Structural and Metabolic Brain Networks in Patients with Mild Cognitive Impairment. *Front. Aging Neurosci.* **2021**, *13*, 774607. [CrossRef]
53. Elder, G.J.; Taylor, J.P. Transcranial Magnetic Stimulation and Transcranial Direct Current Stimulation: Treatments for Cognitive and Neuropsychiatric Symptoms in the Neurodegenerative Dementias? *Alzheimers Res. Ther.* **2014**, *6*, 74. [CrossRef]

Disclaimer/Publisher's Note: The statements, opinions and data contained in all publications are solely those of the individual author(s) and contributor(s) and not of MDPI and/or the editor(s). MDPI and/or the editor(s) disclaim responsibility for any injury to people or property resulting from any ideas, methods, instructions or products referred to in the content.

brain sciences

MDPI

Article

Positive Effect of Super-Resolved Structural Magnetic Resonance Imaging for Mild Cognitive Impairment Detection

Ovidijus Grigas [1], Robertas Damaševičius [1,2,*] and Rytis Maskeliūnas [1]

1 Faculty of Informatics, Kaunas University of Technology, 50254 Kaunas, Lithuania; o.grigas@ktu.edu (O.G.); rytis.maskeliunas@ktu.lt (R.M.)
2 Faculty of Applied Mathematics, Silesian University of Technology, 44-100 Gliwice, Poland
* Correspondence: robertas.damasevicius@polsl.pl

Abstract: This paper presents a novel approach to improving the detection of mild cognitive impairment (MCI) through the use of super-resolved structural magnetic resonance imaging (MRI) and optimized deep learning models. The study introduces enhancements to the perceptual quality of super-resolved 2D structural MRI images using advanced loss functions, modifications to the upscaler part of the generator, and experiments with various discriminators within a generative adversarial training setting. It empirically demonstrates the effectiveness of super-resolution in the MCI detection task, showcasing performance improvements across different state-of-the-art classification models. The paper also addresses the challenge of accurately capturing perceptual image quality, particularly when images contain checkerboard artifacts, and proposes a methodology that incorporates hyperparameter optimization through a Pareto optimal Markov blanket (POMB). This approach systematically explores the hyperparameter space, focusing on reducing overfitting and enhancing model generalizability. The research findings contribute to the field by demonstrating that super-resolution can significantly improve the quality of MRI images for MCI detection, highlighting the importance of choosing an adequate discriminator and the potential of super-resolution as a preprocessing step to boost classification model performance.

Keywords: magneticresonance imaging; super-resolution; mild cognitive impairment; hyperparameter optimization; Pareto optimality; Markov blanket

1. Introduction

Mild cognitive impairment (MCI) is considered as a prodromal stage of Alzheimer's disease based on clinical symptoms [1]. It is also a transitional period between healthy aging, where cognitive decline is a normal phenomena, and dementia [2]. MCI usually impacts cognitive abilities such as reasoning, memory, and logic [3]. People with this condition are usually forgetful, and need more time to think or express certain thoughts. However, they do not need assisted living facilities, because they are able to take care of themselves in everyday life. People with MCI may or may not convert to Alzheimer's disease [4–6] or dementia [4]. The condition every year affects millions of people worldwide and attracts large investments from governments into research and drug production. There is no cure for this disease; however, certain treatments can reduce symptoms if applied on time. Therefore, early diagnosis is crucial, which allows patients and their caregivers enough time to prepare for the future. However, currently, there is no standardized assessment that would allow one to accurately diagnose MCI [7]. Due to this fact, researchers try to find new ways to accurately detect MCI via a vast number of different data modalities, for example, electroencephalogram (EEG) [8], 18F fluoro-deoxy-glucose positron emission tomography (FDG-PET) [9], cerebrospinal fluid (CSF) biomarkers [10], natural language [11], or T1w and T2w MRI [12,13]. Neuroimaging markers are becoming more popular and show great potential towards accurately identifying MCI [14,15]. Certain structural changes in the brain are present when a patient has MCI, for example, a decrease in gray matter volume in the medial temporal lobe [16] and hippocampal, entorhinal cortex atrophy with cortical volume decrease [17,18]. The task of detecting MCI is challenging, because it usually affects elderly people, and it is hard to distinguish if changes in the brain volume are impacted due to normal aging [19] or due to MCI, since some of the regions, for example, the temporal lobe, show a volume decrease in both scenarios. Therefore, it is crucial for the tools to not only focus on the specific known regions of interest (ROI), but also to incorporate other regions of the brain, which may have a correlation to the presence of MCI. Particularly, enhancing smaller regions with finer details in MRI may allow diagnostic tools such as deep learning (DL) models to find other important regions and more accurately detect MCI.

Super-resolution technology has been a helpful tool in many different science areas, for example, hyperspectral imaging [20], nature sciences [21], satellite imagery [22], license plate recognition [23], and medical imaging—this paper. This technology utilizes deep learning models to increase the quality of low-resolution data by upscaling and reconstructing an image, which would be accurate and meaningful. Usually, researchers focus their super-resolution solutions into improvements in a controlled environment, where a small dataset with a highly specialized solution can reach high results, but all of these solutions are impractical in real world scenarios, where data are usually not a controlled factor. A small change in the data domain means the model will be incapable of reconstructing that image. In these challenging scenarios, "real-world" super-resolution solutions become useful. These solutions do not rely on paired image datasets, where a low-resolution image is known for each high-resolution image. Here, low-resolution images are generated randomly by utilizing degradation (augmentation) techniques in a completely random order [24]. By using degradation techniques, we can cover a wider distribution of possible input images, making the model more practical. Therefore, this paper utilizes the real-world super-resolution paradigm. Another problem with super-resolution is that many solutions are not focusing on the perceptual quality of the reconstructed images. Many researchers only focus on peak signal-to-noise ratio (PSNR) and structural similarity index measure (SSIM) to report their results, even though subjectively generated images are blurry and noisy. In the medical imaging field, preserving the structural part of the image quality is as important as the perceptual part. Therefore, just like in our previous paper [25], we maintain the focus to improve the main important aspects of the image quality—structural and perceptual.

Deep learning model hyperparameter optimization plays a crucial role in enhancing the performance and accuracy of diagnostic models in the field of medical imaging [26]. By fine-tuning parameters such as learning rates, layer configurations, and activation functions, these models can be better adapted to the nuances of medical datasets, which often contain complex patterns and subtle features critical for accurate diagnosis [27]. Optimizing hyperparameters enables the models to effectively learn from high-dimensional imaging data, such as MRI, CT scans, and X-rays, leading to improved sensitivity and specificity in detecting and classifying diseases [28].

In medical imaging diagnostics, the stakes are high, as the early and accurate identification of conditions can significantly impact patient outcomes [26]. Hyperparameter optimization ensures that deep learning models are not only tailored to the unique challenges of medical data but also generalized enough to handle variations across different imaging modalities and patient demographics [27]. This process also helps in reducing overfitting, ensuring that the model's performance is robust across unseen data, which is paramount in clinical settings where the model's predictions can directly influence treatment decisions [29].

Bayesian networks, a class of probabilistic graphical models, represent complex relationships between a set of variables using directed acyclic graphs (DAGs) [30]. Each node in a Bayesian network symbolizes a variable, while the edges denote conditional dependencies between them, encapsulating the probabilistic influences of variables on one another [31]. In the context of hyperparameter optimization for machine learning models, Bayesian networks serve as a powerful tool to model and understand the intricate dependencies between various hyperparameters and their impact on model performance metrics [32]. By capturing these relationships, Bayesian networks facilitate a structured exploration of the hyperparameter space, enabling the identification of optimal configurations [33]. This approach not only streamlines the optimization process by focusing on the most influential hyperparameters but also enhances the efficiency and efficacy of the model tuning phase, leveraging probabilistic reasoning to guide the search towards hyperparameter sets that are likely to yield improved performance outcomes [32,33].

The novelty and contribution of this study lie in its innovative integration of super-resolution imaging techniques and advanced machine learning optimization strategies to enhance the detection of MCI from structural MRI scans. Specifically, the study introduces the following novel contributions to the field of medical imaging and diagnostics:

- By employing super-resolution techniques within a generative adversarial network (GAN) framework, this study improves the perceptual quality of structural MRI images. This enhancement is pivotal, as higher-resolution images can reveal subtle brain changes associated with MCI, which are often not discernible in low-resolution scans.
- This research advances the state of the art by incorporating a combination of loss functions, including perceptual loss and adversarial loss, to not only increase the resolution of MRI images but also to maintain their diagnostic integrity. This approach addresses common issues in super-resolution, such as checkerboard artifacts, ensuring that the enhanced images are both high in quality and clinically reliable.
- A key contribution is the application of a POMB approach for hyperparameter optimization in deep learning models used for MCI detection. This method systematically evaluates and selects hyperparameters to balance model complexity and performance, reducing overfitting and improving generalizability. The use of POMB in this context is novel, offering a structured framework for enhancing model accuracy in medical diagnostics.
- This study validates the effectiveness of super-resolution preprocessing on MCI detection across various state-of-the-art deep learning architectures. This empirical evidence supports the premise that super-resolution can serve as a valuable preprocessing step in medical imaging analysis, potentially applicable beyond MCI detection.
- The investigation into the impact of different discriminator architectures within the GAN framework on the quality of super-resolved images underscores the critical role of discriminator choice. This insight contributes to the broader understanding of how GAN components influence the outcome of super-resolution tasks, guiding future research and application in neuroimaging enhancement.

The main purpose of this study is to improve the processing of MRI data and validate the proposed methodology effectiveness in mild cognitive impairment detection.

The rest of the paper is organized as follows: Section 2 discusses the related studies. Section 3 explains the proposed methodology improvements to our previous work to improve perceptual quality of MR images. Section 4 presents the research findings in terms of quantitative and qualitative evaluation of the proposed methodology. Section 5 discusses and summarizes the findings and presents the conclusions.

2. Related Works

Neuroimage enhancement is a compelling field of study that is increasingly gaining traction in research circles. As advancements in imaging technology continue to improve, the need for enhancing neuroimages to extract more accurate diagnostic information becomes more pronounced. For identification of similar studies, we utilized the database engines—Web of Science, Scopus, IEEE Xplore, Springer Link, and Science Direct (Last accessed on 7 March 2024). We constructed the search queries using these keywords: super, resol*, mild*, mci, detect*, class*. We combined the keywords with Boolean operators (AND, OR) and filtered only to articles and conference proceedings. Asterisk (*) was used to include words with different suffixes. Only sources published after 2014 and written in English were included. After the initial screening, 157 sources were identified. After removing duplicates, 86 entries were left. After the title and abstract screening, 22 sources were left. After full-text eligibility review, 6 sources were included in the study, and are compared in Table 1.

Alwakid et al. [34] used ESRGAN [35] to upscale retinal images, and then used the Inception v3 model [36] to classify the images into five different classes of diabetic retinopathy (mild, moderate, proliferative, severe, undetected). The dataset they used was APTOS [37]. Their experiments show that using super-resolution improves baseline accuracy by nearly 18%.

Tan et al. [38] used the SRGAN [39] model to upscale computed tomography (CT) scans of patient lungs, which then were used to classify with the VGG-16 [40] model whether the patient has COVID-19 pneumonia or not. The dataset they used was COVID-CT [41]. Their experiments also show that the super-resolution technique improves baseline accuracy by approximately 8%.

Nagayama et al. [42] utilized super-resolution software PIQE (SR-DLR) [43], which is being sold by Canon alongside their CT scanners. It is a custom 3D CNN trained on CT images. No other details are disclosed by the company. However, validation of the method shows that it improves not only image quality, but also the detection of coronary lumens, calcifications, and non-calcified plaques approximately. The methodology of the source describes using the detectability index to measure performance [44]. The authors have not disclosed the dataset used in their study. The method shows an approximately 5% improvement over the other state-of-the-art solutions.

De Farias et al. [45] slightly modified GAN-CIRCLE [46] and used it to evaluate whether super-resolution improves feature selection in CT scans. For this reason, they used principal component analysis (PCA) with spatial pyramid pooling (SPP), and then checked which features were selected as the most important ones. The authors used the NSCLC [47] dataset. Experiments show that using super-resolution improves feature selection by relatively 2% if ranking by the feature importance using the intraclass correlation coefficient (ICC).

Huang et al. [48] combined wavelet transform with DDGAN [49] to improve the resolution of the ADNI [50] dataset images. They used T1w image slices from the coronal plane and performed $\times 4$ times upscaling from 48×48 to 192×192 resolution. First, they downscaled the original images and then tried to reconstruct them with super-resolution. The experiments with the support vector machine (SVM) as classifier show a relative 2% performance increase by using super-resolution.

Zhang et al. [51] used a custom 3D encoder–decoder GAN with residual connections to super-resolve T2w MRI images. The dataset that they used consisted of 200 patients who went through an inflammatory bowel disease clinical trial, but it is not publicly available. After super-resolving the images, they used ResNet to classify the images, and found no improvement over the baseline.

Table 1. Comparison of different approaches for image super-resolution and classification in medical imaging.

Reference	Super-Resolution Model	Classification Model	Dataset	Improvement
Fundus photography				
Alwakid et al. [34]	ESRGAN	Inception v3	APTOS	18%
CT Scans				
Tan et al. [38]	SRGAN	VGG-16	COVID-CT	8%
Nagayama et al. [42]	PIQE (SR-DLR)	-	-	5%
de Farias et al. [45]	Modified GAN-CIRCLE	PCA+SPP	NSCLC	2%
MRI				
Huang et al. [48]	DDGAN	SVM	ADNI	2%
Zhang et al. [51]	3D Encoder–Decoder GAN	ResNet	-	0%
This paper	Hybrid Transformer GAN	Various Models	ADNI, OASIS-4	1–4%

Naturally, the accuracy varies depending on the application and the size of the dataset used in training, but overall, super-resolution technology improves the accuracy of classification models in the majority of tasks.

3. Materials and Methods

3.1. Experimental Data

For the super-resolution model improvements, we used the same ultra-high-resolution MRI dataset "human phantom" [52] that we used in our previous work [25]. (Dataset available online: https://datadryad.org/stash/dataset/doi:10.5061/dryad.38s74—accessed on 5 March 2024). All of the preprocessing steps were also unchanged.

A short description of both datasets is available in Table 2. More details of how the data were prepared are available in Section 4.1.

Table 2. Description of datasets used in classification of MCI.

Dataset	Description	# of Samples Used
ADNI	First version released in 2004. Focus on Alzheimer's disease and its early-stage MCI. We only used T1w MRI images, although it has many other data modalities	689 MCI, 689 CN
OASIS-4	First version released in 2007. Focus on memory disorders and dementia. We also utilized only T1w MRI images.	47 MCI, 47 CN

CN—Cognitive Normal (Healthy Patient), ADNI—Alzheimer's Disease Neuroimaging Initiative, OASIS—Open Access Series of Imaging Studies.

3.2. Improvement of Super-Resolution Hybrid Transformer GAN

The baseline of the improvements for this study is our previously published method [25], which increases the resolution of structural MRIs while preserving perceptional image quality. It uses hybrid attention transformer (HAT) as a generator and introduces an adversarial training pipeline, which allows one to super-resolve structural MRI and decrease its blurriness and noise. In this study, we employ the following improvements over the previous method: (1) a deeper/denser network for discriminator of hybrid attention transformer (HAT) model generator, (2) use of Wasserstein GAN (WGAN) loss and frequency domain loss, (3) addition of more augmentation techniques, (4) modification of upsampling layer of generator model, and (5) implementation of hyperparameter optimization using POMB.

3.2.1. Usage of Deeper/Denser Network for the Discriminator

To use the deeper model for discriminator, we experimented with various existing model architectures, which are briefly described in Table 3.

Table 3. Model architectures used for discriminator in GAN loss.

Model	Reference	Used Permutations of Model
VGG-16	[40]	With 128 and 256 input features.
ConvMixer	[53]	(width, depth, kernel size, patch size): (1536, 20, 9, 7) (1024, 20, 9, 14)
U-Net	[54]	With 128 and 256 features
ResNet-152	[55]	Only original implementation
ResNext-101	[56]	Only original implementation

3.2.2. Definition of Loss Function

One of the improvements proposed by our previous work was the use of Wasserstein GAN [57] for adversarial training. WGAN proved to make the training of models more stable. Therefore, we replaced vanilla GAN loss with WGAN loss. WGAN loss is defined as in Equations (1) and (2):

$$L_G = \overline{G(z)}, \tag{1}$$

$$L_D = \overline{x} - \overline{G(z)}, \tag{2}$$

where z is a fake image and x is a target image. WGAN discriminator is simply called "critic", because it is only yielding a score of the generated image. The score itself is just a mean value of the tensor.

The next change to our methodology was to swap perceptual-style reconstruction loss with LPIPS loss. It forces generator to focus a bit more on the contents/features of the generated images, rather than on the style, since the loss combines features from multiple layers in the network. The loss is just a LPIPS metric defined in Equation (25) calculation on which gradient descent can then be used.

For pixel-level loss, we used Charbonnier loss for the same reasons that it is a better variant of mean absolute error (MAE) loss, and it is proven to make training more stable and make models produce images with better visual results [58–60]. Charbonnier loss is defined in Equation (3).

$$L_{Charbonnier} = \frac{\sum_{i=1}^{n} \sqrt{(y_i - x_i)^2 + \epsilon^2}}{n}, \tag{3}$$

The last change was to introduce frequency domain-based loss function, which uses Fast Fourier Transform (FFT). FFT is widely used algorithm in many different science fields. It is usually used to reduce noise in images by transforming images from spacial to frequency domain and applying filters [61] to the extracted frequencies. The main idea of frequency domain loss is comparing images pixel-wise like one could do in spacial domain with L1 or L2 loss, but doing so in frequency domain makes the loss slightly more sensitive to blurriness and noise, helps in preserving high-frequency features in images, and overall yields better perceptual quality [62–64]. Loss equation is defined in Equation (6), which is an L1 loss between amplitudes and phases of two distinct images.

$$A_{x_i}, P_{x_i} = FFT(x_i), \tag{4}$$

$$A_{y_i}, P_{y_i} = FFT(y_i), \tag{5}$$

$$L_{FD} = \frac{1}{n}\sum_{i=1}^{n}(\|A_{x_i} - A_{y_i}\| + \|P_{x_i} - P_{y_i}\|), \tag{6}$$

where x is a high-resolution image, y is a generated image, and FFT is a fast Fourier transform applied to 2D image, n is a number of samples in the mini-batch and i is the index of the sample in the mini-batch.

Combined loss for generator is defined in Equation (7). For discriminator, we used defined discriminator adversarial loss Equation (2).

$$L = L_{Charbonnier} + L_{FD} + L_G + L_{LPIPS} \tag{7}$$

3.2.3. Image Augmentation Techniques

Our previous work was following [65]'s described augmentation pipeline, which was developed to train the models to be more generic due to the fact that the training is based on applying various degradation functions to the high-quality images, instead of using paired high-/low-quality images for direct input to the model. The use of randomness in the degradation pipeline trains the model to be more stable given various unknown levels of blurriness, noise, etc., in low-quality images. This branch of super-resolution research is called "real-world" super-resolution. Usually, researchers avoid it because the model performance will be lower than the model trained on paired image dataset. This happens because in controlled environments, models can learn the training set image distribution quite well, but once the low-quality input image is not entirely lying within training set image distribution, generated results will be low-quality.

In our case, a model used for sMRI super-resolution must be practical and capable of dealing with a wider distribution of input images than the training set. Hence, the extensive application of random augmentations (degradations) during training. Original pipeline includes blur, resize, Gaussian noise, Poisson noise, speckle noise, and jpeg compression noise transformations applied in random sequence multiple times. We extended the original pipeline with the additional random augmentations of brightness and contrast jitter, sharpening, gamma, cutout, and random rotation transformations. All used augmentations are depicted in Figure 1.

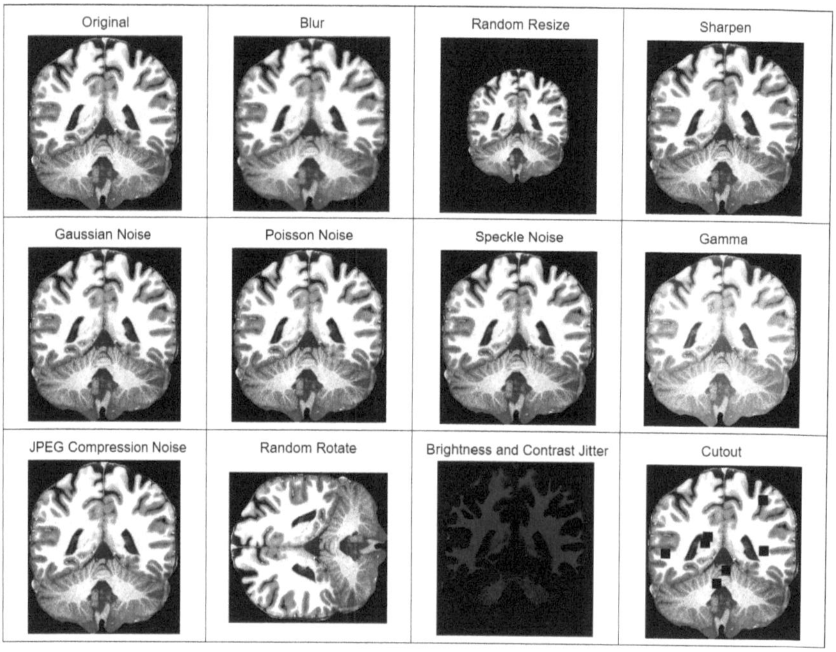

Figure 1. Image augmentations (degradations) used in the training of super-resolution model. Different degradation method outputs are applied to a single extracted slice of T1w MRI of a healthy Caucasian male from "human phantom" dataset [52].

3.2.4. Modified Upsampling Layer of Generator Model

In our methodology, we use HAT generator [66]. Originally, it uses so called "pixel-shuffle" for the upsampling of the tensors, as described in [67]. But this technique is known for being used in classical super-resolution tasks, where perceptual quality is not the main selling point. For real-world super-resolution tasks, the typically used upsampling technique is called "nearest+conv", which uses deconvolution with overlapping to reduce "checkerboard" artifacts in generated images [68].

3.3. Hyperparameter Optimization Using Pareto Optimal Markov Blanket

3.3.1. Types of Hyperparameters

Deep learning model architecture hyperparameters can be intricately described and optimized using the framework of Bayesian networks. This approach uses probabilistic graphical models to represent the conditional dependencies between hyperparameters and the performance metric(s) of interest, enabling systematic exploration and understanding of the hyperparameter space. Four types of hyperparameters are possible in a Bayesian network of hyperparameters:

- A hyperparameter X_i is conditionally independent of the hyperparameter Y_i given S if and only if $P(X_i|Y_i, S) = P(X_i|S)$.
- A hyperparameter $X_i \in \mathbb{R}$ is strongly relevant to the target variable T if and only if $\forall S \subseteq \mathbb{R} \setminus \{X_i\}$, s.t. $P(X_i|S) \neq P(X_i|S, T)$.
- A hyperparameter $X_i \in \mathbb{R}$ is irrelevant to a target variable T if and only if $\forall S \subseteq \mathbb{R} \setminus \{X_i\}$, s.t. $P(X_i|S, T) = P(S|T)$.
- A hyperparameter X_i is redundant for the target variable T if and only if it is weakly relevant to target variable T and has a Markov blanket, $MB(X_i)$, then it is a subset of the Markov blanket of MB_T.

The categorization of hyperparameters as conditionally independent, strongly relevant, irrelevant, and redundant critically informs their inclusion or exclusion for hyperparameter optimization. Conditionally independent hyperparameters are optimized separately; strongly relevant ones are essential and included for optimal performance, while irrelevant and redundant hyperparameters are excluded to streamline the optimization process and avoid overfitting. This selection strategy allows us to achieve an efficient balance between maximizing model performance and maintaining a concise set of hyperparameters, facilitating a targeted and effective tuning process.

3.3.2. Bayesian Network of Hyperparameters

A Bayesian network for the optimization of the hyperparameters of a deep learning model can be represented as a directed acyclic graph (DAG) $G = (V, E)$, where V is the set of nodes and E is the set of directed edges between these nodes.

Let $H = \{h_1, h_2, \ldots, h_n\}$ be the set of hyperparameters of the deep learning model, such as the learning rate, the number of layers, the number of neurons per layer, the type of activation function, and the dropout rate, where each h_i is a hyperparameter subject to optimization.

Let $M = \{m_1, m_2, \ldots, m_k\}$ represent the set of performance metrics, which are the results measured to evaluate the performance of the model under the configuration defined by H. The optimization process seeks to find an optimal configuration $H^* = \{h_1^*, h_2^*, \ldots, h_n^*\}$ such that the performance metrics in M are optimized (maximized or minimized) according to the specified goals of the model.

Directed edges between nodes signify conditional dependencies. For example, if the performance metric node m_i (e.g., validation accuracy) is conditionally dependent on the hyperparameters' nodes H, then there exists a directed edge from each $h_j \in H$ to m_i.

Strongly relevant hyperparameters are directly linked to the performance metrics nodes with directed edges, indicating a direct influence on the model's output. The network highlights these hyperparameters as critical nodes whose values significantly affect the target metrics, necessitating careful optimization.

The Bayesian network helps with conditional independence through the absence of direct paths between certain hyperparameter nodes when conditioned on other nodes. For example, if the hyperparameter X is conditionally independent of Y given Z, the network will not have a direct edge from X to Y when Z is present, highlighting that X's effect on Y is mediated through Z.

Irrelevant hyperparameters do not have direct or indirect paths to the performance metrics nodes, indicating their lack of influence on the model's outcomes. In the Bayesian network, these hyperparameters might be isolated or only connected to other irrelevant hyperparameters, serving as a visual cue for potential exclusion from the optimization process to simplify the model and reduce computational complexity.

Redundant hyperparameters are represented in the network by their connections to the same performance metrics or strongly relevant hyperparameters as other nodes, indicating overlapping influences. Redundant hyperparameters might form clusters within the network, suggesting areas where simplification could occur without loss of predictive power, as their removal or consolidation can lead to a more streamlined and efficient optimization process.

3.4. Conditional Probability Table

Each node $v_i \in V$ is associated with a probability distribution that quantifies the uncertainty about its values. The conditional probability table (CPT) for a performance metric node m_i, given hyperparameters H, quantifies how hyperparameters influence performance metrics, and can be formally defined as $P(m_i|H)$. For instance, the CPT for the performance metric node quantifying accuracy of classification can be represented as

$$P(\text{Accuracy}|h_1, h_2, \ldots, h_n) = p, \tag{8}$$

where p is the probability of achieving a certain level of accuracy given specific values of the hyperparameters $h_1, h_2, \ldots, h_n$.

CPTs provide the quantitative backbone of a Bayesian network, specifying the probabilities of a node given its parents, thereby encapsulating the strength and nature of the dependencies among variables.

3.4.1. Faithfulness of Bayesian Network

Further, we introduce the faithfulness assumption that asserts that all and only the conditional independencies observed in the data are reflected in the network's structure, meaning that the network's edges (or lack thereof) and the CPTs together accurately model the true underlying probabilistic relationships among the variables, which implies that for a Bayesian network to be faithful to its represented domain, its CPTs must not only be consistent with the observed data but also align with the network's structure in portraying the correct dependencies and independencies.

Assume that G denotes a Bayesian network, and P represents a joint probability distribution through the set of hyperparameters $\mathbb{R}$. So, G is faithful to P if P captures all and only the conditional independencies among the hyperparameters in G. The faithfulness condition, a critical assumption in the construction of Bayesian networks, stipulates that all observed conditional independencies in the data are accurately reflected in the network structure. This condition directly impacts the assessment of conditional dependencies among hyperparameters and performance metrics, ensuring that the relationships modeled in the Bayesian network truly represent the underlying data generation process. When identifying the POMB, the faithfulness condition guarantees that the dependencies and independencies inferred from the network are reliable, thereby enabling a more accurate selection of hyperparameters that are genuinely predictive of model performance without being redundant. By adhering to the faithfulness condition, the process of deriving the POMB becomes more robust and grounded in the actual interactions between hyperparameters and outcomes, leading to an optimization strategy that is both effective and reflective of true data-driven insights.

3.4.2. Pareto Optimal Markov Blanket (POMB)

Before defining the Pareto optimal Markov blanket (POMB), we introduce some necessary concepts:

The Markov blanket of a target variable T, denoted as $MB(T)$, is the minimal subset of hyperparameters in a dataset D such that T is conditionally independent of $D \setminus MB(T)$ given $MB(T)$. Formally, for any hyperparameter $X \in D \setminus MB(T)$,

$$P(T|MB(T), X) = P(T|MB(T)). \tag{9}$$

A hyperparameter set S is Pareto optimal if there exists no other hyperparameter set S' such that S' is strictly better than S in at least one criterion (e.g., relevance to T) without being worse in another (e.g., redundancy).

Now, we are ready to define a Pareto optimal Markov blanket: A Markov blanket $MB(T)$ is Pareto optimal if for every hyperparameter $X \in MB(T)$ and any potential hyperparameter $Y \notin MB(T)$, adding Y to or removing X from $MB(T)$ cannot make $MB(T)$ more predictive of T without increasing the redundancy among the hyperparameters in $MB(T)$. Formally, $MB(T)$ is Pareto optimal if for any $X \in MB(T)$ and any $Y \notin MB(T)$,

$$\nexists MB'(T) : (\text{Pred}(MB'(T), T) > \text{Pred}(MB(T), T)) \wedge (\text{Red}(MB'(T)) \leq \text{Red}(MB(T))), \tag{10}$$

where $\text{Pred}(MB, T)$ measures how well MB predicts T, and $\text{Red}(MB)$ quantifies the redundancy within the hyperparameters in MB.

The evaluation process can be formalized using a multi-objective optimization framework, where we define two objective functions: one for predictive performance (f_{Pred}) and another for redundancy (f_{Red}). The goal is to maximize predictive performance while minimizing redundancy.

3.4.3. Pareto Optimality

Given a Markov blanket $MB(T)$ for a target variable T, we define the following optimization problem:

$$\max \quad f_{\text{perf}}(MB(T)) \tag{11}$$

$$\min \quad f_{\text{red}}(MB(T)) \tag{12}$$

subject to $MB(T) \subseteq \mathcal{H}$, where $\mathcal{H}$ is the set of all possible hyperparameters.

$f_{\text{perf}}(MB(T))$ is the predictive performance metric, which could be precision, F1 score, or any other relevant performance metric; and $f_{\text{red}}(MB(T))$ quantifies the redundancy within the Markov blanket, possibly measured by mutual information or correlation among hyperparameters in $MB(T)$.

Pareto optimality comes into play when selecting the optimal $MB(T)$, where a solution $MB^*(T)$ is Pareto optimal if there does not exist another $MB(T)$ such that

$$f_{\text{perf}}(MB(T)) > f_{\text{perf}}(MB^*(T)) \tag{13}$$

$$f_{\text{red}}(MB(T)) < f_{\text{red}}(MB^*(T)) \tag{14}$$

without worsening the other objective. The collection of all Pareto optimal solutions constitutes the Pareto front, from which the optimal Markov blanket can be selected according to specific criteria or preferences.

3.4.4. Ranking Markov Blankets

Ranking Markov blankets by Pareto optimality criteria within a hyperparameter optimization context involves evaluating each Markov blanket according to multiple objectives, aiming to maximize predictive performance while minimizing redundancy. This approach is rooted in multi-objective optimization, where Pareto optimality provides a framework to navigate trade-offs between competing objectives.

A Markov blanket MB_1 is said to Pareto dominate another MB_2 if and only if MB_1 is not worse than MB_2 in all objectives and strictly better in at least one objective. Formally, given two objectives—predictive performance (f_{perf}) and redundancy (f_{red})—MB_1 dominates MB_2 if $f_{\text{perf}}(MB_1) \geq f_{\text{perf}}(MB_2)$ (higher is better for performance) $f_{\text{red}}(MB_1) \leq f_{\text{red}}(MB_2)$ (lower is better for redundancy) At least one of these inequalities is strict.

The Pareto front consists of all non-dominated Markov blankets. These are the MBs for which no other MB exists that Pareto dominates. The Pareto front represents the set of optimal trade-offs between the objectives, where no single MB is universally best, but each is optimal within the context of a specific balance between performance and redundancy.

Ranking Markov blankets (MBs) by Pareto optimality criteria involves a systematic process that can be detailed as follows:

The Pareto front, $\mathcal{PF}$, is made up of non-dominated MBs. An MB, MB_i, is considered non-dominated if there is no other MB_j such that

$$f_{\text{perf}}(MB_j) \geq f_{\text{perf}}(MB_i) \quad \text{and} \quad f_{\text{red}}(MB_j) \leq f_{\text{red}}(MB_i), \tag{15}$$

with at least one inequality being strict. Here, f_{perf} and f_{red} denote the performance and redundancy metrics, respectively.

Within $\mathcal{PF}$, MBs can be further ranked based on secondary criteria. Let $D(MB_i)$ represent the degree of dominance of MB_i, defined as the number of MBs that MB_i dominates. The secondary ranking can then consider $D(MB_i)$, specific preferences, or additional metrics:

$$\text{Rank}(MB_i) = g(D(MB_i), \text{Preferences}, \text{Additional Metrics}), \tag{16}$$

where g is a function that combines these factors into a comprehensive ranking.

The crowding distance, CD_i, for a MB in a dense region of $\mathcal{PF}$, is used to prefer solutions with a broader spread of trade-offs:

$$CD_i = \sum_{k=1}^{K} \left(f_k^{\text{next}}(MB_i) - f_k^{\text{prev}}(MB_i) \right), \tag{17}$$

where K is the number of objectives, and f_k^{next} and f_k^{prev} are the values of the k-th objective for the next and previous MBs in the ranking, respectively.

The ranking of MBs can be dynamically updated as new data or insights become available. Let $\mathcal{PF}_{\text{new}}$ represent the updated Pareto front, then

$$\mathcal{PF}_{\text{new}} = \text{Update}(\mathcal{PF}, \text{New Data}), \tag{18}$$

where $\text{Update}(\cdot)$ is a function that integrates new candidates into $\mathcal{PF}$ and removes dominated ones.

This approach detailed in Algorithm 1 provides a comprehensive framework for ranking MBs in the context of Pareto optimality, balancing between performance optimization and redundancy minimization.

Ranking by Pareto optimality criteria thus involves not only identifying the set of optimal compromises between competing objectives, but also refining within this set based on broader considerations of diversity, dominance, and specific preferences, which ensures a comprehensive exploration of the hyperparameter space, guiding the selection towards solutions that best balance the inherent trade-offs in model optimization.

3.4.5. POMB Construction Criteria

In addition, we introduce two criteria, V-structures and D-separation, which are used to construct the POMB.

In a faithful Bayesian network, an MB of the target variable T, MB_T, in a set $\mathbb{R}$ is an optimal set of hyperparameters, composed of parents, children, and spouses. All other hyperparameters are not conditionally dependent on the target variable T given MB_T, $\forall X_i \in \mathbb{R} \setminus (MB_T \cup T)$, s.t. $X_i \perp T | MB_T$.

A V-structure in a Bayesian network occurs when two nodes (hyperparameters) have arrows pointing to a common child, but there is no direct edge between the two parent nodes. This structure is crucial for understanding conditional independence and dependence relationships because it can introduce conditional dependencies that are not apparent through direct connections alone. If there is no arrow between hyperparameter X_i and hyperparameter Y_i, and hyperparameter Z_i has two incoming arrows from X_i and Y_i, respectively, then X_i, Z_i, and Y_i form a V-structure $X_i \rightarrow Z_i \leftarrow Y_i$. In the context of a POMB, V-structures can influence the determination of which hyperparameters are part of the Markov blanket. Specifically, the spouse (SP) components of a Markov blanket are identified through V-structures, where the spouses are the other parents of the target variable's children. Understanding and identifying V-structures help in correctly identifying these spouses, ensuring the Markov blanket is accurately defined, which is a step toward achieving Pareto optimality by considering redundancy and relevance of hyperparameters.

Algorithm 1 Ranking Markov blankets by Pareto optimality criteria

```
Input: Set of Markov blankets MBs, performance function f_perf, redundancy function f_red
Output: Ranked list of Markov blankets MBs_ranked
procedure IdentifyParetoFront(MBs)
    Initialize ParetoFront ← ∅
    for each MB_i in MBs do
        Dominated ← False
        for each MB_j in MBs do
            if MB_j Pareto dominates MB_i then
                Dominated ← True
                break
            end if
        end for
        if not Dominated then
            Add MB_i to ParetoFront
        end if
    end for
    return ParetoFront
end procedure
procedure SecondaryRanking(ParetoFront)
    Rank ParetoFront based on secondary criteria (degree of dominance, preferences, etc.)
end procedure
procedure ApplyCrowdingDistance(ParetoFront)
    Calculate crowding distance for each MB in ParetoFront
    Re-rank ParetoFront based on crowding distances
end procedure
procedure IterativeRefinement(MBs_ranked)
    while new data or insights available do
        Update MBs_ranked by adding/removing MBs based on new evaluations
        Re-apply procedures for identifying Pareto Front and ranking
    end while
end procedure
ParetoFront ← IdentifyParetoFront(MBs)
SecondaryRanking(ParetoFront)
ApplyCrowdingDistance(ParetoFront)
MBs_ranked ← IterativeRefinement(ParetoFront)
return MBs_ranked
```

D-separation is a criterion used to decide whether a set of hyperparameters is conditionally independent of another set, given a third set of hyperparameters, within a Bayesian network. It systematically checks for blocked paths (considering chains and colliders) to determine independence. A path D between a hyperparameter X_i and hyperparameter Y_i is D-separated by a set of hyperparameters S if and only if the following:

- D includes a chain $X_i \leftarrow Z_i \rightarrow Y_i$ such that the middle hyperparameter Z_i is in S.
- D includes a collider $X_i \rightarrow Z_i \leftarrow Y_i$ such that the middle hyperparameter Z_i is not in S and none of Z_i's successors are in S.

A hyperparameter set S is said to D-separate X_i and Y_i if and only if S blocks every path D from a hyperparameter X_i to a hyperparameter Y_i. D-separation is indirectly related to the identification of a POMB because it provides a methodological way to verify the conditional independencies within the network. When constructing or analyzing the Markov blanket of a target variable, D-separation can be used to validate whether the selected hyperparameters (forming a potential Markov blanket) indeed render the target variable conditionally independent of all hyperparameters not in the blanket. This validation is essential for ensuring that the identified Markov blanket is minimal and optimal, aligning with the goals of Pareto optimality by not including unnecessary (redundant without adding predictive value) hyperparameters. In achieving a Pareto optimal Markov blanket, one must balance between including relevant hyperparameters (those directly influencing or influenced by the target variable and its spouses via V-structures) and avoiding redundancy (ensuring that the inclusion of any hyperparameter does not unnecessarily duplicate information already captured by the blanket, as can be verified through D-separation).

Pareto optimality emphasizes a balance where no hyperparameter can be added to or removed from the Markov blanket without worsening the balance between relevance (predictive power towards the target variable) and redundancy (overlapping information). D-separation helps ascertain the conditional independencies that justify the exclusion of certain hyperparameters from the Markov blanket, while the understanding of V-structures ensures all relevant direct and indirect (through spouses) influences are considered.

Algorithm 2 outlines a structured procedure to find a POMB for hyperparameter optimization. The algorithm starts by identifying potential Markov blankets for each hyperparameter, considering both direct influences (parents and children) and indirect ones (spouses) found through V-structure detection. Each identified Markov Blanket is then evaluated for its predictive performance and redundancy, using D-separation to ensure that included hyperparameters maintain the target performance metric's conditional independence. The final step involves ranking these Markov blankets by their balance of predictive performance against redundancy, selecting the top-ranked set as the POMB.

Algorithm 2 POMB hyperparameter optimization

Input: Bayesian network $\mathcal{B}$ of hyperparameters $\mathcal{H}$ and performance metrics $\mathcal{P}$
Output: Pareto optimal Markov blanket (POMB) for hyperparameters
procedure IDENTIFYPOMB($\mathcal{B}, \mathcal{H}, \mathcal{P}$)
    Initialize $POMB \leftarrow \emptyset$
    for each hyperparameter $h_i \in \mathcal{H}$ **do**
        Identify $PC(h_i)$ and $SP(h_i)$ using V-Structure detection
        $MB(h_i) \leftarrow PC(h_i) \cup SP(h_i)$
        Evaluate $MB(h_i)$ for predictive performance and redundancy
    end for
    Rank $MB(h_i)$ sets by Pareto optimality criteria
    $POMB \leftarrow$ Select top-ranked Markov blankets
    return $POMB$
end procedure
procedure VSTRUCTUREDETECTION($\mathcal{B}, h_i$)
    // Detect V-structures involving h_i
    Identify child nodes C of h_i
    for each pair (c_j, c_k) in C without a direct link **do**
        if c_j and c_k have a common child c_m **then**
            Report V-structure $h_i \rightarrow c_m \leftarrow h_k$
        end if
    end for
end procedure
procedure EVALUATEMARKOVBLANKET($MB, \mathcal{P}$)
    // Evaluate based on D-separation and performance metrics
    Use D-separation to check conditional independencies within MB
    Assess predictive performance using $\mathcal{P}$
    Calculate redundancy score for hyperparameters in MB
    return Combined evaluation score
end procedure

The identification, evaluation, and selection of the POMB are structured around the principles of Bayesian network analysis. Initially, the algorithm employs V-structure detection to meticulously identify potential hyperparameters that directly or indirectly influence the target performance metric, ensuring the inclusion of all relevant and strongly connected hyperparameters. Subsequently, D-separation is utilized to evaluate the conditional independencies among these hyperparameters, refining the initially identified set by removing any hyperparameters that do not contribute to the predictive power or introduce redundancy, thereby ensuring the Markov blanket's minimality and relevance. The selection of the POMB is then carried out by ranking the refined sets of hyperparameters based on their collective predictiveness and non-redundancy, adhering to Pareto optimality criteria, which systematically balances the trade-off between the complexity of the hyperparameter set and the performance of the model, selecting the optimal set that achieves the best performance without unnecessary complexity. Through these steps, the algorithm navigates the hyperparameter space efficiently, ensuring that the selected POMB is both effective in prediction and efficient in configuration.

3.4.6. Refinement and Validation of Markov Blanket

Algorithm 3 outlines a procedure that explicitly utilizes V-structure detection and D-separation to refine and validate the Markov blanket. The process starts with an initial Markov blanket and refines it by ensuring all relevant hyperparameters involved in V-structures pointing to the target variable are included, and those not contributing to such structures or validated dependencies via D-separation are reconsidered for exclusion. This refinement and validation step is crucial for ensuring that the final Markov blanket accurately captures the essential hyperparameters that influence the target variable's performance, adhering to both the structural integrity of the Bayesian network and the underlying data-driven relationships.

Algorithm 3 Refinement and validation of Markov blanket using V-structure detection and D-separation

```
procedure REFINEANDVALIDATEMB(B, MB(T))
    Input: Bayesian network B, initial Markov blanket MB(T) for target T
    Output: Refined and validated Markov blanket MB_refined(T)
    MB_refined(T) ← MB(T)
                                        ▷ Refine MB using V-structure detection
    for each hyperparameter h_i in MB_refined(T) do
        if h_i is part of a V-structure pointing to T then
            Ensure h_i and its spouses are included in MB_refined(T)
        else
            Remove h_i from MB_refined(T) if it only forms V-structures not pointing to T
        end if
    end for
                                        ▷ Validate MB using D-separation
    for each pair of hyperparameters (h_i, h_j) in MB_refined(T) do
        Identify all paths P between h_i and h_j
        for each path p in P do
            if path p is D-separated by MB_refined(T) \ {h_i, h_j} then
                Path p does not introduce dependency; continue
            else
                Path p introduces dependency; refine MB_refined(T) accordingly
            end if
        end for
    end for
    return MB_refined(T)
end procedure
```

Such V-structure detection helps identify cases where two hyperparameters independently influence a third variable (often a performance metric or another hyperparameter), which can signify a critical interaction that should be preserved in the optimization process. Our approach ensures that hyperparameters involved in V-structures are included in the POMB, as the algorithm acknowledges the importance of these conditional dependencies in predicting the target variable, and this helps with the inclusion of hyperparameters that might otherwise be overlooked if only direct dependencies were considered, thereby enhancing the model's predictive performance by capturing more nuanced interactions within the network.

Confirming D-separation between hyperparameters serves to refine the set of optimal hyperparameters by verifying conditional independencies. If a set of hyperparameters is D-separated from the target variable given another set of hyperparameters, this indicates that the former set does not directly influence the target when the latter set's information is available. Thus, hyperparameters that do not contribute additional predictive power or are conditionally independent of the target variable—given the rest of the selected hyperparameters—can be deemed redundant and excluded from the POMB, which reduces the complexity of the hyperparameter set, ensuring that only the most relevant and nonredundant hyperparameters are retained, which simplifies the model and potentially improves generalization by avoiding overfitting.

3.5. Evaluation Metrics

3.5.1. Evaluation of Image Enhancement Results

In our experiments to measure the performance of the models, we used SSIM (structural similarity index measure), PSNR (peak signal-to-noise ratio) and LPIPS (learned perceptual image patch similarity).

Peak signal-to-noise ratio (PSNR) is a image quality metric, which measures difference in decibels between pixel intensity values. Higher metric value indicates better image quality. However, metric does not reflect perceptual image quality. Metric is defined in Equation (19).

$$PSNR = 10\log_{10}(\frac{255^2}{MSE}), \tag{19}$$

where MSE is the mean squared error or L2 loss defined in Equation (20).

$$MSE = \frac{1}{m * n}\sum_{i=0}^{m-1}\sum_{j=0}^{n-1}[I(i,j) - K(i,j)]^2, \tag{20}$$

where an $m \times n$ sized image I is approximated by image K, and i, j are counters for each image dimension.

Structural similarity index measure (SSIM) is another image quality metric, which focuses on visible structure distortions in the image in three channels: luminance, contrast, and structure, which are measured from mean, standard deviation, and cross-covariance between two images. Metric higher value means images are less different. However, metric as well as PSNR are only considering pixel intensities, which means this metric is not capable to capture perceptual quality. Equation of SSIM is noted in Equation (21), the luminance term in Equation (22), the contrast term in Equation (23), and the structure term in Equation (24).

$$SSIM(x,y) = l(x,y)c(x,y)s(x,y), \tag{21}$$

$$l(x,y) = \frac{2\mu_x\mu_y + C_1}{\mu_x^2 + \mu_y^2 + C_1}, \tag{22}$$

$$c(x,y) = \frac{2\sigma_x\sigma_y + C_2}{\sigma_x^2 + \sigma_y^2 + C_2}, \tag{23}$$

$$s(x,y) = \frac{\sigma_{xy} + C_3}{\sigma_x\sigma_y + C_3}, \tag{24}$$

where μ is the mean, σ is the standard deviation, and σ_{xy} is the cross-covariance of images x and y.

Learned perceptual image patch similarity (LPIPS) is a perceptual image quality metric defined in [69]. It is an extension of feature reconstruction loss first described in [70,71]. The difference between the two is that feature reconstruction loss calculates Euclidean distance, whereas LPIPS calculates the MSE distance between feature maps extracted from two images. Another difference is that LPIPS extracts features from multiple layers, whereas feature reconstruction loss uses only one-layer activations. Feature maps are extracted from layers deeper in the model [72], which capture finer details of the images. Originally, VGG-19 was used to retrieve the features, where the model would be trained on ImageNet [73] dataset. LPIPS metric is defined in Equation (25).

$$LPIPS(x,y) = \frac{1}{m}\sum_{j=1}^{m} MSE(\phi_j(x)_{h,w,c}, \phi_j(y)_{h,w,c}), \tag{25}$$

where m is a number of layers, j is a layer index, x is a generated image, y is a target image, j is a convolution layer, ϕ is a feature map, and h, w, c are image height, width and channel dimensions.

3.5.2. Evaluation of Detection of MCI Task

To evaluate models' performance on detection of MCI task, we utilized widely used metrics such as specificity, sensitivity, and accuracy. Metrics are briefly described in Table 4.

Table 4. Metrics used For detection of MCI task.

Metric	Description	Formula
Accuracy	Sum of number N image predictions, where result is 1 if label and prediction match, and 0 otherwise.	$\frac{1}{N}\sum_{i}^{N} 1(y_i = \hat{y}_i)$ (26)
Specificity	Rate of true negative, which describes the probability that a negative prediction is actually negative.	$\frac{TN}{TN + FP}$ (27)
Sensitivity	Rate of true positive, which describes the probability that a positive prediction is actually positive.	$\frac{TP}{TP + FN}$ (28)

4. Results

4.1. Preparation of Datasets Used for Detection of MCI

For the validation of the methodology in the detection of the MCI task, we used ADNI (Alzheimer's Disease Neuroimaging Initiative) [50] and the Open Access Series of Imaging Studies (OASIS) v4 [74] datasets. We combined both datasets to have a broader spectrum of images in our training and validation sets, and we prepared three datasets out of the combined full dataset. Initially, all datasets were preprocessed with our suggested MRI preprocessing pipeline [25], which included spatial normalization, intensity normalization, and skull stripping. Then, we extracted mid slices (sagittal, coronal and axial) of the brain from each patient, which were resized to 256 × 256 resolution. Dataset descriptions are given below:

1. Only preprocessed with the standard pipeline.
2. Additionally using augmentation techniques—affine transformation, color, brightness and contrast jitter, sharpening, blur and motion blur, Gaussian noise, gamma, and image compression transformations. All of the augmentation techniques used are depicted in Figure 2.

3. Additional to augmentations, before applying augmentation, it super-resolves the preprocessed slices to 1024 × 1024 resolution with the improved super-resolution method. An example of a super-resolved image is depicted in Figure 3.

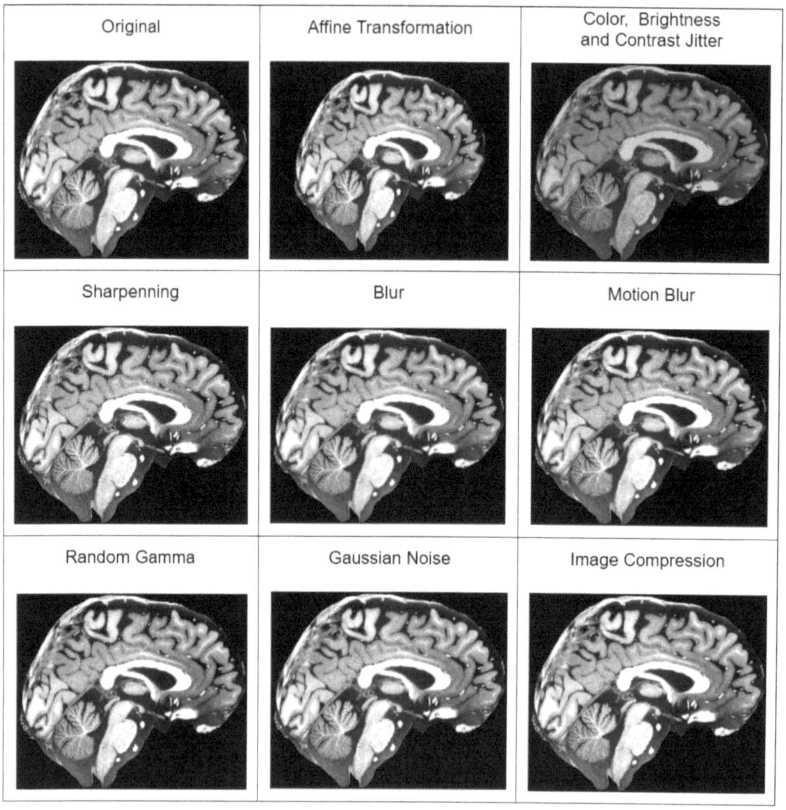

Figure 2. All different augmentation techniques used during training of detection of MCI model. The slice of the brain in this figure is taken from T1w MRI of a healthy 39-year-old male from "human phantom" dataset [52].

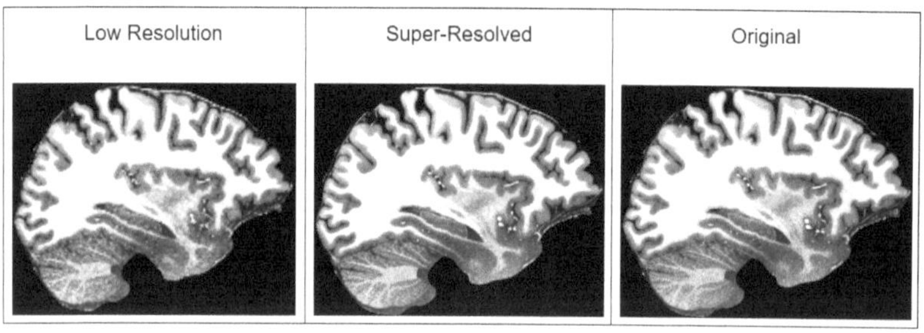

Figure 3. Example of super-resolved low-resolution image with our improved method. The slice of the brain in this figure is taken from T1w MRI of a healthy 39-year-old male from "human phantom" dataset [52].

Each dataset was split in training and validation sets with a proportion of 80/20. Since we only used three slice images of the brain in each plane (sagittal, coronal, axial) for each patient, there was no risk of data leakage. The same patient slices cannot appear in training and in validation.

4.2. Models Used in Detection of MCI

For the model architectures to use in the detection of MCI, we chose some of the state-of-the-art models that are not vision transformers due to the fact that transformers are very resource-hungry. Therefore, all selected models were either based on dense or convolution layers. The evaluated model architectures are listed in Table 5.

Table 5. Model architectures used for detection of MCI task.

Model	Reference	Variations
ConvMixer	[53]	Width = 1536, Depth = 20, Kernel Size = 9, Patch Size = 7.
ResNet	[55]	152.
AlexNet	[75]	No variations.
EfficientNet	[76]	B7.
DenseNet	[77]	201.

4.3. Implementation Details

The training environment is a personal computer with an AMD Ryzen 5900X CPU, RTX 4090 GPU and 32GB RAM.

The super-resolution model was trained with the batch size of 4, cosine annealing learning rate scheduler, 600 k iterations with a minimum learning rate of 1×10^{-7}. The starting learning rate was equal to 1×10^{-4}. For the optimizer, we used Adam with a weight decay of 1×10^{-3}.

The classification model was trained with a batch size of 32, cross-entropy loss for 600 epochs, and an Adam optimizer with fixed learning rate of 2×10^{-5}.

4.4. Results and Discussion of Improved Super-Resolution Method

All of the results that we captured during validation of trained models with different discriminators are listed in Table 6.

Table 6. Objective comparison of models used for discriminator to improve our previous super-resolution HAT model published in [25].

Model	SSIM ↑	PSNR ↑	LPIPS ↓
HAT + ConvMixer1536	88.966	29.621	0.0463
HAT + U-Net 256	88.612	28.809	0.0514
HAT + VGG 256	88.493	28.532	0.0515
HAT + ConvMixer1024	88.695	29.208	0.0519
HAT + U-Net 128 (ours old)	88.585	28.742	0.0529
HAT + VGG 128	88.424	28.366	0.0541
HAT (baseline)	91.406	31.765	0.0984
HAT + ResNet-152	84.460	25.303	0.1189
HAT + ResNext-101	81.170	24.457	0.1883

In Table 6, we can see that the best perceptual quality results are achieved with the ConvMixer1536 model used as discriminator. However, looking at the subjective comparison in Figure 4, it seems that the LPIPS metric does not capture artifacts that are present in images generated by ConvMixer models. Comparing subjectively generated images, images generated using U-Net or VGG are far more close to ground-truth images. This means that LPIPS is unable to correctly quantify perceptual quality of generated images. Similar remarks were made by other researchers, for example, those in [78] (which investigated why artifacts appear and how to reduce them) that all currently used perceptual quality metrics are unable to capture existence of these artifacts in the generated images as a decrease in the metric score.

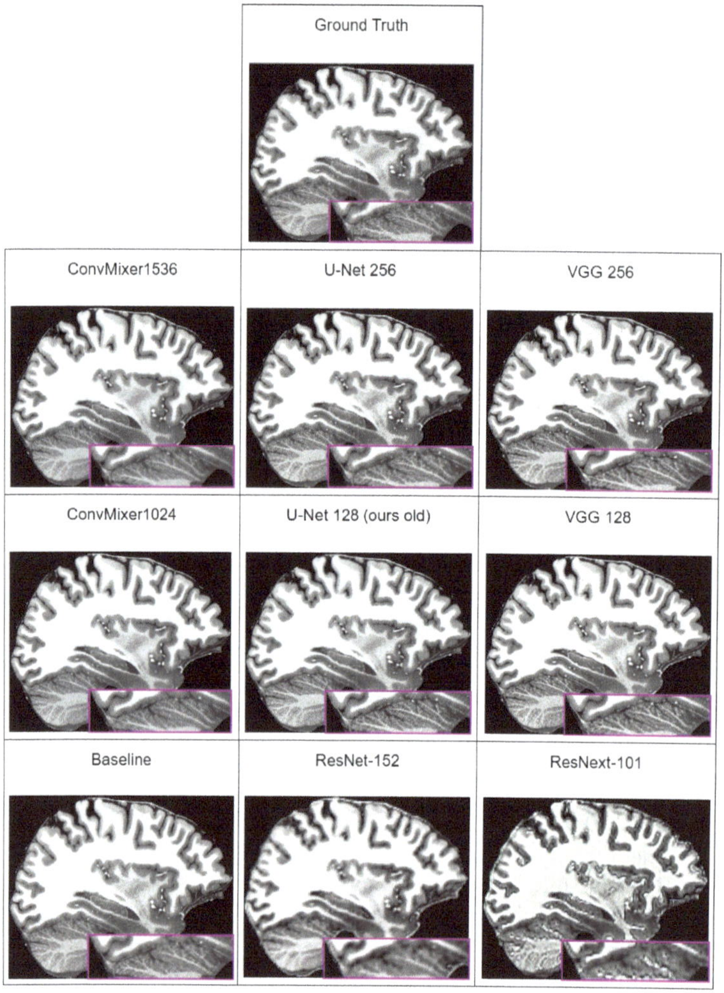

Figure 4. Subjective comparison of super-resolved low-resolution images with our improved method. The ground truth slice of the brain in this figure is taken from MPRAGE T1w MRI that was taken with Siemens 7T Classic MR scanner from "human phantom" dataset [52]. Purple area shows zoomed in section of the brain to better visualize differences between models.

Excluding the fact that LPIPS does not capture artifacts, and therefore, results with ConvMixers are not subjectively best, new methodology improvements increased all of the metric values over the last iteration. The best overall result is achieved with the U-Net discriminator, which uses 256 input features.

4.5. Results and Discussion of Detection of MCI Task

Preparing a third dataset required us to use our new methodology to upscale images into 1024 × 1024 resolution. Initial upscaling finding showed us that we faced a domain shift problem, where our developed model performed poorly on a different dataset used in training. We used the ultra-high-resolution MRI dataset "human phantom" [52]. Our model subjectively was generating good results on the OASIS-4 dataset, but when we tried to run it against ADNI dataset, we found that generated images in some cases contain what we could call "black spot" artifacts Figure 5. This is a typical generalization problem, when the dataset used in real-life usually differs from the one used during training. The best solution in our case is to expose the model to the new data during training using fine-tuning—taking the already-trained model and re-training it with the new data added to the dataset.

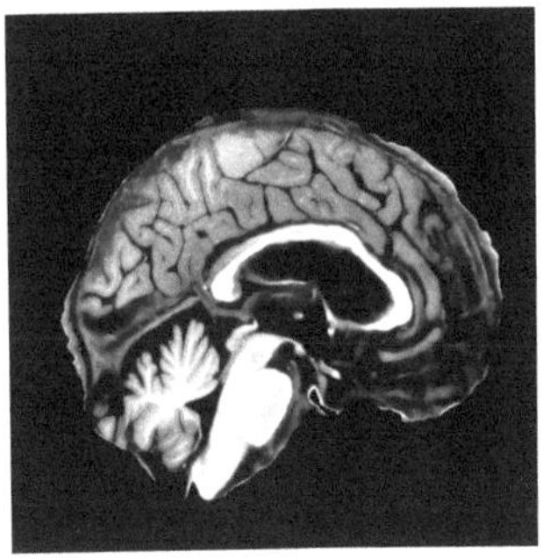

Figure 5. Example of a generated brain image of sagittal plane from ADNI [50] dataset, which contains black spots. The slice of the brain in this figure is taken from MPRAGE T1w MRI, which was taken with 3T MR scanner.

The first step was to upscale all ADNI dataset images and then manually pick those that did not contain "black spot" artifacts, then add those images to the original dataset and fine-tune the already-trained model. After training, the model was able to generate images without "black spot" artifacts.

The second step was to train MCI detection models with three prepared datasets. Validation results are listed in Table 7.

Table 7. Objective comparison of models used for detection of MCI on the first dataset (no augmentation).

Plane	Model	Accuracy	Sensitivity	Specificity
Sagittal	ConvMixer-1536	0.8966	0.8288	0.9641
	AlexNet	0.8876	0.9144	0.8610
	EfficientNet-B7	0.8562	0.8198	0.8923
	ResNet-152	0.8180	0.7117	0.9237
	DenseNet-201	0.7978	0.6261	0.9698
Axial	EfficientNet-B7	0.8899	0.8738	0.9058
	ResNet-152	0.8854	0.8468	0.9238
	AlexNet	0.8539	0.8468	0.8609
	ConvMixer-1536	0.7124	0.5360	0.8878
	DenseNet-201	0.6382	0.3333	0.9417
Coronal	ConvMixer-1536	0.8337	0.7747	0.8923
	ResNet-152	0.8292	0.7072	0.9506
	AlexNet	0.8270	0.8153	0.8385
	EfficientNet-B7	0.8135	0.7027	0.9237
	DenseNet-201	0.7865	0.7387	0.8340

Across a majority of trained models, there were big differences between sensitivity and specificity metrics, which means that models tended to overfit the data. However, in the sagittal and coronal planes, ConvMixer reached the best overall accuracy in the detection of MCI. In the axial plane, the best model was EfficientNet.

The next step was to validate the models against dataset with augmentation techniques. The results are listed in Table 8.

Table 8. Objective comparison of models used for detection of MCI on the second dataset (with augmentation).

Plane	Model	Accuracy	Sensitivity	Specificity
Sagittal	ConvMixer-1536	0.9281	0.8783	0.9775
	EfficientNet-B7	0.9281	0.9369	0.9192
	Resnet-152	0.9236	0.9279	0.9192
	DenseNet-201	0.9101	0.9054	0.9147
	AlexNet	0.8809	0.8603	0.9013
Axial	AlexNet	0.9213	0.9279	0.9147
	ConvMixer-1536	0.9146	0.9730	0.8565
	EfficientNet-B7	0.9146	0.9234	0.9058
	DenseNet-201	0.9079	0.8603	0.9551
	ResNet-152	0.8989	0.9189	0.8789
Coronal	ConvMixer-1536	0.9438	0.9414	0.9461
	ResNet-152	0.9416	0.9820	0.9013
	EfficientNet-B7	0.9371	0.9234	0.9506
	DenseNet-201	0.9101	0.9234	0.8968
	AlexNet	0.9079	0.8513	0.9641

The overall improvement using augmentation was on average around 5%. Here again, ConvMixer showed a lead in the sagittal and coronal planes, whereas on the axial plane, it fell shortly behind AlexNet. The last step to verify the effect of super-resolution on the detection of MCI was to validate models on the third dataset, which used super-resolution and all the augmentation techniques that the second dataset used. The validation results are listed in Table 9.

Table 9. Objective comparison of models used for detection of MCI on the second dataset (with super-resolution and augmentation).

Plane	Model	Accuracy	Sensitivity	Specificity
Sagittal	ResNet-152	0.9371	0.9369	0.9372
	EfficientNet-B7	0.9348	0.9369	0.9327
	ConvMixer-1536	0.9326	0.9459	0.9192
	DenseNet-201	0.9326	0.9369	0.9282
	AlexNet	0.9281	0.9324	0.9237
Axial	EfficientNet-B7	0.9348	0.9549	0.9147
	ConvMixer-1536	0.9326	0.9414	0.9237
	AlexNet	0.9213	0.9099	0.9327
	ResNet-152	0.9213	0.9414	0.9013
	DenseNet-201	0.9191	0.9234	0.9147
Coronal	ResNet-152	0.9573	0.9549	0.9596
	EfficientNet-B7	0.9551	0.9459	0.9641
	ConvMixer-1536	0.9438	0.9414	0.9461
	DenseNet-201	0.9438	0.9324	0.9551
	AlexNet	0.9011	0.8963	0.9058

Comparing results between the second dataset and third, it is obvious that the super-resolution methodology has improved the stability of models, because all models show a small difference between sensitivity and specificity. Additionally, all models across the table show performance improvements of 1–8%, on average 4%, which means that our proposed methodology has a positive effect on the performance of models in the MCI detection task. What is interesting is that in the sagittal and coronal planes with super-resolution, ResNet is showing the best results. This may be due to the fact that the third dataset is using higher-quality images, which yields more features, and it is possible that ResNet residual connections allow the model to retain more important features that are contributing to the accuracy of prediction.

5. Discussion and Conclusions

This study introduces a novel advancement in the detection of mild cognitive impairment (MCI) by applying super-resolution techniques to structural MRI images and optimizing deep learning models using a Pareto optimal Markov blanket (POMB). This approach notably enhances the perceptual quality of MRI images, which subsequently improves the accuracy of various state-of-the-art classifiers in identifying MCI. An improvement in detection accuracy ranging from 1–4% was observed, underscoring the efficacy of super-resolution in enhancing diagnostic models.

The incorporation of a POMB for hyperparameter optimization emerges as a key innovation, streamlining the exploration of complex hyperparameter spaces by focusing on parameters that impact the target variable, either directly or indirectly. This strategy not only accelerates the optimization process but also significantly mitigates the risk of overfitting by ensuring a balance between model complexity and performance. As a result, models demonstrate robustness and generalizability across different datasets, a critical advantage in medical diagnostics.

An important insight from this research is the impact of discriminator choice in generative adversarial network (GAN) setups on the perceptual quality of super-resolved images. The study's comparison reveals that discriminators like VGG and U-Net produce significantly different outcomes, with U-Net marginally superior in PSNR and SSIM metrics. This highlights the profound influence of discriminator selection on both subjective and objective image quality.

A notable discovery pertains to the limitations of the learned perceptual image patch similarity (LPIPS) metric. Despite indicating high perceptual quality for images generated by ConvMixer models, subjective assessments contradicted these findings, revealing poor quality. This discrepancy suggests a pressing need for a new metric capable of accurately detecting "checkerboard" artifacts and properly quantifying perceptual quality differences.

In conclusion, this study advances the field of medical imaging and MCI detection, demonstrating the potent application of super-resolution processing and the crucial role of hyperparameter optimization and discriminator selection in creating accurate and reliable diagnostic models. The findings advocate for ongoing research into more effective perceptual quality metrics, further enhancing the utility of super-resolution in medical diagnostics.

Author Contributions: Conceptualization, R.M.; data curation, O.G.; formal analysis, R.M. and R.D.; funding acquisition, R.D.; investigation, O.G.; methodology, O.G. and R.M.; resources, R.M.; software, O.G.; supervision, R.M.; validation, R.M. and R.D.; visualization, O.G.; writing—original draft, O.G. and R.M.; writing—review and editing, R.D. All authors have read and agreed to the published version of the manuscript.

Funding: This research received no external funding.

Institutional Review Board Statement: Not applicable.

Informed Consent Statement: Not applicable.

Data Availability Statement: We used ADNI (Alzheimer's Disease Neuroimaging Initiative) [50] and the Open Access Series of Imaging Studies (OASIS) v4 [74] datasets, and the "Human Phantom" dataset, available online at https://datadryad.org/stash/dataset/doi:10.5061/dryad.38s74 (accessed on 5 March 2024).

Conflicts of Interest: The authors declare no conflict of interest.

Abbreviations

The following abbreviations are used in this manuscript:

EEG	Electroencephalogram
FDG-PET	Fluoro-deoxy-glucose positron emission tomography
CSF	Cerebrospinal fluid
ROI	Regions of interest
POMB	Pareto optimal Markov blanket
SSIM	Structural similarity index measure
DAG	Directed acyclic graphs
GAN	Generative adversarial network
WGAN	Wasserstein GAN
FFT	Fast Fourier transform
ADNI	Alzheimer's Disease Neuroimaging Initiative
OASIS	Open Access Series of Imaging Studies
PSNR	Peak signal-to-noise ratio
MCI	Mild cognitive impairment
HAT	Hybrid attention transformer
LPIPS	Learned perceptual image patch similarity
HR-MRI-GAN	High-resolution MRI generative adversarial network
CNN	Convolutional neural network
SVM	Support vector machine

References

1. Park, S.; Hong, C.H.; Lee, D.G.; Park, K.; Shin, H. Prospective classification of Alzheimer's disease conversion from mild cognitive impairment. *Neural Netw.* **2023**, *164*, 335–344. [CrossRef] [PubMed]
2. Anderson, N.D. State of the science on mild cognitive impairment (MCI). *CNS Spectrums* **2019**, *24*, 78–87. [CrossRef]
3. Petersen, R.C.; Caracciolo, B.; Brayne, C.; Gauthier, S.; Jelic, V.; Fratiglioni, L. Mild cognitive impairment: a concept in evolution. *J. Intern. Med.* **2014**, *275*, 214–228. [CrossRef] [PubMed]
4. Odusami, M.; Maskeliūnas, R.; Damaševičius, R. Optimized Convolutional Fusion for Multimodal Neuroimaging in Alzheimer's Disease Diagnosis: Enhancing Data Integration and Feature Extraction. *J. Pers. Med.* **2023**, *13*, 1496. [CrossRef] [PubMed]
5. Odusami, M.; Maskeliūnas, R.; Damaševičius, R.; Misra, S. Machine learning with multimodal neuroimaging data to classify stages of Alzheimer's disease: A systematic review and meta-analysis. *Cogn. Neurodyn.* **2023** . [CrossRef]
6. Ramya, J.; Maheswari, B.U.; Rajakumar, M.; Sonia, R. Alzheimer's Disease Segmentation and Classification on MRI Brain Images Using Enhanced Expectation Maximization Adaptive Histogram (EEM-AH) and Machine Learning. *Inf. Technol. Control* **2022**, *51*, 786–800. [CrossRef]
7. Chen, Y.X.; Liang, N.; Li, X.L.; Yang, S.H.; Wang, Y.P.; Shi, N.N. Diagnosis and Treatment for Mild Cognitive Impairment: A Systematic Review of Clinical Practice Guidelines and Consensus Statements. *Front. Neurol.* **2021**, *12*, 719849. [CrossRef] [PubMed]
8. Mitsukura, Y.; Sumali, B.; Watanabe, H.; Ikaga, T.; Nishimura, T. Frontotemporal EEG as potential biomarker for early MCI: A case—Control study. *BMC Psychiatry* **2022**, *22*, 289. [CrossRef]
9. Teng, L.; Li, Y.; Zhao, Y.; Hu, T.; Zhang, Z.; Yao, Z.; Hu, B. Predicting MCI progression with FDG-PET and cognitive scores: A longitudinal study. *BMC Neurol.* **2020**, *20*, 148. [CrossRef]
10. Sonnen, J.A.; Montine, K.S.; Quinn, J.F.; Breitner, J.C.; Montine, T.J. Cerebrospinal Fluid Biomarkers in Mild Cognitive Impairment and Dementia. *J. Alzheimer's Dis.* **2010**, *19*, 301–309. [CrossRef]
11. Ntracha, A.; Iakovakis, D.; Hadjidimitriou, S.; Charisis, V.S.; Tsolaki, M.; Hadjileontiadis, L.J. Detection of Mild Cognitive Impairment through Natural Language and Touchscreen Typing Processing. *Front. Digit. Health* **2020**, *2*, 567158. [CrossRef] [PubMed]
12. Lee, S.N.; Woo, S.H.; Lee, E.J.; Kim, K.K.; Kim, H.R. Association between T1w/T2w ratio in white matter and cognitive function in Alzheimer's disease. *Sci. Rep.* **2024**, *14*, 7228. [CrossRef]
13. Zubrikhina, M.; Abramova, O.; Yarkin, V.; Ushakov, V.; Ochneva, A.; Bernstein, A.; Burnaev, E.; Andreyuk, D.; Savilov, V.; Kurmishev, M.; et al. Machine learning approaches to mild cognitive impairment detection based on structural MRI data and morphometric features. *Cogn. Syst. Res.* **2023**, *78*, 87–95. [CrossRef]
14. Ahmadzadeh, M.; Christie, G.J.; Cosco, T.D.; Arab, A.; Mansouri, M.; Wagner, K.R.; DiPaola, S.; Moreno, S. Neuroimaging and machine learning for studying the pathways from mild cognitive impairment to alzheimer's disease: a systematic review. *BMC Neurol.* **2023**, *23*, 309. [CrossRef] [PubMed]
15. Kung, T.H.; Chao, T.C.; Xie, Y.R.; Pai, M.C.; Kuo, Y.M.; Lee, G.G.C. Neuroimage Biomarker Identification of the Conversion of Mild Cognitive Impairment to Alzheimer's Disease. *Front. Neurosci.* **2021**, *15*, 584641. [CrossRef] [PubMed]

16. Karas, G.; Scheltens, P.; Rombouts, S.; Visser, P.; van Schijndel, R.; Fox, N.; Barkhof, F. Global and local gray matter loss in mild cognitive impairment and Alzheimer's disease. *NeuroImage* **2004**, *23*, 708–716. [CrossRef] [PubMed]
17. Frisoni, G.B.; Fox, N.C.; Jack, C.R.; Scheltens, P.; Thompson, P.M. The clinical use of structural MRI in Alzheimer disease. *Nat. Rev. Neurol.* **2010**, *6*, 67–77. [CrossRef] [PubMed]
18. Bateman, R.J.; Xiong, C.; Benzinger, T.L.; Fagan, A.M.; Goate, A.; Fox, N.C.; Marcus, D.S.; Cairns, N.J.; Xie, X.; Blazey, T.M.; et al. Clinical and Biomarker Changes in Dominantly Inherited Alzheimer's Disease. *N. Engl. J. Med.* **2012**, *367*, 795–804. [CrossRef] [PubMed]
19. Fujita, S.; Mori, S.; Onda, K.; Hanaoka, S.; Nomura, Y.; Nakao, T.; Yoshikawa, T.; Takao, H.; Hayashi, N.; Abe, O. Characterization of Brain Volume Changes in Aging Individuals With Normal Cognition Using Serial Magnetic Resonance Imaging. *JAMA Netw. Open* **2023**, *6*, e2318153. [CrossRef]
20. Chen, C.; Wang, Y.; Zhang, N.; Zhang, Y.; Zhao, Z. A Review of Hyperspectral Image Super-Resolution Based on Deep Learning. *Remote Sens.* **2023**, *15*, 2853, 2853. [CrossRef]
21. Zhao, W.; Zhao, S.; Han, Z.; Ding, X.; Hu, G.; Qu, L.; Huang, Y.; Wang, X.; Mao, H.; Jiu, Y.; et al. Enhanced detection of fluorescence fluctuations for high-throughput super-resolution imaging. *Nat. Photonics* **2023**, *17*, 806–813. [CrossRef]
22. Xiao, Y.; Yuan, Q.; Zhang, Q.; Zhang, L. Deep Blind Super-Resolution for Satellite Video. *IEEE Trans. Geosci. Remote Sens.* **2023**, *61*, 5516316. [CrossRef]
23. Kim, D.; Kim, J.; Park, E. AFA-Net: Adaptive Feature Attention Network in image deblurring and super-resolution for improving license plate recognition. *Comput. Vis. Image Underst.* **2024**, *238*, 103879. [CrossRef]
24. Zhang, R.; Gu, J.; Chen, H.; Dong, C.; Zhang, Y.; Yang, W. Crafting Training Degradation Distribution for the Accuracy-Generalization Trade-off in Real-World Super-Resolution. In Proceedings of the 40th International Conference on Machine Learning, Honolulu, HI, USA, 23–29 July 2023; Volume 202, pp. 41078–41091.
25. Grigas, O.; Maskeliūnas, R.; Damaševičius, R. Improving Structural MRI Preprocessing with Hybrid Transformer GANs. *Life* **2023**, *13*, 1893. [CrossRef] [PubMed]
26. Esteva, A.; Robicquet, A.; Ramsundar, B.; Kuleshov, V.; DePristo, M.; Chou, K.; Cui, C.; Corrado, G.; Thrun, S.; Dean, J. Guide to deep learning in healthcare. *Nat. Med.* **2019**, *25*, 24–29. [CrossRef] [PubMed]
27. Litjens, G.; Kooi, T.; Bejnordi, B.E.; Setio, A.A.A.; Ciompi, F.; Ghafoorian, M.; van der Laak, J.A.; van Ginneken, B.; Sánchez, C.I. A survey on deep learning in medical image analysis. *Med. Image Anal.* **2017**, *42*, 60–88. : 10.1016/j.media.2017.07.005 [CrossRef] [PubMed]
28. Yao, J.; Huang, K.; Zhang, R. A systematic review of deep learning approaches to medical image analysis. *Health Inf. Sci. Syst.* **2018**, *6*, 16. [CrossRef]
29. Bergstra, J.; Bengio, Y. Random Search for Hyper-Parameter Optimization. *Proc. J. Mach. Learn. Res.* **2012**, *13*, 281–305.
30. Koller, D.; Friedman, N. *Probabilistic Graphical Models: Principles and Techniques*; MIT Press: Cambridge, MA, USA, 2009.
31. Heckerman, D.; Geiger, D.; Chickering, D.M. Learning Bayesian Networks: The Combination of Knowledge and Statistical Data. *Proc. Mach. Learn.* **1995**, *20*, 197–243. :1022623210503 [CrossRef]
32. Snoek, J.; Larochelle, H.; Adams, R.P. Practical Bayesian Optimization of Machine Learning Algorithms. In *Advances in Neural Information Processing Systems*; MIT Press: Cambridge, MA, USA, 2012; Volume 25.
33. Bergstra, J.; Bardenet, R.; Bengio, Y.; Kégl, B. Algorithms for Hyper-Parameter Optimization. In *Advances in Neural Information Processing Systems*; MIT Press: Cambridge, MA, USA, 2011; Volume 24.
34. Alwakid, G.; Gouda, W.; Humayun, M. Deep Learning-Based Prediction of Diabetic Retinopathy Using CLAHE and ESRGAN for Enhancement. *Healthcare* **2023**, *11*, 863. [CrossRef]
35. Wang, X.; Yu, K.; Wu, S.; Gu, J.; Liu, Y.; Dong, C.; Loy, C.C.; Qiao, Y.; Tang, X. ESRGAN: Enhanced Super-Resolution Generative Adversarial Networks. *arXiv* **2018**. [CrossRef]
36. Szegedy, C.; Vanhoucke, V.; Ioffe, S.; Shlens, J.; Wojna, Z. Rethinking the Inception Architecture for Computer Vision. *arXiv* **2015**. [CrossRef]
37. Karthik, M.; Sohier, D. APTOS 2019 Blindness Detection. 2019. Available online: https://www.kaggle.com/competitions/aptos2019-blindness-detection/overview (accessed on 10 March 2024).
38. Tan, W.; Liu, P.; Li, X.; Liu, Y.; Zhou, Q.; Chen, C.; Gong, Z.; Yin, X.; Zhang, Y. Classification of COVID-19 pneumonia from chest CT images based on reconstructed super-resolution images and VGG neural network. *Health Inf. Sci. Syst.* **2021**, *9*, 10. [CrossRef] [PubMed]
39. Ledig, C.; Theis, L.; Huszar, F.; Caballero, J.; Cunningham, A.; Acosta, A.; Aitken, A.; Tejani, A.; Totz, J.; Wang, Z.; et al. Photo-Realistic Single Image Super-Resolution Using a Generative Adversarial Network. *arXiv* **2016**. [CrossRef]
40. Simonyan, K.; Zisserman, A. Very Deep Convolutional Networks for Large-Scale Image Recognition. *arXiv* **2014**. [CrossRef]
41. Yang, X.; He, X.; Zhao, J.; Zhang, Y.; Zhang, S.; Xie, P. COVID-CT-Dataset: A CT Scan Dataset about COVID-19. *arXiv* **2020**. [CrossRef]
42. Nagayama, Y.; Emoto, T.; Kato, Y.; Kidoh, M.; Oda, S.; Sakabe, D.; Funama, Y.; Nakaura, T.; Hayashi, H.; Takada, S.; et al. Improving image quality with super-resolution deep-learning-based reconstruction in coronary CT angiography. *Eur. Radiol.* **2023**, *33*, 8488–8500. [CrossRef] [PubMed]
43. Canon Medical. Precise IQ Engine (PIQE): A New Concept in Clarity and Confidence in Cardiac Imaging. 2022. Available online: https://eu.medical.canon/visions-magazine/visionsblog/V38_CTEU220164 (accessed on 10 March 2024).

44. Higaki, T.; Nakamura, Y.; Zhou, J.; Yu, Z.; Nemoto, T.; Tatsugami, F.; Awai, K. Deep Learning Reconstruction at CT: Phantom Study of the Image Characteristics. *Acad. Radiol.* **2020**, *27*, 82–87. [CrossRef] [PubMed]
45. de Farias, E.C.; di Noia, C.; Han, C.; Sala, E.; Castelli, M.; Rundo, L. Impact of GAN-based lesion-focused medical image super-resolution on the robustness of radiomic features. *Sci. Rep.* **2021**, *11*, 21361. [CrossRef]
46. You, C.; Cong, W.; Vannier, M.W.; Saha, P.K.; Hoffman, E.A.; Wang, G.; Li, G.; Zhang, Y.; Zhang, X.; Shan, H.; et al. CT Super-Resolution GAN Constrained by the Identical, Residual, and Cycle Learning Ensemble (GAN-CIRCLE). *IEEE Trans. Med. Imaging* **2020**, *39*, 188–203. [CrossRef]
47. Aerts, H.J.W.L.; Velazquez, E.R.; Leijenaar, R.T.H.; Parmar, C.; Grossmann, P.; Carvalho, S.; Bussink, J.; Monshouwer, R.; Haibe-Kains, B.; Rietveld, D.; et al. Decoding tumour phenotype by noninvasive imaging using a quantitative radiomics approach. *Nat. Commun.* **2014**, *5*, 4006. [CrossRef] [PubMed]
48. Huang, G.; Chen, X.; Shen, Y.; Wang, S., MR Image Super-Resolution Using Wavelet Diffusion for Predicting Alzheimer's Disease. In *Lecture Notes in Computer Science*; Springer Nature: Cham, Switzerland, 2023; pp. 146–157. [CrossRef]
49. Xiao, Z.; Kreis, K.; Vahdat, A. Tackling the Generative Learning Trilemma with Denoising Diffusion GANs. *arXiv* **2021**. [CrossRef]
50. Mueller, S.G.; Weiner, M.W.; Thal, L.J.; Petersen, R.C.; Jack, C.R.; Jagust, W.; Trojanowski, J.Q.; Toga, A.W.; Beckett, L. Ways toward an early diagnosis in Alzheimer's disease: The Alzheimer's Disease Neuroimaging Initiative (ADNI). *Alzheimer's Dement.* **2005**, *1*, 55–66. [CrossRef]
51. Zhang, W.; Basaran, B.; Meng, Q.; Baugh, M.; Stelter, J.; Lung, P.; Patel, U.; Bai, W.; Karampinos, D.; Kainz, B., MoCoSR: Respiratory Motion Correction and Super-Resolution for 3D Abdominal MRI. In *Medical Image Computing and Computer Assisted Intervention – MICCAI 2023*; Springer Nature: Cham, Switzerland, 2023; pp. 121–131. [CrossRef]
52. Lusebrink, F.; Mattern, H.; Yakupov, R.; Acosta-Cabronero, J.; Ashtarayeh, M.; Oeltze-Jafra, S.; Speck, O. Comprehensive ultrahigh resolution whole brain in vivo MRI dataset as a human phantom. *Sci. Data* **2021**, *8*, 138. [CrossRef]
53. Trockman, A.; Kolter, J.Z. Patches Are All You Need? *arXiv* **2022**. [CrossRef]
54. Ronneberger, O.; Fischer, P.; Brox, T. U-Net: Convolutional Networks for Biomedical Image Segmentation. *arXiv* **2015**. [CrossRef]
55. He, K.; Zhang, X.; Ren, S.; Sun, J. Deep Residual Learning for Image Recognition. *arXiv* **2015**. [CrossRef]
56. Xie, S.; Girshick, R.; Dollár, P.; Tu, Z.; He, K. Aggregated Residual Transformations for Deep Neural Networks. *arXiv* **2016**. [CrossRef]
57. Arjovsky, M.; Chintala, S.; Bottou, L. Wasserstein GAN. *arXiv* **2017**. [CrossRef]
58. Wu, B.; Duan, H.; Liu, Z.; Sun, G. SRPGAN: Perceptual generative adversarial network for single image super resolution. *arXiv* **2017**, arXiv:1712.05927.
59. Lai, W.S.; Huang, J.B.; Ahuja, N.; Yang, M.H. Deep Laplacian Pyramid Networks for Fast and Accurate Super-Resolution. In Proceedings of the 2017 IEEE Conference on Computer Vision and Pattern Recognition (CVPR), Honolulu, HI, USA, 21–26 July 2017; IEEE: Piscataway, NJ, USA, 2017. [CrossRef]
60. Anagun, Y.; Isik, S.; Seke, E. SRLibrary: Comparing different loss functions for super-resolution over various convolutional architectures. *J. Vis. Commun. Image Represent.* **2019**, *61*, 178–187. [CrossRef]
61. Lin, Y.; Tan, P.; Li, D.; Wang, X.; Shen, X. An FFT-based beam profile denoising method for beam profile distortion correction. *Nucl. Instruments Methods Phys. Res. Sect. A Accel. Spectrometers Detect. Assoc. Equip.* **2023**, *1047*, 167781. [CrossRef]
62. Liu, J.; Wu, H.; Xie, Y.; Qu, Y.; Ma, L. Trident Dehazing Network. In Proceedings of the 2020 IEEE/CVF Conference on Computer Vision and Pattern Recognition Workshops (CVPRW), Seattle, WA, USA, 14–19 June 2020; IEEE: Piscataway, NJ, USA, 2020. [CrossRef]
63. Kong, L.; Dong, J.; Li, M.; Ge, J.; Pan, J. Efficient Frequency Domain-based Transformers for High-Quality Image Deblurring. *arXiv* **2022**. [CrossRef]
64. Jiang, L.; Dai, B.; Wu, W.; Loy, C.C. Focal Frequency Loss for Image Reconstruction and Synthesis. *arXiv* **2020**. [CrossRef]
65. Zhang, K.; Liang, J.; Van Gool, L.; Timofte, R. Designing a Practical Degradation Model for Deep Blind Image Super-Resolution. *arXiv* **2021**. [CrossRef]
66. Chen, X.; Wang, X.; Zhou, J.; Qiao, Y.; Dong, C. Activating more pixels in image super-resolution Transformer. *arXiv* **2022**, arXiv:2205.04437.
67. Shi, W.; Caballero, J.; Huszár, F.; Totz, J.; Aitken, A.P.; Bishop, R.; Rueckert, D.; Wang, Z. Real-Time Single Image and Video Super-Resolution Using an Efficient Sub-Pixel Convolutional Neural Network. *arXiv* **2016**. [CrossRef]
68. Karras, T.; Aila, T.; Laine, S.; Lehtinen, J. Progressive Growing of GANs for Improved Quality, Stability, and Variation. *arXiv* **2017**. [CrossRef]
69. Zhang, R.; Isola, P.; Efros, A.A.; Shechtman, E.; Wang, O. The Unreasonable Effectiveness of Deep Features as a Perceptual Metric. *arXiv* **2018**. [CrossRef]
70. Gatys, L.A.; Ecker, A.S.; Bethge, M. Texture Synthesis Using Convolutional Neural Networks. *arXiv* **2015**. [CrossRef]
71. Gatys, L.A.; Ecker, A.S.; Bethge, M. A Neural Algorithm of Artistic Style. *arXiv* **2015**. [CrossRef]
72. Zheng, W.; Lu, S.; Yang, Y.; Yin, Z.; Yin, L. Lightweight transformer image feature extraction network. *PeerJ Comput. Sci.* **2024**, *10*, e1755. [CrossRef]
73. Russakovsky, O.; Deng, J.; Su, H.; Krause, J.; Satheesh, S.; Ma, S.; Huang, Z.; Karpathy, A.; Khosla, A.; Bernstein, M.; et al. ImageNet Large Scale Visual Recognition Challenge. *Int. J. Comput. Vis.* **2015**, *115*, 211–252. [CrossRef]

74. Marcus, D.S.; Wang, T.H.; Parker, J.; Csernansky, J.G.; Morris, J.C.; Buckner, R.L. Open Access Series of Imaging Studies (OASIS): Cross-sectional MRI Data in Young, Middle Aged, Nondemented, and Demented Older Adults. *J. Cogn. Neurosci.* **2007**, *19*, 1498–1507. [CrossRef]
75. Krizhevsky, A.; Sutskever, I.; Hinton, G.E. ImageNet classification with deep convolutional neural networks. *Commun. ACM* **2017**, *60*, 84–90. [CrossRef]
76. Tan, M.; Le, Q.V. EfficientNet: Rethinking Model Scaling for Convolutional Neural Networks. *arXiv* **2019**. [CrossRef]
77. Huang, G.; Liu, Z.; van der Maaten, L.; Weinberger, K.Q. Densely Connected Convolutional Networks. *arXiv* **2016**. [CrossRef]
78. Krawczyk, P.; Gaertner, M.; Jansche, A.; Bernthaler, T.; Schneider, G. Artifact generation when using perceptual loss for image deblurring. *TechRxiv* **2023**. [CrossRef]

Disclaimer/Publisher's Note: The statements, opinions and data contained in all publications are solely those of the individual author(s) and contributor(s) and not of MDPI and/or the editor(s). MDPI and/or the editor(s) disclaim responsibility for any injury to people or property resulting from any ideas, methods, instructions or products referred to in the content.

brain sciences

MDPI

Article

Tai Chi Practice Buffers Aging Effects in Functional Brain Connectivity

Jonathan Cerna [1], Prakhar Gupta [2], Maxine He [1], Liran Ziegelman [1], Yang Hu [3] and Manuel E. Hernandez [1,4,5,6,7,*]

1 Neuroscience Program, University of Illinois Urbana-Champaign, Urbana, IL 61801, USA; cerna3@illinois.edu (J.C.); maoyuan2@illinois.edu (M.H.); liran.ziegelman@gmail.com (L.Z.)
2 Department of Electrical and Computer Engineering, University of Illinois Urbana-Champaign, Urbana, IL 61801, USA; prakhar7@illinois.edu
3 Department of Kinesiology, San Jose State University, San Jose, CA 95192, USA; yang.hu@sjsu.edu
4 Department of Biomedical and Translational Sciences, Carle Illinois College of Medicine, University of Illinois Urbana-Champaign, Urbana, IL 61801, USA
5 Department of Kinesiology and Community Health, University of Illinois Urbana-Champaign, Urbana, IL 61801, USA
6 Department of Bioengineering, University of Illinois Urbana-Champaign, Urbana, IL 61801, USA
7 Beckman Institute for Advanced Science and Technology, University of Illinois Urbana-Champaign, Urbana, IL 61801, USA
* Correspondence: mhernand@illinois.edu; Tel.: +1-217-244-8971

Abstract: Tai Chi (TC) practice has been shown to improve both cognitive and physical function in older adults. However, the neural mechanisms underlying the benefits of TC remain unclear. Our primary aims are to explore whether distinct age-related and TC-practice-related relationships can be identified with respect to either temporal or spatial (within/between-network connectivity) differences. This cross-sectional study examined recurrent neural network dynamics, employing an adaptive, data-driven thresholding approach to source-localized resting-state EEG data in order to identify meaningful connections across time-varying graphs, using both temporal and spatial features derived from a hidden Markov model (HMM). Mann–Whitney U tests assessed between-group differences in temporal and spatial features by age and TC practice using either healthy younger adult controls (YACs, $n = 15$), healthy older adult controls (OACs, $n = 15$), or Tai Chi older adult practitioners (TCOAs, $n = 15$). Our results showed that aging is associated with decreased within-network and between-network functional connectivity (FC) across most brain networks. Conversely, TC practice appears to mitigate these age-related declines, showing increased FC within and between networks in older adults who practice TC compared to non-practicing older adults. These findings suggest that TC practice may abate age-related declines in neural network efficiency and stability, highlighting its potential as a non-pharmacological intervention for promoting healthy brain aging. This study furthers the triple-network model, showing that a balancing and reorientation of attention might be engaged not only through higher-order and top-down mechanisms (i.e., FPN/DAN) but also via the coupling of bottom-up, sensory–motor (i.e., SMN/VIN) networks.

Keywords: resting state; electroencephalography; source localization; recurrent neural network dynamics; healthy aging; mind–body practice; Tai Chi

1. Introduction

Given the global socioeconomic challenges posed by an aging population [1,2], there is an urgent need to identify non-pharmacological interventions in order to mitigate age-related multimorbidity and mortality estimates [3]. Aging affects a broad spectrum of functions, including cognition (e.g., executive function, visuospatial processing, memory [4], and fluid intelligence [5,6]) and physical performance (e.g., mobility, agility, strength, and balance [7]). These changes are underpinned by neural factors such as structural [8] and functional [9,10] decline, as well as physical factors like the loss of skeletal muscle mass and mitochondrial capacity [11]. Current trends exacerbate these concerns, as older adults tend to exhibit higher levels of sedentary behavior [12] and lower levels of cognitive engagement [13,14], with research indicating mixed results between different types of sedentary behavior (i.e., passive vs. active) [15] and a heightened risk of cognitive decline [12]. Encouragingly, evidence suggests that physical and cognitive engagement, even when adopted late in life, can have beneficial effects [16–19]. Furthermore, mind–body practices, an umbrella term capturing practices that seek to deliberately integrate the training of the mind and body (e.g., yoga, various forms of meditation, and Tai Chi), have received increasing empirical support as a promising approach to promoting healthy aging and mitigating age-related declines in cognitive and physical function [20–25].

Tai Chi (TC), a mind–body practice steeped in Chinese tradition and philosophy—which is thus culturally rich—has shown preliminary evidence of enhancing cognitive and physical function in older adults [23]. Similar to yoga (and its evidence basis on similar outcomes [26]), TC practice offers a diverse range of approaches to systematically training the mind and body in a holistic fashion. It encourages keen attention while executing slow, deliberate movements that flow in a graceful, dance-like sequence. This mindful movement, combined with controlled breathing exercises and elements of relaxation, makes TC a multi-faceted intervention with the potential to address both cognitive and physical aspects of aging [23,24]. Indeed, mounting evidence suggests that TC might be able to mitigate age-related cognitive [23,27–29] and physical [24] decline. However, the neural basis underlying these salutary effects remains in its infancy.

While the behavioral benefits of TC for older adults are becoming increasingly evident [23,24,28,30–32], the underlying neural mechanisms remain poorly understood [23,25,28]. Traditional neuroimaging approaches have provided valuable insights into brain structure and function with regards to the possible effects of TC practice on brain structure and function [25]. However, these studies often lack the granularity needed to distinguish between the effects of normal aging and those specifically attributable to TC practice. Specifically, there is a tacit assumption in much of the literature that the plasticity induced via TC practice will attenuate aging effects [25,33]. While some morphological findings lend some support to this assumption [25], there is less clarity regarding functional changes [33–35].

Moreover, traditional static approaches often fall short in capturing the dynamic, time-varying nature of neural activity [36,37]. Although various static and dynamic approaches might be able to predict similar outcomes, represent similar information, and consequently offer complementary approaches to studying the brain [38], they also tend to diverge and capture distinctively meaningful patterns [39,40]. Static analyses' primary limitation is their insensitivity to temporal order, meaning that they only provide a snapshot of brain function at a specific moment, potentially overlooking critical temporal fluctuations in neural communication. These fluctuations can be essential for understanding complex neural processes, especially in practices like TC that involve continuous and adaptive interactions between the mind and the body. Dynamic analysis, by contrast, allows researchers to track these temporal changes, offering deeper insights into how such practices may lead to functional improvements in the brain that unravel over time. This limitation is particularly relevant when studying complex mind–body practices like TC, as failing to capture fluctuations in neural communication may cause us to overlook key mechanistic insights into how these practices induce functional changes that result in observable benefits [23,25,28,30,32]. By examining the dynamic nature of whole-brain/network-wide interactions and carefully distinguishing age-related changes from TC-induced effects, we can better understand how TC practice might modulate neural processes and ultimately lead to improved cognitive and physical outcomes in older adults.

It is important to note that the brain likely employs multiple modes of communication [41], including amplitude coupling, phase coupling, and phase–amplitude coupling, among others [42]. Each of these modes can be captured using different metrics, providing insights into various aspects of neural communication. In this study, we chose to focus on amplitude coupling using a neuroelectric analog based on dipole magnitude. This decision was motivated by the prevalence of amplitude-coupling measures in the existing mind–body literature [22,25,26,43,44], allowing for easier comparison across studies. While this approach may not capture all aspects of neural communication, it provides a robust and well-established framework for investigating the effects of TC practice on brain connectivity in older adults [25].

Recent advances in artificial intelligence (AI) offer promising new avenues for neuroimaging analysis, allowing researchers to uncover hidden patterns and temporal dynamics in brain-activity data [39,45]. In particular, unsupervised learning methods have emerged as powerful tools for capturing meaningful fluctuations and connections within these time-varying network configurations [46,47]. When these methods are applied to high-temporal-resolution methods (e.g., magneto-/electroencephalography [M/EEG]), transient brain states and their temporal dynamics can be revealed [48,49], providing a more nuanced understanding of neural activity than traditional static analyses [36]. These advanced techniques not only allow for a more comprehensive examination of brain dynamics but also offer the potential to better differentiate between age-related changes and those specifically induced via TC practice.

In this study, we leveraged an innovative blend of computational approaches to investigate the neural correlates of TC practice in older adults while carefully distinguishing age-related effects from TC-induced changes. We deployed a probabilistic identification of latent brain-state changes via a hidden Markov model (HMM) to extract and explore recurrent neural network dynamics from source-localized, high-density resting-state EEG data. In addition, we thresholded our time-varying graph dynamics using an adaptive, multi-step, data-driven approach that autonomously determines the most appropriate threshold for each network, agnostic to whether weak or strong connections are more relevant, ensuring the retention of statistically significant connections while minimizing spurious links. This decision was prompted by literature that acknowledges the importance of weak connections in neural information processing [50] and cognitive function [51]. In other words, this approach enhanced the robustness of our network analysis by preserving meaningful connections based on their relative importance within the network structure, rather than their absolute strength.

Our primary aims are to explore whether distinct age-related and TC-practice-related relationships can be identified with respect to either temporal or spatial (within/between-network connectivity) differences using features derived from an HMM using source-localized, resting-state EEG data. We hypothesized that aging would be associated with decreased within- and between-network connectivity, while TC practice would partially mitigate these changes, particularly in networks associated with attention, affect, self-related processing, and motor control. We remained agnostic as to what differences would be observed in temporal features, given the paucity of research showing differences based on age or TC practice. By employing this novel analytical approach, we sought to provide a more nuanced understanding of how TC practice might modulate brain function in older adults, potentially informing future interventions aimed at promoting healthy brain aging.

2. Materials and Methods

2.1. Subjects

This cross-sectional study recruited community-dwelling adults (healthy younger adult controls [YACs], $n = 15$; healthy older adult controls [OACs], $n = 15$; and Tai Chi older adult practitioners (TCOAs), $n = 15$) for a single-session experiment. The inclusion criteria were as follows: right-handedness; young adults aged 18–30 and older adults over 65; the absence of acute or chronic neurological disorders such as Parkinson's disease, Huntington's disease, stroke, epilepsy, and seizures; and no severe heart conditions, including heart attack, heart failure, and angina. Further, the following inclusion criteria were applied to select TC practitioners: (1) currently practicing TC (Y/N) and (2) having practiced TC for at least two hours a week in the past 16 weeks (Y/N). Subsequently, accumulated practice hours were derived from the following questions: (3) "How long have you practiced Tai Chi? in weeks or years." and (4) "Currently, on average, how many hours do you practice Tai Chi every week?". From these questions, accumulated practice hours were calculated as follows: total accumulated practice hours = weeks × hours per week. Participants were excluded if they had a cognitive impairment (TICS-M score < 18), a physical disability or the inability to walk independently without an assistive device, or severe chronic pain that limited their physical function. For more details about the demographic information of our cohort, please see Table 1. After providing written, informed consent, the participants were asked to stand as still as possible for 1 min with their eyes closed and for 1 min with their eyes open while high-density EEG data were collected in a controlled laboratory environment that provided a consistent (21.1–21.6 °C) temperature and lighting at approximately 1/3 the level of a typical office, ~150 lux. The study protocol and procedures were approved by the Institutional Review Board of the University of Illinois Urbana-Champaign.

Table 1. Participants' demographic characteristics.

Group	N	Sex (% F)	BMI	Age	Accumulated Practice Hours
YACs	15	20.0%	23.8 ± 5.1	21.5 ± 2.33	
OACS	15	20.0%	24.9 ± 4.9	72.9 ± 4.83	
TCOAs	15	22.2%	22.9 ± 3.0	76.7 ± 5.62	1559 (4 yrs and 3 m) ± 1288 (3 yrs and 6 m)

All values reported represent means ± standard deviations; OACs = older adult controls; YACs = younger adult controls; TCOAs = Tai Chi older adult practitioners. Accumulated practice hours = weeks × hours per week.

2.2. EEG Acquisition and Preprocessing

Please refer to Figure 1 for a visual summary of the entire pipeline outline below. EEG data were recorded using a 64-channel (Ag/AgCl electrode material) active system (ActiCHamp system, Brain Vision LLC, Morrisville, NC, USA) and a sampling rate of 1 kHz. The sensor placement was based on the 10-10 international system. The ground electrode was initially set to the left mastoid, though it is worth noting that, during this period, the lab's data-collection methods varied between using only the left mastoid and using an average of both the left and right mastoids. To ensure consistency across the entire dataset, the data were re-referenced to a common average. Inter-electrode impedance was kept below a threshold of 15 kΩ. To account for eye blinks, electrooculographic activity was captured using two horizontally-placed electrodes in line with the outer canthus of both eyes and a vertically placed electrode below the right orbit.

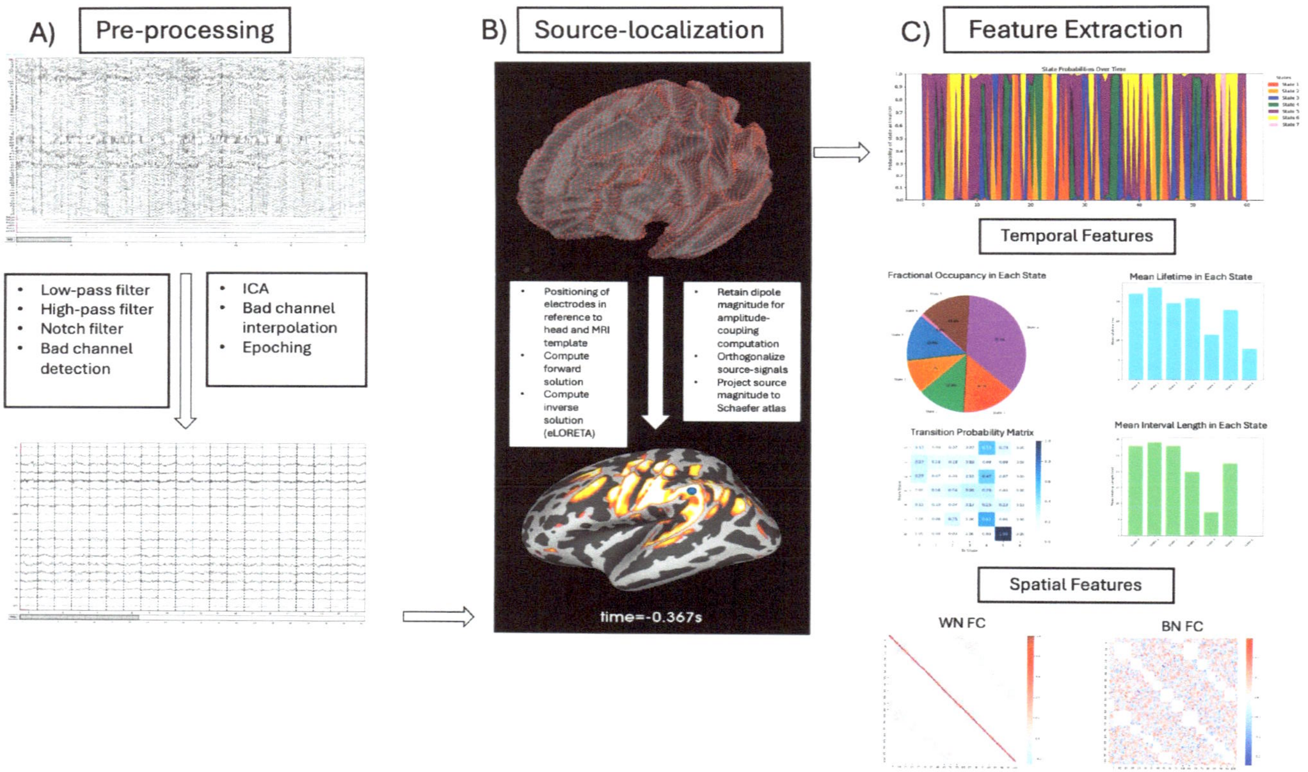

Figure 1. A summary of the processing pipeline used. Panel (**A**) depicts the process through which raw data were pre-processed and prepared for source localization; Panel (**B**) displays the MRI template used for source localization, and it summarizes the processes through which the EEG signal underwent source reconstruction/localization; Panel (**C**) shows a hidden Markov model from which temporal and spatial features were extracted. WN = within network; BN = between network; FC = functional connectivity.

Raw data were loaded into MNE-Python (Python version: 3.10.11; MNE version: 1.6.1) for further processing. A 50-Hz low-pass filter, a 1-Hz high-pass filter, and a notch filter to remove power-line noise at 60 Hz and its harmonics were applied. Bad channels (i.e., channels with excessive drift, with flat or excessive amplitude deflections, etc.) were visually identified, marked, and saved for further processing. Independent component analysis (ICA) was performed on the EEG data to identify and remove artifacts using MNE-ICALabel [52] (for a detailed breakdown of the methodology used in ICALabel, please see Pion-Tonachini et al., 2019 [53]). Before ICA fitting, the data were referenced to a common average. A lower bound for the component number used to fit the ICA was determined by fitting the data to a principal component analysis (PCA), and it was determined to be 15. An upper bound was determined via explained variance, and it was set to 99%. After ICA components were automatically labeled using 1 of 7 categories (i.e., brain, muscle, eye, heart, line noise, channel noise, and other), components were plotted and inspected using time series, an activity-power spectrum, and topographies. Only the "brain" and "other" categories with a predicted probability of >70% were considered for signal reconstruction. Automatic component labeling was revised by trained researchers (i.e., J.C. and M.H.) and corrected as needed. Subsequently, bad channels were interpolated using the interpolate_bads function in MNE, which uses a spherical spline method, projecting the sensor location onto a unit sphere and interpolating the "bad" signal(s) based on the signal at the "good" locations [54]. Interpolated EEG data were epoched into 1-s segments. After z-score normalization, a window-to-window threshold of 6 standard deviations was set to remove unusually high amplitude values. Finally, the preprocessed EEG data were saved for further analysis.

2.3. Source Reconstruction, Parcellation, and Source-Leakage Correction

A custom EEG montage was loaded and adjusted to match the electrode locations of the MRI template used. Specifically, the FreeSurfer average template brain—based on a combination of 40 MRI scans of real brains from healthy adults—was used. To ensure alignment between EEG sensors and the MRI head model, a 3D model was plotted. First, the forward solution was computed, creating a model of how the EEG signals are distributed in the brain, given the electrode locations. Assumptions for the forward model computation included the boundary-element method using a 5120 × 5120 × 5120 volume-conductor model (i.e., brain, skull, and scalp), a minimum distance from the inner skull surface of 5 mm, and a default transformation matrix and source-space estimates. Following forward solution computations, a minimum-norm inverse method was used. An inverse operator was created using the forward model and noise covariance matrix with depth weighting and a loose dipole orientation. Exact low-resolution electromagnetic tomography (eLORETA) [55] was then applied, for which the dipole orientation was discarded and only dipole-magnitude information was retained.

The inverse solution files were utilized in conjunction with a specific brain atlas—the Schaefer atlas with 100 parcels divided into 7 networks [56] (i.e., visual [VIN], somatomotor [SMN], dorsal attention [DAN], ventral attention [VAN], limbic [LIN], frontoparietal [FPN], and default mode network [DMN])—to parcellate brain activity into distinct groups of brain regions with similar network organization to other commonly used atlases (e.g., Yeo's 7-network atlas [57]). This approach facilitates the grouping of source-space EEG data into anatomically and functionally relevant areas, as defined by the atlas. Following the extraction of inverse solutions for each hemisphere and epoch, these were then batch-processed to align with the parcels of the chosen atlas. For both hemispheres, the source estimates were loaded in manageable batches to ensure computational efficiency. The source-estimate files were read sequentially, and their respective time courses were mapped onto the 100-parcel Schaefer atlas. By employing the extract_label_time_course method, the mean activity within each parcel was computed, with careful consideration given to flipping the sign of the time-course data in a manner consistent with the dominant direction of the underlying source space. This step not only ensures that the extracted signal reflects the true neural activity but also corrects for potential source leakage—whereby signals from neighboring regions may contaminate the activity of a given parcel.

Following the initial extraction of the label time courses from the source estimates, the data underwent down-sampling to align with a target frequency of 250 Hz using an anti-aliasing, low-pass filter to prevent the introduction of artifacts. Further, a Hilbert transform was applied to extract the amplitude envelope, representing the instantaneous amplitude of the EEG signal within each parcel. The orthogonalization of the analytic signal's amplitude envelopes was achieved using QR decomposition. Due to the potential for high correlation between neural signals, the QR decomposition algorithm inherently provides a degree of regularization, enhancing numerical stability during the orthogonalization process. If any label pairs were found to be collinear—indicating that source leakage was present—the orthogonalization process aimed to rectify this by creating a set of signals that are orthogonal, meaning they are statistically independent of one another. The procedure used was "symmetric orthogonalization", ensuring that the contribution from one parcel did not erroneously appear in another due to source leakage. This ensured the generation of robust and truly orthogonal components, serving as a solid foundation for subsequent analyses of network dynamics and functional connectivity (FC) [58,59].

2.4. Hidden-Markov-Model-Derived Recurrent State Dynamics

In this study, a hidden Markov model (HMM) was used to identify discrete, recurrent states within EEG source-localized data. This approach rests on the premise that EEG time-series data can be abstracted into a finite sequence of hidden states, each representing distinct patterns of brain connectivity that reoccur over time. HMMs require an a priori selection of states, often named K, to balance model complexity and fit. Previous studies have used either (1) a variational Bayes approach, which approximates the posterior distribution over model parameters and the optimal number of states by minimizing the Kullback–Leibler divergence between the variational distribution and the true posterior distribution [46,48,60,61] or (2) the a priori selection of states with replication to ensure consistent results [62,63].

To determine the optimal number of states, the variance of the orthogonalized data features was computed, and a small fraction of the maximum variance was set as a lower limit to ensure numerical stability. The data underwent PCA for dimensionality reduction to enhance computational efficiency, retaining 95% of the variance. A range of potential states, informed by the previously cited literature, was explored using the Akaike information criterion (AIC) and Bayesian information criterion (BIC) to balance model complexity and fit. The search was repeated for each participant, and the average between AIC and BIC was used to determine the optimal state number for HMM fitting across all participants. The exploration revealed an optimal state count of ~7 for the eyes-closed and eyes-open conditions. These results are consistent with previous EEG and MEG studies using an HMM in which state numbers ranged between 3 and 16 states [48,49,60–66].

To elucidate the dynamic nature of the EEG-derived brain states, we computed several temporal and spatial features from the HMM state sequences. The temporal features included the fractional occupancy, mean lifetime, and mean interval length for each identified state, as well as the transition probability between states. Fractional occupancy quantified the proportion of the total observation time each state occupied, offering insights into the predominance of each state. The mean lifetime, or dwell time, was calculated as the average duration a sequence remained in a particular state before transitioning, reflecting the stability of the state. The mean interval length provided an average measure of the temporal gaps between consecutive appearances of a state, highlighting the recurrence rate of each state. Lastly, transition probability leveraged state-sequence information to calculate the likelihood of transitioning from one state to another (as well as including self-transition probability).

Spatial variables were extracted for each hidden state by computing FC features within and between predefined neural networks. These analyses were predicated on amplitude-coupling correlation matrices derived for each HMM state. Importantly, while the initial data were epoched into 1-s windows, the HMM's state identification process effectively re-windowed the data based on the duration of each identified state. This means that the FC matrices were computed over time windows defined by the duration of each state, not the original 1-s epochs. Within-network connectivity was then calculated by averaging the functional connections among regions within the same network for each state-defined window. Similarly, between-network connectivity was calculated by averaging connections between regions belonging to different networks for each state-defined window. Lastly, to consider the potential influence of changes in FC during state transitions, within- and between-network transition magnitudes were calculated by extracting the difference in FC between consecutive states, weighted by the probability of transitioning between those states. The extraction of these spatial features, rooted in the HMM-derived state durations, allows for a more nuanced understanding of how different brain regions dynamically interact within and across distinct functional networks during specific brain states and while transitioning between them, shedding light on the underlying recurrent neural network dynamics.

2.5. Adaptive Thresholding of Neural Network Graphs

Seeking to identify spurious weak and strong connections, an adaptive thresholding approach was deployed that incorporated (1) edge-weight aggregation, (2) bootstrapping, (3) determination, and (4) the application of an optimal α filter. Each step was as follows:

$$\text{Edge weight aggregation}: \; W = U_{G_i \in G}\left\{ W_{jk} \middle| \left(j,\, k, W_{jk}\right) \in E(G_i) \right\}$$

(1) Where G is the set of all windowed graphs, G_i is a single windowed graph from this set, $E(G_i)$ represents the set of edges in G_i, and W_{jk} is the weight of an edge between nodes j and k.

$$\text{Bootstrapping}: \; W = \{w_1,\, w_2 \cdots w_n\}\,;\; B_i = \{w'_1,\, w'_2 \cdots w'_n\}\; for\; i = 1, 2 \cdots num\; iterations$$

(2) Let W be the set of all aggregated edge weights from the windowed graphs, where n is the total number of aggregated edge weights. For each bootstrap iteration, i, a bootstrap sample, B_i, is created by randomly sampling N weights from W with replacement. Last, the median (M) is taken, and it serves as a statistically robust measure of the central tendency of the edge weights. The number of iterations for the bootstrapping was set to 10,000 to strike a balance between robustness and computational feasibility.

$$\text{Computing } \alpha_{optimal} \text{ iteratively}: \; \alpha_{optimal} = argmin(\alpha \in [\alpha_{start},\, \alpha_{end}] | abs(diff(mean(C_w(G_{filtered}(\alpha)),\; for\; all\; windows\; w)))).$$

(3) First, correlation matrices were converted to NetworkX graphs. Subsequently, the optimal α filter was determined by evaluating a range of α values and selecting the one that minimized the absolute difference in average connectivity across the filtered graphs. To minimize the search space and thus reduce the search time, a golden-section algorithm was implemented to find the $\alpha_{optimal}$. The golden-section search algorithm is a technique for finding the minimum (or maximum) of a unimodal function by successively narrowing the range of values inside which the extremum is known to exist. It works by dividing the interval and evaluating the function at two points, c and d, which are determined by the golden ratio. If $f(c) < f(d)$, the search interval becomes $[a, d]$; otherwise, it becomes $[c, b]$. This process iterates until the interval is sufficiently small. The optimal α was determined as follows: Let $[\alpha_{start},\, \alpha_{end}]$ be the range of α values to be tested (for us $\alpha_{start} = 0.001$, $\alpha_{end} = 0.10$), and let $G_{filtered}(\alpha)$ be the graph filtered using a given α value. For each window w, the mean connectivity $C_w\left(G_{filtered}(\alpha)\right)$ of the filtered graph is calculated.

$$\text{Application of } \alpha \text{ filter}: G_{filtered} = \left\{(u,v) \in E \middle| (w(u,v)/M)^2 / \sum(w(u,k)/M)\right\}^2 \geq \alpha, k \in V, (u,k) \in E$$

(4) To pinpoint meaningful connections within the network, the algorithm employs a disparity filter by evaluating a spectrum of alpha thresholds. Each edge's weight is normalized against the median derived from bootstrapped samples, ensuring uniformity in edge-weight distribution. The disparity filter then examines the relative contribution of an edge's weight to the total weight of connections for a given node. This approach allows for the identification of significant connections by applying a thresholding operation through which an edge is retained if its normalized weight's square, when compared to the sum of squares of all connected edges to that node, meets or exceeds the alpha threshold. Consequently, this method adeptly discerns vital connections, whether inherently weak or strong, by assessing their significance in the context of the node's overall connectivity. The optimal alpha threshold is chosen at the point where the difference in average FC between the input graphs stabilizes or is minimal, ensuring that only connections with substantial relative contributions are preserved and enhancing the network analysis's fidelity. Finally, this optimal threshold is then applied across the dataset, refining the network representation for subsequent analyses.

2.6. Statistical Analyses

Based on limited literature using similar approaches [35], we anticipated a large effect size (rank biserial r $\approx$ 0.75). To achieve 95% power with α = 0.05, a total sample size of 42 participants was needed (computed using G*Power, version 3.1.9.7). Trending significance ($p \leq 0.10$) was also reported. All analyses were conducted using Python (version 3.10.11). Mann–Whitney U tests assessed between-group differences in temporal and spatial features by age and TC practice, with FDR correction for Type 1 errors. Groups were strictly separated to avoid estimate inflation from repeated observations (age effects: OACs vs. YACs; practice effects: OACs vs. TCOAs). Data normality was assessed using the Shapiro–Wilk test, Q–Q plots, histograms, and boxplots. Homoscedasticity was assessed using Levene's test and scatterplots. Normality and variance tests were performed on original variables and residual/predictor plots. A two-tailed approach with α = 0.05 determined statistical significance. Outliers were identified using z-scores and IQR-based rules and qualitatively examined to decide on exclusion or transformation. All scripts generated for this manuscript can be found at the following link: https://github.com/cernajonathan15/Tai-Chi-Practice-Buffers-Aging-Effects-in-Functional-Brain-Connectivity-/tree/5ff84a08d52a5506b09506c66d1239116a6db8eb/Manuscript%20Scripts (accessed on 30 June 2024).

3. Results

Age effects: The analysis showed significant age-related differences in both within-network and between-network mean connectivity. All networks, except for the LIN, had significantly lower within-network FC in older adults, with only the DMN, VAN, and VIN surviving FDR correction. Similarly, all network pairs had significantly lower FC in older adults compared to younger adults, even after FDR correction. Older adults also showed a trend towards a greater between-network transition magnitude for the DAN-LIN, though it did not survive FDR correction, possibly indicating a greater FC needed for equal communication. For detailed within-network and between-network mean connectivity results, see Tables 2 and 3.

Table 2. Within-network mean connectivity differences based on age and practice.

Older Adults	Younger Adults	Dependent Variables	Median1	Median2	Median Diff	U-Statistic	p-Value	FDR-Adjusted p-Value	Rank Biserial Correlation (r)
OACs vs. YACs		DMN	0.054	0.060	−0.006	49	8.97×10^{-3} *	2.38×10^{-2} *	−0.56
		DAN	0.053	0.058	−0.005	59	2.79×10^{-2} *	6.55×10^{-2}	−0.48
		FPN	0.055	0.060	−0.005	61	3.44×10^{-2} *	7.77×10^{-2}	−0.46
		LIN	0.055	0.060	−0.005	82	2.13×10^{-1} *	3.72×10^{-1}	−0.27
		SMN	0.055	0.059	−0.004	57	2.25×10^{-2} *	5.50×10^{-2}	−0.49
		VAN	0.054	0.059	−0.005	49	8.97×10^{-3} *	2.38×10^{-2} *	−0.56
		VIN	0.054	0.060	−0.007	52	1.28×10^{-2} *	3.26×10^{-2} *	−0.54
No Practice	**Practice**	**Dependent Variables**	**Median1**	**Median2**	**Median Diff**	**U-Statistic**	**p-Value**	**FDR-Adjusted p-Value**	**Rank Biserial Correlation (r)**
OACs vs. TCOAs		DMN	0.054	0.069	−0.015	13	4.02×10^{-5} *	1.40×10^{-4}	−0.88
		DAN	0.053	0.069	−0.015	26	3.61×10^{-4} *	9.17×10^{-4} *	−0.77
		FPN	0.055	0.070	−0.014	27	4.22×10^{-4} *	1.03×10^{-3} *	−0.76
		LIN	0.055	0.070	−0.015	37	1.87×10^{-3} *	4.06×10^{-3} *	−0.67
		SMN	0.055	0.069	−0.014	25	3.08×10^{-4} *	8.17×10^{-4} *	−0.78
		VAN	0.054	0.069	−0.015	30	6.71×10^{-4} *	1.52×10^{-3} *	−0.73
		VIN	0.054	0.069	−0.015	30	6.71×10^{-4} *	1.52×10^{-3} *	−0.73

Within-network comparisons by age: OACs vs. YACs and practice OACs vs. TCOAs. *, $p < 0.05$. OACs = older adult controls; YACs = younger adult controls; TCOAs = Tai Chi older adult practitioners; DMN = default mode network; DAN = dorsal attention network; FPN = frontoparietal network; LIN = limbic network; SMN = somatomotor network; VAN = ventral attention network; VIN = visual network.

Table 3. Between-network mean connectivity differences based on age and practice.

Older Adults	Younger Adults	Dependent Variables	Median1	Median2	Median Diff	U-Statistic	*p*-Value	FDR-Adjusted *p*-Value	Rank Biserial Correlation (r)
OACs vs. YACs		DAN-DMN	0.054	0.061	−0.0069	40	2.82×10^{-3} *	1.31×10^{-2} *	−0.64
		DAN-FPN	0.053	0.063	−0.0102	39	2.46×10^{-3} *	1.31×10^{-2} *	−0.65
		DAN-LIN	0.054	0.065	−0.0118	36	1.62×10^{-3} *	1.31×10^{-2} *	−0.68
		DAN-VAN	0.053	0.061	−0.0077	36	1.62×10^{-3} *	1.31×10^{-2} *	−0.68
		FPN-DMN	0.053	0.061	−0.0073	46	6.19×10^{-3} *	1.89×10^{-2} *	−0.59
		LIN-DMN	0.054	0.063	−0.0096	44	4.79×10^{-3} *	1.72×10^{-2} *	−0.61
		LIN-FPN	0.053	0.067	−0.0140	46	6.19×10^{-3} *	1.89×10^{-2} *	−0.59
		SMN-DMN	0.053	0.061	−0.0078	40	2.82×10^{-3} *	1.31×10^{-2} *	−0.64
		SMN-DAN	0.052	0.062	−0.0100	36	1.62×10^{-3} *	1.31×10^{-2} *	−0.68
		SMN-FPN	0.053	0.062	−0.0086	40	2.82×10^{-3} *	1.31×10^{-2} *	−0.64
		SMN-LIN	0.054	0.062	−0.0080	35	1.40×10^{-3} *	1.31×10^{-2} *	−0.69
		SMN-VAN	0.053	0.061	−0.0081	39	2.46×10^{-3} *	1.31×10^{-2} *	−0.65
		VAN-DMN	0.054	0.060	−0.0062	47	7.02×10^{-3} *	2.04×10^{-2} *	−0.58
		VAN-FPN	0.053	0.061	−0.0075	45	5.45×10^{-3} *	1.85×10^{-2} *	−0.60
		VAN-LIN	0.053	0.061	−0.0079	36	1.62×10^{-3} *	1.31×10^{-2} *	−0.68
		VIN-DMN	0.053	0.061	−0.0080	41	3.23×10^{-3} *	1.31×10^{-2} *	−0.64
		VIN-DAN	0.053	0.060	−0.0073	36	1.62×10^{-3} *	1.31×10^{-2} *	−0.68

Table 3. *Cont.*

Older Adults	Younger Adults	Dependent Variables	Median1	Median2	Median Diff	U-Statistic	p-Value	FDR-Adjusted p-Value	Rank Biserial Correlation (r)
OACs vs. YACs		VIN-FPN	0.054	0.064	−0.0101	37	1.87×10^{-3} *	1.31×10^{-2} *	−0.67
		VIN-LIN	0.054	0.065	−0.0109	44	4.79×10^{-3} *	1.72×10^{-2} *	−0.61
		VIN-SMN	0.053	0.062	−0.0092	34	1.22×10^{-3} *	1.31×10^{-2} *	−0.70
		VIN-VAN	0.053	0.061	−0.0084	41	3.23×10^{-3} *	1.31×10^{-2} *	−0.64
OACs vs. TCOAs		DAN-DMN	0.054	0.069	−0.015	13	4.02×10^{-5} *	1.40×10^{-4} *	−0.88
		DAN-FPN	0.053	0.068	−0.015	11	2.80×10^{-5} *	1.40×10^{-4} *	−0.90
		DAN-LIN	0.054	0.069	−0.015	12	3.36×10^{-5} *	1.40×10^{-4} *	−0.89
		DAN-VAN	0.053	0.069	−0.016	14	4.81×10^{-5} *	1.40×10^{-4} *	−0.88
		FPN-DMN	0.053	0.069	−0.016	14	4.81×10^{-5} *	1.40×10^{-4} *	−0.88
		LIN-DMN	0.054	0.069	−0.015	11	2.80×10^{-5} *	1.40×10^{-4} *	−0.90
		LIN-FPN	0.053	0.069	−0.015	14	4.81×10^{-5} *	1.40×10^{-4} *	−0.88
		SMN-DMN	0.053	0.070	−0.016	13	4.02×10^{-5} *	1.40×10^{-4} *	−0.88
		SMN-DAN	0.052	0.070	−0.017	11	2.80×10^{-5} *	1.40×10^{-4} *	−0.90
		SMN-FPN	0.053	0.069	−0.016	12	3.36×10^{-5} *	1.40×10^{-4} *	−0.89
		SMN-LIN	0.054	0.069	−0.014	14	4.80×10^{-5} *	1.40×10^{-4} *	−0.88
		SMN-VAN	0.053	0.069	−0.016	15	5.74×10^{-5} *	1.59×10^{-4} *	−0.87
		VAN-DMN	0.054	0.070	−0.016	14	4.81×10^{-5} *	1.40×10^{-4} *	−0.88
		VAN-FPN	0.053	0.069	−0.015	14	4.81×10^{-5} *	1.40×10^{-4} *	−0.88
		VAN-LIN	0.053	0.068	−0.015	14	4.81×10^{-5} *	1.40×10^{-4} *	−0.88
		VIN-DMN	0.053	0.069	−0.016	13	4.02×10^{-5} *	1.40×10^{-4} *	−0.88
		VIN-DAN	0.053	0.069	−0.016	14	4.81×10^{-5} *	1.40×10^{-4} *	−0.88
		VIN-FPN	0.054	0.068	−0.015	10	2.33×10^{-5} *	1.40×10^{-4} *	−0.91
		VIN-LIN	0.054	0.069	−0.015	6	1.10×10^{-5} *	1.40×10^{-4} *	−0.95
		VIN-SMN	0.053	0.070	−0.017	13	4.02×10^{-5} *	1.40×10^{-4} *	−0.88
		VIN-VAN	0.053	0.070	−0.017	14	4.81×10^{-5} *	1.40×10^{-4} *	−0.88

Between-network comparisons between age: OACs vs. YACs and practice OACs vs. TCOAs. *, $p < 0.05$. OACs = older adult controls; YACs = younger adult controls; TCOAs = Tai Chi older adult practitioners; DMN = default mode network; DAN = dorsal attention network; FPN = frontoparietal network; LIN = limbic network; SMN = somatomotor network; VAN = ventral attention network; VIN = visual network.

Practice effects: TC practice was significantly related to greater within-network and between-network connectivity across all networks and network pairs, even after FDR correction. A trend for within-network transition magnitude in the LIN (Mdn diff = 0.10, U = 163, FDR-adjusted $p = 0.080$, and rank biserial r = 0.45) suggests that TC practice may reduce the FC strength needed for dynamic within-network LIN communication. Trends for a lower mean lifetime, mean interval length, and transition probability, though not surviving FDR correction, might indicate that TC practice is linked to more efficient and stable network communication. Notably, the relationship between TC practice and FC showed a greater effect size than that between age and FC, suggesting that TC practice might compensate for the detrimental effects of age on FC. For detailed mean connectivity results, see Tables 2 and 3.

4. Discussion

This study investigated the distinct relationships between age and TC practice with recurrent neural network dynamics, focusing on both temporal and spatial features. Our results showed that aging is associated with decreased within-network and between-network FC across most brain networks. Conversely, TC practice appears to mitigate these age-related declines, showing increased FC within and between networks in older adults who practice TC compared to non-practicing older adults. These findings suggest that TC practice may abate age-related declines in neural network efficiency and stability, highlighting its potential as a non-pharmacological intervention for promoting healthy brain aging.

4.1. Age-Related Effects

Large-scale, population-based findings by Zonnevald et al. [67] align with our results, indicating significant reductions in within-network and between-network FC in older adults compared to younger adults. For within-network FC, this decline was most pronounced in networks involved in bottom-up attention regulation (VAN), self-related processing (DMN), and visual processing (VIN). With regards to between-network mean FC, this decline was most noticeable in three key areas: (1) between networks responsible for top-down attention regulation and emotional processing (DAN-LIN); (2) between networks involved in motor functions and emotional processing (SMN-LIN); and (3) between networks handling visual processing and motor functions (VIN-SMN).

Previous findings by Ferreira and colleagues [9] were echoed in a recent systematic review by Deery et al. [68], suggesting that normal aging can result in a loss of functional diversity [9], known as the de-differentiation hypothesis [4,69]. In accordance with this hypothesis, we found a trend for a greater between-network transition magnitude between the DAN-LIN. In other words, older adults may require a greater increase in FC when transitioning between states as compared to younger adults, indicative of a loss in amplitude-coupling efficiency with age. These results largely align with previous literature showing a general global decline in FC [9,70], as well as a regional decline in attentional and self-referential/internal processing networks. In addition, we can qualitatively comment that our FC group matrices show a very clear loss of anti-correlations and an increase in positive correlations with age (see Figure 2), aligning with the previously mentioned findings by Zonnevald et al. [67], Ferreira et al. [9], and Deery et al. [68] (among others [4,9,71]). Altogether, these results suggest that normal aging may lead to a network-wide loss of intra-network resource efficiency and specialization and decreased inter-network modularity [9,10]. Interestingly, the FC matrix of TCOAs shows a neural phenotype in between the YACs and OACs: neither a complete loss of anti-correlations nor a total increase in positive correlations.

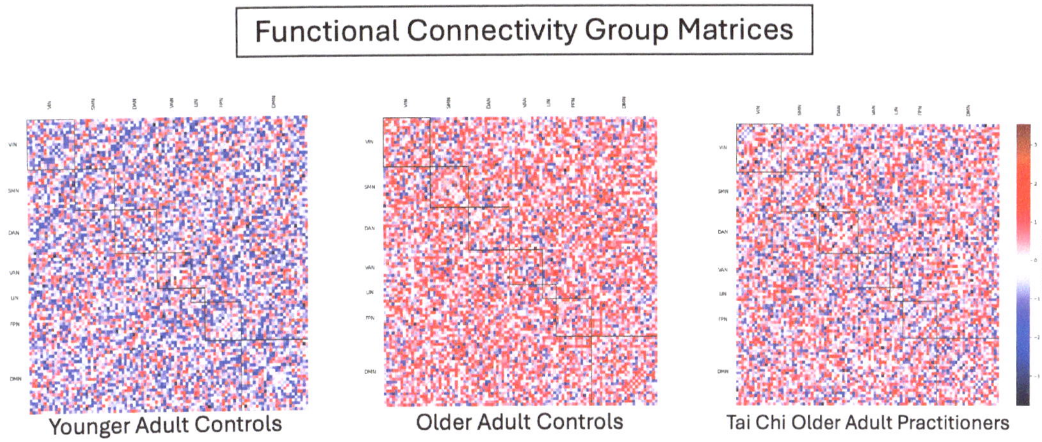

Figure 2. Thresholded functional connectivity matrices for younger adult controls (YACs), older adult controls (OACs), and Tai Chi older adult practitioners (TCOAs). Red indicates positive correlations, and blue indicates negative correlations (z-scored values displayed). Compared to YACs, OACs show reduced negative correlations and increased positive correlations, indicating age-related declines in network specialization. TCOAs exhibit a pattern between YACs and OACs, suggesting that Tai Chi practice may help preserve functional connectivity, maintaining a more balanced network organization despite aging. Networks visualized include visual (VIN), somatomotor (SMN), dorsal attention (DAN), ventral attention (VAN), limbic (LIN), frontoparietal (FPN), and default mode network (DMN).

4.2. *Effects of Tai Chi Practice*

TC practitioners exhibited significantly higher within-network and between-network FC across all examined networks compared to non-practicing older adults. This increase in FC suggests that TC practice may promote neural plasticity and plausibly enhance network efficiency in a network-wide fashion, partially attenuating the declines associated with aging. Notably, when comparing effect sizes between aging and TC practice for within-network FC, the greatest effect size differences were observed in top-down attention regulation and higher-order function (DAN, FPN: r diff = 0.29 and 0.30, respectively), affect (LIN: r diff = 0.40), and self-related processing (DMN: r diff = 0.32) networks, potentially pointing to the underlying neural mechanisms through which TC practice exerts its strongest intra-network effects. In a similar fashion, when comparing effect sizes between aging and TC practice for between-network FC, bottom-up attention regulation and self-related processing (VAN-DMN), higher-order cognitive function and self-related processing (FPN-DMN), and higher-order cognitive function and affect (FPN-LIN) relationships were most prominent. These results suggest that, despite aging-related declines, TC practice may facilitate robust intra- and inter-network communication and integration, which are crucial for maintaining cognitive and affective function, while also facilitating a compensatory response that largely attenuates normal decrements experienced during the aging process (please see Figure 2 for a visual comparison of FC matrices between non-practicing older adults and TC practitioner older adults).

We contextualize the results of TC practice in light of recent studies from the mind–body and meditation literature [25,26,43,72,73], which have lent support to the triple-network model of large-scale communication in the brain, initially proposed by Menon [74]. This framework integrates previously disconnected models of how attentional mechanisms reign in excessive rumination while deploying mindful attention [75,76]. According to this adapted model, mindful attention regulates mind wandering via shifting network dynamics. More specifically, the activity of key nodes within the DMN (e.g., medial prefrontal cortex and posterior cingulate cortex) are known to coordinate stimulus-independent thought processes such as autobiographical memory recall, internal speech, mental time travel, as well as the fundamental differentiation between self and other [77–79]. Although useful and often necessary, excessive internal attention can lead to significant errors caused by a loss of attention to relevant external stimuli [80,81]. These processes can be said to generate a certain level of salience that is monitored and primarily regulated via the dorsal anterior cingulate cortex along with the anterior insular cortex [82], regions known to be involved in performance monitoring and salience detection, respectively [83]. In the process of responding and/or anticipating errors, fronto-insular connections are strengthened to coordinate a beneficially antagonistic process in which DMN regions are downregulated [83] while FPN/DAN regions are upregulated. Consequently, internal attention and external attention are balanced in a way that allows for greater pliancy and responsiveness. Indeed, the VAN and LIN, with extensive connections to the DMN and FPN, form a cortico–striato–thamalo–cortical loop [84] that communicates salient information to the FPN, effectively coordinating between internally and externally oriented attention, as well as the amount of attention that needs to be deployed via the FPN.

A previous study by Liu et al. [34] investigating resting-state fMRI differences between TC practitioners and controls showed that decreased connectivity between the medial frontal gyrus and dorsolateral prefrontal cortex fully mediated the relationship between a mindful, non-judgmental stance and emotional-regulation ability. Although their seed-based analysis did not allow for a more comprehensive evaluation of coordinated large-scale activity, it must be noted that the decoupling observed between the key nodes of the DMN and FPN is a key finding within the mind–body literature at large [26,85,86]. Moreover, the VAN has been observed to be of great importance for the regulation of emotion. Thus, the neural mechanisms and outcomes examined fall squarely within the framework of the triple-network model, as do our results. Moreover, our results add some nuance to the existing framework. Our findings align with the triple-network model, which places a strong emphasis on the dynamics of networks related to top-down regulation of attention, as previously emphasized when highlighting the strongest effect sizes in our results. However, our results also show coupling between sensory–motor networks (both SMN and VIN), top-down and bottom-up attention (DAN and VAN, respectively), and cognitive control (FPN). These results suggest that large-scale networks, including those that comprise the triple-network model, could be influenced by visceral signals [26,33,87]. This possibly alludes to the benefits derived from integrating physical activity with mindful attention, clearly showing how visceral signals may play a regulatory role in the reining in of rumination and, ultimately, the enhancement of cognitive health.

Relatedly, comparing mind–body practices like TC, yoga, and Qigong with traditional exercises such as aerobic and resistance training could highlight both shared and distinct neuroprotective effects on the aging brain. Unfortunately, there are no systematic reviews or meta-analysis to date that allow for such structured comparisons to be made. In fact, we are aware of a single systematic review (i.e., Bray and colleagues) that assessed the possible effects of exercise on FC in older adults with and without cognitive impairment [88]. The inclusion of several multi-domain interventions (which included TC, Qigong, and yoga), however, was telling of the nascent state of the exercise literature with regards to the outcomes of interest to this study. In addition, the inclusion of these studies also makes a differentiation between traditional and non-traditional modes of exercise on the outcomes of interest (i.e., FC in older adults) an intractable issue. Additionally, it is becoming increasingly clear that gross differences in activation and/or connectivity will be insufficient to determine whether and how meaningful distinctions between traditional exercise modalities and mind–body practices exist and how they manifest. Indeed, neither a closer look at the pre–post changes in the study by Bray and colleagues [88], nor a closer examination of related systematic reviews (e.g., Li et al. [89]) reveals clear-cut differences between traditional exercise and non-traditional modes of exercise (i.e., mind–body practices).

Closely inspecting systematic reviews on mind–body practices proves to be similarly insufficient. In particular, recent meta-analyses from Gothe et al. [22] and Pan et al. [25]

describe similar findings: reconfigurations within and between the DMN and FPN occur during exercise, as well as during mind–body practice. In other words, differences in effect may be (a) non-existent, which is unlikely, or (b) subtle, which will require a careful investigation underneath these gross-level FC differences observed in these nascent areas of research. Only a few studies provide preliminary evidence to build upon. Amongst them, structural findings by Villemure and colleagues found that (1) gray-matter volume (GMV) increased with increased time spent practicing yoga; (2) as opposed to controls, GMV was not predicted to follow the classic decline with age in yoga practitioners; (3) poses, breathwork, and meditation all contributed to positive GMV volume, yet different ratios of these three components resulted in distinct areas primarily benefitting [90]. In addition, a study by Sharp et al. compared structural pre–post changes in an intervention comparing a group receiving physical fitness training (i.e., a combination of low- and high-intensity cardiovascular and weight training) and cognitive training (i.e., the Mind Frontiers program) and another group receiving the same intervention, plus a mindfulness intervention (ten 70-min sessions, 11.67 h completed in total) [91]. The added mindfulness group (and not the physical fitness + cognitive training group) showed significantly higher mean right insular connectivity post-training [91]. These two studies clearly show the possibility that combining non-traditional modalities during or apart from exercise (i.e., breathwork and meditation) may contribute to diverging results. These studies also highlight the intertwined nature of movement, breathwork, and mindfulness in practices that do not always neatly separate these components—such as in TC, Qigong, and yoga—which will require methodological dexterity on behalf of researchers who wish to better understand whether and how they may interact.

As previously mentioned, it is important to highlight that our primary metric of choice through which all temporal and spatial features were derived (i.e., amplitude coupling) is only one of the many modes of communication that the brain is hypothesized to use [41,42]. Indeed, our findings are more comprehensive when considering recent complementary findings by studies utilizing similar study designs, such as those by He and Hu [35]. Similar to the current study, He and Hu compared source-localized oscillatory patterns in TC practitioners, age-matched OACs, and YACs. Comparable to our findings, authors found the following pattern: YACs > TCOAs > OACs in alpha 1 (8–10.5 Hz) synchronization and theta desynchronization in central, parietal, and occipital regions. Along with our findings, this evidence provides joint support for a positively altered functional trajectory in TC practitioners that likely buffers the effects of aging. Jointly, our results likely suggest that TC practice might beneficially improve functional brain connectivity through enhanced bidirectional signaling (given greater coupling in top-down and bottom-up pathways in our data) while simultaneously maintaining oscillatory processes supportive of attention and adaptive cognitive control (i.e., alpha 1 synchronization) [92], as well as sensory–motor inhibition [93] and information-specific encoding [94].

4.3. Limitations, Methodological Considerations, and Future Directions

Our study, while providing valuable insights into the effects of TC practice on FC, has several limitations that warrant consideration. Primarily, the cross-sectional nature of our research design limits our ability to draw causal inferences. While we observed significant relationships between TC practice and altered FC patterns, we cannot definitively attribute these changes to the practice itself. Future longitudinal interventions are necessary to establish causality and determine the precise duration of practice required to elicit the neural changes observed in our study and those previously reported in the literature. Furthermore, TC is often considered "mindfulness in motion", which implies that both physical and mental exercises are involved. Our findings should be cautiously interpreted as indicating the overall influence of the two on FC. Future studies should aim to find ways to separate the behavioral, cognitive, and neural influences of the physical and mental aspects of practice to better discern how they may complement or even possibly interfere with each other.

Additionally, our sample size ($n = 15$ per group) was relatively small, and TC practitioners were restricted to a single style practiced (i.e., Yang style), which may limit the generalizability of our findings. The study findings may also have limited generalizability, given the contribution of additional confounding factors such as physical activity levels, sleep quality, or medication use. Larger-scale studies are needed to corroborate and replicate these results, ensuring their robustness across diverse populations. Furthermore, our reliance on an MRI template, rather than individual MRI images, may have introduced some imprecision in our analyses. This is especially relevant in the context of FC, given that age will result in a certain amount of structural atrophy, which has been shown to affect functional outcomes [9]. Therefore, the results from this study should be taken with caution, and future studies should seek to control the effects of overall brain tissue volume on FC whenever possible. While this approach is not uncommon in EEG studies, it is important to note that future investigations, particularly those employing high-temporal resolution methods such as EEG or MEG, would benefit from collecting individual MRI images. This is especially crucial when considering that template models and low-electrode count setups can result in diminished sensitivity and specificity [35,41,42,92–95].

Regarding methodological considerations, we employed a novel unsupervised algorithm to threshold the correlation matrices, aiming to minimize arbitrary decisions in the analytical process. The adaptive nature of this algorithm dynamically adjusts the alpha threshold, tailoring it to the specific characteristics of the cohort being studied. To ensure robustness and generalizability, we employed bootstrapping with replacement over 10,000 iterations. This process involved aggregating edge weights from all participants to create a representative distribution. By resampling from this distribution, we effectively simulated drawing new samples from the same underlying population, allowing us to determine an optimal alpha that is less sensitive to variations within individual datasets and more reflective of the broader population from which the cohort was drawn. While this approach mitigates the risk of overfitting and enhances the specificity of our findings, it is important to note that it does not replace the need for a thorough power analysis. The algorithm itself does not address issues related to statistical power directly related to an insufficiently small sample size, which remains a crucial aspect of the research design. Moreover, a fundamental question is raised in the field of dynamic FC analysis: How can we accurately determine the true number of functional connections within a given cohort?

It is also crucial to acknowledge the inherent limitations of our chosen atlas (i.e., Schaefer atlas, the exclusion of subcortical structures, the lack of individualized parcellation, imprecision with mapping activity due to age-related brain atrophy, etc.) and source-localization method (i.e., eLORETA, which favors distributed sources and provides smoothed/blurred spatial resolution, etc.). These methodological constraints should not be interpreted as evidence for the absence of subcortical contributions to the processes described in our results. Indeed, electrophysiological data have been shown to be affected by subcortical activity [96]. Future studies should aim to expand upon these limitations by exploring the role of subcortical structures in dynamic large-scale communication, providing a more comprehensive understanding of the neural mechanisms underlying TC practice.

While we have addressed several avenues for future research throughout this discussion, additional directions warrant exploration. Given the high dimensionality inherent to dynamic FC analysis, particularly when using EEG, our results provide a broad overview of large-scale communication within this cohort. Future work should strive for a more granular analysis, similar to the approach taken by Ferreira et al. [9], to provide a detailed examination of the nature of correlations comprising the positive and negative connectivity patterns observed in our results. Although we could qualitatively comment on large trends observed, a careful quantitative analysis is still warranted. Furthermore, we aim to delve deeper into the temporal aspects of our findings. By exploiting the Markov-chain dynamics extractable from an HMM, we can gain better insights into the directionality and sequence of interactions within and between networks. This temporal analysis could reveal crucial information about the dynamic nature of neural changes associated with TC practice.

Given the established positive effects of TC on mental health outcomes, such as stress reduction and improvements in anxiety and depression [30,31,34], an intriguing avenue for future research is the exploration of a "network interaction profile" or "neural phenotype" in relation to practitioner expertise. Investigating whether such a profile is predictive of better mental health outcomes could provide valuable insights into the mechanisms underlying the psychophysiological benefits of TC, and it could lead researchers to better understanding how such benefits could be reliably reproduced.

Lastly, it is essential to recognize that TC is a holistic, whole-body practice. To gain a more comprehensive understanding of its benefits, future research should integrate our neuroimaging findings with other physiological measures, such as heart-rate variability [97], respiration patterns, and kinematic data [24,98]. Indeed, our findings clearly show that somatosensory networks may play a regulatory role in attention and affect regulation. However, the nature of the interactions between neural and visceral signals needs to be further explored. In other words, the directionality and temporal dynamics of interactions between visceral signals (e.g., cardiac, respiratory, and kinematic/kinetic) and the neural outcomes reported herein require further exploration. Specifically, future research should investigate how these signals may bidirectionally interact with brain activity to orchestrate the benefits in attention and affect regulation widely reported in the mind–body literature [23,25,26,76,99–101]. This multi-modal approach would provide a more comprehensive understanding of the complex interplay between bodily processes and neural dynamics underlying the effects of TC practice.

5. Conclusions

This study explored the relationships between age and TC practice with recurrent neural network dynamics, focusing on both temporal and spatial features. Our findings revealed that aging is linked to decreased within-network and between-network FC across most brain networks. In contrast, TC practice seems to counteract these age-related declines, showing increased FC within and between networks in older adults who practice TC compared to non-practicing older adults. These results suggest that TC practice may help maintain neural network efficiency and stability, indicating its potential as a non-pharmacological intervention for promoting healthy brain aging.

Our study adds support and nuance to the triple-network model showing that a balancing and reorientation of attention might be engaged not only through a higher-order and top-down mechanism (i.e., FPN/DAN) but also via the coupling of bottom-up, sensory–motor (i.e., SMN/VIN) networks. Future work should seek to unpack the nature of the intra- and inter-network couplings found, as well as the temporal directionality in which the couplings occur, to further elucidate the neural mechanisms through which TC practice may exert its neuroprotective effects.

Author Contributions: Conceptualization, J.C. and M.E.H.; methodology, J.C., P.G., M.H., Y.H., L.Z. and M.E.H.; formal analysis, J.C. and P.G.; data curation, J.C., P.G., M.H. and Y.H.; writing—original draft preparation, J.C.; writing—review and editing, J.C., P.G., M.H., Y.H., L.Z. and M.E.H.; visualization, J.C. and P.G.; supervision and funding acquisition, M.E.H. All authors have read and agreed to the published version of the manuscript.

Funding: This research was funded, in part, by the Jump ARCHES endowment through the Health Care Engineering Systems Center.

Institutional Review Board Statement: The study was conducted in accordance with the Declaration of Helsinki and approved by the Institutional Review Board (or Ethics Committee) of the University of Illinois Urbana-Champaign (IRB Protocol No. 15317, approved 15 August 2023).

Informed Consent Statement: Informed consent was obtained from all subjects involved in the study.

Data Availability Statement: The raw data supporting the conclusions of this article will be made available by the authors without undue reservation.

Acknowledgments: We thank members of the Mobility and Fall Prevention Research Lab who assisted with data collection and the participants who made this study possible. We would like to thank the administrators and staff of the National Center for Supercomputing Applications (NCSA) at the University of Illinois Urbana-Champaign, especially those who support the Hardware-Accelerated Learning (HAL) cluster.

Conflicts of Interest: The authors declare no conflicts of interest. The funders of the study had no role in the design of the study, in the collection, analyses, or interpretation of data, in the writing of the manuscript, or in the decision to publish the results.

References

1. World Health Organization. *Decade of Healthy Ageing: Baseline Report*; World Health Organization: Geneva, Switzerland, 2020.
2. Hong, C.; Sun, L.; Liu, G.; Guan, B.; Li, C.; Luo, Y. Response of Global Health Towards the Challenges Presented by Population Aging. *China CDC Wkly.* **2023**, *5*, 884. [PubMed]
3. Arshadipour, A.; Thorand, B.; Linkohr, B.; Ladwig, K.-H.; Heier, M.; Peters, A. Multimorbidity patterns and mortality in older adults: Results from the KORA-Age study. *Front. Nutr.* **2023**, *10*, 1146442. [CrossRef] [PubMed]
4. Park, D.C.; Reuter-Lorenz, P. The adaptive brain: Aging and neurocognitive scaffolding. *Annu. Rev. Psychol.* **2009**, *60*, 173–196. [CrossRef] [PubMed]
5. Loaiza, V.M. An overview of the hallmarks of cognitive aging. *Curr. Opin. Psychol.* **2024**, *56*, 101784. [CrossRef]
6. Kievit, R.A.; Fuhrmann, D.; Borgeest, G.S.; Simpson-Kent, I.L.; Henson, R.N.A. The neural determinants of age-related changes in fluid intelligence: A pre-registered, longitudinal analysis in UK Biobank. *Wellcome Open Res.* **2018**, *3*, 38. [CrossRef]
7. Cadore, E.L.; Rodríguez-Mañas, L.; Sinclair, A.; Izquierdo, M. Effects of different exercise interventions on risk of falls, gait ability, and balance in physically frail older adults: A systematic review. *Rejuvenation Res.* **2013**, *16*, 105–114. [CrossRef]
8. Oschwald, J.; Guye, S.; Liem, F.; Rast, P.; Willis, S.; Röcke, C.; Jäncke, L.; Martin, M.; Mérillat, S. Brain structure and cognitive ability in healthy aging: A review on longitudinal correlated change. *Rev. Neurosci.* **2019**, *31*, 1–57. [CrossRef]
9. Ferreira, L.K.; Regina, A.C.B.; Kovacevic, N.; Martin, M.d.G.M.; Santos, P.P.; Carneiro, C.d.G.; Kerr, D.S.; Amaro, E.; McIntosh, A.R.; Busatto, G.F. Aging effects on whole-brain functional connectivity in adults free of cognitive and psychiatric disorders. *Cereb. Cortex* **2016**, *26*, 3851–3865. [CrossRef]
10. Escrichs, A.; Biarnes, C.; Garre-Olmo, J.; Fernández-Real, J.M.; Ramos, R.; Pamplona, R.; Brugada, R.; Serena, J.; Ramió-Torrentà, L.; Coll-De-Tuero, G.; et al. Whole-Brain Dynamics in Aging: Disruptions in Functional Connectivity and the Role of the Rich Club. *Cereb. Cortex* **2021**, *31*, 2466–2481. [CrossRef]
11. Grevendonk, L.; Connell, N.J.; McCrum, C.; Fealy, C.E.; Bilet, L.; Bruls, Y.M.H.; Mevenkamp, J.; Schrauwen-Hinderling, V.B.; Jörgensen, J.A.; Moonen-Kornips, E.; et al. Impact of aging and exercise on skeletal muscle mitochondrial capacity, energy metabolism, and physical function. *Nat. Commun.* **2021**, *12*, 4773. [CrossRef]
12. Copeland, J.L.; Ashe, M.C.; Biddle, S.J.; Brown, W.J.; Buman, M.P.; Chastin, S.; A Gardiner, P.; Inoue, S.; Jefferis, B.J.; Oka, K.; et al. Sedentary time in older adults: A critical review of measurement, associations with health, and interventions. *BMJ Publ. Group* **2017**, *51*, 1539. [CrossRef] [PubMed]
13. Hess, T.M. Selective Engagement of Cognitive Resources: Motivational Influences on Older Adults' Cognitive Functioning. *Perspect. Psychol. Sci.* **2014**, *9*, 388–407. [CrossRef]
14. Ennis, G.E.; Hess, T.M.; Smith, B.T. The impact of age and motivation on cognitive effort: Implications for cognitive engagement in older adulthood. *Psychol. Aging* **2013**, *28*, 495–504. [CrossRef] [PubMed]
15. Wanders, L.; Bakker, E.A.; van Hout, H.P.; Eijsvogels, T.M.; Hopman, M.T.; Visser, L.N.; Wouters, H.; Thijssen, D.H. Association between sedentary time and cognitive function: A focus on different domains of sedentary behavior. *Prev. Med.* **2021**, *153*, 106731. [CrossRef] [PubMed]
16. Manning, K.M.; Hall, K.S.; Sloane, R.; Magistro, D.; Rabaglietti, E.; Lee, C.C.; Castle, S.; Kopp, T.; Giffuni, J.; Katzel, L.; et al. Longitudinal analysis of physical function in older adults: The effects of physical inactivity and exercise training. *Aging Cell* **2024**, *23*, e13987. [CrossRef] [PubMed]
17. Anguera, J.A.; Boccanfuso, J.; Rintoul, J.L.; Al-Hashimi, O.; Faraji, F.; Janowich, J.; Kong, E.; Larraburo, Y.; Rolle, C.; Johnston, E.; et al. Video game training enhances cognitive control in older adults. *Nature* **2014**, *501*, 97–101. [CrossRef]
18. Rebok, G.W.; Ball, K.; Guey, L.T.; ScD, R.N.J.; DrPH, H.K.; King, J.W.; Marsiske, M.; Morris, J.N.; Tennstedt, S.L.; Unverzagt, F.W.; et al. Ten-year effects of the advanced cognitive training for independent and vital elderly cognitive training trial on cognition and everyday functioning in older adults. *J. Am. Geriatr. Soc.* **2014**, *62*, 16–24. [CrossRef]
19. Hinton, C.; Caban, S.; Dent, K.; Wicke, R.; Pool, K.; Robertson, J.; Goodman, S.; Frye, J.; Vetter, N.; Chukwu, C.; et al. Physical Activity and Older Adults Systematic Literature Review. Office of Disease Prevention and Health Promotion, Office of the Assistant Secretary for Health, Office of the Secretary, U.S. Department of Health and Human Services: Rockville, MD, USA, 2023.

20. Gothe, N.P.; McAuley, E. Yoga and Cognition: A Meta-Analysis of Chronic and Acute Effects. *Psychosom. Med.* **2015**, *77*, 784–797. [CrossRef]
21. Bhattacharyya, K.K.; Liu, Y.; Gothe, N.P.; Fauth, E.B. Mind-Body Practice and Family Caregivers' Subjective Well-Being: Findings From the Midlife in the United States (MIDUS) Study. *Gerontol. Geriatr. Med.* **2023**, *9*, 1–9. [CrossRef]
22. Gothe, N.P.; Khan, I.; Hayes, J.; Erlenbach, E.; Damoiseaux, J.S. Yoga Effects on Brain Health: A Systematic Review of the Current Literature. *Brain Plast.* **2019**, *5*, 105–122. [CrossRef]
23. Wayne, P.M.; Walsh, J.N.; Taylor-Piliae, R.E.; Wells, R.E.; Papp, K.V.; Donovan, N.J.; Yeh, G.Y. Effect of tai chi on cognitive performance in older adults: Systematic review and meta-analysis. *J. Am. Geriatr. Soc.* **2014**, *62*, 25–39. [CrossRef] [PubMed]
24. Hu, Y.; Kattan, C.; Kontos, D.; Zhu, W.; Hernandez, M.E. Benefits of tai ji quan practice on neuromuscular functions in older adults: A Systematic Review and meta-analysis. *Churchill Livingstone* **2021**, *42*, 101295. [CrossRef] [PubMed]
25. Pan, Z.; Su, X.; Fang, Q.; Hou, L.; Lee, Y.; Chen, C.C.; Lamberth, J.; Kim, M.-L. The effects of Tai Chi intervention on healthy elderly by means of neuroimaging and EEG: A systematic review. *Front. Aging Neurosci.* **2018**, *10*, 110. [CrossRef]
26. Voss, S.; Cerna, J.; Gothe, N.P. Yoga Impacts Cognitive Health: Neurophysiological Changes and Stress Regulation Mechanisms. *Exerc. Sport. Sci. Rev.* **2023**, *51*, 73–81. [CrossRef] [PubMed]
27. Zhang, Y.; Li, C.; Zou, L.; Liu, X.; Song, W. The effects of mind-body exercise on cognitive performance in elderly: A systematic review and meta-analysis. *Int. J. Environ. Res. Public Health* **2018**, *15*, 2791. [CrossRef] [PubMed]
28. Jasim, N.; Balakirishnan, D.; Zhang, H.; Steiner-Lim, G.Z.; Karamacoska, D.; Yang, G.-Y. Effects and mechanisms of Tai Chi on mild cognitive impairment and early-stage dementia: A scoping review. *Syst. Rev.* **2023**, *12*, 200. [CrossRef]
29. Wang, X.; Si, K.; Gu, W.; Wang, X. Mitigating effects and mechanisms of Tai Chi on mild cognitive impairment in the elderly. *Front. Aging Neurosci.* **2023**, *14*, 1028822. [CrossRef]
30. Wang, F.; Lee, E.-K.O.; Wu, T.; Benson, H.; Fricchione, G.; Wang, W.; Yeung, A.S. The effects of tai chi on depression, anxiety, and psychological well-being: A systematic review and meta-analysis. *Int. J. Behav. Med.* **2014**, *21*, 605–617. [CrossRef]
31. Sani, N.A.; Yusoff, S.S.M.; Norhayati, M.N.; Zainudin, A.M. Tai Chi Exercise for Mental and Physical Well-Being in Patients with Depressive Symptoms: A Systematic Review and Meta-Analysis. *Int. J. Environ. Res. Public Health* **2023**, *20*, 2828. [CrossRef]
32. Park, M.; Song, R.; Ju, K.; Shin, J.C.; Seo, J.; Fan, X.; Gao, X.; Ryu, A.; Li, Y. Effects of Tai Chi and Qigong on cognitive and physical functions in older adults: Systematic review, meta-analysis, and meta-regression of randomized clinical trials. *BMC Geriatr.* **2023**, *23*, 352. [CrossRef]
33. Wei, G.-X.; Dong, H.-M.; Yang, Z.; Luo, J.; Zuo, X.-N. Tai Chi Chuan optimizes the functional organization of the intrinsic human brain architecture in older adults. *Front. Aging Neurosci.* **2014**, *6*, 74. [CrossRef] [PubMed]
34. Liu, Z.; Wu, Y.; Li, L.; Guo, X. Functional Connectivity Within the Executive Control Network Mediates the Effects of Long-Term Tai Chi Exercise on Elders' Emotion Regulation. *Front. Aging Neurosci.* **2018**, *10*, 315. [CrossRef]
35. He, T.; Hu, Z. Effects of Tai Chi Chuan on cortical sources of EEG rhythms in the resting state in elderly individuals: A cross-sectional study. *Neuroreport* **2022**, *33*, 180–185. [CrossRef]
36. Hutchison, R.M.; Womelsdorf, T.; Allen, E.A.; Bandettini, P.A.; Calhoun, V.D.; Corbetta, M.; Della Penna, S.; Duyn, J.H.; Glover, G.H.; Gonzalez-Castillo, J.; et al. Dynamic functional connectivity: Promise, issues, and interpretations. *Neuroimage* **2013**, *80*, 360–378. [CrossRef] [PubMed]
37. Kopell, N.J.; Gritton, H.J.; Whittington, M.A.; Kramer, M.A. Beyond the connectome: The dynome. *Cell Press.* **2014**, *83*, 1319–1328. [CrossRef] [PubMed]
38. Matkovič, A.; Anticevic, A.; Murray, J.D.; Repovš, G. Static and dynamic functional connectomes represent largely similar information. *bioRxiv* **2023**. [CrossRef]
39. Guidotti, R.; D'andrea, A.; Basti, A.; Raffone, A.; Pizzella, V.; Marzetti, L. Long-Term and Meditation-Specific Modulations of Brain Connectivity Revealed Through Multivariate Pattern Analysis. *Brain Topogr.* **2023**, *36*, 409–418. [CrossRef]
40. Park, J.E.; Jung, S.C.; Ryu, K.H.; Oh, J.Y.; Kim, H.S.; Choi, C.-G.; Kim, S.J.; Shim, W.H. Differences in dynamic and static functional connectivity between young and elderly healthy adults. *Neuroradiology* **2017**, *59*, 781–789. [CrossRef]
41. Mostame, P.; Sadaghiani, S. Phase- and amplitude-coupling are tied by an intrinsic spatial organization but show divergent stimulus-related changes. *Neuroimage* **2020**, *219*, 117051. [CrossRef]
42. Vinck, M.; Uran, C.; Spyropoulos, G.; Onorato, I.; Broggini, A.C.; Schneider, M.; Canales-Johnson, A. Principles of large-scale neural interactions. *Cell Press.* **2023**, *111*, 987–1002. [CrossRef]
43. Shen, Y.-Q.; Zhou, H.-X.; Chen, X.; Castellanos, F.X.; Yan, C.-G. Meditation effect in changing functional integrations across large-scale brain networks: Preliminary evidence from a meta-analysis of seed-based functional connectivity. *J. Pac. Rim Psychol.* **2020**, *14*, e10. [CrossRef]
44. Ganesan, S.; Beyer, E.; Moffat, B.; Van Dam, N.T.; Lorenzetti, V.; Zalesky, A. Focused attention meditation in healthy adults: A systematic review and meta-analysis of cross-sectional functional MRI studies. *Neurosci. Biobehav. Rev.* **2022**, *141*, 104846. [CrossRef]
45. Monsour, R. Neuroimaging in the Era of Artificial Intelligence: Current Applications. *Fed. Pract.* **2022**, *141*, 104846. [CrossRef]
46. Vidaurre, D.; Smith, S.M.; Woolrich, M.W. Brain network dynamics are hierarchically organized in time. *Proc. Natl. Acad. Sci. USA* **2017**, *114*, 12827–12832. [CrossRef]

47. Higgins, C.; Liu, Y.; Vidaurre, D.; Kurth-Nelson, Z.; Dolan, R.; Behrens, T.; Woolrich, M. Replay bursts in humans coincide with activation of the default mode and parietal alpha networks. *Neuron* **2021**, *109*, 882–893. [CrossRef] [PubMed]
48. Hunyadi, B.; Woolrich, M.; Quinn, A.; Vidaurre, D.; De Vos, M. A dynamic system of brain networks revealed by fast transient EEG fluctuations and their fMRI correlates. *Neuroimage* **2019**, *185*, 72–82. [CrossRef] [PubMed]
49. Vidaurre, D.; Quinn, A.J.; Baker, A.P.; Dupret, D.; Tejero-Cantero, A.; Woolrich, M.W. Spectrally resolved fast transient brain states in electrophysiological data. *Neuroimage* **2016**, *126*, 81–95. [CrossRef] [PubMed]
50. Ren, H.-P.; Bai, C.; Baptista, M.S.; Grebogi, C. Weak connections form an infinite number of patterns in the brain. *Sci. Rep.* **2017**, *7*, 46472. [CrossRef]
51. Santarnecchi, E.; Galli, G.; Polizzotto, N.R.; Rossi, A.; Rossi, S. Efficiency of weak brain connections support general cognitive functioning. *Hum. Brain Mapp.* **2014**, *35*, 4566–4582. [CrossRef]
52. Li, A.; Feitelberg, J.; Saini, A.P.; Höchenberger, R.; Scheltienne, M. MNE-ICALabel: Automatically annotating ICA components with ICLabel in Python. *J. Open Source Softw.* **2022**, *7*, 4484. [CrossRef]
53. Pion-Tonachini, L.; Kreutz-Delgado, K.; Makeig, S. ICLabel: An automated electroencephalographic independent component classifier, dataset, and website. *Neuroimage* **2019**, *198*, 181–197. [CrossRef] [PubMed]
54. Perrin, F.; Pernier, J.; Bertrand, O.; Echallier, J. Spherical splines for scalp potential and current density mapping. *Electroencephalogr. Clin. Neurophysiol.* **1989**, *72*, 184–187. [CrossRef] [PubMed]
55. Pascual-Marqui, R.D.; Lehmann, D.; Koukkou, M.; Kochi, K.; Anderer, P.; Saletu, B.; Tanaka, H.; Hirata, K.; John, E.R.; Prichep, L.; et al. Assessing interactions in the brain with exact low-resolution electromagnetic tomography. *Philos. Trans. R. Soc. A Math. Phys. Eng. Sci.* **2011**, *369*, 3768–3784. [CrossRef] [PubMed]
56. Schaefer, A.; Kong, R.; Gordon, E.M.; Laumann, T.O.; Zuo, X.-N.; Holmes, A.J.; Eickhoff, S.B.; Yeo, B.T.T. Local-Global Parcellation of the Human Cerebral Cortex from Intrinsic Functional Connectivity MRI. *Cereb. Cortex* **2018**, *28*, 3095–3114. [CrossRef] [PubMed]
57. Thomas Yeo, B.T.; Krienen, F.M.; Sepulcre, J.; Sabuncu, M.R.; Lashkari, D.; Hollinshead, M.; Roffman, J.L.; Smoller, J.W.; Zöllei, L.; Polimeni, J.R.; et al. The organization of the human cerebral cortex estimated by intrinsic functional connectivity. *J. Neurophysiol.* **2011**, *106*, 1125–1165. [CrossRef]
58. Colclough, G.; Brookes, M.; Smith, S.; Woolrich, M. A symmetric multivariate leakage correction for MEG connectomes. *Neuroimage* **2015**, *117*, 439–448. [CrossRef]
59. O'Neill, G.C.; Tewarie, P.; Vidaurre, D.; Liuzzi, L.; Woolrich, M.W.; Brookes, M.J. Dynamics of large-scale electrophysiological networks: A technical review. *NeuroImage* **2018**, *180*, 559–576. [CrossRef]
60. Baker, A.P.; Brookes, M.J.; A Rezek, I.; Smith, S.M.; Behrens, T.; Smith, P.J.P.; Woolrich, M.; Kingdom, U. Fast transient networks in spontaneous human brain activity. *elife* **2014**, *3*, e01867. [CrossRef]
61. Quinn, A.J.; Vidaurre, D.; Abeysuriya, R.; Becker, R.; Nobre, A.C.; Woolrich, M.W. Task-evoked dynamic network analysis through Hidden Markov Modeling. *Front. Neurosci.* **2018**, *12*, 603. [CrossRef]
62. Jun, S.; Alderson, T.H.; Malone, S.M.; Harper, J.; Hunt, R.H.; Thomas, K.M.; Iacono, W.G.; Wilson, S.; Sadaghiani, S. Rapid dynamics of electrophysiological connectome states are heritable. *Netw. Neurosci.* **2024**, 1–50. [CrossRef]
63. Jun, S.; Alderson, T.H.; Altmann, A.; Sadaghiani, S. Dynamic trajectories of connectome state transitions are heritable. *bioRxiv* **2021**. [CrossRef] [PubMed]
64. Vidaurre, D.; Hunt, L.T.; Quinn, A.J.; Hunt, B.A.E.; Brookes, M.J.; Nobre, A.C.; Woolrich, M.W. Spontaneous cortical activity transiently organises into frequency specific phase-coupling networks. *Nat. Commun.* **2018**, *9*, 2987. [CrossRef]
65. Coquelet, N.; De Tiège, X.; Roshchupkina, L.; Peigneux, P.; Goldman, S.; Woolrich, M.; Wens, V. Microstates and power envelope hidden Markov modeling probe bursting brain activity at different timescales. *Neuroimage* **2022**, *247*, 118850. [CrossRef]
66. Stevner, A.B.A.; Vidaurre, D.; Cabral, J.; Rapuano, K.; Nielsen, S.F.V.; Tagliazucchi, E.; Laufs, H.; Vuust, P.; Deco, G.; Woolrich, M.W.; et al. Discovery of key whole-brain transitions and dynamics during human wakefulness and non-REM sleep. *Nat. Commun.* **2019**, *10*, 1035. [CrossRef]
67. Zonneveld, H.I.; Pruim, R.H.; Bos, D.; Vrooman, H.A.; Muetzel, R.L.; Hofman, A.; Rombouts, S.A.; van der Lugt, A.; Niessen, W.J.; Ikram, M.A.; et al. Patterns of functional connectivity in an aging population: The Rotterdam Study. *Neuroimage* **2019**, *189*, 432–444. [CrossRef] [PubMed]
68. Deery, H.A.; Di Paolo, R.; Moran, C.; Egan, G.F.; Jamadar, S.D. The older adult brain is less modular, more integrated, and less efficient at rest: A systematic review of large-scale resting-state functional brain networks in aging. *Psychophysiology* **2023**, *60*, e14159. [CrossRef] [PubMed]
69. Reuter-Lorenz, P.A.; Park, D.C. How Does it STAC Up? Revisiting the Scaffolding Theory of Aging and Cognition. *Neuropsychol. Rev.* **2014**, *24*, 355–370. [CrossRef]
70. Farras-Permanyer, L.; Mancho-Fora, N.; Montalà-Flaquer, M.; Bartrés-Faz, D.; Vaqué-Alcázar, L.; Peró-Cebollero, M.; Guàrdia-Olmos, J. Age-related changes in resting-state functional connectivity in older adults. *Neural Regen. Res.* **2019**, *14*, 1544–1555. [CrossRef]
71. Santaella, D.F.; Balardin, J.B.; Afonso, R.F.; Giorjiani, G.M.; Sato, J.R.; Lacerda, S.S.; Amaro, E., Jr.; Lazar, S.; Kozasa, E.H. Greater anteroposterior default mode network functional connectivity in long-term elderly yoga practitioners. *Front. Aging Neurosci.* **2019**, *10*, 158. [CrossRef]

72. Bremer, B.; Wu, Q.; Álvarez, M.G.M.; Hölzel, B.K.; Wilhelm, M.; Hell, E.; Tavacioglu, E.E.; Torske, A.; Koch, K. Mindfulness meditation increases default mode, salience, and central executive network connectivity. *Sci. Rep.* **2022**, *12*, 13219. [CrossRef]
73. Cui, L.; Tao, S.; Yin, H.-C.; Shen, Q.-Q.; Wang, Y.; Zhu, L.-N.; Li, X.-J. Tai Chi Chuan Alters Brain Functional Network Plasticity and Promotes Cognitive Flexibility. *Front. Psychol.* **2021**, *12*, 665419. [CrossRef]
74. Menon, V. Large-scale brain networks and psychopathology: A unifying triple network model. *Trends Cogn. Sci.* **2011**, *15*, 483–506. [CrossRef] [PubMed]
75. Feruglio, S.; Matiz, A.; Pagnoni, G.; Fabbro, F.; Crescentini, C. The Impact of Mindfulness Meditation on the Wandering Mind: A Systematic Review. *Neurosci. Biobehav. Rev.* **2021**, *131*, 313–330. [CrossRef] [PubMed]
76. Chiesa, A.; Serretti, A.; Jakobsen, J.C. Mindfulness: Top-down or bottom-up emotion regulation strategy? *Clin. Psychol. Rev.* **2023**, *33*, 82–96. [CrossRef] [PubMed]
77. Østby, Y.; Walhovd, K.B.; Tamnes, C.K.; Grydeland, H.; Westlye, L.T.; Fjell, A.M. Mental time travel and default-mode network functional connectivity in the developing brain. *Proc. Natl. Acad. Sci. USA* **2012**, *109*, 16800–16804. [CrossRef] [PubMed]
78. Raichle, M.E. The Brain's Default Mode Network. *Annu. Rev. Neurosci.* **2015**, *38*, 433–447. [CrossRef] [PubMed]
79. Xu, X.; Yuan, H.; Lei, X. Activation and Connectivity within the Default Mode Network Contribute Independently to Future-Oriented Thought. *Sci. Rep.* **2016**, *6*, 21001. [CrossRef]
80. Weissman, D.H.; Roberts, K.C.; Visscher, K.M.; Woldorff, M.G. The neural bases of momentary lapses in attention. *Nat. Neurosci.* **2006**, *9*, 971–978. [CrossRef]
81. Mittner, M.; Hawkins, G.E.; Boekel, W.; Forstmann, B.U. A Neural Model of Mind Wandering. *Trends Cogn. Sci.* **2016**, *20*, 570–578. [CrossRef]
82. Carter, C.S.; Braver, T.S.; Barch, D.M.; Botvinick, M.M.; Noll, D.; Cohen, J.D. Anterior Cingulate Cortex, Error Detection, and the Online Monitoring of Performance. *Science* **1998**, *280*, 747–749. [CrossRef]
83. Sridharan, D.; Levitin, D.J.; Menon, V. A critical role for the right fronto-insular cortex in switching between central-executive and default-mode networks. *Natl. Acad. Sci.* **2008**, *105*, 12569–12574. [CrossRef] [PubMed]
84. Peters, S.K.; Dunlop, K.; Downar, J. Cortico-striatal-thalamic loop circuits of the salience network: A central pathway in psychiatric disease and treatment. *Front. Syst. Neurosci.* **2016**, *10*, 104. [CrossRef] [PubMed]
85. Garrison, K.A.; Zeffiro, T.A.; Scheinost, D.; Constable, R.T.; Brewer, J.A. Meditation leads to reduced default mode network activity beyond an active task. *Cogn. Affect. Behav. Neurosci.* **2015**, *15*, 712–720. [CrossRef] [PubMed]
86. Brewer, J.A.; Worhunsky, P.D.; Gray, J.R.; Tang, Y.-Y.; Weber, J.; Kober, H. Meditation experience is associated with differences in default mode network activity and connectivity. *Proc. Natl. Acad. Sci. USA* **2011**, *108*, 20254–20259. [CrossRef]
87. Azzalini, D.; Rebollo, I.; Tallon-Baudry, C. Visceral Signals Shape Brain Dynamics and Cognition. *Trends Cogn. Sci.* **2019**, *23*, 488–509. [CrossRef]
88. Bray, N.W.; Pieruccini-Faria, F.; Bartha, R.; Doherty, T.J.; Nagamatsu, L.S.; Montero-Odasso, M. The effect of physical exercise on functional brain network connectivity in older adults with and without cognitive impairment. A systematic review. *Mech. Ageing Dev.* **2021**, *196*, 111493. [CrossRef]
89. Li, M.-Y.; Huang, M.-M.; Li, S.-Z.; Tao, J.; Zheng, G.-H.; Chen, L.-D. The effects of aerobic exercise on the structure and function of DMN-related brain regions: A systematic review. *Int. J. Neurosci.* **2017**, *127*, 634–649. [CrossRef]
90. Villemure, C.; Äœeko, M.; Cotton, V.A.; Bushnell, M.C.; Čeko, M. Neuroprotective effects of yoga practice: Age-, experience-, and frequency-dependent plasticity. *Front. Hum. Neurosci.* **2015**, *9*, 281. [CrossRef]
91. Sharp, P.B.; Sutton, B.P.; Paul, E.J.; Sherepa, N.; Hillman, C.H.; Cohen, N.J.; Kramer, A.F.; Prakash, R.S.; Heller, W.; Telzer, E.H.; et al. Mindfulness training induces structural connectome changes in insula networks. *Sci. Rep.* **2018**, *8*, 7929. [CrossRef]
92. Sadaghiani, S.; Dombert, P.L.; Løvstad, M.; Funderud, I.; Meling, T.R.; Endestad, T.; Knight, R.T.; Solbakk, A.-K.; D'esposito, M. Lesions to the Fronto-Parietal Network Impact Alpha-Band Phase Synchrony and Cognitive Control. *Cereb. Cortex* **2019**, *29*, 4143–4153. [CrossRef]
93. Pscherer, C.; Mückschel, M.; Summerer, L.; Bluschke, A.; Beste, C. On the relevance of EEG resting theta activity for the neurophysiological dynamics underlying motor inhibitory control. *Hum. Brain Mapp.* **2019**, *40*, 4253–4265. [CrossRef] [PubMed]
94. Pscherer, C.; Mückschel, M.; Bluschke, A.; Beste, C. Resting-state theta activity is linked to information content-specific coding levels during response inhibition. *Sci. Rep.* **2022**, *12*, 4530. [CrossRef] [PubMed]
95. Brodbeck, V.; Spinelli, L.; Lascano, A.M.; Wissmeier, M.; Vargas, M.-I.; Vulliemoz, S.; Pollo, C.; Schaller, K.; Michel, C.M.; Seeck, M. Electroencephalographic source imaging: A prospective study of 152 operated epileptic patients. *Brain* **2011**, *134*, 2887–2897. [CrossRef]
96. Seeber, M.; Cantonas, L.-M.; Hoevels, M.; Sesia, T.; Visser-Vandewalle, V.; Michel, C.M. Subcortical electrophysiological activity is detectable with high-density EEG source imaging. *Nat. Commun.* **2019**, *10*, 753. [CrossRef] [PubMed]
97. Wei, G.; Li, Y.; Yue, X.; Ma, X.; Chang, Y.; Yi, L.; Li, J.; Zuo, X. Tai Chi Chuan modulates heart rate variability during abdominal breathing in elderly adults. *PsyCh J.* **2015**, *5*, 69–77. [CrossRef]
98. Leung, E.S.F.; Tsang, W.W.N. Comparison of the kinetic characteristics of standing and sitting Tai Chi forms. *Disabil. Rehab.* **2008**, *30*, 1891–1900. [CrossRef]
99. Chiesa, A.; Calati, R.; Serretti, A. Does mindfulness training improve cognitive abilities? A systematic review of neuropsychological findings. *Clin. Psychol. Rev.* **2011**, *31*, 449–464. [CrossRef]

100. Pascoe, M.C.; de Manincor, M.J.; Hallgren, M.; Baldwin, P.A.; Tseberja, J.; Parker, A.G. Psychobiological mechanisms underlying the mental health benefits of yoga-based interventions: A narrative review. *Mindfulness* **2021**, *12*, 2877–2889. [CrossRef]
101. Schmalzl, L.; Powers, C.; Blom, E.H. Neurophysiological and neurocognitive mechanisms underlying the effects of yoga-based practices: Towards a comprehensive theoretical framework. *Front. Hum. Neurosci.* **2015**, *9*, 235. [CrossRef]

Disclaimer/Publisher's Note: The statements, opinions and data contained in all publications are solely those of the individual author(s) and contributor(s) and not of MDPI and/or the editor(s). MDPI and/or the editor(s) disclaim responsibility for any injury to people or property resulting from any ideas, methods, instructions or products referred to in the content.

brain sciences

MDPI

Article

Estimated Disease Progression Trajectory of White Matter Disruption in Unilateral Temporal Lobe Epilepsy: A Data-Driven Machine Learning Approach

Daichi Sone [1,2,*], Noriko Sato [1], Yoko Shigemoto [1], Iman Beheshti [3], Yukio Kimura [1] and Hiroshi Matsuda [1]

1 Department of Radiology, National Center of Neurology and Psychiatry, Tokyo 187-8551, Japan; snoriko@ncnp.go.jp (N.S.); yokos@ncnp.go.jp (Y.S.); yukio-k01@ncnp.go.jp (Y.K.); hiroshi.matsuda@mt.strins.or.jp (H.M.)

2 Department of Psychiatry, Jikei University School of Medicine, Tokyo 105-8461, Japan

3 Department of Human Anatomy and Cell Science, Rady Faculty of Health Sciences, Max Rady College of Medicine, University of Manitoba, Winnipeg, MB R3E 0J9, Canada; iman.beheshti@umanitoba.ca

* Correspondence: daichisone@gmail.com; Tel.: +81-042-341-2711; Fax: +81-042-344-6745

Abstract: Background/Objectives: Although the involvement of progressive brain alterations in epilepsy was recently suggested, individual patients' trajectories of white matter (WM) disruption are not known. Methods: We investigated the disease progression patterns of WM damage and its associations with clinical metrics. We examined the cross-sectional diffusion tensor imaging (DTI) data of 155 patients with unilateral temporal lobe epilepsy (TLE) and 270 age/gender-matched healthy controls, and we then calculated the average fractional anisotropy (FA) values within 20 WM tracts of the whole brain. We used the Subtype and Stage Inference (SuStaIn) program to detect the progression trajectory of FA changes and investigated its association with clinical parameters including onset age, disease duration, drug-responsiveness, and the number of anti-seizure medications (ASMs). Results: The SuStaIn algorithm identified a single subtype model in which the initial damage occurs in the ipsilateral uncinate fasciculus (UF), followed by damage in the forceps, superior longitudinal fasciculus (SLF), and anterior thalamic radiation (ATR). This pattern was replicated when analyzing TLE with hippocampal sclerosis (n = 50) and TLE with no lesions (n = 105) separately. Further-progressed stages were associated with longer disease duration ($p < 0.001$) and a greater number of ASMs ($p = 0.001$). Conclusions: the disease progression model based on WM tracts may be useful as a novel individual-level biomarker.

Keywords: temporal lobe epilepsy; white matter; diffusion tensor imaging; machine learning

1. Introduction

Epilepsy is a common chronic neurological disorder and is characterized by recurrent seizures caused by abnormal and excessive neural activities [1]. The psychosocial and economic burdens of epilepsy on patients and their caregivers are significant [2,3]. In light of these serious conditions, epilepsy was selected as the target of the World Health Organization's Intersectional Global Action Plan in 2022 [4]. In fact, problems in epilepsy care include not only seizure control, but also comorbidities and psychosocial issues [5]. To address these complex issues, various advanced biomarkers, including brain imaging, are expected to be developed [6].

In recent years, the disease progression of epilepsy has been a matter of controversy. It is well known that brain atrophy and white matter (WM) damage in epilepsy can extend beyond the epileptogenic foci [7,8], and it has also been suggested that abnormal brain networks are involved in such neuronal damage [9]. A 2019 study using longitudinal brain MRI data showed that in individuals with epilepsy, the rate of cortical thinning over time is higher than that in healthy aging [10]. However, even if epilepsy is progressive, not all patients progress uniformly, and it is not clear in what order the damage progresses. In this regard, estimating the pattern of disease progression in each patient may lead to the development of novel individual-level biomarkers for epilepsy.

To address this issue, another study applying brain morphology MRI reported that the use of an unsupervised machine learning analysis, i.e., the Subtype and Stage Inference (SuStaIn) algorithm [11,12], has made it possible to classify the progressive subtypes and stages of individual brain atrophy in epilepsy [13,14]. In the study, the patterns of brain morphological changes in patients with focal epilepsy were classified into three subtypes: the cortical type, starting with reduced cortical thickness; the basal ganglia type, starting with basal ganglia atrophy; and the hippocampal type, starting with hippocampal atrophy; the hippocampal type was reported to be the most frequent in temporal lobe epilepsy (TLE) [13].

TLE is the most prevalent form of focal epilepsy and is often refractory to drug treatment [15]. Not only is brain morphology atrophy known to occur in TLE, but so is WM microstructural damage [16]. Since brain morphological alterations are expected to progress in TLE, we hypothesized that WM tract damage may also be progressive along with some specific trajectories. In addition, given the role of WM tracts in connecting different brain regions and the recent concept of epilepsy as a brain network disorder [17], the patterns of WM damage progression could be highly relevant. We speculated that the subtyping and staging of the progression of WM damage over time in TLE may be clinically useful as an individual-level biomarker for categorizing and monitoring disease progression. We thus conducted the present study to identify the subtypes and staging patterns of WM microstructural alterations in TLE, using diffusion tensor imaging (DTI) and data-driven machine learning algorithms. The SuStaIn algorithm was applied to DTI data in 155 unilateral TLE patients and it estimated the progression trajectories of WM disruption. The flow of analysis is shown in Figure 1. We further discussed the potential utilities of the subtyping and staging as a novel individual-level imaging biomarker.

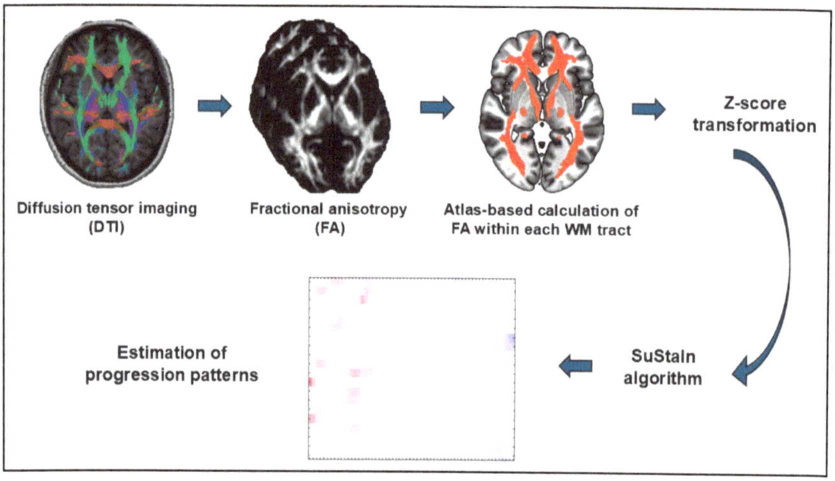

Figure 1. The flow of analysis in this study. The DTI data were processed by tract-based spatial statistics (TBSS) and atlas-based calculation of fractional anisotropy (FA) within each WM tract. The Z-scores were analyzed by SuStaIn algorithm to estimate disease progression patterns.

2. Materials and Methods

2.1. Subjects

We recruited 155 patients with unilateral TLE who were examined at our epilepsy center in Tokyo, Japan between December 2013 and March 2017. Board-certified epileptologists made the diagnosis of TLE based on (i) the presence of focal seizures consistent with TLE, and (ii) focal epileptiform discharge predominantly in unilateral temporal areas as revealed by conventional scalp electroencephalography (EEG). Long-term video-EEG monitoring and/or interictal ^{18}F-FDG PET were also performed when needed. High-resolution MRI scans of all patients were visually inspected by experienced neuroradiologists.

Patients with the following criteria were excluded: those with a significant medical history of acute encephalitis, meningitis, severe head trauma, or ischemic encephalopathy; suspicious epileptogenic lesions (e.g., tumor, cortical dysplasia or vascular malformation) on MRI other than ipsilateral hippocampal sclerosis (HS) at the abnormal EEG side; or epileptic paroxysms in extra-temporal regions on EEG.

Two hundred seventy age/gender-matched healthy controls (HCs) without any history of neurological or psychiatric disorders and any use of central nervous system medication were also recruited. All of the subjects provided written informed consent to participate in accordance with the Declaration of Helsinki. This study was approved by the Institutional Review Board at National Center of Neurology and Psychiatry Hospital, Tokyo, Japan.

2.2. MRI Acquisitions

All subjects underwent 3.0-T MRI scans with a 32-channel coil (Philips Medical System, Best, The Netherlands). The parameters of the 3D T1-weighted image were the following: repetition time (TR), 7.12 ms; echo time (TE) 3.4 ms; flip angle, 10°; number of excitations (NEX), 1; effective slice thickness, 0.6 mm with no gap; slices, 300; matrix, 260 × 320; and field of view (FOV), 26 × 24 cm. The DTI sequence was obtained with the following parameters: TR, 6700 ms; TE) 58 ms; flip angle, 90°; NEX, 2; effective slice thickness, 3.0 mm with no gap; slices, 60; matrix, 80 × 78; and FOV, 24 × 24 cm. The DTI was acquired along 15 non-collinear directions with a diffusion-weighted b-factor of 1000 s/mm^2, and one image was acquired without a diffusion gradient. Coronal fluid-attenuated inversion recovery (FLAIR) imaging and transverse 2D turbo spin echo T2-weighted imaging were also obtained for visual inspection.

2.3. MRI Processing

The DTI data were initially preprocessed with tract-based spatial statistics (TBSS) with the use of the PANDA toolbox v.1.3.1 (https://www.nitrc.org/projects/panda/ (accessed on 20 January 2023)) [18] running on MATLAB (MathWorks, Natick, MA, USA) and the FMRIB Software Library (FSL) ver. 5.0.11. Eddy current correction and brain extraction were performed, and then the TBSS pipeline provided an atlas-based region-of-interest (ROI) analysis using all tracts of the Johns Hopkins University (JHU) atlas. The automated ROI locations were visually checked for anatomical accuracy. The FA threshold for the TBSS was set at 0.20. The pipeline calculated mean FA values within each tract of the atlas in each patient [19]. We visually confirmed no problematic error or artifact on the quality of the raw and processed DTI data.

2.4. Subtype and Stage Inference (SuStaIn) Analysis

First, all of the mean FA values within each tract were corrected for age and sex using a linear regression model as in our previous study [20]. As the SuStaIn algorithm requires Z-scores for the machine learning analysis [11], we calculated Z-scores for each tract's FA values of the patients by using the data of the 270 healthy controls. Since WM damage in TLE is known to be more profound on the focus side [8], we investigated the WM changes in consideration of the focal side; to analyze left and right TLE together, we reclassified the Z-score of each tract to the ipsilateral and contralateral sides, except for the midline structures, i.e., major and minor forceps.

The Z-scores of all 20 ROIs of the 155 patients with unilateral TLE were entered into the SuStaIn algorithm (https://github.com/ucl-pond/SuStaInMatlab (accessed on 20 January 2023)) as described in our previous study [20]. Although an excessive number of biomarkers may cause problems in this analysis, we considered 20 ROIs would be acceptable based on similar previous studies [20,21]. As a SuStaIn analysis performs an unsupervised machine learning strategy, any information other than the Z-scores, e.g., the anatomy of each ROI or clinical data, was not taken into account. The linear Z-score model and mathematical model underlying the SuStaIn algorithm have been described [11]; the steps include model-fitting, convergence, uncertainty estimation, cross-validation, and similarity between subtypes. As described [11,21,22], the SuStaIn algorithm categorized our individual patients into subtypes and estimated the most likely sequence in which the selected ROIs reached different progression stages over time. While each subject's stage was estimated as probability values of weighted staging, we utilized the stage with the maximum likelihood as the subject's progression stage. The optimal number of subtypes was estimated using the cross-validation information criterion (CVIC) to balance model complexity [11,13].

2.5. Separate Analyses for the TLE Patients with and without Hippocampal Sclerosis

Although our primary analysis aimed to identify progression patterns in TLE both with and without HS, there could be differences between these two categories, and we therefore separately performed additional SuStaIn analyses for the 50 TLE patients with HS (TLE-HS) and the 105 TLE patients without HS (i.e., TLE with no visible lesions [TLE-NL]).

2.6. Statistical Analyses

The Shapiro–Wilk test revealed non-parametric distributions for most of the clinical continuous variables in this study. We investigated the relationships of the disease subtypes and stages derived from the SuStaIn analysis with the following clinical data: focus side, onset age, disease duration, presence of HS, number of antiseizure medications (ASMs), and pharmaco-resistance. We used the χ^2 test for categorical data, the Mann–Whitney U-test for group comparisons with continuous variables, and Spearman's rank test for the correlation analysis. A p-value < 0.05 was deemed significant. The statistical analyses were performed by SPSS software ver. 25.0 (IBM Corp., Armonk, NY, USA).

3. Results

3.1. Clinical Demographics

The demographic data of the patients with TLE and the HCs are summarized in Table 1. There was no significant difference in age or sex between the TLE and HC groups. Compared to the TLE-NL patients, the TLE-HS patients had younger onset ages and longer durations of disease, and they used a greater number of ASMs.

Table 1. Demographics of the patients with temporal lobe epilepsy and the healthy controls.

	TLE	HC	*p*-Value	TLE-HS	TLE-NL	*p*-Value
N	155	270	NA	50	105	NA
Age (yrs) median (IQR)	42 (26)	45 (16)	0.354	44 (21)	40 (27)	0.997
Gender (M:F)	68:87	119:151	0.968	18:32	50:55	0.173
Onset age (yrs) median (IQR)	20 (22)	NA	NA	10 (15)	24 (30)	<0.001
Duration (yrs) median (IQR)	17 (24)	NA	NA	28 (20)	9 (19)	<0.001
Laterality	L = 107, R = 48	NA	NA	L = 32, R = 18	L = 75, R = 30	0.35
Etiology	HS = 50, NL = 105	NA	NA	NA	NA	NA
Number of ASMs median (IQR) *	2 (2)	NA	NA	2 (1)	2 (1)	0.002
Seizure freedom	SF = 14, not SF = 141	NA	NA	SF = 2, not SF = 48	SF = 12, not SF = 93	0.131

TLE: temporal lobe epilepsy, HC: healthy controls, HS: hippocampal sclerosis, NA: not available, NL: no lesion. ASMs: antiseizure medications, SF: seizure freedom. * missing in 5 patients.

3.2. SuStaIn Algorithm Results

The SuStaIn algorithm identified a single subtype from the WM tract-based mean FA data of the 155 patients with unilateral TLE. In the progression model of this subtype, the initial damage occurs in the ipsilateral uncinate fasciculus (UF), followed by damage in the forceps, superior longitudinal fasciculus (SLF), and anterior thalamic radiation (ATR)

(Figure 2A). The cingulum, inferior longitudinal fasciculus (ILF), inferior fronto-occipital fasciculus (IFOF), and corticospinal tract would be disrupted in the middle disease stages.

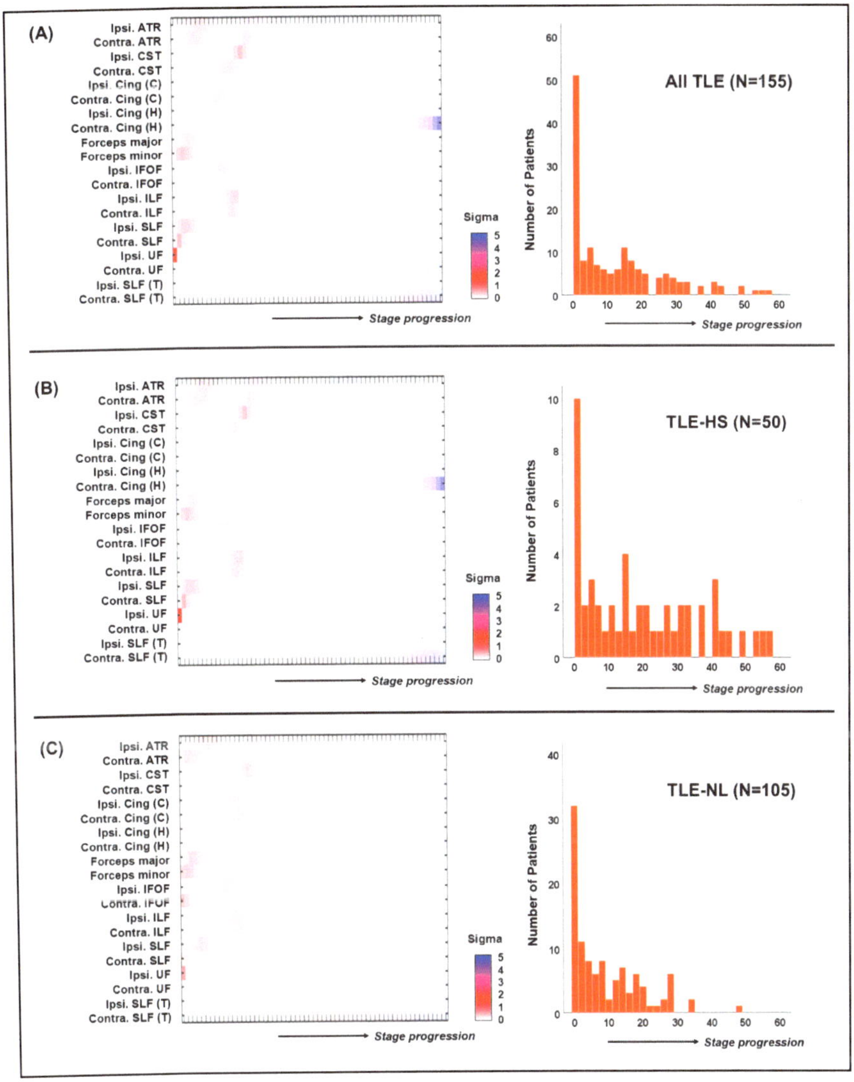

Figure 2. The progression pattern of white matter (WM) tract disruption in temporal lobe epilepsy (TLE) (left) and the number of patients at each progression stage. Results of (**A**) all 155 patients with TLE, (**B**) the 50 patients with TLE with hippocampal sclerosis (HS), and (**C**) the 105 patients with TLE with no visible lesions. ATR: anterior thalamic radiation, CST: corticospinal tract, Cing (C): cingulum (cingulate gyrus), Cing (H): cingulum hippocampus, IFOF: inferior fronto-occipital fasciculus, ILF, inferior longitudinal fasciculus, SLF: superior longitudinal fasciculus, UF: uncinate fasciculus, SLF (T): superior longitudinal fasciculus (temporal projection).

3.3. Associations with Clinical Parameters

As the SuStaIn algorithm detected just one subtype, we analyzed the relationships between the staging results and clinical parameters (Table 2). We observed that the staging was not significantly associated with gender, side of focus, or seizure freedom. The TLE-HS group showed significantly more progressed stages than the TLE-NL group ($p < 0.001$). Stage progression was also correlated with the disease duration and the number of ASMs (Figure 3).

Table 2. Associations between progression stages and clinical parameters in patients with temporal lobe epilepsy.

Categorical Comparison		
Categories and median (IQR) Stages		*p*-value
Male 5.5 (18)	Female 9 (21)	0.382
HS 16 (28)	NL 5 (15)	<0.001
Left TLE 7 (17)	Right TLE 11.5 (24)	0.205
SF 6.5 (13)	not SF 8 (19)	0.427
Correlation analysis		
Parameters	Spearman's rs	*p*-value
Age	0.102	0.207
Onset age	−0.191	0.017
Duration	0.330	<0.001
Number of ASMs	0.269	0.001

HS: hippocampal sclerosis, NL: no lesion, TLE: temporal lobe epilepsy, SF: seizure freedom, ASMs: anti-seizure medications.

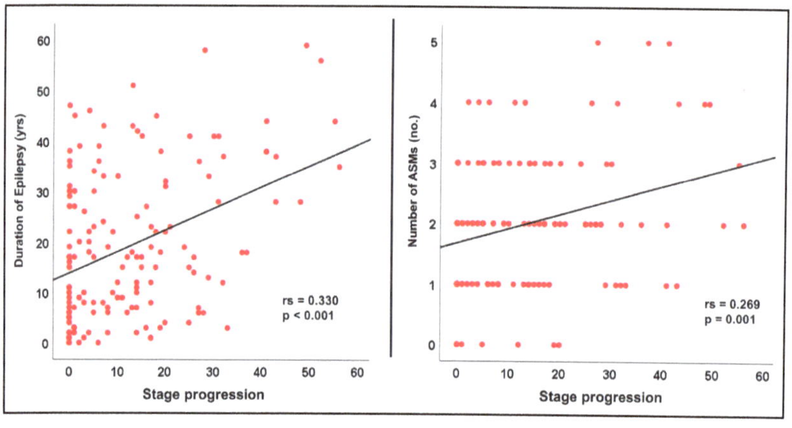

Figure 3. Significant correlations of stage progression with disease duration (**left**) and the number of antiseizure medications (ASMs) used (**right**).

3.4. Separate Analyses for the TLE-HS and TLE-NL Patients

Similar progression patterns were reproduced by the separate analyses for the patients with TLE-HS (Figure 2B) and those with TLE-NL (Figure 2C). In both analyses, one subtype was identified by the SuStaIn algorithm, in which the ipsilateral UF was damaged first and the forceps, SLF, and ATR were damaged at later timepoints (Figure 2B,C). Regarding the clinical associations with staging, similar results, i.e., correlations with disease duration, were observed (Supplement Table S1).

4. Discussion

We calculated the progression models of WM damage in patients with TLE, using an unsupervised machine learning algorithm. As a result, the SuStaIn algorithm identified a single subtype in which the ipsilateral UF damage occurred first, and the forceps, SLF, and ATR were damaged subsequently. Since the UF is a part of the limbic system, connecting the anterior temporal lobe and the orbitofrontal cortex [23], our findings are consistent with the anatomical pathophysiology in TLE. This progression pattern model was replicated in the separate analyses for the TLE-HS and TLE-NL groups, indicating that WM changes in TLE may share a similar progression trajectory. Regarding the clinical correlates, further-progressed stages were associated with longer disease durations and the use of a greater number of antiseizure medications. In addition, the patients with TLE with HS showed more advanced stages compared to the TLE patients with no lesions. Although many epilepsy neuroimaging studies have used machine learning, most were supervised learning studies using clinically labeled data, with few reports of unsupervised learning [24]. The advantage of unsupervised learning is that it can be used to find hidden patterns in unlabeled data that are difficult to notice clinically and may thus lead to new discoveries [24].

The white matter damage in TLE is extensive [8,16], but it has not been known when and in what order this damage occurs. The progression of WM disruption over time in TLE has not yet been clearly demonstrated with the use of longitudinal data. However, a 2019 longitudinal morphological MRI study demonstrated that the progression of brain atrophy over time in focal epilepsy exceeds that of normal aging [10], and it is conceivable that white matter damage may also progress over time. The WM damage progression pattern model in TLE that was identified in our present investigation can be used to identify the disease progression stages in individual patients and may serve as a novel clinical biomarker. WM is the structure that communicates between brain regions and serves as the base of the brain network, and has potential for a variety of future studies, which may include epilepsy types other than TLE, relevance to clinical outcomes such as postsurgical seizure freedom, or associations with brain network metrics.

Xiao et al. investigated disease progression patterns of brain atrophy in focal epilepsy and idiopathic generalized epilepsy (IGE) by using cross-sectional MRI data and the SuStaIn algorithm [13]. According to their findings, although IGE presented two different trajectories, i.e., the basal ganglia atrophy type and the cortical thinning type, the brain morphological changes in focal epilepsy were classified into three subtypes: the cortical type, starting with reduced cortical thickness; the basal ganglia type, starting with basal ganglia atrophy; and the hippocampal type, starting with hippocampal atrophy; in addition, the hippocampal type was reported to be the most frequent in TLE [13]. Our present analyses identified only one subtype for WM progression, possibly because we selected a relatively homogeneous clinical group, i.e., patients with unilateral TLE. Another possible explanation might be the use of a tract-level evaluation. Using tract-based mean FA values alone may not assess white matter damage in sufficient anatomical detail and might warrant further investigation using a better methodology beyond a tract-level analysis. Conversely, if only one subtype actually exists, a more specific method for time-based modeling, rather than the spatiotemporal heterogeneity approach [25], may be useful for further detailed investigation.

We also detected several clinical correlates with disease progression stages. The TLE-HS patients presented more progressed stages compared to the TLE-NL patients, and this may reflect more severe WM damage in the TLE-HS group. It has been repeatedly confirmed that the integrity of the white matter in individuals with TLE-HS is more profoundly impaired [8,16]. We also observed a positive correlation between staging and disease duration (Spearman's rs = 0.330, $p < 0.001$), which is consistent with the recent study using morphological brain MRI [13]. In TLE, both gray matter atrophy and WM fiber damage may progress over time along with the duration of disease. The number of ASMs used may also be an important factor affecting WM disruption. As our cohort was mostly drug-resistant cases, caution should be used when considering the nonsignificant results between staging and seizure freedom, considering the small sample of seizure-free patients. In addition, due to the cross-sectional design, causal relationships between these associations cannot be addressed. We did not investigate the effect of seizure burden. While no significant correlations between disease stages and seizure frequency were found in the previous study [13], further investigations would be warranted for these issues.

This study has several limitations. The sample size was medium (155 patients with TLE and 270 healthy controls) from a single epilepsy center, and careful interpretation would be needed for sub-analyses with a small sample size, e.g., seizure-free patients (N = 14 in total). This study lacked external validation, although the results were generally replicated by the additional analyses performed separately for the TLE-HS and TLE-NL groups. It should also be noted that our findings are based solely on cross-sectional data and theoretical models, and thus our results must be tested in studies with larger cohorts and longitudinal investigations. Our clinical data were also limited, lacking more detailed examinations, e.g., cognitive dysfunction or surgical outcomes. More detailed clinical data could be useful in the future to further explore the potential utility of SuStaIn results as a clinical biomarker. There might be other unknown or unevaluated confounders, e.g., the effect of medications, which should be considered for careful interpretations of the results of this study.

5. Conclusions

Using a data-driven machine learning analysis, we identified the white matter disease progression trajectory in patients with unilateral TLE, in which the initial damage occurs in the ipsilateral UF, followed by damage in the forceps, SLF, and ATR. More progressed stages of TLE were associated with the presence of hippocampal sclerosis, longer disease duration, and a greater number of ASMs used. These findings may contribute to the better pathophysiological understanding of the progression of temporal lobe epilepsy as well as the establishment of novel imaging biomarkers.

Supplementary Materials: The following supporting information can be downloaded at: https://www.mdpi.com/article/10.3390/brainsci14100992/s1, Table S1: Associations between progression stages and clinical parameters derived from the separate analyses for the TLE-HS and TLE-NL groups.

Author Contributions: D.S.: Conceptualization, Data curation, Formal analysis, Writing—original draft, N.S.: Supervision, Writing—review and editing, Y.S.: Resources, Supervision, Writing—review and editing, I.B.: Supervision, Writing—review and editing, Y.K.: Resources, Supervision, Writing-review and editing, H.M.: Supervision, Writing—review and editing. All authors have read and agreed to the published version of the manuscript.

Funding: This work was supported by grants from the Japan Society for the Promotion of Science (KAKENHI; no. JP21K15720), the Japan Epilepsy Research Foundation (JERF TENKAN 22007), and the Uehara Memorial Foundation (all to D.S.).

Institutional Review Board Statement: This study was approved by the Institutional Review Board at National Center of Neurology and Psychiatry Hospital, Tokyo, Japan (no. A2013-039, approval on 7 August 2013).

Informed Consent Statement: All of the subjects gave written informed consent to participate in accordance with the Declaration of Helsinki.

Data Availability Statement: Data not included in the article will be made available from the corresponding author to qualified researchers on reasonable request subject to ethics approval.

Conflicts of Interest: The authors declare no conflicts of interest.

References

1. Thijs, R.D.; Surges, R.; O'Brien, T.J.; Sander, J.W. Epilepsy in adults. *Lancet* **2019**, *393*, 689–701. [CrossRef] [PubMed]
2. Collaborators, G.B.D.E. Global, regional, and national burden of epilepsy, 1990–2016: A systematic analysis for the Global Burden of Disease Study 2016. *Lancet Neurol.* **2019**, *18*, 357–375. [CrossRef]

3. Spiciarich, M.C.; von Gaudecker, J.R.; Jurasek, L.; Clarke, D.F.; Burneo, J.; Vidaurre, J. Global Health and Epilepsy: Update and Future Directions. *Curr. Neurol. Neurosci. Rep.* **2019**, *19*, 30. [CrossRef]
4. Reynolds, E.H. The origins and early development of the ILAE/IBE/WHO global campaign against epilepsy: Out of the shadows. *Epilepsia Open* **2024**, *9*, 77–83. [CrossRef]
5. Keezer, M.R.; Sisodiya, S.M.; Sander, J.W. Comorbidities of epilepsy: Current concepts and future perspectives. *Lancet Neurol.* **2016**, *15*, 106–115. [CrossRef] [PubMed]
6. Wykes, R.C.; Khoo, H.M.; Caciagli, L.; Blumenfeld, H.; Golshani, P.; Kapur, J.; Stern, J.M.; Bernasconi, A.; Dedeurwaerdere, S.; Bernasconi, N. WONOEP appraisal: Network concept from an imaging perspective. *Epilepsia* **2019**, *60*, 1293–1305. [CrossRef] [PubMed]
7. Whelan, C.D.; Altmann, A.; Botia, J.A.; Jahanshad, N.; Hibar, D.P.; Absil, J.; Alhusaini, S.; Alvim, M.K.M.; Auvinen, P.; Bartolini, E.; et al. Structural brain abnormalities in the common epilepsies assessed in a worldwide ENIGMA study. *Brain J. Neurol.* **2018**, *141*, 391–408. [CrossRef]
8. Hatton, S.N.; Huynh, K.H.; Bonilha, L.; Abela, E.; Alhusaini, S.; Altmann, A.; Alvim, M.K.M.; Balachandra, A.R.; Bartolini, E.; Bender, B.; et al. White matter abnormalities across different epilepsy syndromes in adults: An ENIGMA-Epilepsy study. *Brain J. Neurol.* **2020**, *143*, 2454–2473. [CrossRef]
9. Lariviere, S.; Rodriguez-Cruces, R.; Royer, J.; Caligiuri, M.E.; Gambardella, A.; Concha, L.; Keller, S.S.; Cendes, F.; Yasuda, C.; Bonilha, L.; et al. Network-based atrophy modeling in the common epilepsies: A worldwide ENIGMA study. *Sci. Adv.* **2020**, *6*, eabc6457. [CrossRef]
10. Galovic, M.; van Dooren, V.Q.H.; Postma, T.; Vos, S.B.; Caciagli, L.; Borzi, G.; Rosillo, J.C.; Vuong, K.A.; de Tisi, J.; Nachev, P.; et al. Progressive Cortical Thinning in Patients with Focal Epilepsy. *JAMA Neurol.* **2019**, *76*, 1230–1239. [CrossRef]
11. Young, A.L.; Marinescu, R.V.; Oxtoby, N.P.; Bocchetta, M.; Yong, K.; Firth, N.C.; Cash, D.M.; Thomas, D.L.; Dick, K.M.; Cardoso, J.; et al. Uncovering the heterogeneity and temporal complexity of neurodegenerative diseases with Subtype and Stage Inference. *Nat. Commun.* **2018**, *9*, 4273. [CrossRef] [PubMed]
12. Young, A.L.; Oxtoby, N.P.; Garbarino, S.; Fox, N.C.; Barkhof, F.; Schott, J.M.; Alexander, D.C. Data-driven modelling of neurodegenerative disease progression: Thinking outside the black box. *Nat. Rev. Neurosci.* **2024**, *25*, 111–130. [CrossRef]
13. Xiao, F.; Caciagli, L.; Wandschneider, B.; Sone, D.; Young, A.L.; Vos, S.B.; Winston, G.P.; Zhang, Y.; Liu, W.; An, D.; et al. Identification of different MRI atrophy progression trajectories in epilepsy by subtype and stage inference. *Brain J. Neurol.* **2023**, *146*, 4702–4716. [CrossRef]
14. Jiang, Y.; Li, W.; Li, J.; Li, X.; Zhang, H.; Sima, X.; Li, L.; Wang, K.; Li, Q.; Fang, J.; et al. Identification of four biotypes in temporal lobe epilepsy via machine learning on brain images. *Nat. Commun.* **2024**, *15*, 2221. [CrossRef]
15. Engel, J., Jr. Introduction to temporal lobe epilepsy. *Epilepsy Res.* **1996**, *26*, 141–150. [CrossRef] [PubMed]
16. Otte, W.M.; van Eijsden, P.; Sander, J.W.; Duncan, J.S.; Dijkhuizen, R.M.; Braun, K.P. A meta-analysis of white matter changes in temporal lobe epilepsy as studied with diffusion tensor imaging. *Epilepsia* **2012**, *53*, 659–667. [CrossRef] [PubMed]
17. Royer, J.; Bernhardt, B.C.; Lariviere, S.; Gleichgerrcht, E.; Vorderwulbecke, B.J.; Vulliemoz, S.; Bonilha, L. Epilepsy and brain network hubs. *Epilepsia* **2022**, *63*, 537–550. [CrossRef]
18. Cui, Z.; Zhong, S.; Xu, P.; He, Y.; Gong, G. PANDA: A pipeline toolbox for analyzing brain diffusion images. *Front. Hum. Neurosci.* **2013**, *7*, 42. [CrossRef]
19. Wakana, S.; Caprihan, A.; Panzenboeck, M.M.; Fallon, J.H.; Perry, M.; Gollub, R.L.; Hua, K.; Zhang, J.; Jiang, H.; Dubey, P.; et al. Reproducibility of quantitative tractography methods applied to cerebral white matter. *NeuroImage* **2007**, *36*, 630–644. [CrossRef]
20. Sone, D.; Young, A.; Shinagawa, S.; Tsugawa, S.; Iwata, Y.; Tarumi, R.; Ogyu, K.; Honda, S.; Ochi, R.; Matsushita, K.; et al. Disease Progression Patterns of Brain Morphology in Schizophrenia: More Progressed Stages in Treatment Resistance. *Schizophr. Bull.* **2024**, *50*, 393–402. [CrossRef]
21. Young, A.L.; Bocchetta, M.; Russell, L.L.; Convery, R.S.; Peakman, G.; Todd, E.; Cash, D.M.; Greaves, C.V.; van Swieten, J.; Jiskoot, L.; et al. Characterizing the Clinical Features and Atrophy Patterns of MAPT-Related Frontotemporal Dementia with Disease Progression Modeling. *Neurology* **2021**, *97*, e941–e952. [CrossRef] [PubMed]
22. Vogel, J.W.; Young, A.L.; Oxtoby, N.P.; Smith, R.; Ossenkoppele, R.; Strandberg, O.T.; La Joie, R.; Aksman, L.M.; Grothe, M.J.; Iturria-Medina, Y.; et al. Four distinct trajectories of tau deposition identified in Alzheimer's disease. *Nat. Med.* **2021**, *27*, 871–881. [CrossRef] [PubMed]
23. Von Der Heide, R.J.; Skipper, L.M.; Klobusicky, E.; Olson, I.R. Dissecting the uncinate fasciculus: Disorders, controversies and a hypothesis. *Brain J. Neurol.* **2013**, *136*, 1692–1707. [CrossRef] [PubMed]
24. Sone, D.; Beheshti, I. Clinical Application of Machine Learning Models for Brain Imaging in Epilepsy: A Review. *Front. Neurosci.* **2021**, *15*, 684825. [CrossRef]
25. Liu, L.; Sun, S.; Kang, W.; Wu, S.; Lin, L. A review of neuroimaging-based data-driven approach for Alzheimer's disease heterogeneity analysis. *Rev. Neurosci.* **2024**, *35*, 121–139. [CrossRef]

Disclaimer/Publisher's Note: The statements, opinions and data contained in all publications are solely those of the individual author(s) and contributor(s) and not of MDPI and/or the editor(s). MDPI and/or the editor(s) disclaim responsibility for any injury to people or property resulting from any ideas, methods, instructions or products referred to in the content.

brain sciences

MDPI

Article

Biomarkers of Immersion in Virtual Reality Based on Features Extracted from the EEG Signals: A Machine Learning Approach

Hamed Tadayyoni [1,†], Michael S. Ramirez Campos [2,†], Alvaro Joffre Uribe Quevedo [3] and Bernadette A. Murphy [1,*]

1 Faculty of Health Sciences, Ontario Tech University, Oshawa, ON L1G 0C5, Canada; hamed.tadayyoniahrab@ontariotechu.net
2 Faculty of Biomedical Engineering, Universidad Escuela Colombiana de Ingeniería Julio Garavito, AK 45 #205-59, Bogotá 111166, Colombia; michael.ramirez@mail.escuelaing.edu.co
3 Faculty of Business and Information Technology, Ontario Tech University, Oshawa, ON L1G 0C5, Canada; alvaro.quevedo@ontariotechu.ca
* Correspondence: bernadette.murphy@ontariotechu.ca
† These authors contributed equally to this work.

Abstract: Virtual reality (VR) enables the development of virtual training frameworks suitable for various domains, especially when real-world conditions may be hazardous or impossible to replicate because of unique additional resources (e.g., equipment, infrastructure, people, locations). Although VR technology has significantly advanced in recent years, methods for evaluating immersion (i.e., the extent to which the user is engaged with the sensory information from the virtual environment or is invested in the intended task) continue to rely on self-reported questionnaires, which are often administered after using the virtual scenario. Having an objective method to measure immersion is particularly important when using VR for training, education, and applications that promote the development, fine-tuning, or maintenance of skills. The level of immersion may impact performance and the translation of knowledge and skills to the real-world. This is particularly important in tasks where motor skills are combined with complex decision making, such as surgical procedures. Efforts to better measure immersion have included the use of physiological measurements including heart rate and skin response, but so far they do not offer robust metrics that provide the sensitivity to discriminate different states (idle, easy, and hard), which is critical when using VR for training to determine how successful the training is in engaging the user's senses and challenging their cognitive capabilities. In this study, electroencephalography (EEG) data were collected from 14 participants who completed VR jigsaw puzzles with two different levels of task difficulty. Machine learning was able to accurately classify the EEG data collected during three different states, obtaining accuracy rates of 86% and 97% for differentiating easy versus hard difficulty states and baseline vs. VR states. Building on these results may enable the identification of robust biomarkers of immersion in VR, enabling real-time recognition of the level of immersion that can be used to design more effective and translative VR-based training. This method has the potential to adjust aspects of VR related to task difficulty to ensure that participants are immersed in VR.

Keywords: virtual reality; immersion; task difficulty; electroencephalography (EEG); biomarkers; machine learning

1. Introduction

Virtual reality (VR) allows the delivery of novel solutions in various domains such as entertainment [1], simulations [2], tele-rehabilitation [3,4], and training [5]. In particular, VR training applications not only provide the opportunity to experience scenarios that impose high physical or hygienic risks [6], but also allow trainees to practice the module as many times as necessary without being limited by fear of wasting real resources [7]. Despite its potential, VR's limitations include physical drawbacks such as VR-induced motion sickness [5] and the weight of the head-mounted device (HMD) [8]. Furthermore, VR-based training may not accurately simulate the level of tactile, haptic, or proprioceptive feedback with which users need to be trained to develop the required kinaesthetic skills [9]. Additionally, virtual environments may fail to accurately represent the real-world scenario in terms of visual and auditory cues and fidelity [10]. These restrictions may decrease the level of effectiveness of VR-based training and must be studied and addressed to optimize VR for training in certain applications [5].

As a result of these limitations, the success of VR training can depend on how successful it is in engaging the user's senses and cognitive capabilities to the same level as its real-world counterpart. In the literature, engagement is defined in terms of different quantities such as presence, flow, fidelity, and immersion [11]. Flow is defined as the process of optimal experience [12], presence refers to the psychological sense of being in the virtual environment [13], and immersion is defined as the degree to which the user feels engaged and absorbed in the environment and attends to the planned task [14]. Immersion encompasses different aspects of the sense of 'being there' [15], including being caught up in the sensory input of the virtual environment, as well as being mentally and cognitively invested in the intended task. Immersion that refers to the sensory information received by the user from the virtual environment is called sensory immersion [16], while cognitive immersion is defined by the degree of engagement of the user caused by the task's demands [1]. Although the former is mostly constrained by technology-related aspects of the virtual environment and how well the software and hardware provide the required levels of different real-world sensory information [4], the latter is dependent on how much the designed task engages the user [17]. Immersion provides a better quantification of engagement in the evaluation of a virtual training designed to replicate the real-world experience, as its definition encompasses both sensory and cognitive components of VR training [11].

Research on immersion has been crucial to determine the impact and success of VR experiences in the translation of cognitive and motor learning [18]. There are different subjective and objective methods proposed in the literature to study immersion. Subjective methods strongly rely on participants' opinions and self-reported data [13,19] while considering the sense of immersion tied to the phenomenological experience of the user [1]. These measures rely on the understanding that the user has of the concept of immersion [19] and are impacted by the inherent subjectivity of the measured quantity. Additionally, asking about immersion while the user is inside the virtual environment breaks the immersion, as it distracts the user from their subjective experience [20], and asking about it afterwards makes the results highly dependent on the recollection of the user's experience [21]. Therefore, quantifying immersion in a consistent and objective manner that enables researchers to compare their findings and investigate the difference between immersion levels resulting from different tasks, environments, levels of difficulty, circumstances, etc., is necessary. Researchers have investigated various objective methods of measuring immersion that do not require conscious deliberation from the participants [11,22], using performance-based and physiological-based points of view. Physiological measures have included eye tracking [11], galvanic skin response [23], electrocardiogram [24], and electroencephalography (EEG) [2,25], among others.

In the literature, to our knowledge, the use of EEG for studying immersion has been limited to measuring the amplitude of event-related potentials (ERPs), evoked in response to a stimulus that is not related to the task in which the immersion of the participant is studied. This is followed by a statistical analysis of ERP amplitudes to study the differences between different levels of immersion and/or presence [1,2,23,25,26]. Although this method is more promising than other physiological measures in terms of accuracy and resistance to confounding variables (including being influenced by how virtual environments represent information, boredom, and exhaustion), it still lags in offering a robust marker for identifying immersion that is not influenced by potential confounding variables, and it has resulted in heterogeneous, and in some cases contradictory findings [1,25]. It also suffers from an inability to identify and differentiate low and high levels of immersion in real time. Machine learning (ML) methods for classifying EEG signals can offer the ability to differentiate between different levels of immersion in real time.

In the literature, EEG-based machine learning and other classification approaches have been used in various paradigms to extract insightful meaning from different mathematical features of the signals. Kamińska et al. [27] and Aliyari et al. [28] were able to classify different levels of stress imposed on the users in the virtual environment. Deep learning has been used to extract information from EEG for stroke patients performing a real-time rehabilitation experiment [29]. Moncada et al. proposed a method for a VR-based protocol to classify important characteristics related to epilepsy [30], while Yildrim has reviewed ML-based methods used to classify EEG characteristics attributed to cybersickness [31]. Hekmatmanesh et al. investigated the use of different methods based on EEG (based on a common spatial pattern algorithm) to improve the detection of motor imagery patterns in EEG signals in brain–computer interface applications by evaluating the efficiency of various types of classifiers [32]. Other work has investigated the possibility of using brain–computer interfaces to control movements in VR based on ML-based movement prediction [33], and other work has investigated the applications of machine learning approaches for EEG-based emotion recognition [34].

These studies show that the potential for extracting relevant features for classification of EEG recordings is promising, with the potential to identify biomarkers of sensory processing in EEG recordings of a VR-based task. These methods introduce more robust biomarkers for their corresponding applications, where more accurate and homogeneous results are obtained, but also offer the potential for automatic recognition and classification of EEG data in real time. If they can progress to real-time measurement, machine learning approaches have the potential to address the limitations of VR-based training on the performance and transfer of skills to the real world and contribute to improving the design of VR-based training. Additionally, ML approaches might enable real-time customization of various features of training according to the individual characteristics of a user.

In this study, immersion was attributed to the level of difficulty of the task, based on the past literature [35,36]. Therefore, different levels of task difficulty were used, which included sitting idle and solving a jigsaw puzzle in easy and hard conditions in VR, where the number of pieces determined the difficulty of the task. Machine learning algorithms (stochastic gradient descent (SGD), support vector classifier (SVC), decision tree (DT), Gaussian naive Bayes (GNB), k-nearest neighbors (KNN), random forest (RF), and a multilayer perceptron (MLP)) were used to classify the EEG signals recorded during these states. Various temporal, frequency-domain, and non-linear features were used for analysing the EEG signals and in total two sets of features were tested (10 features for three or nine central channels and four frequency bands). The combination of a novel design protocol (which has shown its robustness in a recent study [25]) and machine learning approaches was used in the current study. The study aimed to determine whether machine learning approaches could accurately classify the three states based on the features extracted from EEG data, in addition to determining which features best represent different states of immersion.

2. Materials and Methods

2.1. Overall Experimental Procedure

A total of 14 right-handed individuals (7 male, 6 female, 1 preferred not to say) between the ages of 18 and 35 participated in this study. The dominance of the right hand was determined by a score of above 40 in the Edinburgh handedness inventory [37]. The study exclusion criteria required all participants not to have any neurological conditions (such as epilepsy, multiple sclerosis, skull fracture or serious head injury, attention deficit hyperactivity disorder, etc.), and not to have recurrent or chronic neck pain, and not to take any tricyclic antidepressants, neuroleptic or antipsychotic medications, or recreational drugs, as they can alter EEG suitability. Furthermore, to avoid hearing and severe visual conditions as well as motion sickness, which could compromise the results, the participants were asked if they had hearing problems, stereo blindness, or had reported previous VR-induced motion sickness; participants reporting any of these were excluded from the study. This study was approved by the research ethics board of the University of Ontario Institute of Technology (Ontario Tech University) (REB #17351).

Prior to the main study, we conducted various preliminary studies [1–3,23,26] and developed a protocol [25] to investigate the feasibility of the chosen task for discriminating between low and high levels of immersion. A VR jigsaw puzzle was selected for the study because it enables potential confounding variables, not related to immersion, to be minimized. This is described in greater detail below (Section 2.2).

The main study started with a calibration stage in which participants sat on a chair and wore both the EEG cap and the Meta Quest Pro VR headset. The calibration focused on collecting a 'baseline' data set with the participants watching a 360° pre-recorded video of the real study room while remaining idle for two 6 min blocks. After completing the baseline collection, the participants played through the jigsaw puzzles for four 6 min blocks of easy, hard, hard, and easy levels. The overall experimental protocol is depicted in Figure 1. The participants were instructed to use controllers to select, pick, reorient, and place pieces. The participants were allowed to interact with the game through a familiarization block with the objective of reducing the cognitive load that would be required when familiarizing with the controllers while solving the puzzle at the same time. A short 2 min break was anticipated in which the headset (and not the EEG cap) was removed, enforced to avoid exhaustion from wearing the headset, which weighs 722 g.

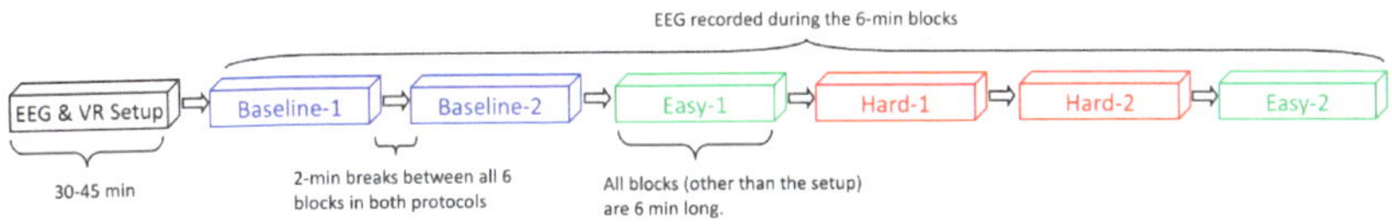

Figure 1. Overall experimental protocol.

The 'Jigsaw Puzzle VR' (available through https://www.meta.com/experiences/5080756015327836/?utm_source=altlabvr.com (accessed on 9 July 2023)) game was chosen because it provided the closest experience to solving a puzzle in real life. This game allows users to use the controllers to move and put together the pieces (Figure 2). In this case, difficulty refers to how complex it is to complete the puzzle according to the number of pieces and the time required to complete the puzzle [25]. Two levels of difficulty were chosen: one with 24 pieces, set as easy difficulty; and a 60-piece puzzle selected for the hard difficulty. Each component of this procedure is defined in detail in the following subsections.

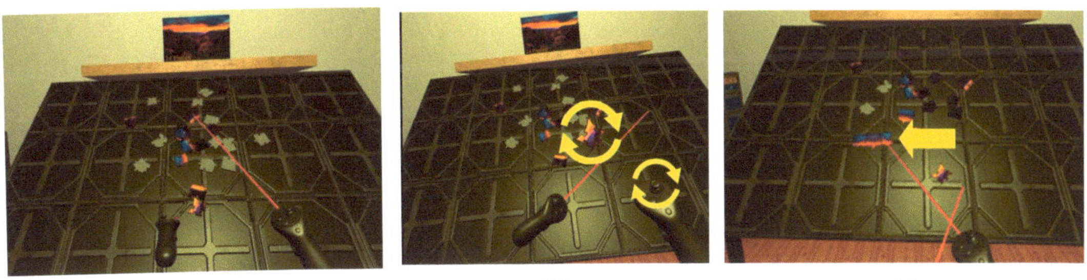

(a) (b) (c)

Figure 2. 'Jigsaw Puzzle VR' game interactions: (**a**) Picking up puzzle pieces by pointing and selecting them using the trigger button; (**b**) rotating the puzzle piece with the thumb sticks; (**c**) the pieces are joined together when matched.

2.2. Choice of the Experimental Task

Our proposed protocol employing a jigsaw puzzle provides a suitable testbed with the following highlights:

- The similarity between the easy and hard levels in terms of interactions highlights that the main difference between the difficulty levels is only related to the cognitive demand. The scenes for the easy and hard puzzles were chosen from very similar natural and 'unfamous' landscapes, similar in color and pattern, so that the participants were not stimulated by possible memories, emotions, and thoughts induced by other types of pictures. The images used for different blocks of playing the jigsaw puzzle are presented in Figure 3.
- The number of pieces for the puzzles was adjusted in our pilot studies to ensure that the easy and hard puzzles could be completed within the allocated study time. Furthermore, ensuring that the puzzle can be completed minimizes the risk of participants feeling demotivated, according to the motivational intensity model (MIM) [38]. Therefore, during the pilot phase of the study, several permutations of duration and number of pieces were tested to find the optimum combination [25]. We came up with the final number of pieces for easy and hard levels through multiple rounds of piloting in which different skilled and unskilled participants played the game with different number of pieces, puzzle scenes, and lengths. We tested durations as short as 3 min and as long as 12 min, together with the number of pieces as low as 20 pieces and as high as 96 pieces. Most participants could complete two easy puzzles (each with 24 pieces) or one hard puzzle (with 60 pieces) in the two 6 min blocks allocated to each condition.

(**a**) (**b**)

Figure 3. Photos of similar landscapes used for 2 difficulty levels of the jigsaw puzzle game: (**a**) used for the easy level and (**b**) used for the hard level. To have control over the difficulty level of the puzzles, the photos were chosen to resemble the same color distribution and scenery, so that the only difference between the levels was the number of the pieces chosen for each level of difficulty. (photo sources: ((**a**)—top) image from wallpapers.com, "Beautiful Scenery Trees Wallpaper", accessed on 13 October 2023, © 2023 wallpapers.com; ((**a**)—bottom) Peakpx, "Shenandoah National Park", accessed on 13 October 2023, © 2023 peakpx.com; (**b**) Peakpx, "view nature, bonito, flowers", accessed on 13 October 2023, © 2023 peakpx.com).

2.3. Choice of Rest State (Baseline Collection)

During baseline data collection, the participant wears the VR HMD on top of the EEG cap. Additionally, the headset is powered during the baseline collection to have all possible confounding parameters caused by wearing the HMD exactly consistent between the easy and hard difficulties. Acknowledging that visual cues can influence cognitive load, we explored using a 180° version of the fixation cross (e.g., reticle) [39] in VR, and playing a 360° video of the same environment where the visual stimuli matched the same environment in which the participant was currently in. The 360° video was chosen over the fixation cross, since participants found that the latter was boring and monotonous, creating mental distractions that could impact the EEG [25].

2.4. EEG Recording

The EEG signals were recorded using a Waveguard™ 64-electrode EEG cap (manufactured by ANT Neuro, Hengelo, The Netherlands), following the 10–20 electrode placement system [40] (as shown in Figure 2). We used a TMSi REFA-8 amplifier (TMSi, Oldenzaal, The Netherlands) for EEG recording. Throughout the EEG recording, we ensured that electrode impedances remained below 10 kΩ. The EEG data were collected using Advanced Source Analysis Lab™ (ANT Neuro, Hengelo, The Netherlands) at a sampling frequency of 2048 Hz. In this study, features were extracted from the EEG data recorded from the three midline frontal, central, and parietal electrodes (lines 3, 4, and z shown in Figure 4).

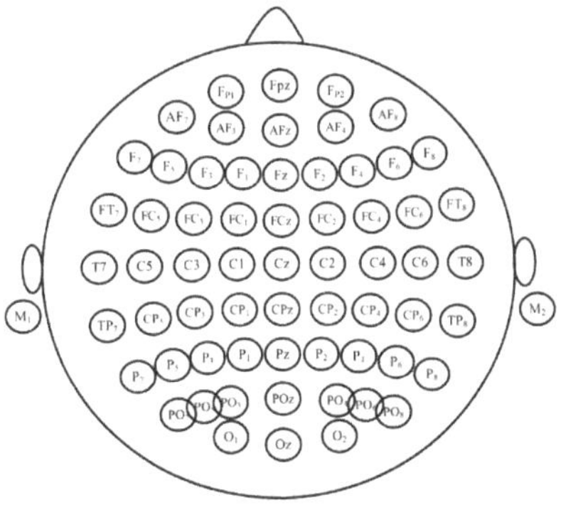

Figure 4. Layout of the locations of EEG channels according to the international 10–20 system.

2.5. EEG Signals Pre-Processing

The EEG data were pre-processed offline using ASA 4.10.1 and later using Python in Google Collaboratory, through which the artifacts from muscle activity and/or blinking were removed. Eyeblinks were removed through the artifact removal feature of ASA. A bandpass filter of low cut-off frequency of 0.1 Hz and high cut-off frequency of 30 Hz with a steepness slope of 24 dB/octave was used to remove the amplifier, environment, and connection noise. Artifacts with amplitude outside the region of [−100, 100] μv were also removed. Later, the EMG artifacts were removed from the signal through independent component analysis (ICA) in Python. In this study, interpolation was never required to substitute signals from a noisy channel.

2.6. General Machine Learning Pipeline

All EEG signals were segmented into 4 s windows. This was performed so that in future analyses the data could be grouped to see if the level of immersion changed over time. Then, all windows are grouped and labeled according to the level of immersion for which they were recorded (i.e., three states of baseline, easy, and hard). The temporal, frequency-domain, and non-linear features were then extracted from each 4 s EEG window. According to previous work related to the use of ERPs to identify different levels of immersion during VR tasks, midline channels (Fz, Cz, and Pz) can provide relevant information about immersion levels [1–3,23]. In this sense, two global groups of features were generated; the first were features only extracted from the midline channels and the second were features extracted from the midline and adjacent channels (F3, F4, C3, C4, P3, P4). The reason for choosing the first group of features is for consistency with what has been previously reported in the literature [3,26]. Subsequently, feature selection was performed through two methods: one using the maximum relevance minimum redundancy

(MRMR) method, and the other using the combination of MRMR with a statistical test of independence (Mann–Whitney U test). Afterwards, eight machine learning classifications were performed using different feature sets, with the first through fourth classifications using the features of the midline channels as input. The fifth through eighth classifications used the midline and adjacent channels' features as input. The first, second, fifth, and sixth classifications differentiated the easy from hard VR states. The third, fourth, seventh, and eighth differentiated the baseline state from the difficulty. Finally, the related biomarkers were identified through EEG characterization of the best two classifiers to identify the differences between the baseline and VR states. The detailed pipeline of the data analysis and machine learning process is depicted in Figure 5.

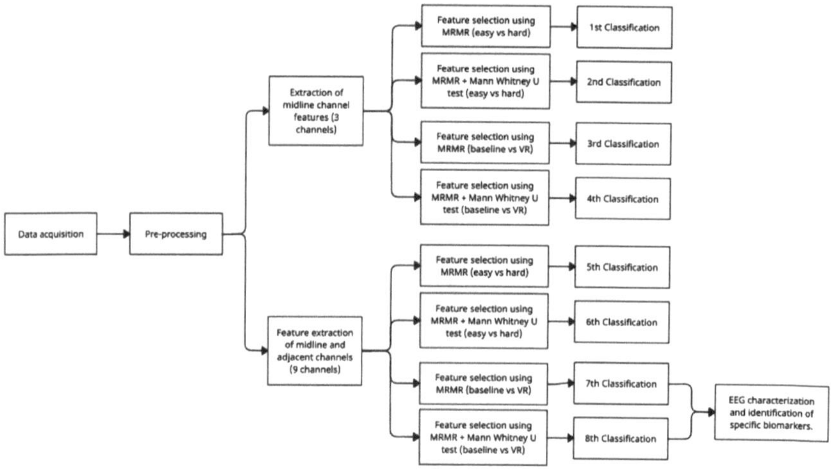

Figure 5. Machine learning pipeline used in this study.

2.7. Introducing the Primary Features

The features used in this study were selected primarily based on previous work that showed success in defining optimal features for ML-based approaches for the classification of EEG data for other applications [41,42]. Table 1 shows the different features that were used in this study. In total, these 10 features were used for a group of 3 and 9 channels of EEG filtered into 4 frequency bands (delta (0.2–4 Hz), theta (4–8 Hz), alpha (8–12 Hz) and beta (12–30 Hz)), resulting in the final counts of 120 and 360 for channel-band-feature trios.

Table 1. Features used in this study.

Type of Feature	Features
Temporal	Activity (variance) [43] Mobility [43] Complexity [43]
Frequency-domain	Power spectral density (PSD)
Entropy	Permutation Spectral Entropy
Non-linear	Higuchi's fractal dimension [44] Hurst's exponent [45]
Statistical	Kurtosis Skewness

2.8. Methods for Feature Selection

As mentioned earlier, two techniques were used for feature selection: MRMR and MRMR combined with the Mann–Witney U statistical test [46]. For the second technique, the Mann–Whitney U test was applied to the MRMR results to select the features that showed the greatest statistical difference. The MRMR approach evaluates the significance of each feature by considering two key relationships: the F statistic between each feature and the target variable or label, and the Pearson correlation between each feature and the remaining features in the data set. Consequently, a higher score indicates a greater relevance of a feature [47]. In contrast to principal component analysis (PCA), which produces principal components that are linear combinations of all original features, and linear discriminant analysis (LDA), which focuses on maximizing separability between classes based on the projection of the data on a new orthogonal basis and does not directly consider the class labels or target variable, MRMR selects a subset of original features that are directly interpretable. This can be advantageous in situations such as this study, where interpretation and understanding of the selected features (and not their combinations or projections) in relation to the problem under study are the main focus [48].

2.9. Classification Methods and EEG Characterization

The following classification methods were implemented and used: SGD, SVC, DT, GNB, KNN, RF, and MLP. A heuristic method was then applied to find the training hyperparameters of the models. A total of 80% of the data were used for training, and the remaining data were used to test the models. Following the classification, the channel-band-feature trios that provide the most relevant information through specific features for identifying the level of immersion are recognized and introduced as relevant markers. In this study, we evaluate the performance of the classifiers based on the accuracy percentage metric (defined as the proportion of the number of correct predictions in all predictions [49]). The parameters used for running the classification methods are summarized in Table A1 in the Appendix A to this paper.

3. Results

Two groups of features were generated: 120 features extracted from the midline channels and 360 features extracted from the midline and adjacent channels. The best classifier method was random forest, which obtained accuracies above 85%. With respect to the features, the most relevant channels were Fz, Cz, Pz, F3, P3, C3, F4, P4, and C4.

Tables 2–5 show the accuracy of the tested model for each classification performed during this approach. In Tables 2 and 4, we are using a total of 120 features (3 channels, 4 frequency bands, 10 basic features), and in Tables 3 and 5, we are using a total of 360 features (9 channels, 4 frequency bands, 10 basic features). Tables 2 and 3 show the accuracy percentages for classification between the easy and hard states, while Tables 4 and 5 show the accuracy percentages for classification of baseline vs. VR state (easy and hard together). In all tables, the second column lists the accuracy percentages for the most relevant and statistically significant features obtained from the MRMR method and Mann–Whitney test, respectively, and the third column shows the accuracy percentages of the classifiers for the most relevant features resulting from only the MRMR.

All classifications were performed using different sets of data (batches) to train and test the model: all features; 10% of the total features using the MRMR method; and the features selected using the MRMR complemented by the Mann–Whitney U test. The batches for the classifications which used the midline channels' features as input were 120 features, 12 most relevant features (according to MRMR relevance score), and 6 most relevant features (MRMR + Mann–Whitney). On the other hand, the batches for the classifications that used the features of the midline and adjacent channels were 360 features, 36 most relevant features (according to MRMR relevance score), and 20 most relevant features (MRMR + Mann–Whitney).

Table 2. Percentage accuracy for each classifier using the midline channels' features as inputs differentiating the easy and hard puzzles as classes.

Percentage of Classification Accuracy (Easy vs. Hard) 3 Channels			
Classifier	**6 Best Features**	**12 Features**	**All Features**
SGD (stochastic gradient descent)	59.47	57.23	63.14
SVC (support vector classifier)	57.84	58.04	69.86
DT (decision tree)	59.27	54.79	67.01
GNB (Gaussian naive Bayes)	56.82	54.79	52.75
KNN (k-nearest neighbors)	59.27	59.06	71.69
RF (random forest)	61.30	59.06	76.37
MLP (multilayer perceptron)	59.47	60.90	73.93

Table 3. Percentage of accuracy for each classifier using the midline and adjacent channels' features as input differentiating the easy and hard puzzles as classes.

Percentage of Classification Accuracy (Easy vs. Hard) 9 Channels			
Classifier	**20 Features**	**36 Features**	**All Features**
SGD	58.83	59.02	71.62
SVC	70.86	73.68	84.21
DT	66.73	70.11	75.19
GNB	55.08	56.20	53.76
KNN	72.74	75.75	86.09
RF	71.24	79.70	86.65
MLP	76.50	80.26	86.09

Table 4. Percentage accuracy for each classifier using the midline channels' features as inputs differentiating the baseline and VR (easy and hard together) as classes.

Percentage of Classification Accuracy (Baseline vs. VR) 3 Channels			
Classifier	**6 Features**	**12 Features**	**All Features**
SGD	70.38	73.51	83.70
SVC	74.18	76.09	89.67
DT	73.10	72.83	81.93
GNB	67.93	68.07	75.68
KNN	74.32	75.95	87.91
RF	75.41	78.26	89.81
MLP	75.27	77.31	91.98

Table 5. Percentage accuracy for each classifier using the midline and adjacent channels' features as inputs differentiating the baseline and VR (easy and hard together) as classes.

Percentage of Classification Accuracy (Baseline vs. VR) 9 Channels			
Classifier	**20 Features**	**36 Features**	**All Features**
SGD	85.84	87.09	93.23
SVC	86.72	88.85	96.12
DT	82.46	85.71	89.85
GNB	83.46	83.58	81.45
KNN	86.09	87.72	97.37
RF	86.34	87.22	96.87
MLP	86.22	88.35	96.49

In general, the performance of most classifiers when all features of the batch are used as input is promising. However, when the batch contains fewer features, the performance is observed to drop, as expected. This implies that by decreasing the number of features below 5%, this trend would continue, and there would be no point in performing any analysis based on the features used if the performance of the classifiers does not even exceed 75% accuracy percentage. This trend is also shown in Table 6, where the accuracy of classifiers is being reported using the best 36 features (chosen by MRMR only) and the best 5, 10, or 20 features (chosen by MRMR and Mann–Whitney together). Figure 6 shows the relevance score for the best 20 features (with the highest relevance) after applying MRMR, and Table 7 presents the *p*-value of these 20 most relevant features resulting after applying MRMR + Mann–Whitney for the fourth set of features (extracted from the midline and adjacent channels and used to classify the baseline and VR states). To better understand the association of the best features with different brain regions, Figure 7 depicts the mean of the z-normalized values of the most relevant features in different electrodes.

Table 6. Percentage accuracy for each classifier that uses the features of the midline and adjacent channels as inputs differentiating the baseline and VR (easy and hard together) as classes.

Percentage of Classification Accuracy (Baseline vs. VR) 9 Channels					
Classifier	5 Features	10 Features	20 Features	36 Features	All Features
SGD	84.09	85.34	85.84	87.09	93.23
SVC	84.09	86.22	86.72	88.85	96.12
DT	82.46	84.84	82.46	85.71	89.85
GNB	82.08	83.58	83.46	83.58	81.45
KNN	82.21	85.71	86.09	87.72	97.37
RF	83.21	85.84	86.34	87.22	96.87
MLP	84.96	86.22	86.22	88.35	96.49

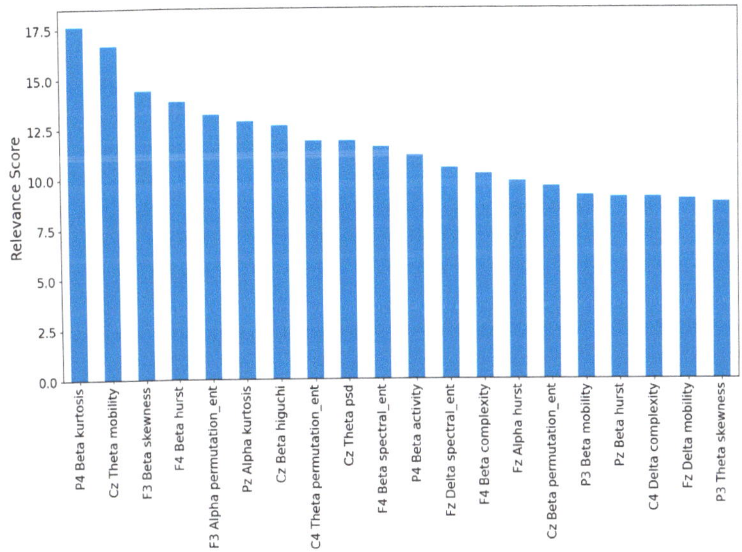

Figure 6. MRMR scores for the best features for baseline vs. VR classification using features of the 9 channels.

Based on this preliminary analysis, the EEG signal characterization and identification of possible biomarkers was accomplished using the approach that classified the baseline and VR states (easy and hard), using the features of the EEG signals of the midline and adjacent channels as input parameters.

Table 7. p-value for the most relevant features based on MRMR results (Figure 6) used to obtain percentage of accuracy for baseline vs. VR in 9 channels (to obtain results in the third column of Table 6).

Feature Name	p-Value	Feature Name	p-Value
P4 Beta kurtosis	7.37×10^{-200}	Cz Theta psd	9.82×10^{-148}
Cz Theta mobility	3.31×10^{-188}	Cz Beta permutation entropy	2.06×10^{-146}
F3 Beta skewness	1.21×10^{-185}	F4 Beta spectral entropy	6.07×10^{-144}
F3 Alpha permutation entropy	1.91×10^{-179}	Fz Delta mobility	1.14×10^{-140}
F4 Beta hurst	9.89×10^{-172}	F4 Alpha hurst	3.00×10^{-140}
Pz Alpha kurtosis	1.02×10^{-165}	Pz Beta activity	3.43×10^{-137}
C4 Theta permutation entropy	2.86×10^{-164}	Pz Alpha activity	2.33×10^{-128}
P4 Beta activity	1.24×10^{-161}	Fz Delta spectral entropy	6.89×10^{-131}
Fz Alpha hurst	4.15×10^{-157}	Pz Beta hurst	3.10×10^{-126}
Cz Beta higuchi	3.52×10^{-156}	F4 Beta complexity	5.28×10^{-125}

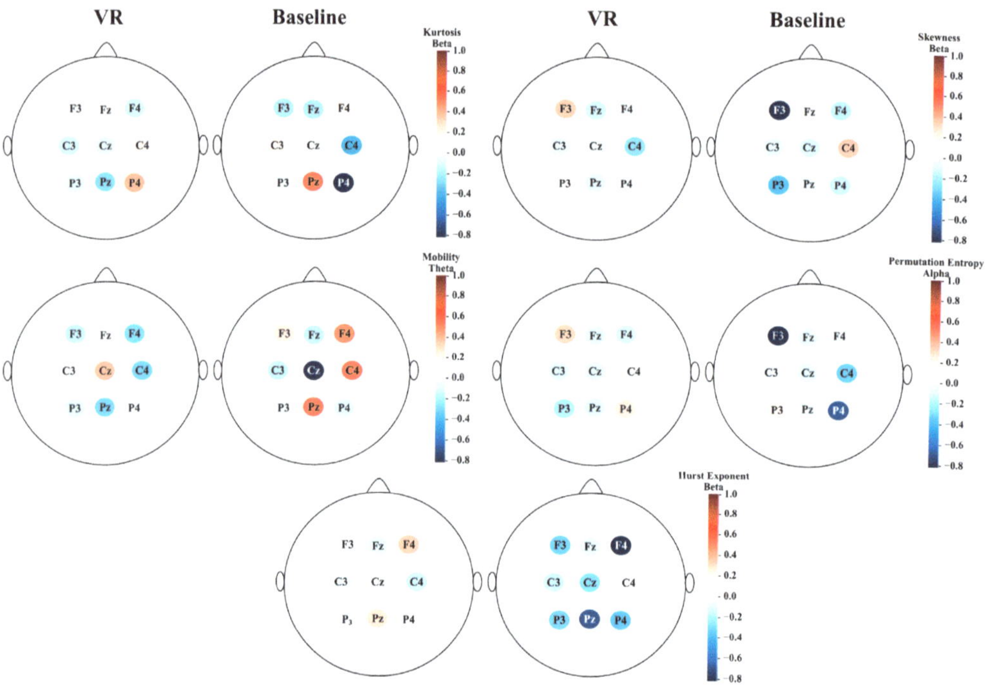

Figure 7. Topographic map of z-normalized mean value for most relevant features on selected electrodes.

4. Discussion

4.1. Biomarkers of Immersion in VR

To the best of our knowledge, this study is the first to use machine learning methods to classify features computed from EEG signals extracted during the performance of VR tasks. This approach was able to differentiate EEG during two levels of puzzle difficulty (easy or hard), and to differentiate the baseline state from the VR states (easy and hard together), obtaining accuracy scores above 86% and 97%, respectively.

It is important to note that the classification performance was better when more information was available (Tables 3 and 5), which indicates that the percentage of accuracy presented here could be increased by adding more EEG channels adjacent to the midline.

In addition, feature selection methods prove to be of great importance when generating more efficient classifiers without largely affecting their performance, and to perform more specific analyses on the features that provide relevant information, thus enabling the characterization of the signals under study. In this case, the combination of MRMR and the Mann–Whitney U test [50] proved to be of great help in selecting not only the most relevant features but also those that showed statistical difference between the classes (Table 7). For this reason, the order of the relevant features shown in Figure 6 is not the same as that shown in Table 7. This allowed us to obtain classifiers that still reflect promising performance using less than 5% of the total features as input (Table 6). Thus, the need for a smaller number of features implies an increase in computational efficiency when training and testing artificial intelligence models. This may prove valuable in future studies or applications that require real-time processing.

Comparing the results from Tables 2–5 shows that while the accuracy percentage of 86% is obtained using only 10 features for classification between the baseline and VR states, such accuracy rates are obtainable only using all possible features (i.e., 360 features from all nine studied channels) for differentiating the easy and hard states, which makes a specific analysis difficult given the nature of the results obtained for this particular case. So, as a first contribution we propose possible biomarkers to differentiate between a baseline (idle) state and states related to the VR-based task (easy and hard), which is a first step towards obtaining reliable biomarkers to measure immersion.

Table 6 shows that when using the best 10 features (the first 10 features of Table 7 with the best p-values), five of the seven classifiers used achieved accuracy percentages higher than 85%. In the case of this particular approach, the best classifiers were SVC, RF, and MLP, with MLP being the most accurate. This may represent an opportunity for deep learning models to be included in the future to meet the same objective. Table 7 presents the most relevant final features, i.e., the features recorded in this table were the ones used to obtain the results shown in Table 6. Consequently, Figure 6 and Table 7 allow us to propose the following biomarkers to differentiate the level of immersion between a baseline state and a VR task state in a virtual reality environment: the kurtosis of the P4 and Pz channels in the beta and alpha frequency ranges, respectively, the mobility in the Cz channel in theta band, the skewness for F3 in beta band, the permutation entropy in F3 and C4 in the alpha and theta bands, respectively, the value of the Hurst exponent for F4 and Fz in beta and alpha bands, respectively, the activity in P4 in beta band, and finally, the Higuchi exponent value for Cz in beta band.

4.2. Association of Biomarkers of Immersion in VR and Neurophysiological Findings

A correlation between attention allocation and engagement level of immersion has been found in previous work [51]. Given the association between frontal cortex and attentional control [52], the sensitivity of features corresponding to the three frontal electrodes in the current study to the sense of immersion is unsurprising (F3 Beta skewness, F3 Alpha permutation entropy, F4 Beta hurst, and Fz Alpha hurst). This association has also been studied in the context of using auditory ERPs to investigate immersion in VR [3]. More specifically, there is a strong correlation between dorsolateral prefrontal cortex activity and planning [53], which is one of the cognitive skills involved in solving a jigsaw puzzle. The right and left prefrontal regions are associated with different functions [54,55]. While the right prefrontal cortex is more involved in strategic construction of plans, the left prefrontal cortex is more engaged in supervising the execution of the plans and control processes [53]. Fz activity has also been found to be related to the difficulty level of the task in VR [1].

This is supported by the frontal-related biomarkers of immersion found in our study (F3 Beta skewness, F3 Alpha permutation entropy, and F4 Beta hurst). As seen in Figure 7, the mean z-normalized permutation entropy of the EEG signals from the F3 channel in the beta band is relatively higher than other channels as well as the same channel in the baseline state. Permutation entropy quantifies the amount of uncertainty and unpredictability in an EEG signal [56]. Therefore, the higher permutation entropy in the F3 channel suggests that the neural activities of the left prefrontal cortex were forced to change as a result of cognitive demands related to the execution of plans to solve the puzzle. Moreover, having a relatively higher mean skewness of F3 EEG signals in the beta band (as seen in Figure 7) may be indicative of changes in the amplitude of the signals related to execution of plans. Mathematically, a highly skewed distribution may indicate the presence of outliers or rare events [57]. In contrast, Figure 7 also shows that the Hurst exponent for EEG signals recorded at F4 is relatively larger than that of the other electrodes and for the same electrode in baseline state. A greater Hurst exponent suggests more pronounced long-term correlations or persistence, where the signal tends to exhibit trends or patterns that persist over time [45]. This may be related to the association of the right prefrontal cortex with the strategic planning necessary to integrate and maintain information while solving the puzzle [54].

On the other hand, the superior parietal region has been associated with the visuospatial and visuomotor functions [58,59]. While some studies suggest that visuospatial functions should not be considered as primarily right-lateralized, the fact that the right superior parietal lobe is also involved in attention processes [53,60] might be the reason why two features related to P4 and one related to Pz appeared in the final best features, rather than a feature related to P3. The relatively higher kurtosis of EEG signals for P4 in Figure 7, compared to other electrodes, likely reflects the difference in complexity of neural dynamics underlying cognitive processes in this electrode in comparison to other ones [61].

5. Limitations

This is a proof-of-concept study that suggests that EEG combined with machine learning approaches may have the potential to create a real-time measure of immersion. We attempted to make the puzzle versions as similar as possible so that factors such as effort, motivation, engagement, mental exertion, cognitive demand, and interest would be similar for both puzzles; however, it is possible that these factors did vary between puzzle versions, and thus, impacted the results of the machine learning approaches.

6. Conclusions

To the best of our knowledge, this study is the first to introduce a machine-learning-based approach to identify markers of virtual reality immersion in EEG signals. Subjective methods of studying immersion in virtual reality do not always provide reliable results and cannot be administered in real time, while objective methods such as auditory event-related potentials have provided heterogeneous and, in some cases, contradictory results. The machine learning method used in the current study shows promising results in the test bed of a protocol that attributes immersion to the difficulty level of the task in virtual reality.

The ML approach was able to classify the EEG data collected during three different states (idle, easy, and hard) with accuracy rates of 86% and 97% for differentiating easy vs. hard difficulty states and baseline vs. VR states. Utilizing more EEG channels and features is recommended for future work in order to propose relevant biomarkers to differentiate between high and low immersion levels related to the difficulty of the VR task and cognitive load of a VR training. Similarly, in the future, we plan to include deep learning models in order to compare their performance with the classical machine learning models used in this paper.

Author Contributions: This work was completed in the Human Neurophysiology and Rehabilitation Laboratories at Ontario Tech University. All persons who meet authorship criteria are listed as authors, and all authors certify that they have participated sufficiently in the work to take public responsibility for the content, including participation in the concept, design, analysis, writing, or revision of the manuscript. The following is a breakdown of the individual contributions of each author. Conceptualization, H.T., M.S.R.C., A.J.U.Q. and B.A.M.; methodology, H.T., M.S.R.C., A.J.U.Q. and B.A.M.; validation, H.T. and M.S.R.C.; formal analysis, H.T. and M.S.R.C.; investigation, H.T. and M.S.R.C.; data curation: H.T. and M.S.R.C.; writing—original draft preparation, H.T. and M.S.R.C.;

writing—review and editing, H.T., M.S.R.C., A.J.U.Q. and B.A.M.; supervision, A.J.U.Q. and B.A.M. All authors have read and agreed to the published version of the manuscript.

Funding: This work was supported by the National Sciences and Engineering Research Council of Canada (NSERC) through NSERC Discovery Grant (BM): 2022-04777 and NSERC Discovery Grant RGPIN-2018-05917 (AQ) as well as an Ontario Tech University Graduate Scholarship (HT).

Institutional Review Board Statement: The study was conducted in accordance with the Declaration of Helsinki and approved by the Institutional Review Board (or Ethics Committee) of University of Ontario Institute of Technology (Ontario Tech University), REB #17351.

Informed Consent Statement: Informed consent was obtained from all subjects involved in the study. Written informed consent has been obtained from the participant(s) to publish this paper.

Data Availability Statement: The data sets generated during and/or analyzed during the current study are available from the corresponding author on reasonable request.

Acknowledgments: The research team would like to acknowledge all individuals who took part in this study, thank you for making this possible.

Conflicts of Interest: All authors certify that they have no affiliations with or involvement in any organization or entity with any financial or non-financial interest in the subject matter or materials discussed in this manuscript. The funders had no role in the design of the study; in the collection, analyses, or interpretation of data; in the writing of the manuscript; or in the decision to publish the results.

Appendix A

The following tables summarize the parameters used for running different classifiers in this study.

Table A1. Parameters used for running classifier differentiating the easy and hard puzzle as classes (3 channels).

Classification Parameters—(Easy vs. Hard) 3 Channels			
Classifier	**6 Best Features**	**12 Features**	**All Features**
SGD	alpha = 0.01 loss = squared_error max_iter = 100 tol = 0.0001	loss = log max_iter = 10 penalty = elasticnet tol = 10	loss = huber max_iter = 100 penalty = elasticnet tol = 0.0001
SVC	C = 100 kernel = linear tol = 0.01	C = 1 kernel = linear tol = 0.01	C = 1 kernel = poly tol = 0.01
DT	ccp_alpha = 0.001 criterion = entropy max_features = auto	ccp_alpha = 0.001 criterion = entropy max_features = auto	ccp_alpha = 0.001 max_features = auto
GNB	var_smoothing = 1	var_smoothing = 0.01	var_smoothing = 1
KNN	leaf_size = 10 metric = euclidean weights = distance	leaf_size = 10 metric = cityblock n_neighbors = 7	leaf_size = 10 metric = euclidean n_neighbors = 17
RF	max_depth = 10 max_features = auto n_estimators = 500	max_depth = 5 max_features = auto	max_depth = 10 max_features = auto n_estimators = 500

Table A1. *Cont.*

Classification Parameters—(Easy vs. Hard) 3 Channels			
Classifier	6 Best Features	12 Features	All Features
MLP	activation = tanh alpha = 0.001 hidden_layer_sizes = 500 max_iter = 5000	alpha = 0.001 hidden_layer_sizes = 500 max_iter = 5000 solver = sgd	activation = logistic alpha = 0.001 hidden_layer_sizes = 500 max_iter = 5000

Table A2. Parameters used for running classifier differentiating the easy and hard puzzle as classes (9 channels).

Classification Parameters—(Easy vs. Hard) 9 Channels			
Classifier	20 Best Features	36 Features	All Features
SGD	alpha = 0.01 loss = perceptron max_iter = 10 penalty = elasticnet tol = 0.0001	alpha = 0.01 loss = modified_huber max_iter = 100 penalty = l1 tol = 0.01	loss = modified_huber penalty = l1 tol = 0.0001
SVC	C = 100 kernel = poly tol = 0.01	C = 100 kernel = linear tol = 0.01	C = 100 kernel = poly tol = 0.01
DT	ccp_alpha = 0.0001 criterion = entropy max_features = auto	ccp_alpha = 0.001 criterion = entropy max_features = auto	ccp_alpha = 0.001 max_features = auto
GNB	var_smoothing = 1	var_smoothing = 0.1	var_smoothing = 0.01
KNN	leaf_size = 10 metric = cityblock n_neighbors = 7 weights = distance	leaf_size = 10 metric = cityblock n_neighbors = 13	leaf_size = 10 metric = cityblock n_neighbors = 7 weights = distance
RF	max_depth = 10 max_features = auto n_estimators = 500	max_depth = 10 max_features = auto n_estimators = 200	max_depth = 10 max_features = auto n_estimators = 1000
MLP	activation = tanh alpha = 0.001 hidden_layer_sizes = 500 max_iter = 5000	alpha = 0.001 hidden_layer_sizes = 500 max_iter = 5000 solver = sgd	activation = logistic alpha = 0.001 hidden_layer_sizes = 500 max_iter = 5000

Table A3. Parameters used for running classifier differentiating the Baseline and difficulty (easy and hard) as classes (3 channels).

Classification Parameters—(Baseline vs. VR) 3 Channels			
Classifier	6 Best Features	12 Features	All Features
SGD	alpha = 0.01 loss = squared_error max_iter = 10 tol = 0.0001	alpha = 0.01 loss = log max_iter = 100 penalty = elasticnet tol = 0.0001	alpha = 0.01 penalty = elasticnet max_iter = 100
SVC	C = 10 kernel = linear tol = 0.01	C = 1 kernel = linear tol = 0.01	C = 100 kernel = linear tol = 0.01

Table A3. *Cont.*

Classification Parameters—(Baseline vs. VR) 3 Channels			
Classifier	**6 Best Features**	**12 Features**	**All Features**
DT	ccp_alpha = 0.001 max_features = auto	ccp_alpha = 0.001 max_features = auto splitter = random	ccp_alpha = 0.001 criterion = entropy max_features = auto
GNB	var_smoothing = 1	var_smoothing = 1	var_smoothing = 10
KNN	leaf_size = 10 metric = cityblock n_neighbors = 25	leaf_size = 10 metric = cityblock n_neighbors = 27	leaf_size = 10 metric = cityblock n_neighbors = 7
RF	max_depth = 7 max_features = auto n_estimators = 1000	criterion = entropy max_depth = 10 max_features = auto n_estimators = 10	max_depth = 10 max_features = auto n_estimators = 50
MLP	alpha = 0.001 hidden_layer_sizes = 200 max_iter = 5000	alpha = 0.001 hidden_layer_sizes = 500 max_iter = 5000 solver = sgd	activation = logistic alpha = 0.001 hidden_layer_sizes = 500 max_iter = 5000

Table A4. Parameters used for running classifier differentiating the baseline and difficulty (easy and hard) as classes (9 channels).

Classification Parameters—(Baseline vs. VR) 9 Channels					
Classifier	**5 Best Features**	**10 Best Features**	**20 Best Features**	**36 Features**	**All Features**
SGD	max_iter = 100 tol = 0.0001	alpha = 0.01 max_iter = 100 penalty = l1	alpha = 0.01 loss = epsilon_insensitive max_iter = 10 penalty = elasticnet tol = 0.0001	alpha = 0.01 max_iter = 10 penalty = elasticnet tol = 0.01	alpha = 0.01 max_iter = 100 tol = 0.0001
SVC	C = 100 kernel = linear tol = 0.01	C = 100 kernel = linear tol = 0.01	C = 10 kernel = linear tol = 0.01	C = 10 kernel = linear tol = 0.01	C = 10 kernel = linear tol = 0.01
DT	ccp_alpha = 0.01 criterion = entropy max_features = auto splitter = random	ccp_alpha = 0.001 max_features = auto	ccp_alpha = 0.01 criterion = entropy max_features = auto splitter = random	ccp_alpha = 0.001 max_features = auto	ccp_alpha = 0.001 max_features = auto
GNB	var_smoothing = 1	var_smoothing = 1	var_smoothing = 1	var_smoothing = 0.1	var_smoothing = 10
KNN	leaf_size = 10 metric = euclidean n_neighbors = 11	leaf_size = 10 metric = euclidean n_neighbors = 17 weights = distance	leaf_size = 10 metric = euclidean n_neighbors = 11	leaf_size = 10 metric = euclidean n_neighbors = 17	leaf_size = 10 metric = cityblock
RF	criterion = entropy max_depth = 5 max_features = auto n_estimators = 50	max_depth = 10 max_features = auto n_estimators = 1000	criterion = entropy max_depth = 10 max_features = auto n_estimators = 50	criterion = entropy max_depth = 10 max_features = auto n_estimators = 10	criterion = entropy max_depth = 10 max_features = auto n_estimators = 1000
MLP			alpha = 0.001 hidden_layer_sizes = 200 max_iter = 5000	alpha = 0.001 hidden_layer_sizes = 500 max_iter = 5000 solver = sgd	activation = logistic alpha = 0.001 hidden_layer_sizes = 500 max_iter = 5000

References

1. Burns, C.G.; Fairclough, S.H. Use of auditory event-related potentials to measure immersion during a computer game. *Int. J. Hum. Comput. Stud.* **2015**, *73*, 107–114. [CrossRef]
2. Kober, S.E.; Neuper, C. Using auditory event-related EEG potentials to assess presence in virtual reality. *Int. J. Hum. Comput. Stud.* **2012**, *70*, 577–587. [CrossRef]
3. Ghani, U.; Signal, N.; Niazi, I.K.; Taylor, D. Efficacy of a Single-Task ERP Measure to Evaluate Cognitive Workload During a Novel Exergame. *Front. Hum. Neurosci.* **2021**, *15*, 742384. [CrossRef]

4. Rose, T.; Nam, C.S.; Chen, K.B. Immersion of virtual reality for rehabilitation-Review. *Appl. Ergon.* **2018**, *69*, 153–161. [CrossRef]
5. Carruth, D.W. Virtual reality for education and workforce training. In Proceedings of the 2017 15th International Conference on Emerging eLearning Technologies and Applications (ICETA), Stary Smokovec, Slovakia, 26–27 October 2017; pp. 1–6.
6. Gibson, J.; Quevedo, A.U.; Genco, F.; Tokuhiro, A. A Review of Applications of Virtual Reality and Serious Games in Nuclear Industry Training Scenarios. *Oper. New Build* **2024**, *69*, 29–43.
7. De Ribaupierre, S.; Kapralos, B.; Haji, F.; Stroulia, E.; Dubrowski, A.; Eagleson, R. Healthcare training enhancement through virtual reality and serious games. In *Virtual, Augmented Reality and Serious Games for Healthcare*; Springer: Berlin/Heidelberg, Germany, 2014; pp. 9–27.
8. Renganayagalu, S.K.; Mallam, S.C.; Nazir, S. Effectiveness of VR head mounted displays in professional training: A systematic review. *Technol. Knowl. Learn.* **2021**, *26*, 999–1041. [CrossRef]
9. Valori, I.; McKenna-Plumley, P.E.; Bayramova, R.; Zandonella Callegher, C.; Altoè, G.; Farroni, T. Proprioceptive accuracy in Immersive Virtual Reality: A developmental perspective. *PLoS ONE* **2020**, *15*, e0222253. [CrossRef]
10. Hendrix, C.; Barfield, W. Presence in virtual environments as a function of visual and auditory cues. In Proceedings of the Virtual Reality Annual International Symposium, Research Triangle Park, NC, USA, 11–15 March 1995; pp. 74–82.
11. Jennett, C.; Cox, A.L.; Cairns, P.; Dhoparee, S.; Epps, A.; Tijs, T.; Walton, A. Measuring and defining the experience of immersion in games. *Int. J. Hum. Comput. Stud.* **2008**, *66*, 641–661. [CrossRef]
12. Csikszentmihalyi, M.; Csikzentmihaly, M. *Flow: The psychology of Optimal Experience*; Harper & Row: New York, NY, USA, 1990; Volume 1990.
13. Witmer, B.G.; Singer, M.J. Measuring presence in virtual environments: A presence questionnaire. *Presence* **1998**, *7*, 225–240. [CrossRef]
14. LaViola, J.J., Jr.; Kruijff, E.; McMahan, R.P.; Bowman, D.; Poupyrev, I.P. *3D User Interfaces: Theory and Practice*; Addison-Wesley Professional: Boston, MA, USA, 2017.
15. Pausch, R.; Proffitt, D.; Williams, G. Quantifying immersion in virtual reality. In Proceedings of the 24th Annual Conference on Computer Graphics and Interactive Techniques, Los Angeles, CA, USA, 3–8 August 1997; pp. 13–18.
16. Agrawal, S.; Simon, A.; Bech, S.; Bærentsen, K.; Forchhammer, S. Defining immersion: Literature review and implications for research on immersive audiovisual experiences. *J. Audio Eng. Soc.* **2019**, *68*, 404–417. [CrossRef]
17. Fairclough, S.H.; Gilleade, K.; Ewing, K.C.; Roberts, J. Capturing user engagement via psychophysiology: Measures and mechanisms for biocybernetic adaptation. *Int. J. Auton. Adapt. Commun. Syst.* **2013**, *6*, 63–79. [CrossRef]
18. Slater, M.; Linakis, V.; Usoh, M.; Kooper, R. Immersion, presence and performance in virtual environments: An experiment with tri-dimensional chess. In Proceedings of the ACM Symposium on Virtual Reality Software and Technology, Hong Kong, China, 1–4 July 1996; pp. 163–172.
19. Slater, M. Measuring presence: A response to the Witmer and Singer presence questionnaire. *Presence Teleoper Virtual Environ.* **1999**, *8*, 560–565. [CrossRef]
20. Putze, S.; Alexandrovsky, D.; Putze, F.; Höffner, S.; Smeddinck, J.D.; Malaka, R. Breaking The Experience: Effects of Questionnaires in VR User Studies. In Proceedings of the 2020 CHI Conference on Human Factors in Computing Systems, Honolulu, HI, USA, 25–30 April 2020; pp. 1–15.
21. Eggemeier, F.T. Properties of workload assessment techniques. In *Human Mental Workload*; North-Holland: Oxford, UK, 1988; pp. 41–62. [CrossRef]
22. Darken, R.P.; Bernatovich, D.; Lawson, J.P.; Peterson, B. Quantitative measures of presence in virtual environments: The roles of attention and spatial comprehension. *Cyberpsychol. Behav.* **1999**, *2*, 337–347. [CrossRef]
23. Terkildsen, T.; Makransky, G. Measuring presence in video games: An investigation of the potential use of physiological measures as indicators of presence. *Int. J. Hum. Comput. Stud.* **2019**, *126*, 64–80. [CrossRef]
24. Perrin, A.-F.N.M.; Xu, H.; Kroupi, E.; Řeřábek, M.; Ebrahimi, T. Multimodal Dataset for Assessment of Quality of Experience in Immersive Multimedia. In Proceedings of the 23rd ACM International Conference on Multimedia, Brisbane, Australia, 26–30 October 2015; pp. 1007–1010.
25. Ramirez, M.; Tadayyoni, H.; McCracken, H.; Quevedo, A.J.U.; Murphy, B.A. Identifying Markers of Immersion Using Auditory Event-Related EEG Potentials in a VR Jigsaw Puzzle. In Proceedings of the 2024 IEEE Conference on Virtual Reality and 3D User Interfaces Abstracts and Workshops (VRW), Orlando, FL, USA, 16–21 March 2024; pp. 1033–1034.
26. Grassini, S.; Laumann, K.; Thorp, S.; Topranin, V.M. Using electrophysiological measures to evaluate the sense of presence in immersive virtual environments: An event-related potential study. *Brain Behav.* **2021**, *11*, e2269. [CrossRef]
27. Kamińska, D.; Smółka, K.; Zwoliński, G. Detection of mental stress through EEG signal in virtual reality environment. *Electronics* **2021**, *10*, 2840. [CrossRef]
28. Aliyari, H.; Golabi, S.; Sahraei, H.; Daliri, M.R.; Minaei-Bidgoli, B.; Tadayyoni, H.; Kazemi, M. Evaluation of Stress and Cognition Indicators in a Puzzle Game: Neuropsychological, Biochemical and Electrophysiological Approaches. *Arch. Razi Inst.* **2022**, *77*, 1397–1403. [CrossRef]
29. Karácsony, T.; Hansen, J.P.; Iversen, H.K.; Puthusserypady, S. Brain computer interface for neuro-rehabilitation with deep learning classification and virtual reality feedback. In Proceedings of the 10th Augmented Human International Conference 2019, Reims, France, 11–12 March 2019; pp. 1–8.

30. Moncada, F.; Martín, S.; González, V.M.; Álvarez, V.M.; García-López, B.; Gómez-Menéndez, A.I.; Villar, J.R. Virtual reality and machine learning in the automatic photoparoxysmal response detection. *Neural Comput. Appl.* **2023**, *35*, 5643–5659. [CrossRef]
31. Yildirim, C. A review of deep learning approaches to EEG-based classification of cybersickness in virtual reality. In Proceedings of the 2020 IEEE International Conference on Artificial Intelligence and Virtual Reality (AIVR), Utrecht, The Netherlands, 14–18 December 2020; pp. 351–357.
32. Hekmatmanesh, A.; Wu, H.; Jamaloo, F.; Li, M.; Handroos, H. A combination of CSP-based method with soft margin SVM classifier and generalized RBF kernel for imagery-based brain computer interface applications. *Multimed. Tools Appl.* **2020**, *79*, 17521–17549. [CrossRef]
33. Kritikos, J.; Makrypidis, A.; Alevizopoulos, A.; Alevizopoulos, G.; Koutsouris, D. Can Brain–Computer Interfaces Replace Virtual Reality Controllers? A Machine Learning Movement Prediction Model during Virtual Reality Simulation Using EEG Recordings. *Virtual Worlds* **2023**, *2*, 182–202. [CrossRef]
34. Chen, T.; Ju, S.; Ren, F.; Fan, M.; Gu, Y. EEG emotion recognition model based on the LIBSVM classifier. *Measurement* **2020**, *164*, 108047. [CrossRef]
35. Qin, H.; Rau, P.-L.P.; Salvendy, G. Effects of different scenarios of game difficulty on player immersion. *Interact. Comput.* **2010**, *22*, 230–239. [CrossRef]
36. Nilsson, N.C.; Nordahl, R.; Serafin, S. Immersion revisited: A review of existing definitions of immersion and their relation to different theories of presence. *Hum. Technol.* **2016**, *12*, 108–134. [CrossRef]
37. Oldfield, R.C. The assessment and analysis of handedness: The Edinburgh inventory. *Neuropsychologia* **1971**, *9*, 97–113. [CrossRef]
38. Wright, R.A. Refining the Prediction of Effort: Brehm's Distinction between Potential Motivation and Motivation Intensity. *Soc. Personal. Psychol. Compass* **2008**, *2*, 682–701. [CrossRef]
39. Tauscher, J.P.; Schottky, F.W.; Grogorick, S.; Bittner, P.M.; Mustafa, M.; Magnor, M. Immersive EEG: Evaluating Electroencephalography in Virtual Reality. In Proceedings of the 2019 IEEE Conference on Virtual Reality and 3D User Interfaces (VR), Osaka, Japan, 23–27 March 2019; pp. 1794–1800.
40. Homan, R.W. The 10-20 Electrode System and Cerebral Location. *Am. J. EEG Technol.* **1988**, *28*, 269–279. [CrossRef]
41. Stancin, I.; Cifrek, M.; Jovic, A. A review of EEG signal features and their application in driver drowsiness detection systems. *Sensors* **2021**, *21*, 3786. [CrossRef]
42. Zhao, Q.; Jiang, H.; Hu, B.; Li, Y.; Zhong, N.; Li, M.; Lin, W.; Liu, Q. Nonlinear dynamic complexity and sources of resting-state EEG in abstinent heroin addicts. *IEEE Trans. Nanobiosci.* **2017**, *16*, 349–355. [CrossRef] [PubMed]
43. Hjorth, B. EEG analysis based on time domain properties. *Electroencephalogr. Clin. Neurophysiol.* **1970**, *29*, 306–310. [CrossRef] [PubMed]
44. Higuchi, T. Approach to an irregular time series on the basis of the fractal theory. *Phys. D Nonlinear Phenom.* **1988**, *31*, 277–283. [CrossRef]
45. Hurst, H.E. Long-term storage capacity of reservoirs. *Trans. Am. Soc. Civ. Eng.* **1951**, *116*, 770–799. [CrossRef]
46. Engelbrecht, H.; Lindeman, R.W.; Hoermann, S. A SWOT analysis of the field of virtual reality for firefighter training. *Front. Robot. AI* **2019**, *6*, 101. [CrossRef]
47. Zhao, Z.; Anand, R.; Wang, M. Maximum Relevance and Minimum Redundancy Feature Selection Methods for a Marketing Machine Learning Platform. In Proceedings of the 2019 IEEE International Conference on Data Science and Advanced Analytics (DSAA), Washington, DC, USA, 5–8 October 2019; pp. 442–452.
48. Bishop, C.M. *Pattern Recognition and Machine Learning*; Springer: New York, NY, USA, 2006.
49. Belyadi, H.; Haghighat, A. *Machine Learning Guide for Oil and Gas Using Python: A Step-By-Step Breakdown with Data, Algorithms, Codes, and Applications*; Gulf Professional Publishing: Oxford, UK, 2021.
50. Ramirez, M.; McCracken, H.; Grant, B.; Yielder, P.; Quevedo, A.J.U.; Murphy, B.A. Using Machine Learning to Classify EEG Data Collected with or without Haptic Feedback During a Simulated Drilling Task. In Proceedings of the 2024 IEEE Conference on Virtual Reality and 3D User Interfaces Abstracts and Workshops (VRW), Orlando, FL, USA, 16–21 March 2024; pp. 769–770.
51. Souza, R.H.C.E.; Naves, E.L.M. Attention detection in virtual environments using EEG signals: A scoping review. *Front. Physiol.* **2021**, *12*, 727840. [CrossRef]
52. Posner, M.I.; Petersen, S.E. The attention system of the human brain. *Annu. Rev. Neurosci.* **1990**, *13*, 25–42. [CrossRef]
53. Newman, S.D.; Carpenter, P.A.; Varma, S.; Just, M.A. Frontal and parietal participation in problem solving in the Tower of London: fMRI and computational modeling of planning and high-level perception. *Neuropsychologia* **2003**, *41*, 1668–1682. [CrossRef]
54. Prabhakaran, V.; Narayanan, K.; Zhao, Z.; Gabrieli, J. Integration of diverse information in working memory within the frontal lobe. *Nat. Neurosci.* **2000**, *3*, 85–90. [CrossRef]
55. Braver, T.S.; Bongiolatti, S.R. The role of frontopolar cortex in subgoal processing during working memory. *Neuroimage* **2002**, *15*, 523–536. [CrossRef]
56. Berger, S.; Schneider, G.; Kochs, E.F.; Jordan, D. Permutation entropy: Too complex a measure for EEG time series? *Entropy* **2017**, *19*, 692. [CrossRef]
57. Groeneveld, R.A.; Meeden, G. Measuring skewness and kurtosis. *J. R. Stat. Soc. Ser. D Stat.* **1984**, *33*, 391–399. [CrossRef]
58. Seydell-Greenwald, A.; Ferrara, K.; Chambers, C.E.; Newport, E.L.; Landau, B. Bilateral parietal activations for complex visual-spatial functions: Evidence from a visual-spatial construction task. *Neuropsychologia* **2017**, *106*, 194–206. [CrossRef]

59. Culham, J.C.; Cavina-Pratesi, C.; Singhal, A. The role of parietal cortex in visuomotor control: What have we learned from neuroimaging? *Neuropsychologia* **2006**, *44*, 2668–2684. [CrossRef] [PubMed]
60. Corbetta, M.; Miezin, F.M.; Shulman, G.L.; Petersen, S.E. A PET study of visuospatial attention. *J. Neurosci.* **1993**, *13*, 1202–1226. [CrossRef] [PubMed]
61. Inuso, G.; La Foresta, F.; Mammone, N.; Morabito, F.C. Brain activity investigation by EEG processing: Wavelet analysis, kurtosis and Renyi's entropy for artifact detection. In Proceedings of the 2007 International Conference on Information Acquisition, Jeju City, Republic of Korea, 8–11 July 2007; pp. 195–200.

Disclaimer/Publisher's Note: The statements, opinions and data contained in all publications are solely those of the individual author(s) and contributor(s) and not of MDPI and/or the editor(s). MDPI and/or the editor(s) disclaim responsibility for any injury to people or property resulting from any ideas, methods, instructions or products referred to in the content.

brain sciences

MDPI

Article

The Effects of Distancing Design Collaboration Necessitated by COVID-19 on Brain Synchrony in Teams Compared to Co-Located Design Collaboration: A Preliminary Study

Yi-Teng Shih [1,*], Luqian Wang [1], Clive H. Y. Wong [2], Emily L. L. Sin [1], Matthias Rauterberg [3], Zhen Yuan [4] and Leanne Chang [5]

1 School of Design, The Hong Kong Polytechnic University, Hong Kong
2 Department of Psychology, The Education University of Hong Kong, Hong Kong
3 Department of Industrial Design, Eindhoven University of Technology, 5612 AZ Eindhoven, The Netherlands
4 Faculty of Health Sciences, University of Macau, Macau
5 School of Communication, Hong Kong Baptist University, Hong Kong
* Correspondence: yi-teng.shih@polyu.edu.hk

Abstract: Due to the widespread involvement of distributed collaboration triggered by COVID-19, it has become a new trend that has continued into the post-pandemic era. This study investigated collective performance within two collaborative environments (co-located and distancing settings) by assessing inter-brain synchrony patterns (IBS) among design collaborators using functional near-infrared spectroscopy. The preliminary study was conducted with three dyads who possessed 2–3 years of professional product design experience. Each dyad completed two designated design tasks in distinct settings. In the distributed condition, participants interacted through video conferencing in which they were allowed to communicate by verbalization and sketching using a shared digital whiteboard. To prevent the influences of different sketching tools on design outputs, we employed digital sketching for both environments. The interactions between collaborators were identified in three behaviors: verbal only, sketch only, and mixed communication (verbal and sketch). The consequences revealed a higher level of IBS when mixed communication took place in distributed conditions than in co-located conditions. Comparably, the occurrence of IBS increased when participants solely utilized sketching as the interaction approach within the co-located setting. A mixed communication method combining verbalization and sketching might lead to more coordinated cognitive processes when in physical isolation. Design collaborators are inclined to adjust their interaction behaviors in order to adapt to different design environments, strengthen the exchange of ideas, and construct design consensus. Overall, the present paper discussed the performance of virtual collaborative design based on a neurocognitive perspective, contributing valuable insights for the future intervention design that promotes effective virtual teamwork.

Keywords: collaborative design; inter-brain synchrony (IBS); hyper-scanning; design cognition; COVID-19

1. Introduction

Teamwork innovation has long been recognized as a core competitiveness in an organization's ability to address complex problems. Social distancing restrictions during the COVID-19 pandemic have enforced traditional co-located collaborative mode into virtual teamwork in an accelerative way, resulting in great transformation for design collaborators that largely influence their way of communicating and interacting. To adapt to this COVID-19-related disruption, organizations were striving to embrace information and communication technologies (ICTs), such as video conferencing platforms, web-based tools, and computer-aided systems, in order to facilitate efficient virtual teamwork. However, the surge in ICT utilization poses a major challenge to the digital resilience of both individuals and organizations. Previous studies [1–5] have argued the impairments in collaborators' cognition and communication within distributed collaborative design processes, leading to a deterioration of group performance. Researchers generally recognized that distributed teams reduced the awareness of collaborators [6–8] and the abundance of information [9], as well as aggravated miscommunication and conflicts [10,11]. Although it is widely accepted that co-located teams outperformed virtual teams, several studies suggested minor or insignificant correlations between teamwork design processes and collaborative (distributed or co-located) environments [12–14].

A considerable body of the literature has explored the implications of distributed design collaboration for design outcomes, collaboration efficiency, and overall group performance. Although several researchers have started to examine the effects of online collaboration on design activities, the predominant research methods employed continue to be self-reported questionnaires, interviews, and observations. Such traditional research methods are deficient in explaining the underlying factors that affect group design activities and interactions between design partners in different types of environments: co-located and distributed settings. Therefore, there is a need to gain insight into the neural activities and inter-brain connectivity during collaborative design processes, which showcases the potential to offer more objective evidence and demystify how team interactivity operates in various contexts.

A new technology from cognitive neuroscience, termed hyper scanning, has been developed and widely utilized to investigate inter-brain synchrony (IBS), a potential indicator for collective performance among teams [15,16]. IBS refers to the degree to which the brains of two or more individuals are synchronized. Reinero and colleagues [17] suggested that IBS can be a complementary approach for understanding collective performance among teams where self-report surveys are limited to capture design behavior. Another study, conducted by Lu et al. [18], examined the occurrence of IBS during collaborative tasks and interactive activities over time and observed a positive association between collaborative behavior and IBS. However, most hyper-scanning studies of interacting individuals are conducted in a face-to-face situation in the same room, where subjects can communicate mutually based on both verbal cues and non-verbal cues, such as facial expressions and body movements. A limited hyper-scanning study explores the effects of different collaborative environments on the degree of IBS, thereby impacting communication effectiveness and collective performance. Additionally, meager research focuses on design-related collaborations, which is a dynamic process involving various design behaviors to formulate design requirements, build design goals, and construct design solutions jointly. Only one relevant study [19] focused on the real-life creative problem-solving processes among teams, which is yet merely focused on the measurement of the left hemisphere of the brain.

In this study, we aimed to address three research questions. Firstly, we examined the design activities and interactions that occur in two distinct collaborative environments, co-located and distributed settings. Next, we explored the similarities and differences in IBS patterns when multiple design partners engage in design problem-solving processes within these two types of environments. Lastly, we investigated the correlations between the design collaboration environments and brain synchrony patterns, which in turn influence the design outputs and team performance. This study has the potential to unravel the neural underpinnings affecting design collaboration and its correlations with collective performance, as well as contribute new insights into the intervention design that promotes effective virtual teamwork, both in the context of design education and design practices.

2. Literature Review

2.1. Distributed Design Collaboration and Digital Resilience

The concept of collaborative design, as presented by Lahti et al. [20], entails an interactive and cooperative process in which participants engage in active communication to collectively establish a design objective, explore problem and solution spaces, and construct design solutions. Establishing effective communication between interactive individuals to exchange ideas during the concept generation process from diverse perspectives is a key element of a successful design collaboration driving product innovation [21]. The rapid development of the pandemic has forced designers to adapt to virtual teamwork; all design collaborations take place remotely using online video conferencing platforms, which has accumulatively become a trend that may continue during the post-pandemic era. Thus, design practitioners are required to increase their competencies of resilience to integrate technology into the collaborative experience so as to increase remote working benefits and mitigate digital stressors [22]. Digital stressors are commonly defined as any adverse effects that technology may have on users. Resilience refers to a process that enables people to effectively navigate and manage stressors, allowing them to bounce back from adversity [23]. The term digital resilience describes specific knowledge, skills, attitudes, competencies, and behaviors that individuals must acquire so that digital stressors can be counteracted. In this study, we defined digital resilience as the ability of collaborators to overcome technical difficulties and continuously adapt to online collaboration, even achieving collaborative effectiveness and design outcomes comparable to that of co-located collaboration.

Effective communication in design collaborations is featured by real-time interactions involving verbalization and the utilization of various visual techniques. In terms of the influences of virtual collaboration on design tasks, a variety of prior studies observed the overperformance of co-located collaborations compared to distributed teams. Based on the consequences of Liska's research [24], virtual teams required approximately one-third (33.32%) more time to address the same assigned works and encountered a higher incidence of revising their solutions compared to co-located teams. Moreover, Hammond et al. [25] pointed out that even though design collaborators spend more time on the assignment, fewer design alternatives were delivered within such a distributed collaboration process. In addition, distributed collaboration can even induce specific interactive behaviors, as Kvan [26] and Lee & Do [27] propose, designers are prone to compromise in design decisions and showcase less willingness to explore the best solutions within virtual collaborative settings. Likewise, in another analysis [28], distributed collaborators were observed to exhibit a lower inclination towards using gestures, allocate more time towards sketching, and participate in fewer studies and discussions with respect to design problems. Several protocol studies [12,14] indicated no significant differences or even better performance in quality or novelty of design solutions within distancing cooperation. In addition, Yang et al. [29] found that in the context of online design collaboration, students tend to allocate more time to sketching compared to the co-present design environment. However, contrary to previous research, the researchers revealed a positive impact whereby increased sketching behaviors reduced cognitive load for students, facilitated the better expression of ideas, and promoted mutual understanding among interactive individuals.

Protocol studies, retrospective reviews, and observations alone are insufficient to explore how different collaboration environments impact the interaction behavior and collective performance of designers. Moreover, there is a lack of effective research on whether the changes in design behavior result in a weakening or compensating effect on collaborative performance. Therefore, in this study, we investigated the relationship between design collaborative behavior and collaborative performance from a brain-based perspective, focusing on brain movements and connectivity and brain synchrony, in various collaborative settings.

2.2. IBS and Brain Regions Relevant to Design Activities

Neuroimaging technology is a widely utilized technique that can capture brain information of interactive individuals within a non-invasive manner, thereby contributing to the study regarding interpersonal social interactions. However, due to the prior related works studying neurocognition that have focused on isolated individuals, the enigmatic box regarding how the brain engages in dynamic group collaborations has failed to be fully unraveled. An emerging technique termed hyper-scanning has been devised to concurrently capture and measure brain activations of multiple collaborative individuals [30]. Compared to conventional neuroimaging study designs [31], hyper-scanning experiments provide a more realistic approximation of interactions between individuals. The degree of IBS, the coordination of brain activity among collaborators, can be measured by the hyper-scanning method. IBS serves as a neuro mechanism that aids scientists in identifying brain regional connectivity and dynamics during social interaction tasks. Functional Near-infrared Spectroscopy (fNIRS) and Electroencephalography (EEG) have been more frequently applied than functional magnetic resonance imaging (fMRI) for measuring IBS, due to their reasonable spatial resolution, greater resilience to body movements and less limitation of experimental setting. As a result, fNIRS and EEG are arguably more suitable for studying IBS within naturalistic interactive environments [32,33].

Numerous studies have generally observed that IBS could be an objective and reliable indicator of collective performance. For instance, the occurrence of IBS often increases when team members communicate or infer intentions mutually [34]. Another study also observed a close relationship between group identification and IBS when individuals worked together to complete problem-solving tasks [17]. Likewise, a study carried out by Hsu et al. [35] revealed a stronger IBS among subjects in cooperative mode compared to single-player mode. Moreover, there was a noticeable decrease in the strength of IBS when subjects switched from being collaborators to competitors.

To the best of our knowledge, the majority of hyper-scanning studies examining interactions among individuals are always conducted in a co-located environment, featured by sufficient verbal and non-verbal cues. Merely a limited number of studies have investigated group interactions in distributed collaborative settings, where individuals exert greater efforts in deducing and predicting partners' intentions. One EEG study undertook an experiment in which each pair of participants collaboratively played an online car racing game within a physically isolated environment [36]. The researchers found significant positive relations between better collective performance and increased brain synchrony. Another study also illustrated that face-to-face conditions promoted more cooperation and a higher IBS compared to face-blocked interactions. However, the tasks conducted in the above studies are a far cry from real-world collaboration and team interactions. Scientists still know little about temporal brain dynamics and how different cooperative environments affect IBS and collective performance among real-world teamworks.

Additionally, to date, very few research studies have studied real design collaborations from the neurocognition perspective. In design teamwork, team members often utilize communication via various ways for idea exchange and mutual understanding establishment, especially in problem-solving and concept-generation processes. One of the fNIRS-based hyper-scanning studies examined real-world creative problem-solving processes in teams and explored the temporal changes in IBS over time [19]. The main limitation of this study is that they restricted their study to measurements of the left hemisphere of the brain. The previous literature has shown that multiple areas of the brain are activated when performing activities similar to those design tasks, especially the prefrontal cortex (PFC) area [37,38]. The PFC is associated with multiple cognitive processes, including but not limited to planning, maintaining focus, information filtering, and executive function [39]. Within the realm of design creative tasks, the PFC plays a crucial role in various cognitive functions. Specifically, the PFC on the right is often involved in divergent thinking, while the opposite hemisphere is more active in rule-based design, goal-oriented planning, and analytical judgment [40]. Strong synchrony observed in the right PFC is linked to an increased level of ingenuity in generated solutions [41].

Furthermore, during the execution of creative tasks, the left and right dorsolateral prefrontal cortical areas (DLPFC) are both active [42]. Increased activation in the right DLPFC is typically associated with the performance of creative problem-solving and visual–spatial thinking [43]. The left DLPFC is also involved in creative tasks and exhibits greater activation when engaged in goal-oriented planning for innovative solutions. In addition, the right ventrolateral PFC (VLPFC) contributes to evaluating problems instead of solving problems, aiding in generating alternative assumptions in the problem space search [44]. By employing neuroscience methodologies to investigate design cognition, we can enhance comprehension of the neurocognitive processes associated with design and refine design thinking theory [45].

3. Research Methodology

This study investigated how distributed design collaborations impact design collaboration behaviors, as well as the associations between specific design activities and underlying neural activities involving IBS as a critical predictor. In light of the aims of this study, think-aloud protocol analysis was employed to analyze and identify design interaction behaviors into three interactive behaviors: verbal only, sketch only, and mixed communication (a combination of verbalization and sketching). According to these three design interaction approaches, recorded video data were segmented into smaller episodes, which are used as critical timecodes for subsequent brain activity segmentation and brain-to-brain synchrony analysis. Hence, this study commonly consists of five components: (i) experiment settings, (ii) data collection, (iii) interaction segmentation, (iv) brain activity segmentation, and (v) inter-brain connectivity analysis.

3.1. Participants

The preliminary study was conducted with three dyads of volunteers (1 female–female, 1 male–male, and 1 female–male) who were equipped with 2–3 years of professional product design experience. All subjects self-identified as right-handed, healthy, and reported no visual impairments or neurological conditions. The age range of participants varied between 22 and 25 years (Mean = 23.3, SD = 0.943). Participants paired in the same dyad were previously acquainted, so that they could conduct the design process quickly and smoothly after a warm-up session. Informed consent was obtained from both dyad members prior to participation. The overarching aim was to design a paradigm that closely resembled real-world design collaboration scenarios. Therefore, dyads were asked to work on design problems for a continuous time of 25–30 min with little instruction and no interventions. All dyads received consistent design briefs and instructions. Ethical approval was obtained for this project on 14 September 2021 (approval number: HSEARS20210914003).

3.2. Experimental Settings and Procedures

This study was conducted in carefully configured design studio spaces in order to create a controlled environment that is as close to a real-world setting as possible. The experimental procedure includes two tasks, requiring participants to undertake two separate conceptual design tasks within different design collaboration environments: co-located and distributed. In terms of task 1, each pair of participants was seated together on the same side of a rectangular table within the same room (see Figure 1), and a fNIRS cap was fitted over the forehead of each participant. After subjects filled in the consent form, the design brief was provided and elaborated to the participants prior to the start of the experiment. Dyads were asked to work together to design a toy and collaboratively define the target groups and contexts. Participants were then provided with a five-minute warm-up session for a brief discussion to determine their specific design scope. No fNIRS scanning happened during the warm-up session. Subsequently, a 25–30 min design session commenced, yet participants had the flexibility to end their design activities earlier or later based on their design progress. All pairs of designers were required to develop at least one final deliverable at the end of the design session. After a five-minute break, participants were placed in separate rooms without any communication before task 2 commenced (see Figure 2). Participants were instructed to join a ZOOM meeting and enabled their camera and microphone for virtual communication. They were also asked to change their displayed names to their assigned identification numbers. The design requirement for task 2 is to cooperate on a conceptual design for multi-functional furniture that could be used indoors and outdoors. Repeating the same steps of task 1, dyads were told to undertake a five-minute virtual warm-up session for design brief exploration and another 25–30 min design session employing the whiteboard feature in the ZOOM meeting, and participants were also allowed to end the design activities earlier or later accordingly. Figure 3 well illustrates the designated experimental sequences and time frames.

Figure 1. Co-located design collaboration: each dyad was seated together on the same side of a rectangular table within the same room.

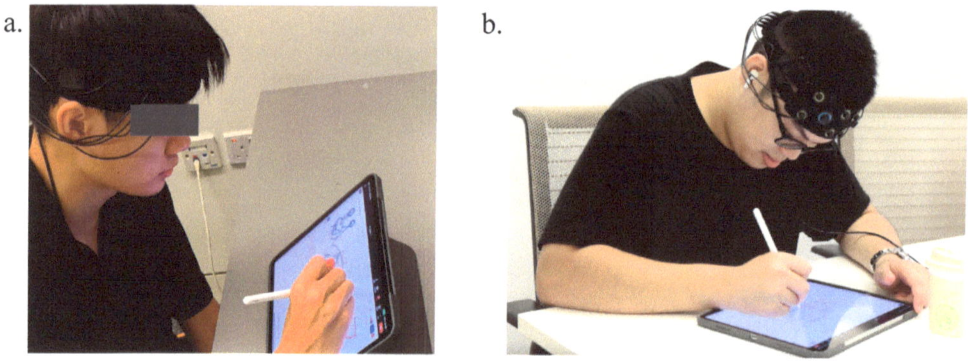

Figure 2. Distributed design collaboration, two subjects were situated in separate rooms. (**a**) The view from camera A; (**b**) the view from camera B.

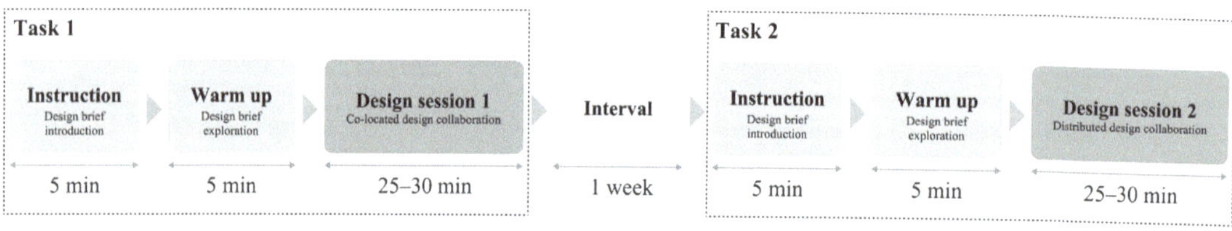

Figure 3. Sequence and duration of experimental sessions.

In this study, digital sketching using the ZOOM whiteboard feature was utilized in both collaborative contexts (co-located and distributed), aiming to eliminate the influence of different sketching tools (pen-and-paper sketching and digital sketching) on the design outputs [46,47]. In order to record participants' design activities and interactions, ZOOM recording was conducted while completing design sessions for capturing verbalization and sketching activities. In addition, other video cameras were installed in front of each dyad for identifying non-verbal design behaviors and interactions, such as eye contact and body language. Figure 4 demonstrates specific cameras' fields of view.

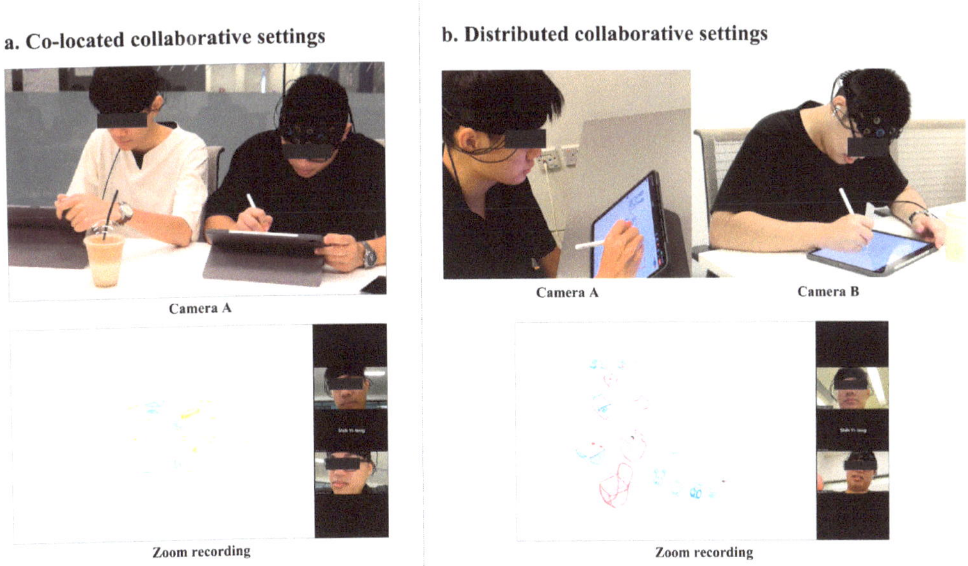

Figure 4. (**a**) Zoom recording and one camera's fields of view for co-located collaboration contexts. (**b**) Zoom recording and another two cameras' fields of view for distributed collaboration environment.

3.3. Instruments and Computational Tools

One prominent technique used in hyper-scanning research is fNIRS, a non-invasive neuroimaging method that utilizes near-infrared light to penetrate the scalp and skull, enabling the monitoring of hemodynamic responses in specific brain regions. Correlative neurocognition reviews [30,48] have highlighted the wide use of fNIRS in investigations focusing on brain-to-brain communication during social interaction tasks, especially during interpersonal cooperation. fNIRS has been used as a dominant complement to fMRI and EEG to measure IBS, as its reasonable spatial resolution, greater resilience to body movement, and less experimental settings limits frequently applied for IBS measurement within naturalistic interactive environments. Therefore, we conducted a fNIRS-based hyper-scanning study. Each participant was fitted with fNIRS (OctaMon, Artinis Medical Systems, the Netherlands, as shown in Figure 5a) headcap on the forehead for the assessment of cerebral blood flow (CBF) changes in the prefrontal cortex. Scanning data were recorded using OxySoft 3D software 4.0.6.1 x64, which supports recording two individuals' changes in oxy-hemoglobin (HbO) and deoxy-hemoglobin (HbR) levels on one laptop simultaneously in both co-present and distributed settings. Figure 6 presents the instance of the signal extracted from one of the dyads with a time window of 400–800 s.

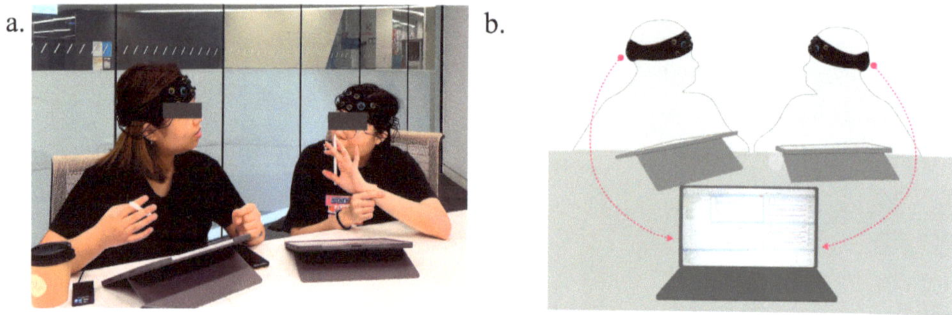

Figure 5. (**a**) fNIRS headcap settings for data collection during co-located design collaboration; (**b**) scanning data were recorded through OxySoft 3D software, supporting the recording of two individuals' brain activities on one laptop concurrently.

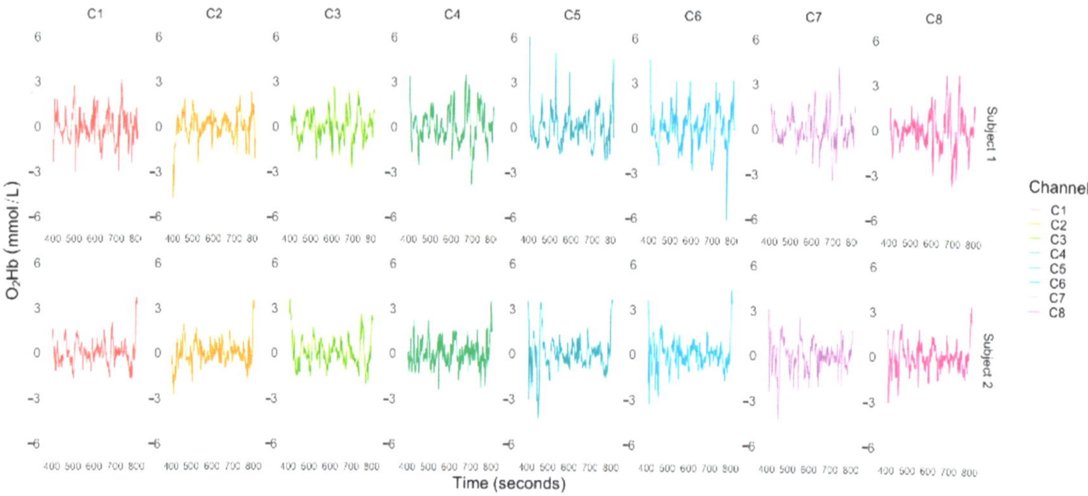

Figure 6. Example of fNIRS data collected from one of the dyads. Notes: due to the length and drifting of the signal, the signal presented above was extracted from one of the dyads with a time window of 400–800 s.

All signal processing and statistical analyses were performed using the R programming (Version 4.3.1) language, a powerful tool for statistical computing and graphics. To facilitate these computations, we utilized a variety of relevant R packages designed for data manipulation, signal processing, and statistical modeling. These tools allowed us to process the fNIRS data, perform the necessary statistical tests, and derive meaningful results about the patterns of IBS under different conditions and behaviors in the context of design collaborations.

3.4. Data Analysis

3.4.1. Interaction Segmentation

The video recording data were initially filtered by coding for off-task behaviors (e.g., jokes, banter between the designers, and conversation of events unrelated to the design problem). Subsequently, the video data was segmented into small episodes and coded for three design interaction behaviors: verbal-only, sketch-only, and mixed communication (a combination of verbal and sketch). Verbal-only means that within a certain period, the design ideas are only proposed and transmitted through verbal communication. Similarly, sketch-only means that only sketch activities take place during a certain period of time, as the only methods of conceptual exchange. In terms of mixed communication, which means that verbalization and sketching occur simultaneously during a period or quickly alternate. Table 1 presents specific instances collected from one of the dyads, elaborating on each defined design behavior observed during the design collaboration process. Two well-trained investigators conducted the episode segmentation separately aligning with the same criteria. By comparing the segments classified by the 2 investigators, 23 controversial segments were excluded. Overall, 432 segments were extracted, of which 250 episodes occurred within the co-located context and 182 were distributed collaborations.

Table 1. Examples of detailed transcripts and sketching activities (screenshots) in each design condition: verbal only, sketch only, and mixed communication (sketch and verbal).

No.	Condition	Specific Behaviour	Instances (Scripts and Screenshots)
1	Verbal only	Participant A explained ideas by verbalization only. Participant B plays as an audience.	A: "What do you think about this, like this, stacking all the modules." A: "It's a bit like Noah's Ark. Or it can also be stacked like a pyramid." B: "I think it looks great."
		Participant B explained ideas by verbalization only. Participant A plays as an audience.	B: "I'm thinking we can keep the under layer as a circle shape." B: "Because if the shape is too flat, it may not float on the water, or maybe it could be just like a little boat." A: "I can picture what you are describing."
		Participants exchange design ideas alternately and finally reach a consensus.	A: "But the size of this ball cannot be too small" B: "But if the shape is a ball, they might fall easily" A: "I think it's okay, because they can float on the water" B: "Oh! You're right."
2	Sketch only	Participant A explains ideas by sketching only. Participant B plays as an information receiver.	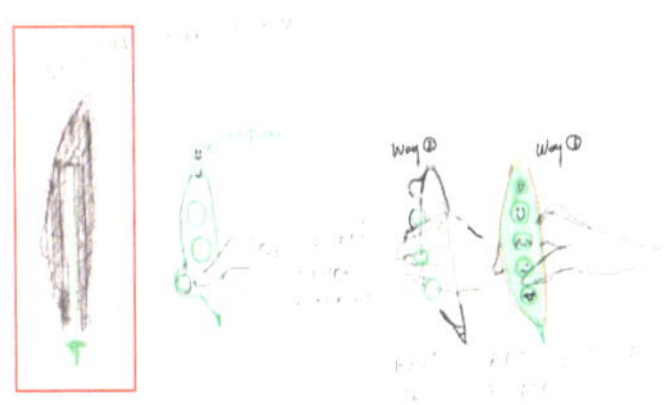
		Participant B explains ideas by sketching only. Participant A plays as an information receiver.	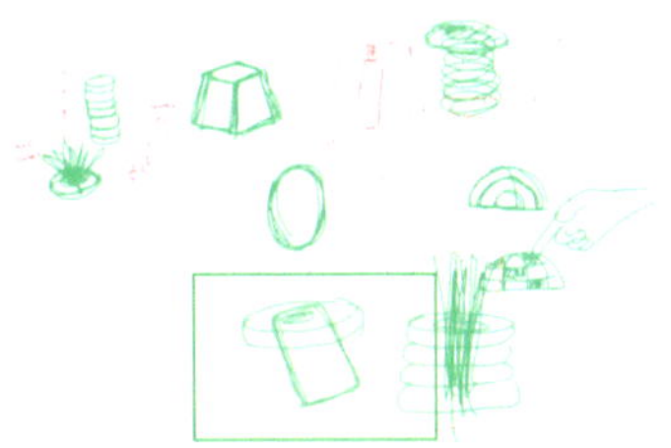

Table 1. *Cont.*

No.	Condition	Specific Behaviour	Instances (Scripts and Screenshots)
2	Sketch only	Participants design by sketching collaboratively.	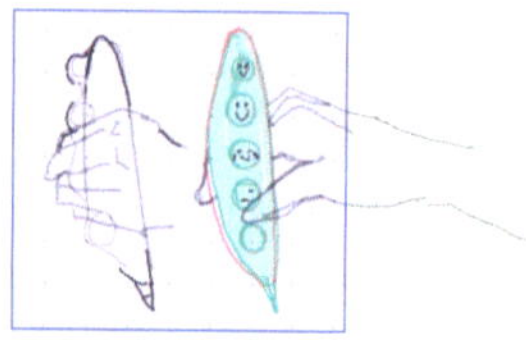
3	Mixed communication (Sketch + Verbal)	Participant A is information provided by think aloud and sketching concurrently. Participant B plays as an information receiver.	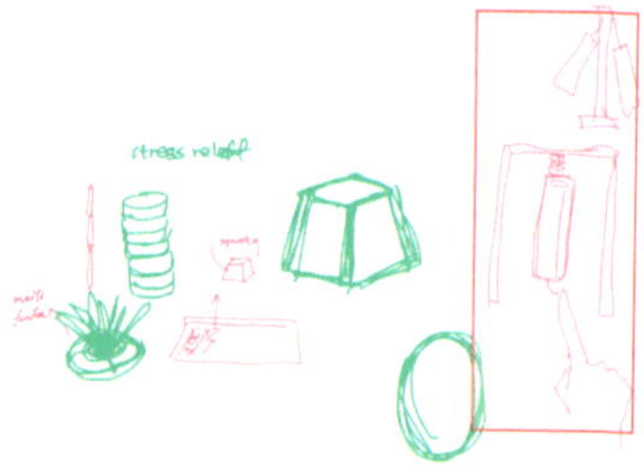
		Participant B is information provided by think aloud and sketching concurrently. Participant A plays as an information receiver.	
		Participants A and B think aloud and sketch collaboratively.	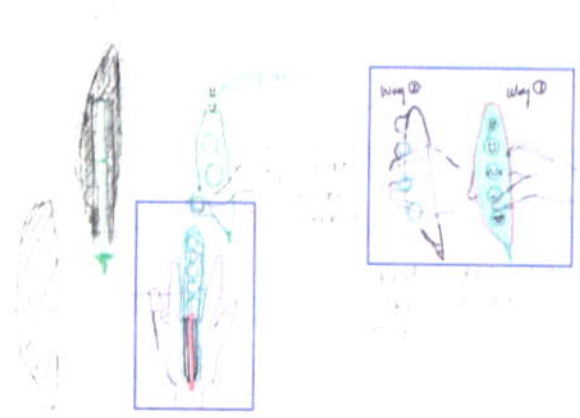

3.4.2. IBS Analysis

fNIRS Data Segmentation and Variance Estimation

The continuous fNIRS data were divided into 15 s windows according to those behavior segments defined in Table 1. For each of these time windows and each channel, the variance was calculated. To ensure the quality of the signals and eliminate outliers, time windows with variance values above or below 2.5 standard deviations from the mean variance calculated across all time windows and channels were excluded. This step was crucial to filter out periods with potential motion artifacts, which could result in high variance, and dead periods (where no signal was captured), which would result in low variance. Since the behaviors of each pair of participants varied (i.e., some pairs may exhibit more verbal behavior, while others may exhibit more sketching behavior), the selected time windows were randomly sampled to avoid bias. For each condition (face to face and remote) and each behavior (verbal only, sketch only, and simultaneous verbal and sketch), 10 times windows were selected.

Establishment of Synchrony Measurement

The fNIRS device used in this study was capable of capturing data from eight channels per participant. Four of these channels were situated on the left frontal region of the brain and four on the right frontal region, thereby allowing for a comprehensive capture of brain activity across these vital areas. After the data collection, the channels were aggregated for each side of the brain for each participant. This process resulted in four distinct data sets: Participant 1's left frontal activity, Participant 1's right frontal activity, Participant 2's left frontal activity, and Participant 2's right frontal activity. Synchrony measures were then established around the two regions of interest—left and right frontal regions—for each participant. This resulted in four distinct paths for IBS analysis: (i) Participant 1 Left Frontal to Participant 2 Left Frontal; (ii) Participant 1 Left Frontal to Participant 2 Right Frontal; (iii) Participant 1 Right Frontal to Participant 2 Left Frontal; (iv) Participant 1 Right Frontal to Participant 2 Right Frontal. These paths provide a comprehensive framework for analyzing the interplay and synchrony of brain activities between the participants during their design collaboration under various conditions and modes of communication.

IBS between any pair of sites were measured with the average length of the Kuramoto Order Parameter (KOP). The KOP measures the phase synchrony between two signals by calculating the vector average of phase angles over time (see Figure 7). A value of 1 indicates perfect phase synchrony, while a value near 0 indicates no phase synchrony. The KOP was calculated for each pair of brain sites in each experimental condition. The average KOP length across time was then used as the index of IBS between those two sites. Higher average KOP lengths indicate greater IBS.

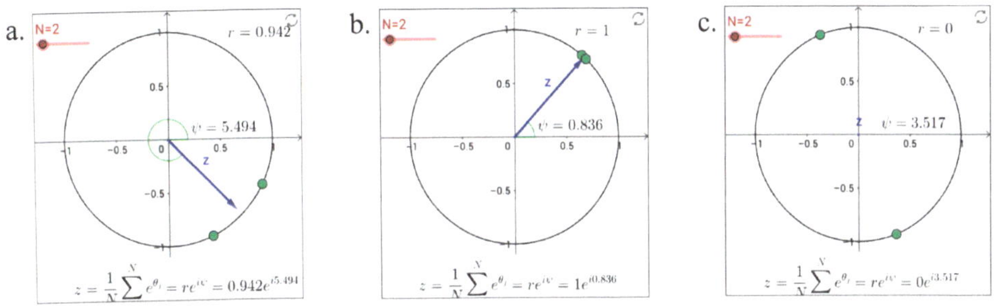

Figure 7. Illustration of Kuramoto Order Parameter (the phase angles for two signal sources are depicted by green dots, originating from their respective unit vectors, the blue arrows represent the mean direction of these unit vectors). (**a**) the proximity of phase angles between the two signals results in a magnitude nearly equal to 1; (**b**) shows that the phase angles from both sources are aligned, producing a magnitude of exactly 1; (**c**) illustrates that the sources are in antiphase, leading to a magnitude of 0.

IBS Calculation

To calculate IBS, we extracted 20 non-overlapping 15 s time windows from the brain signal data timed to the interaction between the two participants as shown in the video. Within each window, we calculated the instantaneous Kuramoto Order Parameter (KOP), denoted r, between the two brain sites at each time point. For example, with 150 time points, this gave 150 r values. We averaged these r values to obtain a "window-level" synchrony value representing the phase synchrony during that 15 s period. We then averaged the 20 "window-level" r values within each experimental condition to obtain a "dyad-level" mean KOP, denoted $\bar{r}$, for that condition. Since there were 20 window-level values per condition, each dyad-level $\bar{r}$ represented the mean synchrony across those 20 time periods. The synchrony index $\bar{r}$ ranges from 0 to 1. A value of 0 indicates completely out-of-phase signals, while 1 indicates perfect in-phase synchrony. Intermediate $\bar{r}$ values indicate partial synchrony. Thus, the dyad-level $\bar{r}$ reflected the average phase synchrony between the two brain sites during a given experimental condition.

4. Results

4.1. IBS Analysis

To understand the effects of different conditions (co-located vs. distancing) and behaviors (verbal only, sketch only, mixed interaction (verbal + sketch)), we employed a linear mixed model. This model allowed us to establish the main effects of condition and behavior, as well as their interaction effects. Following this, post hoc pairwise comparisons were calculated where appropriate to further delve into the differences between the conditions and behaviors in terms of their influence on IBS. Given the small sample size of this preliminary study, we refrained from reporting the statistical results at the individual channel-to-channel synchrony level. However, to provide insights into the patterns of IBS, we still present the mean values of synchrony for each of the four established paths: (i) Participant 1 Left Frontal to Participant 2 Left Frontal; (ii) Participant 1 Left Frontal to Participant 2 Right Frontal; (iii) Participant 1 Right Frontal to Participant 2 Left Frontal; and (iv) Participant 1 Right Frontal to Participant 2 Right Frontal. These mean values offer a preliminary view of the patterns of IBS under different conditions and behaviors, further contributing to our understanding of collaborative cognition in design tasks.

Our preliminary study revealed several findings that highlight the differences in IBS among designers collaborating in a face-to-face (F2F) setting compared with a remote setting (see Figure 8). The interactions were categorized into three design behaviors: verbal communication only, sketching only, and mixed communication (V + S). The IBS was higher during the sketch-only behavior in the F2F condition compared to the remote condition. Conversely, during the V + S behavior, the IBS was higher in the remote condition than in the F2F condition. In addition, in the F2F condition, IBS was greater during the sketch-only behavior than during the V + S behavior. In the remote condition, however, the IBS was higher during the V + S behavior than during the sketch-only behavior. In the F2F condition, the IBS was smallest during the V + S behavior compared to both verbal-only and sketch-only behaviors.

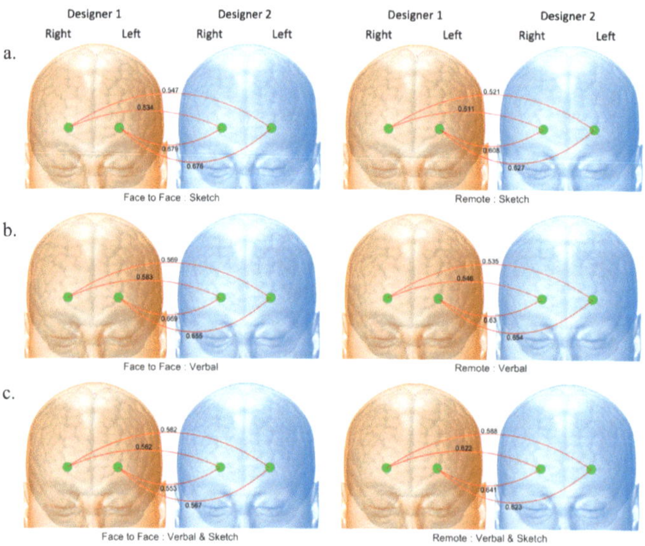

Figure 8. Average IBS by condition, behavior, and inter-brain connectivity pathways. (**a**) the IBS of the first dyad (female-female); (**b**) the IBS of the second dyad (male-male); (**c**) the IBS of the third dyad(female-male).

4.2. Statistical Analysis

To examine the influence of experimental conditions and behaviors on inter-brain synchrony (IBS), we specified a linear mixed-effects model with the formula IBS~Condition × Behavior + (1 | Dyad) + (1 | Path). In this model, IBS is the dependent variable, reflecting the inter-brain synchrony coefficient. Condition and behavior are treated as fixed effects, with their interaction term, Condition × Behavior, investigating whether the effect of one factor is contingent on the level of the other. Random effects terms (1 | Dyad) and (1 | Path) introduce random intercepts for each dyad and each path, respectively, which allow for the modeling of variability within dyads and paths that are not captured by the fixed effects.

Model fitting was conducted using the 'lme4' package in R. To determine the significance of the fixed effects, we performed an Analysis of Variance (ANOVA) using the ANOVA function from the stats package, which yielded an ANOVA table presenting the degrees of freedom, the sum of squares, mean squares, F-statistics, and associated *p*-values for each fixed effect (see Table 2). To ascertain the necessity of including random effects in our model, we compared it to simpler nested models with different random effects structures. Specifically, we compared our full model (IBS~Condition × Behavior + (1 | Dyad) + (1 | Path)) to a model with random intercepts for dyads only (IBS~Condition Behavior + (1 | Dyad)) and to a linear model without random effects (IBS~Condition × Behavior). These comparisons were made using chi-square tests (Figures 9 and 10), which are appropriate for comparing nested models differing in complexity. Additionally, the chi-square test results indicated that the full model with both (1 | Dyad) and (1 | Path) random effects provided a significantly better fit to the data than the models with fewer random effects, justifying the inclusion of both random intercepts in our analysis. For post hoc analysis (see Table 3), pairwise comparisons of the estimated marginal means for each pair of conditions within behavior levels and each pair of behaviors within condition levels were executed using the 'emmeans' package. We addressed the multiple comparison issue by applying the False Discovery Rate (FDR) correction using the Benjamini–Hochberg procedure to control for type I errors.

Table 2. ANOVA test for the interaction effect between condition and behavior.

Variable	Sum Sq	Mean Sq	NumDF	DenDF	F Value	*p*-Value
Condition	0.00901	0.009011	1	1073.8	0.172	0.678
Behavior	0.05676	0.028382	2	1073.8	0.5417	0.582
Interaction	0.47281	0.236405	2	1073.8	4.5124	0.011

Notes: Sum Sq: Sum of Square; Mean Sq: Mean Sum of Square; numDF = numerator degrees of freedom; denDF = denominator degrees of freedom.

Table 3. Post hoc analysis of pairwise comparisons at each level of condition and behavior.

Condition	Behavior	Contrast	Estimate	SE	df	T Ratio	*p*-Value	fdr *p*
F2F	/	Sk − Vb	−0.010	0.024	1082.02	−0.393	0.691	0.691
F2F	/	Sk − VS	0.043	0.024	1082.02	1.775	0.073	0.143
F2F	/	Vb − VS	0.053	0.024	1082.02	2.168	0.029	0.097
Remote	/	Sk − Vb	−0.024	0.024	1082.02	−1.001	0.311	0.350
Remote	/	Sk − VS	−0.052	0.024	1082.02	−2.120	0.032	0.097
Remote	/	Vb − VS	−0.027	0.024	1082.02	−1.119	0.258	0.332
/	Sk	F2F − remote	0.042	0.024	1082.02	1.737	0.079	0.143
/	Vb	F2F − remote	0.028	0.024	1082.02	1.129	0.254	0.332
/	VS	F2F − remote	−0.053	0.024	1082.02	−2.158	0.029	0.097

Notes: Sk = sketch only; Vb = verbal only; VS = verbalization + sketch; F2F: co-located interaction; Remote: distancing interaction.

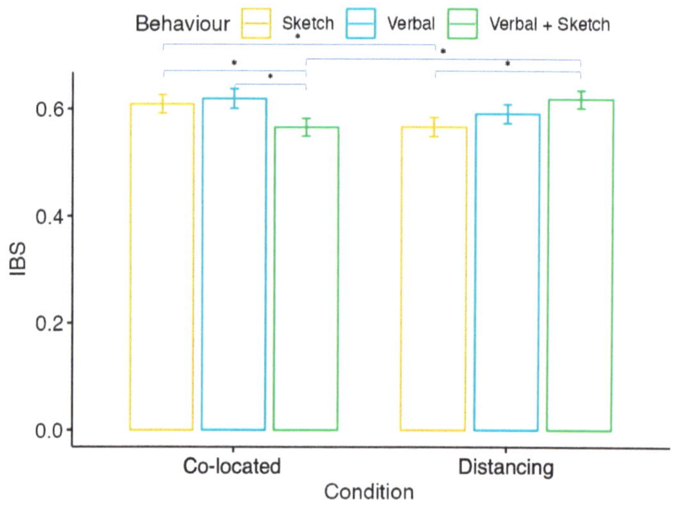

Figure 9. IBS by condition and behavior. Note: Asterisks (*) denote statistical significance with a *p*-value less than 0.05.

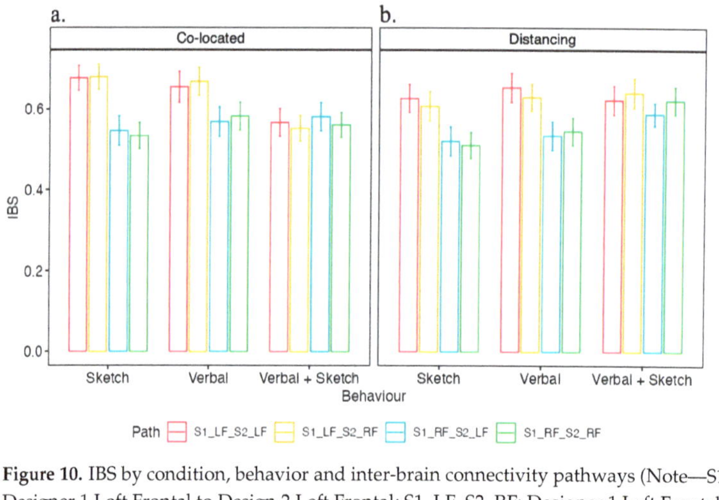

Figure 10. IBS by condition, behavior and inter-brain connectivity pathways (Note—S1_LF_S2_LF: Designer 1 Left Frontal to Design 2 Left Frontal; S1_LF_S2_RF: Designer 1 Left Frontal to Design 2 Right Frontal; S1_RF_S2_LF: Designer 1 Right Frontal to Design 2 Left Frontal; and S1_RF_S2_RF: Designer 1 Right Frontal to Design 2 Right Frontal). (**a**) illustrates the Inter-Brain Synchrony (IBS) occurring in a co-located setting, where two designers are seated together, engaging in face-to-face communication during the design discussion; (**b**) illustrates the distancing condition, the designers are situated in separate rooms, with communication enabled through video conferencing software that allows screen sharing and collaborative drawing.

4.3. Design Outcome Evaluation

The three design teams were able to satisfy both toy design and multifunctional chair tasks between co-located and distributed modes. Table 4 shows the evaluation results of the digital sketches by the four design experts. The scores in Table 5 are the average scores of the four reviewers. The fourth column (average score) in each mode shows the average performance of the three design teams for each criterion.

Table 4. Screenshot of the final design solutions by digital sketches of each team within different collaborative environments.

	Co-Located Mode	Distributed Mode
Team 1	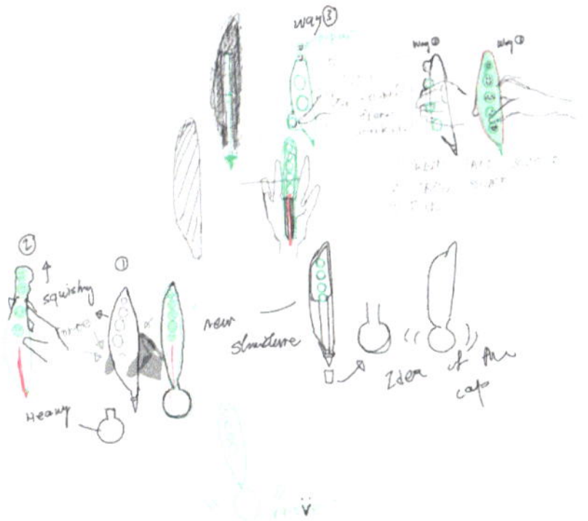 An office toy used for hand relaxing	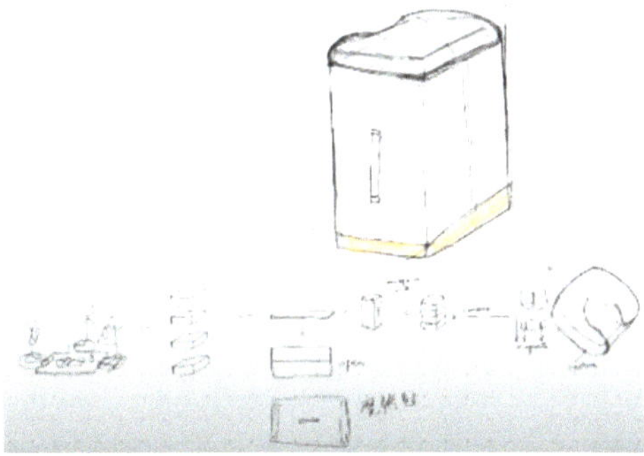 A versatile chair can be used as a furniture stool at home or as a picnic blanket outdoors.
Team 2	 A block toy to play with during the bath, designed for kids aged ranged between 3-6 years.	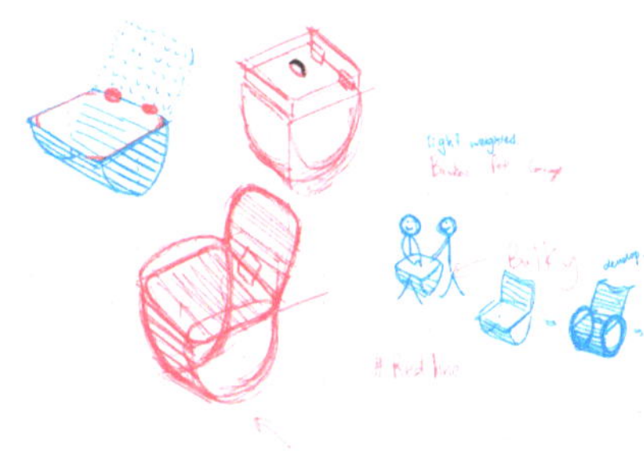 A multifunctional DIY outdoor chair for elderly.
Team 3	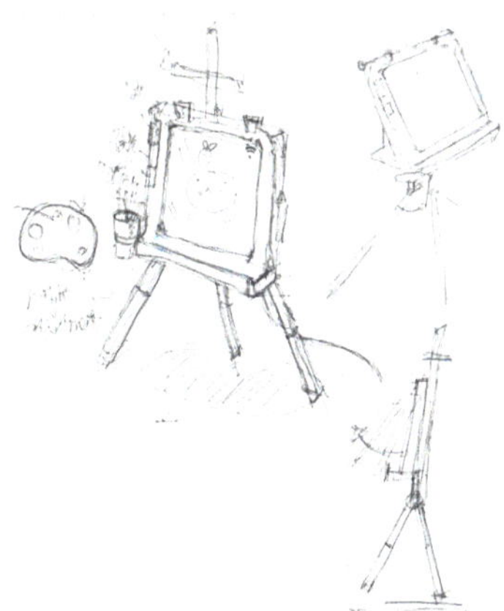 A multifunctional magic drawing board for early learning.	 A multifunctional dining table designed for two cartoon characters.

Table 5. Scores for the design outcomes within different design conditions.

Criteria	Co-Located Mode				Distributed Mode			
	Team 1	Team 2	Team 3	Av	Team 1	Team 2	Team 3	Av
How innovative	6.1	5.5	4.8	5.5	5.3	5.1	4.5	5.0
How creative	6.3	6.0	5.3	5.9	5.8	5.6	6.1	5.8
Satisfying design task	7.1	6.7	6.0	6.6	6.2	6.6	6.8	6.5
Practical solution	7.3	6.5	6.7	6.8	6.0	6.4	5.7	6.0
Flexibility of the design	6.2	6.4	7.1	6.6	6.3	6.6	7.0	6.6
Av	6.6	6.2	6.0	6.3	5.9	6.1	6.0	6.0

Team 1's co-located mode design outcome received higher scores in terms of satisfying the design task (7.1 vs. 6.6) and practical solution (7.3 vs. 6.4). The criterion of flexibility of the design score was closer for the two design outcomes (6.2 vs. 6.3). In addition, the average scores for both collaboration modes were very similar for Team 2 and Team 3 (6.2 vs. 6.1 and 6.0 vs. 6.0). Overall, the three design teams in both collaboration modes produced very similar design outcomes.

5. Discussions

Our study provides valuable insights into the nuances of collaborative design processes under different conditions, and how these conditions can influence IBS. The increased IBS during the sketch-only behavior in the F2F setting suggests that co-located interactions might facilitate a better shared understanding when designers are expressing their ideas purely through sketches. This could be attributed to the immediate and unfiltered feedback made possible by real-time, physical interactions. In this setting, non-verbal cues such as body language or facial expression might also play a significant role. In contrast, the higher IBS observed during the mixed communication (verbal and sketch) in the distributed condition indicates that this combination of communication modes might be more effective in synchronizing the designers' cognitive processes when working remotely. This might be due to the increased reliance on verbal communication to form a shared understanding in the absence of physical presence. The need to articulate thoughts clearly and concisely during remote collaboration might lead to a more coordinated cognitive process.

Interestingly, IBS was greater during sketch-only behavior compared to mixed verbal and sketching communication in the co-located condition. Conversely, within the remote collaboration setting, IBS was elevated during mixed communication versus sketch-only behavior. This suggests the form of interaction that best facilitates cognitive alignment may heavily depend on whether design partners share physical space. Notably, the lowest IBS in face-to-face collaboration occurred with simultaneous verbalization and sketching, potentially indicating heightened cognitive demands that desynchronize neural processes. The richness of contextual cues in physical proximity may further challenge integration across multiple communication modes. Furthermore, the highest IBS took place when collaborators communicated in verbal-only within the co-located condition, while the mixed communication (verbal and sketch) behavior promoted the highest IBS during online design collaboration. This finding supports the prior discoveries [29] of increased time allocated to sketching in virtual teams. These preliminary findings could profoundly influence the development of optimally collaborative work environments and digital platforms. Further research should elucidate the precise mechanisms relating design team synchrony to performance across contexts, providing actionable direction for enhancing collective innovation.

The limitation of this preliminary study constrains the generalizability of the findings and conclusions. Firstly, the small sample size of the three dyads restricts the statistical power and precludes drawing definitive conclusions regarding the impact of different collaborative settings on IBS patterns and design outcomes. Additional participants are necessary to quantitatively discern such effects. Additionally, the limited age range and design experience level of the participants may not represent the true diversity of collaborative teams in real-world design practices. Broader sampling would augment ecological validity. Therefore, future studies will be conducted on larger and more diverse samples, considering additional confounding variables, such as gender, age ranges, and years of design experience.

6. Conclusions

This study investigated the patterns of brain synchrony among design collaborators during the conceptual design process within two collaborative environments: distributed and co-located settings. The consequences based on the preliminary study emphasize several variations in IBS among designers collaborating in these two settings. Through protocol analysis, interactions between each dyad were classified into three categories: verbal-only, sketch-only, and mixed interaction (verbal and sketch). Subsequently, according to the hyper-scanning analysis, the increased IBS was observed during the sketch-only behavior in the co-located setting, suggesting that sketching might be a facilitator for better mutual understanding when design collaboration occurs face to face. This could be attributed to the immediate and unfiltered feedback made possible by real-time, physical interactions. Comparably, our results revealed a higher level of IBS when subjects employed mixed communication (verbal and sketch) in distributed conditions, demonstrating the combination of verbal communication and sketching might lead to a more coordinated cognitive process when physical isolation.

Moreover, the IBS was greater during the sketch-only behavior than during the mixed communication behavior within the co-present setting. Interestingly, the level of IBS was found to be higher when participants performed sketch-only behavior compared to mixed communication behavior in the co-present settings, while the IBS was higher during the combination of verbal and sketching behavior within remote settings. This finding illustrates the close associations between the utilization of communication methods improving cognitive synchrony and collaborative environments. Design collaborators are inclined to adjust their interaction behaviors in order to adapt to different design environments and strengthen the exchange of opinions and the construction of consensus. Furthermore, the results indicate that there were no significant differences in overall collective performance and design outputs between these two collaboration contexts.

To draw statistical conclusions on the impact of IBS on team behavior and performance, it is suggested that future studies be conducted with a larger sample size along the same framework. The preliminary study demonstrated how neuroimaging can be used to analyze behavioral patterns in two different collaboration environments. It could be a step towards building effective virtual teamwork beyond the design realm. Furthermore, these findings could have important implications for the design of collaborative workspaces with digital tools. Further study is needed to better understand the underlying mechanisms and how these insights could be applied to optimize team performance in design contexts. In subsequent research, interventions that promote IBS can be tested, such as team training, introducing diversity within groups, and assessing their impact on IBS.

Author Contributions: Conceptualization, Y.-T.S. and C.H.Y.W.; methodology, E.L.L.S. and L.W.; formal analysis, C.H.Y.W. and L.W.; investigation, Y.-T.S.; data curation, E.L.L.S. and L.W.; writing—original draft preparation, L.W. and C.H.Y.W.; writing—review and editing, M.R. and Y.-T.S.; visualization, L.W. and C.H.Y.W.; supervision, Z.Y. and M.R.; project administration, L.C. and Y.-T.S.; funding acquisition, Y.-T.S., Z.Y. and L.C. All authors have read and agreed to the published version of the manuscript.

Funding: The work described in this paper was funded by CRF PolyU from the Research Grants Council of Hong Kong (Project No. C5048-21G).

Institutional Review Board Statement: This study was conducted according to the guidelines of the Declaration of Helsinki and approved by the PolyU Institutional Review Board (HSEARS20210914003). Ethics approval date is 14 September 2021.

Informed Consent Statement: Informed consent was obtained from all subjects involved in this study.

Data Availability Statement: The datasets generated and/or analyzed during the current study are not publicly available due to privacy but are available from the corresponding author upon reasonable request.

Acknowledgments: The authors thank John Gero for his valuable comments on this study.

Conflicts of Interest: The authors declare no conflicts of interest.

References

1. Rice, D.J.; Davidson, B.D.; Dannenhoffer, J.F.; Gay, G.K. Improving the effectiveness of virtual teams by adapting team processes. *Comput. Support. Coop. Work* **2017**, *16*, 567–594. [CrossRef]
2. Sawyer, R.K.; DeZutter, S. Distributed creativity: How collective creations emerge from collaboration. *Psychol. Aesthet. Creat. Arts* **2009**, *3*, 81. [CrossRef]
3. Cho, J.Y.; Cho, M.H. Student perceptions and performance in online and offline collaboration in an interior design studio. *Int. J. Technol. Des. Educ.* **2014**, *24*, 473–491. [CrossRef]
4. Turana, Y.; Nathaniel, M.; Shen, R.; Ali, S.; Aparasu, R.R. Citicoline and COVID-19-Related Cognitive and Other Neurologic Complications. *Brain Sci.* **2022**, *12*, 59. [CrossRef] [PubMed]
5. Heilmann, F.; Weinberg, H.; Wollny, R. The Impact of Practicing Open- vs. Closed-Skill Sports on Executive Functions—A Meta-Analytic and Systematic Review with a Focus on Characteristics of Sports. *Brain Sci.* **2022**, *12*, 1071. [CrossRef] [PubMed]
6. Martins, L.L.; Gilson, L.L.; Maynard, M.T. Virtual Teams: What Do We Know and Where Do We Go From Here? *J. Manag.* **2004**, *30*, 805–835. [CrossRef]
7. Premeti, A.; Bucci, M.P.; Isel, F. Evidence from ERP and Eye Movements as Markers of Language Dysfunction in Dyslexia. *Brain Sci.* **2022**, *12*, 73. [CrossRef] [PubMed]
8. Schmidt, K. The Problem with 'Awareness'. *Comput. Support. Coop. Work* **2002**, *11*, 285–298. [CrossRef]
9. Graveline, A.; Geisler, C.; Danchak, M. *Teaming Together Apart: Emergent Patterns of Media Use in Collaboration at a Distance*; IEEE: Piscataway, NJ, USA, 2000; pp. 381–393.
10. Hinds, P.J.; Bailey, D.E. Out of Sight, Out of Sync: Understanding Conflict in Distributed Teams. *Organ. Sci.* **2003**, *14*, 615–632. [CrossRef]
11. Montoya-Weiss, M.M.; Massey, A.P.; Song, M. Getting it Together: Temporal Coordination and Conflict Management in Global Virtual Teams. *Acad. Manag. J.* **2001**, *44*, 1251–1262. [CrossRef]
12. Tang, H.; Lee, Y.; Gero, J. Comparing collaborative co-located and distributed design processes in digital and traditional sketching environments: A protocol study using the function–behaviour structure coding scheme. *Des. Stud.* **2011**, *32*, 1–29. [CrossRef]
13. González-Ibáñez, R.; Haseki, M.; Shah, C. Let's search together, but not too close! An analysis of communication and performance in collaborative information seeking. *Inf. Process. Manag.* **2013**, *49*, 1165–1179. [CrossRef]
14. Mulet, E.; Chulvi, V.; Royo, M.; Galán, J. Influence of the dominant thinking style in the degree of novelty of designs in virtual and traditional working environments. *J. Eng. Des.* **2016**, *27*, 413–437. [CrossRef]
15. Crivelli, D.; Balconi, M. Near-infrared spectroscopy applied to complex systems and human hyperscanning networking. *Appl. Sci.* **2017**, *7*, 922. [CrossRef]
16. Czeszumski, A.; Eustergerling, S.; Lang, A.; Menrath, D.; Gerstenberger, M.; Schuberth, S.; Schreiber, F.; Rendon, Z.Z.; König, P. Hyperscanning: A valid method to study neural inter-brain underpinnings of social interaction. *Front. Hum. Neurosci.* **2020**, *14*, 39. [CrossRef] [PubMed]
17. Reinero, D.A.; Dikker, S.; Van Bavel, J.J. Inter-brain synchrony in teams predicts collective performance. *Soc. Cogn. Affect. Neurosci.* **2021**, *16*, 43–57. [CrossRef] [PubMed]
18. Lu, K.; Hao, N. When do we fall in neural synchrony with others? Social Cognitive and Affect. *Neuroscience* **2019**, *14*, 253–261.
19. Naama, M.; Grace, H.; Allan, L.R. Real-life creative problem solving in teams: fNIRS based hyperscanning study. *NeuroImage* **2019**, *203*, 116161.
20. Lahti, H.; Seitamaa-Hakkarainen, P.; Hakkarainen, K. Collaboration patterns in computer supported collaborative designing. *Des. Stud.* **2004**, *25*, 351–371. [CrossRef]
21. Dreamson, N. Online collaboration in design education: An experiment in real-time manipulation of prototypes and communication. *Int. J. Art Des. Educ.* **2017**, *36*, 188–199. [CrossRef]
22. Grant, C.; Clarke, C. Digital Resilience: A Competency Framework for Agile Workers. In *Agile Working and Well-Being in the Digital Age*; Grant, C., Russell, E., Eds.; Palgrave Macmillan: Cham, Switzerland, 2020; pp. 117–130. [CrossRef]
23. Windle, G.; Bennett, K.M.; Noyes, J.A. Methodological review of resilience measurement scales. *Health Qual Life Outcomes* **2011**, *9*, 8. [CrossRef] [PubMed]

24. Liska, R. Can performance of modern virtual teams measure up to co-located teams. *Team Perform. Manag. Int. J.* **2022**, *28*, 205–222. [CrossRef]
25. Hammond, J.M.; Harvey, C.M.; Richard, J.K.; Compton, W.D.; Darisipudi, A. Distributed Collaborative Design Teams: Media Effects on Design Processes. *Int. J. Hum.-Comput. Interact.* **2005**, *18*, 145–165. [CrossRef]
26. Kvan, T. Collaborative design: What is it? *Autom. Constr.* **2000**, *9*, 409–415. [CrossRef]
27. Lee, S.; Do, E.Y.-L. The effects of computing technology in creative design tasks: A case study of design collaboration. In Proceedings of the Seventh ACM Conference on Creativity and Cognition, San Diego, CA, USA, 23–26 June 2009; pp. 387–388.
28. Eris, O.; Martelaro, N.; Badke-Schaub, P. A comparative analysis of multimodal communication during design sketching in co-located and distributed environments. *Des. Stud.* **2014**, *35*, 559–592. [CrossRef]
29. Yang, Z.; Xiang, W.; You, W.; Sun, L. The influence of distributed collaboration in design processes: An analysis of design activity on information, problem, and solution. *Int. J. Technol. Des. Educ.* **2021**, *31*, 587–609. [CrossRef]
30. Babiloni, F.; Astolfi, L. Social neuroscience and hyperscanning techniques: Past, present and future. *Neurosci. Biobehav. Rev.* **2014**, *44*, 76–93. [CrossRef]
31. Dikker, S.; Wan, L.; Davidesco, I.; Kaggen, L.; Oostrik, M.; McClintock, J.; Rowland, J.; Michalareas, G.; Van Bavel, J.J.; Ding, M.; et al. Brain-to-Brain Synchrony Tracks Real-World Dynamic Group Interactions in the Classroom. *Curr. Biol.* **2017**, *27*, 1375–1380. [CrossRef]
32. Jiang, J.; Dai, B.; Peng, D.; Zhu, C.; Liu, L.; Lu, C. Neural synchronization during face-to-face communication. *J. Neurosci.* **2012**, *32*, 16064–16069. [CrossRef]
33. Li, R.; Rui, G.; Zhao, C.; Wang, C.; Fang, F.; Zhang, Y. Functional network alterations in patients with amnestic mild cognitive impairment characterized using functional near-infrared spectroscopy. *IEEE Trans. Neural Syst. Rehabil. Eng.* **2019**, *28*, 123–132. [CrossRef]
34. Cui, X.; Bryant, D.M.; Reiss, A.L. NIRS-based hyperscanning reveals increased interpersonal coherence in superior frontal cortex during cooperation. *Neuroimage* **2012**, *59*, 2430–2437. [CrossRef] [PubMed]
35. Hsu, C.; Peng, P.H.; Peng, P.C.; Hsu, T.Y.; Chuang, C.H. Cooperative and Competitive-related Inter-Brain Synchrony during Gaming. In Proceedings of the IEEE International Conference on Systems, Man, and Cybernetics (SMC), Melbourne, Australia, 17–20 October 2021; pp. 3391–3395.
36. Wikström, V.; Saarikivi, K.; Falcon, M.; Makkonen, T.; Martikainen, S.; Putkinen, V.; Cowley, B.C.; Tervaniemi, M. Inter-brain synchronization occurs without physical co-presence during cooperative online gaming. *Neuropsychologia* **2022**, *174*, 108316. [CrossRef] [PubMed]
37. Alexiou, K.; Zamenopoulos, T.; Johnson, J.H.; Gilbert, S.J. Exploring the neurological basis of design cognition using brain imaging: Some preliminary results. *Des. Stud.* **2009**, *30*, 623–647. [CrossRef]
38. Shealy, T.; Gero, J.S. The neurocognition of three engineering concept generation techniques. In Proceedings of the Design Society: International Conference on Engineering Design, Delft, The Netherlands, 5–8 August 2019; Volume 1, pp. 1833–1842.
39. Lara, A.H.; Wallis, J.D. The role of prefrontal cortex in working memory: A mini review. *Front. Syst. Neurosci.* **2015**, *9*, 173. [CrossRef] [PubMed]
40. Gabora, L. Revenge of the 'Neurds': Characterizing creative thought in terms of the structure and dynamics of memory. *Creat. Res. J.* **2010**, *22*, 1–13. [CrossRef]
41. Fink, A.; Grabner, R.H.; Benedek, M.; Reishofer, G.; Hauswirth, V.; Fally, M.; Neuper, C.; Ebner, F.; Neubauer, A.C. The creative brain: Investigation of brain activity during creative problem solving by means of EEG and FMRI. *Hum. Brain Mapp.* **2009**, *30*, 734–748. [CrossRef] [PubMed]
42. Aziz-Zadeh, L.; Liew, S.-L.; Dandekar, F. Exploring the neural correlates of visual creativity. *Soc. Cogn. Affect. Neurosci.* **2013**, *8*, 475–480. [CrossRef]
43. Kleibeuker, S.W.; Koolschijn, P.C.M.P.; Jolles, D.D.; Schel, M.A.; De Dreu, C.K.W.; Crone, E.A. Prefrontal cortex involvement in creative problem solving in middle adolescence and adulthood. *Dev. Cogn. Neurosci.* **2013**, *5*, 197–206. [CrossRef]
44. Goel, V.; Vartanian, O. Dissociating the roles of right ventral lateral and dorsal lateral prefrontal cortex in generation and maintenance of hypotheses in set-shift problems. *Cereb. Cortex* **2005**, *15*, 1170–1177. [CrossRef]
45. Grohs, J.; Shealy, T.; Maczka, D.; Hu, M.; Panneton, R.; Yang, X. Evaluating the potential of fNIRS neuroimaging to study engineering problem solving and design. In Proceedings of the ASEE Annual Conference, Columbus, OH, USA, 25 June 2017.
46. Jorge, D.C.; Mark, K.; EunSook, K. Conceptual product design in digital and traditional sketching environments: A comparative exploratory study. *J. Des. Res.* **2018**, *16*, 131–154.
47. Zhang, Q.; Li, X.; Liu, X.; Liu, S.; Zhang, M.; Liu, Y.; Zhu, C.; Wang, K. The Effect of Non-Invasive Brain Stimulation on the Downregulation of Negative Emotions: A Meta-Analysis. *Brain Sci.* **2022**, *12*, 786. [CrossRef] [PubMed]
48. Balters, S.; Weinstein, T.; Mayseless, N.; Auernhammer, J.; Hawthorne, G.; Steinert, M.; Meinel, C.; Leifer, L.J.; Reiss, A.L. Design science and neuroscience: A systematic review of the emergent field of Design Neurocognition. *Des. Stud.* **2023**, *84*, 101148. [CrossRef]

Disclaimer/Publisher's Note: The statements, opinions and data contained in all publications are solely those of the individual author(s) and contributor(s) and not of MDPI and/or the editor(s). MDPI and/or the editor(s) disclaim responsibility for any injury to people or property resulting from any ideas, methods, instructions or products referred to in the content.

brain sciences

MDPI

Article

The Use of Generative Adversarial Network and Graph Convolution Network for Neuroimaging-Based Diagnostic Classification

Nguyen Huynh [1], Da Yan [2], Yueen Ma [3], Shengbin Wu [4], Cheng Long [5], Mirza Tanzim Sami [6], Abdullateef Almudaifer [6,7], Zhe Jiang [8], Haiquan Chen [9], Michael N. Dretsch [10], Thomas S. Denney [1,11,12,13], Rangaprakash Deshpande [14] and Gopikrishna Deshpande [1,11,12,13,15,16,*]

1 Auburn University Neuroimaging Center, Department of Electrical and Computer Engineering, Auburn University, Auburn, AL 36849, USA; nph0013@auburn.edu (N.H.); dennets@auburn.edu (T.S.D.)
2 Department of Computer Sciences, Indiana University Bloomington, Bloomington, IN 47405, USA; yanda@iu.edu (D.Y.)
3 Department of Computer Sciences, The Chinese University of Hong Kong, Shatin, Hong Kong; yema21@cse.cuhk.edu.hk
4 Department of Mechanical Engineering, University of California, Berkeley, CA 94720, USA; shengbin_wu@berkeley.edu
5 School of Computer Science and Engineering, Nanyang Technological University, Singapore 639798, Singapore; c.long@ntu.edu.sg
6 Department of Computer Sciences, University of Alabama at Birmingham, Birmingham, AL 35294, USA; mtsami@uab.edu (M.T.S.); lateef11@uab.edu (A.A.)
7 College of Computer Science and Engineering, Taibah University, Yanbu 41477, Saudi Arabia
8 Department of Computer and Information Science and Engineering, University of Florida, Gainesville, FL 32611, USA; zhe.jiang@ufl.edu
9 Department of Computer Sciences, California State University, Sacramento, CA 95819, USA; haiquan.chen@csus.edu
10 Walter Reed Army Institute of Research-West, Joint Base Lewis-McChord, WA 98433, USA; dretschphd@gmail.com
11 Department of Psychological Sciences, Auburn University, Auburn, AL 36849, USA
12 Alabama Advanced Imaging Consortium, Birmingham, AL 36849, USA
13 Center for Neuroscience, Auburn University, Auburn, AL 36849, USA
14 Athinoula A. Martinos Center for Biomedical Imaging, Massachusetts General Hospital, Harvard Medical School, Charlestown, MA 02129, USA; rdeshpande3@mgh.harvard.edu
15 Department of Psychiatry, National Institute of Mental Health and Neurosciences, Bangalore 560030, India
16 Department of Heritage Science and Technology, Indian Institute of Technology, Hyderabad 502285, India
* Correspondence: gzd0005@auburn.edu

Abstract: Functional connectivity (FC) obtained from resting-state functional magnetic resonance imaging has been integrated with machine learning algorithms to deliver consistent and reliable brain disease classification outcomes. However, in classical learning procedures, custom-built specialized feature selection techniques are typically used to filter out uninformative features from FC patterns to generalize efficiently on the datasets. The ability of convolutional neural networks (CNN) and other deep learning models to extract informative features from data with grid structure (such as images) has led to the surge in popularity of these techniques. However, the designs of many existing CNN models still fail to exploit the relationships between entities of graph-structure data (such as networks). Therefore, graph convolution network (GCN) has been suggested as a means for uncovering the intricate structure of brain network data, which has the potential to substantially improve classification accuracy. Furthermore, overfitting in classifiers can be largely attributed to the limited number of available training samples. Recently, the generative adversarial network (GAN) has been widely used in the medical field for its generative aspect that can generate synthesis images to cope with the problems of data scarcity and patient privacy. In our previous work, GCN and GAN have been designed to investigate FC patterns to perform diagnosis tasks, and their effectiveness has been tested on the ABIDE-I dataset. In this paper, the models will be further applied to FC data derived from more public datasets (ADHD, ABIDE-II, and ADNI) and our in-house dataset (PTSD) to justify their generalization on all types of data. The results of a number of experiments show the powerful characteristic of GAN to mimic FC data to achieve high performance in disease prediction. When employing GAN for data augmentation, the diagnostic accuracy across ADHD-200, ABIDE-II, and ADNI datasets surpasses that of other machine learning models, including results achieved with BrainNetCNN. Specifically, in ADHD, the accuracy increased from 67.74% to 73.96% with GAN, in ABIDE-II from 70.36% to 77.40%, and in ADNI, reaching 52.84% and 88.56% for multiclass and binary classification, respectively. GCN also obtains decent results, with the best accuracy in ADHD datasets at 71.38% for multinomial and 75% for binary classification, respectively, and the second-best accuracy in the ABIDE-II dataset (72.28% and 75.16%, respectively). Both GAN and GCN achieved the highest accuracy for the PTSD dataset, reaching 97.76%. However, there are still some limitations that can be improved. Both methods have many opportunities for the prediction and diagnosis of diseases.

Keywords: resting-state functional magnetic resonance imaging; resting-state functional connectivity; deep learning; graph convolution network; generative adversarial network

1. Introduction

Functional magnetic resonance imaging (fMRI) is a neuroimaging tool that measures changes in cerebral blood flow to provide a visual representation of brain activity, allowing researchers to study brain function. The use of functional connectivity (FC) obtained from resting-state fMRI (rs-fMRI) enables imaging of temporal interaction between brain regions and has therefore been extensively employed in the classification of brain disorders and the identification of objective biomarkers associated with the underlying disorders. FC is a connectivity matrix representing functional communication between different brain regions, and the strength of connection between region i and region j is represented as the value of row i and column j in the matrix. The value is calculated using Pearson's correlation between the time series representing region i and j; however, other metrics of association between time series can also be used [1,2]. Considerable evidence from rs-fMRI studies has shown the alteration or disruption of FC in individuals with neuropsychiatric and neurodegenerative disorders [3–7]. Several recent works have applied convolutional neural networks (CNNs) that incorporate these altered brain FC patterns as relevant features for rapid and reliable classification of brain disorders. However, these models are constrained by two challenges. First, although traditional CNNs can extract local meaningful features from order and grid-like data (such as images), the spatial features learned in CNN may not be optimal for graph structure data (such as networks), which are invariant to node ordering and have irregular relationships between nodes. Second, patient fMRI data used for training is currently limited in its sample size because of a range of factors, such as the exorbitant expense of data acquisition, barriers to standardized data acquisition across different sites, and consequent open sharing of data. The relatively small sample size of patient data often leads to models being overfit. When relatively smaller samples of patient data are used with larger samples of healthy controls in the same model, it also causes the problem of class imbalance. To overcome those issues, graph convolutional networks (GCNs), an extended version of CNN, are proposed to deal with graph-structure data, while generative adversarial networks (GANs) can deal with data scarcity in neuroimaging due to their ability to generate additional data for training purposes.

The brain can be conceptualized as a network where the specialized regions are represented as nodes, and the pathways of communication or links between these regions are regarded as edges. By analyzing the patterns of FC, we can gain valuable insight into the temporal properties and dynamic interplay between the brain regions, revealing a more comprehensive view of the brain network. Therefore, graph theoretical analysis may be an ideal tool to investigate the organizational mechanisms underlying brain networks. Several complex graph theoretic algorithms have been applied to study the pathophysiology of various diseases [8–10]. The brain graph is a network representation of the intricate interactions between N distinct regions of the brain and therefore can be captured by the $N \times N$ matrix. The elements in the matrix capture the strength or degree of correlation between each pair of nodes in the network. In general, brain graphs can be categorized as functional connectivity or effective connectivity, where the former captures the strength of statistical associations or correlation between brain regions and the latter represents the directionality of information flow. Networks can also be grouped as unweighted or weighted, depending on whether the edges are assigned a binary or continuous value. In functional brain networks, the edges can be estimated by various statistical methods, such as Pearson's correlation coefficients, Spearman's correlation, or Kendall rank correlation coefficients.

Our research aims to design an end-to-end GCN model that can be applied to functional graphs (here, constructed from rs-fMRI data) for distinguishing healthy controls from those with brain disorders. Similar to CNN, the proposed GCN also includes a convolution operation that learns localized patterns from the networks and a pooling operation that can not only downsample the graph but also increase the receptive field, allowing the graph to learn global graph-level patterns. The model learns features from each node and its relationship with neighboring nodes to generate new feature maps via the spectral-based convolution method. The spectral convolution operation [11] can transform complex node representations to low-dimensional representations to tackle graph-structure data more easily.

To solve the problem of small sample sizes and class imbalance, we recently proposed a modified version of the existing GAN model to be able to generate realistic FC correlation matrices [12]. Generally, GAN consists of two main models that are trained in the adversarial optimization process: a generator G is designed to generate outputs that can mislead the discriminator into treating them as authentic. Unconditioned GAN or unsupervised GAN can discover the nature of data distribution and their latent structure to produce synthetic data. By utilizing those characteristics, conditional GAN and auxiliary classifier GAN have been used to allow GAN to perform classification tasks [13,14]. The classification performance can be improved by adding synthetic data to the classifier [15,16]. The proposed GAN model adapted these ideas to perform semi-supervised tasks. One of the issues involved in training GANs is the phenomenon called mode collapse, where the model only produces data belonging to a specific class. To prevent mode collapse, the proposed model utilizes supplementary information such as class category or phenotypic features to enhance the variety of the dataset. The generator of GAN will receive random noise combined with additional attributions, such as gender or age, to generate a synthetic FC matrix. The discriminator D will adopt the architecture of BrainNetCNN [17], where filters are customized to function well with the connectivity matrix. Our previous paper [12] also utilizes the inner product operation to embedding vectors to quantify the statistical link between two brain regions. Thus, we utilize the GAN we previously developed, which is an improvement over existing GAN-based methods for neuroimaging data.

We have reported on the designs of GCN and GAN needed to work on FC data and tested them on the ABIDE-I dataset [12,18]. However, there is a need to examine the generalizability of these models to other datasets derived from different patient populations. Therefore, here we will test the applicability of GCN and GAN based models on FC-based brain networks for discriminating healthy subjects from individuals diagnosed with ADHD (ADHD-200 [19] dataset), autism (ABIDE-II [20] dataset instead of ABIDE-I used in our previous work), PTSD (acquired in-house but publicly shared [21]), and Alzheimer's (ADNI [22]) datasets. We have reported the utility of traditional machine learning models on these datasets before, and here we used those results to compare them with those obtained from GCN and GAN. We also compared the proposed models with BrainNetCNN [17] to evaluate the efficacy of GCN for extracting structural features and GAN for data augmentation. The statistical tests were also conducted to determine which models achieved superior performance.

2. Related Work

Deep learning has attracted considerable attention for its potential to automatically detect and classify neurological diseases at an early stage. Specifically, convolutional neural networks (CNN) have been successful in using high-dimensional medical imaging data to predict diagnostic status. Kawahara et al. [17] proposed the BrainNetCNN in 2017, which is a class of CNNs that can be used to predict non-imaging variables (such as diagnostic status) using brain networks as input features. Another study [23] improves the detection of epileptic seizures using electroencephalogram (EEG) data by applying variable-frequency complex demodulation (VFCDM) and CNNs. Building on basic CNNs, researchers have improved the classification performance by applying transfer learning, a technique that utilizes the pre-trained models to enable models to leverage knowledge gained from one dataset to perform well on different datasets [24–26]. This method has the advantage of allowing the model to train on image data acquired at multiple sites.

GCN is able to model the complex interconnections between nodes in a graph, making it particularly well-suited for analyzing the irregular structure of brain network data. Therefore, it has been employed for diagnostic classification using functional brain networks. Prior works proposed different GCN-based architectures to distinguish between healthy and unhealthy subjects that can be categorized as individual-based graph architecture and population-based graph architecture. The main difference between these two methods is the representation of a node, wherein nodes in the individual-based graph represent brain regions while nodes in the population-based graph denote subjects. For instance, Ktena et al. [27] proposed Siamese GCN that analyzes brain functional connectivity networks by exploiting the similarities between two brain networks with the assumption that the classification task can be significantly improved with more accurate similarity metrics. Another study used varied templates to generate brain functional/structural connectivity networks for individuals subject and then trained a triplet graph convolutional network to learn the relationship at multiple scales [28]. The proposed model achieved high performance in the classification of mild cognitive impairment and attention-deficit/hyperactivity disorder with healthy controls. On the other hand, Parisot et al. [29] considered implementing spectral GCN on a population-based graph where each subject is considered a node. The model leverages the relevant features from both rs-fMRI and non-imaging data to discriminate between nodes of healthy control and nodes of individuals with autism disorder. Kim et al. [30] introduced the spatio-temporal attention graph isomorphism network (STAGIN) model, which addresses dynamic graphs by employing two spatial attention READOUT mechanisms (Graph-Attention READOUT (GARO) and Squeeze-Excitation READOUT (SERO)) to capture spatial features at each time point and employing a transformer encoder to learn temporal attended features. Zhao et al. [31] introduced a data augmentation approach combining a "sliding window" strategy with the self-attention mechanism GCN (SA-GCN) for autism classification, utilizing time series subsegments to construct correlation matrices, and introducing both low-order and high-order functional graphs to enable the model to exploit features from various perspectives. Another study [32] proposed a model that comprises two distinct GCNs, f-GCN and p-GCN, where f-GCN analyzes individual brain networks within subjects by utilizing stacked GCNs and eigenpooling for coarsened graph generation, employing max pooling for node representation aggregation, while p-GCN, a population-based model, treats each subject as a graph node and utilizes f-GCN output as a node feature.

Researchers have applied the generative aspect of GAN to various tasks in medical image analysis, including classification [33], segmentation [34], de-noising [35], image reconstruction [36], and image synthesis [37]. The use of GAN as a data augmentation method has been shown to outperform various traditional augmentation methods. GAN with feature matching has been proposed to discriminate psychiatric patients from controls [38]. The model learns to generate functional network connectivity that is constructed by independent component analysis, and the feature matching technique was used to stabilize the training process. The paper shows that GAN performs better than other traditional machine learning methods, such as support vector machine or nearest neighbors, with more than 6% higher accuracy. Barile et al. [39] utilized GAN with an autoencoder to generate brain connectivity for multiple sclerosis (MS) classification, ensuring that the model's training prevents collapse by producing synthetic data matching real data statistics. Cao et al. [40] introduced a multiloop algorithm aimed at improving the quality of generated data by enabling the assessment and ranking of sample distribution in each iteration, facilitating the selection of high-quality samples for training. While many studies have focused on generating realistic 3D brain images, only a few studies have developed GAN models to learn to mimic functional connectivity networks. This is not only computationally less demanding but also helpful in understanding brain network anomalies and underlying brain disorders.

3. Material and Methods

3.1. Data

Attention deficit hyperactivity disorder (ADHD) ADHD is a prevalent neurobehavioral disorder in childhood that is typically characterized by symptoms of inattention, hyperactivity, and impulsivity. Children with ADHD are classified into three separate categories: ADHD-I (inattention), ADHD-H (hyperactive/impulsive), and ADHD-C (combination of both symptoms). The ADHD-200 Global Competition was held in summer 2011 and challenged teams to provide the best performance for diagnosing individuals with ADHD from their resting-state fMRI scans [19]. There are 929 subjects in the dataset, which consists of 573 healthy controls, 207 individuals with ADHD-C, 13 individuals with ADHD-H, and 136 individuals with ADHD-I. Scanning for each participant took place at one of seven distinct sites, namely Peking University, Kennedy Krieger Institute, NeuroIMAGE Sample, New York University Child Study Center, Oregon Health & Science University, University of Pittsburgh, and Washington University. For more information regarding the acquisition parameters and site distribution, please refer the webpage http://fcon_1000.projects.nitrc.org/indi/adhd200/, accessed on 19 March 2024. Since there are fewer subjects diagnosed with subtype ADHD-H in comparison with the other classes, we combined subjects with ADHD-H into ADHD-C, which makes the problem into a 3-way diagnosis classification.

Autism Spectrum Disorder (ASD) ASD is a clinical term that encompasses a range of neurodevelopmental disorders marked by deficits in social behavior and communication skills, along with repeated behaviors and restricted interests. The classification of ASD individuals was carried out using an rs-fMRI image from the Austim Brain Imaging Data Exchange Data (ABIDE). ABIDE is a group of organizations that has collected and distributed datasets containing rs-fMRI, alongside additional clinical and demographic information from both individuals with ASD and those who are typically developing [20,41]. The initial ABIDE data, or ABIDE I, have been experimented with by the two models in the papers. In this work, the algorithms were extended to apply to ABIDE II, a new multi-site open data resource that was established to increase the sample size. Data for the imaging were obtained from 11 different facilities and involved a total of 623 participants. Of these, 356 were considered to be healthy conhorts, 214 had been diagnosed with autism patients, and 53 had been diagnosed with Asperger's syndrome (a mild symptom of autism).

Post-traumatic stress disorder (PTSD) & post-concussive syndrome (PCS) PTSD is a psychological disorder that develops in some individuals who have experienced shocking, horrifying, or life-threatening events. PCS is a condition in which symptoms or other functional difficulties persist for a period of time after sustaining a concussion or a mild traumatic brain injury. Such disorders often co-occur in individuals serving in the military. This study investigating PTSD/PCS involved 87 active-duty US solders recruited from Fort Moore, GA and Fort Novosel, AL, USA. Data collection was approved by the Institutional Review Board (IRB) at Auburn University and the U.S. Army Medical Research and Development Command IRB (HQ USAMRDC IRB). This sample included 28 combat controls, 17 individuals diagnosed with PTSD, and 42 individuals who had both PTSD/PCS. The imaging data for the study were obtained exclusively at the Auburn University Neuroimaging Center. Information about screening procedures to diagnose PTSD/PCS symptoms and acquisition parameters can be found in the paper [21]. Since each subject has 2 runs, we will treat each run as 1 subject, resulting in a dataset with 174 subjects in total.

Mild cognitive impairment (MCI) & Alzheimer's disease (AD) As people age, the risk of developing AD increases, and this condition is the primary cause of dementia in the US. When an individual experiences mild cognitive dysfunction in the memory domain, they may be diagnosed with MCI, and it is believed that people who are diagnosed with MCI are at an increased risk of developing AD later in life. Diagnosis and treatment of the condition remain challenging, with no definitive diagnostic test and cure available at present. Therefore, accurate detection of MCI can aid in preventing further deterioration and slowing the progression of AD. The imaging data was sampled from the Alzheimer's disease neuroimaging initiative (ADNI) database to perform a 4-way multiclass classification: healthy controls, early MCI (EMCI), late MCI (LMCI), and AD. In particular, 35 matched healthy controls, 34 subjects with EMCI, 34 subjects with LMCI, and 29 subjects with AD were collected from the database. The data acquisition process used for this study can be found in the paper [22].

3.2. Data Preprocessing

FC was derived with the assistance of Data Processing Assistant for Resting-state MRI (DPARSF, version V5.3_210101) and functional connectivity toolboxes (CONN) softwares, version v.22.a (https://web.conn-toolbox.org/, accessed on 19 March 2024). Firstly, to minimize subject motion artifacts during the scanning process, motion correction techniques were performed to align each image to a standard reference point in time. Then, slice time correction was performed, and after that, the subject's data underwent a nonlinear transformation to align it with a common reference MNI152 (Montreal Neurological Institute) space, which facilitates group-level analysis. The preprocessing pipeline also includes regressing out nuisance variables, such as six head motion parameters, the mean white matter, and the cerebrospinal fluid (CSF) signal, in order to minimize confounding effects. Then, the estimation of the underlying neural time series was carried out using the blind deconvolution method proposed by Wu et al. [42]. The deconvolved data was then achieved by the Wiener filter. We applied a temporal band-pass filter with a bandwidth of 0.01–0.1 Hz to the data. Mean time series was extracted from defined 200 regions of interest provided by Craddock (known as the CC200 template) [43]. Pearson's correlations between the mean time series of two brain regions were established, resulting in the FC for each subject with shape 200 × 200. However, due to incomplete brain coverage in the ADHD data, only 190 out of 200 regions were captured using the Craddock atlas. Similar to the ADHD dataset, the PTSD dataset suffered from incomplete data coverage and was only able to cover 125 out of 200 regions.

3.3. Graph Convolutional Network

The GCN architecture is depicted in Figure 1. For each subject, we define an undirected graph $G \equiv \{V, E\}$ as a functional brain network, where $V = \{v_1, \ldots v_i\}$ is a set of N nodes (N may vary depending on the number of regions of interests) and $E = \{e_{ij}\}$ represents a collection of connectivity edges from node v_i to node v_j. The graph was represented by an adjacency matrix $\mathbf{A} \in \mathbb{R}^{N \times N}$, where each element $a_{ij} = 1$ if the value of the corresponding position of the mean matrix $\bar{A}$ is greater than the cutoff threshold τ and $a_{ij} = 0$ otherwise. The mean matrix $\bar{A}$ was determined by the mean of all the functional connectivity matrices in the training dataset, and the threshold τ was decided by the percentage of positive connections that we need to keep. One of the reasons that support this idea is that by taking the mean, we can sparsify the data to different degrees by varying the threshold. Furthermore, by keeping only relevant connections between regions, we can detect abnormal changes in meaningful patterns or connections that can effectively separate healthy subjects and subjects with brain disorders [3–7].

In this work, the graph convolutional layer was implemented from the spectral perspective. In the process of spectral graph convolution, the graph signals are transformed from node domain to frequency domain using the graph Fourier transform. Then, to reduce the computational complexity and enable the graph to learn locally, the K-polynomial filters were used in ChebNet; this approach can be simplified by taking only the first order approximation [11]. Hence at layer l, the output representation node was computed as:

$$\mathbf{H}^{(1)} = \sigma(\tilde{\mathbf{D}}^{-\frac{1}{2}}\tilde{\mathbf{A}}\tilde{\mathbf{D}}^{-\frac{1}{2}}\mathbf{H}^{(l-1)}\mathbf{W}^{(l)}) \tag{1}$$

where $\tilde{\mathbf{A}} = \mathbf{I} + \mathbf{A}$ is equivalent to adding self-loops to the adjacency matrix and $\tilde{\mathbf{D}}$ is the diagonal degree matrix of $\tilde{\mathbf{A}}$, i.e., $\tilde{\mathbf{D}}_{i,i} = \sum_j \tilde{\mathbf{A}}_{ij}$. σ is activation function (Rectified Linear Unit (ReLU) or linear activation function). In this work, ReLU activation was chosen. Furthermore, $\mathbf{H}^{(l-1)} \in \mathbb{R}^{N\times d}$ represents d attributes of the N nodes, and $\mathbf{W} \in \mathbb{R}^{d\times m}$ refers to a learnable matrix used at layer l that transforms the input node representation $\mathbf{H}^{(l-1)}$ from d to m feature dimensions. The initial node representations $\mathbf{H}^{(0)}$ are just the original input features or functional connectivity of each subject: $\mathbf{H}^{(0)} = \mathbf{X}$. As evident, we employed an individual-based graph architecture. Equation (1) aggregates node representations in their direct neighborhood, helping to gain more information after each iteration for the purpose of learning the graph.

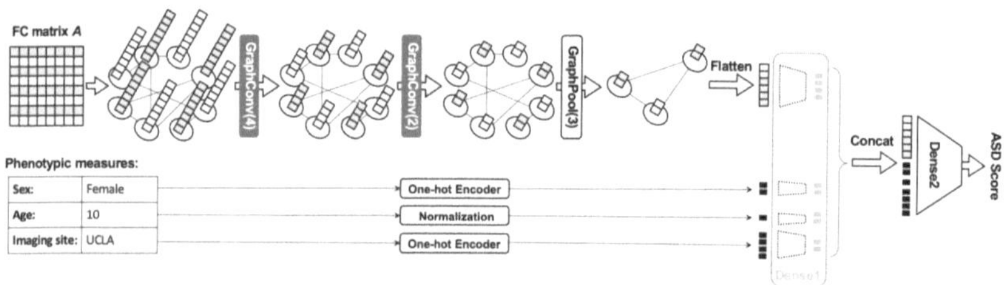

Figure 1. Illustration of the GCN architecture proposed in our previous work [18] that we have applied here. In the figure, the model consists of two convolutional layers that transforms the number of node features from 8 to 2 and one pooling layer that pools the number of nodes from 8 to 3. The output of GCN was also concatenated with subject's attribute data (gender, age, imaging site) and then the combined input was passed to the classifier. The results reported in this paper were generated by this GCN architecture with a slight changes in parameters in each layer (as described in methods).

To apply GCN to the graph classification task, a graph-level representation is needed. Similar to conventional CNNs where pooling method is applied to reduce the spatial resolution, many methods of pooling for GCNs have been proposed with the aim of decreasing the number of nodes to obtain coarser graphs while preserving important graph properties. One of the graph pooling approaches is self-attention graph pooling (SAGPool), which is a technique that utilizes a graph neural network to produce a score for each node based on its features, and subsequently selects the K nodes with the highest score [44]. Specially, the self-attention scores $\mathbf{z}$ for each node is calculated as:

$$\mathbf{z} = \tanh(\tilde{\mathbf{D}}^{-\frac{1}{2}}\tilde{\mathbf{A}}\tilde{\mathbf{D}}^{-\frac{1}{2}}\mathbf{H}^{(l-1)}\mathbf{\Theta}^{(l)}) \tag{2}$$

where $\tilde{\mathbf{A}} = \mathbf{A}^{(l-1)} + \mathbf{I}$, which depends on the adjacency matrix of the previous layer, and $\mathbf{\Theta} \in \mathbb{R}^{d\times 1}$ is the weight of the pooling layer. Because graph pooling changes the graph or particularly the adjacency matrix $\mathbf{A}$, the shape of adjacency matrix $\mathbf{A}$ and the output node representation after pooling will change based on the top-k nodes we want to keep. To update those variables, first the top-k nodes were obtained as the following steps:

$$\text{idx} = \text{top-rank}(\mathbf{z}, k) \tag{3}$$

$$\mathbf{z}_{mask} = \mathbf{z}(\text{idx}) \tag{4}$$

The outputs of graph pooling were then determined as:

$$\mathbf{H}^{(l)} = \mathbf{H}^{(l-1)}(\text{idx}, :) \odot \mathbf{z}_{mask} \tag{5}$$

$$\mathbf{A}^{(l)} = \mathbf{A}^{(l-1)}(\text{idx}, \text{idx}) \tag{6}$$

where $\mathbf{H}^{(l-1)}(\text{idx}, :)$ contains node-specific features that are indexed, $\odot$ performs element-wise multiplication, and $\mathbf{A}^{(l-1)}(\text{idx}, \text{idx})$ is an adjacency matrix that is indexed by both rows and columns.

Non-imaging measures that contribute variance to the imaging data, such as gender, age, and imaging site, can also combine with the extracted features from GNN to boost the prediction performance. To guarantee that all feature values are bounded in the interval [0, 1], gender and imaging site features were first encoded to one-hot vectors, while the age feature was normalized by dividing by 100. All non-imaging features were also transformed to the vector of length 2 by the dense layer, and 1 dense layer was also used to transform the output of the GNN model to the vector of length 15. Those vectors were then concatenated and used as input for the classifier that consists of one dense layer with a softmax activation function to compute the likelihood of each subject's network belonging to a particular class label.

3.4. Generative Adversarial Network

Generative adversarial network (GAN) comprises two different functional models, namely the discriminator (D) and the generator (G). The two models can be trained simultaneously, in which the generator takes random variable z from a prior distribution (usually Gaussian noise or uniform distribution) to generate new images, while the discriminator focuses on distinguishing whether the image is authentic or not. For supervised learning, the output of the discriminator will also include the probabilities of the class label in addition to its validity output. GAN is able to generate synthetic data that are of high quality and closely resemble real data by using an iterative adversarial approach. The specific designs of the discriminator and the generator are demonstrated in the following (and visually illustrated in Figure 2):

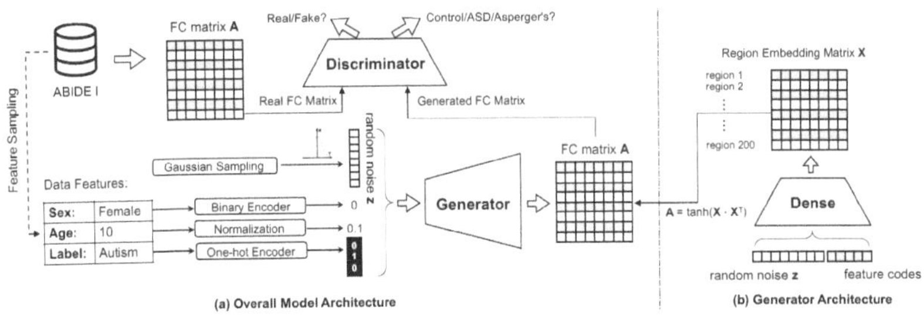

Figure 2. Illustration of the GAN model proposed by using previously [12], which we have used in this work. The generator produces a synthetic functional connectivity matrix via the combined input of random noise and feature codes (gender, age, and label). The discriminator was trained on both real FC data and synthesized FC data generated from the generator.

Generator architecture: The generator collects the random noise vector **z** drawn from a uniform distribution to produce synthetic functional connectivity data. One of the issues of the generator is mode collapse, which occurs when there is only a limited set of samples that the generator can generate. To mitigate this problem, we use ideas from conditional GAN (CGAN) [13] and InfoGAN [45], which integrate more attribute data into the latent input, including category labels and phenotypic measures (such as age, gender, etc).

Typically, the generator will directly output the image from the latent input, which will violate the nature of functional connectivity, where each entry in the matrix corresponds to the correlation coefficients between the average time series of pairs of brain regions i and j. By transforming the latent vector **z** to a **X** matrix where $\mathbf{X} \in \mathbb{R}^{N\times d}$, we will have each row in **X** representing the embedding vector of one brain region (N is the number of ROIs and d is the dimension of the embedded region). Then the generated output **A** is determined by taking the inner product of **X** with tanh activation function to ensure each value in **A** will have a range from -1 and 1:

$$\mathbf{A} = \tanh(\mathbf{X}\mathbf{X}^T) \tag{7}$$

Discriminator architecture: The discriminator is provided with both types of inputs—the original image or a synthesized one—and decides whether the input is real or not. To boost the performance of the discriminator, phenotypic features for each subject were also included as input besides the FC matrix. Similar to the design of deep convolutional GAN (DCGAN) [45], which uses multiple convolution layers to extract features, we employed BrainNetCNN, which was proposed as specifically designed convolutional filters for modeling brain networks. The BrainNetCNN consists of three special convolution layers: the edge-to-edge layer (ECE), the edge-to-node layer (ECN), and the node-to-graph layer (NCG). The ECE layer used cross-shaped filters to calculate the weighted sum of all the neighboring edges that results in a new edge value. On the other hand, regarding edge-to-node layer, given one node, we do the convolution for all the edges that connect to that node. If the number of ROIs is N, then the output of the ECE layer will have the shape of $N \times N$, while the shape of the output of the ECN layer is $N \times 1$. Finally, the NCG layer acts as a fully connected layer, which summarizes all the nodes into a single graph.

Then the dense layers were used to convert the output of the NCG layer and phenotypic features to a new feature space. These two vectors were then concatenated and fed to the dense layer with two heads, one with sigmoid activation for validity classification and another with softmax activation for label classification.

4. Experimental Setting

The architectures and hyper-parameters of both GAN and GCN were adopted from our previous papers [12,18] based on their highest performances on the ABIDE-I dataset.

In particular, the GCN model that was tested on the datasets has the following structure: 2 convolution layers, followed by 1 pooling layer. In particular, the first and second convolution layers transformed feature vectors to have sizes of 25 and 10, respectively, then the pooling layer was applied to downsample the graph from N nodes to 10 nodes. The shallow GCN was selected because the model performance tends to decrease with an increase in the number of layers. This phenomenon is known as over-smoothing, where through many messages passing steps, all node representations may become similar to each other, making it infeasible to identify discriminant features. The output of the pooling layer is then flattened and integrated with normalized age, one-hot coding of gender, and the imaging site (only available for ADHD and ABIDE-II datasets). One classifier layer was used to directly read out the combined inputs to produce the probability for each class by using the softmax activation function.

Regarding GAN, the discriminator has three type of layers similar to BrainNetCNN, which include an ECE layer with 16 feature maps, followed by an ECN layer with 64 filters, and an NCG layer with 128 filters to extract all the nodes' features. The BatchNormalization, the LeakyReLU activation function, and the Dropout function with a dropout rate of 0.5

were used consecutively after each layer. The dense layer with 64 hidden units continues to extract features from the flattened output of the NCG layer. To combine with phenotypic features, the age and gender of one individual are first concatenated to a vector of length 2, and this vector is then transformed into a vector of length 16 by a dense layer. The fully-connected output is then merged with this feature vector. The combined input is passed through one more dense layer with 32 perceptrons before being fed to the classification layer that predicts the class label for the subject as well as the validity of the FC (real or fake). As for the generator part, a random vector of length 50 (including gender, age, and label) is fed into the embedding layer, which has the function to turn the input into an $N \times d$ matrix, where N corresponds to the number of regions and d represents the embedded dimension. N are equal to 190, 200, 125, and 200 for the ADHD, ABIDE-II, PTSD, and ADNI datasets, respectively, while d is selected to be 10. Since not all subjects in the ADHD and PTSD datasets had usable data from all 200 ROIs (either because of data quality or a lack of whole-brain coverage), the values of N for these datasets are not equal to 200. Nonetheless, the left-out ROIs corresponded to the cerebellum, and subcortex and cortical ROIs were present in all datasets. For every region, its feature representation is stored in a single row of the matrix. The inner product is then taken to output the functional connectivity matrix.

A test dataset consisting of 10% of the data was created for each dataset to assess the model's performance. After leaving out 10% of the data for testing, a 5-fold cross-validation approach was used to split the remaining data into training and validation sets. Therefore, each model was trained five times, and the cross-validation performance of each model is the average of these repeated runs. The model that had the best performance on the validation set was chosen for assessment on the test set. The test accuracy is, of course, obtained by using the test data on the trained model once. For the GAN model, validity accuracy is also considered to select the model besides its performance on the validation set (note that in GANs, the discriminator has two outputs: one for the probability of validity to test the authenticity of the FC (real or fake) and one for classification (HC or patients)). We applied the Adam algorithm as an optimization method with a learning rate of 0.01 for GCN and a learning rate of 0.0001 and $\beta_1 = 0.5$ for GAN.

Other models: For comparison purposes, 18 traditional machine learning models used by Lanka et al. [21] were also trained on all the datasets by the default hyper-parameters from Scikit-learn and Matlab tools provided in the paper. These models include probabilistic or Bayesian methods. In the probabilistic framework, the models were assumed with some prior belief in the data distribution, and then the model parameters were selected to maximize the probability of the observed data, given particular parameter settings. The representatives of the probabilistic models were Gaussian Naïve Bayes (GNB), linear discriminant analysis (LDA), quadratic discriminant analysis (QDA), sparse logistic regression (SLR), and ridge logistic regression (RLR). The kernel-based models utilize kernel functions to transfer the input into a different space, and then the models can be trained on the new feature space, including support vector machines with linear functions (LinearSVM), radial basis functions (RBF-SVM), and relevance vector machines (RVM). Some traditional neural networks are also involved, namely the multilayer perceptron neural net (MLP-Net), the fully-connected neural net (FC-Net), the extreme learning machine (ELM), and the linear vector quantization net (LVQNET). Also, k-nearest neighbors (kNN) is an instance-based learning model that assigns the unknown data to the appropriate categories based on the distances between the unknown data and the data points that have been labeled. Finally, ensemble learning is the technique that allows multiple classifiers to solve a problem with the belief that multiple classifiers can provide a better result than a single classifier. Using a decision tree as a base classifier, several methods were used to train ensemble classifiers, namely bagged trees, boosted stumps, random forest, and rotation forest. Further details regarding these models can be found in Lanka et al. [21]. Additionally, BrainNetCNN, which is the top-performing method for connectome classification, was also trained with the same 5-fold CV, and the hyper-parameters and training process are similar to the settings of the discriminator in GAN.

To evaluate the models, using only accuracy may not be appropriate for imbalanced classification scenarios. Therefore, other metrics such as precision score, recall score/sensitivity, specificity, F1 score, and area under the curve (AUC) are also reported. Those metrics often apply to binary classification problem; therefore, to deal with multiclass classification, the one-vs-rest (OvR) algorithm (with a macro-averaging strategy) was used.

5. Results

5.1. Cutoff Threshold

The binary adjacency matrix representing the graph for each dataset was built by thresholding the values of the mean matrix derived from the training data. In particular, if the correlation coefficient between region i and region j is greater than cutoff threshold τ, the value of the adjacency matrix at (i, j) is equal to 1 and 0 otherwise. In order to choose the appropriate threshold, we plotted the percentages of preserved edges against the cutoff threshold and chose the elbow of the curve as the cutoff, as in previous work [46,47]. The mean matrix was derived from the average of all the training data across the 5-fold CV. Figure 3a–d shows the appropriate cutoff thresholds that can preserve meaningful edges for the ADHD, ABIDE-II, PTSD, and ADNI datasets, respectively. The cutoff threshold for ADHD, ABIDE-II, and ADNI datasets is 0.15, which maintains 13.17%, 20.60% and 14,80% of the total edges in each dataset, respectively, while the threshold for the PTSD dataset is 0.2, which keeps 16.19% of edges.

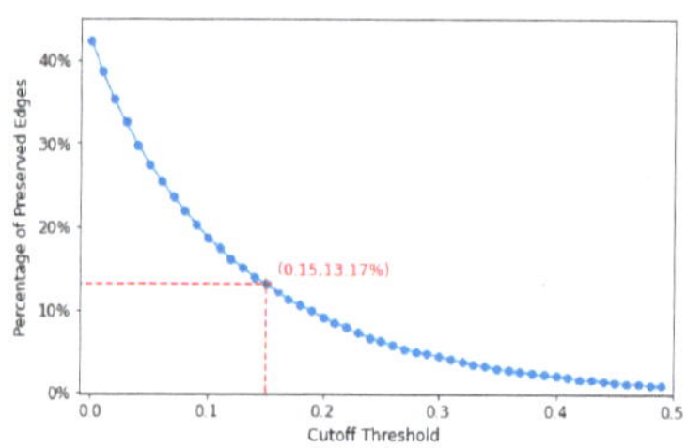

(**a**) ADHD dataset

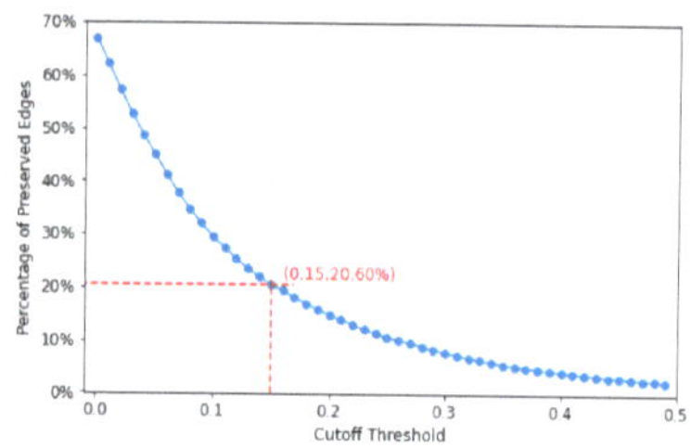

(**b**) ABIDE-II dataset

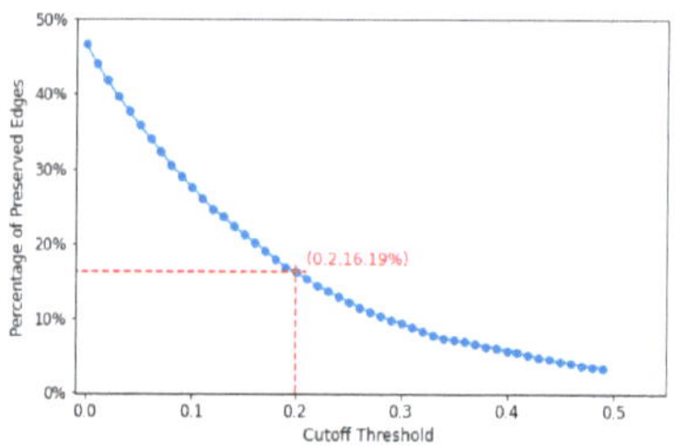

(**c**) PTSD dataset

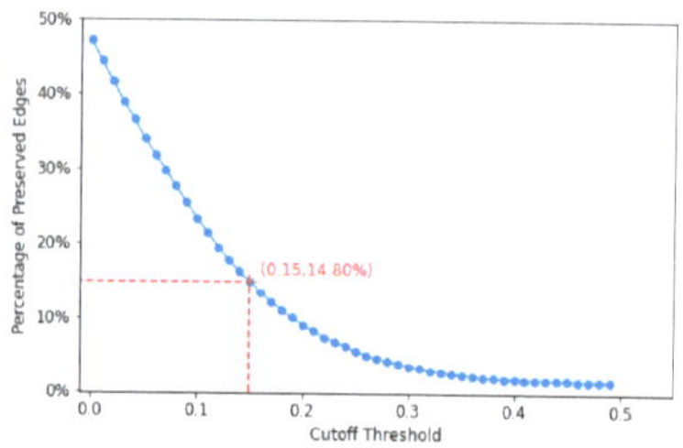

(**d**) ADNI dataset

Figure 3. Percentages of edges preserved when the cutoff threshold is varied for each dataset.

5.2. Model Comparison

The outcomes of all the models for multinomical classification are presented in Table 1 (a), Table 2 (a), Table 3 (a), and Table 4 (a) for the ADHD, ABIDE-II, PTSD, and ADNI datasets, respectively, while Table 1 (b), Table 2 (b), Table 3 (b), and Table 4 (b) demonstrate the results of those respective datasets in binary classification scenario. The value highlighted with red color represents the top performing result across all the models, while the blue highlight indicates the second highest result. In Figure 4, the models have been sorted from worst to best performance. We can observe that some models may perform very well for some metrics or datasets, but the deep learning models (including GCN and GAN) generally perform well across all metrics and datasets.

Table 1. Performance comparison of models on ADHD dataset for multinomial (a) and binary (b) classification (Red color indicates best performance, while blue color denotes second best performance).

(a)

Model	Accuracy	Precision	Recall	Specificity	F1 Score	AUC
GNB	54.19%	33.72%	47.86%	56.49%	39.56%	68.48%
LDS	50.32%	19.55%	13.51%	72.28%	15.47%	55.81%
QDA	44.52%	17.47%	18.31%	63.51%	13.15%	49.89%
SLR	59.35%	24.93%	22.08%	80.00%	23.18%	75.42%
RLR	62.15%	35.18%	37.99%	73.68%	36.34%	75.31%
Linear SVM	41.72%	33.67%	51.49%	31.93%	40.58%	68.13%
RBF_SVM	61.94%	30.00%	1.36%	100.00%	4.35%	82.28%
RVM	63.44%	42.24%	22.86%	86.67%	29.31%	–
MLP-Net	52.47%	32.62%	50.19%	50.88%	39.34%	71.49%
FC-Net	45.38%	22.96%	33.34%	49.47%	26.09%	61.38%
ELM	57.63%	34.43%	32.21%	71.58%	33.24%	–
KNN	33.76%	13.41%	50.00%	16.49%	21.16%	71.25%
Bagged Trees	57.42%	14.52%	3.44%	91.23%	6.91%	57.46%
Boosted Trees	57.42%	20.41%	15.45%	81.75%	17.49%	57.81%
Boosted Stumps	57.63%	28.97%	14.74%	83.86%	19.36%	63.52%
Random Forest	61.29%	0.00%	0.00%	100.00%	–	59.80%
Rotation Forest	61.29%	22.67%	2.73%	97.89%	7.82%	–
BrainNetCNN	67.74%	53.32%	42.60%	82.44%	46.08%	74.96%
GAN	68.16%	41.16%	34.82%	85.96%	36.82%	74.46%
GCN	71.38%	59.52%	45.00%	84.58%	49.86%	75.94%

(b)

Model	Accuracy	Precision	Recall	Specificity	F1 Score	AUC
GNB	63.23%	51.78%	73.89%	56.49%	60.88%	69.38%
LDS	54.84%	38.17%	27.22%	72.28%	31.76%	54.11%
QDA	52.47%	37.79%	35.00%	63.51%	36.16%	49.25%
SLR	62.80%	52.97%	35.56%	80.00%	42.53%	73.68%
RLR	66.02%	56.48%	53.89%	73.68%	55.10%	73.95%
Linear SVM	50.11%	42.36%	78.89%	31.93%	55.09%	63.65%
RBF_SVM	61.94%	60.00%	1.67%	100%	5.41%	82.89%
RVM	64.73%	58.94%	30.00%	86.67%	39.57%	–
MLP-Net	61.94%	50.56%	79.44%	50.88%	61.57%	69.92%
FC-Net	57.20%	46.18%	69.44%	49.47%	54.91%	60.65%
ELM	63.01%	52.40%	49.44%	71.58%	50.82%	–
KNN	47.31%	42.10%	96.11%	16.49%	58.55%	66.45%
Bagged Trees	60.22%	44.09%	11.11%	91.23%	17.45%	57.53%
Boosted Trees	60.00%	46.42%	25.56%	81.75%	32.85%	57.58%

Table 1. *Cont.*

Model	Accuracy	Precision	Recall	Specificity	F1 Score	AUC
Boosted Stumps	60.00%	44.84%	22.22%	83.86%	29.48%	58.62%
Random Forest	61.29%	0%	0%	100%	_	58.04%
Rotation Forest	61.72%	56.00%	4.44%	97.89%	10.05%	_
BrainNetCNN	71.62%	66.56%	54.44%	82.44%	58.50%	74.74%
GAN	73.96%	72.80%	55.02%	85.96%	61.22%	76.34%
GCN	75.50%	71.66%	61.12%	84.58%	65.48%	78.80%

Table 2. Performance comparison of models on ABIDE-II dataset for multinomial (a) and binary (b) classification (Red color indicates best performance, while blue color denotes second best performance).

(a)

Model	Accuracy	Precision	Recall	Specificity	F1 Score	AUC
GNB	66.13%	47.83%	41.90%	73.89%	44.54%	68.13%
LDS	64.52%	46.19%	31.33%	81.67%	37.25%	65.89%
QDA	46.45%	21.91%	27.05%	55.56%	24.18%	53.09%
SLR	71.29%	43.23%	33.90%	85.00%	37.14%	77.96%
RLR	70.97%	49.86%	40.29%	80.56%	43.68%	77.96%
Linear SVM	71.29%	47.21%	40.29%	81.11%	43.07%	75.13%
RBF_SVM	63.23%	38.12%	10.48%	96.67%	16.32%	72.00%
RVM	69.68%	72.68%	33.24%	88.33%	45.16%	_
MLP-Net	65.16%	34.72%	39.81%	71.11%	36.89%	74.56%
FC-Net	56.13%	17.78%	24.76%	67.78%	24.50%	63.67%
ELM	58.71%	27.45%	33.05%	66.11%	29.98%	_
KNN	59.68%	37.00%	4.76%	97.22%	8.13%	58.99%
Bagged Trees	55.81%	18.52%	11.90%	82.22%	14.27%	54.14%
Boosted Trees	57.42%	22.17%	14.76%	81.67%	17.49%	59.26%
Boosted Stumps	60.03%	27.18%	19.05%	81.67%	22.32%	59.44%
Random Forest	60.32%	34.29%	6.19%	96.67%	10.23%	61.84%
Rotation Forest	59.03%	22.90%	12.38%	87.22%	15.89%	_
BrainNetCNN	70.36%	39.28%	28.20%	90.02%	33.12%	70.5%
GAN	73.56%	34.7%	32.88%	88.34%	33.60%	68.26%
GCN	72.28%	38.78%	32.02%	88.90%	34.96%	72.68%

(b)

Model	Accuracy	Precision	Recall	Specificity	F1 Score	AUC
GNB	69.35%	63.65%	63.08%	73.89%	63.33%	72.29%
LDS	68.06%	65.99%	49.23%	81.67%	56.29%	71.60%
QDA	56.45%	48.20%	57.69%	55.56%	52.48%	56.62%
SLR	73.55%	73.62%	57.69%	85.00%	64.65%	81.11%
RLR	74.52%	71.05%	66.15%	80.56%	68.50%	80.34%

Table 2. *Cont.*

Model	Accuracy	Precision	Recall	Specificity	F1 Score	AUC
Linear SVM	74.52%	71.55%	65.38%	81.11%	68.19%	81.54%
RBF_SVM	63.55%	79.10%	17.69%	96.67%	28.74%	80.21%
RVM	71.94%	75.48%	49.23%	88.33%	59.41%	_
MLP-Net	70.32%	63.98%	69.23%	71.11%	66.04%	77.28%
FC-Net	60.00%	53.84%	49.23%	67.78%	44.79%	65.19%
ELM	66.13%	58.51%	66.15%	66.11%	62.04%	_
KNN	59.68%	74.00%	7.69%	97.22%	13.51%	58.53%
Bagged Trees	58.71%	51.06%	26.15%	82.22%	34.09%	57.79%
Boosted Trees	59.03%	51.78%	27.69%	81.67%	35.62%	59.17%
Boosted Stumps	61.29%	57.26%	33.08%	81.67%	41.84%	53.95%
Random Forest	61.29%	79.43%	12.31%	96.67%	20.88%	65.38%
Rotation Forest	60.97%	56.69%	24.61%	87.22%	33.95%	_
BrainNetCNN	73.56%	78.64%	50.58%	90.02%	61.54%	75.84%
GAN	77.40%	79.62%	62.30%	88.34%	69.62%	75.90%
GCN	75.16%	78.44%	56.12%	88.90%	65.06%	74.12%

Table 3. Performance comparison of models on PTSD dataset for multinomial (a) and binary (b) classification (Red color indicates best performance, while blue color denotes second best performance).

(a)

Model	Accuracy	Precision	Recall	Specificity	F1 Score	AUC
GNB	82.22%	81.89%	78.75%	80%	80.29%	92.75%
LDS	50.00%	49.27%	57.50%	43.33%	52.96%	68.35%
QDA	47.78%	44.44%	40.00%	53.33%	41.67%	58.79%
SLR	88.89%	90.83%	81.25%	93.33%	85.57%	98.81%
RLR	95.56%	94.53%	93.33%	93.33%	95.29%	99.53%
Linear SVM	96.64%	97.78%	96.25%	96.67%	96.95%	99.53%
RBF_SVM	68.89%	59.45%	57.50%	63.33%	56.66%	97.94%
RVM	68.89%	75.00%	67.50%	56.67%	70.31%	_
MLP-Net	92.22%	91.75%	96.25%	86.67%	93.78%	98.56%
FC-Net	68.89%	52.61%	48.75%	86.67%	48.10%	94.01%
ELM	36.67%	44.09%	45.00%	23.33%	43.97%	_
KNN	48.89%	23.52%	48.75%	16.67%	31.71%	73.63%
Bagged Trees	83.33%	90.02%	77.50%	86.67%	83.08%	91.72%
Boosted Trees	70.00%	80.46%	68.75%	56.67%	74.00%	85.88%
Boosted Stumps	60.00%	66.10%	65.00%	30.00%	64.34%	76.87%
Random Forest	81.11%	85.76%	77.5%	73.33%	81.12%	97.51%
Rotation Forest	83.33%	87.71%	78.75%	80.00%	82.49%	_
BrainNetCNN	97.76%	98.88%	97.50%	96.67%	98.08%	98.44%
GAN	96.64%	95.76%	98.76%	93.33%	97.20%	98.98%
GCN	95.56%	95.76%	95%	93.33%	95.32%	96.96%

Table 3. *Cont.*

(b)						
Model	**Accuracy**	**Precision**	**Recall**	**Specificity**	**F1 Score**	**AUC**
GNB	90.00%	90.51%	95.00%	80.00%	92.67%	94.72%
LDS	68.89%	74.49%	81.67%	43.33%	77.81%	64.72%
QDA	64.44%	74.62%	70.00%	53.33%	71.94%	61.67%
SLR	96.67%	96.79%	98.33%	93.33%	97.53%	98.61%
RLR	97.76%	96.92%	100.00%	93.33%	98.40%	99.44%
Linear SVM	97.76%	98.46%	98.33%	96.67%	98.33%	99.44%
RBF_SVM	87.78%	84.57%	100.00%	63.33%	91.62%	98.33%
RVM	80.00%	80.95%	91.67%	56.67%	85.90%	–
MLP-Net	94.44%	94.33%	98.33%	86.67%	96.11%	98.33%
FC-Net	75.56%	94.18%	70.00%	86.67%	76.09%	93.06%
ELM	54.44%	64.94%	70.00%	23.33%	66.78%	–
KNN	70.00%	69.90%	96.67%	16.67%	81.06%	83.06%
Bagged Trees	90.00%	93.85%	91.67%	86.67%	92.51%	92.78%
Boosted Trees	80.00%	81.42%	91.67%	56.67%	85.92%	86.11%
Boosted Stumps	66.67%	68.75%	91.67%	16.67%	78.57%	75.00%
Random Forest	90.00%	88.22%	98.33%	73.33%	92.92%	99.44%
Rotation Forest	90.00%	90.58%	95.00%	80.00%	92.59%	–
BrainNetCNN	97.76%	98.46%	98.33%	96.67%	98.34%	98.60%
GAN	97.76%	96.92%	100.00%	93.33%	98.40%	99.16%
GCN	97.76%	96.92%	100.00%	93.33%	98.40%	96.38%

Table 4. Performance comparison of models on ADNI dataset for multinomial (a) and binary (b) classification (Red color indicates best performance, while blue color denotes second best performance).

(a)						
Model	**Accuracy**	**Precision**	**Recall**	**Specificity**	**F1 Score**	**AUC**
GNB	37.14%	38.00%	27.78%	55.00%	31.82%	55.85%
LDS	30.00%	40.78%	32.78%	25.00%	36.15%	57.00%
QDA	22.86%	25.52%	28.89%	10.00%	26.49%	49.22%
SLR	32.86%	23.22%	21.67%	65.00%	21.88%	58.34%
RLR	32.86%	28.78%	28.89%	45.00%	27.86%	62.16%
Linear SVM	35.71%	29.89%	29.44%	50.00%	29.45%	57.95%
RBF_SVM	30.00%	24.02%	17.78%	55.00%	19.26%	63.80%
RVM	37.14%	40.33%	32.78%	50.00%	35.95%	–
MLP-Net	37.14%	32.78%	36.67%	35.00%	34.49%	59.52%
FC-Net	35.71%	23.94%	31.11%	50.00%	26.84%	66.11%
ELM	17.14%	21.44%	21.67%	5.00%	20.06%	–
KNN	24.29%	23.00%	30.56%	5.00%	26.11%	50.59%
Bagged Trees	24.29%	10.89%	13.33%	50.00%	19.95%	54.45%
Boosted Trees	25.71%	29.75%	26.67%	25.00%	34.00%	52.33%

Table 4. *Cont.*

Model	Accuracy	Precision	Recall	Specificity	F1 Score	AUC
Boosted Stumps	30.00%	36.83%	39.44%	10.00%	36.33%	52.33%
Random Forest	37.14%	41.22%	29.44%	55.00%	34.15%	54.57%
Rotation Forest	30.00%	42.00%	25.00%	40.00%	31.16%	–
BrainNetCNN	38.02%	21.50%	23.34%	50.00%	21.66%	58.86%
GAN	52.84%	42.42%	41.66%	80.00%	41.20%	66.42%
GCN	44.28%	37.56%	29.46%	55.00%	31.82%	62.46%

(b)

Model	Accuracy	Precision	Recall	Specificity	F1 Score	AUC
GNB	65.71%	79.72%	70.00%	55.00%	74.50%	59.00%
LDS	58.57%	70.73%	72.00%	25.00%	71.33%	74.50%
QDA	54.29%	66.57%	72.00%	10.00%	68.99%	41.00%
SLR	74.29%	84.67%	78.00%	65.00%	81.16%	85.00%
RLR	75.71%	80.51%	88.00%	45.00%	83.86%	87.00%
Linear SVM	71.43%	80.41%	80.00%	50.00%	79.94%	81.00%
RBF_SVM	65.71%	79.72%	70.00%	55.00%	74.50%	70.50%
RVM	70.00%	79.78%	78.00%	50.00%	78.84%	–
MLP-Net	78.57%	79.34%	96.00%	35.00%	86.60%	88.00%
FC-Net	74.29%	81.14%	84.00%	50.00%	82.22%	80.00%
ELM	50.00%	63.84%	68.00%	5.00%	65.58%	–
KNN	55.71%	66.73%	76.00%	5.00%	70.97%	59.50%
Bagged Trees	60.00%	77.17%	64.00%	50.00%	69.60%	70.00%
Boosted Trees	65.71%	73.41%	82.00%	25.00%	76.20%	69.00%
Boosted Stumps	65.71%	71.00%	88.00%	10.00%	78.36%	53.50%
Random Forest	65.71%	79.43%	70.00%	55.00%	73.88%	70.75%
Rotation Forest	60.00%	74.11%	68.00%	40.00%	70.81%	–
BrainNetCNN	82.86%	82.88%	96.00%	50.00%	88.80%	82.00%
GAN	88.56%	92.66%	92.00%	80.00%	91.96%	84.00%
GCN	80.00%	83.47%	90.00%	55.00%	86.34%	84.18%

ADHD For multinominal classification, GCN achieves the highest values for the accuracy score, precision score, and f1 score and the second highest for AUC. GAN also achieves the second highest accuracy score with 68.16%, which is only 3% less than the accuracy of GCN. The results remain the same in the binary classification scenario, with the only exception in the precision score where the GAN model takes the first place while GCN has the second place. Although the RBF-SVM model has the highest performance for specificity and AUC scores, its recall score is rather low with only 1.67%, which fails to predict the actual patients with disease. GAN and GCN therefore achieve better performance overall among all the models.

ABIDE-II GAN and GCN outperform the other models in accuracy for both multinomial classification (73.56% and 72.28%) and binary classification (77.40% and 75.16%). GAN also shows the highest results in precision score and f1 score. kNN, RBF-SVM, and random rorest classifiers obtained the highest and second highest specificity; however, their recall scores are rather low. On the other hand, the specificity scores of GAN and GCN are relatively high (88.34% and 88.9% respectively).

PTSD This is a homogeneous dataset wherein the scanning of all subjects was carried out on a single scanner using the same sequence. Since the sources of non-neural variability are minimized relatively in this dataset, most models performed very well (AUC > 90%). Therefore, it is not very informative to evaluate various classification models against one another. Nevertheless, BrainNetCNN outperforms GAN and GCN in terms of accuracy, precision, and f1 score for 3-way classification. Also in 3-way classification, while the evaluation results of GCN were outperformed by Linear SVM and BrainNetCNN, the model still has better performance than the others do (by a margin of 1% to 4%). As for binary classification, it can be seen that GAN and GCN have approximately similar patterns where they achieve the highest accuracy, highest recall, highest f1 score (97.76%, 100% and 98.40% respectively), and second highest precision score (96.92%) and specificity (93.33%). The best performance on this dataset also includes RLR, Linear SVM, and BrainNetCNN.

ADNI GAN appeared to reach the top level of performance in both 4-way classification and binary classification, particularly the accuracy score where the value is higher than the second highest value by large margins (52.84% vs. 44.28% and 88.56% vs. 82.86%). GCN displays only the second highest result in accuracy for multinomial classification. The reasons for this issue may be due to the limited sample dataset for training and the fact that the cut-off threshold may remove some important features in the graph.

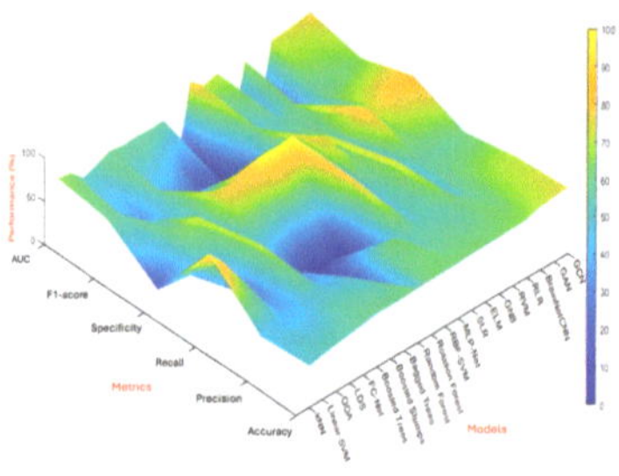

(**a**) ADHD dataset

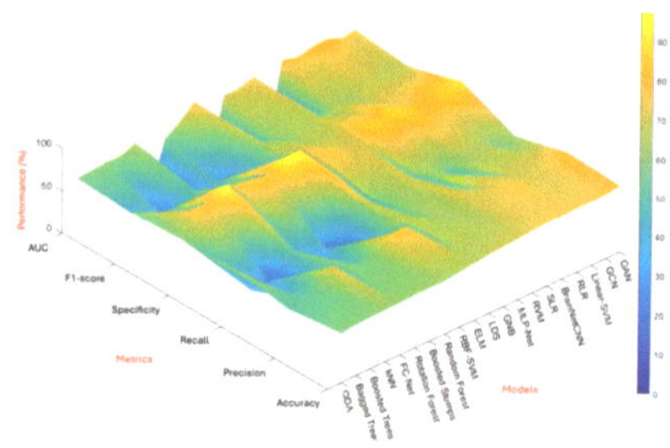

(**b**) ABIDE-II dataset

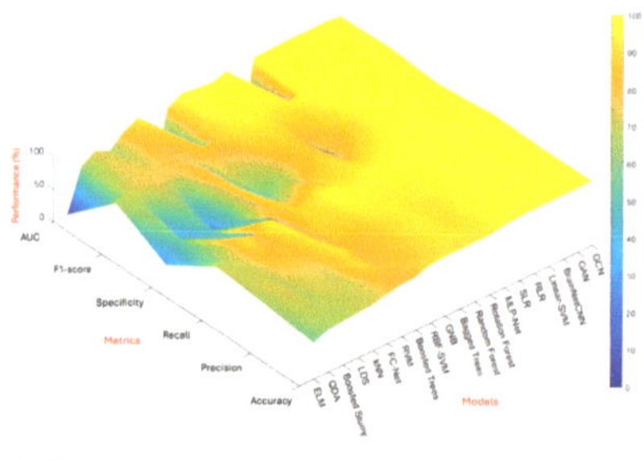

(**c**) PTSD dataset

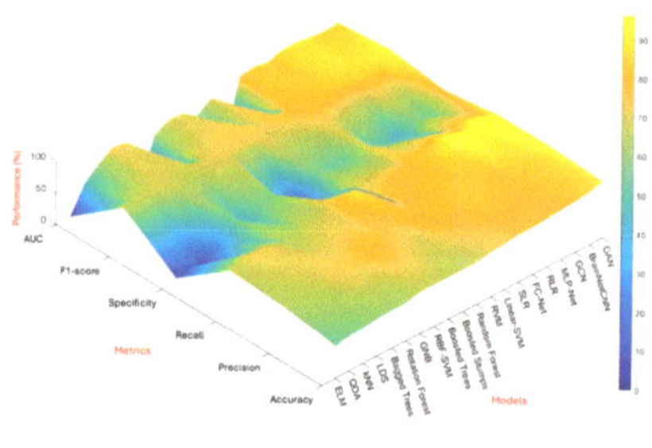

(**d**) ADNI dataset

Figure 4. Illustration of the models' performance sorted from worst to best for each dataset.

5.3. *Effect of Different Thresholds on GCN's Performance*

Even though we have used a criterion for threshold selection that has been widely reported before, we want to ensure that our choices do not remove any important connections that may negatively impact the model's performance. Therefore, we estimated binary classification for the four datasets and plotted against different cutoff thresholds. As we can see in Figure 5a–d, all the accuracy results for all four datasets peak at our choices of thresholds, justifying the selection of thresholds based on the elbow cutoff criterion.

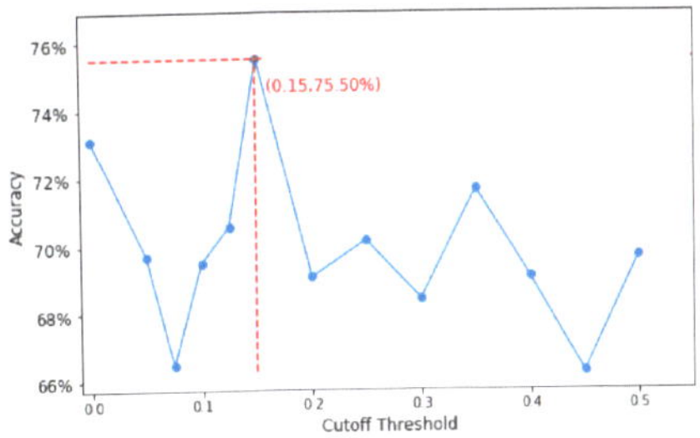

(**a**) ADHD dataset

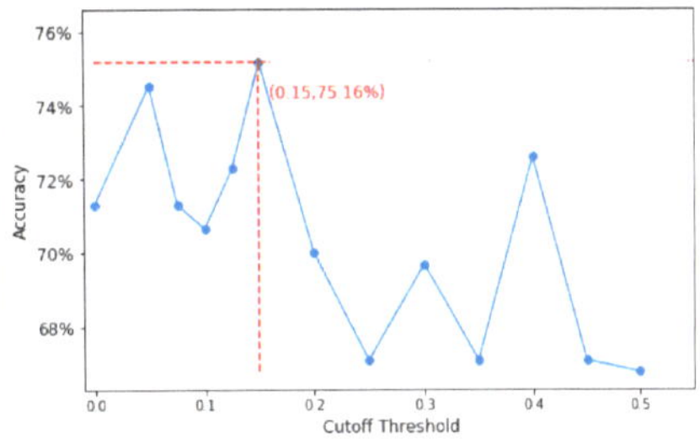

(**b**) ABIDE-II dataset

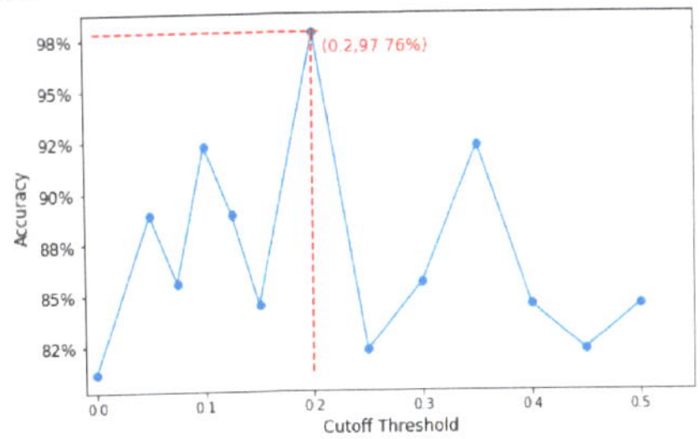

(**c**) PTSD dataset

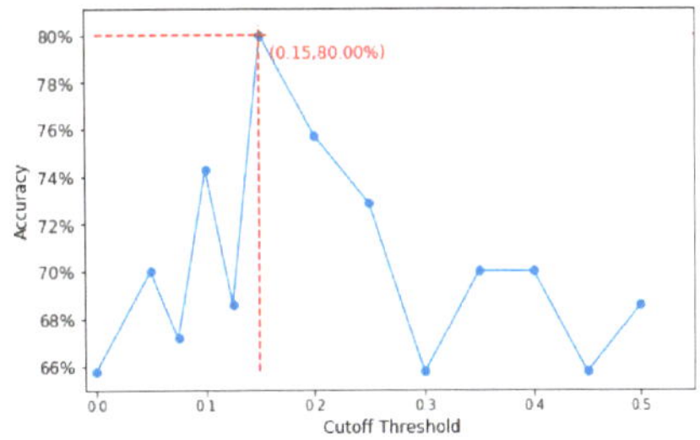

(**d**) ADNI dataset

Figure 5. GCN's performance on different thresholds for each dataset.

5.4. Statistical Significance

A random classifier for the binary classification problem would have the probability of 50% to predict the label correctly. A model with a prediction below that expectation cannot be used [48]. Therefore, we modeled the outcomes of each classifier as a Bernoulli process B(n,p), where n is a total number of subjects from the test samples and p is the probability of success. Then we want to test whether the probability of correctly predicted labels by the classifiers could surpass the expected probability. The results of all the models on all the datasets are shown in Table 5. GAN and GCN appear to achieve significant results on all the datasets.

Table 5. The p-values of the Bernoulli test for all the models. Significance was defined at $\alpha = 0.05$.

Model	Dataset			
	ADHD	ABIDE-II	PTSD	ADNI
GNB	0.005	0.001	4.84×10^{-4}	0.042
LDA	0.175	0.003	0.079	0.168
QDA	0.302	0.155	0.079	0.282
SLR	0.008	6.95×10^{-5}	8.12×10^{-5}	0.006
RLR	0.001	6.95×10^{-5}	1.10×10^{-5}	0.006
LinearSVM	0.459	6.95×10^{-5}	1.10×10^{-5}	0.017
RBF-SVM	0.009	0.021	4.84×10^{-4}	0.042
RVM	0.003	1.88×10^{-4}	0.009	0.017
MLP-Net	0.008	4.80×10^{-4}	8.12×10^{-5}	0.002
FC-Net	0.089	0.064	0.009	0.006
ELM	0.005	0.005	0.319	0.424
kNN	0.698	0.064	0.030	0.282
Bagged Tree	0.024	0.102	4.84×10^{-4}	0.168
Boosted Tree	0.024	0.064	0.009	0.042
Boosted Stump	0.024	0.038	0.003	0.042
Random Forest	0.015	0.038	4.84×10^{-4}	0.042
Rotation Forest	0.015	0.038	4.84×10^{-4}	0.168
BrainNetCNN	1.06×10^{-5}	6.95×10^{-5}	1.10×10^{-5}	5.35×10^{-5}
GCN	5.48×10^{-7}	2.41×10^{-5}	1.10×10^{-5}	5.35×10^{-5}
GAN	1.53×10^{-6}	7.87×10^{-6}	1.10×10^{-5}	2.66×10^{-5}

5.5. Statistical Comparison

To test the hypothesis that GAN and GCN generalize better than the other models, all the accuracy scores generated by the CV method were collected as samples for a statistical test. In particular, we made the assumption of the null hypothesis that the performances of GAN and GCN are worse than those of the other models, and we would like to check whether there is enough evidence to reject the null hypothesis. The Wilcoxon rank-sum test was applied to compare the performances of GAN and GCN with other models. The Wilcoxon technique, as an alternative approach to the Student's t-test, can be more appropriate when the sample is small because we cannot assume the data are normally distributed [49]. The level of significance was selected at $\alpha = 0.05$.

Table 6 (a) and (b) show the statistical results (p-value) of the Wilcoxon test for the comparison of GAN and GCN, respectively, with the other models on all the datasets. The tests indicated that GAN and GCN statistically have greater accuracy scores than almost all the traditional ML models on all the datasets (p-value < 0.05). We also do not have enough evidence to conclude that GAN and GCN statistically perform better than BrainNetCNN, although the test suggests that GAN has a better performance than BrainNetCNN for the ABIDE-II dataset (p-value = 0.02).

Table 6. The p-value of the Wilcoxon rank-sum test for the comparisons of GAN with the other models (a) and GCN with the other models (b) on all the datasets. Significance was defined at $\alpha < 0.05$.

(a)

Model	Dataset			
	ADHD	ABIDE-II	PTSD	ADNI
GNB	0.004	0.004	0.04	0.004
LDA	0.004	0.004	0.004	0.004
QDA	0.004	0.004	0.004	0.004
SLR	0.004	0.032	0.579	0.020
RLR	0.004	0.032	0.738	0.004
LinearSVM	0.004	0.059	0.738	0.004
RBF-SVM	0.004	0.004	0.004	0.004
RVM	0.004	0.004	0.004	0.004
MLP-Net	0.004	0.044	0.341	0.171
FC-Net	0.004	0.004	0.004	0.004
ELM	0.004	0.004	0.004	0.004
kNN	0.004	0.004	0.004	0.004
Bagged Tree	0.004	0.004	0.087	0.004
Boosted Tree	0.004	0.004	0.004	0.004
Boosted Stump	0.004	0.004	0.004	0.004
Random Forest	0.004	0.004	0.012	0.004
Rotation Forest	0.004	0.004	0.04	0.004
BrainNetCNN	0.206	0.020	0.738	0.198
GCN	0.794	0.187	0.738	0.059

(b)

Model	Dataset			
	ADHD	ABIDE-II	PTSD	ADNI
GNB	0.004	0.004	0.04	0.008
LDA	0.004	0.004	0.004	0.008
QDA	0.004	0.004	0.004	0.004
SLR	0.004	0.14	0.579	0.159
RLR	0.004	0.38	0.738	0.048
LinearSVM	0.004	0.556	0.738	0.044
RBF-SVM	0.004	0.004	0.004	0.008

Table 6. *Cont.*

(**b**)

Model	Dataset			
	ADHD	**ABIDE-II**	**PTSD**	**ADNI**
RVM	0.004	0.016	0.004	0.044
MLP-Net	0.004	0.194	0.341	0.567
FC-Net	0.004	0.004	0.004	0.044
ELM	0.004	0.008	0.004	0.004
kNN	0.004	0.004	0.004	0.004
Bagged Tree	0.004	0.004	0.087	0.008
Boosted Tree	0.004	0.004	0.004	0.016
Boosted Stump	0.004	0.004	0.004	0.012
Random Forest	0.004	0.004	0.012	0.016
Rotation Forest	0.004	0.004	0.04	0.004
BrainNetCNN	0.095	0.258	0.738	0.825
GAN	0.270	0.877	0.738	1

6. Discussion

GAN shows excellent results on independent test data on both large and small datasets, where the model had the best performance for the ABIDE-II, PTSD, and ADNI datasets and the second best performance for the ADHD dataset. The improvement of GAN using BrainNetCNN as the backbone network over using just BrainNetCNN alone demonstrates the benefits of data augmentation by GAN. This could potentially address the problem of data scarcity for neuroimaging based diagnostic prediction in patient populations in neurology and psychiatry.

Table 7 shows the computational time required for each model to complete training across datasets. Generally, all three deep learning models require more time to train than the traditional method, which can be attributed to their complexity and larger number of trainable parameters. We can observe that the GAN exhibits the longest training time. This is because the GAN model needs to learn the data distribution to synthesize data, in addition to the time required for training the classifier. Despite this extended training time, GAN achieves the best performance among all models across the four datasets. Notably, GCN requires less training time than BrainNetCNN across the three datasets (ABIDE-II, PTSD, and ADNI), yet it achieves better performance in ABIDE-II and ADNI and equivalent performance in PTSD. This suggests that, despite requiring fewer trainable parameters, GCN is a superior tool for capturing the complex structure of brain networks. Some traditional models require very little training time, sometimes as low as 0.01 s. However, their performance does not match that of GAN and GCN. This indicates a trade-off between training time and performance across traditional and deep learning models. In future research, there is a need to decrease the training time of GAN and GCN while maintaining satisfactory accuracy results to enhance their practical applicability in real-world clinical settings.

In Figure 3a–d, we can see that each dataset has a different cut-off threshold. As mentioned above, we aim to retain only the strong connections in the backbone network crucial for identifying abnormal patterns in individuals with brain disorders. Therefore, we intend to prune the low tail of the curve, which comprises solely low connection values. However, selecting an excessively high threshold may result in the elimination of many relevant connections, thereby negatively impacting accuracy performance (as demonstrated by examples in Figure 5a–d, where accuracy decreases with increasing thresholds). To strike a balance, we opt to set the threshold at the elbow of each curve distribution, which shares a similar concept with the elbow criterion used in k-means clustering. This choice allows for the retention of meaningful connections while removing redundant, noisy ones. Our hypothesis is validated by the accuracy results presented in Figure 5. Additionally, since each dataset exhibits distinct distributions in connection values, the selection of the elbow must vary accordingly. This accounts for differences in cut-off threshold selection across datasets.

Table 7. The comparison of computational time (in seconds) required to train each model.

Model	Dataset			
	ADHD	ABIDE-II	PTSD	ADNI
GNB	0.12	0.11	0.01	0.01
LDA	1.65	1.49	0.22	0.34
QDA	6.28	3.09	0.07	0.1
SLR	44.18	29.14	2.18	5.35
RLR	21.29	14.88	1.41	3.54
LinearSVM	67.83	4.22	3.08	0.48
RBF-SVM	5.13	1.61	0.05	0.3
RVM	242.32	92.47	35.31	23.24
MLP-Net	24.09	19.55	10.77	8.19
FC-Net	18.86	17.26	10.17	9.42
ELM	2.02	0.08	0.17	0.17
kNN	0.409	0.23	0.01	0.01
Bagged Tree	52.74	35.92	1.32	2.79
Boosted Tree	5.06	4.40	0.388	0.63
Boosted Stump	4.02	3.99	0.41	0.55
Random Forest	5.20	3.23	0.29	0.30
Rotation Forest	304.66	201.79	19.89	34.10
BrainNetCNN	114.42	133.79	38.74	132.46
GCN	144.6	110.57	34.13	90.76
GAN	194.98	236.23	83.29	260.87

7. Limitations and Future Research

The hyperparameters used in this paper were obtained from our previous works [12,18], where a hyperparameter tuning approach was employed to select the optimal parameters yielding the best results. Therefore, we applied the same parameters to this paper and achieved good results. However, it must be noted that extensive tuning of hyperparameters to a given dataset makes the model overfit the data and hence makes it less generalizable. This is not desirable in clinical diagnostic applications since there is wide variability in the human population, and we want these models to be generally applicable.

Ensemble methods can combine multiple deep neural networks to achieve more stable and generalizable predictions by mitigating variance and reducing generalization errors. However, due to the distinct characteristics and nature of GANs and GCNs, the development of ensemble frameworks for these techniques remains incomplete. While implementing this method requires careful planning and a significant time investment, its potential benefits are substantial. In our future work, we aim to explore the integration of GANs and GCNs to investigate whether this combination can lead to further performance improvements in terms of accuracy.

Interpretability is considered a crucial factor when integrating deep learning into clinical practice. In our study, we employed GCN coupled with a top-k pooling method. This approach offers interpretability by selecting a set (k) of the most relevant brain regions most predictive of brain disorders. These identified regions have the potential to serve as biomarkers, helping in the early detection of diseases. Although the paper has not presented the results, the methods hold significant potential, and we plan to implement them in future work.

GCN illustrates the effectiveness of applying graph neural networks to graph-structure data by achieving the highest performance in the ADHD dataset and also comparatively good results in other datasets. One of the ways to improve GCN is to train embedding of nodes in a space that has fewer dimensions instead of directly using row vectors as feature vectors [50]. This technique utilizes a framework from an encoder-decoder perspective that can better capture the information contained in the data. The design of the adjacency matrix also plays an essential role. Instead of static non-directional graphs obtained from FC, directional graphs can be obtained using effective connectivity [51]. The graphs could also be computed across different blocks of time to estimate the dynamics [52]. These types of advanced graphical features, when used with GCN, have the potential to improve our understanding of the mechanisms underlying neuronal dynamics by examining alterations between patients and healthy controls.

8. Conclusions

We identified two major challenges for the application of deep learning for neuroimaging-based diagnostic classification: small sample sizes of patients and incompatibility of graphical features of brain networks and architectures of traditional deep learning models. We have illustrated how these issues can be addressed using brain connectivity features from four different clinical datasets. The patient data scarcity issue was addressed using GANs, while GCNs allowed us to conveniently handle graph-based features within a deep learning framework. Both GAN and GCN provided the best and second best accuracy for the four clinical datasets we used.

Author Contributions: Conceptualization, N.H., T.S.D., M.N.D. and G.D.; methodology, N.H., D.Y., Y.M. and G.D.; software, S.W., C.L., M.T.S. and A.A.; validation, N.H. and G.D.; formal analysis, N.H. and D.R.; investigation, N.H. and G.D.; data curation, D.R.; writing—original draft preparation, All authors; writing—review and editing, all authors, visualization, N.H. and D.R.; supervision, G.D., T.S.D., M.N.D. and D.Y.; project administration, G.D., T.S.D. and M.N.D.; funding acquisition, G.D., T.S.D. and M.N.D. All authors have read and agreed to the published version of the manuscript.

Funding: Attention deficit hyperactivity disorder (ADHD) data acquisition was supported by NIMH (National Institute of Mental Health, Bethesda, MD, USA) grant # R03MH096321. Alzheimer's disease neuroimaging initiative (ADNI) data acquisition was funded by multiple agencies and the list can be obtained from http://adni.loni.usc.edu/wp-content/uploads/how_to_apply/ADNI_Acknowledgement_List.pdf, accessed on 19 March 2024. As such, the investigators within the ADNI contributed to the design and implementation of ADNI and/or provided data but did not participate in analysis or writing of this report. Autism brain imaging data exchange (ABIDE) data acquisition was supported by NIMH grant # K23MH087770. The authors acknowledge financial support for this work from the U.S. Army Medical Research and Development Command (MRDC) (Grant number 00007218). The authors would also like to thank the personnel at the traumatic brain injury (TBI) clinic and behavioral health clinic, Fort Moore, GA, USA and the US Army Aeromedical Research Laboratory, Fort Novosel, AL, USA, and most of all, the Soldiers who participated in the study.

Institutional Review Board Statement: The procedure and the protocols in this study were approved by the Auburn University Institutional Review Board (IRB) and the Headquarters U.S. Army Medical Research and Development Command, IRB (HQ USAMRDC IRB). The ethical approval for the project was granted on 8 August 2013.

Informed Consent Statement: Informed consent was obtained from all subjects involved in the study.

Data Availability Statement: The data from ADHD (https://fcon_1000.projects.nitrc.org/indi/adhd200/, 19 March 2024), Autism (https://fcon_1000.projects.nitrc.org/indi/abide/, accessed on 19 March 2024) and Alzheimer's (https://adni.loni.usc.edu/, accessed on 19 March 2024) is available publicly and we have used those public datasets. The PTSD data were acquired in-house and were funded by the US Department of Defense. Contractual obligations do not allow us to publicly share the raw data; however, we are happy to share processed data with individual investigators upon request.

Acknowledgments: The authors thank Julie Rodiek and Wayne Duggan for facilitating post-traumatic stress disorder (PTSD) data acquisition.

Conflicts of Interest: The authors declare no conflicts of interest.

Disclaimer: Material has been reviewed by the Walter Reed Army Institute of Research. There is no objection to its presentation and/or publication. The opinions or assertions contained herein are the private views of the authors, and are not to be construed as official, or as reflecting true views of the Department of the Army or the Department of Defense or the United States Government. The investigators have adhered to the policies for protection of human subjects as prescribed in AR 70–25.

References

1. Su, L.; Wang, L.; Shen, H.; Feng, G.; Hu, D. Discriminative analysis of non-linear brain connectivity in schizophrenia: An fmri study. *Front. Hum. Neurosci.* **2013**, *7*, 702. [CrossRef] [PubMed]
2. Wang, Y.; Kang, J.; Kemmer, P.B.; Guo, Y. An efficient and reliable statistical method for estimating functional connectivity in large scale brain networks using partial correlation. *Front. Neurosci.* **2016**, *10*, 123. [CrossRef] [PubMed]
3. Damoiseaux, J.S.; Prater, K.E.; Miller, B.L.; Greicius, M.D. Functional connectivity tracks clinical deterioration in alzheimer's disease. *Neurobiol. Aging* **2012**, *33*, 828-e19. [CrossRef] [PubMed]
4. Hull, J.V.; Dokovna, L.B.; Jacokes, Z.J.; Torgerson, C.M.; Irimia, A.; Horn, J.D.V. Resting-state functional connectivity in autism spectrum disorders: A review. *Front. Psychiatry* **2017**, *7*, 205. [CrossRef] [PubMed]
5. Lanius, R.A.; Williamson, P.C.; Bluhm, R.L.; Densmore, M.; Boksman, K.; Neufeld, R.W.J.; Gati, J.S.; Menon, R.S. Functional connectivity of dissociative responses in posttraumatic stress disorder: A functional magnetic resonance imaging investigation. *Biol. Psychiatry* **2005**, *57*, 873–884. [CrossRef] [PubMed]
6. Tomasi, D.; Volkow, N.D. Abnormal functional connectivity in children with attention-deficit/hyperactivity disorder. *Biol. Psychiatry* **2012**, *71*, 443–450. [CrossRef] [PubMed]
7. Zhang, H.-Y.; Wang, S.-J.; Liu, B.; Ma, Z.-L.; Yang, M.; Zhang, Z.-J.; Teng, G.-J. Resting brain connectivity: Changes during the progress of alzheimer disease. *Radiology* **2010**, *256*, 598–606. [CrossRef] [PubMed]
8. Brier, M.R.; Thomas, J.B.; Fagan, A.M.; Hassenstab, J.; Holtzman, D.M.; Benzinger, T.L.; Morris, J.C.; Ances, B.M. Functional connectivity and graph theory in preclinical alzheimer's disease. *Neurobiol. Aging* **2014**, *35*, 757–768. [CrossRef]
9. Guye, M.; Bettus, G.; Bartolomei, F.; Cozzone, P.J. Graph theoretical analysis of structural and functional connectivity mri in normal and pathological brain networks. *Magn. Reson. Mater. Phys. Biol. Med.* **2010**, *23*, 409–421. [CrossRef]
10. Keown, C.L.; Datko, M.C.; Chen, C.P.; Maximo, J.O.; Jahedi, A.; Müller, R.-A. Network organization is globally atypical in autism: A graph theory study of intrinsic functional connectivity. *Biol. Psychiatry: Cogn. Neurosci. Neuroimaging* **2017**, *2*, 66–75. [CrossRef]
11. Kipf, T.N.; Welling, M. Semi-supervised classification with graph convolutional networks. *arXiv* **2016**, arXiv:1609.02907.
12. Yan, D.; Wu, S.; Sami, M.T.; Almudaifer, A.; Jiang, Z.; Chen, H.; Rangaprakash, D.; Deshpande, G.; Ma, Y. Improving brain dysfunction prediction by gan: A functional-connectivity generator approach. In Proceedings of the 2021 IEEE International Conference on Big Data (Big Data), Orlando, FL, USA, 15–18 December 2021 ; IEEE: Piscataway, NJ, USA, 2021; pp. 1514–1522.
13. Mirza, M.; Osindero, S. Conditional generative adversarial nets. *arXiv* **2014**, arXiv:1411.1784.
14. Odena, A.; Olah, C.; Shlens, J. Conditional image synthesis with auxiliary classifier gans. In Proceedings of the International Conference on Machine Learning, PMLR, Sydney, Australia, 6–11 August 2017; pp. 2642–2651.
15. Li, W.; Wang, Y.; Cai, Y.; Arnold, C.; Zhao, E.; Yuan, Y. Semi-supervised rare disease detection using generative adversarial network. *arXiv* **2018**, arXiv:1812.00547.
16. Yang, Y.; Nan, F.; Yang, P.; Meng, Q.; Xie, Y.; Zhang, D.; Muhammad, K. Gan-based semi-supervised learning approach for clinical decision support in health-iot platform. *IEEE Access* **2019**, *7*, 8048–8057. [CrossRef]
17. Kawahara, J.; Brown, C.J.; Miller, S.P.; Booth, B.G.; Chau, V.; Grunau, R.E.; Zwicker, J.G.; Hamarneh, G. Brainnetcnn: Convolutional neural networks for brain networks; towards predicting neurodevelopment. *NeuroImage* **2017**, *146*, 1038–1049. [CrossRef] [PubMed]
18. Ma, Y.; Yan, D.; Long, C.; Rangaprakash, D.; Deshpande, G. Predicting autism spectrum disorder from brain imaging data by graph convolutional network. In Proceedings of the 2021 International Joint Conference on Neural Networks (IJCNN), Shenzhen, China, 18–22 July 2021; IEEE: Piscataway, NJ, USA, 2021; pp. 1–8.
19. ADHD-200 Consortium. The adhd-200 consortium: A model to advance the translational potential of neuroimaging in clinical neuroscience. *Front. Syst. Neurosci.* **2012**, *6*, 62.
20. Martino, A.D.; Yan, C.; Li, Q.; Denio, E.; Castellanos, F.X.; Alaerts, K.; Anderson, J.S.; Assaf, M.; Bookheimer, S.Y.; Dapretto, M.; et al. The autism brain imaging data exchange: Towards a large-scale evaluation of the intrinsic brain architecture in autism. *Mol. Psychiatry* **2014**, *19*, 659–667. [CrossRef]
21. Lanka, P.; Rangaprakash, D.; Dretsch, M.N.; Katz, J.S.; Denney, T.S.; Deshpande, G. Supervised machine learning for diagnostic classification from large-scale neuroimaging datasets. *Brain Imaging Behav.* **2020**, *14*, 2378–2416. [CrossRef] [PubMed]
22. Petersen, R.C.; Aisen, P.S.; Beckett, L.A.; Donohue, M.C.; Gamst, A.C.; Harvey, D.J.; Jack, C.R.; Jagust, W.J.; Shaw, L.M.; Toga, A.W.; et al. Alzheimer's disease neuroimaging initiative (adni): Clinical characterization. *Neurology* **2010**, *74*, 201–209. [CrossRef]
23. Veeranki, Y.R.; McNaboe, R.; Posada-Quintero, H.F. Eeg-based seizure detection using variable-frequency complex demodulation and convolutional neural networks. *Signals* **2023**, *4*, 816–835. [CrossRef]
24. Basaia, S.; Agosta, F.; Wagner, L.; Canu, E.; Magnani, G.; Santangelo, R.; Filippi, M.; Alzheimer's Disease Neuroimaging Initiative. Automated classification of alzheimer's disease and mild cognitive impairment using a single mri and deep neural networks. *NeuroImage Clin.* **2019**, *21*, 101645. [CrossRef] [PubMed]
25. Li, H.; Parikh, N.A.; He, L. A novel transfer learning approach to enhance deep neural network classification of brain functional connectomes. *Front. Neurosci.* **2018**, *12*, 491. [CrossRef]

26. Zeng, L.; Wang, H.; Hu, P.; Yang, B.; Pu, W.; Shen, H.; Chen, X.; Liu, Z.; Yin, H.; Tan, Q.; et al. Multi-site diagnostic classification of schizophrenia using discriminant deep learning with functional connectivity mri. *EBioMedicine* **2018**, *30*, 74–85. [CrossRef]
27. Ktena, S.I.; Parisot, S.; Ferrante, E.; Rajchl, M.; Lee, M.; Glocker, B.; Rueckert, D. Metric learning with spectral graph convolutions on brain connectivity networks. *NeuroImage* **2018**, *169*, 431–442. [CrossRef]
28. Yao, D.; Sui, J.; Wang, M.; Yang, E.; Jiaerken, Y.; Luo, N.; Yap, P.; Liu, M.; Shen, D. A mutual multi-scale triplet graph convolutional network for classification of brain disorders using functional or structural connectivity. *IEEE Trans. Med. Imaging* **2021**, *40*, 1279–1289. [CrossRef] [PubMed]
29. Parisot, S.; Ktena, S.I.; Ferrante, E.; Lee, M.; Guerrero, R.; Glocker, B.; Rueckert, D. Disease prediction using graph convolutional networks: Application to autism spectrum disorder and alzheimer's disease. *Med. Image Anal.* **2018**, *48*, 117–130. [CrossRef] [PubMed]
30. Kim, B.; Ye, J.C.; Kim, J.-J. Learning dynamic graph representation of brain connectome with spatio-temporal attention. *Adv. Neural Inf. Process. Syst.* **2021**, *34*, 4314–4327.
31. Zhao, F.; Li, N.; Pan, H.; Chen, X.; Li, Y.; Zhang, H.; Mao, N.; Cheng, D. Multi-view feature enhancement based on self-attention mechanism graph convolutional network for autism spectrum disorder diagnosis. *Front. Hum. Neurosci.* **2022**, *16*, 918969. [CrossRef] [PubMed]
32. Li, L.; Jiang, H.; Wen, G.; Cao, P.; Xu, M.; Liu, X.; Yang, J.; Zaiane, O. Te-hi-gcn: An ensemble of transfer hierarchical graph convolutional networks for disorder diagnosis. *Neuroinformatics* **2022**, *2*, 353–375. [CrossRef]
33. Yerukalareddy, D.R.; Pavlovskiy, E. Brain tumor classification based on mr images using gan as a pre-trained model. In Proceedings of the 2021 IEEE Ural-Siberian Conference on Computational Technologies in Cognitive Science, Genomics and Biomedicine (CSGB), Yekaterinburg, Russia, 26–28 May 2021; IEEE: Piscataway, NJ, USA, 2021; pp. 380–384.
34. Mondal, A.K.; Dolz, J.; Desrosiers, C. Few-shot 3d multi-modal medical image segmentation using generative adversarial learning. *arXiv* **2018**, arXiv:1810.12241.
35. Ran, M.; Hu, J.; Chen, Y.; Chen, H.; Sun, H.; Zhou, J.; Zhang, Y. Denoising of 3d magnetic resonance images using a residual encoder–decoder wasserstein generative adversarial network. *Med. Image Anal.* **2019**, *55*, 165–180. [CrossRef] [PubMed]
36. Quan, T.M.; Nguyen-Duc, T.; Jeong, W. Compressed sensing mri reconstruction using a generative adversarial network with a cyclic loss. *IEEE Trans. Med. Imaging* **2018**, *37*, 1488–1497. [CrossRef] [PubMed]
37. Dar, S.U.H.; Yurt, M.; Karacan, L.; Erdem, A.; Erdem, E.; Cukur, T. Image synthesis in multi-contrast mri with conditional generative adversarial networks. *IEEE Trans. Med. Imaging* **2019**, *38*, 2375–2388. [CrossRef]
38. Zhao, J.; Huang, J.; Zhi, D.; Yan, W.; Ma, X.; Yang, X.; Li, X.; Ke, Q.; Jiang, T.; Calhoun, V.D.; et al. Functional network connectivity (fnc)-based generative adversarial network (gan) and its applications in classification of mental disorders. *J. Neurosci. Methods* **2020**, *341*, 108756. [CrossRef]
39. Barile, B.; Marzullo, A.; Stamile, C.; Durand-Dubief, F.; Sappey-Marinier, D. Data augmentation using generative adversarial neural networks on brain structural connectivity in multiple sclerosis. *Comput. Methods Programs Biomed.* **2021**, *206*, 106113. [CrossRef] [PubMed]
40. Cao, Y.; Kuai, H.; Liang, P.; Pan, J.-S.; Yan, J.; Zhong, N. Bnloop-gan: A multi-loop generative adversarial model on brain network learning to classify alzheimer's disease. *Front. Neurosci.* **2023**, *17*, 1202382. [CrossRef] [PubMed]
41. Traut, N.; Heuer, K.; Lemaître, G.; Beggiato, A.; Germanaud, D.; Elmaleh, M.; Bethegnies, A.; Bonnasse-Gahot, L.; Cai, W.; Chambon, S.; et al. Insights from an autism imaging biomarker challenge: Promises and threats to biomarker discovery. *NeuroImage* **2022**, *255*, 119171. [CrossRef] [PubMed]
42. Wu, G.-R.; Liao, W.; Stramaglia, S.; Ding, J.-R.; Chen, H.; Marinazzo, D. A blind deconvolution approach to recover effective connectivity brain networks from resting state fmri data. *Med. Image Anal.* **2013**, *17*, 365–374. [CrossRef] [PubMed]
43. Craddock, R.C.; James, G.A.; Holtzheimer, P.E., III; Hu, X.P.; Mayberg, H.S. A whole brain fmri atlas generated via spatially constrained spectral clustering. *Hum. Brain Mapp.* **2012**, *33*, 1914–1928. [CrossRef]
44. Lee, J.; Lee, I.; Kang, J. Self-attention graph pooling. In Proceedings of the International Conference on Machine Learning, PMLR, Long Beach, CA, USA, 9–15 June 2019; pp. 3734–3743.
45. Radford, A.; Metz, L.; Chintala, S. Unsupervised representation learning with deep convolutional generative adversarial networks. *arXiv* **2015**, arXiv:1511.06434.
46. Garrison, K.A.; Scheinost, D.; Finn, E.S.; Shen, X.; Constable, R.T. The (in) stability of functional brain network measures across thresholds. *Neuroimage* **2015**, *118*, 651–661. [CrossRef] [PubMed]
47. van den Heuvel, M.P.; de Lange, S.C.; Zalesky, A.; Seguin, C.; Yeo, B.T.T.; Schmidt, R. Proportional thresholding in resting-state fmri functional connectivity networks and consequences for patient-control connectome studies: Issues and recommendations. *Neuroimage* **2017**, *152*, 437–449. [CrossRef] [PubMed]
48. Pereira, F.; Mitchell, T.; Botvinick, M. Machine learning classifiers and fmri: A tutorial overview. *Neuroimage* **2009**, *45*, S199–S209. [CrossRef]
49. Demšar, J. Statistical comparisons of classifiers over multiple data sets. *J. Mach. Learn. Res.* **2006**, *7*, 1–30.
50. Xu, M. Understanding graph embedding methods and their applications. *SIAM Rev.* **2021**, *63*, 825–853. [CrossRef]

51. Zhao, S.; Rangaprakash, D.; Liang, P.; Deshpande, G. Deterioration from healthy to mild cognitive impairment and alzheimer's disease mirrored in corresponding loss of centrality in directed brain networks. *Brain Inform.* **2019**, *6*, 8. [CrossRef]
52. Rangaprakash, D.; Odemuyiwa, T.; Dutt, D.N.; Deshpande, G.; Initiative, A.D.N. Density-based clustering of static and dynamic functional mri connectivity features obtained from subjects with cognitive impairment. *Brain Inform.* **2020**, *7*, 19. [CrossRef]

Disclaimer/Publisher's Note: The statements, opinions and data contained in all publications are solely those of the individual author(s) and contributor(s) and not of MDPI and/or the editor(s). MDPI and/or the editor(s) disclaim responsibility for any injury to people or property resulting from any ideas, methods, instructions or products referred to in the content.

brain sciences

MDPI

Article

The Commonality and Individuality of Human Brains When Performing Tasks

Jie Huang

Department of Radiology, Michigan State University, East Lansing, MI 48824, USA; huangj@msu.edu;
Tel.: +1-517-884-3246

Abstract: It is imperative to study individual brain functioning toward understanding the neural bases responsible for individual behavioral and clinical traits. The complex and dynamic brain activity varies from area to area and from time to time across the entire brain, and BOLD-fMRI measures this spatiotemporal activity at large-scale systems level. We present a novel method to investigate task-evoked whole brain activity that varies not only from person to person but also from task trial to trial within each task type, offering a means of characterizing the individuality of human brains when performing tasks. For each task trial, the temporal correlation of task-evoked ideal time signal with the time signal of every point in the brain yields a full spatial map that characterizes the whole brain's functional co-activity (FC) relative to the task-evoked ideal response. For any two task trials, regardless of whether they are the same task or not, the spatial correlation of their corresponding two FC maps over the entire brain quantifies the similarity between these two maps, offering a means of investigating the variation in the whole brain activity trial to trial. The results demonstrated a substantially varied whole brain activity from trial to trial for each task category. The degree of this variation was task type-dependent and varied from subject to subject, showing a remarkable individuality of human brains when performing tasks. It demonstrates the potential of using the presented method to investigate the relationship of the whole brain activity with individual behavioral and clinical traits.

Keywords: human brain function; whole brain activity; individuality

1. Introduction

Our perception, cognition and action are mediated by brain function. Brain functional organization consists of multiple functional systems from simple systems such as sensorimotor and visual systems to complex cognitive systems such as language. These separated systems seem to suggest a functional segregation of brain function, but human behavior is the result of an integrated functioning of the whole brain's activity. For example, performing a simple visually cued finger-tapping (FT) task evokes both visual and sensorimotor systems. The information of visual cue is first processed through the visual system and then triggers the motor system to plan and execute the task of tapping fingers, which consequently evoke the somatosensory system. This performance may vary from trial to trial due to possible attention variation and interaction among these systems, resulting in a task-evoked whole brain activity that may vary from trial to trial. Investigating this trial-by-trial whole brain activity may provide insight to understand the relationship of brain activity with individual behavior.

Even without performing any specific task, human brain intrinsic activity accounts for 20% of all the energy consumed by the body to maintain the operations of the brain, and these operations involve the acquisition and maintenance of information for interpreting, responding to and predicting environmental demands [1]. This intrinsic activity, i.e., the resting-state (rs) activity, is spontaneous but exhibits a surprising level of spatial and temporal organization across the entire brain [2,3]. Numerous rs-fMRI studies demonstrate the existence of multiple functional connectivity networks (FCNs) within the entire brain [4–6]. The sliding window approach of analyzing rs-fMRI data reveals the time-varying behavior of these FCNs, demonstrating dynamic FCN from time to time [7]. These rs-fMRI studies, however, are group-based studies that analyze the fMRI data in a standard template space. It remains to be explored how to extend the rs-fMRI technique to investigate the relationship of window-by-window activity of FCNs with individual behavior.

A recent combined rs- and task-fMRI study revealed the relationship of functional connectivity of the sensorimotor and visual cortical networks between resting and task states [8]. The study showed that the intrinsic and task-evoked FCNs shared a common network and the task enhanced the coactivity within that common network in comparison to the intrinsic activity. However, the task activated only partial but not whole of the intrinsic FCN. The task also activated substantially additional areas outside the intrinsic FCN, demonstrating the different functioning of the intrinsic FCNs compared to the task-evoked FCNs. Another combined rs- and task-fMRI study compared the intrinsic activity with the activity evoked by tasks at several levels of analysis from an FT-activated area within the primary sensorimotor cortex to the entire brain [9]. Contrary to our intuition, the intrinsic activity was found to be substantially larger than the task activity at all levels of analysis. The study also found that, for the task state, the brain controlled the intrinsic activity not only during the task period but also during the rest between tasks. The brain activated a task-specific network only when the task was performed but kept it relatively "silent" for other different tasks, and at the same time, it simultaneously controlled the activation of all task-specific networks during the performance of each task. These results demonstrate a dynamic whole brain activity that may depend on each individual brain's controlling of its activity, and consequently, the whole brain activity may vary from task trial to trial for each individual brain. Accordingly, investigating this trial-by-trial whole brain activity may provide insight to understand the relationship of brain activity with individual behavior.

The complex and dynamic brain activity varies from area to area and from time to time across the entire brain. BOLD-fMRI measures this spatiotemporal activity at large-scale systems level [10,11]. Numerous fMRI studies have demonstrated its effectiveness and reliability in investigating the common features of human brain functional organization at a group level (i.e., the commonality across the subjects within a group) and the effects of brain disorders on brain activity. It is imperative, however, to study individual brain functioning for understanding the neural bases responsible for individual behavioral and clinical traits. Person-specific neuroimaging approaches in investigating individual brain functioning have been reported in the literature [12–15]. In this study we present a novel method to investigate task-evoked whole brain activity that varies not only from person to person but also from task trial to trial within each task type, offering a means of characterizing the individuality of human brains when performing tasks.

2. Materials and Methods

We extend our previous four studies [9,16–18]. This study analyzed the same fMRI data. It used the same subjects, same image acquisition, and similar image preprocessing procedures. We briefly describe each paragraph. For more information, refer to our previous study [16].

Participants: 9 healthy subjects (4 female and 5 male, ages 21–55 years old) participated in the study.

Image acquisition: functional brain images were acquired on a GE 3.0 T clinical scanner with an 8-channel head coil using a gradient echo Echo-Planar-Imaging pulse sequence (TE/TR = 28/2500 ms, flip angle 80°, FOV 224 mm, matrix 64 × 64, slice thickness 3.5 mm, and spacing 0.0 mm). Thirty-eight axial slices to cover the whole brain were scanned, and the first three volume images were discarded. Each subject undertook a 12 min task-fMRI scan while performing three different tasks. Each task was presented eight times, for a total of 24 task trials, and the task presentation was interleaved. Each trial comprised a 6 s task period followed by a 24 s rest period, resulting in 12 volume images for each task trial. Task

1 was a word-reading (WR) paradigm: subjects silently read English words. Task 2 was a pattern-viewing (PV) paradigm: subjects viewed a black-and-white striped pattern with a spatial frequency of 2.8 cycles per degree. Task 3 was a visually cued FT paradigm: each subject tapped the five fingers of their right hand as quickly as possible in a random order. During the 24 s rest period, subjects were asked to focus their eyes on a small fixation mark at the screen center and try not to think of anything. After the task-fMRI scan, T1-weighted whole brain MR images were also acquired using a 3D IR-SPGR pulse sequence.

Image preprocessing: image preprocessing of the functional images was performed using AFNI (analysis of functional neuro images) software (http://afni.nimh.nih.gov/afni, accessed on 11 December 2023, Version AFNI_2011_12_21_1014) [16,19]. It included removing spikes, slice-timing correction, motion correction, spatial filtering with a Gaussian kernel with a full-width half-maximum of 4.0 mm, computing the mean volume image, bandpassing the signal intensity time courses to the range of 0.009–0.08 Hz, and computing the relative signal change (%) of the bandpassed signal intensity time courses. After these preprocessing steps, further image analysis was carried out using in-house developed Matlab-based software (MATLAB R2019b) algorithms.

Quantification of trial-by-trial brain activity within each subject: task-evoked brain activity can be characterized by an ideal BOLD response time signal [20]. This ideal response was generated by convolving the 6 s task on and 24 s task off temporal paradigm with a hemodynamic response function, using the 3dDeconvolve program in AFNI with the convolution kernel SPMG3. For each task trial, the temporal correlation (TC) r of this ideal time signal with the time signal of every point in the brain yields a full spatial map that characterizes the whole brain's functional co-activity (FC) relative to the task-evoked ideal response. This computation results in 8 FC maps for each of the three task categories and each subject. A given task should evoke similar FC maps by repeating the task. For any two task trials, regardless of whether they are the same task or not, the spatial correlation (SC) R of their corresponding two FC maps over the entire brain quantifies the similarity between these two maps, offering a means of investigating the variation in the whole brain activity trial to trial. For each individual subject, the SC R values of all pairwise FC maps for all task trials measure the variations in these FC maps and therefore quantify the individuality of that subject in performing these tasks.

For each subject, each FC map uniquely characterizes the whole brain's activity when performing a given task trial for that subject, offering a marker to distinguish tasks based on their FC maps. To test this prediction, we choose one FC map from each task category and use these three FC maps as their corresponding task markers to predict the task type of each trial for the remaining 21 trials. For a given test trial, the predicted task type is the one with the largest SC R among the three chosen FC maps. There are a total of 512 combinations in choosing three FC maps from the three task categories and 21 test trials for each choice, resulting in a total of 10,752 tests for each individual subject. The correct rate of identifying these task trials further quantifies the individuality of that subject in performing these tasks.

The commonality of brain activity across the subjects: To examine this commonality, for each subject, we first compute the task-mean FC map averaged over the 8 FC maps for each task category and use this task-mean FC map to represent the whole brain's FC in performing that task. Then, using AFNI, we convert all 27 task-mean FC maps from the 9 subjects to a standard template space (icbm452) for group analysis. In this standard template space, for each task category, the SC R of any two paired FC maps over the entire brain measures the similarity of brain activity between the corresponding two subjects in performing that task, offering a means of quantifying the commonality of brain activity across the subjects in performing these tasks.

3. Results

For each subject, based on the T1 and EPI images, in the original MRI space, we generated a mask to cover the entire brain. For each subject and each task trial, we computed the TC r of the ideal BOLD response with the time signal of every voxel within the brain mask to yield the FC map for that subject and that task. The trial-by-trial variation in this TC r map across the brain for a representative subject is illustrated in Figure 1. Then, for each subject, we computed the SC R for (1) all pairwise FC maps within each task category (a total of 28 paired FC maps for each task category) and (2) all pairwise FC maps between any two task categories (a total of 64 paired FC maps between two task categories) (Table 1). The mean R within the FT category had the largest value among all categories for each individual subject, showing the greatest similarity of the whole brain's activity when performing the FT task (Figure 2). The mean R within each of the other two tasks (WR and PV) was substantially reduced for every subject, demonstrating that the whole brain's activity varied substantially from trial to trial when performing these tasks. The mean R of paired FC maps between two task categories was relatively smaller in comparison to that within a task category and varied substantially from subject to subject, consistent with the expectation that the difference in the brain's activity of performing two different tasks should be larger than that of performing the same task repeatedly.

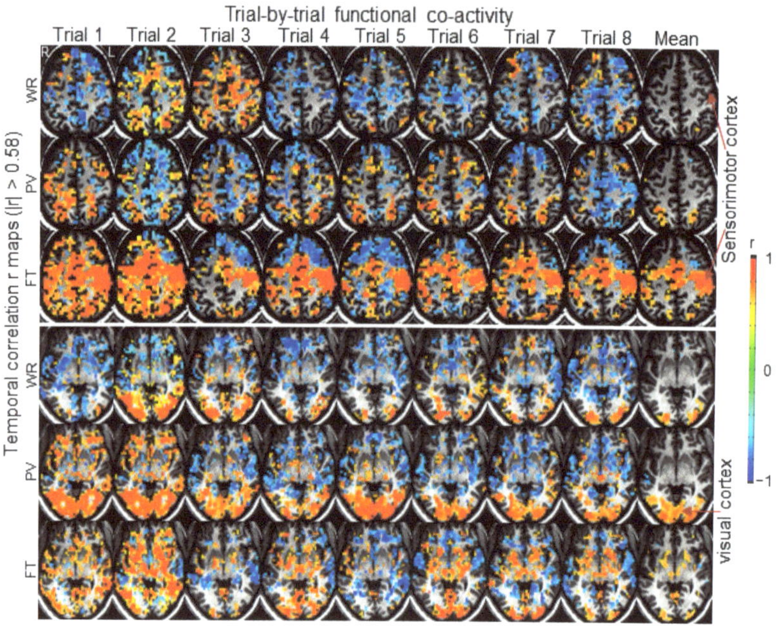

Figure 1. Illustration of the variation in trial-by-trial whole brain FC relative to the task-evoked ideal response for a representative subject. For the illustration purpose, these TC r maps were presented with threshold $|r| > 0.58$ ($N = 12$, $p < 0.05$). The right-hand FT-evoked activity in both the left sensorimotor cortex and supplementary motor area was consistent for all 8 trials, but the FC for other cortical areas within the selected slice varied substantially from trial to trial (the third row in the top panel). Similarly, the PV-evoked activity in the visual cortex was also consistent for all 8 trials, though its degree varied substantially from trial to trial (the second row in the bottom panel). WR: word reading; PV: pattern viewing; FT: finger tapping; R: right; L: left.

Table 1. Similarity of trial-by-trial whole brain FC within each task category and between any two task categories for each individual subject. This similarity was measured with the SC R of pairwise FC maps over the brain mask. The number of voxels within the brain mask varied from subject to subject with a mean brain size of 1085 ± 96 cm^3. WR: word reading; PV: pattern viewing; FT: finger tapping; Min: minimum; Max: maximum; MN: mean; SD: standard deviation.

Subject	Number of Voxels	R within WR Category				R within PV Category				R within FT Category			
		Min	Max	MN	SD	Min	Max	MN	SD	Min	Max	MN	SD
1	23,542	0.12	0.55	0.35	0.13	0.11	0.36	0.22	0.07	0.25	0.53	0.41	0.07
2	27,035	0.10	0.44	0.27	0.09	0.05	0.36	0.20	0.09	0.19	0.57	0.43	0.10
3	29,249	0.03	0.40	0.21	0.09	0.04	0.29	0.18	0.07	0.15	0.42	0.31	0.08
4	22,005	−0.05	0.41	0.15	0.13	0.05	0.48	0.28	0.11	0.20	0.55	0.45	0.09
5	25,877	−0.08	0.31	0.14	0.10	−0.04	0.47	0.27	0.12	0.30	0.63	0.45	0.09
6	23,951	0.06	0.52	0.26	0.12	0.06	0.55	0.31	0.12	0.13	0.64	0.40	0.11
7	23,681	0.00	0.47	0.24	0.13	−0.06	0.41	0.17	0.13	0.12	0.61	0.36	0.11
8	26,840	0.01	0.40	0.16	0.09	0.05	0.42	0.25	0.09	0.05	0.59	0.32	0.15
9	25,528	−0.01	0.48	0.23	0.14	−0.10	0.54	0.20	0.17	0.16	0.47	0.30	0.09
MN	25,301	0.02	0.44	0.22	0.11	0.02	0.43	0.23	0.11	0.17	0.56	0.38	0.10
SD	2229	0.06	0.07	0.07	0.02	0.07	0.09	0.05	0.03	0.07	0.07	0.06	0.02
Subject	**Number of voxels**	**R between WR and PV**				**R between WR and FT**				**R between PV and FT**			
		Min	Max	MN	SD	Min	Max	MN	SD	Min	Max	MN	SD
1	23,542	−0.03	0.36	0.19	0.09	0.01	0.43	0.22	0.10	−0.05	0.41	0.14	0.10
2	27,035	−0.07	0.35	0.14	0.09	−0.10	0.27	0.13	0.09	−0.27	0.28	0.06	0.12
3	29,249	−0.09	0.43	0.14	0.09	−0.00	0.35	0.18	0.10	−0.10	0.29	0.09	0.10
4	22,005	−0.20	0.43	0.11	0.13	−0.28	0.25	−0.04	0.14	−0.22	0.21	−0.00	0.12
5	25,877	−0.16	0.43	0.15	0.14	−0.26	0.34	0.04	0.13	−0.22	0.39	0.09	0.14
6	23,951	−0.07	0.56	0.25	0.13	−0.06	0.49	0.18	0.12	−0.10	0.35	0.14	0.12
7	23,681	−0.16	0.36	0.09	0.11	−0.27	0.47	0.12	0.15	−0.28	0.34	0.02	0.13
8	26,840	−0.18	0.33	0.10	0.11	−0.20	0.27	0.06	0.10	−0.23	0.23	0.00	0.10
9	25,528	−0.23	0.32	0.04	0.12	−0.18	0.38	0.02	0.11	−0.39	0.35	−0.00	0.16
MN	25,301	−0.13	0.40	0.13	0.11	−0.15	0.36	0.10	0.12	−0.20	0.32	0.06	0.12
SD	2229	0.07	0.08	0.06	0.02	0.11	0.09	0.09	0.02	0.11	0.07	0.06	0.02

Each FC map uniquely characterized the whole brain's activity in performing that task trial for that subject. Using FC map as a marker to distinguish tasks based on their FC maps, for each individual subject, the correct rate of identifying these task trials was higher than that of random selection correct rate of 33.3% for each of the three task categories (Figure 3). This correct rate was substantially and consistently higher for the FT task than that for the other two tasks of WR and PV, independent of the subjects. For all subjects, the correct rate of identifying these task trials ranged from 41.2% to 77.4% with a mean of 62.3 ± 13.4% (SD) for the WR trials, 50.0% to 84.5% with a mean of 66.9 ± 10.9% for the PV trials and 83.9% to 99.8% with mean 92.7 ± 5.8% for the FT trials, respectively. A paired t-test analysis showed that this correct rate was significantly larger than that of random selection for each task category (largest $p < 0.0002$). For each subject, we computed the mean SC R within each task category and investigated the association of the correct rate of identifying that task with this mean SC R value. A significant correlation between the R and correct rate was observed across all subjects (r = 0.83, $p = 1.9 \times 10^{-5}$ for N = 27) (Figure 3).

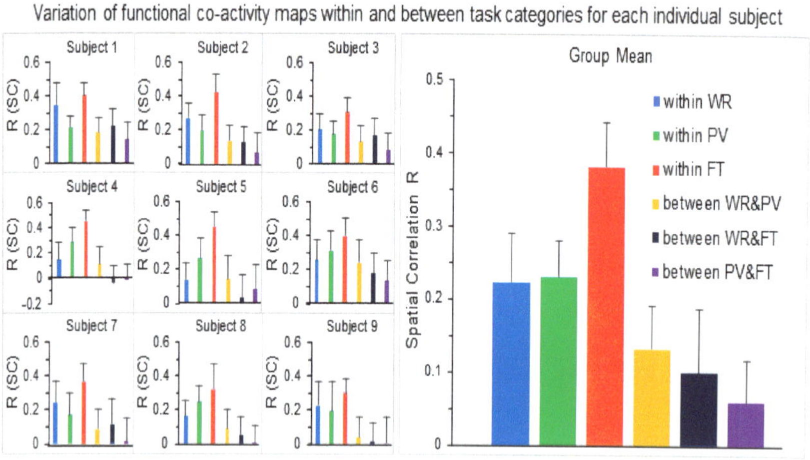

Figure 2. Comparison of the mean spatial correlation (SC) R of pairwise FC maps within each task category and between two task categories for each individual subject (left three columns) and the group-mean values averaged over the nine subjects (right plot). WR: word reading; PV: pattern viewing; FT: finger tapping. The error bars indicate the standard deviations.

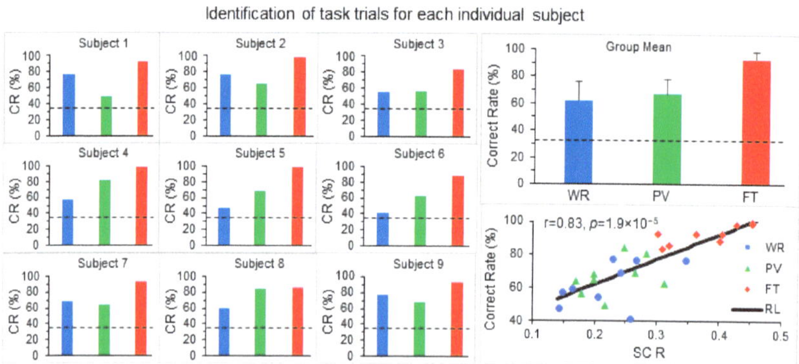

Figure 3. The correct rate (CR) of identifying task trials based on their FC maps for each individual subject (left three columns) and the group mean averaged over the nine subjects (right top plot). The dash lines indicate the random selection CR of 33.3% (1 out of 3 choices). The right bottom plot illustrates the association of the correct rate with the SC R across the subjects. WR: word reading; PV: pattern viewing; FT: finger tapping; RL: regression line. The error bars indicate the standard deviations.

The task-mean FC map for each task category and each subject is illustrated in Figure 4. This task-mean FC map showed a substantial variation not only between different tasks but also from subject to subject (Figure 5). The group-mean SC R was larger within each task category than that between task categories, showing the commonality of these task-evoked FC maps across all subjects. Using each subject's three task-mean FC maps as the three task markers to identify the 24 tasks for the rest eight subjects, the correct rate of task identification was 65.3% for WR, 90.3% for PV and 100% for FT, respectively, substantially higher than the correct rate of 33.3% for random selection.

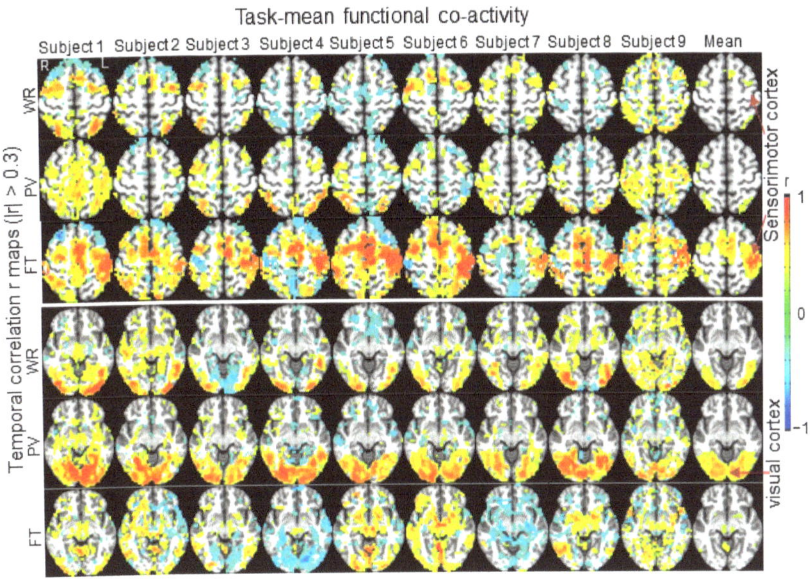

Figure 4. Illustration of the whole brain task-mean FC for each of the three task categories and each subject. For the illustration purpose, these task-mean TC r maps were presented with threshold $|r| > 0.3$. The right-hand FT-evoked activity in both the left sensorimotor cortex and supplementary motor area was consistent for all 9 subjects, though its degree varied substantially from subject to subject (the third row in the top panel). Similarly, the PV-evoked activity in the visual cortex was also consistent for all 9 subjects (the second row in the bottom panel). This whole brain task-mean FC showed a large variation not only between different task types but also from subject to subject. WR: word reading; PV: pattern viewing; FT: finger tapping; R: right; L: left.

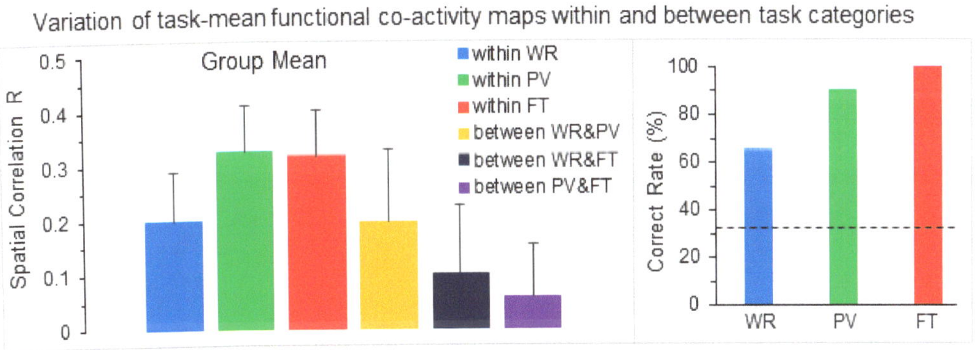

Figure 5. Comparison of the group-mean spatial correlation (SC) R of pairwise task-mean FC maps within each task category and between two task categories averaged over all subjects (left plot). The correct rate of identifying tasks using each subject's three task-mean FC maps as the three task markers to identify the task for the rest eight subjects (right plot). The dash lines indicate the random selection CR of 33.3% (1 out of 3 choices). WR: word reading; PV: pattern viewing; FT: finger tapping. The error bars indicate the standard deviations.

4. Discussion and Conclusions

This study examined trial-by-trial whole brain activity for each individual subject. As expected, the right-hand FT task activated the left sensorimotor cortex and supplementary motor area consistently across all eight trials for each individual subject. The size of this activation in these areas, however, varied not only from trial to trial (Figure 1) but also from subject to subject (Figure 4). Outside the sensorimotor system, the cortical activity varied substantially from trial to trial for all subjects; i.e., some areas showed a positive activity relative to the FT-evoked ideal response for one trial but a negative activity for another trial, demonstrating a varied whole brain activity when performing these repeated FT tasks. This variation in the whole brain activity from trial to trial characterizes the individuality of the human brains in performing these repeated FT tasks. Similar results were observed for the other two tasks of WR and PV with the same conclusion (Figures 1 and 4). The SC R of two FC r maps quantifies the degree of the similarity of the whole brain activity in performing the two tasks, regardless of whether they are the same task or not; i.e., the larger the R value, the smaller the variation in the whole brain activity. Although the FT task showed the smallest variation consistently across all nine subjects, this variation varied substantially from trial to trial for every subject as reflected in their corresponding large values of standard deviation (Figure 2), providing evidence to show the individuality of the human brains in performing these repeated FT tasks. In comparison to the FT task, the WR and PV tasks showed larger variations that also varied from subject to subject, providing further evidence to demonstrate the individuality of the human brains in performing these tasks.

For a given task, the FC r map across the entire brain reflects the whole brain's activity in performing that task and therefore provides a marker to identify the task based on its FC r map. The correct rate of identifying these tasks was higher than that of random selection for each individual subject (Figure 3), and as a group, this correct rate was significantly higher than that of random selection for each task category (largest $p < 0.0002$). As the SC R of any two FC r maps over the entire brain measures the similarity between these two maps and the correct rate of identifying these two tasks depends on this similarity, as expected, the correct rate of identifying these tasks was found to be positively associated with the SC R ($p = 1.9 \times 10^{-5}$) (Figure 3). Among the three tasks of WR, PV and FT, the FT task had the largest R value followed by PV and then WR, indicating a possible inverse relationship of this R value with the degree of simplicity of the task. These results demonstrate the potential of using the presented method to investigate the relationship of the whole brain activity with individual behavioral and clinical traits.

For each subject, the task-mean FC r map of each task category reflects the common brain activity in performing that task. This mean FC map substantially reduced the trial-by-trial variation in the whole brain activity (last column in Figure 1). However, it varied substantially from subject to subject for each of the three tasks (Figure 4), showing a large variation in the whole brain activity from subject to subject when performing the same task. This large variation was also reflected in the large value of standard deviation of the SC R values for both within each task category and between any two task categories (left plot in Figure 5), demonstrating a limited commonality of the whole brain activity across these subjects when performing the same task. It provides further evidence to demonstrate the imperative of developing novel method to investigate the relationship of the whole brain activity with individual behavioral and clinical traits.

It may be worth comparing our presented method with those approaches reported in the literature in regard to the person-specific neuroimaging approach for studying individual brain functioning and its relationship to personal traits. First, to the best of our knowledge, we have not seen any method that can measure trial-by-trial whole brain activity within each task category for each individual subject. Second, most task-fMRI studies comprise group-based analysis aiming to identify regions of common activation or common functional networks across participants. Such an analysis requires the transference of each individual data to a standard template and then their analysis of as a group. This approach is effective and reliable in identifying the commonality of brain functional organization across a group as demonstrated by numerous fMRI studies. However, it may ignore important differences across the participants that might be responsible for individual traits. This is because individual brains may differ in size and shape, functional areas may vary in anatomical location across individuals, and abnormal brain structure may be associated with neurological disorders [21–25]. Accordingly, it is imperative to be able to analyze the fMRI data for each individual subject. Third, although person-specific approaches can effectively and reliably identify individual from group, they use either a pre-defined functional brain atlas or group-based parcellations and/or functional networks defined in a standard template space as their frameworks to carry out their analyses [12,26–30]. In comparison, the analysis of our presented method is conducted in the original MRI space for each individual participant, which might be crucial for applying the BOLD-fMRI technique to daily clinical practice.

In clinical practice, fMRI has been applied to presurgical planning and preoperative risk assessment for brain tumor and epilepsy surgeries [31–33]. To preserve language from surgical damage is a challenging but crucial task. It requires a precise mapping of language areas and associated networks. One main challenge is to dissociate task-associated from language-essential neural activity with fMRI because even a simple task may evoke multiple networks. One language fMRI mapping study with direct cortical stimulation of 40 consecutive patients with gliomas showed a 37.1% sensitivity and 83.4% specificity of the fMRI mapping in identifying the language areas, demonstrating the demand of substantially improved language fMRI mapping in clinical practice [34]. This result is consistent with our observed large variation in the WR task in the whole brain activity for both within each subject (Figures 1 and 2) and between subjects (Figures 4 and 5). As our presented method enables us to analyze trial-by-trial whole brain activity for each individual subject, it may improve the precision of language fMRI mapping. Furthermore, combining artificial intelligence with this method may develop a more effective and reliable method to examine individual human brain functioning that is crucial in daily clinical practice.

5. Conclusions

This study presented a novel method to examine trial-by-trial whole brain activity for each individual subject, providing insights for investigating the individuality of human brains when performing tasks. The results demonstrated a substantially varied whole brain activity from trial to trial for each task category. The degree of this variation was task type-dependent and varied from subject to subject, showing a remarkable individuality of human brains when performing tasks. It demonstrates the potential of using the presented method to investigate the relationship of the whole brain activity with individual behavioral and clinical traits.

Funding: This research received no external funding.

Institutional Review Board Statement: The Institutional Review Board at Michigan State University approved the study (IRB # 03-818, approved on 6 July 2015, and all methods were performed in accordance with the institution's relevant guidelines and regulations.

Informed Consent Statement: Written informed consent was obtained from all subjects prior to the study.

Data Availability Statement: Data are available on request due to restrictions of protecting the privacy of the research data. The data presented in this study are available on request from the corresponding author. The data are not publicly available as they are stored on a publicly inaccessible hard drive.

Acknowledgments: This work was supported by the Michigan State University Radiology Pilot Scan Program.

Conflicts of Interest: The author declares no conflicts of interest.

References

1. Raichle, M.E. Two views of brain function. *Trends Cogn. Sci.* **2010**, *14*, 180–190. [CrossRef]
2. Biswal, B.; Yetkin, F.Z.; Haughton, V.M.; Hyde, J.S. Functional connectivity in the motor cortex of resting human brain using echo-planar MRI. *Magn. Reson. Med.* **1995**, *34*, 537–541. [CrossRef] [PubMed]
3. Raichle, M.E. The restless brain. *Brain Connect* **2011**, *1*, 3–12. [CrossRef] [PubMed]

4. Fox, M.D.; Snyder, A.Z.; Vincent, J.L.; Corbetta, M.; Van Essen, D.C.; Raichle, M.E. The human brain is intrinsically organized into dynamic, anticorrelated functional networks. *Proc. Natl. Acad. Sci. USA* **2005**, *102*, 9673–9678. [CrossRef] [PubMed]
5. Thomas Yeo, B.T.; Krienen, F.M.; Sepulcre, J.; Sabuncu, M.R.; Lashkari, D.; Hollinshead, M.; Roffman, J.L.; Smoller, J.W.; Zöllei, L.; Polimeni, J.R.; et al. The organization of the human cerebral cortex estimated by intrinsic functional connectivity. *J. Neurophysiol.* **2011**, *106*, 1125–1165. [CrossRef]
6. Buckner, R.L.; Krienen, F.M.; Castellanos, A.; Diaz, J.C.; Yeo, B.T.T. The organization of the human cerebellum estimated by intrinsic functional connectivity. *J. Neurophysiol.* **2011**, *106*, 2322–2345. [CrossRef]
7. Calhoun, V.D.; Miller, R.; Pearlson, G.; Adalı, T. The chronnectome: Time-varying connectivity networks as the next frontier in fMRI data discovery. *Neuron* **2014**, *84*, 262–274. [CrossRef]
8. Xiong, Z.; Tian, C.; Zeng, X.; Huang, J.; Wang, R. The Relationship of Functional Connectivity of the Sensorimotor and Visual Cortical Networks Between Resting and Task States. *Front. Neurosci.* **2020**, *14*, 592720. [CrossRef]
9. Huang, J. Greater brain activity during the resting state and the control of activation during the performance of tasks. *Sci. Rep.* **2019**, *9*, 5027. [CrossRef]
10. Ogawa, S.; Lee, T.M.; Kay, A.R.; Tank, D.W. Brain magnetic resonance imaging with contrast dependent on blood oxygenation. *Proc. Natl. Acad. Sci. USA* **1990**, *87*, 9868–9872. [CrossRef] [PubMed]
11. Kwong, K.K.; Belliveau, J.W.; Chesler, D.A.; Goldberg, I.E.; Weisskoff, R.M.; Poncelet, B.P.; Kennedy, D.N.; Hoppel, B.E.; Cohen, M.S.; Turner, R. Dynamic magnetic resonance imaging of human brain activity during primary sensory stimulation. *Proc. Natl. Acad. Sci. USA* **1992**, *89*, 5675–5679. [CrossRef]
12. Finn, E.S.; Shen, X.; Scheinost, D.; Rosenberg, M.D.; Huang, J.; Chun, M.M.; Papademetris, X.; Constable, R.T. Functional connectome fingerprinting: Identifying individuals using patterns of brain connectivity. *Nat. Neurosci.* **2015**, *18*, 1664–1671. [CrossRef] [PubMed]
13. Kong, R.; Li, J.; Orban, C.; Sabuncu, M.R.; Liu, H.; Schaefer, A.; Sun, N.; Zuo, X.-N.; Holmes, A.J.; Eickhoff, S.B.; et al. Spatial Topography of Individual-Specific Cortical Networks Predicts Human Cognition, Personality, and Emotion. *Cereb. Cortex* **2019**, *29*, 2533–2551. [CrossRef] [PubMed]
14. Salehi, M.; Karbasi, A.; Barron, D.S.; Scheinost, D.; Constable, R.T. Individualized functional networks reconfigure with cognitive state. *Neuroimage* **2020**, *206*, 116233. [CrossRef]
15. Michon, K.J.; Khammash, D.; Simmonite, M.; Hamlin, A.M.; Polk, T.A. Person-specific and precision neuroimaging: Current methods and future directions. *Neuroimage* **2022**, *263*, 119589. [CrossRef]
16. Huang, J. Human brain functional areas of unitary pooled activity discovered with fMRI. *Sci. Rep.* **2018**, *8*, 2388. [CrossRef]
17. Huang, J. Dynamic activity of human brain task-specific networks. *Sci. Rep.* **2020**, *10*, 7851. [CrossRef] [PubMed]
18. Huang, J. A Holistic Analysis of Individual Brain Activity Revealed the Relationship of Brain Areal Activity with the Entire Brain's Activity. *Brain Sci.* **2022**, *13*, 6. [CrossRef]
19. Cox, R.W. AFNI: Software for analysis and visualization of functional magnetic resonance neuroimages. *Comput. Biomed. Res.* **1996**, *29*, 162–173. [CrossRef]
20. Friston, K.J.; Holmes, A.P.; Worsley, K.J.; Poline, J.-P.; Frith, C.D.; Frackowiak, R.S.J. Statistical parametric maps in functional imaging: A general linear approach. *Hum. Brain Mapp.* **1995**, *2*, 189–210. [CrossRef]
21. Amunts, K.; Zilles, K. Architectonic Mapping of the Human Brain beyond Brodmann. *Neuron* **2015**, *88*, 1086–1107. [CrossRef] [PubMed]
22. Malikovic, A.; Amunts, K.; Schleicher, A.; Mohlberg, H.; Eickhoff, S.B.; Wilms, M.; Palomero-Gallagher, N.; Armstrong, E.; Zilles, K. Cytoarchitectonic analysis of the human extrastriate cortex in the region of V5/MT+: A probabilistic, stereotaxic map of area hOc5. *Cereb. Cortex* **2007**, *17*, 562–574. [CrossRef] [PubMed]
23. Frost, M.A.; Goebel, R. Measuring structural-functional correspondence: Spatial variability of specialised brain regions after macro-anatomical alignment. *Neuroimage* **2012**, *59*, 1369–1381. [CrossRef] [PubMed]
24. Datta, R.; Detre, J.A.; Aguirre, G.K.; Cucchiara, B. Absence of changes in cortical thickness in patients with migraine. *Cephalalgia* **2011**, *31*, 1452–1458. [CrossRef] [PubMed]
25. Özkan, E.; Gürsoy-Özdemir, Y. Occipital bending in migraine with visual aura. *Headache* **2021**, *61*, 1562–1567. [CrossRef]
26. Liu, J.; Liao, X.; Xia, M.; He, Y. Chronnectome fingerprinting: Identifying individuals and predicting higher cognitive functions using dynamic brain connectivity patterns. *Hum. Brain Mapp.* **2018**, *39*, 902–915. [CrossRef]
27. Miranda-Dominguez, O.; Feczko, E.; Grayson, D.S.; Walum, H.; Nigg, J.T.; Fair, D.A. Heritability of the human connectome: A connectotyping study. *Netw. Neurosci.* **2018**, *2*, 175–199. [CrossRef]
28. Wang, X.; Li, Q.; Zhao, Y.; He, Y.; Ma, B.; Fu, Z.; Li, S. Decomposition of individual-specific and individual-shared components from resting-state functional connectivity using a multi-task machine learning method. *Neuroimage* **2021**, *238*, 118252. [CrossRef]
29. Ooi, L.Q.R.; Chen, J.; Zhang, S.; Kong, R.; Tam, A.; Li, J.; Dhamala, E.; Zhou, J.H.; Holmes, A.J.; Yeo, B.T.T. Comparison of individualized behavioral predictions across anatomical, diffusion and functional connectivity MRI. *Neuroimage* **2022**, *263*, 119636. [CrossRef] [PubMed]
30. Domhof, J.W.; Eickhoff, S.B.; Popovych, O.V. Reliability and subject specificity of personalized whole-brain dynamical models. *Neuroimage* **2022**, *257*, 119321. [CrossRef] [PubMed]

31. Black, D.; Vachha, B.; Mian, A.; Faro, S.; Maheshwari, M.; Sair, H.; Petrella, J.; Pillai, J.; Welker, K. American Society of Functional Neuroradiology-Recommended fMRI Paradigm Algorithms for Presurgical Language Assessment. *AJNR Am. J. Neuroradiol.* **2017**, *38*, E65–E73. [CrossRef] [PubMed]
32. Benjamin, C.F.A.; Li, A.X.; Blumenfeld, H.; Constable, R.T.; Alkawadri, R.; Bickel, S.; Helmstaedter, C.; Meletti, S.; Bronen, R.; Warfield, S.K.; et al. Presurgical language fMRI: Clinical practices and patient outcomes in epilepsy surgical planning. *Hum. Brain Mapp.* **2018**, *39*, 2777–2785. [CrossRef] [PubMed]
33. Agarwal, S.; Sair, H.I.; Gujar, S.; Pillai, J.J. Language Mapping With fMRI: Current Standards and Reproducibility. *Top. Magn. Reson. Imaging* **2019**, *28*, 225–233. [CrossRef] [PubMed]
34. Kuchcinski, G.; Mellerio, C.; Pallud, J.; Dezamis, E.; Turc, G.; Rigaux-Viodé, O.; Malherbe, C.; Roca, P.; Leclerc, X.; Varlet, P.; et al. Three-tesla functional MR language mapping: Comparison with direct cortical stimulation in gliomas. *Neurology* **2015**, *84*, 560–568. [CrossRef]

Disclaimer/Publisher's Note: The statements, opinions and data contained in all publications are solely those of the individual author(s) and contributor(s) and not of MDPI and/or the editor(s). MDPI and/or the editor(s) disclaim responsibility for any injury to people or property resulting from any ideas, methods, instructions or products referred to in the content.

brain sciences

MDPI

Article

Distinguishing Laparoscopic Surgery Experts from Novices Using EEG Topographic Features

Takahiro Manabe [1], F.N.U. Rahul [2], Yaoyu Fu [3], Xavier Intes [2,4], Steven D. Schwaitzberg [5], Suvranu De [6], Lora Cavuoto [3] and Anirban Dutta [1,*]

1 School of Engineering, University of Lincoln, Lincoln LN6 7TS, UK; tmanabe@u.northwestern.edu
2 Centre for Modeling, Simulation, and Imaging in Medicine, Rensselaer Polytechnic Institute, Troy, MI 12180, USA; rahul@rpi.edu (F.R.); intesx@rpi.edu (X.I.)
3 Department of Industrial and Systems Engineering, University at Buffalo, Buffalo, NY 14260, USA; yaoyufu@buffalo.edu (Y.F.); loracavu@buffalo.edu (L.C.)
4 Department of Biomedical Engineering, Rensselaer Polytechnic Institute, Troy, MI 12180, USA
5 School of Medicine and Biomedical Sciences, University at Buffalo, Buffalo, NY 14203, USA; schwaitz@buffalo.edu
6 College of Engineering, Florida A&M University-Florida State University, Tallahassee, FL 32310, USA; sde@eng.famu.fsu.edu
* Correspondence: adutta@case.edu

Abstract: The study aimed to differentiate experts from novices in laparoscopic surgery tasks using electroencephalogram (EEG) topographic features. A microstate-based common spatial pattern (CSP) analysis with linear discriminant analysis (LDA) was compared to a topography-preserving convolutional neural network (CNN) approach. Expert surgeons (N = 10) and novice medical residents (N = 13) performed laparoscopic suturing tasks, and EEG data from 8 experts and 13 novices were analysed. Microstate-based CSP with LDA revealed distinct spatial patterns in the frontal and parietal cortices for experts, while novices showed frontal cortex involvement. The 3D CNN model (ESNet) demonstrated a superior classification performance (accuracy > 98%, sensitivity 99.30%, specificity 99.70%, F1 score 98.51%, MCC 97.56%) compared to the microstate based CSP analysis with LDA (accuracy ~90%). Combining spatial and temporal information in the 3D CNN model enhanced classifier accuracy and highlighted the importance of the parietal–temporal–occipital association region in differentiating experts and novices.

Keywords: fundamentals of laparoscopic surgery; electroencephalogram; skill classification; common spatial pattern; temporal–spatial pattern recognition; deep neural networks

1. Introduction

Laparoscopic surgery training is a comprehensive module under the Fundamentals of Laparoscopic Surgery (FLS) curriculum, aimed at equipping medical professionals, scientists, and doctors with basic surgical skills required for successful laparoscopic procedures. FLS is a joint program by the American Gastrointestinal and Surgery Association and the American Academy of Surgery for general surgery [1]. FLS certification involves five psychomotor tasks of increasing complexity: pegboard transfer, pattern cutting, placement of a ligating loop, suturing with extracorporeal knot tying, and suturing with intracorporeal knot tying. This training focuses on cognitive and psychological abilities essential for minimally invasive surgery and serves as a standardised assessment of physicians' capabilities where brain correlates are important to robustly identify expertise [2].

To evaluate brain correlates of FLS skills, it is proposed that the brain forms a cognitive-perceptual mental model [3,4] during the initial stages of the skill acquisition in a novel laparoscopy environment [5–8]. Here, Fitts and Posner proposed a three-stage model for motor skill acquisition, comprising the cognitive stage, the associative stage, and the autonomous stage [9]. During these stages for motor skill acquisition, the brain–behaviour relationship can be explored based on portable brain imaging. Brain circuit mechanisms, driven by motor skill proficiency, involve selective attention and cortical alterations in motor planning and execution [6]. For example, specific brain mechanisms [10] subserved by motor skill proficiency may represent dissociable selective attention or local excitability alterations in the cortex during motor planning and execution that are postulated to be driven by a supplementary motor area, premotor cortex, and cerebellum [11]—all communicating via the thalamus [12] and the corticothalamic loops [13,14]. In this study, we hypothesised that these semi-stable brain states involving selective attention and cortical alterations in motor planning and execution can be estimated based on the topography of electroencephalogram (EEG). The majority of contemporary brain–computer interfaces utilizing EEG rely on machine learning algorithms [15] and a wide array of classifier types is employed within this domain including facial expressions as control commands [16].

In this study, it is postulated that while experts will already have a cognitive perceptual model for FLS task performance based on their prior experience, the novices will start building the cognitive perceptual model on their first exposure to the FLS task [3,4]. Semi-stable brain states have been analysed in prior studies based on microstates [17], which can be estimated based on the scalp potential field or EEG topography [18], and are differentially modulated by the vigilance level [19]. Microstates approach to analyse brain states has an a priori assumption that only one spatial map accurately defines the brain's global state at a given time and that the residuals are considered noise [18]. This microstate-based analysis has been applied to error-based learning using EEG in conjunction with functional near-infrared spectroscopy during a complex surgical motor task [20]. Based on related prior studies [14,21], we postulated in this study that the EEG topography during FLS suturing with intracorporal knot tying task will differ between experts and novices. First, we applied conventional common spatial pattern (CSP) approach, one of the most common methods for feature extraction in brain–computer interfaces [22], to classify two skill levels, experts and novices. We improved the traditional CSP method that is known to suffer from noise sensitivity due to the L2 norm in its optimisation problem to find a spatial filter [23]. We developed a microstate-based CSP approach that performed better due to a metacriterion that favours the highest signal-to-noise ratio [24]. We presented these preliminary results using microstate-based CSP approach at the Interservice/Industry Training, Simulation, and Education Conference (I/ITSEC) 2022 [21]. In our I/ITSEC presentation, we focused on a cohort of 10 expert surgeons and 10 novice medical residents. Through the application of a linear discriminant analysis with 10-fold cross-validation, we successfully attained a classification accuracy exceeding 90%, utilizing spatial pattern vectors extracted from the scalp. In this paper, we present a more advanced convolutional neural network (CNN) based approach with Grad-CAM analysis [25] and compare the results with our microstate-based CSP approach.

Our current study is motivated by prior studies that show non-Markovian and nonstationary microstates [26] can classify cognitive states using the attention-based time series deep learning framework [27]. However, the challenge remains in pre-selecting scalp potential topographies (microstates) that are considered stable [18], while short periods of unstable EEG topographies may occur, e.g., during errors. Instead of preselecting EEG microstates, one can use EEG topography as 3D tensor input for attention features in a CNN, e.g., see ESNet [28], where topography-preserving EEG-based temporal attentive pooling may be neurophysiologically interpretable [29] using Grad-CAM analysis [25]. Therefore, we adapted ESNet [28] to classify experts versus novices and compared the temporally important topography-preserving time segments with the microstate-based CSP approach [21] for mechanistic insights into skill learning [30]. Mechanistic insights were guided by prior studies [30,31] using functional near-infrared spectroscopy (fNIRS) that found cortical activation in the right prefrontal cortex, the right precentral gyrus, and the right postcentral gyrus at the start of the FLS task. Then, the left inferior frontal gyrus, the optical part, the left superior frontal gyrus, the medial orbital, the left postcentral gyrus, the gyrus, the left superior temporal gyrus, right superior frontal gyrus, and the medial orbital cortical areas of the cortical areas of the orbital showed significant differences between experts and novices in the error epochs [20]. In the current study, we analysed a subset of participants from prior studies [20,30] where simultaneous EEG measurements were conducted for our EEG topographic feature analysis.

2. Methods

2.1. Subjects and Experimental Setup

The study received approval from the Institutional Review Board of the University at Buffalo, USA, and all procedures adhered to local research regulations for human subjects. Thirteen neurologically normal novice medical students (seven females) and ten experienced surgeons (five females), all right-handed, participated after providing written informed consent. The EEG data utilised in this study are a subset of a previously published study [20,30] where multimodal fNIRS-EEG data were collected.

The experienced surgeons, with 1 to 25 years of expertise in FLS laparoscopic suturing tasks, were compared to novices new to FLS suturing with intracorporal knot tying. A prior study [30] demonstrated a statistically significant superior performance of experienced surgeons (overall score: 370.4, SD: 61.3) compared to novices (overall score: 84.2, SD: 65.3). Participants received verbal instructions and were equipped with laparoscopic tools for the task, which involved suturing through two marks in a Penrose drain and tying specific knots using needle drivers operated by both hands. The task began with the 'start' command, recorded in the multimodal data, and concluded when the subject cut both ends of the suture within a 180 s timeframe.

A customised multimodal fNIRS-EEG montage with 32 active gel electrodes (Figure 1A) was used to record brain activation signals. The EEG signals were captured by a wireless LiveAmp system (Brain Vision, Brain Vision, LLC-515 N. Greenfield Parkway, Suite 100, Garner, NC 27529, USA) at a rate of 500 Hz through 32 channels, as indicated by the grey 'E' discs in Figure 1A.

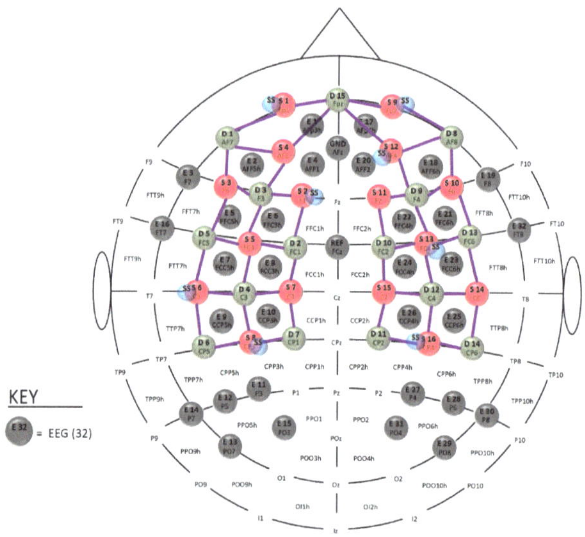

(A)

Figure 1. *Cont.*

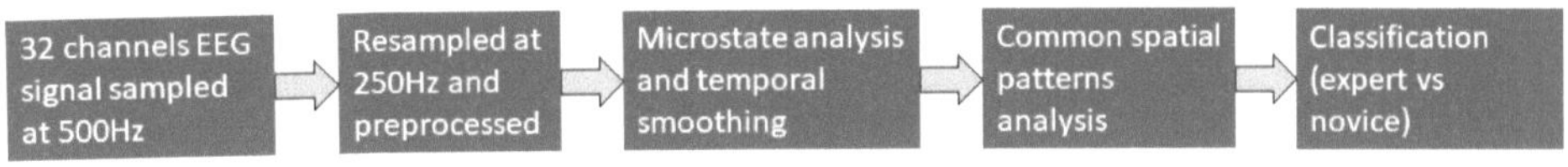

(**B**)

2 mins Rest	3 mins Task	2 mins Rest	3 mins Task	2 mins Rest	3 mins Task	2 mins Rest

(**C**)

Figure 1. (**A**) Multimodal sensor montage where the 32 active EEG gel electrodes (E1–E32) are shown with grey discs. The fNIRS source (S1–S16) and detectors (D1–D15) were not used in the current study. (**B**) EEG data processing pipeline in EEGLab and BCILab for the CSP-based classification of experts versus novices. (**C**) Repeated measures of FLS task (3 min) with rest periods (2 min).

2.2. Data Preprocessing in EEGLab

The EEG data underwent comprehensive pre-processing and offline analysis using the EEGLab toolbox, an open-source software (https://sccn.ucsd.edu/eeglab/index.php accessed on 27 November 2023), designed for microstate analysis [18]. Initially, the data were downsampled to 250 Hz and high pass filtered at 1 Hz. To eliminate line noise, the 'cleanline' function was applied, followed by the 'clean_rawdata' function to identify and reject problematic channels. The interpolation of bad channels was accomplished using spherical splines [32] within the 'clean_rawdata' function, followed by re-referencing the EEG time series to the global average.

Task epochs were defined from the 'start' trigger by the experimenter, marking the initiation of the FLS task for each subject. The data then underwent artefact subspace reconstruction (ASR) using default settings in EEGLab, followed by re-referencing the EEG time series to the global average. ASR, an automated method, effectively removed transient EEG artefacts [33]. The default ASR parameter value of 20 was used, balancing the removal of non-brain signals with retaining brain activity, with the optimal range typically between 20 and 30 [33].

To focus on cortical sources corresponding with fNIRS HbO activity [20], a Laplacian spatial filter was applied to eliminate volume conduction from subcortical sources. Two expert subjects were excluded from the analysis due to the presence of $\geq$5 bad channels, as reliable microstate analysis requires the maximum number of bad channels to be less than five per subject [34]. Consequently, eight expert subjects remained in the study.

2.3. Data Processing of EEGLab and BCILab for Microstate-Based CSP Analysis

Microstate analysis was performed using the EEGlab toolbox [35] after aggregating EEG data during the FLS task from all experts (N = 8) and novices (N = 13), which is detailed in our published study [20]. In this study, we investigated the FLS complex task onset response where a previous study [36] demonstrated that the concentration of oxyhemoglobin peaked within 10 seconds during complex motor actions. Therefore, a 10 s duration was deemed sufficient for investigating the FLS complex task onset response using EEG and functional near-infrared spectroscopy [20]. FLS task related EEG dynamics will continue beyond the initial 10 seconds, which was not investigated in this study. First, we identified EEG microstate prototypes based on modified K-means clustering in EEGlab. The modified clustering of K-means was based on the goodness of fit of the microstate segmentation determined from the global explained variance (GEV) and the cross-validation criterion (CV). Here, the GEV criterion should theoretically become monotonically larger with increasing number of clusters [35]. The modified clustering of K-means in EEGlab found topographical maps of polarity-invariant microstate prototypes [35] from spontaneous EEG data during the FLS task (and the rest periods between the trials). Here, global field power (GFP) peaks are used to segment the EEG time series. The minimum peak distance was set at 10 ms (default) and 1000 randomly selected peaks (default) per subject were used for segmentation. Then, we rejected the GFP peaks that exceeded the standard deviation of all GFPs of all maps one time to segment the EEG data into a predefined number (2 to 8) of microstates. Here, the goal is to maximise the similarity between the EEG samples and the prototypes of the microstates they are assigned to using the modified K-means algorithm [35]. The modified K-means algorithm also sorts the microstate prototypes in decreasing GEV. We had set 100 random numbers of initialisations and 1000 maximum iterations for the modified K-means algorithm with 1×10^{-6} (default) as the relative threshold of convergence [35]. These microstates provided prototypes for subsequent microstate-based CSP analysis [21].

Microstate labels were applied to EEG samples from experts and novices based on topographical similarity (called backfitting) using the EEGlab toolbox [35]. Modified K-means algorithm [35] benefits of using k-means++ [37] for initialisation and the squared Euclidean metric for similarity calculation. Since short periods of unstable EEG topographies can occur, we applied temporal smoothing. Then, the temporally smoothed EEG topographies of experts (N = 8) and novices (N = 13) at the start of the FLS task in a 10 s time window were subjected to CSP analysis and classification using BCILab [38]. Here, if X_1 and X_2 are the EEG topographies from the experts and novices at the start of the FLS task, viz., X_1 is a matrix of rows 250 Hz × 10 s (=2500 data points) and columns 32 channels, then, the desired spatial filter is obtained by, $\underset{w}{\text{argmax}} J(w) = \frac{w^T X_1^T X_1 w}{w^T X_2^T X_2 w} = \frac{w^T C_1 w}{w^T C_2 w}$, where w denotes the spatial filter, and C_1 and C_2 represent the covariance matrices of X_1 and X_2, respectively. Using the Lagrange multiplier approach, the optimisation problem can be written as, $L(\lambda, w) = w^T C_1 w - \lambda(w^T C_2 w)$, where λ is the Lagrange multiplier. The optimisation problem to find the spatial filter, w, requires the derivative set to zero, i.e., $\frac{\delta L}{\delta w} = 2w^T C_1 - 2\lambda w^T C_2 = 0$. The solution to this optimisation problem are the eigenvectors, $M = C_2^{-1} C_1$, representing the spatial pattern vectors on the scalp. Here, the regularised CSP can improve robustness in small sample setting [39], and the largest eigenvector from, $M_1 = (C_2 + \alpha K)^{-1} C_1$ and $M_2 = (C_1 + \alpha K)^{-1} C_2$, represent the spatial pattern vectors on the scalp with K assumed as an identity matrix [40]. Then, the classification was performed using a simple linear discriminant analysis (LDA) with a 10-fold cross-validation. The computational pipeline, starting from the raw EEG data to the classification, is shown in Figure 1B. Figure 1C shows the repeated measure design with 3 min for the FLS task and 2 min for the rest period.

2.4. Data Processing for Topography-Preserving CNN Approach

The procedure to convert the EEG data into a cuboid tensor is represented in Figure 2. Since spatiotemporal patterns were considered distinctive between experts and novices, spatiotemporal patterns were represented as 3D data that contained spatial information in two dimensions as well as temporal information in the third dimension. The EEG time series obtained from each channel was first downsampled at 120 Hz [28] and then projected to the corresponding position (from the scalp EEG montage; see Figure 1A) into a 2D image of a 16 × 16 square grid (height × width) using an azimuthal equidistant projection. We followed [28] so the EEG data during the FLS task from 2 s before the start trigger was divided into 3 s segments using a 1-second sliding window. The process was repeated in all sliding time steps, and the empty locations on the 16 × 16 grid between the projected electrode locations were interpolated using the griddata() function, Matlab (Mathworks, Inc., Natick, MA, USA) built-in function. Here, the griddata() function grids process 2D or 3D scattered data with a desired interpolation method. We used the v4 interpolation method in Matlab (Mathworks, Inc., USA) for better quality instead of cubic spline interpolation in ESNet [28]. Finally, the EEG data was shaped as a 3D tensor that included spatio-temporal information (that is, height × width × time). Here, we generated $X^{eeg} \in \mathbb{R}^{16 \times 16 \times 360}$ 3D EEG image for each 3-seconds (360 data points) EEG time window according to ESNet [28]. Therefore, 21 subjects (8 Experts and 13 Novices), with each subject performing the task three times (trials or reps), provided 21 subjects × 3 reps × 180 time windows (=11,340 cuboid tensors).

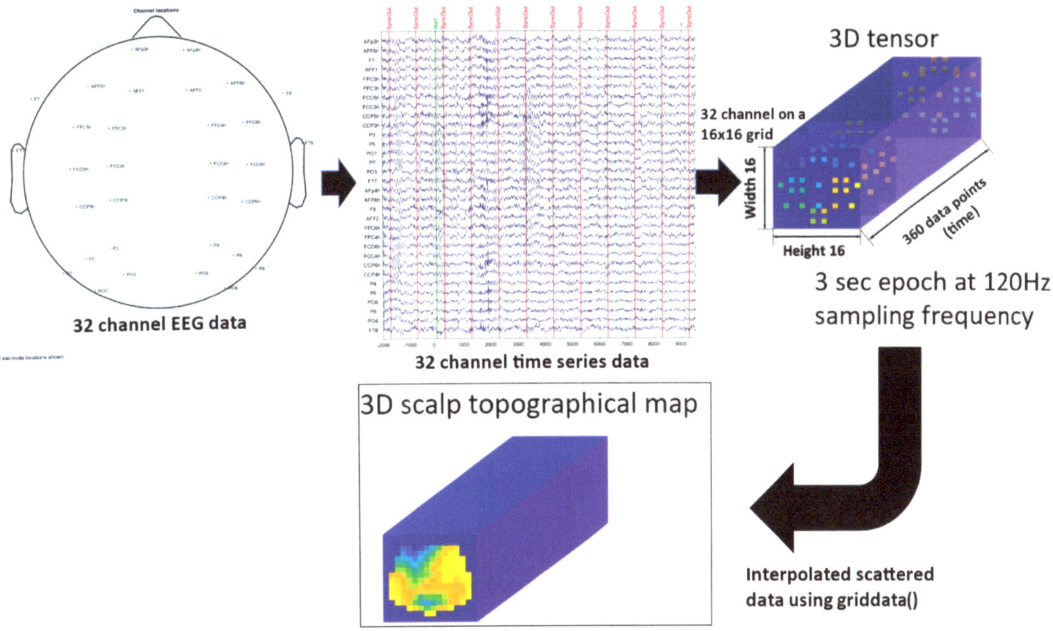

Figure 2. Transformation of 3 s of EEG time window into a 3D tensor for CNN analysis.

2.5. CNN for the 3D-EEG Tensor Classification of Expert versus Novice

A 3D CNN model, called ESNet [28], takes into account both spatial and temporal information by implementing a specific pooling layer called temporal attentive pooling (TAP) layer that compresses temporal information efficiently. The structure of the 3D CNN model is shown in Figure 3, which we adapted from ESNet [28]. The model consisted of three convolutional layers, and each of them is followed by a rectified linear unit (ReLU) activation function. Each layer inputs the channel information and doubles it as an output. Short-length kernels and strides were used for spatial information (i.e., the first and second axes) in each convolutional layer. Then, for temporal information (i.e., the third axis), short length kernels and stride were used in the second and third convolutional layers, while longer kernels and stride lengths were used in the first convolutional layer [28]. In summary, we determined the size of [kernel, stride] = [(2, 2, 10), (2, 2, 4)] for the first layer, [(2, 2, 2), (2, 2, 2)] for the second layer, and [(2, 2, 3), (2, 2, 2)] for the third layer. After the three convolutional layers, the TAP layer followed an efficient pooling process in the CNN model. The TAP layer first conducts Spatial Attentive Pooling (SAP), where the characteristic after the third convolutional layer is multiplied element by element by a trainable parameter, $\varphi \in \mathbb{R}^{2\times2\times46\times64}$, and then computes the sum along the spatial axis for the characteristic, resulting in the SAP feature shape of $\mathbb{R}^{1\times1\times46\times64}$. Then, the SAP feature was classified by a Fully Connected (FC) layer, followed by the Softmax activation function, and multiplied element by the original feature after the third convolutional layer, and then, the sum along the temporal axis for the result was calculated. In total, the entire TAP process converted the shape of the original feature $\mathbb{R}^{2\times2\times46\times64}$ to $\mathbb{R}^{2\times2\times1\times64}$, providing a larger weight to the relevant temporal information and, therefore, compressing it efficiently. The detailed structure and concept of the TAP layer are described in the original paper [28]. Then, the feature after the TAP layer was passed through the FC layer, followed by the ReLU function, Dropout, and Softmax layer. In addition to the dropout layer, we further implemented the batch normalisation between each convolutional layer and the ReLU function, after the TAP layer and FC layer and the ReLU function. The L2 regularisation was also adapted in a kernel and bias at each FC layer with a regularisation factor of 0.01 to prevent overfitting. The mechanistic insights were based on Gradient-weighted Class Activation Mapping (Grad-CAM) for "visual explanations" of decisions from our CNN-based model [25]. GradCAM uses the gradients of the EEG map flowing into the final convolutional layer to produce a coarse localisation map highlighting the salient regions for expert versus novice classification.

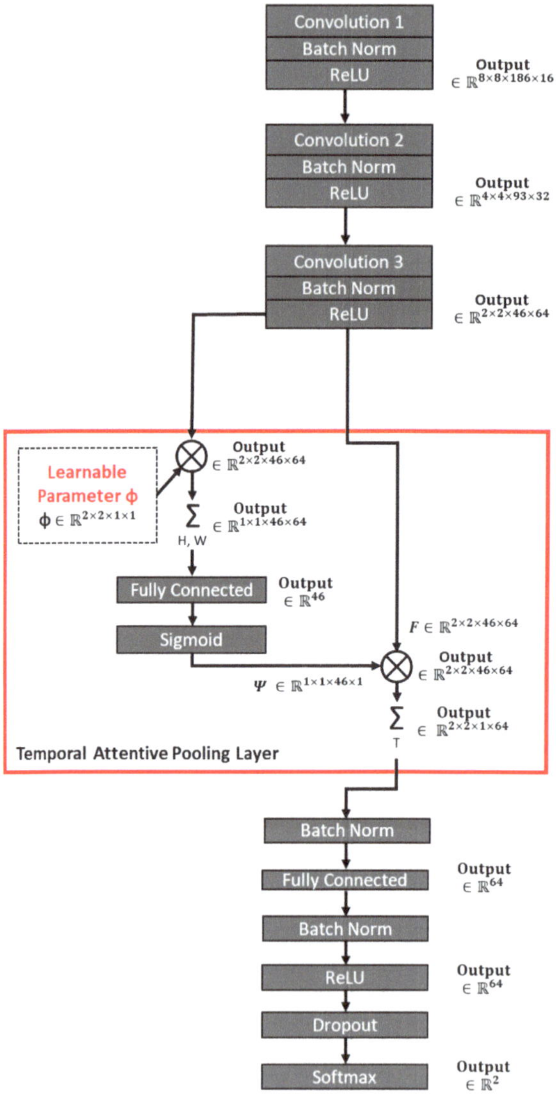

Figure 3. Our customised ESNet [28] architecture. The red box shows a temporal attentive pooling layer that was designed to compress temporal information extracted by consecutive convolutional layers efficiently. This pooling layer assigns higher weights to crucial time segments, enhancing the model's focus on temporally significant features within the 3D feature representation.

2.6. CNN Classification & Evaluation Criteria

We applied our customised ESNet [28], as shown in Figure 3, to classify experts versus novices with a five-fold cross-validation. In the five-fold cross-validation and testing, we divided the participants data in the 9:1 ratio, in which 10% of the total experts (8 subjects × 3 reps × 180 time windows) and novices (13 subjects × 3 reps × 180 time windows) data were used as holdout test data, and 90% of the total data were used for ten repeats of five-fold cross-validation. In each five-fold cross-validation, we trained the model using 80% of the 90% of total experts (8 subjects × 3 reps × 180 time windows) and novices (13 subjects × 3 reps × 180 time windows) data and cross-validated the model using 20% of the 90% total data, as shown in Figure 4. In each training epoch, the batch size was set at 32, and the training epoch was repeated 200 times, with five iterations within a five-fold cross-validation, with the learning rate set at 0.001. Then, for testing, this five-fold cross-validation was repeated 10 times that generated a new training and validation splits of the trials, at random, where we initialised the weights each time using the Keras initialiser function 'glorot_uniform', in which random values are pulled as initialised variables. The results of each iteration were evaluated with the holdout test data (10% of the total data) using indices: accuracy, F1 score, Mathews correlation coefficient (MCC), sensitivity, and specificity. The definition of F1 score, MCC, sensitivity, and specificity are as follows:

$$F1 = \frac{(precision) \times (recall)}{(precision) + (recall)} \times 2$$

$$MCC = \frac{(TP \times TN - FP \times FN)}{\sqrt{(TP+FP)(TP+FN)(TN+FP)(TN+FN)}}$$

$$Sensitivity = Recall = \frac{TP}{TP+FN}$$

$$Specificity = \frac{TN}{FP+TN}$$

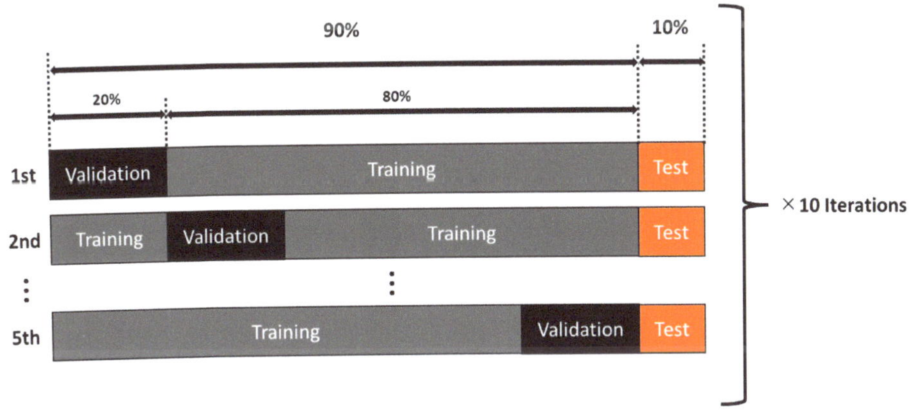

Figure 4. Data distribution for the five-fold cross-validation procedure that was repeated 10 times that generated a new training and validation splits of the trials, at random. Test data, shown in orange, remained the same for all the 10 repeats of the five-fold cross-validation.

Here, precision is shown as follows:

$$Precision = \frac{TP}{FP+FP}$$

Here, TP, FP, FN, and TN are the elements of the confusion matrix for binary classification.

$$C = [TP,\ FP;\ FN,\ TN]$$

Moreover, TP (true positive) and FP (false positive) are the ratios of data correctly and falsely classified as positive data (i.e., Expert), respectively. Then, FN (false negative) and TN (true negative) are the numbers of data correctly and falsely classified as negative data (i.e., Novice), respectively.

3. Results

3.1. Microstate-Based CSP Classification of Expert versus Novice

We selected six microstate EEG prototypes based on the global explained variance (GEV) and the cross-validation criterion (CV) that was published earlier [20]. Here, the CV criterion, which points to the best clustering solution at its smallest value, reaches the minimum value for six microstates that are shown in Figure 5, sorted in decreasing GEV. As expected for a visuomotor task, the highest GEV is for microstate 1, corresponding to activation of the visual cortex (visual imagery [41]). The six microstate prototypes were backfitted to the EEG for 10 s at the start of the FLS task where it is postulated to be the start of building a cognitive-perceptual model [3,4] by the novices [6].

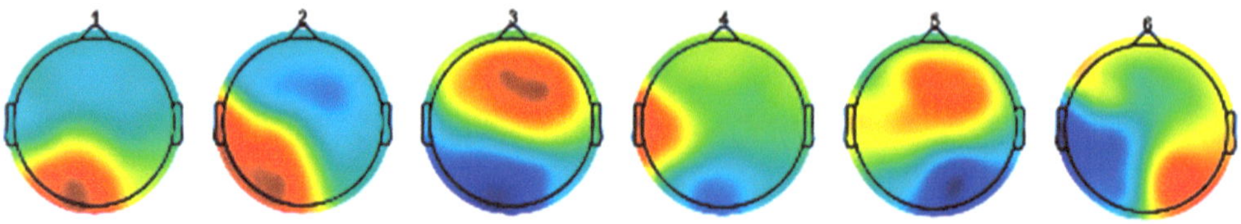

Figure 5. The 1–6 EEG microstate prototypes are sorted by decreasing global explained variance. These six EEG microstates are thought to represent basic building blocks of cognitive and perceptual processes during FLS skill learning [20].

The global field power (GFP) of the first active microstates at the start of the FLS task was subjected to CSP analysis to find the spatial filters. Then, after applying spatial filters to the expert and novice EEG data and extracting features from them, the experts and novices were classified by LDA. We compared our microstate-based regularised CSP approach with conventional regularised CSP, where the microstate-based regularised CSP approach achieved a classification accuracy of 90.84% compared to 82.26% with conventional regularised CSP. The scalp topography for the first spatial filter using microstate based regularised CSP approach identified topographical maps from microstates 2 and 4 as the most significant eigenvectors. Also, our microstate based regularised CSP approach achieved classification accuracy greater than 90%. Here, microstate analysis applied a meta-criterion favouring the highest signal-to-noise ratio [24] that improved the accuracy when compared to that of conventional regularised CSP. Furthermore, microstates 2 and 4 as the most significant eigenvectors illustrated the importance of EEG electrodes in the parietal–temporal–occipital region for the classification of experts and novices during the FLS task. Microstate 2 was dominant in novices, while microstate 4 was dominant in the experts. We also computed the Kappa coefficient, which is a statistical method to measure the degree of agreement between classes. The Kappa coefficient method assigns zero to random classification and one to perfect classification [42], which is a more robust criterion than classification accuracy by considering random agreement. The microstate based regularised CSP approach outperformed conventional regularised CSP with a Kappa coefficient of more than 0.9. Importantly, the regularised CSP approach identified topographical maps from microstates 2 and 4 as the largest eigenvectors (from $M_2 = (C_1 + \alpha K)^{-1}C_2$ and $M_1 = (C_2 + \alpha K)^{-1}$, respectively).

3.2. *CNN for EEG 3D Tensor Classification of Expert versus Novice*

Five-Fold Cross-Validation

Figures 6 and 7 show the loss function and accuracy of the model, respectively, during 200 epochs of training and validation processes. The learning curve converges at the middle (100th epoch) of the training epochs, and the accuracy performance gap between training and validation stays within 2.5% by the end. Table 1 shows the average and maximum accuracies during the learning phase are shown for each of the 20 epochs.

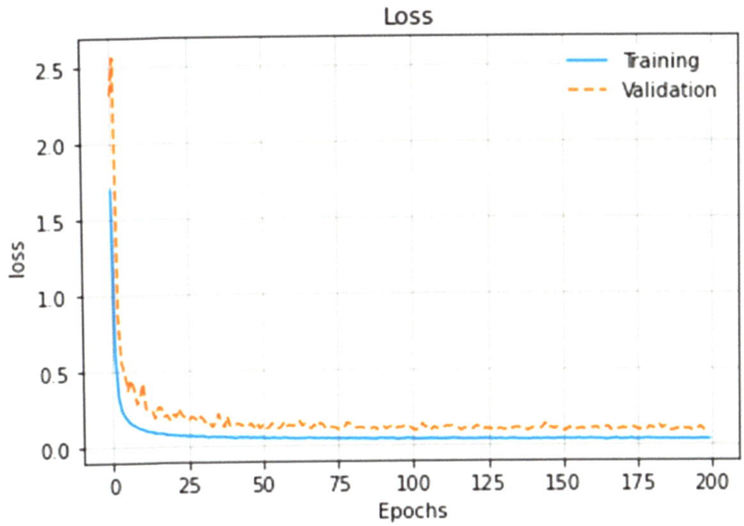

Figure 6. Training and validation loss function performance of the model.

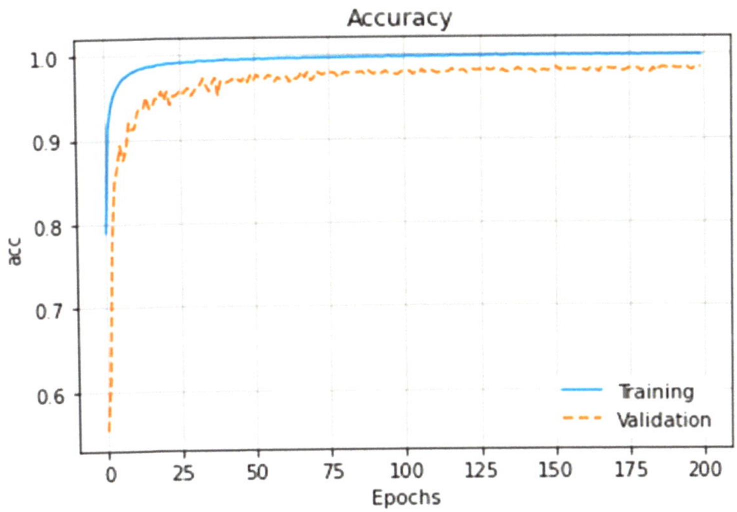

Figure 7. Accuracy performance of model training and validation.

Table 1. Training and validation results: mean ± standard deviation and maximum accuracy during training and validation.

Epoch	Training Accuracy		Validation Accuracy	
	Mean ± Standard Deviation	Maximum	Mean ± Standard Deviation	Maximum
1	0.7895 ± 0.0157	0.8369	0.5522 ± 0.0398	0.7339
20	0.9883 ± 0.0016	0.9927	0.9570 ± 0.0140	0.9889
40	0.9934 ± 0.0013	0.9974	0.9685 ± 0.0099	0.9912
60	0.9952 ± 0.0008	0.9980	0.9699 ± 0.0126	0.9918
80	0.9956 ± 0.0011	0.9994	0.9709 ± 0.0105	0.9924
100	0.9962 ± 0.0010	0.9988	0.9779 ± 0.0080	0.9924
120	0.9966 ± 0.0009	0.9990	0.9796 ± 0.0062	0.9936
140	0.9973 ± 0.0008	0.9990	0.9794 ± 0.0070	0.9912
160	0.9972 ± 0.0008	0.9994	0.9793 ± 0.0065	0.9912
180	0.9971 ± 0.0008	0.9991	0.9778 ± 0.0096	0.9936
200	0.9975 ± 0.0008	0.9996	0.9836 ± 0.0038	0.9936

3.3. Ten Evaluations with the Holdout Test Dataset

Table 2 shows the mean ± standard deviation and maximum for F1, MCC, precision, sensitivity, and specificity for the holdout test dataset over 10 repetitions of five-fold cross-validation. In Table 2, the highest values of each assessment (F1, MCC, accuracy, sensitivity, and specificity) are highlighted in red. Since our previous results of the classification accuracy using microstate-based CSP and LDA were 90.53%, so the topography-preserving CNN resulted is a significant improvement with >98% classification accuracy. The highest sensitivity, which indicates the percentage of correct predictions in the data labelled as positive (i.e., Expert), is 99.30% maximum. Then, the specificity, the rate of correct predictions in data labelled as negative (i.e., Novice), is 99.70% maximum. Furthermore, the F1 score, which evaluates the trade-off between recall and precision, reached 98.51%, indicating the equivalence of the model classification. Finally, the Matthews correlation coefficient (MCC), which evaluates the trade-off between the precision of positive and negative classifications (ranging from −100% to 100%), had a maximum of 97.56%. This implied that there was almost no classification bias among novices and experts even after five-fold cross-validation was repeated 10 times that generated a new training and validation splits of the trials, at random—see Table 2.

3.4. Gradient-Weighted Class Activation Mapping (Grad-CAM) Assessment of the CNN

The input of 16 × 16 EEG grid data to CNN (see Figure 3) is shown in the supplementary materials in Figure S1A for experts and novices. Then, the Grad-CAM heatmap for the convolutional layer 1 is shown in Figure S1B, for convolutional layer 2 is shown in Figure S1C, for the convolutional layer 3 is shown in Figure S1D, and for the TAP layer is shown in Figure 8. Note that the TAP layer first conducts Spatial Attentive Pooling which can provide insights into salient brain areas distinctive between experts and novices. The heatmap shows the salient regions in the topography-preserving convolutional layers from 1 to 3 (see Figure 3) where the time compressed central tendency of the heatmap for the TAP layer is shown in the top panel of Figure 8. The bottom left quadrant of the 16 × 16 EEG grid data is the discriminating salient region between experts and the novices. This bottom left quadrant is denoted by '2′ on the 1D x-axis in the bottom panel of Figure 8 showing temporal activation with flattened 2D space. The discriminating salient regions from the TAP layer corresponded (see E9, E10, E11, E12, E13, E14, and E15 in Figure 1A) with the centro-parietal (CCP5h, CCP3h), parietal (P3, P5, P7), and parieto–occipital (PO3,

PO7) regions that partly overlap with the significantly different regions between experts and novices in our prior study [20].

Table 2. Test results with the holdout test data (five-fold cross-validation repeated 10 times that generated a new training and validation splits of the trials): mean ± standard deviation and maximum for F1, MCC, precision, sensitivity, and specificity (confusion matrix for each iteration is shown in Table S1 in the supplementary materials). Numbers in **Bold** are highest across iterations.

Iteration	F1		MCC		Accuracy		Sensitivity		Specificity	
	Mean ± Standard Deviation	Maximum	Mean ± Standard Deviation	Maximum	Mean ± Standard Deviation	Maximum	Mean ± Standard Deviation	Maximum	Mean ± Standard Deviation	Maximum
1	0.9843 ± 0.0162	0.9928	**0.9756 ± 0.0221**	0.9887	0.9886 ± 0.0126	0.9947	**0.9930 ± 0.0197**	1.0000	0.9863 ± 0.0229	1.0000
2	**0.9851 ± 0.0171**	0.9913	0.9765 ± 0.0237	0.9864	**0.9891 ± 0.0138**	0.9937	0.9824 ± 0.0330	0.9942	0.9931 ± 0.0130	0.9983
3	0.9784 ± 0.0239	0.9869	0.9660 ± 0.0334	0.9796	0.9842 ± 0.0193	0.9905	0.9822 ± 0.0401	0.9971	0.9855 ± 0.0109	0.9882
4	0.9767 ± 0.0278	0.9871	0.9633 ± 0.0382	0.9796	0.9828 ± 0.0225	0.9905	0.9783 ± 0.0525	1.0000	0.9860 ± 0.0300	0.9950
5	0.9792 ± 0.0142	0.9843	0.9674 ± 0.0197	0.9754	0.9849 ± 0.0110	0.9884	0.9799 ± 0.0236	0.9940	0.9878 ± 0.0213	0.9983
6	0.9746 ± 0.0228	0.9843	0.9600 ± 0.0304	0.9752	0.9813 ± 0.0174	0.9884	0.9707 ± 0.0350	0.9908	0.9880 ± 0.0333	0.9967
7	0.9821 ± 0.0144	0.9871	0.9719 ± 0.0193	0.9796	0.9870 ± 0.0110	0.9905	0.9861 ± 0.0192	0.9940	0.9876 ± 0.0223	0.9950
8	0.9745 ± 0.0403	0.9942	0.9594 ± 0.0552	0.9909	0.9804 ± 0.0335	0.9958	0.9550 ± 0.0692	0.9942	**0.9970 ± 0.0117**	1.0000
9	0.9829 ± 0.0167	0.9871	0.9730 ± 0.0232	0.9798	0.9874 ± 0.0136	0.9905	0.9758 ± 0.0340	0.9912	0.9944 ± 0.0139	0.9983
10	0.9758 ± 0.0366	0.9899	0.9618 ± 0.0491	0.9841	0.9821 ± 0.0284	0.9926	0.9741 ± 0.0425	0.9912	0.9874 ± 0.0402	1.0000

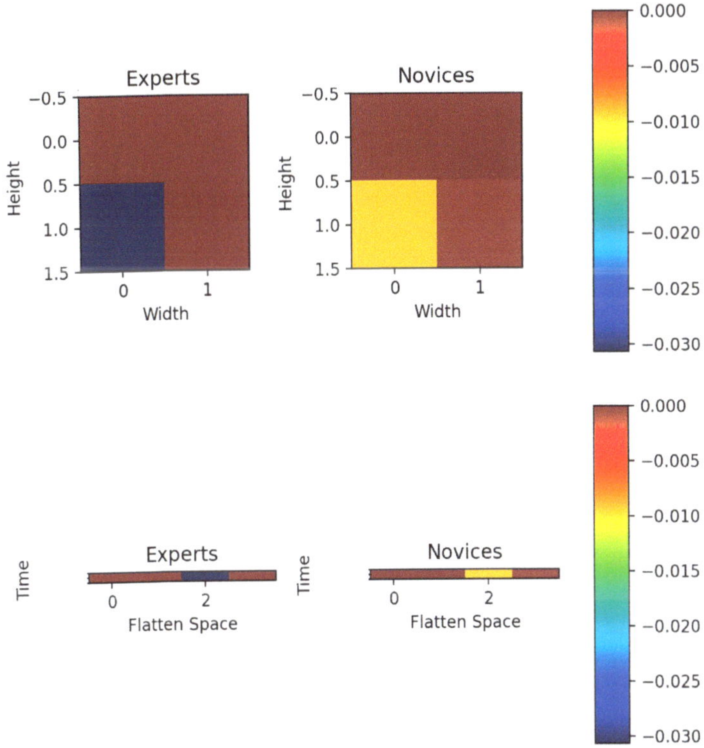

Figure 8. Spatial and temporal information are integrated through the incorporation of a dedicated pooling layer known as the temporal attentive pooling (TAP) layer, designed to efficiently condense temporal information. An illustrative Gradient-weighted Class Activation Mapping (Grad-CAM) assessment of TAP layer is shown where the top panel shows the compressed central tendency, while the bottom panel shows temporal activation (time in seconds) with flattened 2D grid (256 = 16 × 16) on the 1D x-axis.

4. Discussion

In this study, the novice trainees attempted a complex visuomotor task in a novel laparoscopic environment; therefore, they had to start building the perceptual model of the novel 3D environment based on 2D video and tactile feedback [43]. EEG topography, for example, microstate topographies, can be used as a marker of proficiency such that FLS psychomotor tasks with increasing task complexity can progress in the simulator as the novice trainee achieves proficiency towards FLS certification. For example, microstate 4 (see Figure 5) has been associated with the activation of the left inferior parietal lobe [44] related to the level of expert skill [45]. In our previous study [20], the microstate 4 was found to be more common in experts who are expected to have the action semantic knowledge [45]. Furthermore, global gestalt perception [46] is postulated to be present in experts due to their experience. Here, EEG topography can provide neurophysiological insights [20], e.g., microstate 1 (corresponding to visual cortex [41]), microstate 3 (corresponding to attention reorientation [41] and medial frontal cortex activation [47], and microstates 5 (topography comparable to microstate 3) during task performance can be considered markers of expertise. Then, the sequential flow of information between different brain states can be related to microstate sequences corresponding to the perception–action coupling [20].

We postulated that the CNN approach can learn the underlying temporal dynamics and provide latent representations that can be sensitive to other factors such as mental stress [26]. In this study, the ESNet approach [28] using EEG topography was adapted to classify experts from novices that provided a significant improvement with the highest sensitivity of 99.30% and the highest specificity at 99.70%. Since our CNN is topography-preserving, the Grad-CAM heatmap highlighting the bottom left quadrant of the TAP layer aligned with microstate 2 (see Figure 5) was found dominant in the novices from microstate-based CSP analysis. Here, microstate 2 is comparable to right-frontal left-posterior microstate A of the prototypical microstate classes [18,48], whereas microstate 4 hotspot that overlies the temporoparietal junction and the left inferior parietal lobe [44] may be related to the intact perception of global gestalt [49]. In particular, the Grad-CAM heatmap in the bottom panel of Figure 8D highlighted the parietal–occipital association area in novices (when compared to experts) at the beginning of the FLS task. This requires further investigation based on higher density EEG source localisation, since parietal hotspot was also found to be important for discrimination (relevant for spatial binding [46] based on CSP analysis which aligns well with the cognitive perception models [3,4]). Then, the supplementary motor area complex (SMA) is postulated to play a central role in the descent from the prefrontal to the motor cortex for the flow of skill-related information [7]. Here, SMA is known to be involved in planning complex motor finger tasks [50], and considered the programming area for motor effector subroutines in bimanual coordination tasks. Additionally, SMA has been suggested to form a queue of time-ordered motor commands before voluntary movement is executed via the descending pathways of the primary motor cortex (M1). In the current study, microstate 5 is postulated to capture SMA-related brain activity, which was found to be more frequent in experts than novices.

In the context of the perception–action cycle [51], investigation of motor skill acquisition with different virtual and physical simulation technologies [52] can provide insights into the neurophysiology of skill learning. Specifically, perception and action form a functional system through which behaviour is adapted in novices during exploratory actions to develop perceptual memory at the beginning in a novel environment. Then, perceptual memory allows action planning for improved skilled behaviour by updating the action parameters and refining them in executive memory, a continuous process of exploitative learning to reduce task variability. The two crucial attributes of the perception–action cycle are perceptual and executive memory [53], which are subserved by the frontoparietal network [54]. Here, the EEG-based analysis using microstate-based CSP and ESNet identified primarily the parietal–temporal–occipital EEG electrodes (microstates 2 and 4, the most significant eigenvectors) that illustrated the importance of the parietal–temporal–occipital association region for the classification of experts and novices.

In our previous study [55], we found that average fNIRS HbO-based cortical activation in novices was mainly in the left pars opercularis of the inferior frontal gyrus involved in cognitive control [56]. The inferior frontal gyrus is postulated to be crucial for error-based learning [20] since published studies have shown that the inferior frontal gyrus and the presupplementary motor area (pre-SMA) are involved in stop signal task performance [57] that is relevant in error correction. Then, the prefrontal area [20,58] was found to be more active based on the activation of fNIRS HbO, which may be related to the manipulation of structured information [59]. Therefore, the fNIRS-guided attention network (FGANet) [28] may improve neurophysiological interpretation by capturing the frontoparietal hemodynamic network [54]. Specifically, neuroimaging of the rostrocaudal characteristics of the frontal lobes that are associated with varying degrees of information processing complexity [60] can be improved with fNIRS-EEG fusion where spatially important regions can be identified from fNIRS signals while temporally detailed neuronal activation, e.g., microstates, can be extracted from the EEG signals [20].

The main limitation of the current study is the low-density EEG montage since microstate analysis is more reliable with higher electrode densities [34,61,62]. Furthermore, a higher EEG electrode density can allow robust source localisation [63] to establish the regions of the brain underlying salient microstates that support skilled behaviour. Also, the limited number of subjects (8 experts and 13 novices) did not allow classification of individual skill level. Here, we conducted group comparison of EEG topography that may be too nonspecific to support clear conclusions about the skill level of individual subjects [64]. Therefore, the current study showed the feasibility of the CNN approach that substantially improved (>98%) EEG topography-based group classification of experts versus novices for FLS suturing with intracorporeal knot tying task when compared to microstate-based CSP analysis with LDA (~90%). Here, the accuracy performance gap between training and validation stayed within 2.5% by the end due to a limited number of subjects (see Figures 6 and 7), and that gap did not lead to classification bias even after five-fold cross-validation was repeated 10 times and generated new training and validation splits, at random—see Table 2. A potential pitfall in using artifact removal using ICA in EEGlab is a decrease in rank that can cause decreased accuracy in the CSP implementation in BCIlab used in the current study [65]. Therefore, we have verified the spatial filters that they are not complex numbers in the current CSP analysis with LDA. Task onset trigger was set manually by the experimenter when the start command was assigned by him/her to the subject to start the FLS task, which can affect CSP analysis with LDA; however, the temporal attentive pooling layer of ESNet [28] can find temporally important time segments despite small (<10 s) misalignments. Then, a weakness of Grad-CAM used in this study is its partial derivative approach that can miss multiple occurrences of the same class and/or can lead to inaccurate localisation of a heatmap; therefore, Grad-CAM++ may be preferred in the future [66].

5. Conclusions and Future Research

We postulated that testing ESNet [28] for our application can provide mechanistic insights from EEG topography-preserving CNN approach that can be enhanced with a temporal attentive pooling layer using simultaneous fNIRS signals (see FGANet [28]). In the future research, FGANet [28] approach of online fNIRS-EEG fusion may drive closed-loop adaptive FLS simulators in virtual reality such that task difficulty may be individually paced according to brain-based metrics to develop "coping" to handle cognitive stress response (sympathetic vasoconstriction or 'choking' [67,68] monitored with portable neuroimaging [26]. Furthermore, subject-specific portable neuroimaging skill learning may provide brain-based error prediction [20] that can be compared with actual task errors from 3D (behaviour) video data (from FLS box trainer) to develop predictive fNIRS-EEG-video fusion. An expected task error can be highlighted in the 2D video feedback to novices to facilitate visuospatial attention for corrective action in the early stage of skill learning. Here, a distinction is necessary between sensory prediction error [69], which is postulated to be important at the initial perceptual-cognitive stage of skill learning [70], and task error which is postulated to be important in the later stages for strategy learning [9] to achieve expert performance. Then, the CNN with Grad-CAM approach provided insights into the main brain areas that differentiated experts from novices, which may be facilitated with neuroimaging-guided non-invasive brain stimulation—[58,71]. For example, non-invasive cerebellar stimulation may facilitate sensory prediction error and/or non-invasive frontal stimulation may facilitate task error feedback to improve FLS task performance and demonstrate brain-behaviour causality [72]. Also, a simultaneous multimodal EEG-fNIRS approach to measure task and/or non-invasive brain stimulation related brain response can provide important mechanistic insights, e.g., during non-invasive brain stimulation facilitated skill learning, where neurovascular coupling may be modulated by endogenous [73] and exogenous [74] arousals, e.g., due to sympathetic vasoconstriction [20,67,75].

Supplementary Materials: The following supporting information can be downloaded at: https://www.mdpi.com/article/10.3390/brainsci13121706/s1.

Author Contributions: Conceptualization, A.D.; methodology, T.M. and A.D.; software, T.M.; validation, T.M., F.N.U.R. and A.D.; formal analysis, A.D.; investigation, T.M. and Y.F.; resources, L.C. and S.D.S.; data curation, T.M.; writing—original draft preparation, T.M.; writing—review and editing, T.M., F.N.U.R., L.C. and A.D.; visualization, T.M.; supervision, A.D. and L.C.; project administration, A.D., L.C., S.D.S. and S.D.; funding acquisition, X.I., S.D.S., L.C., A.D. and S.D. All authors have read and agreed to the published version of the manuscript.

Funding: The authors appreciate the support of this study through the Medical Technology Enterprise Consortium (MTEC) award, #W81XWH2090019 (2020-628), and the US Army Futures Command, Combat Capabilities Development Command Soldier Centre STTC cooperative research agreement, #W912CG-21-2-0001. T.M. was funded by the pump priming grant from the school of engineering, University of Lincoln, UK for the writing—review and editing.

Institutional Review Board Statement: The study was conducted in accordance with the Declaration of Helsinki and approved by the Institutional Review Board of the University at Buffalo, USA. Approval code STUDY00004789. Approval date 26 August 2020.

Informed Consent Statement: Informed consent was obtained from all subjects involved in the study.

Data Availability Statement: Data available on request due to privacy/ethical restrictions.

Acknowledgments: The authors appreciate the support of pump priming from the school of engineering, University of Lincoln, UK for 2023 summer internship of Takahiro Manabe.

Conflicts of Interest: All authors declare that they have no conflict of interest.

References

1. Birkmeyer, J.D.; Finks, J.F.; O'Reilly, A.; Oerline, M.; Carlin, A.M.; Nunn, A.R.; Dimick, J.; Banerjee, M.; Birkmeyer, N.J.O. Surgical Skill and Complication Rates after Bariatric Surgery. *N. Engl. J. Med.* **2013**, *369*, 1434–1442. [CrossRef] [PubMed]
2. Dehabadi, M.; Fernando, B.; Berlingieri, P. The Use of Simulation in the Acquisition of Laparoscopic Suturing Skills. *Int. J. Surg.* **2014**, *12*, 258–268. [CrossRef] [PubMed]
3. Cioffi, D. Beyond Attentional Strategies: Cognitive-Perceptual Model of Somatic Interpretation. *Psychol. Bull.* **1991**, *109*, 25–41. [CrossRef] [PubMed]
4. Renner, R.S.; Velichkovsky, B.M.; Helmert, J.R. The Perception of Egocentric Distances in Virtual Environments—A Review. *ACM Comput. Surv.* **2013**, *46*, 23:1–23:40. [CrossRef]
5. Marucci, M.; Di Flumeri, G.; Borghini, G.; Sciaraffa, N.; Scandola, M.; Pavone, E.F.; Babiloni, F.; Betti, V.; Aricò, P. The Impact of Multisensory Integration and Perceptual Load in Virtual Reality Settings on Performance, Workload and Presence. *Sci. Rep.* **2021**, *11*, 4831. [CrossRef] [PubMed]
6. Kamat, A.; Makled, B.; Norfleet, J.; Schwaitzberg, S.D.; Intes, X.; De, S.; Dutta, A. Directed Information Flow during Laparoscopic Surgical Skill Acquisition Dissociated Skill Level and Medical Simulation Technology. *NPJ Sci. Learn.* **2022**, *7*, 1–13. [CrossRef]
7. Kamat, A.; Intes, X.; De, S.; Dutta, A. Efference Information Flow during Skill Acquisition Mediates Its Interaction with Medical Simulation Technology. In Proceedings of the Biophotonics Congress: Biomedical Optics 2022 (Translational, Microscopy, OCT, OTS, BRAIN), Fort Lauderdale, FL, USA, 24–27 April 2022; paper JTu3A.33. Optica Publishing Group: Washington, DC, USA, 2022.

8. Riener, R.; Harders, M. *Virtual Reality in Medicine*; Springer: London, UK, 2012; ISBN 978-1-4471-4010-8.
9. Taylor, J.A.; Ivry, R.B. The Role of Strategies in Motor Learning. *Ann. N. Y. Acad. Sci.* **2012**, *1251*, 1–12. [CrossRef] [PubMed]
10. Gu, Q.L.; Lam, N.H.; Wimmer, R.D.; Halassa, M.M.; Murray, J.D. *Computational Circuit Mechanisms Underlying Thalamic Control of Attention*; Tufts University: Medford, MA, USA, 2021.
11. Guillot, A.; Collet, C.; Nguyen, V.A.; Malouin, F.; Richards, C.; Doyon, J. Brain Activity during Visual versus Kinesthetic Imagery: An fMRI Study. *Hum. Brain Mapp.* **2009**, *30*, 2157–2172. [CrossRef]
12. Crick, F. Function of the Thalamic Reticular Complex: The Searchlight Hypothesis. *Proc. Natl. Acad. Sci. USA* **1984**, *81*, 4586–4590. [CrossRef]
13. Collins, D.P.; Anastasiades, P.G. Cellular Specificity of Cortico-Thalamic Loops for Motor Planning. *J. Neurosci.* **2019**, *39*, 2577–2580. [CrossRef]
14. Guo, K.; Yamawaki, N.; Svoboda, K.; Shepherd, G.M.G. Anterolateral Motor Cortex Connects with a Medial Subdivision of Ventromedial Thalamus through Cell Type-Specific Circuits, Forming an Excitatory Thalamo-Cortico-Thalamic Loop via Layer 1 Apical Tuft Dendrites of Layer 5B Pyramidal Tract Type Neurons. *J. Neurosci.* **2018**, *38*, 8787–8797. [CrossRef] [PubMed]
15. Lotte, F.; Bougrain, L.; Cichocki, A.; Clerc, M.; Congedo, M.; Rakotomamonjy, A.; Yger, F. A Review of Classification Algorithms for EEG-Based Brain-Computer Interfaces: A 10 Year Update. *J. Neural. Eng.* **2018**, *15*, 031005. [CrossRef] [PubMed]
16. Pawuś, D.; Paszkiel, S. BCI Wheelchair Control Using Expert System Classifying EEG Signals Based on Power Spectrum Estimation and Nervous Tics Detection. *Appl. Sci.* **2022**, *12*, 10385. [CrossRef]
17. Pascual-Marqui, R.D.; Michel, C.M.; Lehmann, D. Segmentation of Brain Electrical Activity into Microstates: Model Estimation and Validation. *IEEE Trans. Biomed. Eng.* **1995**, *42*, 658–665. [CrossRef] [PubMed]
18. Michel, C.M.; Koenig, T. EEG Microstates as a Tool for Studying the Temporal Dynamics of Whole-Brain Neuronal Networks: A Review. *NeuroImage* **2018**, *180*, 577–593. [CrossRef]
19. Krylova, M.; Alizadeh, S.; Izyurov, I.; Teckentrup, V.; Chang, C.; van der Meer, J.; Erb, M.; Kroemer, N.; Koenig, T.; Walter, M.; et al. Evidence for Modulation of EEG Microstate Sequence by Vigilance Level. *NeuroImage* **2021**, *224*, 117393. [CrossRef]
20. Walia, P.; Fu, Y.; Norfleet, J.; Schwaitzberg, S.D.; Intes, X.; De, S.; Cavuoto, L.; Dutta, A. Error-Related Brain State Analysis Using Electroencephalography in Conjunction with Functional near-Infrared Spectroscopy during a Complex Surgical Motor Task. *Brain Inform.* **2022**, *9*, 29. [CrossRef]
21. Manabe, T.; Walia, P.; Fu, Y.; Intes, X.; De, S.; Schwaitzberg, S.; Cavuoto, L.; Dutta, A. EEG Topographic Features for Assessing Skill Levels during Laparoscopic Surgical Training. *Res. Sq.* **2022**. [CrossRef]
22. Yu, H.; Lu, H.; Wang, S.; Xia, K.; Jiang, Y.; Qian, P. A General Common Spatial Patterns for EEG Analysis with Applications to Vigilance Detection. *IEEE Access* **2019**, *7*, 111102–111114. [CrossRef]
23. Koles, Z.J. The Quantitative Extraction and Topographic Mapping of the Abnormal Components in the Clinical EEG. *Electroencephalogr. Clin. Neurophysiol.* **1991**, *79*, 440–447. [CrossRef] [PubMed]
24. Custo, A.; Van De Ville, D.; Wells, W.M.; Tomescu, M.I.; Brunet, D.; Michel, C.M. Electroencephalographic Resting-State Networks: Source Localization of Microstates. *Brain Connect* **2017**, *7*, 671–682. [CrossRef] [PubMed]
25. Selvaraju, R.R.; Cogswell, M.; Das, A.; Vedantam, R.; Parikh, D.; Batra, D. Grad-CAM: Visual Explanations from Deep Networks via Gradient-Based Localization. *Int. J. Comput. Vis.* **2020**, *128*, 336–359. [CrossRef]
26. Sikka, A.; Jamalabadi, H.; Krylova, M.; Alizadeh, S.; van der Meer, J.N.; Danyeli, L.; Deliano, M.; Vicheva, P.; Hahn, T.; Koenig, T.; et al. Investigating the Temporal Dynamics of Electroencephalogram (EEG) Microstates Using Recurrent Neural Networks. *Hum. Brain Mapp.* **2020**, *41*, 2334–2346. [CrossRef] [PubMed]
27. Agrawal, S.; Chinnadurai, V.; Sharma, R. Hemodynamic Functional Connectivity Optimization of Frequency EEG Microstates Enables Attention LSTM Framework to Classify Distinct Temporal Cortical Communications of Different Cognitive Tasks. *Brain Inform.* **2022**, *9*, 25. [CrossRef]
28. Kwak, Y.; Song, W.-J.; Kim, S.-E. FGANet: fNIRS-Guided Attention Network for Hybrid EEG-fNIRS Brain-Computer Interfaces. *IEEE Trans. Neural. Syst. Rehabil. Eng.* **2022**, *30*, 329–339. [CrossRef]
29. Kumar, N.; Michmizos, K.P. A Neurophysiologically Interpretable Deep Neural Network Predicts Complex Movement Components from Brain Activity. *Sci. Rep.* **2022**, *12*, 1101. [CrossRef]
30. Walia, P.; Fu, Y.; Schwaitzberg, S.D.; Intes, X.; De, S.; Dutta, A.; Cavuoto, L. Portable Neuroimaging Differentiates Novices from Those with Experience for the Fundamentals of Laparoscopic Surgery (FLS) Suturing with Intracorporeal Knot Tying Task. *Surg. Endosc.* **2022**. [CrossRef]
31. Fu, Y.; Walia, P.; Schwaitzberg, S.D.; Intes, X.; De, S.; Dutta, A.; Cavuoto, L. Changes in Functional Neuroimaging Measures as Novices Gain Proficiency on the Fundamentals of Laparoscopic Surgery Suturing Task. *Neurophotonics* **2023**, *10*, 023521. [CrossRef]
32. Perrin, F.; Pernier, J.; Bertrand, O.; Echallier, J.F. Spherical Splines for Scalp Potential and Current Density Mapping. *Electroencephalogr. Clin. Neurophysiol.* **1989**, *72*, 184–187. [CrossRef]
33. Chang, C.-Y.; Hsu, S.-H.; Pion-Tonachini, L.; Jung, T.-P. Evaluation of Artifact Subspace Reconstruction for Automatic Artifact Components Removal in Multi-Channel EEG Recordings. *IEEE Trans. Biomed. Eng.* **2020**, *67*, 1114–1121. [CrossRef] [PubMed]
34. Zhang, K.; Shi, W.; Wang, C.; Li, Y.; Liu, Z.; Liu, T.; Li, J.; Yan, X.; Wang, Q.; Cao, Z.; et al. Reliability of EEG Microstate Analysis at Different Electrode Densities during Propofol-Induced Transitions of Brain States. *NeuroImage* **2021**, *231*, 117861. [CrossRef] [PubMed]

35. Poulsen, A.T.; Pedroni, A.; Langer, N.; Hansen, L.K. Microstate EEGlab Toolbox: An Introductory Guide. *bioRxiv* **2018**. [CrossRef]
36. Li, X.; Krol, M.A.; Jahani, S.; Boas, D.A.; Tager-Flusberg, H.; Yücel, M.A. Brain Correlates of Motor Complexity during Observed and Executed Actions. *Sci. Rep.* **2020**, *10*, 10965. [CrossRef]
37. Arthur, D.; Vassilvitskii, S. K-Means++: The Advantages of Careful Seeding. In Proceedings of the Eighteenth Annual ACM-SIAM Symposium on Discrete Algorithms, New Orleans, LA, USA, 7–9 January 2007; Society for Industrial and Applied Mathematics: Philadelphia, PA, USA, 2007; pp. 1027–1035.
38. Kothe, C.A.; Makeig, S. BCILAB: A Platform for Brain-Computer Interface Development. *J. Neural. Eng.* **2013**, *10*, 056014. [CrossRef] [PubMed]
39. Lu, H.; Eng, H.-L.; Guan, C.; Plataniotis, K.N.; Venetsanopoulos, A.N. Regularized Common Spatial Pattern with Aggregation for EEG Classification in Small-Sample Setting. *IEEE Trans. Biomed. Eng.* **2010**, *57*, 2936–2946. [CrossRef] [PubMed]
40. Lotte, F.; Guan, C. Regularizing Common Spatial Patterns to Improve BCI Designs: Unified Theory and New Algorithms. *IEEE Trans. Biomed. Eng.* **2011**, *58*, 355–362. [CrossRef]
41. Britz, J.; Van De Ville, D.; Michel, C.M. BOLD Correlates of EEG Topography Reveal Rapid Resting-State Network Dynamics. *Neuroimage* **2010**, *52*, 1162–1170. [CrossRef]
42. Townsend, G.; Graimann, B.; Pfurtscheller, G. A Comparison of Common Spatial Patterns with Complex Band Power Features in a Four-Class BCI Experiment. *IEEE Trans. Biomed. Eng.* **2006**, *53*, 642–651. [CrossRef]
43. Tanagho, Y.S.; Andriole, G.L.; Paradis, A.G.; Madison, K.M.; Sandhu, G.S.; Varela, J.E.; Benway, B.M. 2D versus 3D Visualization: Impact on Laparoscopic Proficiency Using the Fundamentals of Laparoscopic Surgery Skill Set. *J. Laparoendosc. Adv. Surg. Tech. A* **2012**, *22*, 865–870. [CrossRef]
44. Numssen, O.; Bzdok, D.; Hartwigsen, G. Functional Specialization within the Inferior Parietal Lobes across Cognitive Domains. *eLife* **2021**, *10*, e63591. [CrossRef] [PubMed]
45. van Elk, M. The Left Inferior Parietal Lobe Represents Stored Hand-Postures for Object Use and Action Prediction. *Front. Psychol.* **2014**, *5*. [CrossRef] [PubMed]
46. Zaretskaya, N.; Anstis, S.; Bartels, A. Parietal Cortex Mediates Conscious Perception of Illusory Gestalt. *J. Neurosci.* **2013**, *33*, 523–531. [CrossRef] [PubMed]
47. Gehring, W.J.; Fencsik, D.E. Functions of the Medial Frontal Cortex in the Processing of Conflict and Errors. *J. Neurosci.* **2001**, *21*, 9430–9437. [CrossRef] [PubMed]
48. Khanna, A.; Pascual-Leone, A.; Michel, C.M.; Farzan, F. Microstates in Resting-State EEG: Current Status and Future Directions. *Neurosci. Biobehav. Rev.* **2015**, *49*, 105–113. [CrossRef] [PubMed]
49. Rennig, J.; Bilalic, M.; Huberle, E.; Karnath, H.-O.; Himmelbach, M. The Temporo-Parietal Junction Contributes to Global Gestalt Perception—Evidence from Studies in Chess Experts. *Front. Hum. Neurosci.* **2013**, *7*. [CrossRef] [PubMed]
50. Roland, P.E.; Larsen, B.; Lassen, N.A.; Skinhoj, E. Supplementary Motor Area and Other Cortical Areas in Organization of Voluntary Movements in Man. *J. Neurophysiol.* **1980**, *43*, 118–136. [CrossRef]
51. Fuster, J.M. Chapter 8—Prefrontal Cortex in Decision-Making: The Perception–Action Cycle. In *Decision Neuroscience*; Dreher, J.-C., Tremblay, L., Eds.; Academic Press: San Diego, CA, USA, 2017; pp. 95–105. ISBN 978-0-12-805308-9.
52. Dutta, A.; Kamat, A.; Makled, B.; Norfleet, J.; Intes, X.; De, S. Interhemispheric Functional Connectivity in the Primary Motor Cortex Distinguishes between Training on a Physical and a Virtual Surgical Simulator. In Proceedings of the Medical Image Computing and Computer Assisted Intervention—MICCAI 2021, Strasbourg, France, 27 September–1 October 2021; de Bruijne, M., Cattin, P.C., Cotin, S., Padoy, N., Speidel, S., Zheng, Y., Essert, C., Eds.; Springer International Publishing: Cham, Switzerland, 2021; pp. 636–644.
53. Fuster, J.M. Upper Processing Stages of the Perception-Action Cycle. *Trends Cogn. Sci.* **2004**, *8*, 143–145. [CrossRef]
54. Marek, S.; Dosenbach, N.U.F. The Frontoparietal Network: Function, Electrophysiology, and Importance of Individual Precision Mapping. *Dialogues Clin. Neurosci.* **2018**, *20*, 133–140. [CrossRef]
55. Walia, P.; Fu, Y.; Schwaitzberg, S.D.; Intes, X.; De, S.; Cavuoto, L.; Dutta, A. Neuroimaging Guided tES to Facilitate Complex Laparoscopic Surgical Tasks—Insights from Functional Near-Infrared Spectroscopy. In Proceedings of the 2021 43rd Annual International Conference of the IEEE Engineering in Medicine & Biology Society (EMBC), Guadalajara, Mexico, 1–5 November 2021.
56. Levy, B.J.; Wagner, A.D. Cognitive Control and Right Ventrolateral Prefrontal Cortex: Reflexive Reorienting, Motor Inhibition, and Action Updating. *Ann. N. Y. Acad. Sci.* **2011**, *1224*, 40–62. [CrossRef]
57. Seidler, R.D.; Kwak, Y.; Fling, B.W.; Bernard, J.A. *Neurocognitive Mechanisms of Error-Based Motor Learning*; Advances in Experimental Medicine and Biology; Springer: New York, NY, USA, 2013; Volume 782. [CrossRef]
58. Walia, P.; Kumar, K.N.; Dutta, A. Neuroimaging Guided Transcranial Electrical Stimulation in Enhancing Surgical Skill Acquisition. Comment on Hung et al. The Efficacy of Transcranial Direct Current Stimulation in Enhancing Surgical Skill Acquisition: A Preliminary Meta-Analysis of Randomized Controlled Trials. *Brain Sci.* **2021**, *11*, 707. *Brain Sci.* **2021**, *11*, 1078. [CrossRef]
59. Kroger, J.; Kim, C. Frontopolar Cortex Specializes for Manipulation of Structured Information. *Front. Syst. Neurosci.* **2022**, *16*. [CrossRef] [PubMed]
60. Thiebaut de Schotten, M.; Urbanski, M.; Batrancourt, B.; Levy, R.; Dubois, B.; Cerliani, L.; Volle, E. Rostro-Caudal Architecture of the Frontal Lobes in Humans. *Cereb. Cortex* **2017**, *27*, 4033–4047. [CrossRef] [PubMed]

61. Bréchet, L.; Michel, C.M. EEG Microstates in Altered States of Consciousness. *Front. Psychol.* **2022**, *13*, 856697. [CrossRef] [PubMed]
62. Dinov, M.; Leech, R. Modeling Uncertainties in EEG Microstates: Analysis of Real and Imagined Motor Movements Using Probabilistic Clustering-Driven Training of Probabilistic Neural Networks. *Front. Hum. Neurosci.* **2017**, *11*. [CrossRef] [PubMed]
63. Michel, C.M.; Brunet, D. EEG Source Imaging: A Practical Review of the Analysis Steps. *Front. Neurol.* **2019**, *10*, 325. [CrossRef] [PubMed]
64. Cook, D.A. Much Ado about Differences: Why Expert-Novice Comparisons Add Little to the Validity Argument. *Adv. Health Sci. Educ. Theory Pract.* **2015**, *20*, 829–834. [CrossRef]
65. Rybar, M.; Daly, I.; Poli, R. Potential Pitfalls of Widely Used Implementations of Common Spatial Patterns. *Annu. Int. Conf. IEEE Eng. Med. Biol. Soc.* **2020**, *2020*, 196–199. [CrossRef]
66. Chattopadhay, A.; Sarkar, A.; Howlader, P.; Balasubramanian, V.N. Grad-CAM++: Generalized Gradient-Based Visual Explanations for Deep Convolutional Networks. In Proceedings of the 2018 IEEE Winter Conference on Applications of Computer Vision (WACV), Lake Tahoe, NV, USA, 12–15 March 2018; pp. 839–847.
67. Hannah, T.C.; Turner, D.; Kellner, R.; Bederson, J.; Putrino, D.; Kellner, C.P. Neuromonitoring Correlates of Expertise Level in Surgical Performers: A Systematic Review. *Front. Hum. Neurosci.* **2022**, *16*, 705238. [CrossRef]
68. Modi, H.N.; Singh, H.; Orihuela-Espina, F.; Athanasiou, T.; Fiorentino, F.; Yang, G.-Z.; Darzi, A.; Leff, D.R. Temporal Stress in the Operating Room: Brain Engagement Promotes "Coping" and Disengagement Prompts "Choking". *Ann. Surg.* **2018**, *267*, 683–691. [CrossRef]
69. Schlerf, J.; Ivry, R.B.; Diedrichsen, J. Encoding of Sensory Prediction Errors in the Human Cerebellum. *J. Neurosci.* **2012**, *32*, 4913–4922. [CrossRef] [PubMed]
70. Broadbent, D.P.; Causer, J.; Williams, A.M.; Ford, P.R. Perceptual-Cognitive Skill Training and Its Transfer to Expert Performance in the Field: Future Research Directions. *Eur. J. Sport Sci.* **2015**, *15*, 322–331. [CrossRef] [PubMed]
71. Rahul, F.N.U.; Dutta, A.; Subedi, A.; Makled, B.; Norfleet, J.; Intes, X.; De, S. A Deep Learning Model for a Priori Estimation of Spatiotemporal Regions for Neuroimaging Guided Non-Invasive Brain Stimulation. *Brain Stimul. Basic Transl. Clin. Res. Neuromodulation* **2021**, *14*, 1689. [CrossRef]
72. Brain-Behavior Analysis of Transcranial Direct Current Stimulation Effects on a Complex Surgical Motor Task. Available online: https://www.researchsquare.com (accessed on 4 October 2023).
73. Han, F.; Gu, Y.; Liu, X. A Neurophysiological Event of Arousal Modulation May Underlie fMRI-EEG Correlations. *Front. Neurosci.* **2019**, *13*. [CrossRef]
74. Arora, Y.; Dutta, A. Human-in-the-Loop Optimization of Transcranial Electrical Stimulation at the Point of Care: A Computational Perspective. *Brain Sci.* **2022**, *12*, 1294. [CrossRef]
75. Arora, Y.; Dutta, A. Perspective: Disentangling the Effects of tES on Neurovascular Unit. *Front. Neurol.* **2023**, *13*, 1038700. [CrossRef]

Disclaimer/Publisher's Note: The statements, opinions and data contained in all publications are solely those of the individual author(s) and contributor(s) and not of MDPI and/or the editor(s). MDPI and/or the editor(s) disclaim responsibility for any injury to people or property resulting from any ideas, methods, instructions or products referred to in the content.

brain sciences

MDPI

Review

Artificial Intelligence as A Complementary Tool for Clincal Decision-Making in Stroke and Epilepsy

Smit P. Shah [1,*] and John D. Heiss [2]

[1] Resident Physician, University of South Carolina School of Medicine, PRISMA Health Richland, Columbia, SC 29203, USA
[2] Senior Clinician and Neurosurgical Residency Director, Surgical Neurology Branch [SNB], Building 10, Room 3D20, 10 Center Drive, Bethesda, MD 20814, USA; john.heiss@nih.gov
* Correspondence: spshah031591@gmail.com

Abstract: Neurology is a quickly evolving specialty that requires clinicians to make precise and prompt diagnoses and clinical decisions based on the latest evidence-based medicine practices. In all Neurology subspecialties—Stroke and Epilepsy in particular—clinical decisions affecting patient outcomes depend on neurologists accurately assessing patient disability. Artificial intelligence [AI] can predict the expected neurological impairment from an AIS [Acute Ischemic Stroke], the possibility of ICH [IntraCranial Hemorrhage] expansion, and the clinical outcomes of comatose patients. This review article informs readers of artificial intelligence principles and methods. The article introduces the basic terminology of artificial intelligence before reviewing current and developing AI applications in neurology practice. AI holds promise as a tool to ease a neurologist's daily workflow and supply unique diagnostic insights by analyzing data simultaneously from several sources, including neurological history and examination, blood and CSF laboratory testing, CNS electrophysiologic evaluations, and CNS imaging studies. AI-based methods are poised to complement the other tools neurologists use to make prompt and precise decisions that lead to favorable patient outcomes.

Keywords: artificial; intelligence; neurology; stroke; epilepsy; neuroimaging

1. Introduction

In the coming years, the complexity of data used in Neurology's clinical and research aspects will proliferate. Electronic medical records hold vast amounts of information. Major health systems rely on data-heavy technology to analyze clinical and genomic information. Computer analysis of digital medical data could aid the neurologist in making diagnoses, detecting disease patterns, and detecting health vulnerabilities. With its sophisticated machine learning algorithms, AI offers efficient and practical tools to clinicians to better interpret, access, and understand clinical information and narrow differential diagnoses in simple and complex cases [1,2]. AI has demonstrated great clinical utility in the management of Migraines as demonstrated by Torrente A. et al. [3]. Due to a high incidence of Stroke and Epilepsy in United States, which have been leading causes of morbidity and mortality, we would like to focus, exhibit, and discuss potential applications of AI in these two fields specifically by presenting our literature review and innovations so far, which can serve as great clinical adjuncts for clinicians which, in turn, can help deliver excellent patient care. Artificial intelligence could aid the neurology subspecialties of stroke and epilepsy by increasing the speed and consistency of analysis of clinical imaging studies and other data and clinical decision-making. Artificial intelligence can use evidence-based medicine practices to assure that the most modern and accepted medicine is being delivered. Artificial intelligence systems draw on extensive data sets of clinical information and are less prone than humans to have recency, recall, and other biases that can lead to inaccurate conclusions or ranking of the likelihood of the various diagnoses in a differential diagnosis. AI can help usher the era of personalized medicine into routine neurology clinical practice.

2. Basic Terminology and Concepts of AI

Key AI terms include 'Machine Learning', 'Supervised Learning', 'Unsupervised Learning', 'Model and Training', 'Artificial Neural Network', 'Deep Neural Network', 'Convolutional Neural Network', 'Black Box' and 'Reinforcement Learning' [4,5].

Machine Learning: Machine Learning [ML] is a field of AI associated with developing, studying, and generalizing statistical algorithms over time to perform tasks without specific instructions. A developed algorithm encodes statistical regularities extrapolated inherently from a database of examples to assess parameters for future predictions [4,6].

Supervised Learning: Supervised Learning [SL] uses previously established expert-labeled training examples to create an algorithm to assess parameters for future predictions. Its paradigm is analogous to machine learning because input and output values are used to train the algorithm model and derive the function relating input to output values. The SL function analyzes new data and derives the expected output values. Because SL creates a learning algorithm from training data, it may misinterpret data related to situations or diagnoses not present in the training data. SL is susceptible to errors from incomplete training data, so-called generalization errors [4,7].

Unsupervised Learning: Unsupervised Learning [UL] is less constrained than Supervised Learning because algorithms are learned and developed from the patterns in unlabeled data. In UL, machine learning algorithms discover patterns or data groupings without human intervention [4,8].

Modeling and Training: Modeling trains a machine-learning algorithm to make predictions from unseen data. Training coincides with modeling, where machine learning algorithms are fed examples from a training data set to update and calibrate parameters for future predictions. In model training, information types and their weights and bias fit into a machine learning algorithm to improve function over the predictive range [4].

Artificial Neural Network [ANN]: A machine learning technique that amalgamates and processes many layers of information, each holding essential parameters extracted incrementally from training data. Brain neuron network organization inspired this concept. Signals travel from input to output after traversing all layers multiple times [4,9].

Deep Neural Network: A deep neural network [DNN] is an artificial neural network [ANN] with multiple layers between the input and output layers. The various types of neural networks share these components: neurons, synapses, weights, biases, and functions. These components function together like brain neural networks. A DNN can be trained like other ML algorithms [4,10].

Convolutional Neural Network: Like the human visual cortex, the convolutional neural network displays connectivity patterns. It is a feed-forward neural network that learns feature engineering via filter optimization [4,11].

Black Box: Black box AI models arrive at conclusions or decisions without explaining how they were reached. The precise steps leading to the Black Box model's predictions cannot be explained because the predictions arise from unexplained parameters being processed by a highly complex analysis maze that is machine-derived and not a direct product of human consciousness and thought processes [4].

Reinforcement Learning

Reinforcement learning [RL] is a machine learning training method that develops decision algorithms by rewarding desired behaviors and punishing undesired ones. RL depends on environmental interactions. The algorithm receives rewards or penalties according to the desirability of behaviors and learns through this editing to make better decisions over time. The RL algorithm completes tasks without earlier instructions. It can learn while failing to complete the task. It derives basic rules guiding future predictions from experience performing the task [5].

3. Methods

To write this review, we searched PubMed using the key words "Artificial Intelligence", "Acute Ischemic Stroke", "Epilepsy", "Clinical Decision Making" and "Intracranial Hemorrhage (ICH)" for articles published on these subjects between 2000 and 2023 (Figure 1). From these articles, we decided which papers utilized AI in their decision-making. Articles describing studies that answered research questions about the clinical utility of AI methods were then selected and reported in tabular format (Tables 1–3). The Quality Improvement method of the Plan-Do-Check-Act was suggested as a way for ongoing testing and improving of AI algorithms used in clinical practice (Table 4).

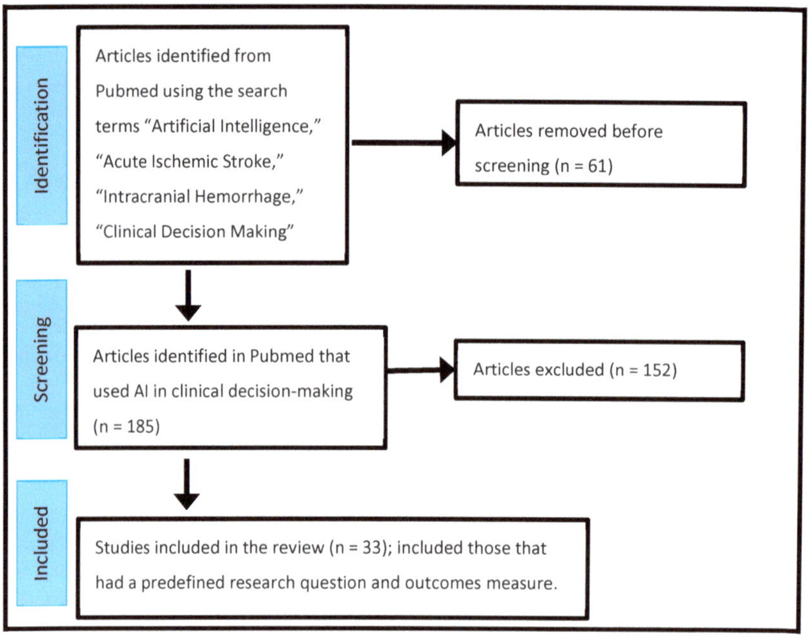

Figure 1. Flow diagram of the search strategy.

Table 1. Summary of some studies showing the application of AI for initial neuroimaging in AIS [Acute Ischemic Stroke] between 2000 and 2023.

Year	Authors	Research Question	Outcomes Measures/Conclusions
2023 [12]	Field N. et al.	Does supplying an LVO detection algorithm notification to the thrombectomy team's cell phone improve ischemic stroke workflow?	Transfer time and Mechanical Thrombectomy [MT] Initiation time decreased.
2023 [13]	Zhaou X. et al.	Does CTA derived from CT Perfusion [CTA-DF-CTP] give better image quality and diagnostic accuracy than traditional CTA in AIS?	CTA derived from CTA-DF-CTP had diagnostic accuracy comparable to traditional CTA and CTA-DF-CTP.
2023 [14]	Xiang et al.	Is it feasible to apply computed tomography perfusion [CTP] imaging-guided mechanical thrombectomy in acute ischemic stroke patients with LVO beyond the therapeutic time window?	NIHSS of MT group-CTP guided [at 6 h, 24 h, 7 days, and 30 days] was significantly better [$p < 0.05$]; however, infarct core volume approximation was too high or too low for this group.

Table 1. *Cont.*

Year	Authors	Research Question	Outcomes Measures/Conclusions
2023 [15]	Du B. et al.	In patients with ICAS [Intracranial Atherosclerotic Stenosis] in the anterior circulation, is AI based on CBF [Cerebral Blood Flow] or sCoV [Spatial Coefficient of Variation] better for predicting vascular cognitive impairment?	Cognitive impairment seems better predicted by AI analysis of sCoV than CBF.
2023 [16]	Farsani S. et al.	Can AG-DCNN [Attention Gated Deep Convoluted Neural Network] predict infarct volume and size?	AG-DCNN, using only admission DWI, predicted infarct volumes at 3–7 days after stroke onset with accuracy like models using DWI and PWI.
2022 [17]	Kossen T. et al.	How can modern machine learning methods such as generative adversarial networks [GANs] automate perfusion map generation from [DSC-MR] Dynamic Susceptibility Contrasted MR in AIS on an expert level without manual validation?	DSC-MR using machine learning can speed up patient stratification by perfusion mapping in AIS.
2022 [18]	Long Le et al.	Can an advanced deep learning-based method accurately and rapidly assess collateral perfusion in AIS by automatically generating a multiphase collateral imaging map from dynamic susceptibility contrast-enhanced MR perfusion [DSC-MRP] images?	DSC-Enhanced MR Perfusion improved accuracy and sped the assessment of the collateral perfusion.
2021 [19]	Neeves G et al.	Can a machine-learning [ML] algorithm grade digital subtraction angiograms [DSA] by the mTICI scale?	ML of complete cerebral DSA predicted mTICI scores following EVT of MCA occlusions.
2020 [20]	Grosser M. et al.	In AIS patients, how do predictions of machine learning models based on local [regional] tissue susceptibility to ischemia compare with those of machine learning models based on global brain imaging?	Compared to single global machine learning models, locally trained machine learning models can lead to better prediction of lesion outcomes in AIS patients.
2019 [21]	Satish R. et al.	Can Convolutional Neural Network analysis of Multisequence MRI in AIS predict the ischemic core and penumbra?	CNN analysis experimentally confirmed local changes.
2019 [22]	Reid M. et al.	For detecting early severe ischemia, how does NCCT compare with multiphase computed tomography angiography [mCTA] regional leptomeningeal score [mCTA-rLMC] and an mCTA venous [mCTA-venous] perfusion lesion?	An assessment blinded to clinical information in patients undergoing endovascular therapy [EVT] showed that mCTA-venous more accurately detected early ischemia and predicted clinical outcomes than NCCT and the mCTA-rLMC score.
2018 [23]	Nielsen A. et al.	In AIS, can Deep Learning improve Tissue Outcome and Treatment Effect predictions?	Deep Learning improves predictions of final neurological outcome and lesion volume.
2018 [24]	Chung-Ho. et al.	Can imaging features and advanced machine learning use the TSS [Time Since Stroke] classification to characterize the Acute Ischemic Stroke Onset Time?	Demonstrates the potential benefit of using advanced machine learning methods in TSS classification.
2017 [25]	Yu. Y. et al.	Can machine learning models trained on perfusion-weighted magnetic resonance imaging [PWI] and diffusion-weighted MRI scans predict HT [hemorrhagic transformation] occurrence and location in AIS?	HT prediction was a machine-learning problem. Specifically, the model learned to extract imaging markers of HT directly from source PWI images.

Table 1. *Cont.*

Year	Authors	Research Question	Outcomes Measures/Conclusions
2016 [26]	Tian X. et al.	Can clinically acceptable PCT [dynamic cerebral Perfusion Computed Tomography] images be created from low-dose CT images restored with a coupled dictionary learning [CDL] method in chronic and AIS patients?	CDL increased kinetic enhanced details and improved diagnostic hemodynamic parameter maps
2013 [27]	Fang R. et al.	Will the robust sparse perfusion deconvolution method [SPD] accurately estimate cerebral blood flow [CBF] in CTP performed at a low radiation dose?	SPD was superior to existing methods for CBF and helped differentiate normal and ischemic brain tissue.
2010 [28]	Mendrick A. et al.	Can the diagnostic yield of CTP in cerebrovascular diseases be expanded by combining arterial and venous segmentation and vessel-enhanced volume?	This artery and vein segmentation method was accurate for arteries and veins with normal perfusion. Combining the artery and vein segmentation with the vessel-enhanced volume produced an arteriogram and venogram, extending the diagnostic yield of CTP scans and making a CTA scan unnecessary.
2007 [29]	Meyer-Baese A. et al.	Do five unsupervised clustering techniques help analyze dynamic susceptibility contrast MRI time series?	Clustering is a valuable tool for analyzing and visualizing brain regional perfusion properties.

Table 2. Studies applying AI to diagnosing and managing ICH [IntraCranial Hemorrhage] between 2000 and 2023.

Year	Authors	Research Question	Outcome Measures/Conclusions
2023 [30]	Feng H. et al.	Can AI use the GCS score, NIH stroke scale, INR, BUN, hemorrhage location, hematoma volume, modified Rankin score, and other risk factors to construct a prediction model for the prognosis of ICH at discharge, 3 months, and 12 months?	The study showed that prediction models for modified Rankin scores showed a relatively high predictive performance. Also, the study found risk factors and constructed a prediction model to predict poor modified-Rankin score outcomes and mortality at discharge, 3 months, and 12 months in ICH patients.
2023 [31]	Maghami M. et al.	Are machine learning methods for detecting ICH from non-contrast CT scans sufficiently precise to be considered acceptable diagnostic tests of accuracy [DTA]?	This meta-analysis showed that assessing noncontract CT scans using ML algorithms for detecting ICH had acceptable DTA.
2023 [32]	Vacek A. et al.	Can E-ASPECTS delineate the extent and distribution of ICH from brain CT?	AI software-Brainomix Ltd. (Oxford, UK) excellently delineated ICH extent- on stroke CTs by AI software in about 71% of cases. ICH extent was more likely to be over or underestimated when ICH was extensive, intraventricular, or extra-axial.
2023 [33]	Chen Y. et al.	Can a convolutional neural network [CNN] create a clinical imaging perfusion model predicting the short-term neurological outcomes of ICH patients?	The CNN prognostication prediction model was more effective than ICH scales in predicting neurological outcomes and ICH patients at discharge. Predictions improved slightly after including clinical data.

Table 2. *Cont.*

Year	Authors	Research Question	Outcome Measures/Conclusions
2023 [34]	MacIntosh B. et al.	Can Viola AI estimate the number and volume of hematoma clusters in traumatic brain injury and ICH patients?	The automated total hemorrhage volume estimate correlated with the per-participant hemorrhage cluster count. This tool may help evaluate various types of ICH in the future.
2023 [35]	Kotovich D. et al.	Did implementing a commercial artificial intelligence solution in a level 1 trauma center emergency room affect ICH's clinical outcome?	Artificial intelligence computer-aided triage and prioritization software in the emergency room setting was associated with a significant reduction in 30 day and 120 day all-cause mortality and morbidity in ICH patients. It was also associated with a significant reduction in modified Rankin score on discharge.
2023 [36]	Li. Y. et al.	Can ML predict early perihematomal edema expansion [PHE] from non-contrast CT scan data in patients with spontaneous ICH?	This model was the best marker for predicting prior hematoma edema expansion in patients with ICH. It could predict early perihematomal edema expansion and improve the discrimination of early identification of spontaneous ICH in patients at risk of PHE expansion.
2023 [37]	Mastoukas S., et al.	What are AI methods' reported sensitivity, specificity, and accuracy for detecting ICH and chronic cerebral microbleeds?	In 40 studies, overall sensitivity, specificity, and accuracy were more than 90% for ICH and cerebral microbleed detection. AI algorithms were developed from large data sets, volumetric analysis of imaging examinations, fine-tuning, and false-positivity reduction.
2022 [38]	Lim M. et al.	How do deep neural networks [DNN] and support vector machines [SVM] compare with clinical prognostic scores for prognosticating 30-day mortality and 90-day poor functional outcome [PFO] in spontaneous intracerebral hemorrhage [SICH]?	The SVM model performed significantly better than clinical prognostic scores in predicting 90-day PFO in SICH.
2021 [39]	Heit J. et al.	What is the accuracy of RAPID ICH, 2D/3D, a volitional neural network application designed to detect ICH, in detecting and measuring ICH volume?	Rapid ICH was highly accurate in detecting ICH and quantifying the volume of intraparenchymal and intraventricular hemorrhages.

Table 3. Studies applying AI to diagnosing and managing Epilepsy between 2000 and 2023.

Year	Authors	Research Questions	Outcome Measures/Conclusions
2023 [40]	Zheng Z. et al.	Can EEG Deep Features and Machine Learning Classifiers assess and prognostically analyze KCNQ2 patients by combining the two well-trained models, RESNET-15 and RESNET-18, to extract deep features of EEG?	An outcome of 79% accuracy was reported in pediatric patients.
2023 [41]	Wang H. et al.	Can the multi-technique deep learning method WAE-Net use clinical data and multi-contrast MR imaging [T2WI and FLAIR images combined as FLAIR3 images] to forecast antiseizure medication treatment in a retrospective study involving 300 children with tuberous sclerosis complex-related epilepsy?	The hybrid technique of FLAIR3 could accurately localize tuberous sclerosis complex lesions, and the proposed method achieved the best performance [area under the curve = 0.908 and accuracy of 0.847] in the testing cohort among the compared methods.

Table 3. *Cont.*

Year	Authors	Research Questions	Outcome Measures/Conclusions
2023 [42]	Asadi-Pooya A. et al.	Can AI machine learning methods reliably differentiate idiopathic generalized epilepsy from focal epilepsy using easily accessible and applicable clinical history and physical examination data?	This algorithm aimed at easing epilepsy classification for individuals whose epilepsy began at age 10 and older. The stacking classifier led to better results than the base classifier in general. Precision was 81%, sensitivity was 81%, and specificity was close to 77%.
2023 [43]	Tveit J. et al.	Can the artificial intelligence program SCORE-AI [Standardized Computer-based Organizing Reporting of EEG] be developed and validated to distinguish abnormal from normal EEGs, detect focal epilepsy epileptiform discharges and generalized epilepsy, and distinguish focal nonepileptiform and diffuse nonepileptiform EEGs?	SCORE-AI accuracy approached human expert-level and fully automated interpretation of routine EEGs. Accuracy was approximately 88.3%, significantly higher than the three previously published models comparing EEG interpretation to human experts.
2023 [44]	Gustavo T. et al.	In patients diagnosed with epilepsy wearing the mjn-SERAS brain activity sensor, can AI create a personalized mathematical model for the programmed recognition of oncoming seizures before they start using patient-specific EEG training data?	The AI program accurately detected pre- and interictal EEG segments in drug-resistant epilepsy patients.

Table 4. PDCA [Plan-Do-Check-Act] Concept Extrapolation for AI [45].

Extrapolation of PDCA in AI
Plan Explore and discuss the question, assess the potential solution, and make use of the various machine learning models or methods as described above, set the endpoint in the objectives and goals, identify the potential metrics to use for implementation and quality measurement, prepare the action plan which includes implementation along with a potential route to reevaluate as needed.
Do Evaluate earlier models; train or retrain and test different machine learning models; assess and see if known machine learning solutions and components of the AI protocol can be improved or changed; test the overall solution to assess its integrity; review the code and filter out older ML models which did not work.
Check Monitor the model for fairness; assess for bias and variance; monitor the stability precisely to ascertain clarity and results; implement split testing of two methodologies; compare them head-to-head and assess to see which performs better.
Act The goal is standardization and continuous improvement, deploying the solution and continuing to monitor for biasing and variance, evaluating for areas of improvement in active machine learning algorithms and machine learning components, standardizing data, and features, and continuing the PDCA cycle accordingly.

4. Discussion

A growing body of literature suggests that artificial intelligence is becoming an invaluable tool for stroke and epilepsy clinicians. Studies report AI applications complementing traditional neurological care and improving diagnostic accuracy and clinical outcomes. As discussed above, early AI applications in the 2000s used clustering to analyze MRI sequences for regional brain perfusion properties. AI applications are standard care tools at the major level in CSCs [Comprehensive Stroke Centers] for analyzing CT perfusion studies and detecting large vessel occlusion [LVO]. The field of Stroke Neurology has improved its care systems by perfecting diagnostics and hastening stroke care. For example, AI tools can help minimize transfer time and improve outcomes by shortening the time to treatment with thrombolytics or mechanical thrombectomy. CT perfusion studies hold data critical to evaluating the cerebral vascular physiology after a stroke. A fundamental measure is rCBF [relative Cerebral Blood Flow], the flow rate through the vasculature in the brain region of interest [ROI]. Other measures include rCBV [relative Cerebral Blood Volume], the volume of blood within the ROI vasculature; MTT [Mean Transit Time], the average time for arterial-to-venous blood transit through infarcted tissue; and TTP [Time-To-Peak] the time interval between first appearance to peak enhancement of contrast-containing blood in the arterial vessels [46]. These CT perfusion imaging factors help assess the Mismatch Ratio and the infarct Core. Clinical decisions on the likelihood of improvement with mechanical thrombectomy consider these measures and the Modified Ranking Score [mRS]. AI assures clinical decisions are evidence-based, consistent with diagnostic and treatment guidelines, and give proper weight to relevant diagnostic and prognostic factors.

Acute decision-making in AIS uses AI for rapid and reliable analysis of perfusion and vessel imaging [Table 1—via PubMed search]. AI has vessel-imaging applications beyond the AIS setting. For example, in the setting of intracranial atheromatous disease or multiple vascular risk factors, AI can help predict cognitive impairment and other patient outcomes in a patient. Physicians can explore the nonemergent role of AI in vessel imaging by using Deep Convoluted Neural Networks and Generative Adversarial Networks to generate automated perfusion maps that stratify a patient's AIS risk.

Convoluted Deep Neural Networks have been used extensively to predict the prognosis of ICH patients [Table 2—via PubMed search]. In addition, AI software can detect ICH and chronic cerebral microbleeds, ascertain ICH volume, and predict the rate of ICH expansion. AI can aid in emergency room intake neuroimaging of patients with suspected ICH. AI methods give clinicians precise volumetric and quantitative analysis of ICH's intraparenchymal and intraventricular components, guiding treatment that may lower the morbidity and mortality of ICH in these patients. Additionally, AI analysis of serial imaging in an ICU-level setting may guide physician prognostication of ICH expansion or stability and patient outcome. Some AI studies estimate the functional outcomes of ICH patients. A physician knowing the outcome AI predicts and the relevant prognostic clinical information not considered by the AI can give patients' families an evidence-based view of the expected ICH outcome that aids decision-making.

In Epilepsy, AI can detect ictal and interictal patterns in routine and long-term EEGs. AI-based EEG analysis can be applied to adult and pediatric epilepsy patients [Table 3—via PubMed search]. AI programs may provide clinicians with information about which AED regimen would lead to better seizure control for patients with known epilepsy syndromes or genetic mutations predisposing patients to epilepsy. Also, using AI, the risk of epileptogenicity of focal MRI lesions can be predicted by routine or 1 h EEGs. This information can guide the decision for advanced neuroimaging for epilepsy patients who are epilepsy surgery candidates. This would be key in the current era given the significant evolution of surgical application in treatment refractory epilepsy patients and severely morbid conditions leading to epilepsy including Tuberous Sclerosis and Rasmussen's Encephalitis.

Artificial intelligence's continued adoption in neurology depends on clinicians and researchers continuing to test and improve AI prediction models. The quality improvement models used in industry can be used to continually improve AI by reducing diagnostic and other experience-based prediction errors. As new AI methods and protocols evolve, medical experts should iteratively compare expected and actual results to judge their validity, accuracy, and clinical value. Designing an AI algorithm is a plan, or hypothesis, that the algorithm will be of clinical value. However, testing an AI algorithm allows iterative scientific hypothesis testing and revision until the hypothesis fits the data. After the final version of the algorithm fits the practice data set, the algorithm is tested with new data to assess its accuracy and error rate. After that, the algorithm is revised as necessary using quality improvement methods. The quality improvement steps are [1] Plan, [4] Do, [6] Check, and [7] Act- PDCA cycle [Table 4] [45].

A sole human clinician can only see a tiny fraction of the patients covered by an extensive healthcare system and knows his patient outcomes, those reported by his colleagues, and those reported in the clinical literature. AI can potentially draw upon data from the entire healthcare system to derive diagnostic and prognostic information that can fill gaps in a neurologist's experience or serve as reminders before decision-making. AI can retrospectively mine data for suspected and unsuspected factors leading to an AIS or ICH that could inform future medical treatment of at-risk individuals in a neurologist's and primary care physician's practice.

The PDCA quality improvement cycle rigorously reviews the predicted and actual outcomes of AI-based methods, leading to their progressive updating and improvement. The AI models from practice data sets are tested with new clinical information and revised appropriately. Testing of mature AI models with new data assesses their clinical value and error rate. AI models can be revised and re-tested iteratively until their accuracy is clinically valuable. Many organizations and companies adopted the Deming PDCA cycle to improve their systems and functional outcomes. Implementing the PDCA concept can ensure AI-based protocols have continued quality improvement, regular checks to assess their outcomes, and are developed into clinically valuable and reliable products.

5. Conclusions

AI is a diagnostic and prognostic tool to help neurologists assess patients more efficiently and treat them more effectively. AI can usher in a new era in clinical neurology by supplying a complementary tool in stroke and epilepsy that improves diagnostics and systemic efficiency, enabling better and more predictable functional patient outcomes. From a futuristic standpoint, as more data is collected by various systems-based practices in the field of medicine, with the implementation of PDCA and more efficient AI-based stroke and epilepsy protocols, implementation systems can be utilized as adjuncts to clinical evaluation in the field of Neurology.

Author Contributions: Conceptualization, S.P.S. and J.D.H.; methodology, S.P.S. and J.D.H.; Software, S.P.S. and J.D.H. used PUBMED search; validation, S.P.S. and J.D.H.; formal analysis, S.P.S. and J.D.H.; investigation, S.P.S. and J.D.H.; resources, S.P.S. and J.D.H.; data curation, S.P.S. and J.D.H.; writing—original draft preparation, S.P.S. and J.D.H.; writing—review and editing, S.P.S. and J.D.H.; visualization, S.P.S. and J.D.H.; supervision, S.P.S. and J.D.H.; project administration, S.P.S. and J.D.H. All authors have read and agreed to the published version of the manuscript.

Funding: This work was supported by intramural research funds from the National Institute of Neurological Disorders and Stroke [ZIANS003052], National Institutes of Health.

Conflicts of Interest: The authors declare no conflict of interest.

References

1. Auger, S.D.; Jacobs, B.M.; Dobson, R.; Marshall, C.R.; Noyce, A.J. Big data, machine learning and artificial intelligence: A neurologist's guide. *Pract. Neurol.* **2020**, *21*, 4–11. [CrossRef]
2. Singh, A.; Velagala, V.R.; Kumar, T.; Dutta, R.R.; Sontakke, T. The Application of Deep Learning to Electroencephalograms, Magnetic Resonance Imaging, and Implants for the Detection of Epileptic Seizures: A Narrative Review. *Cureus* **2023**, *15*, e42460. [CrossRef]
3. Torrente, A.; Maccora, S.; Prinzi, F.; Alonge, P.; Pilati, L.; Lupica, A.; Di Stefano, V.; Camarda, C.; Vitabile, S.; Brighina, F. The Clinical Relevance of Artificial Intelligence in Migraine. *Brain Sci.* **2024**, *14*, 85. [CrossRef]
4. Vinny, P.; Vishnu, V.; Srivastava, M.P. Artificial Intelligence shaping the future of neurology practice. *Med. J. Armed. Forces India* **2021**, *77*, 276–282. [CrossRef] [PubMed]
5. Miceli, G.; Basso, M.G.; Rizzo, G.; Pintus, C.; Cocciola, E.; Pennacchio, A.R.; Tuttolomondo, A. Artificial Intelligence in Acute Ischemic Stroke Subtypes According to Toast Classification: A Comprehensive Narrative Review. *Biomedicines* **2023**, *11*, 1138. [CrossRef]
6. Koza, J.R.; Bennett, F.H.; Andre, D.; Keane, M.A. Automated Design of Both the Topology and Sizing of Analog Electrical Circuits Using Genetic Programming. In *Artificial Intelligence in Design '96*; Gero, J.S., Sudweeks, F., Eds.; Springer: Dordrecht, The Netherlands, 1996; pp. 151–170. ISBN 978-94-010-6610-5. [CrossRef]
7. Mohri, M.; Rostamizadeh, A.; Talwalkar, A. *Foundations of Machine Learning*; The MIT Press: Cambridge, MA, USA, 2012; ISBN 9780262018258.

8. Buhmann, J.; Kuhnel, H. Unsupervised and supervised data clustering with competitive neural networks. In Proceedings of the IJCNN International Joint Conference on Neural Networks, Baltimore, MD, USA, 7–11 June 1992; Volume 4, pp. 796–801. [CrossRef]
9. Brahme, A. *Comprehensive Biomedical Physics*; Elsevier: Boca Raton, FL, USA, 2014; p. 1, ISBN 978-0-444-53633-4.
10. LeCun, Y.; Bengio, Y.; Hinton, G. Deep learning. *Nature* **2015**, *521*, 436–444. [CrossRef] [PubMed]
11. Venkatesan, R.; Li, B. *Convolutional Neural Networks in Visual Computing: A Concise Guide*; CRC Press: Boca Raton, FL, USA, 2017; ISBN 978-1-351-65032-8.
12. Field, N.C.; Entezami, P.; Boulos, A.S.; Dalfino, J.; Paul, A.R. Artificial intelligence improves transfer times and ischemic stroke workflow metrics. *Interv. Neuroradiol.* **2023**, *epub ahead of print*. [CrossRef]
13. Zhou, X.-Z.; Lu, K.; Zhai, D.-C.; Cui, M.-M.; Liu, Y.; Wang, T.-T.; Shi, D.; Fan, G.-H.; Ju, S.-H.; Cai, W. The image quality and diagnostic performance of CT perfusion-derived CT angiography versus that of conventional CT angiography. *Quant. Imaging Med. Surg.* **2023**, *13*, 7294–7303. [CrossRef]
14. Wu, Y.-P.; Xiang, S.-F.; Su, Y.; Li, S.-Y.; Yang, S.-J. Application of Computed Tomography Perfusion Imaging-guided Mechanical Thrombectomy in Ischemic Stroke Patients with Large Vessel Occlusion beyond the Therapeutic Time Window. *Curr. Med. Imaging*, **2023**, *epub ahead of print*. [CrossRef]
15. Du, B.; Yin, S.; Cao, S.; Mo, Y.; Liu, Y.; Zhang, Y.; Qiu, B.; Wu, X.; Hu, P.; Wang, K.; et al. Intracranial Atherosclerotic Stenosis Is Associated with Cognitive Impairment in Patients with Non-Disabling Ischemic Stroke: A pCASL-Based Study. *Brain Connect.* **2023**, *13*, 508–518. [CrossRef] [PubMed]
16. Nazari-Farsani, S.; Yu, Y.; Armindo, R.D.; Lansberg, M.; Liebeskind, D.S.; Albers, G.; Christensen, S.; Levin, C.S.; Zaharchuk, G. Predicting final ischemic stroke lesions from initial diffusion-weighted images using a deep neural network. *NeuroImage Clin.* **2023**, *37*, 103278. [CrossRef]
17. Kossen, T.; Madai, V.I.; Mutke, M.A.; Hennemuth, A.; Hildebrand, K.; Behland, J.; Aslan, C.; Hilbert, A.; Sobesky, J.; Bendszus, M.; et al. Image-to-image generative adversarial networks for synthesizing perfusion parameter maps from DSC-MR images in cerebrovascular disease. *Front. Neurol.* **2023**, *13*, 1051397. [CrossRef] [PubMed]
18. Le, H.L.; Roh, H.G.; Kim, H.J.; Kwak, J.T. A 3D Multi-task Regression and Ordinal Regression Deep Neural Network for Collateral Imaging from Dynamic Susceptibility Contrast-Enhanced MR perfusion in Acute Ischemic Stroke. *Comput. Methods Programs Biomed.* **2022**, *225*, 107071. [CrossRef] [PubMed]
19. Neves, G.; Warman, P.; Bueso, T.; Duarte-Celada, W.; Windisch, T. Identification of successful cerebral reperfusions [mTICI $\geq$ 2b] using an artificial intelligence strategy. *Neuroradiology* **2022**, *64*, 991–997. [CrossRef] [PubMed]
20. Grosser, M.; Gellißen, S.; Borchert, P.; Sedlacik, J.; Nawabi, J.; Fiehler, J.; Forkert, N.D. Localized prediction of tissue outcome in acute ischemic stroke patients using diffusion- and perfusion-weighted MRI datasets. *PLoS ONE* **2020**, *15*, e0241917. [CrossRef] [PubMed]
21. Sathish, R.; Rajan, R.; Vupputuri, A.; Ghosh, N.; Sheet, D. Adversarially Trained Convolutional Neural Networks for Semantic Segmentation of Ischaemic Stroke Lesion using Multisequence Magnetic Resonance Imaging. In Proceedings of the2019 41st Annual International Conference of the IEEE Engineering in Medicine & Biology Society (EMBC), Berlin, Germany, 23–27 July 2019; pp. 1010–1013.
22. Reid, M.; Famuyide, A.O.; Forkert, N.D.; Talai, A.S.; Evans, J.W.; Sitaram, A.; Hafeez, M.; Najm, M.; Menon, B.K.; Demchuk, A.; et al. Accuracy and Reliability of Multiphase CTA Perfusion for Identifying Ischemic Core. *Clin. Neuroradiol.* **2019**, *29*, 543–552. [CrossRef] [PubMed]
23. Nielsen, A.; Hansen, M.B.; Tietze, A.; Mouridsen, K. Prediction of Tissue Outcome and Assessment of Treatment Effect in Acute Ischemic Stroke Using Deep Learning. *Stroke* **2018**, *49*, 1394–1401. [CrossRef] [PubMed]
24. Ho, K.C.; Speier, W.; El-Saden, S.; Arnold, C.W. Classifying Acute Ischemic Stroke Onset Time using Deep Imaging Features. *AMIA Annu. Symp. Proc.* **2018**, *2017*, 892–901.
25. Yu, Y.; Guo, D.; Lou, M.; Liebeskind, D.S.; Scalzo, F. Prediction of Hemorrhagic Transformation Severity in Acute Stroke from Source Perfusion MRI. *IEEE Trans. Biomed. Eng.* **2017**, *65*, 2058–2065. [CrossRef]
26. Tian, X.; Zeng, D.; Zhang, S.; Huang, J.; Zhang, H.; He, J.; Lu, L.; Xi, W.; Ma, J.; Bian, Z. Robust low-dose dynamic cerebral perfusion CT image restoration via coupled dictionary learning scheme. *J. X-ray Sci. Technol.* **2016**, *24*, 837–853. [CrossRef]
27. Fang, R.; Chen, T.; Sanelli, P.C. Towards robust deconvolution of low-dose perfusion CT: Sparse perfusion deconvolution using online dictionary learning. *Med. Image Anal.* **2013**, *17*, 417–428. [CrossRef]
28. Mendrik, A.; Vonken, E.; van Ginneken, B.; Smit, E.; Waaijer, A.; Bertolini, G.; Viergever, M.A.; Prokop, M. Automatic segmentation of intracranial arteries and veins in four-dimensional cerebral CT perfusion scans. *Med. Phys.* **2010**, *37*, 2956–2966. [CrossRef]
29. Meyer-Baese, A.; Lange, O.; Wismueller, A.; Hurdal, M.K. Analysis of Dynamic Susceptibility Contrast MRI Time Series Based on Unsupervised Clustering Methods. *IEEE Trans. Inf. Technol. Biomed.* **2007**, *11*, 563–573. [CrossRef]
30. Feng, H.; Wang, X.; Wang, W.; Zhao, X. Risk factors and a prediction model for the prognosis of intracerebral hemorrhage using cerebral microhemorrhage and clinical factors. *Front. Neurol.* **2023**, *14*, 1268627. [CrossRef]
31. Maghami, M.; Sattari, S.A.; Tahmasbi, M.; Panahi, P.; Mozafari, J.; Shirbandi, K. Diagnostic test accuracy of machine learning algorithms for the detection intracranial hemorrhage: A systematic review and meta-analysis study. *Biomed. Eng. Online* **2023**, *22*, 114. [CrossRef]

32. Vacek, A.; Mair, G.; White, P.; Bath, P.M.; Muir, K.W.; Salman, R.A.-S.; Martin, C.; Dye, D.; Chappell, F.M.; von Kummer, R.; et al. Evaluating artificial intelligence software for delineating hemorrhage extent on CT brain imaging in stroke. *J. Stroke Cerebrovasc. Dis.* **2024**, *33*, 107512. [CrossRef]
33. Chen, Y.; Jiang, C.; Chang, J.; Qin, C.; Zhang, Q.; Ye, Z.; Li, Z.; Tian, F.; Ma, W.; Feng, M.; et al. An artificial intelligence-based prognostic prediction model for hemorrhagic stroke. *Eur. J. Radiol.* **2023**, *167*, 111081. [CrossRef] [PubMed]
34. MacIntosh, B.J.; Liu, Q.; Schellhorn, T.; Beyer, M.K.; Groote, I.R.; Morberg, P.C.; Poulin, J.M.; Selseth, M.N.; Bakke, R.C.; Naqvi, A.; et al. Radiological features of brain hemorrhage through automated segmentation from computed tomography in stroke and traumatic brain injury. *Front. Neurol.* **2023**, *14*, 1244672. [CrossRef] [PubMed]
35. Kotovich, D.; Twig, G.; Itsekson-Hayosh, Z.; Klug, M.; Ben Simon, A.; Yaniv, G.; Konen, E.; Tau, N.; Raskin, D.; Chang, P.J.; et al. The impact on clinical outcomes after 1 year of implementation of an artificial intelligence solution for the detection of intracranial hemorrhage. *Int. J. Emerg. Med.* **2023**, *16*, 50. [CrossRef] [PubMed]
36. Li, Y.-L.; Chen, C.; Zhang, L.-J.; Zheng, Y.-N.; Lv, X.-N.; Zhao, L.-B.; Li, Q.; Lv, F.-J. Prediction of Early Perihematomal Edema Expansion Based on Noncontrast Computed Tomography Radiomics and Machine Learning in Intracerebral Hemorrhage. *World Neurosurg.* **2023**, *175*, e264–e270. [CrossRef]
37. Matsoukas, S.; Scaggiante, J.; Schuldt, B.R.; Smith, C.J.; Chennareddy, S.; Kalagara, R.; Majidi, S.; Bederson, J.B.; Fifi, J.T.; Mocco, J.; et al. Accuracy of artificial intelligence for the detection of intracranial hemorrhage and chronic cerebral microbleeds: A systematic review and pooled analysis. *Radiol. Med.* **2022**, *127*, 1106–1123. [CrossRef]
38. Lim, M.J.R.; Quek, R.H.C.; Ng, K.J.; Loh, N.-H.W.; Lwin, S.; Teo, K.; Nga, V.D.W.; Yeo, T.T.; Motani, M. Machine Learning Models Prognosticate Functional Outcomes Better than Clinical Scores in Spontaneous Intracerebral Haemorrhage. *J. Stroke Cerebrovasc. Dis.* **2021**, *31*, 106234. [CrossRef]
39. Heit, J.; Coelho, H.; Lima, F.; Granja, M.; Aghaebrahim, A.; Hanel, R.; Kwok, K.; Haerian, H.; Cereda, C.; Venkatasubramanian, C.; et al. Automated Cerebral Hemorrhage Detection Using RAPID. *Am. J. Neuroradiol.* **2020**, *42*, 273–278. [CrossRef] [PubMed]
40. Zeng, Z.; Xu, Y.; Zhou, Y.; Su, R.; Tao, L.; Wang, Z.; Chen, C.; Chen, W. Prognostic Analysis of KCNQ2 Patients via Combining EEG Deep Features and Machine Learning Classifiers. In Proceedings of the 2023 45th Annual International Conference of the IEEE Engineering in Medicine & Biology Society (EMBC), Sydney, Australia, 24–27 July 2023; pp. 1–4.
41. Wang, H.; Hu, Z.; Jiang, D.; Lin, R.; Zhao, C.; Zhao, X.; Zhou, Y.; Zhu, Y.; Zeng, H.; Liang, D.; et al. Predicting Antiseizure Medication Treatment in Children with Rare Tuberous Sclerosis Complex–Related Epilepsy Using Deep Learning. *Am. J. Neuroradiol.* **2023**, *44*, 1373–1383. [CrossRef] [PubMed]
42. Asadi-Pooya, A.A.; Fattahi, D.; Abolpour, N.; Boostani, R.; Farazdaghi, M.; Sharifi, M. Epilepsy classification using artificial intelligence: A web-based application. *Epilepsia Open* **2023**, *8*, 1362–1368. [CrossRef] [PubMed]
43. Tveit, J.; Aurlien, H.; Plis, S.; Calhoun, V.D.; Tatum, W.O.; Schomer, D.L.; Arntsen, V.; Cox, F.; Fahoum, F.; Gallentine, W.B.; et al. Automated Interpretation of Clinical Electroencephalograms Using Artificial Intelligence. *JAMA Neurol.* **2023**, *80*, 805–812. [CrossRef]
44. Torres-Gaona, G.; Aledo-Serrano, Á.; García-Morales, I.; Toledano, R.; Valls, J.; Cosculluela, B.; Munsó, L.; Raurich, X.; Trejo, A.; Blanquez, D.; et al. Artificial intelligence system, based on mjn-SERAS algorithm, for the early detection of seizures in patients with refractory focal epilepsy: A cross-sectional pilot study. *Epilepsy Behav. Rep.* **2023**, *22*, 100600. [CrossRef]
45. QA for Machine Learning Models With the PDCA Cycle. Available online: https://dzone.com/articles/qa-for-machine-learning-models-with-the-pdca-cycle (accessed on 1 February 2024).
46. Khandelwal, N. CT perfusion in acute stroke. *Indian J. Radiol. Imaging* **2008**, *18*, 281–286. [CrossRef]

Disclaimer/Publisher's Note: The statements, opinions and data contained in all publications are solely those of the individual author(s) and contributor(s) and not of MDPI and/or the editor(s). MDPI and/or the editor(s) disclaim responsibility for any injury to people or property resulting from any ideas, methods, instructions or products referred to in the content.

brain sciences

MDPI

Systematic Review

Limitations in Evaluating Machine Learning Models for Imbalanced Binary Outcome Classification in Spine Surgery: A Systematic Review

Marc Ghanem [1,2,3], Abdul Karim Ghaith [1,2], Victor Gabriel El-Hajj [1,2,4], Archis Bhandarkar [1,2], Andrea de Giorgio [5], Adrian Elmi-Terander [4,6,*] and Mohamad Bydon [1,2]

1 Mayo Clinic Neuro-Informatics Laboratory, Mayo Clinic, Rochester, MN 55902, USA; marc.ghanem01@lau.edu (M.G.); ghaith.abdulkarim@mayo.edu (A.K.G.); victor.gabriel.elhajj@stud.ki.se (V.G.E.-H.); archis.bhandarkar@gmail.com (A.B.); bydon.mohamad@mayo.edu (M.B.)
2 Department of Neurological Surgery, Mayo Clinic, Rochester, MN 55902, USA
3 School of Medicine, Lebanese American University, Byblos 4504, Lebanon
4 Department of Clinical Neuroscience, Karolinska Institutet, 17177 Stockholm, Sweden
5 Artificial Engineering, Via del Rione Sirignano, 80121 Naples, Italy; andrea@degiorgio.info
6 Department of Surgical Sciences, Uppsala University, 75236 Uppsala, Sweden
* Correspondence: adrian.elmi.terander@ki.se

Abstract: Clinical prediction models for spine surgery applications are on the rise, with an increasing reliance on machine learning (ML) and deep learning (DL). Many of the predicted outcomes are uncommon; therefore, to ensure the models' effectiveness in clinical practice it is crucial to properly evaluate them. This systematic review aims to identify and evaluate current research-based ML and DL models applied for spine surgery, specifically those predicting binary outcomes with a focus on their evaluation metrics. Overall, 60 papers were included, and the findings were reported according to the PRISMA guidelines. A total of 13 papers focused on lengths of stay (LOS), 12 on readmissions, 12 on non-home discharge, 6 on mortality, and 5 on reoperations. The target outcomes exhibited data imbalances ranging from 0.44% to 42.4%. A total of 59 papers reported the model's area under the receiver operating characteristic (AUROC), 28 mentioned accuracies, 33 provided sensitivity, 29 discussed specificity, 28 addressed positive predictive value (PPV), 24 included the negative predictive value (NPV), 25 indicated the Brier score with 10 providing a null model Brier, and 8 detailed the F1 score. Additionally, data visualization varied among the included papers. This review discusses the use of appropriate evaluation schemes in ML and identifies several common errors and potential bias sources in the literature. Embracing these recommendations as the field advances may facilitate the integration of reliable and effective ML models in clinical settings.

Keywords: machine learning; artificial intelligence; deep learning; predictive modeling; spine surgery

1. Introduction

In recent years, the integration of machine learning (ML) into spine surgery has shown promise in enabling personalized risk predictions [1,2]. These advancements could improve patient outcomes, streamline surgical decision-making, reduce costs, and optimize medical management [3]. ML, a subset of artificial intelligence (AI), utilizes computer algorithms to efficiently solve intricate tasks. A notable advantage lies in its adaptability, enabling models to continually learn and be redesigned by incorporating new data and modifying their underlying knowledge.

Machine learning has witnessed significant advancements, notably in the realm of deep learning (DL)—an advanced subset that involves neural networks with multiple layers, enabling more intricate data processing and abstraction. This structure contributes to its capability to automatically learn and extract features from complex datasets [4]. The accumulation of advancements has garnered strong support from the industry, recognizing the substantial potential of ML and DL in enhancing medical research and clinical care [5]. However, despite the developments made in prediction models, their effective application in predicting uncommon outcomes remains limited in the literature. This brings attention to the class imbalance challenge in ML, where certain classes of interest occur far less frequently than others [6].

Imbalanced data essentially means that a dataset is skewed, leading to challenges with data generalizability, inadequate training of the ML model, and false positive readings. This issue is particularly relevant in medical ML models, where only a small proportion of individuals may experience a certain event, such as a specific condition or complication. In spine surgery, the outcomes of interest, such as readmission, extended length of stay, or specific complications, are considered infrequent events. In such cases, the integration of ML for personalized risk predictions becomes trickier, as the rarity of these specific events adds complexity to predictive modeling. If ML models lack design considerations for tackling class imbalance, they may become skewed towards one end of the spectrum, making their predictions unreliable. This underscores the significance of addressing the class imbalance challenge within ML. Hence, this review highlights the importance of refining our understanding and application of evaluation methods to navigate the complexities of uncommon outcome predictions more effectively.

2. Inadequate Evaluation Metrics

A classifier can only be as effective as the metric used to assess it. Selecting the wrong metric for model evaluation can lead to suboptimal model training or even mislead the authors into selecting a poor model instead of a better-performing one. Below are metrics that should not be solely relied on for imbalanced classification.

2.1. *Accuracy*

Accuracy measures how well a model predicts the correct class. It is calculated as the ratio of correct predictions to the total number of predictions. However, when evaluating a binary classification model on an imbalanced dataset, accuracy can be misleading. This is because it only considers the total number of correct predictions without weighing the dataset's imbalance.

In scenarios with imbalanced datasets, a model consistently predicting the majority class can exhibit high accuracy but may struggle to accurately identify the minority class. When accuracy closely aligns with the class imbalance rate, it suggests the model might be predicting the majority class for all instances. In such cases, the accuracy is driven by the class imbalance, hindering the model's ability to distinguish between positive and negative classes. Therefore, it is crucial to employ multiple metrics for a comprehensive evaluation of the model's performance.

2.2. *The Area under the ROC Curve (AUROC)*

AUROC is calculated as the area under the curve of the true positive rate (TPR) versus the false positive rate (FPR). A no-skill classifier will have a score of 0.5, whereas a perfect classifier will have a score of 1.0.

While AUROC is useful for comparing the performance of different models, it can be misleading with class imbalance as the TPR and FPR are affected by the class distribution.

For instance, in a model predicting a specific disease on an imbalanced dataset, the TPR may be low as the model struggles to predict sick cases, while the FPR may be high because the model accurately predicts healthy cases. In such instances, the AUROC may yield falsely high-performance results.

2.3. Adequate Evaluation Metrics

In assessing a binary classification model on an imbalanced dataset, key metrics include the confusion matrix (CM), F1 score, Matthews correlation coefficient (MCC), and area under the precision-recall curve (AUPRC).

2.4. Confusion Matrix

The CM matrix delineates true positive, true negative, false positive, and false negative in model predictions [7]. This matrix is particularly useful for imbalanced classes, offering insights into the model's performance on each class separately. It also facilitates the calculations of various metrics such as precision, recall, and F1 score.

As mentioned earlier, relying solely on accuracy is advised against in imbalanced cases, with the confusion matrix providing a strong rationale for that. Researchers can use it to visualize the model's performance, pinpoint common errors, and make the necessary adjustments to enhance overall performance. Table 1 displays the metrics provided by the CM.

Table 1. Metrics Provided by the Confusion Matrix.

Metrics Provided by the Confusion Matrix.	
True Positive (TP)	The number of predictions where the classifier correctly predicts the positive class as positive.
True Negative (TN)	The number of predictions where the classifier correctly predicts the negative class as negative.
False Positive (FP)	The number of predictions where the classifier incorrectly predicts the negative class as positive.
False Negative (FN)	The number of predictions where the classifier incorrectly predicts the positive class as negative.
Recall/Sensitivity	The proportion of true positive predictions to all actual positive cases TP/(TP + FN).
Specificity	The proportion of all negative samples that are correctly predicted as negative by the classifier TN/(TN + FP).
Precision/Positive predictive value (PPV)	The proportion of true positive predictions to all positive predictions TP/(TP + FP).
Negative predictive value (NPV)	The proportion of true negative predictions to all negative predictions made by the model TN/(TN + FN).

2.5. F1 Score

Improving the model's performance often involves aiming for a balance between precision and recall. However, it is essential to acknowledge that there is a trade-off between these two metrics, where enhancement of one metric score can lead to a reduction in the other. The correct balance is highly reliant on the model's objective and is referred to as the F1 score. The F1 score is particularly useful when faced with imbalanced classes as it emphasizes the harmonic mean between precision and recall [8].

2.6. Matthews Correlation Coefficient (MCC)

The Matthews correlation coefficient (MCC) stands out as a robust metric, especially when dealing with imbalanced class data. MCC is a balanced metric that takes into account all four components of the CM. It is defined as $(TP \times TN - FP \times FN)/\text{sqrt}((TP + FP) \times (TP + FN) \times (TN + FP) \times (TN + FN))$. The MCC tends to approach +1 in cases of perfect classification and −1 in instances of entirely incorrect classification (inverted classes). When facing class-imbalanced data, the MCC is considered a strong metric due to its effectiveness in capturing various aspects of classification performance. Notably, it remains close to 0 for completely random classifications.

2.7. Informedness (Youden's J Statistic)

Informedness, also known as Youden's J statistic, quantifies the difference between the true positive rate (Recall) and the false positive rate (FPR). It is computed as Recall + Specificity − 1, with values ranging from −1 to +1. A higher informedness value signifies a superior classifier [9].

2.8. Markedness

Markedness gauges the difference between the PPV and NPV. The calculation involves adding PPV and NPV, then subtracting 1, resulting in a range from −1 to +1. A higher markedness value suggests a better overall performance in predictive values [9].

2.9. The Area under the Precision-Recall Curve (AUPRC)

AUPRC is a valuable metric when working with imbalanced datasets as it considers precision and recall in its calculation [10]. This is important when dealing with imbalanced datasets where the focus is on identifying positive cases and minimizing false positives. The AUPRC is derived by plotting precision and recall values at various thresholds and then computing the area under the resulting curve.

The resulting curve is formed by different points, and classifiers performing better under different thresholds will be ranked higher. On the plot, a no-skill classifier manifests as a horizontal line with precision proportional to the number of positive examples in the dataset. Conversely, a point in the top right corner signifies a perfect classifier.

2.10. Brier Score (BS)

The Brier Score (BS) serves as a metric for assessing the accuracy of a probabilistic classifier and is used to evaluate the performance of binary classification models [11]. It is determined by calculating the mean squared difference between the predicted probabilities for the positive class and the true binary outcomes. The BS ranges from 0 to 1, with a score of 0 indicating a perfect classifier, while 1 suggests predicted probabilities completely discordant with actual outcomes.

It is important to note that while the BS possesses desirable properties, it does have limitations. For instance, it may favor tests with high specificity in situations where the clinical context requires high sensitivity, especially when the prevalence is low [12].

To address these limitations, a model's BS evaluation should consider the outcome prevalence in the patient sample, prompting the computation of the null BS. The null BS acts as a benchmark for evaluating a model's performance by always predicting the most prevalent outcome in the dataset. The model's BS is then compared to that of the null model, and ΔBrier is calculated by subtracting the null BS from that of the model under evaluation. The ΔBrier is a scalar value and indicates the extent to which the model outperforms the null model. The formula follows ΔBrier = BS of the model − BS of the null model.

2.11. Additional Evaluation Metrics and Graphical Tools

2.11.1. Calibration Curves

A calibration plot is a graphical tool used to evaluate a probabilistic model. The curve illustrates the alignment between the model's predicted probabilities and the observed frequencies of the positive class in the test set. A perfect model would exhibit an intercept value of 0 and a slope value of 1. These plots are particularly valuable for evaluating models trained on imbalanced data, offering insights into the model's ability to predict the positive class.

Addressing imbalanced data involves using techniques such as undersampling and oversampling to achieve classification balance and alleviate classifier bias. However, determining the optimal sample size for training remains a significant challenge. An alternative strategy is to leverage learning curves, which provide insights into reducing error probability as the training set size increases. One example is a theoretical learning curve for the multi-class Bayes classifier, considering general multivariate parametric models of class-conditional probability density [13]. This curve offers an estimate of the reduction in the excess probability of error without relying on specific model parameters. Learning curves contribute to an essential understanding of the model's behavior and its performance improvements with increased data. Table 1 outlines the metrics derived from the confusion matrix.

2.11.2. Decision Curve

A decision curve is a graphical tool used to evaluate a classifier's performance by examining the trade-off between sensitivity and 1-specificity across varying thresholds for classifying an instance as positive. The optimal threshold is the one that maximizes the net benefit. By convention, the model's benefit strategy at each threshold is compared to the treat-all and treat-none strategies. The decision curve analysis stands out from other statistical methods by its ability to evaluate the clinical value of a predictor. Figure 1A–D depicts the AUROC, AUPRC, calibration, and decision curve figures.

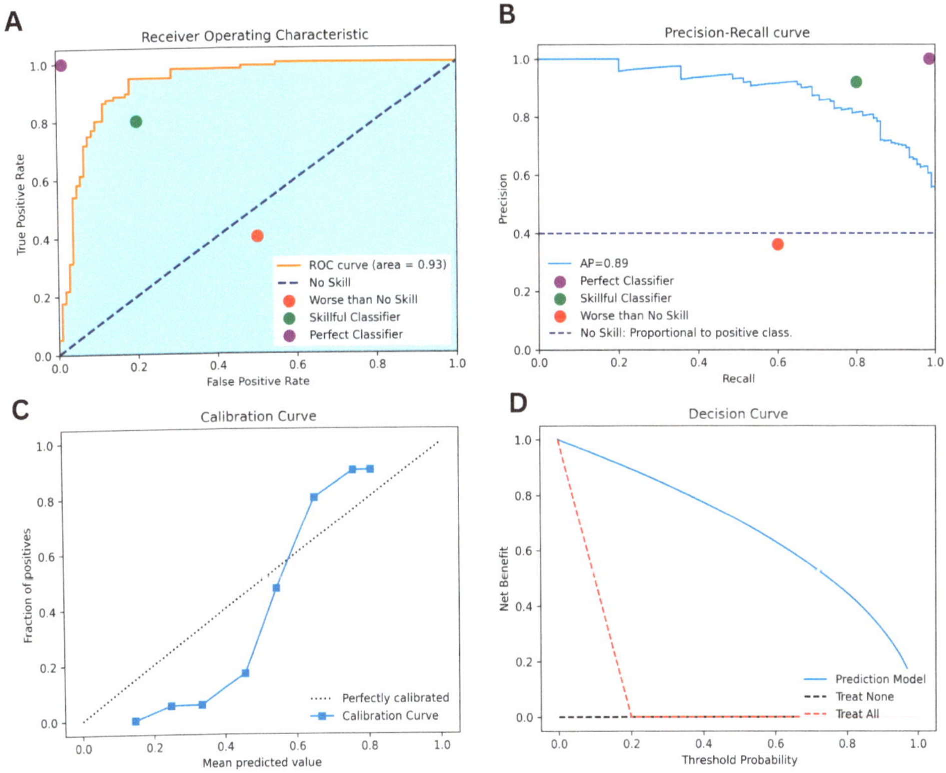

Figure 1. Illustrations of Various Performance Metrics for the Same Classifier: (**A**) Area Under the Receiver Operating Characteristic Curve, (**B**) Area Under the Precision-Recall Curve, (**C**) Calibration Curve, (**D**) Decision Curve.

With that in mind, this systematic review of the literature aims to provide a comprehensive summary of the state of AI within the field of spine surgery. The focus will be on reporting metrics, data visualization, and common errors, including inappropriate handling of imbalanced datasets and incomplete reporting of model performance metrics.

3. Materials and Methods

3.1. Data Sources and Search Strategies

A comprehensive search of several databases was performed on 28 February 2023. Results were limited to the English language but had no date limitations. The databases included Ovid MEDLINE(R), Ovid Embase, Ovid Cochrane Central Register of Controlled Trials, Ovid Cochrane Database of Systematic Reviews, Web of Science Core Collection via Clarivate Analytics, and Scopus via Elsevier. The search strategies were designed and conducted by a medical librarian in collaboration with the study investigators (Table S1). Controlled vocabulary supplemented with keywords was used. The actual strategies listing all search terms used and how they are combined are available in the Supplemental Material. Ultimately, 3340 papers and 121 full-text articles were assessed, resulting in the inclusion of 60 studies (Figure 2) [14–72]. This review was conducted in accordance with the PRISMA guidelines (Table S2).

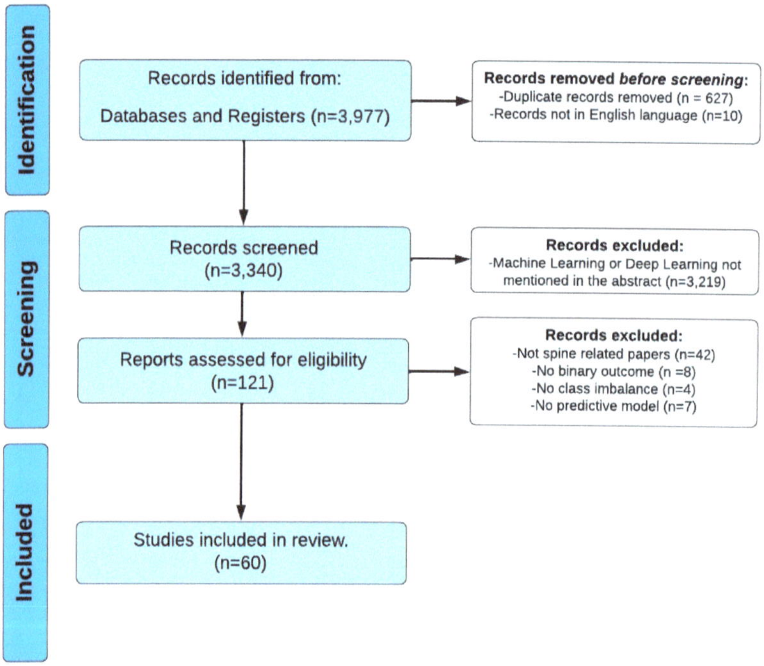

Figure 2. PRISMA Flowchart Illustrating Systematic Review Search Strategy.

3.2. Eligibility Criteria and Data Extraction

Inclusion criteria encompass studies focusing on ML-based prediction models pertaining to binary surgical outcomes following spine surgery. Both intraoperative and postoperative outcomes were eligible. Exclusion criteria comprised studies predicting nonbinary outcomes (e.g., 3+ categorical or numeric outcomes), those predicting non-spine surgical outcomes, studies with balanced outcomes, and those lacking predictive models.

The extracted data from all studies included the first author, paper title, year of publication, spinal pathology and surgery type, sample size, outcome variable (the primary result being measured), imbalance percentage, accuracy, AUROC (area under the receiver operating characteristic curve), sensitivity, specificity, PPV (positive predictive value), NPV (negative predictive value), Brier score (BS), other metrics, dataset, performance, journal, and error type (Table 2).

Table 2. Performance Metrics, Datasets, and Outcome Variables in Reviewed ML Studies on Imbalanced Binary Classification in Spine Surgery.

Author	Year	Primary Pathology and Surgery Type	Sample Size	Outcome Variable	Imbalance	Accuracy	AUROC	Sensitivity	Specificity	PPV	NPV	Brier	Other Metric	Dataset	Performance Related Figures	Journal	Error Type
Cabrera	2022	Posterior Cervical Decompression with Instrumented Fusion	29,949	>4 days LOS	18.21% (5454)	0.781	0.781	0.4978	0.842	-	-	-	-	NSQIP 2008–2018	AUROC Calibration plot	Journal of Clinical Neuroscience	I and II
				Readmission	4.4% (1318)	0.9512	0.791	0.4615	0.9718			-					
				Reoperation	2.51% (752)	0.9559	0.781	0.4333	0.9683			-					
				Infection	4.4% (1318)	0.9311	0.724	0.1695	0.9676			-					
				Transfusion	2.6% (779)	0.7577	0.902	0.8864	0.7532			-					
Han	2019	Spine Surgery	345,510 * 760,724 **	Pulmonary complications	4.7% (16,138) * 5.3% 40,046) **	-	0.75	0.82	0.52	-	-	0.044	-	MKS */CMS **	AUROC Calibration plot	The Spine Journal	I and II
				Congestive heart failure	1.0% (3538) * 3.6% 26,989) **	-	0.75	0.84	0.51	-	-	0.026					
				Pneumonia	1.9% (6629) * 2.9% 21,861) **	-	0.74	0.81	0.51	-	-	0.024					
				Urinary tract infections	3.3% (11,410) * 6.2% 46,786) **	-	0.71	0.78	0.52	-	-	0.075					
				Neurologic complications	2.1% (7317) * 4.0% 29,462) **	-	0.69	0.76	0.51	-	-	0.032					
				Cardiac dysrhythmia	4.3% (14,689) * 10.6% (80,822) **	-	0.72	0.78	0.53	-	-	0.53					
				Overall adverse events	18.0% (60,958) * 27.6% 209,646) **	-	0.7	0.71	0.57	-	-	0.166					
				Overall medical complications	-	-	0.7	-	-	-	-	-					
				Overall surgical complications	-	-	0.69	-	-	-	-	-					
Kuris	2021	Anterior, Posterior, and Posterior Interbody Lumbar Spinal Fusion	63,533 ALIF: 12,915 PLIF: 27,212 PSF:23,406	Readmission	ALIF: 4.92% (635) PLIF: 4.41% (1200) PSF: 4.49% (1051)	0.94–0.95	0.64–0.65	-	-	-	-	0.048–0.052	-	NSQIP 2009–2018	Visualization of BS Calibration plot	World Neurosurgery	I

Table 2. *Cont.*

Author	Year	Primary Pathology and Surgery Type	Sample Size	Outcome Variable	Imbalance	Accuracy	AUROC	Sensitivity	Specificity	PPV	NPV	Brier	Other Metric	Dataset	Performance Related Figures	Journal	Error Type
Shah	2021	Lumbar Spinal Fusion	38,788	Readmission or Major Complication	11.5% (4470)	-	0.686	-	-	-	-	0.094	AUPRC: 0.283	All California hospitals 2015–2017	AUROC PR-curve	World Neurosurgery	I
Valliani	2022	Thoracolumbar Spine Surgery	SCDW: 5224	Non-home discharge	SCDW: 23.28% (1216)	-	0.81	-	-	0.64	0.83	-	-	Algorithm development: SCDW *** 2008–2019	AUROC Calibration plot	World Neurosurgery	I
			NIS:492,312		NIS: 20.64% (101,613)	-	0.77	-	-	0.6	0.82	-	-	Out-of-sample validation: National Inpatient Sample 2009–2017			
Gowd	2022	Anterior Cervical Discectomy and Fusion	42,194	Any adverse event	3.14% (1327)	-	0.73	0.029	0.9994	0.615	0.966	-	-	NSQIP 2011–2017	AUROC Confusion matrix	World Neurosurgery	II
				Extended length of stay	16.36% (6905)	-	0.73	0.1821	0.9793	0.65	0.85	-	-				
				Transfusion	0.44% (184)	-	0.9	0.0294	0.9998	0.4	0.996	-	-				
				Surgical site infection	058% (243)	-	0.63	0	1	0	0.993	-	-				
				Return to OR	1.58% (667)	-	0.64	0	1	0	0.982	-	-				
				Pneumonia	0.76% (3210)	-	0.8	0.0102	0.9989	0.067	0.992	-	-				
Ogink	2019	Spondylolisthesis Surgery	9338	Non-home discharge	18.6% (1737)	-	0.753	-	-	-	-	0.132 Null: 0.152	-	NSQIP 2009–2016	AUROC Calibration plot	European Spine Journal	I
Karhade	2018	Lumbar Degenerative Disc Disorders Elective Surgery	26,364	Non-routine discharge	9.28% (2447)	-	0.823	-	-	0.33	0.54	0.0713 Null: 0.086	-	NSQIP 2011–2016	AUROC Calibration plot Decision curve	Neurosurgical Focus	I
Kalagara	2019	Lumbar Laminectomy	26,869	Unplanned readmission	5.59% (1502)	0.950/ 0.796	0.801 / 0.690	0.496/ 0.405	-	-	-	-	-	NSQIP 2011–2014	-	J Neurosurg Spine	I and II
Hopkins	2020	Posterior Lumbar Fusion	23,264	Readmission	5.15% (1198)	0.962	0.812	0.355	0.995	0.785	0.97	-	-	NSQIP 2011–2016	AUROC	J Neurosurg Spine	II

Table 2. *Cont.*

Author	Year	Primary Pathology and Surgery Type	Sample Size	Outcome Variable	Imbalance	Accuracy	AUROC	Sensitivity	Specificity	PPV	NPV	Brier	Other Metric	Dataset	Performance Related Figures	Journal	Error Type
Goyal	2019	Spinal Fusion	59,145	Discharge to non-home facility	12.6% (7452)	0.77–0.79	0.85–0.87	0.77–0.80	0.77–0.79	0.32–0.35	0.96	-	-	NSQIP 2012–2013	-	J Neurosurg Spine	II
				30-day unplanned readmission	4.5% (2662)	0.59–0.71	0.63–0.66	0.46–0.63	0.59–0.72	0.07	0.97	-	-				
Stopa	2019	Elective Spine Surgery	144	Non-routine discharge	6.[illegible]% (10)	-	0.89	0.6	0.95	0.5	0.97	0.049	-	**** 2013–2015	AUROC Calibration plot Decision curve Confusion matrix	J Neurosurg Spine	II
Li	2022	Single-Level Laminectomy Surgery	35,644	Discharged on day of surgery	37.1% (13,230)	0.69/0.70	0.77/0.77	0.83/0.58	0.55/0.80	0.77/0.69	0.64/0.70	-	-	NSQIP 2017–2018	-	Global Spine Journal	II
Veeramani	2022	Anterior Cervical Discectomy and Fusion	54,502	Unplanned re-intubation	0.5 % (278)	72–99.6	0.52–0.77	-	-	-	-	0.04–0.18	-	NSQIP 2010–2018	AUROC Calibration plot	Global Spine Journal	I
DiSilvestro	2020	Metastatic Intraspinal Neoplasm Excision	2094	Mortality	5.1[illegible]% (108)	-	0.898	-	-	-	-	-	-	NSQIP 2006–2018	AUROC	World Neurosurgery	I
Zhang	2021	Posterior Spine Fusion Surgery	1281	Short LOS	20.5% (262)	0.68–0.83	0.566–0.821	-	-	-	-	0.13–0.29	-	NSQIP 2006–2018	AUROC Calibration plot	Journal of Clinical Medicine	I
Kim	2018	Posterior Lumbar Spine Fusion	22,629	Cardiac complications	0.4[illegible]% (100)	-	0.71	0	0.9997	0	0.9985	-	-	NSQIP 2010–2014	AUROC Confusion matrix	Spine (Phila Pa 1976)	I and II
				VTE complications	1.0[illegible]% (242)	-	0.588	-	-	-	-	-	-				
				Wound complications	1.8[illegible]% (420)	-	0.613	0	0.9999	0	0.9785	-	-				
				Mortality	0.15% (34)	-	0.703	-	-	-	-	-	-				
Arvind	2018	Anterior Cervical Discectomy	20,879	Mortality	0.[illegible]% (21)	-	0.979	0.1667	0.9943	0.0278	0.9992	-	-	Multicenter data set & NSQIP 2010–2014	AUROC Confusion matrix	Spine Deformity	I and II
				Wound complications	0.5% (105)	-	0.518	0.5429	0.4458	0.0055	0.9943	-	-				
				VTE complications	0.[illegible]% (63)	-	0.656	-	-	-	-	-	-				
				Cardiac complications	0.2% (42)	-	0.772	-	-	-	-	-	-				

Table 2. *Cont.*

Author	Year	Primary Pathology and Surgery Type	Sample Size	Outcome Variable	Imbalance	Accuracy	AUROC	Sensitivity	Specificity	PPV	NPV	Brier	Other Metric	Dataset	Performance Related Figures	Journal	Error Type
Arora	2022	Elective Spine Surgery	3678	Discharged to rehabilitation	22% (809)	-	0.79	0.8	0.64	-	-	-	-	Single academic institution	AUROC	Spine Epidemiology	I
Ogink	2019	Lumbar spinal stenosis	28,600	Non-home discharge	18.2% (5205)	-	0.751	-	-	-	-	0.131 Null: 0.15	-	NSQIP 2009–2016	AUROC Calibration plot	European Spine Journal	I
Kim	2018	Spinal Deformity Procedures	4073	Mortality	0.5% (29)	-	0.844	0	1	0	0.9937	-	-	NSQIP 2010–2014	AUROC Confusion matrix	Spine Deformity	I & II
				Wound complications	2.4% (139)	-	0.606	0.6579	0.5871	0.0343	0.9872	-	-				
				VTE complications	1.8% (105)	-	0.547	-	-	-	-	-	-				
				Cardiac complications	0.7% (39)	-	0.768	-	-	-	-	-	-				
Zhang	2022	Degenerative spinal disease surgery	663	Postop Delerium	27.45% (182)	0.77	0.87	0.861	0.773	-	-	-	F1: 0.673 Youden: 0.34	Single academic institution	Calibration plots Decision curve	CNS Neuroscience & Therapeutics	I
Yang	2022	Thoracolumbar burst fracture	161	Perioperative blood loss	38.5% (62)	0.783	0.864	0.867	0.814	0.741	0.826	-	F1: 0.793	Single academic institution	AUROC	Frontiers in Public Health	None
Xiong	2022	Posterior Lumbar Interbody Fusion	584	Surgical site infection	5.65% (33)	0.9107	0.8726	0.3333	0.974	0.625	0.9184	-	F3: 0.5747	Single academic institution	AUROC Confusion matrix	Computational & Mathematical Methods in Medicine	II
Wang	2020	Microvascular decompression	912	Postop Delerium	24.2% (221)	0.923	0.962	0.788	-	0.881	-	-	F1: 0.832	Single academic institution	AUROC	Journal of Clinical Anesthesia	I
Wang	2021	Posterior Lumbar Fusion	13,500	Venous thromboembolism	0.95% (1283)	-	0.709	-	-	-	-	-	-	NSQIP 2010–2017	-	Global Spine Journal	I
Wang	2021	Posterior laminectomy and fusion with cervical myelopathy	184	C5 palsy	14.13% (26)	0.918	0.923	0.6667	0.9677	0.8	0.9375	-	-	Single academic institution	AUROC Confusion matrix	Journal of Orthopaedic Surgery and Research	None

Table 2. *Cont.*

Author	Year	Primary Pathology and Surgery Type	Sample Size	Outcome Variable	Imbalance	Accuracy	AUROC	Sensitivity	Specificity	PPV	NPV	Brier	Other Metric	Dataset	Performance Related Figures	Journal	Error Type
Wang	2021	Minimally Invasive Transforaminal Lumbar Interbody Fusion	705	Surgical site infections	4.68% (33)	0.9	0.78	-	-	-	-	-	-	Single academic institution	AUROC	Frontiers in Medicine	I
Zhang	2021	Posterior Spine Fusion Surgery	1281	Short length of stay	20.5% (262)	0.831	0.814	-	-	-	-	0.13	-	NSQIP 2006–2018	AUROC Calibration plots	Journal of neurosurgery	I
Valliani	2022	Cervical Spine Surgery	SAI: 4342 NIS: 311,582	Extended length of stay	25% (1086/77,896)	-	0.87/0.84	0.70/0.57	0.89/0.92	0.75/0.75	0.86/0.83	-	-	Single academic institution National Inpatient Sample	AUROC	Neurosurgery	None
Stopa	2019	Elective Spine Surgery	144	Non-routine discharge	6.9% (10)	-	0.89	-	-	0.5	0.97	-	-	**** 2013–2015	AUROC Calibration plot	Neurosurgery	I
Siccoli	2019	Lumbar spinal stenosis	635	Reoperation Overall	9.5% (60)	0.69	0.66	0.32	0.69	0.1	0.9	0.09	F1: 0.15	Single academic institution	AUROC	Neurosurgical Focus	II
			635	Reoperation at Index	4.3% (27)	0.63	0.61	0.5	0.64	0.07	0.96	0.05	F1: 0.12				
			451	Prolonged Operation	15% (68)	0.78	0.54	0.85	0.23	0.91	0.14	0.13	F1: 0.88				
			633	Extended Hospital Stay	15% (95)	0.77	0.58	0.27	0.87	0.28	0.86	0.13	F1: 0.27				
Shah	2022	Posterior cervical spinal fusion	6822	Major complication or 30-day readmission	18.8% (1279)	0.7214	0.679	0.5117	0.7699	0.3394	0.8722	0.4081	AUPRC: 0.377	California hospitals 2015–2017	AUROC PR-curve Confusion matrix	European Spine Journal	II
Saravi	2022	Lumbar Decompression Surgery	236	Extended length of stay	25% (59)	0.814	0.814	-	-	-	-	-	-	Single academic institution	AUROC	Journal of Clinical Medicine	I
Russo	2021	Anterior Cervical Discectomy and Fusion	1516	Extended length of stay	42.4% (643)	0.66/0.69	0.68/0.68	0.52/0.49	0.72/0.78	0.44/0.48	0.78/0.78	-	-	Single academic institution	AUROC Confusion matrix Decision curve	Journal of the American Academy of Orthopaedic Surgeons	II

Table 2. *Cont.*

Author	Year	Primary Pathology and Surgery Type	Sample Size	Outcome Variable	Imbalance	Accuracy	AUROC	Sensitivity	Specificity	PPV	NPV	Brier	Other Metric	Dataset	Performance Related Figures	Journal	Error Type
Rodrigues	2022	Anterior Cervical Discectomy and Fusion	176,816	2-yr reoperation	5.6% (9956))	-	0.671	-	-	-	-	-	-	^ 2007 to 2016	AUROC Calibration plot	Spine	I
				90-day complication	7.5% (13,254)		0.823										
				90-day readmission	6.3% (11,192)		0.713										
Ren	2022	Lumbar Discectomy	1159	Recurrent lumbar disc herniation	11.22% (130)	0.8641	-	0.8269	-	0.8958	-	-	F1: 0.86	Single academic institution	AUROC	Global Spine Journal	I
Porche	2022	Lumbar surgery	231	Urinary retention	25.9% (60)	-	0.737	0.954	0.254	0.6	0.79	-	-	Single academic institution	AUROC Confusion matrix Calibration plot	Journal of Neurosurgery Spine	I
Pedersen	2022	Lumbar Disc Herniation	1988	EuroQol	36.5% (726)	0.79	0.84	0.7	0.84	0.83	0.71	-	MCC ^^: 0.54 F1: 0.83	Danish national registry for spine surgery	-	Global Spine Journal	None
				Oswestry Disability Index	36.3% (721)	0.69	0.74	0.67	0.7	0.71	0.65	-	MCC ^^: 0.37 F1: 0.71				
				Visual Analog Scale Leg	32.3% (643)	0.64	0.65	0.43	0.8	0.66	0.6	-	MCC ^^: 0.25 F1: 0.57				
				Visual Analog Scale Back	32.3% (643)	0.72	0.78	0.64	0.77	0.79	0.61	-	MCC ^^: 0.41 F1: 0.78				
				Ability to return to work (1 year)	14.2% (282)	0.86	0.81	0.61	0.92	0.91	0.63	-	MCC ^^: 0.53 F1: 0.91				
Nunes	2022	Thoracolumbar fractures surgery	215,999	30-day readmission	8.8% (19,148)	0.575	0.743	0.776	0.556	0.145	0.962	-	F1: 0.245	HCUP and SID in 187 hospitals in Florida 2014 to 2018	-	International Journal of Health Planning & Management	II

Table 2. *Cont.*

Author	Year	Primary Pathology and Surgery Type	Sample Size	Outcome Variable	Imbalance	Accuracy	AUROC	Sensitivity	Specificity	PPV	NPV	Brier	Other Metric	Dataset	Performance Related Figures	Journal	Error Type
Merali	2019	Degenerative cervical myelopathy	605	6 Month: SF-6D	-	0.718	0.71	0.75	0.5	0.9	0.25	-	-	Multicenter AOSpine CSM North America	AUROC Confusion matrix	PLoS ONE	II
				12 Month: SF-6D		0.77	0.7	0.78	0.63	0.98	0.12						
				24 Month: SF-6D		0.708	0.73	0.74	0.47	0.92	0.17						
				6 Month: mJOA		0.667	0.73	0,7	0.59	0.82	0.43						
				12 Month: mJOA		0.713	0.73	0.7	0.59	0.82	0.43						
				24 Month: mJOA		0.649	0.67	0.63	0.8	0.96	0.23						
Martini	2021	Spine Surgery	11,150	Non-home discharge	15.8% (1764)	-	0.91	-	-	-	-	-	-	Single academic institution	AUROC	Spine	I
Khan	2020	Degenerative Cervical Myelopathy	702	Worsening functional status	12.1% (85)	0.714	0.788	0.779	0.704	-	-	-	-	Multicenter	AUROC Calibration plot	Neurosurgery	I
Karhade	2019	Spinal metastasis	1790	30-day mortality	8.4% (152)	-	0.769	-	-	-	-	0.0706 Null: 0.079	-	NSQIP 2009 through 2016	AUROC Calibration plot Decision curve	Neurosurgery	I
Karhade	2019	Lumbar disc herniation	5413	Sustained postoperative opioid prescription	7.7% (416)	-	0.79	-	-	-	-	0.065 Null: 0.071	-	Multicenter	AUROC Calibration plot Decision curve	The Spine Journal	I
Karhade	2019	Anterior cervical discectomy and fusion	2737	Sustained postoperative opioid prescription	9.9% (270)	-	0.8	-	-	-	-	0.075 Null: 0.089	-	Multicenter	AUROC Calibration plot Decision curve	The Spine Journal	I
Karhade	2022	Spinal metastasis	4303	6-week mortality	14.1% (610)	-	0.84	-	-	-	-	0.1 Null: 0.12	-	Multicenter	AUROC Calibration plot Decision curve	The Spine Journal	I

Table 2. *Cont.*

Author	Year	Primary Pathology and Surgery Type	Sample Size	Outcome Variable	Imbalance	Accuracy	AUROC	Sensitivity	Specificity	PPV	NPV	Brier	Other Metric	Dataset	Performance Related Figures	Journal	Error Type
Karhade	2019	Lumbar spine surgery	8435	Sustained postoperative opioid prescription	2.5% (82)	-	0.7	-	-	-	-	0.039 Null: 0.041	-	Multicenter	AUROC Calibration plot Decision curve	The Spine Journal	I
Karhade	2021	Anterior lumbar spine surgery	1035	Intraoperative vascular injury	7.2% (75)	-	0.92	0.86	0.93	0.52	0.99	0.04 Null: 0.077	F1: 0.44 AUPRC: 0.74	Multicenter	AUROC Calibration plot Decision curve	The Spine Journal	II
							0.75	-	-	-	-	0.072 Null: 0.077	-				I
Karhadea	2021	Anterior cervical discectomy and fusion	2917	Length of stay greater than one day	35.2% (1027)	-	0.68	-	-	-	-	0.21	-	-	AUROC Calibration plot	Seminars in Spine Surgery	I
Karabacak	2023	Spinal Tumor Resections	3073	Prolonged length of stay	25% (769)	0.804	0.745	0.618	-	0.478	-	-	F1: 0.538 MCC: 0.422 AUPRC: 0.602	NSQIP 2015 through 2020	AUROC PR-curve	Cancers	II
				Non-home discharge	23.4% (718)	0.75	0.701	0.442	-	0.375	-	-	F1: 0.405 MCC: 0.250 AUPRC: 0.408				II
				Major complications	12.33% (379)	0.856	0.73	0.383	-	0.221	-	-	F1: 0.279 MCC: 0.216 AUPRC: 0.309				II
Jin	2022	Intradural Spinal Tumors	4488	Readmission	11.7% (524)	-	0.693/ 0.525/ 0.643	-	-	-	-	0.093/ 0.093/ 0.099	-	IBM MarketScan Claims Database 2007–2016	AUROC Calibration plots	Neurospine	I
				Non-home discharge	18.9% (956)	-	0.786	-	-	-	-	0.155					

Table 2. *Cont.*

Author	Year	Primary Pathology and Surgery Type	Sample Size	Outcome Variable	Imbalance	Accuracy	AUROC	Sensitivity	Specificity	PPV	NPV	Brier	Other Metric	Dataset	Performance Related Figures	Journal	Error Type
Jain	2020	Long Segment Posterior Lumbar Spine Fusion	37,852	Discharge-to-facility	35.4% (13,400)	-	0.77	-	-	-	-	-	-	State Inpatient Database 2005–2010	AUROC	The Spine Journal	I
				90-day readmission	19.0% (7192)	-	0.65	-	-	-	-	-	-				
				90-day major medical complications	13.0% (4921)	-	0.7	-	-	-	-	-	-				
Hopkins	2020	Posterior spinal fusions	4046	Surgical Site Infection	1.[illegible]% (61)	-	0.775	0.4955	0.9988	0.9256	0.985	-	-	Single academic institution	AUROC	Clinical Neurology & Neurosurgery	II
Fatima	2020	Lumbar Degenerative Spondylolisthesis	80,610	Overall adverse events	4.9% (3965)	-	0.7	-	-	-	-	-	-	NSQIP 2005–2016	AUROC Calibration plot Decision curve	World Neurosurgery	I & II
				Medical adverse events	10.1% (8165)	-	0.7	-	-	-	-	0.02	-				
				Surgical adverse events	1.9% (1518)	-	0.69	-	-	-	-	0.07	-				
				Pneumonia	0.6% (450)	-	0.71	0.95	0.91	0.26	-	0.04	-				
				Bleeding transfusion	5.3% (4268)	-	0.7	0.98	0.95	0.24	-	0.05	-				
				Urinary tract infection	1.3% (1074)	-	0.7	-	-	-	-	0.01	-				
				Superficial wound infection	0.9% (750)	-	0.62	0.97	0.95	0.23	-	-	-				
				Sepsis	0.6% (473)	-	0.63	-	-	-	-	-	-				
Etzel	2022	Lumbar Arthrodesis	ALIF:12,915 PLIF/TLIF: 27,212 PSF: 23,406	Prolonged length of stay	-	0.799/ 0.813/ 0.804	0.752/ 0.723/ 0.753	-	-	-	-	0.15/ 0.15 0.14	-	NSQIP 2009–2018	AUROC Calibration plots	Journal of the American Academy of Orthopaedic Surgeons	I

Table 2. *Cont.*

Author	Year	Primary Pathology and Surgery Type	Sample Size	Outcome Variable	Imbalance	Accuracy	AUROC	Sensitivity	Specificity	PPV	NPV	Brier	Other Metric	Dataset	Performance Related Figures	Journal	Error Type
Elsamadicy	2022	Metastatic Spinal Column Tumors	4346	Readmission	22.8% (991)	-	0.59	-	-	-	-	-	-	Nationwide Readmission Database 2016–2018	AUROC	Global Spine Journal	I
Dong	2022	Minimally Invasive Kyphoplasty in Osteoporotic Vertebral Compression Fractures	346	Risk of Recollapse	11.56% (40)	0.8844	0.81	0.875	0.8856	0.5	0.9819	-	-	Single academic institution	AUROC Confusion matrix	Frontiers in Public Health	II
Dong	2022	Lumbar Interbody Fusion	157	Short Term Unfavorable Clinical Outcomes	16.56% (26)	0.9367	0.88	0.7667	0.9766	0.8846	0.947	-	-	Single academic institution	AUROC Confusion matrix	BMC Musculoskeletal Disorders	None
				Long Term Unfavorable Clinical Outcomes	5.7% (9)	0.9459	0.78	0.9291	0.9776	0.9874	0.8792	-	-				
Yen	2022	Lumbar disc herniation	1316	Sustained postoperative opioid prescription	3.1% (41)	-	0.76	-	-	-	-	0.028	AUPRC: 0.33	Single academic institution	AUROC AUPRC Calibration plot Decision curve	The Spine Journal	I

* Truven MarketScan (MKS) and MarketScan Medicaid Databases; ** Centers for Medicare and Medicaid Services (CMS) Medicare database. *** Single-center data warehouse; **** Transitional Care Program at Brigham and Women's Hospital. ^ IBM MarketScan Commercial Claims and Encounters Database and Medicare Supplement; ^^ Matthews's correlation coefficient. HCUP: Healthcare Cost and Utilization Project; PR: Precision-Recall; SID: State Inpatient Database; AUROC: Area under the ROC curve; AUPRC: Area under the PR curve; BS: Brier Score.

3.3. Data Synthesis and Risk of Bias Assessment

Our aim was to investigate the methodologies employed by the included studies, emphasizing the process rather than the outcomes or findings themselves. Accordingly, we refrained from engaging in narrative synthesis, data pooling, risk of bias assessment, or evidence certainty determination. Instead, our review specifically addressed methodologies related to models handling class imbalance.

3.4. Statistical Analysis

Given the considerable heterogeneity between studies, we did not perform a meta-analysis and opted for a qualitative and comprehensive analysis instead. Study characteristics are presented using frequencies and percentages for categorical variables. In cases where studies reported multiple results within a single outcome (e.g., different AUCs per type of complication), the top scores were taken. Metrics were computed for studies that provided a confusion matrix.

4. Results

4.1. Characteristics of the Included Studies

The selected papers cover a variety of outcomes, some focusing on a single target while others address multiple targets. Table 2 outlines the metrics derived from the confusion matrix. Among the 60 papers, 12 focused on readmissions, 13 predicted lengths of stay (LOS), 12 addressed non-home discharge, 6 estimated mortality, and 5 anticipated reoperations. The models also forecasted a variety of medical and surgical outcomes, as detailed in Table 3. The target outcomes exhibited data imbalances ranging from 0.44% to 42.4%. Figure 3 illustrates the growing number of papers in the field over time.

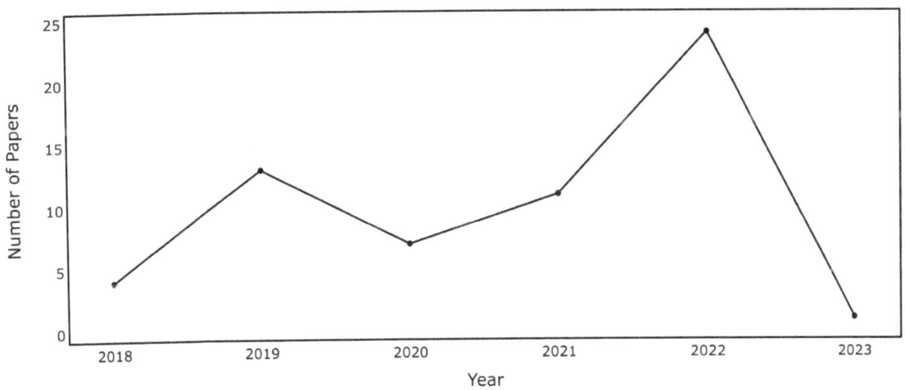

Figure 3. Annual Count of ML and DL Papers on Binary Outcome Prediction in Spine Surgery Included in the Review.

In the analysis of the 60 included papers, 59 reported the model's AUROC, 28 mentioned accuracies, 33 provided sensitivity, 29 discussed specificity, 28 addressed PPV, 24 considered NPV, 25 indicated BS (with 10 providing null model Brier), and 8 detailed the F1 score. Additionally, a variety of representations and visualizations were presented in these papers: 52 included an AUROC figure, 27 featured a calibration curve, 13 displayed a confusion matrix, 12 showcased decision curves, 3 incorporated PR curves, and only 1 offered a precision-recall curve. Moreover, to train their models, 23 studies utilized NSQIP data, and 19 used single-center data, while the rest used multicenter data or other national datasets. In the following sections, we explore prevalent errors observed in the reviewed articles, highlighting key areas for improvement in the evaluation and reporting of machine learning models in spine surgery applications.

Table 3. Outcome variables predicted by ML models in reviewed studies.

Topic	Complication	Number
Infection	Surgical site infection	5
	Wound complications	3
	Infection	1
	Sepsis	1
General Adverse Events	Surgical adverse events	2
	Any adverse event	4
	Major complications	1
	Medical adverse events	5
	Mortality	6
	Readmission	12
	Reoperation	5
Quality of Life/Pain	Visual Analog Scale Back	1
	Visual Analog Scale Leg	1
	6 Month: mJOA	1
	6 Month: SF-6D	1
	12 Month: mJOA	1
	12 Month: SF-6D	1
	Sustained postoperative opioid prescription	4
	24 Month: mJOA	1
	24 Month: SF-6D	1
	EuroQol	1
	Ability to return to work (1 year)	1
	Worsening functional status	1
	Oswestry Disability Index	1
Surgical	Risk of Recollapse	1
	Prolonged Operation	1
	Recurrent lumbar disc herniation	1
	Intraoperative vascular injury	1
Cardiac	Cardiac complications	3
	Cardiac dysrhythmia	1
	Congestive heart failure	1
Pulmonary	Pulmonary complications	1
	Unplanned re-intubation	1
	Pneumonia	3
Length of Stay	Extended length of stay	10
	Short length of stay	3
Neurology	C5 palsy	1
	Neurologic complications	1
	Postop delerium	2

Table 3. *Cont.*

Topic	Complication	Number
Other	VTE complications	4
	Transfusion	3
	Perioperative blood loss	1
	Urinary retention	1

4.2. Error Type I: Incomplete Reporting of Performance Metrics

Han et al. presented models predicting various medical and surgical complications, demonstrating strong performance metrics such as AUROCs, BS, sensitivity, and acceptable specificity [15]. Similarly, Arora et al. developed a well-performing model that predicts patient discharge to rehabilitation, achieving high AUROC, sensitivity, and specificity with an adjusted threshold of 0.16 [32]. Both studies also demonstrated well-calibrated models through calibration plots.

Shah et al. developed models predicting readmission or major complications, achieving satisfactory AUROC, AUPRC, and BS while outperforming the baseline AUPRC, indicating its effectiveness in predicting true positives well [17]. Valliani et al. predicted non-home discharge with remarkable AUROCs, PPV, and NPV. The study also presented a well-calibrated model through a calibration plot, although the plot did not display true probability and predicted risks greater than 0.8 [18]. Despite these models' solid performance on the metrics reported, studies in this category failed to report other metrics crucial for model evaluation. While some omitted the PPV and NPV, others failed to mention baseline AUPRC, sensitivity, specificity, and the null model BS. Without the inclusion of all the necessary evaluation metrics, the assessment lacks validity, even when reported metrics show high performance.

4.3. Error Type IIA: Metric Optimization at the Expense of Others

Li et al. developed artificial neural networks (ANN) and random forest (RF) models for predicting day-of-surgery patient discharge. The ANN model exhibited high sensitivity but low specificity, while the RF model showed the opposite [26]. Kim et al. and Arvind et al. presented models predicting mortality, wound complications, venous thromboembolism, and cardiac complications [30,31,34]. The Linear regression (LR) models exhibited high specificities at the expense of extremely low sensitivities. In contrast, ANN displayed high sensitivities and specificities but low PPVs. Goyal et al. developed models predicting non-home discharge and 30-day unplanned readmission [24]. The models predicting non-home discharge achieved high AUROCs, accuracies, sensitivity, specificity, and NPV but low PPV, leading to many false positives. This training method is advised only when the target is critically important and should not be missed, even if it means encountering many false positives.

Stopa et al. and Karhade et al. trained models to predict non-routine discharge, presenting high AUROC, BS, specificity, and NPV but low sensitivity and PPV [21,25]. Although both models demonstrated well-calibrated performance via calibration plots, they struggled to detect positive cases correctly, facing low sensitivity scores and PPVs. Moreover, both papers presented a decision curve demonstrating that their models are better than the treat-all or the treat-non approach.

4.4. Error Type IIB: High Accuracy and AUROC but Poor Sensitivity

Cabrera et al. developed models that predict extended LOS, readmission, reoperation, infection, and transfusion. Although these models achieved high accuracies, their sensitivities were generally low, except for the model predicting transfusion [14]. Gowd et al. predicted multiple surgical outcomes with high AUROCs and NPV but low PPV and extremely low sensitivity scores [19]. Kalagara et al. trained models to predict unplanned readmission, reporting high accuracies but low sensitivities, while specificity, PPV, and NPV were not provided [22]. Hopkins et al. developed a readmission prediction model with high accuracy, AUROC, specificity, PPV, and NPV but low sensitivity, indicating an inability to identify a significant proportion of true positive instances [23].

4.5. Other Errors

In addition to the previously mentioned errors, some papers provided poor calibration plots and omitted essential metrics. Kuris et al., Veeramani et al., and Zhang et al. presented models predicting readmission, unplanned re-intubation, and short LOS, respectively, with acceptable AUROCs, accuracies, and BSs [16,27,29]. However, all three studies provided calibration plots indicating poor calibration, as the calibration curves were not in proximity to the near-perfect prediction diagonal. Moreover, the null model BS was not reported. Ogink et al. developed models predicting non-home discharge displaying adequate AUROCs and BSs [33]. Nevertheless, the calibration plots in both studies revealed that the models were not well-calibrated for larger observed proportions and predicted probabilities, as the calibration curves drifted away from the near-perfect prediction diagonal. Furthermore, these five papers failed to report sensitivities, specificities, PPVs, and NPVs.

5. Discussion

ML's ability to predict future events by training on vast healthcare data has attracted substantial interest [73]. Nevertheless, predicting rare events poses significant challenges attributed to the skewed data distribution. To address this issue, techniques for imbalanced class learning have been designed. This paper focuses on showcasing the application of ML in predicting uncommon patterns or events within the realm of spinal surgeries. These surgeries encompass various risks and require a thorough assessment of potential outcomes, such as readmission, reoperation, ELOS, and discharges to non-home settings [74,75].

We reviewed 60 papers addressing post-spinal surgery outcome predictions, examining specific elements of spinal surgeries such as pathologies, surgical procedures, and spinal levels. However, a limited number of these studies adequately evaluated their models using suitable metrics for imbalanced data binary classification tasks. This observation highlights the need for more rigorous model evaluation methods to ensure their clinical reliability and effectiveness in rare-event predictions. In a study by Haixiang et al., it was revealed that 38% of the 517 papers addressing imbalanced classification across various domains used accuracy as an evaluation metric despite the authors' awareness of dealing with an imbalanced problem [76]. In some instances, the accuracy of a proposed method might be lower than the class imbalance ratio, implying that a dummy classifier solely predicting the majority class would yield better performance.

The importance of appropriate evaluation metrics for imbalanced classification problems in machine learning cannot be overstated. Our analysis revealed that many papers relied on inadequate evaluation metrics. Moreover, our review identified instances where models optimized one metric at the expense of others. These practices can lead to misinterpretation of model performance and hinder clinical applicability. Therefore, it is crucial to conduct a comprehensive evaluation of classifier performance, addressing all relevant metrics rather than focusing on only one or two. Additionally, striking a balance between the various performance metrics is essential to ensure that models can be effectively employed in clinical decision-making. By emphasizing the need for a holistic approach to classifier evaluation, our study encourages the development of more robust and reliable ML models for predicting rare outcomes in spinal surgery and other healthcare applications.

Training a binary classification model on an imbalanced dataset, where one class significantly outnumbers the other, poses challenges as the model may be biased towards the more prevalent class. Most strategies addressing this issue can be applied in the preprocessing stage prior to model training. These strategies include undersampling the majority class, oversampling the minority class, modifying weights, and optimizing thresholds.

Undersampling involves reducing instances of the majority class in the training sample to equalize the classes. Various undersampling techniques, such as random undersampling, NearMiss, cluster-based undersampling, and Tomek links, can balance a dataset. Random undersampling selects a subset of majority class examples randomly, while NearMiss retains examples from the majority class closest to the minority class [77]. Cluster-based undersampling sorts majority class examples into clusters and selects a representative subset from each cluster. Tomek links remove examples from the majority class closely related to minority class examples, increasing the space between classes and facilitating classification [78].

Another method for balancing classes is oversampling, which entails adding more minority class examples to the training dataset. For binary classification, strategies such as random oversampling, the synthetic minority over-sampling technique (SMOTE), and adaptive synthetic sampling (ADASYN) can be employed. Random oversampling adds random minority class samples to the training set until classes are equal, potentially leading to overfitting if the oversampled data does not represent the original minority class distribution. SMOTE, a more advanced technique, creates synthetic samples using the k-nearest neighbors algorithm to ensure new samples resemble original minority class samples [79]. ADASYN is similar to SMOTE but generates synthetic samples more representative of the feature space region where the minority class is under-represented. While oversampling techniques appear more promising than undersampling ones, especially with small datasets, it is important to note that oversampling involves the addition of synthetic data that might not correspond to the real data. Given this constraint, advanced generative deep-learning algorithms were developed [80,81]. One such advancement is generative adversarial network synthesis for oversampling (GANSO), which has demonstrated superior performance compared to the synthetic minority oversampling technique (SMOTE) [82].

In addition to the sampling methods discussed, threshold optimization can enhance classification model performance by adjusting the decision threshold for identifying positive category cases [83]. This involves calculating the model's performance at various thresholds and selecting the one with the best performance. It is essential to conduct this optimization on a separate validation set to avoid overfitting. Once the optimal threshold is determined, it can be applied to a model's predictions on new data.

It is good practice to systematically test various suitable algorithms for the task at hand. Decision tree algorithms, such as random forest (RF), classification and regression tree (CART), and C4, perform well with imbalanced datasets. Additionally, classifiers' performance can be enhanced by assigning weights based on the inverse of class frequencies or using advanced techniques like cost-sensitive learning. In place of traditional classification models, anomaly detection models can also be used. Ensemble methods, such as bagging and boosting, are also effective in handling imbalanced data. Finally, it is crucial to evaluate using appropriate metrics for imbalanced classification tasks, such as MCC, CM, precision, recall, F1 score, and AUPRC. By employing a diverse set of metrics and considering the unique characteristics of each dataset, researchers can avoid being misled by metrics like accuracy and AUROC.

6. Conclusions

This systematic review summarizes the current literature on ML and DL in spine surgery outcome prediction. Evaluating these models is crucial for their successful integration into clinical practice, especially given the imbalanced nature of spine surgery predicted outcomes. The 60 papers reviewed focused on binary outcomes such as ELOS, readmissions, non-home discharge, mortality, and reoperations. The review highlights the prevalent use of the AUROC metric in 59 papers. Other metrics like sensitivity, specificity, PPV, NPV, Brier score, and F1 score were inconsistently reported.

Based on the findings of this review, our recommendations for future research in ML applications for spine surgery are threefold. First, we advocate for the comprehensive use and reporting of all appropriate evaluation metrics to ensure a holistic assessment of model performance. Second, developing strategies to optimize classifier performance on imbalanced data is crucial. Third, we stress the necessity of increasing awareness among researchers, reviewers, and editors about the pitfalls associated with inadequate model evaluation. To improve peer review quality, we suggest including at least one ML specialist in the review process of medical AI papers, as a high level of model design scrutiny is not a realistic demand from clinician reviewers.

The significance of proper evaluation schemes in applied ML cannot be overstated. Embracing these recommendations as the field advances will undoubtedly facilitate the integration of reliable and effective ML models in clinical settings. Ultimately, integrating such models in the clinical setting will contribute to improved patient outcomes, surgical decision-making, and medical management in spine surgery.

Supplementary Materials: The following supporting information can be downloaded at https://www.mdpi.com/article/10.3390/brainsci13121723/s1, Table S1: Search strategy; Table S2: PRISMA 2020 checklist.

Author Contributions: Conceptualization, M.G.; methodology, M.G.; formal analysis, M.G.; investigation, M.G., V.G.E.-H. and A.K.G.; resources, M.G., V.G.E.-H. and A.K.G.; data curation, M.G., V.G.E.-H. and A.K.G.; writing—original draft preparation, M.G., V.G.E.-H. and A.K.G.; writing—review and editing, M.G., V.G.E.-H., A.K.G., A.B., A.d.G., A.E.-T. and M.B.; visualization, M.G.; supervision, A.E.-T. and M.B.; project administration, M.B. All authors have read and agreed to the published version of the manuscript.

Funding: This research received no external funding.

Institutional Review Board Statement: Not applicable.

Informed Consent Statement: Not applicable.

Data Availability Statement: No new data were created or analyzed in this study. Data sharing is not applicable to this article.

Conflicts of Interest: Author Andrea de Giorgio was employed by the company Artificial Engineering. The company had no role in the conceptualization, data handling, drafting, or revision of the manuscript. The remaining authors declare that the research was conducted in the absence of any commercial or financial relationships that could be construed as a potential conflict of interest.

References

1. Chang, M.; Canseco, J.A.; Nicholson, K.J.; Patel, N.; Vaccaro, A.R. The Role of Machine Learning in Spine Surgery: The Future Is Now. *Front. Surg.* **2020**, *7*, 54. [CrossRef] [PubMed]
2. El-Hajj, V.G.; Gharios, M.; Edström, E.; Elmi-Terander, A. Artificial Intelligence in Neurosurgery: A Bibliometric Analysis. *World Neurosurg.* **2023**, *171*, 152–158.e4. [CrossRef] [PubMed]
3. Harris, E.P.; MacDonald, D.B.; Boland, L. Personalized perioperative medicine: A scoping review of personalized assessment and communication of risk before surgery. *Can. J.* **2019**, *66*, 1026–1037. [CrossRef] [PubMed]
4. LeCun, Y.; Bengio, Y.; Hinton, G. Deep learning. *Nature* **2015**, *521*, 436–444. [CrossRef] [PubMed]
5. Saravi, B.; Hassel, F.; Ülkümen, S.; Zink, A.; Shavlokhova, V.; Couillard-Despres, S.; Boeker, M.; Obid, P.; Lang, G. Artificial intelligence-driven prediction modeling and decision making in spine surgery using hybrid machine learning models. *J. Pers. Med.* **2022**, *12*, 509. [CrossRef]
6. Guo, X.; Yin, Y.; Dong, C.; Yang, G.; Zhou, G. On the Class Imbalance Problem. In Proceedings of the 2008 Fourth International Conference on Natural Computation, Jinan, China, 18–20 October 2008; pp. 192–201.
7. Hong, C.S.; Oh, T.G. TPR-TNR plot for confusion matrix. *Commun. Stat. Appl. Methods* **2021**, *28*, 161–169. [CrossRef]
8. Van Rijsbergen, C.J.; Van Rijsbergen, C.J.K. Information Retrieval, Butterworth-Heinemann. *J. Librariansh.* **1979**, *11*, 237.
9. Ruopp, M.D.; Perkins, N.J.; Whitcomb, B.W.; Schisterman, E.F. Youden Index and Optimal Cut-Point Estimated from Observations Affected by a Lower Limit of Detection. *Biom. J.* **2008**, *50*, 419–430. [CrossRef]
10. Davis, J.; Goadrich, M. The Relationship Between Precision-Recall and ROC Curves. In Proceedings of the 23rd International Conference on Machine Learning, ACM, Pittsburgh, PA, USA, 25–29 June 2006. [CrossRef]
11. Huang, C.; Li, S.-X.; Caraballo, C.; Masoudi, F.A.; Rumsfeld, J.S.; Spertus, J.A.; Normand, S.-L.T.; Mortazavi, B.J.; Krumholz, H.M. Performance Metrics for the Comparative Analysis of Clinical Risk Prediction Models Employing Machine Learning. *Circ. Cardiovasc. Qual. Outcomes* **2021**, *14*, 1076–1086. [CrossRef]

12. Assel, M.; Sjoberg, D.D.; Vickers, A.J. The Brier score does not evaluate the clinical utility of diagnostic tests or prediction models. *Diagn. Progn. Res.* **2017**, *1*, 19. [CrossRef]
13. Salazar, A.; Vergara, L.; Vidal, E. A proxy learning curve for the Bayes classifier. *Pattern Recognit.* **2023**, *136*, 109240. [CrossRef]
14. Cabrera, A.; Bouterse, A.; Nelson, M.; Razzouk, J.; Ramos, O.; Chung, D.; Cheng, W.; Danisa, O. Use of random forest machine learning algorithm to predict short term outcomes following posterior cervical decompression with instrumented fusion. *J. Clin. Neurosci.* **2023**, *107*, 167–171. [CrossRef] [PubMed]
15. Han, S.S.; Azad, T.D.; Suarez, P.A.; Ratliff, J.K. A machine learning approach for predictive models of adverse events following spine surgery. *Spine J.* **2019**, *19*, 1772–1781. [CrossRef] [PubMed]
16. Kuris, E.O.; Veeramani, A.; McDonald, C.L.; DiSilvestro, K.J.; Zhang, A.S.; Cohen, E.M.; Daniels, A.H. Predicting Readmission After Anterior, Posterior, and Posterior Interbody Lumbar Spinal Fusion: A Neural Network Machine Learning Approach. *World Neurosurg.* **2021**, *151*, e19–e27. [CrossRef] [PubMed]
17. Shah, A.A.; Devana, S.K.; Lee, C.; Bugarin, A.; Lord, E.L.; Shamie, A.N.; Park, D.Y.; van der Schaar, M.; SooHoo, N.F. Prediction of Major Complications and Readmission After Lumbar Spinal Fusion: A Machine Learning–Driven Approach. *World Neurosurg.* **2021**, *152*, e227–e234. [CrossRef]
18. Valliani, A.A.; Kim, N.C.; Martini, M.L.; Gal, J.S.; Neifert, S.N.; Feng, R.; Geng, E.A.; Kim, J.S.; Cho, S.K.; Oermann, E.K.; et al. Robust Prediction of Non-home Discharge After Thoracolumbar Spine Surgery With Ensemble Machine Learning and Valida-tion on a Nationwide Cohort. *World Neurosurg.* **2022**, *165*, e83–e91. [CrossRef]
19. Gowd, A.K.; O'Neill, C.N.; Barghi, A.; O'Gara, T.J.; Carmouche, J.J. Feasibility of Machine Learning in the Prediction of Short-Term Outcomes Following Anterior Cervical Discectomy and Fusion. *World Neurosurg.* **2022**, *168*, e223–e232. [CrossRef]
20. Ogink, P.T.; Karhade, A.V.; Thio, Q.C.B.S.; Hershman, S.H.; Cha, T.D.; Bono, C.M.; Schwab, J.H. Development of a machine learning algorithm predicting discharge placement after surgery for spondylolisthesis. *Eur. Spine J.* **2019**, *28*, 1775–1782. [CrossRef]
21. Karhade, A.V.; Ogink, P.; Thio, Q.; Broekman, M.; Cha, T.; Gormley, W.B.; Hershman, S.; Peul, W.C.; Bono, C.M.; Schwab, J.H. Development of machine learning algorithms for prediction of discharge disposition after elective inpatient surgery for lumbar degenerative disc disorders. *Neurosurg. Focus* **2018**, *45*, E6. [CrossRef]
22. Kalagara, S.; Eltorai, A.E.M.; Durand, W.M.; DePasse, J.M.; Daniels, A.H. Machine learning modeling for predicting hospital re-admission following lumbar laminectomy. *J. Neurosurg. Spine* **2018**, *30*, 344–352. [CrossRef]
23. Hopkins, B.S.; Yamaguchi, J.T.; Garcia, R.; Kesavabhotla, K.; Weiss, H.; Hsu, W.K.; Smith, Z.A.; Dahdaleh, N.S. Using machine learning to predict 30-day readmissions after posterior lumbar fusion: An NSQIP study involving 23,264 patients. *J. Neurosurg. Spine* **2019**, *32*, 399–406. [CrossRef] [PubMed]
24. Goyal, A.; Ngufor, C.; Kerezoudis, P.; McCutcheon, B.; Storlie, C.; Bydon, M. Can machine learning algorithms accurately predict discharge to nonhome facility and early unplanned readmissions following spinal fusion? Analysis of a national surgical registry. *J. Neurosurg. Spine* **2019**, *31*, 568–578. [CrossRef] [PubMed]
25. Stopa, B.M.; Robertson, F.C.; Karhade, A.V.; Chua, M.; Broekman, M.L.D.; Schwab, J.H.; Smith, T.R.; Gormley, W.B. Predicting nonroutine discharge after elective spine surgery: External validation of machine learning algorithms. *J. Neurosurg. Spine* **2019**, *31*, 742–747. [CrossRef] [PubMed]
26. Li, Q.; Zhong, H.; Girardi, F.P.; Poeran, J.; Wilson, L.A.; Memtsoudis, S.G.; Liu, J. Machine Learning Approaches to Define Candidates for Ambulatory Single Level Laminectomy Surgery. *Glob. Spine J.* **2022**, *12*, 1363–1368. [CrossRef] [PubMed]
27. Veeramani, A.; Zhang, A.S.; Blackburn, A.Z.; Etzel, C.M.; DiSilvestro, K.J.; McDonald, C.L.; Daniels, A.H. An Artificial Intelligence Approach to Predicting Unplanned Intubation Following Anterior Cervical Discectomy and Fusion. *Glob. Spine J.* **2022**, *13*, 1849–1855. [CrossRef] [PubMed]
28. DiSilvestro, K.J.; Veeramani, A.; McDonald, C.L.; Zhang, A.S.; Kuris, E.O.; Durand, W.M.; Cohen, E.M.; Daniels, A.H. Predicting Postoperative Mortality After Metastatic Intraspinal Neoplasm Excision: Development of a Machine-Learning Approach. *World Neurosurg.* **2021**, *146*, e917–e924. [CrossRef] [PubMed]
29. Zhang, A.S.; Veeramani, A.; Quinn, M.S.; Alsoof, D.; Kuris, E.O.; Daniels, A.H. Machine Learning Prediction of Length of Stay in Adult Spinal Deformity Patients Undergoing Posterior Spine Fusion Surgery. *J. Clin. Med.* **2021**, *10*, 4074. [CrossRef]
30. Kim, J.S.; Merrill, R.K.; Arvind, V.; Kaji, D.; Pasik, S.D.; Nwachukwu, C.C.; Vargas, L.; Osman, N.S.; Oermann, E.K.; Caridi, J.M.; et al. Examining the Ability of Artificial Neural Networks Machine Learning Models to Accurately Predict Complications Following Posterior Lumbar Spine Fusion. *Spine* **2018**, *43*, 853–860. [CrossRef]
31. Arvind, V.; Kim, J.S.; Oermann, E.K.; Kaji, D.; Cho, S.K. Predicting Surgical Complications in Adult Patients Undergoing Anterior Cervical Discectomy and Fusion Using Machine Learning. *Neurospine* **2018**, *15*, 329–337. [CrossRef]
32. Arora, A.B.; Lituiev, D.; Jain, D.; Hadley, D.; Butte, A.J.; Berven, S.; Peterson, T.A. Predictive Models for Length of Stay and Discharge Disposition in Elective Spine Surgery: Development, Validation, and Comparison to the ACS NSQIP Risk Calculator. *Spine* **2023**, *48*, E1–E13. [CrossRef]
33. Ogink, P.T.; Karhade, A.V.; Thio, Q.C.B.S.; Gormley, W.B.; Oner, F.C.; Verlaan, J.J.; Schwab, J.H. Predicting discharge placement after elective surgery for lumbar spinal stenosis using machine learning methods. *Eur. Spine J.* **2019**, *28*, 1433–1440. [CrossRef] [PubMed]
34. Kim, J.S.; Arvind, V.; Oermann, E.K.; Kaji, D.; Ranson, W.; Ukogu, C.; Hussain, A.K.; Caridi, J.; Cho, S.K. Predicting Surgical Complications in Patients Undergoing Elective Adult Spinal Deformity Procedures Using Machine Learning. *Spine Deform.* **2018**, *6*, 762–770. [CrossRef] [PubMed]

35. Zhang, Y.; Wan, D.; Chen, M.; Li, Y.; Ying, H.; Yao, G.; Liu, Z.; Zhang, G. Automated machine learning-based model for the prediction of delirium in patients after surgery for degenerative spinal disease. *CNS Neurosci. Ther.* **2023**, *29*, 282–295. [CrossRef] [PubMed]
36. Yang, B.; Gao, L.; Wang, X.; Wei, J.; Xia, B.; Liu, X.; Zheng, P. Application of supervised machine learning algorithms to predict the risk of hidden blood loss during the perioperative period in thoracolumbar burst fracture patients complicated with neurological compromise. *Front. Public Health* **2022**, *10*, 969919. [CrossRef] [PubMed]
37. Xiong, C.; Zhao, R.; Xu, J.; Liang, H.; Zhang, C.; Zhao, Z.; Huang, T.; Luo, X. Construct and Validate a Predictive Model for Surgical Site Infection after Posterior Lumbar Interbody Fusion Based on Machine Learning Algorithm. *Comput. Math. Methods Med.* **2022**, *2022*, 2697841. [CrossRef] [PubMed]
38. Wang, Y.; Lei, L.; Ji, M.; Tong, J.; Zhou, C.-M.; Yang, J.-J. Predicting postoperative delirium after microvascular decompression surgery with machine learning. *J. Clin. Anesth.* **2020**, *66*, 109896. [CrossRef] [PubMed]
39. Wang, K.Y.; Ikwuezunma, I.; Puvanesarajah, V.; Babu, J.; Margalit, A.; Raad, M.; Jain, A. Using Predictive Modeling and Supervised Machine Learning to Identify Patients at Risk for Venous Thromboembolism Following Posterior Lumbar Fusion. *Glob. Spine J.* **2021**, *13*, 1097–1103. [CrossRef]
40. Wang, H.; Tang, Z.-R.; Li, W.; Fan, T.; Zhao, J.; Kang, M.; Dong, R.; Qu, Y. Prediction of the risk of C5 palsy after posterior laminectomy and fusion with cervical myelopathy using a support vector machine: An analysis of 184 consecutive patients. *J. Orthop. Surg. Res.* **2021**, *16*, 332. [CrossRef]
41. Wang, H.; Fan, T.; Yang, B.; Lin, Q.; Li, W.; Yang, M. Development and Internal Validation of Supervised Machine Learning Algo-rithms for Predicting the Risk of Surgical Site Infection Following Minimally Invasive Transforaminal Lumbar Interbody Fusion. *Front. Med.* **2021**, *8*, 771608. [CrossRef]
42. Valliani, A.A.; Feng, R.; Martini, M.L.; Neifert, S.N.; Kim, N.C.; Gal, J.S.; Oermann, E.K.; Caridi, J.M. Pragmatic Prediction of Excessive Length of Stay After Cervical Spine Surgery With Machine Learning and Validation on a National Scale. *Neurosurgery* **2022**, *91*, 322–330. [CrossRef]
43. Siccoli, A.; de Wispelaere, M.P.; Schröder, M.L.; Staartjes, V.E. Machine learning–based preoperative predictive analytics for lumbar spinal stenosis. *Neurosurg. Focus* **2019**, *46*, E5. [CrossRef] [PubMed]
44. Shah, A.A.; Devana, S.K.; Lee, C.; Bugarin, A.; Lord, E.L.; Shamie, A.N.; Park, D.Y.; van der Schaar, M.; SooHoo, N.F. Machine learning-driven identification of novel patient factors for prediction of major complications after posterior cervical spinal fusion. *Eur. Spine J.* **2022**, *31*, 1952–1959. [CrossRef] [PubMed]
45. Saravi, B.; Zink, A.; Ülkümen, S.; Couillard-Despres, S.; Hassel, F.; Lang, G. Performance of Artificial Intelligence-Based Algorithms to Predict Prolonged Length of Stay after Lumbar Decompression Surgery. *J. Clin. Med.* **2022**, *11*, 4050. [CrossRef]
46. Russo, G.S.; Canseco, J.A.; Chang, M.; Levy, H.A.; Nicholson, K.; Karamian, B.A.; Mangan, J.; Fang, T.; Vaccaro, A.R.; Kepler, C.K. A Novel Scoring System to Predict Length of Stay After Anterior Cervical Discectomy and Fusion. *J. Am. Acad. Orthop. Surg.* **2021**, *29*, 758–766. [CrossRef] [PubMed]
47. Rodrigues, A.J.B.; Schonfeld, E.B.; Varshneya, K.B.; Stienen, M.N.M.; Staartjes, V.E.; Jin, M.C.B.; Veeravagu, A. Comparison of Deep Learning and Classical Machine Learning Algorithms to Predict Postoperative Outcomes for Anterior Cervical Discectomy and Fusion Procedures With State-of-the-art Performance. *Spine* **2022**, *47*, 1637–1644. [CrossRef] [PubMed]
48. Ren, G.; Liu, L.; Zhang, P.; Xie, Z.; Wang, P.; Zhang, W.; Wang, H.; Shen, M.; Deng, L.; Tao, Y.; et al. Machine Learning Predicts Recurrent Lumbar Disc Herniation Following Percutaneous Endoscopic Lumbar Discectomy. *Glob. Spine J.* **2022**, *14*, 25. [CrossRef] [PubMed]
49. Porche, K.; Maciel, C.B.; Lucke-Wold, B.; Robicsek, S.A.; Chalouhi, N.; Brennan, M.; Busl, K.M. Preoperative prediction of postoperative urinary retention in lumbar surgery: A comparison of regression to multilayer neural network. *J. Neurosurg. Spine* **2022**, *36*, 32–41. [CrossRef]
50. Pedersen, C.F.; Andersen, M.; Carreon, L.Y.; Eiskjær, S. Applied Machine Learning for Spine Surgeons: Predicting Outcome for Patients Undergoing Treatment for Lumbar Disc Herniation Using PRO Data. *Glob. Spine J.* **2022**, *12*, 866–876. [CrossRef]
51. Nunes, A.A.; Pinheiro, R.P.; Costa, H.R.T.; Defino, H.L.A. Predictors of hospital readmission within 30 days after surgery for thoracolumbar fractures: A mixed approach. *Int. J. Health Plan. Manag.* **2022**, *37*, 1708–1721. [CrossRef]
52. Merali, Z.G.; Witiw, C.D.; Badhiwala, J.H.; Wilson, J.R.; Fehlings, M.G. Using a machine learning approach to predict outcome after surgery for degenerative cervical myelopathy. *PLoS ONE* **2019**, *14*, e0215133. [CrossRef]
53. Martini, M.L.; Neifert, S.N.B.; Oermann, E.K.; Gilligan, J.T.; Rothrock, R.J.; Yuk, F.J.; Gal, J.S.; Nistal, D.A.B.; Caridi, J.M. Application of Cooperative Game Theory Principles to Interpret Machine Learning Models of Nonhome Discharge Following Spine Surgery. *Spine* **2021**, *46*, 803–812. [CrossRef] [PubMed]
54. Khan, O.; Badhiwala, J.H.; A Akbar, M.; Fehlings, M.G. Prediction of Worse Functional Status After Surgery for Degenerative Cervical Myelopathy: A Machine Learning Approach. *Neurosurgery* **2021**, *88*, 584–591. [CrossRef] [PubMed]
55. Barber, S.M.; Fridley, J.S.; Gokaslan, Z.L. Commentary: Development of Machine Learning Algorithms for Prediction of 30-Day Mortality After Surgery for Spinal Metastasis. *Neurosurgery* **2019**, *85*, E92–E93. [CrossRef] [PubMed]
56. Karhade, A.V.; Thio, Q.C.B.S.; Ogink, P.T.; A Shah, A.; Bono, C.M.; Oh, K.S.; Saylor, P.J.; Schoenfeld, A.J.; Shin, J.H.; Harris, M.B.; et al. Development of Machine Learning Algorithms for Prediction of 30-Day Mortality After Surgery for Spinal Metastasis. *Neurosurgery* **2019**, *85*, E83–E91. [CrossRef] [PubMed]

57. Karhade, A.V.; Ogink, P.T.; Thio, Q.C.; Cha, T.D.; Gormley, W.B.; Hershman, S.H.; Smith, T.R.; Mao, J.; Schoenfeld, A.J.; Bono, C.M.; et al. Development of machine learning algorithms for prediction of prolonged opioid prescription after surgery for lumbar disc herniation. *Spine J.* **2019**, *19*, 1764–1771. [CrossRef] [PubMed]
58. Karhade, A.V.; Ogink, P.T.; Thio, Q.C.; Broekman, M.L.; Cha, T.D.; Hershman, S.H.; Mao, J.; Peul, W.C.; Schoenfeld, A.J.; Bono, C.M.; et al. Machine learning for prediction of sustained opioid prescription after anterior cervical discectomy and fusion. *Spine J.* **2019**, *19*, 976–983. [CrossRef] [PubMed]
59. Karhade, A.V.; Fenn, B.; Groot, O.Q.; Shah, A.A.; Yen, H.-K.; Bilsky, M.H.; Hu, M.-H.; Laufer, I.; Park, D.Y.; Sciubba, D.M.; et al. Development and external validation of predictive algorithms for six-week mortality in spinal metastasis using 4,304 patients from five institutions. *Spine J.* **2022**, *22*, 2033–2041. [CrossRef]
60. Karhade, A.V.; Cha, T.D.; Fogel, H.A.; Hershman, S.H.; Tobert, D.G.; Schoenfeld, A.J.; Bono, C.M.; Schwab, J.H. Predicting prolonged opioid prescriptions in opioid-naïve lumbar spine surgery patients. *Spine J.* **2020**, *20*, 888–895. [CrossRef]
61. Karhade, A.V.; Bongers, M.E.; Groot, O.Q.; Cha, T.D.; Doorly, T.P.; Fogel, H.A.; Hershman, S.H.; Tobert, D.G.; Srivastava, S.D.; Bono, C.M.; et al. Development of machine learning and natural language processing algorithms for preoperative prediction and automated identification of intraoperative vascular injury in anterior lumbar spine surgery. *Spine J.* **2021**, *21*, 1635–1642. [CrossRef]
62. Karhade, A.V.; Shin, D.; Florissi, I.; Schwab, J.H. Development of predictive algorithms for length of stay greater than one day after one- or two-level anterior cervical discectomy and fusion. *Semin. Spine Surg.* **2021**, *33*, 100874. [CrossRef]
63. Karabacak, M.; Margetis, K. A Machine Learning-Based Online Prediction Tool for Predicting Short-Term Postoperative Outcomes Following Spinal Tumor Resections. *Cancers* **2023**, *15*, 812. [CrossRef]
64. Jin, M.C.; Ho, A.L.; Feng, A.Y.; Medress, Z.A.; Pendharkar, A.V.; Rezaii, P.; Ratliff, J.K.; Desai, A.M. Prediction of Discharge Status and Readmissions after Resection of Intradural Spinal Tumors. *Neurospine* **2022**, *19*, 133–145. [CrossRef] [PubMed]
65. Jain, D.; Durand, W.B.; Burch, S.; Daniels, A.; Berven, S. Machine Learning for Predictive Modeling of 90-day Readmission, Major Medical Complication, and Discharge to a Facility in Patients Undergoing Long Segment Posterior Lumbar Spine Fusion. *Spine* **2020**, *45*, 1151–1160. [CrossRef] [PubMed]
66. Hopkins, B.S.; Mazmudar, A.; Driscoll, C.; Svet, M.; Goergen, J.; Kelsten, M.; Shlobin, N.A.; Kesavabhotla, K.; A Smith, Z.; Dahdaleh, N.S. Using artificial intelligence (AI) to predict postoperative surgical site infection: A retrospective cohort of 4046 posterior spinal fusions. *Clin. Neurol. Neurosurg.* **2020**, *192*, 105718. [CrossRef] [PubMed]
67. Fatima, N.; Zheng, H.; Massaad, E.; Hadzipasic, M.; Shankar, G.M.; Shin, J.H. Development and Validation of Machine Learning Algorithms for Predicting Adverse Events After Surgery for Lumbar Degenerative Spondylolisthesis. *World Neurosurg.* **2020**, *140*, 627–641. [CrossRef] [PubMed]
68. Etzel, C.M.; Veeramani, A.; Zhang, A.S.; McDonald, C.L.; DiSilvestro, K.J.; Cohen, E.M.; Daniels, A.H. Supervised Machine Learning for Predicting Length of Stay After Lumbar Arthrodesis: A Comprehensive Artificial Intelligence Approach. *J. Am. Acad. Orthop. Surg.* **2022**, *30*, 125–132. [CrossRef]
69. Elsamadicy, A.A.; Koo, A.B.; Reeves, B.C.; Cross, J.L.; Hersh, A.; Hengartner, A.C.; Karhade, A.V.; Pennington, Z.; Akinduro, O.O.; Lo, S.-F.L.; et al. Utilization of Machine Learning to Model Important Features of 30-day Readmissions following Surgery for Metastatic Spinal Column Tumors: The Influence of Frailty. *Glob. Spine J.* **2022**, *2022*. *190*, 13. [CrossRef]
70. Dong, S.-T.; Zhu, J.; Yang, H.; Huang, G.; Zhao, C.; Yuan, B. Development and Internal Validation of Supervised Machine Learning Algorithm for Predicting the Risk of Recollapse Following Minimally Invasive Kyphoplasty in Osteoporotic Vertebral Com-pression Fractures. *Front. Public Health* **2022**, *10*, 874672. [CrossRef]
71. Dong, S.; Zhu, Y.; Yang, H.; Tang, N.; Huang, G.; Li, J.; Tian, K. Evaluation of the Predictors for Unfavorable Clinical Outcomes of Degenerative Lumbar Spondylolisthesis After Lumbar Interbody Fusion Using Machine Learning. *Front. Public Health* **2022**, *10*, 835938. [CrossRef]
72. Yen, H.-K.; Ogink, P.T.; Huang, C.-C.; Groot, O.Q.; Su, C.-C.; Chen, S.-F.; Chen, C.-W.; Karhade, A.V.; Peng, K.-P.; Lin, W.-H.; et al. A machine learning algorithm for predicting prolonged postoperative opioid prescription after lumbar disc herniation surgery. An external validation study using 1316 patients from a Taiwanese cohort. *Spine J.* **2022**, *22*, 1119–1130. [CrossRef]
73. Weiss, P. Rare Events. *Sci. News* **2003**, *163*, 227. [CrossRef]
74. Reis, R.C.; de Oliveira, M.F.; Rotta, J.M.; Botelho, R.V. Risk of Complications in Spine Surgery: A Prospective Study. *Open Orthop. J.* **2015**, *9*, 20–25. [CrossRef] [PubMed]
75. Licina, A.; Silvers, A.; Laughlin, H.; Russell, J.; Wan, C. Pathway for enhanced recovery after spinal surgery-a systematic review of evidence for use of individual components. *BMC Anesthesiol.* **2021**, *21*, 74. [CrossRef] [PubMed]
76. Guo, H.; Li, Y.; Shang, J.; Gu, M.; Huang, Y.; Gong, B. Learning from class-imbalanced data: Review of methods and applications. *Expert Syst. Appl.* **2017**, *73*, 220–239. [CrossRef]
77. Tanimoto, A.; Yamada, S.; Takenouchi, T.; Sugiyama, M.; Kashima, H. Improving imbalanced classification using near-miss instances. *Expert Syst. Appl.* **2022**, *201*, 117130. [CrossRef]
78. Zeng, M.; Zou, B.; Wei, F.; Liu, X.; Wang, L. Effective prediction of three common diseases by combining SMOTE with Tomek links technique for imbalanced medical data. In Proceedings of the 2016 IEEE International Conference of Online Analysis and Computing Science (ICOACS), Chongqing, China, 28–29 May 2016; pp. 225–228.
79. Blagus, R.; Lusa, L. SMOTE for high-dimensional class-imbalanced data. *BMC Bioinform.* **2013**, *14*, 106. [CrossRef]
80. Figueira, A.; Vaz, B. Survey on Synthetic Data Generation, Evaluation Methods and GANs. *Mathematics* **2022**, *10*, 2733. [CrossRef]

81. de Giorgio, A.; Cola, G.; Wang, L. Systematic review of class imbalance problems in manufacturing. *J. Manuf. Syst.* **2023**, *71*, 620–644. [CrossRef]
82. Salazar, A.; Vergara, L.; Safont, G. Generative Adversarial Networks and Markov Random Fields for oversampling very small training sets. *Expert Syst. Appl.* **2020**, *163*, 113819. [CrossRef]
83. Yogi, A.; Dey, R. Class Imbalance Problem in Data Science: Review. *Int. Res. J. Comput. Sci.* **2022**, *9*, 56–60. [CrossRef]

Disclaimer/Publisher's Note: The statements, opinions and data contained in all publications are solely those of the individual author(s) and contributor(s) and not of MDPI and/or the editor(s). MDPI and/or the editor(s) disclaim responsibility for any injury to people or property resulting from any ideas, methods, instructions or products referred to in the content.

brain sciences

MDPI

Perspective

Artificial Intelligence's Transformative Role in Illuminating Brain Function in Long COVID Patients Using PET/FDG

Thorsten Rudroff [1,2]

[1] Department of Health and Human Physiology, University of Iowa, Iowa City, IA 52242, USA; thorsten-rudroff@uiowa.edu; Tel.: +1-(319)-467-0363; Fax: +1-(319)-355-6669
[2] Department of Neurology, University of Iowa Hospitals and Clinics, Iowa City, IA 52242, USA

Abstract: Cutting-edge brain imaging techniques, particularly positron emission tomography with Fluorodeoxyglucose (PET/FDG), are being used in conjunction with Artificial Intelligence (AI) to shed light on the neurological symptoms associated with Long COVID. AI, particularly deep learning algorithms such as convolutional neural networks (CNN) and generative adversarial networks (GAN), plays a transformative role in analyzing PET scans, identifying subtle metabolic changes, and offering a more comprehensive understanding of Long COVID's impact on the brain. It aids in early detection of abnormal brain metabolism patterns, enabling personalized treatment plans. Moreover, AI assists in predicting the progression of neurological symptoms, refining patient care, and accelerating Long COVID research. It can uncover new insights, identify biomarkers, and streamline drug discovery. Additionally, the application of AI extends to non-invasive brain stimulation techniques, such as transcranial direct current stimulation (tDCS), which have shown promise in alleviating Long COVID symptoms. AI can optimize treatment protocols by analyzing neuroimaging data, predicting individual responses, and automating adjustments in real time. While the potential benefits are vast, ethical considerations and data privacy must be rigorously addressed. The synergy of AI and PET scans in Long COVID research offers hope in understanding and mitigating the complexities of this condition.

Keywords: AI; Long COVID; neuroimaging; cognition; non-invasive brain stimulation

1. Introduction

The COVID-19 pandemic has fundamentally changed the way we view healthcare, leaving us with a plethora of unanswered questions and emerging challenges. Long COVID, also known as post-acute sequelae of COVID-19, refers to the persistent symptoms experienced by some patients after recovering from an initial COVID-19 infection. There has been much discussion around the terminology used to describe the extended health effects of COVID-19 infection. Terms such as "Long COVID", "COVID long-haulers", "post-acute COVID-19", and "late sequelae of COVID-19" have all been proposed. However, for consistency in this perspective, we will use the term "Long COVID". The WHO defines Long COVID as a condition occurring in those with a confirmed or probable history of SARS-CoV-2 infection, typically 3 months from initial COVID-19 onset [1]. While the respiratory and cardiovascular aspects of COVID-19 have been widely studied, less attention has been paid to its effects on the brain. Recently, researchers have begun employing cutting-edge imaging techniques, such as positron emission tomography with fluorodeoxyglucose (PET/FDG), in conjunction with artificial intelligence (AI), to delve into the intricate world of brain function in Long COVID patients. This innovative approach has the potential to shed light on the neurological symptoms of Long COVID and may pave the way for more effective treatments.

2. The Enigma of Long COVID and Brain Function

There is increasing concern about the potential effects of Long COVID on brain function and cognition. Many Long COVID patients report neurological symptoms including fatigue, headache, loss of taste and smell, impaired concentration and mental fog, forgetfulness, anxiety, and depression. Studies have found objective cognitive deficits in some Long COVID patients, including impaired performance on tests of processing speed, executive function, verbal learning, and episodic memory [2–6]. Neuropsychiatric disorders like anxiety, depression [7], and post-traumatic stress disorder (PTSD) [8] also appear to be more common following COVID-19. The biological mechanisms underlying these cognitive and neuropsychiatric effects are still under investigation but likely involve neuroinflammation, microvascular changes, and neural network dysregulation.

Several theories have been proposed regarding the pathophysiology of Long COVID neurological effects [9]:

- Direct viral invasion of the brain.
- Neurotoxic effects of inflammatory mediators.
- Autoantibodies against neural antigens.
- Microvascular pathology and blood–brain barrier disruption.
- Mitochondrial dysfunction and cellular bioenergetics issues.
- Neuroplasticity changes due to illness stressors.

The neurological manifestations of Long COVID have puzzled researchers, as the virus primarily affects the respiratory system. In an effort to understand the underlying mechanisms, the focus has shifted towards brain imaging techniques like PET/FDG and the power of AI.

3. PET/FDG Imaging: A Window into Brain Function

Emerging brain imaging studies are providing insights into potential neurological changes associated with Long COVID. Positron emission tomography imaging with fluorodeoxyglucose (PET/FDG) is emerging as a promising tool for illuminating brain abnormalities associated with Long COVID. PET/FDG scans involve the injection of a radioactive tracer into the body, which accumulates in areas with high metabolic activity, such as the brain. The PET scanner then detects the gamma rays emitted by the tracer, creating a detailed image of the brain's metabolic activity. PET/FDG provides a non-invasive way to measure glucose metabolism in the brain.

Details on the PET/FDG imaging techniques and protocols typically used to assess brain function in Long COVID studies [10–12]:

- Radiotracer used: 18F-fluorodeoxyglucose (FDG), a glucose analog, is the standard radiotracer used to image glucose metabolism in the brain.
- PET scanner types: These studies generally use whole-body PET/CT scanners or dedicated brain PET scanners with a resolution around 4–6 mm.
- Patient preparation: Patients are asked to fast for 4–6 h before the scan to stabilize metabolic state. Serum glucose levels are checked prior to radiotracer injection.
- FDG Dose: 5–10 mCi of FDG is injected intravenously. Scanning begins 30–60 min post-injection when radiotracer accumulation in brain reaches equilibrium.
- Scan duration: 15–30 min per PET acquisition. Longer scans can improve image statistics and allow for full brain coverage.
- Image reconstruction: Iterative reconstruction algorithms like ordered subset expectation maximization (OSEM) used.
- Image processing: Standardized uptake value (SUV) metrics calculated in regions of interest. AI algorithms applied for advanced analyses.
- Control groups: Age-matched healthy controls are scanned using the same protocol for comparison.

Standardization of imaging protocols is important to obtain reproducible quantitative results across subjects and follow-up scans. The combination of PET with AI and MRI scans provides complimentary information on neural inflammation, network disruption, and atrophy patterns in Long COVID.

Areas of decreased metabolism on PET/FDG imaging have been linked to inflammation and neurodegeneration. PET/FDG allows for measurement of glucose metabolism as an indicator of inflammation and cellular activity [10]. It can identify affected brain regions in Long COVID patients. PET/FDG studies have found reduced metabolic activity and hypometabolism in certain brain areas of Long COVID patients, including the frontal and temporal lobe, limbic system, and brainstem. This suggests inflammation preferentially targeting these regions. The brain hypometabolism patterns are associated with neuropsychiatric disorders and could underline cognitive/neurological symptoms in Long COVID [11,12]. The neuropsychologic test battery comprises the Hopkins Verbal Learning Test-Revised, Brief Visuospatial-Memory Test-Revised, Digit Span forward/revers, Trail Making Test part A/B, Color-Word Interference Test, Symbol-Digit Modalities Test, and a semantic and letter fluency test. However, PET/FDG requires interpretation by specialists in nuclear medicine and neuroimaging to make pattern recognition decisions mostly using qualitative readings. Thus, the challenge lies in interpreting the complex data generated by these scans, and this is where AI comes into play.

4. Artificial Intelligence (AI) as the Cognitive Enhancer

In this quest for understanding, the marriage of PET/FDG and AI stands out as a transformative force, offering a beacon of hope in our battle against Long COVID. AI has revolutionized the healthcare industry, and its applications extend to the interpretation of medical images. In the case of PET/FDG scans, AI algorithms have demonstrated remarkable capabilities in detecting subtle changes in brain metabolism that might be challenging for human experts to identify. These algorithms can process vast amounts of data quickly and efficiently, increasing the accuracy and reliability of results.

Matsubara et al. [13] reviewed recent studies applying AI, especially deep learning techniques, for PET image generation. For denoising, convolutional neural networks (CNNs) like U-Net [14,15] and generative adversarial networks (GANs) [16,17] have been applied to recover standard dose/duration PET from low-dose/short scans. CNNs have become the predominant deep learning approach for recovering full PET data from low-dose or abbreviated scans. Xiang et al. [18] pioneered the use of CNNs for this application, training a model to generate standard 12 min brain fluorodeoxyglucose (FDG) PET images from 3 min scans. Their auto-context CNN architecture, comprising three 4-layer CNN blocks with skip connections, achieved results comparable to the previous state-of-the-art method. Subsequently, U-Net, a U-shaped CNN with built-in skip connections, has proven highly effective for full PET data recovery across various tracers and scan types. For example, Chen et al. [19] showed a U-Net trained on multi-contrast MRI could recover full-dose amyloid PET scans from just 1/100 of the radiotracer dose. Recovered images enabled accurate visual assessment of amyloid status. U-Net has also been successfully applied to reconstruct full-dose whole body and cardiac PET/FDG images from abbreviated scans.

4.1. CNNs and GANs for PET Image Generation

CNNs and GANs are types of deep neural networks with different architectures and applications.

4.2. CNN Architectures for PET Image Generation

CNNs are a specialized type of artificial neural network commonly used for image processing and computer vision tasks. Here is a quick explanation of how CNNs work:

- Convolutional layers—These layers perform convolutions over the input image to extract features. The convolution is performed by sliding filters or kernels over the image and computing dot products between the filter and image patch. Different filters detect different types of features like edges, colors, textures, etc.

- Pooling layers—These layers downsample the image representation to reduce computational load and overfitting. Max pooling takes the maximum within filter regions while average pooling takes the average.
- Fully connected layers—These classic neural network layers connect the extracted features to the output nodes for classification. They help combine the features and make predictions.
- Non-linear activations—Non-linear activation functions like ReLU are applied after each convolution and fully connected layer to introduce non-linearity in the model.

Some key advantages of CNNs are the ability to automatically learn relevant features from training data, invariance to translations, rotations and distortions, and capability to exploit spatial structure. CNNs have revolutionized computer vision and are also very effective for neuroimaging analysis and diagnosis. However, they require large-labeled datasets for training. Overall, CNNs provide a powerful tool for automated feature learning from neuroimages. CNN architectures, especially U-Net, have become the dominant deep learning approach for recovering complete PET data from low-dose or short-duration scans. CNNs can generate full dynamic range, standard duration PET images from truncated scans across brain, whole body, and cardiac imaging.

4.3. GANs as an Alternative Approach

GANs have emerged as an alternative deep learning approach for recovering full dose, standard-duration PET images from truncated scans. Wang et al. [20] first applied adversarial training between a generator network to produce 12 min brain PET/FDG scans from 3 min scans, and a discriminator network to classify images as real or generated. Their 3D conditional GAN architecture outperformed 3D U-Net in terms of peak signal-to-noise ratio, normalized mean squared error, and standard uptake value bias. Subsequently, Lu et al. [21] demonstrated GANs could reconstruct whole-body PET/FDG images to standard dose levels from just 10% dose scans. The GAN achieved comparable performance to U-Net in terms of signal-to-noise ratio and standard uptake value biases.

Here is a simplified explanation of how GANs work:

- Generator network—This network generates new synthetic data instances (images, audio, etc.) that are similar to the training data. It starts from random noise and transforms it to match the data distribution.
- Discriminator network—This network tries to distinguish between real training data and the synthetic data created by the generator. It estimates the probability that a sample came from the real training data.
- Adversarial training—The generator and discriminator networks are trained together in an adversarial manner. The generator tries to better fool the discriminator, while the discriminator tries to properly classify real vs. fake data.
- Nash equilibrium—The training reaches equilibrium when the generator produces such realistic data that the discriminator cannot differentiate it from real data. At this point, both models have maximized their objectives.

The key advantages of GANs include the ability to generate novel realistic data, learn meaningful latent representations, and model complex high-dimensional distributions. In neuroimaging, GANs can be used for data augmentation, image synthesis, and modeling brain data distributions. In summary, alongside CNNs, GAN frameworks show promise for reconstructing complete, full-dynamic range PET scans from low-dose or short acquisition protocols across brain and whole-body imaging. Adversarial training provides an alternative deep learning strategy to CNNs for PET image recovery tasks. However, training stability can be an issue with GANs. Overall, they are a powerful generative modeling framework with many applications in medical imaging and healthcare.

So, in summary, CNNs are optimized for discriminative tasks while GANs are optimized for generative modeling and synthetic data generation. CNNs classify data while GANs create new data, but they can complement each other in certain applications.

4.4. CNNs and GANs for Image Translation and Synthesis

The application of deep learning (CNN, GAN) in medical imaging extends to the challenging tasks of intra- and inter-modality image translation and image synthesis. Techniques like CNN and GAN have successfully tackled these previously daunting endeavors within the medical imaging domain [22]. An illustrative example of this progress is the use of deep learning to create computed tomography (CT) images from magnetic resonance (MR) images, which has been employed to enhance PET attenuation correction in hybrid PET/MR scanners, as elaborated in the "PET attenuation correction" section.

The utilization of deep learning (CNN, GAN) for image translation and synthesis in medical imaging offers three significant advantages for PET imaging:

1. Supplement Missing Data: In medical imaging, missing data can occur due to various reasons. For example, the acquisition of thin-sliced MR images is often omitted from clinical routines due to lengthy scan durations, even though these thin-sliced MR images are essential for quantitative analysis of brain PET images. Deep learning can be employed to synthesize thin-sliced MR images, thus enabling quantitative analysis of PET images even when MR acquisitions are not available.
2. Reduction in Scans: Deep learning-driven image translation and synthesis allow for the avoidance of acquiring specific target images, leading to a reduction in the total acquisition time. This reduction not only alleviates the burden on patients but also minimizes their exposure to radiation.
3. Data Augmentation: Image translation and synthesis play a vital role in data augmentation, addressing issues related to insufficient training data and data imbalance in machine learning applications. This approach is especially valuable in the computer-aided diagnosis of rare diseases where collecting large amounts of data is a formidable challenge. Deep learning-based data augmentation through image translation and synthesis enhances the performance of machine learning models in such cases.

4.5. CNNs and GANs for Diagnosis and Prediction

CNNs (convolutional neural networks) and GANs (generative adversarial networks) are two types of deep learning architectures that show promising applications for helping with diagnosis and prediction in Long COVID patients:

1. CNNs for Diagnostic Pattern Recognition: CNNs can be trained on medical imaging datasets like PET, MRI, or CT scans to recognize unique radiographic signatures associated with post-COVID neurological, cardiovascular, or respiratory damage. This allows for automated diagnosis aid systems to be developed for detecting Long COVID sequalae.

For example, brain PET scans analyzed by a CNN could identify distinct patterns of inflammation or glucose hypometabolism that characterize memory and cognitive dysfunction in long haulers.

2. GANs for Synthetic Data Augmentation: A major barrier in applying deep learning is limited patient data. GANs can generate synthetic PET scans that emulate Long COVID-specific abnormalities like neurological inflammation. This artificially expanded dataset helps train CNN diagnostic models to be more robust and generalizable with less real-world examples.
3. CNNs for Prognostic Risk Stratification: Analyzing temporal sequences of scans from confirmed Long COVID patients, CNN algorithms can discover prognostic imaging biomarkers linked to disease recovery trajectories. Such predictive models can guide treatment personalization and follow-up care.

Overall, CNNs and GANs have exciting utilities in harnessing medical imaging data to assist detection, prognosis, and management of Long COVID afflictions. Larger multi-center studies are needed to assemble diverse training data to implement these AI technologies.

4.6. Further Readings on CNNS and GANs

Review articles that provide an overview and survey of CNNs and GANs: "Optimizing Image Captioning using Deep Learning based Object Detection" by Sahu et al. [23] provides a thorough review of CNN architectures like VGGNet, ResNet, Inception, etc., for image captioning. "Generative Adversarial Networks: An Overview" by Creswell et al. [24] reviews the basic framework, theory, types of GANs, training methods, evaluation metrics, and applications. "A review of convolutional neural networks for inverse problems in imaging" [25] focuses on CNN methods for image denoising, super-resolution, inpainting, artifact removal, etc. "Convolutional Neural Networks for Medical Image Analysis: Full Training or Fine Tuning?" [26] discusses CNN training techniques for medical imaging—full training vs. fine tuning. "Recent advances in deep learning for medical image segmentation" [27] surveys deep learning especially CNNs for medical image segmentation tasks.

These review papers provide a broad overview of key CNN and GAN methodologies, architectures, applications, and trends within computer vision and medical imaging. They serve as a good starting point to better understand these widely used deep learning techniques.

In summary, deep learning's ability to perform image translation and synthesis in the field of medical imaging has opened up new avenues for improving the quality and efficiency of various medical procedures, including PET imaging. These advancements have the potential to enhance patient care, accelerate diagnoses, and facilitate the development of more effective treatments. Limitations include lack of large PET datasets and evaluation metrics for generated images. Future directions include unsupervised learning and transformer models. Deep learning has brought advances in PET image generation and will likely be commonly used in clinical practice for image quality improvement and scan burden reduction.

5. The Transformative Role of AI in Long COVID Research

AI possesses a unique ability to analyze intricate patterns and subtle changes in PET/FDG data that might evade human recognition. By identifying regions of the brain with altered metabolic activity, AI can offer a deeper understanding of how Long COVID affects the brain. These findings help pinpoint areas of concern, such as inflammation or reduced blood flow, providing a more precise view of the neurological changes associated with the condition.

Where AI truly shines is in its capacity to discern patterns and correlations in vast datasets. Researchers can use AI to compare the PET scans of Long COVID patients with those of healthy individuals, thus revealing specific brain regions that exhibit abnormal activity. These discoveries hold the promise of identifying novel biomarkers associated with Long COVID, allowing for early diagnosis and the development of targeted treatment strategies.

Furthermore, AI can help predict the progression of neurological symptoms in Long COVID patients. By analyzing PET scan data alongside clinical information and genetics, AI models can provide insights into the likelihood of severe cognitive impairment or mental health issues. This proactive approach to patient care offers an invaluable opportunity to manage Long COVID 's long-term effects.

AI-powered computational approaches can integrate diverse datasets from omics to imaging to glean new mechanistic insights into Long COVID pathophysiology. For example, deep learning algorithms applied to high-dimensional molecular data may uncover novel biological pathways underlying lingering symptoms. AI-enabled analysis of medical imaging could identify distinct radiographic phenotypes and signatures of organ dysfunction.

Advanced analytics using natural language processing and machine learning on enormous sets of healthcare data can unravel risk factors and subtypes of Long COVID. AI tools can rapidly mine electronic health records, insurance claims data, digital biomarker wearables, and more to find clinical, demographic, and social determinants that predispose patients to Long COVID or its most severe presentations. These big data analytics can guide prognosis, treatment, and study design.

Another application is the accelerated identification of new therapeutics for Long COVID using AI-based drug discovery and repurposing platforms. By screening libraries of molecules, predicting compound–target interactions, and modeling drug response, AI can fast-track the development of novel treatments to alleviate stubborn Long COVID symptoms. AI can also identify promising repurposing opportunities for existing drugs.

AI promises to transform Long COVID clinical trials through better participant stratification and outcome measurement. It also enables tailored interventions via individualized predictions. In the clinic, AI augmentation can help multidisciplinary Long COVID care teams deliver coordinated, evidence-based services. Chatbots and virtual assistants provide accessible support.

Summary points:

1. Early Detection: AI can help in the early identification of abnormal brain metabolism patterns in Long COVID patients, potentially allowing for timely interventions and personalized treatment plans.
2. Precision Medicine: By analyzing PET/FDG scans alongside other clinical and genetic data, AI can facilitate the development of more precise treatment strategies tailored to each patient's unique profile.
3. Monitoring Disease Progression: Long COVID can manifest differently in various individuals, and its symptoms may evolve over time. AI can continuously monitor brain function and adapt treatment plans accordingly.
4. Accelerating Research: AI-powered analysis of PET/FDG data from a large number of patients can speed up research into Long COVID, enabling a better understanding of the condition and potential therapies.
5. Uncovering New Insights: AI can identify patterns and correlations that might go unnoticed by human researchers, leading to the discovery of previously unknown factors contributing to Long COVID.

AI is a disruptive technology that can substantially advance every aspect of Long COVID research and care—from elucidating biological mechanisms to validating treatments. By leveraging the power of AI, researchers seek to unravel the mysteries of this confounding condition and substantially improve patient outcomes. The full benefits have yet to be realized; however, the future looks bright at the intersection of AI and Long COVID research.

Nonetheless, as we embrace AI's transformative role in illuminating brain function with PET scans in Long COVID patients, we must also consider the ethical implications. Safeguarding patient data privacy and ensuring responsible AI usage is paramount. Strict measures and regulations should be in place to protect individuals' rights and personal information.

6. Challenges for Clinical Transformation: Beyond Performance Validation

There is a significant challenge in translating AI innovations into routine patient care. The transformational gap refers to the gap between developing an artificial intelligence/machine learning model in a research setting and successfully deploying it in real-world clinical practice. Some key aspects of the transformational gap include (Figure 1):

- Performance gap—Models often perform worse in real-world settings compared to research environments due to differences in data distribution, population characteristics, clinical workflows, etc. Bridging this gap requires extensive validation and testing.
- Utility gap—Even accurate models may not improve meaningful clinical outcomes, quality of care, or costs. Clinical utility needs to be proven through randomized trials or comparative effectiveness studies.

- Usability gap—Integration into clinical workflows is non-trivial. Factors like user interfaces, interpretability, interoperability, and physician acceptance determine real-world adoption.
- Regulatory gap—Lack of regulatory frameworks for AI/ML model approval and governance creates uncertainty around safe and ethical deployment.
- Implementation gap—Organizational barriers around costs, liability, reimbursement, training, and IT infrastructure can prevent adoption. Planning for sustainability is crucial.

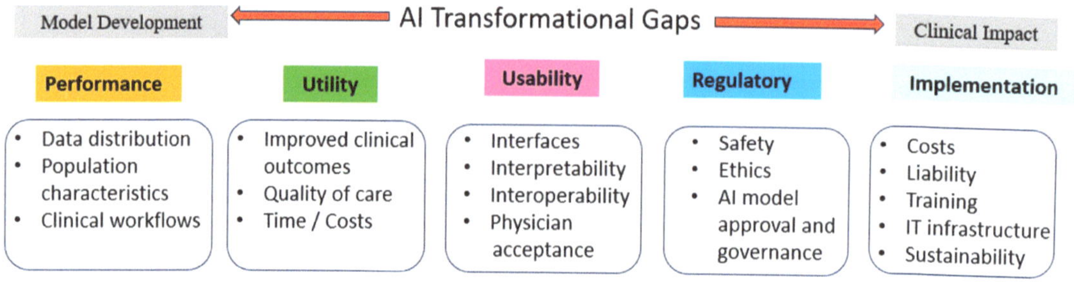

Figure 1. Navigating the AI transformational gap between initial model development and routine clinical Long COVID care by emphasizing and demonstrating five essential concepts: performance, utility, usability, regulatory, and implementation.

7. Potential Future Research Avenues

7.1. Assessing Cognitive Impairment in Long COVID Patients

As discussed above, cognitive impairments like brain fog, difficulty concentrating, and memory issues have emerged as common Long COVID symptoms [2–9]. Assessing cognitive impairment in Long COVID patients is crucial for prognosis and guiding treatment. FDG/PET imaging provides a quantitative means to measure brain metabolism and has shown utility in evaluating neurodegenerative disorders like Alzheimer's disease [28]. AI techniques like deep learning algorithms offer new opportunities to analyze FDG/PET data to predict cognitive decline.

7.2. Using PET/FDG and AI for Early Prediction

PET/FDG brain scans analyzed by convolutional neural networks (CNNs) can be used to predict future cognitive impairment in Long COVID patients. CNNs can extract spatial features from PET images relevant to brain metabolism patterns linked to cognitive decline. By training CNN models on labeled FDG/PET data from cognitively normal and impaired populations, the networks can learn to classify scans based on disease-related metabolic patterns. Long COVID patients, especially those over age 50, complaining of brain fog [28] would undergo FDG/PET scans at baseline. A pretrained CNN classifier would analyze the PET data to generate predictions on the patient's risk of developing mild cognitive impairment or dementia within 1–2 years. High-risk patients could then potentially be selected for early interventions or clinical trials for Alzheimer's prevention. The AI could also help uncover why COVID-19 might raise dementia risk in some patients.

Key challenges include curating multi-institutional labeled PET datasets for model training and validation. Physician assessments of cognitive function using standard tests like the Montreal Cognitive Assessment [29] would provide ground truth labels. Extensive testing is essential to establish the predictive performance and clinical utility of the AI methodology.

This AI-powered FDG/PET approach could enable early identification of Long COVID patients at risk for cognitive decline. Early interventions could then be explored to halt further deterioration. With Long COVID affecting millions globally, tools to assess long-term neurological impacts are urgently needed.

7.3. Enhancing Non-Invasive Brain Stimulation with AI

Furthermore, non-invasive brain stimulation (NIBS) techniques like transcranial.

Direct-Current Stimulation (tDCS), transcranial Alternating Current Stimulation (tACS), and transcutaneous Vagus Nerve Stimulation (tVNS) can modulate brain activity and connectivity. They are safe, well-tolerated options for neurological disorders. tDCS studies show reduced fatigue and improved cognition in Long COVID patients when applied to frontal and parietal areas [30]. tACS may counteract abnormal brain oscillations underlying fatigue [31]. Early data show cognitive improvements in Alzheimer's patients. tVNS activated cholinergic anti-inflammatory pathways and reduced fatigue in a Long COVID pilot study [32]. It has anti-inflammatory effects relevant to post-viral immune dysfunction. NIBS provides a promising non-pharmacological approach to target proposed mechanisms underlying Long COVID fatigue like inflammation, hypofrontality, and network dysfunction. More research is needed on optimal NIBS protocols and sham-controlled trials in Long COVID patients, but early findings suggest these techniques could alleviate persistent neurological symptoms.

AI could be utilized to advance NIBS techniques. Machine learning algorithms can analyze neuroimaging scans (PET/FDG, fMRI, EEG) before stimulation to identify optimal target regions for each patient based on their unique brain connectivity patterns.

- AI models can be trained on large datasets to predict individual treatment response and side effects based on demographic, clinical, and neuroimaging variables. This allows for personalized, precision medicine approaches.
- Closed-loop systems can track physiological signals during stimulation and automatically adjust stimulation parameters in real time to optimize effects.
- Reinforcement learning algorithms can iteratively adjust stimulation settings across sessions to maximize therapeutic benefits and minimize side effects for each patient.
- Advanced neural networks and deep learning models can help automate analysis of complex physiological signals acquired during and after stimulation.
- AI planning can design optimal stimulation protocols involving scheduling, electrode placement, and dosage to efficiently achieve treatment goals.
- Big data analytics can identify patterns, correlations, and subgroups across diverse patient populations that inform individualized stimulation protocols.
- Simulations of brain network dynamics can model effects of stimulation on connectivity. This allows for in silico optimization before delivering it to patients.
- Natural language processing can extract clinically meaningful insights from patient reports on symptoms over the course of therapy.

In summary, AI has diverse applications spanning predictive modeling, closed-loop control systems, large-scale analytics, simulations, and adaptive learning algorithms that can enhance development of non-invasive brain stimulation as a precision medicine for neurological disorders.

8. Limitations

Evaluating the quantitative accuracy of PET images generated by deep learning is important, but there is currently a lack of consensus on the best methods. Commonly used measures like peak signal-to-noise ratio (PSNR) and structural similarity index (SSIM) reflect perceptual similarity but not quantitative accuracy. Some studies have evaluated quantitative accuracy by comparing radioactivity concentration, SUV, contrast recovery, etc. However, more work is needed to establish standardized evaluation methods. A limitation is the lack of large PET image datasets to train deep learning models. Creating shared public databases could enable more transfer learning. However, given how emergent this post-COVID neurological dysfunction phenomenon is, such repositories are simply not available yet. As with many cutting edge applications of AI to new medical contexts, progress often starts from limited datasets. Efforts like the UK Biobank imaging dataset [33–35] on post-COVID neurological deficits demonstrate feasibility. With more patients being scanned, open data sharing and global coordination amongst researchers are absolutely key—and achievable. For optimal AI development, consolidated image repositories must be the crucial first step. Alternative techniques like unsupervised, self-supervised, and weakly supervised learning may help with limited data. Transformers have potential for breakthroughs in PET image generation, as they have in natural language processing. Attention-based models like BERT and XLNet could be applied to PET images. Multimodal PET/MR data alignment can introduce errors. Systematic evaluation of the effect of PET-MR alignment errors on deep learning performance is needed.

In summary, key challenges are developing standardized quantitative evaluation methods, creating large public PET image datasets, and exploring alternative deep learning techniques that require less data. Evaluating the impacts of multimodal data alignment is also important in future work.

9. Conclusions

Cutting-edge PET/FDG neuroimaging combined with AI analysis offers tremendous potential to elucidate the neurological impacts of Long COVID. AI techniques including CNNs and GANs can detect subtle patterns in PET data that provide insights into brain inflammation, hypometabolism, network dysfunction, and cognitive decline associated with Long COVID. Although still an emerging application, the integration of AI and advanced imaging could transform our understanding of Long COVID's effects on the brain, enabling better diagnosis, prognostics, treatments, and eventually prevention. However, rigorous validation and attention to responsible and ethical AI development remain imperative as these technologies progress from bench to bedside. By harnessing the synergy between AI and neuroimaging, researchers seek to unravel the neurological complexities of Long COVID and meaningfully improve patient outcomes.

Funding: This research received no external funding.

Institutional Review Board Statement: Not applicable.

Informed Consent Statement: Not applicable.

Data Availability Statement: Not applicable.

Conflicts of Interest: The author declares no conflicts of interest.

References

1. WHO. *Coronavirus (COVID-19) a Clinical Case Definition of Post COVID-19 Condition by a Delphi Consensus*; World Health Organization: Geneva, Switzerland, 2021.
2. Ceban, F.; Ling, S.; Lui, L.M.W.; Lee, Y.; Gill, H.; Teopiz, K.M.; Rodrigues, N.B.; Subramaniapillai, M.; Di Vincenzo, J.D.; Cao, B.; et al. Fatigue and cognitive impairment in Post-COVID-19 Syndrome: A systematic review and meta-analysis. *Brain Behav. Immun.* **2022**, *101*, 93–135. [CrossRef]
3. Mazza, M.G.; Palladini, M.; De Lorenzo, R.; Bravi, B.; Poletti, S.; Furlan, R.; Ciceri, F.; Vai, B.; Bollettini, I.; Melloni, E.M.T.; et al. One-year mental health outcomes in a cohort of COVID-19 survivors. *J. Psychiatr. Res.* **2022**, *145*, 118–124. [CrossRef]
4. Ortelli, P.; Ferrazzoli, D.; Sebastianelli, L.; Engl, M.; Romanello, R.; Nardone, R.; Bonini, I.; Koch, G.; Saltuari, L.; Quartarone, A.; et al. Neuropsychological and neurophysiological correlates of fatigue in post-acute patients with neurological manifestations of COVID-19: Insights into a challenging symptom. *J. Neurol. Sci.* **2021**, *420*, 117271. [CrossRef] [PubMed]
5. Krishnan, K.; Miller, A.K.; Reiter, K.; Bonner-Jackson, A. Neurocognitive profiles in patients with persisting cognitive symptoms associated with COVID-19. *Arch. Clin. Neuropsychol.* **2022**, *37*, 729–737. [CrossRef] [PubMed]
6. Ortelli, P.; Ferrazzoli, D.; Sebastianelli, L.; Maestri, R.; Dezi, S.; Spampinato, D.; Saltuari, L.; Alibardi, A.; Engl, M.; Kofler, M.; et al. Altered motor cortex physiology and dysexecutive syndrome in patients with fatigue and cognitive difficulties after mild COVID-19. *Eur. J. Neurol.* **2022**, *29*, 1652–1662. [CrossRef] [PubMed]
7. Mazza, M.G.; De Lorenzo, R.; Conte, C.; Poletti, S.; Vai, B.; Bollettini, I.; Melloni, E.M.T.; Furlan, R.; Ciceri, F.; Rovere-Querini, P.; et al. Anxiety and depression in COVID-19 survivors: Role of inflammatory and clinical predictors. *Brain Behav. Immun.* **2020**, *89*, 594–600. [CrossRef]
8. Chamberlain, S.R.; Grant, J.E.; Trender, W.; Hellyer, P.; Hampshire, A. Post-traumatic stress disorder symptoms in COVID-19 survivors: Online population survey. *BJ Psych. Open* **2021**, *7*, e4. [CrossRef]
9. Davis, H.E.; McCorkell, L.; Moore Vogel, J.; Topol, E.J. Long COVID: Major findings, mechanisms and recommendations. *Nat. Rev. Microbiol.* **2023**, *21*, 133–146. [CrossRef]

10. Rudroff, T.; Workman, C.D.; Ponto, L.L.B. ^{18}F-FDG-PET Imaging for Post-COVID-19 Brain and Skeletal Muscle Alterations. *Viruses* **2021**, *13*, 2283. [CrossRef]
11. Guedj, E.; Million, M.; Dudouet, P.; Tissot-Dupont, H.; Bregeon, F.; Cammilleri, S.; Raoult, D. 18F-FDG brain PET hypometabolism in post-SARS-CoV-2 infection: Substrate for persistent/delayed disorders? *Eur. J. Nucl. Med. Mol. Imaging* **2021**, *48*, 592–595. [CrossRef]
12. Dressing, A.; Bormann, T.; Blazhenets, G.; Schroeter, N.; Walter, L.I.; Thurow, J.; August, D.; Hilger, H.; Stete, K.; Gerstacker, K.; et al. Neuropsychological profiles and cerebral glucose metabolism in neurocognitive Long-Covid-syndrome. *J. Nucl. Med.* **2021**, *63*, 1058–1063. [CrossRef] [PubMed]
13. Matsubara, K.; Ibaraki, M.; Nemoto, M.; Watabe, H.; Kimura, Y. A review on AI in PET imaging. *Ann. Nucl. Med.* **2022**, *36*, 133–143. [CrossRef]
14. Kang, E.; Min, J.; Ye, J.C. A deep convolutional neural network using directional wavelets for low-dose X-ray CT reconstruction. *Med. Phys.* **2017**, *44*, e360–e375. [CrossRef]
15. Shan, H.; Padole, A.; Homayounieh, F.; Kruger, U.; Khera, R.D.; Nitiwarangkul, C.; Kalra, M.K.; Wang, G. Competitive performance of a modularized deep neural network compared to commercial algorithms for low-dose CT image reconstruction. *Nat. Mach. Intell.* **2019**, *1*, 269–276. [CrossRef] [PubMed]
16. Wolterink, J.M.; Leiner, T.; Viergever, M.A.; Isgum, I. Generative adversarial networks for noise reduction in low-dose CT. *IEEE Trans. Med. Imaging* **2017**, *36*, 2536–2545. [CrossRef] [PubMed]
17. Yi, X.; Babyn, P. Sharpness-aware low-dose CT denoising using conditional generative adversarial network. *J. Digit. Imaging* **2018**, *31*, 655–669. [CrossRef]
18. Xiang, L.; Qiao, Y.; Nie, D.; An, L.; Wang, Q.; Shen, D. Deep autocontext convolutional neural networks for standard-dose PET image estimation from low-dose PET/MRI. *Neurocomputing* **2017**, *267*, 406–416. [CrossRef] [PubMed]
19. Chen, K.T.; Gong, E.; de Carvalho Macruz, F.B.; Xu, J.; Boumis, A.; Khalighi, M.; Poston, K.L.; Sha, S.J.; Greicius, M.D.; Mormino, E.; et al. Ultra-low-dose (18)F-Florbetaben amyloid PET imaging using deep learning with multi-contrast MRI inputs. *Radiology* **2019**, *290*, 649–656. [CrossRef]
20. Wang, Y.J.; Baratto, L.; Hawk, K.E.; Theruvath, A.J.; Pribnow, A.; Thakor, A.S.; Gatidis, S.; Lu, R.; Gummidipundi, S.E.; Garcia-Diaz, J.; et al. Artificial intelligence enables whole-body positron emission tomography scans with minimal radiation exposure. *Eur. J. Nucl. Med. Mol. Imaging* **2021**, *48*, 2771–2781. [CrossRef]
21. Liu, H.; Wu, J.; Lu, W.; Onofrey, J.A.; Liu, Y.H.; Liu, C. Noise reduction with cross-tracer and cross-protocol deep transfer learning for low-dose PET. *Phys. Med. Biol.* **2020**, *65*, 185006. [CrossRef]
22. Wang, T.; Lei, Y.; Fu, Y.; Wynne, J.F.; Curran, W.J.; Liu, T.; Yang, X. A review on medical imaging synthesis using deep learning and its clinical applications. *J. Appl. Clin. Med. Phys.* **2021**, *22*, 11–36. [CrossRef] [PubMed]
23. Sahu, R.; Dash, M.K.; Verra, D. Optimizing Image Captioning using Deep Learning based Object Detection. In Proceedings of the Fifth International Conference on Computational Intelligence and Communication Technologies (CCICT), Sonepat, India, 8–9 July 2022.
24. Creswell, A.; White, T.; Dumoulin, V.; Arulkumaran, K.; Sengupta, B.; Anil, A.; Bharath, A.A. Generative Adversarial Networks: An Overview. *IEEE Signal Process. Mag.* **2017**, *35*, 53–65. [CrossRef]
25. McCann, M.T.; Jin, K.H.; Unser, M.A. Review of Convolutional Neural Networks for Inverse Problems. *IEEE Signal Process. Mag.* **2017**, *34*, 85–95. [CrossRef]
26. Tajbakhsh, N.; Shin, J.Y.; Gurudu, S.; Hurst, R.T.; Kendall, C.B.; Gotway, M.B.; Liang, J. Convolutional neural networks for medical image analysis: Full training or fine tuning? *IEEE Trans. Med. Imaging* **2016**, *35*, 1299–1312. [CrossRef]
27. Chen, X.; Wang, X.; Zhang, K.; Fung, K.M.; Theresa, C.; Thai, T.C.; Moore, K.; Mannel, R.S.; Liu, H.; Zheng, B.; et al. Recent advances and clinical applications of deep learning in medical image analysis. *Med. Image Anal.* **2022**, *79*, 102444. [CrossRef] [PubMed]
28. Newberg, A.B.; Coble, R.; Khosravis, M.; Alavi, A. Positron Emission Tomography-Based Assessment of Cognitive Impairment and Dementias, Critical Role of Fluorodeoxyglucose in such Settings. *PET Clin.* **2022**, *17*, 479–494. [CrossRef] [PubMed]
29. Rogers, C.J.; Ayuso, J.; Hackney, M.E.; Penza, C. Alzheimer Disease and Related Cognitive Impairment in Older Adults: A Narrative Review of Screening, Prevention, and Management for Manual Therapy Providers. *J. Chiropr. Med.* **2023**, *22*, 148–156. [CrossRef]
30. Santana, K.; Franca, E.; Sato, J.; Silva, A.; Queiroz, M.; de Farias, J.; Rodrigues, D.; Souza, I.; Ribeiro, V.; Caparelli-Dáquer, E.; et al. Non-invasive brain stimulation for fatigue in post-acute sequelae of SARS-CoV-2 (PASC). *Brain Stimul.* **2023**, *16*, 100–107. [CrossRef]
31. Linnhoff, S.; Koehler, L.; Haghikia, A.; Zaehle, T. The therapeutic potential of non-invasive brain stimulation for the treatment of Long-COVID-related cognitive fatigue. *Front. Immunol.* **2022**, *13*, 935614. [CrossRef]
32. Badran, B.W.; Huffman, S.M.; Morgan, D.; Austelle, C.W.; Bikson, M.; Kautz, S.A.; George, M.S. A pilot randomized controlled trial of supervised, at-home, self-administered transcutaneous auricular vagus nerve stimulation (taVNS) to manage long COVID symptoms. *Bioelectron. Med.* **2022**, *8*, 13. [CrossRef]
33. Miller, K.L.; Alfaro-Almagro, F.; Bangerter, N.K.; Thomas, D.L.; Yacoub, E.; Xu, J.; Bartsch, A.J.; Jbabdi, S.; Sotiropoulos, S.N.; Andersson, J.L.; et al. Multimodal population brain imaging in the UK Biobank prospective epidemiological study. *Nat. Neurosci.* **2016**, *19*, 1523–1536. [CrossRef] [PubMed]

34. Alfaro-Almagro, F.; Jenkinson, M.; Bangerter, N.K.; Andersson, J.L.; Griffanti, L.; Douaud, G.; Sotiropoulos, S.N.; Jbabdi, S. Hernandez-Fernandez, M.; Vallee, E.; et al. Image processing and quality control for the first 10,000 brain imaging datasets from UK Biobank. *Neuroimage* **2018**, *166*, 400–424. [CrossRef] [PubMed]
35. Littlejohns, T.J.; Holliday, J.; Gibson, L.M.; Garratt, S.; Oesingmann, N.; Alfaro-Almagro, F.; Bell, J.D.; Boultwood, C.; Collins, R.; Conroy, M.C.; et al. The UK Biobank imaging enhancement of 100,000 participants: Rationale, data collection, management and future directions. *Nat. Commun.* **2020**, *11*, 2624. [CrossRef] [PubMed]

Disclaimer/Publisher's Note: The statements, opinions and data contained in all publications are solely those of the individual author(s) and contributor(s) and not of MDPI and/or the editor(s). MDPI and/or the editor(s) disclaim responsibility for any injury to people or property resulting from any ideas, methods, instructions or products referred to in the content.

MDPI AG
Grosspeteranlage 5
4052 Basel
Switzerland
Tel.: +41 61 683 77 34

Brain Sciences Editorial Office
E-mail: brainsci@mdpi.com
www.mdpi.com/journal/brainsci

Disclaimer/Publisher's Note: The title and front matter of this reprint are at the discretion of the Guest Editors. The publisher is not responsible for their content or any associated concerns. The statements, opinions and data contained in all individual articles are solely those of the individual Editors and contributors and not of MDPI. MDPI disclaims responsibility for any injury to people or property resulting from any ideas, methods, instructions or products referred to in the content.

www.ingramcontent.com/pod-product-compliance
Lightning Source LLC
Chambersburg PA
CBHW041419210926
51850CB00013B/3320
* 9 7 8 3 7 2 5 8 4 0 5 4 0 *